Electronic Democracy

Electronic Democracy examines a range of key actors within representative democracy – political parties, pressure groups, new social movements and government bodies – and assesses how they are using new information and communication technologies (ICTs) to fulfil their traditional roles.

While political parties and local government have been the subject of increasing empirical investigation, interest groups, international organisations and new social movements have not attracted significant scholarly attention until now. The authors investigate issues such as how far the Internet will reform and revitalise political organisations and institutions, and whether or not representative democracy is under threat from the direct communication offered by these new technologies.

The book features comparative studies focusing on the United Kingdom, the United States, Sweden, Germany and Australia. It will interest both students and researchers of political communication, organisations, participation and institutions.

Rachel K. Gibson is Deputy Director of the Centre for Social Research in the Research School of Social Sciences (RSSS) at the Australian National University, Australia.

Andrea Römmele is Senior Research Fellow at the Mannheim Centre for European Social Research (MZES) at the University of Mannheim, Germany.

Stephen J. Ward is Senior Lecturer in Politics at the European Studies Research Institute, University of Salford, UK.

Routledge/ECPR Studies in European Political Science
Edited by Thomas Poguntke
Keele University, UK and

Jan W. van Deth
University of Mannheim, Germany on behalf of the European Consortium for Political Research

The Routledge/ECPR Studies in European Political Science series is published in association with the European Consortium for Political Research – the leading organisation concerned with the growth and development of political science in Europe. The series presents high-quality edited volumes on topics at the leading edge of current interest in political science and related fields, with contributions from European scholars and others who have presented work at ECPR workshops or research groups.

Electronic Democracy

Mobilisation, organisation
and participation via new ICTs

**Edited by Rachel K. Gibson,
Andrea Römmele and
Stephen J. Ward**

LONDON AND NEW YORK

First published 2004
by Routledge
11 New Fetter Lane, London EC4P 4EE

Simultaneously published in the USA and Canada
by Routledge
29 West 35th Street, New York, NY 10001

Routledge is an imprint of the Taylor & Francis Group

© 2004 Rachel K. Gibson, Andrea Römmele and Stephen J. Ward for
selection and editorial matter; individual contributors their contributions

Typeset in Baskerville MT by
Newgen Imaging Systems (P) Ltd, Chennai, India
Printed and bound in Great Britain by
Antony Rowe Ltd, Chippenham, Wiltshire

British Library Cataloguing in Publication Data
A catalogue record for this book is available from the British Library

Library of Congress Cataloging in Publication Data
  Electronic democracy : mobilisation, organisation and participation
via new ICTs / edited by Rachel K. Gibson, Andrea Römmele,
Stephen J. Ward.
    p. cm.
  Includes bibliographical references and index.
    1. Political participation–Computer network resources. 2. Political
campaigns–Computer network resources. 3. Internet in political
campaigns. 4. Internet in public administration. I. Gibson, Rachel Kay.
II. Römmele, Andrea, 1967– III. Ward, Stephen, 1965– IV. Title.

JF799.E44 2004
320'.0285'4678–dc21   2003012387

ISBN 0–415–32482–3

Contents

Figures

Tables

Contributors

Joachim Åström, University of Örebro, Sweden

Christine Bellamy, Nottingham Trent University, UK

Rachel K. Gibson, Australian National University, Canberry, Australia

Jennifer D. Greer, University of Nevada-Reno, Nevada, USA

Stuart Hodkinson, University of Leeds, UK

Mark E. LaPointe, University of Washington, USA

Wainer Lusoli, London School of Economics, UK

Catherine Needham, Oxford University, UK

Oren Perez, London School of Economics, UK and Bar Ilan University, Israel

Jenny Pickerill, Curtin University, Perth, Australia

Charles D. Raab, University of Edinburgh, UK

Andrea Römmele, Mannheim Centre for European Social Research, University of Mannheim, Germany

Stephen J. Ward, University of Salford, UK

Thomas Zittel, Mannheim Centre for European Social Research, University of Mannheim, Germany

Series editor's preface

One doesn't have to be a Marxist to accept the notion that technology shapes our world and determines the opportunities for social change and the ways people define their positions. This platitude can be easily illustrated by pointing out to the impact of the spread of television or the usage of modern survey techniques on political campaigning. Less well known is the fact that the introduction of air-condition devices transformed political decision-making processes in Washington. In the last few years, political parties and interest groups in each and every country opened their own websites with easy accessible information. Politicians like the German chancellor Gerhard Schröder answered questions of citizens using the Internet, and all over the world members of parliaments can be contacted directly by sending an email message from the living room.

This volume does not constitute yet another fashionable account of the blessings of modern communication and information technologies. Neither does it present a simple solution for the traditional practical problems of democratic decision-making procedures by substituting the crowded marketplace of ancient Greek city-states by some multi-choice-vote-at-home referendum at the start of the New Millennium. As the editors point out in their introduction, the contributions to this volume are based on the presumption that any political use of new technologies takes place within existing institutional frameworks of parliaments, executive branches, and political parties. It is this combination of discussions about these existing institutions of representative democracies on the one hand, and the opportunities of new technologies on the other, which define the unique character of the collection of essays presented in this volume. While there is certainly no lack of research on either of these two topics, only few publications aim explicitly at the relationships between these two areas in a systematic way.

Before the opportunities for new technologies in different political contexts are examined, Rachel Gibson, Wainer Lusoli, Andrea Römmele and Stephen Ward offer an overview of the main aspects of the use of these technologies in representative democracies (Chapter 1). The following four chapters deal with the problems and prospects of information technologies in several countries. In Chapter 1, Charles Raab and Christine Bellamy discuss the changes in parliamentary decision-making processes and the use of new technologies from a theoretical perspective. The core chapters of this part consist of comparative studies of the ways technologies are used in different contexts. Catherine Needham compares the integration of new technologies in the working of central governing institutions in the United States and the United Kingdom (Chapter 3), while Thomas Zittel focuses on the parliaments in the United States, Sweden and Germany (Chapter 4). The gap between expressed intentions of politicians and the actual initiatives to use new technologies to improve democratic decision-making processes is clearly illustrated by Joachim Åström in his analysis of Swedish local governments. The second set of four contributions is addressed to the meso level. Jennifer Greer and Mark LaPointe analyse the use of web communication in US-Senate and gubernatorial elections (Chapter 6). The opportunities for involvement in international organisations are, first, shown by Oren Perez in his analyses of participation experimentation processes in organisations like WTO or ISO (Chapter 7) and, second, by Stuart Hodkinson in his study of the impact of the Internet on labour organisations (Chapter 8). From Jenny Pickerill's enquiry into the differences between Australian and British political-action groups it is clear that especially activists organised in small autonomous groups can use new technologies more effectively than established lobby groups (Chapter 9). The editors' summary and interpretations of the main findings are presented in Chapter 10 and do not have to be reproduced here.

Despite the limited number of cases investigated, the contributions to this volume show that the chances for the use of new technologies depend heavily on existing political institutions and the way they function. Several important questions arise from reading the contributions to this volume and the concluding chapter by the editors. As with every technology, the use of new technologies cannot be restricted to benevolent improvements of representative democracies or the strengthening of social and political involvement only. For instance, Dutch hooligans already discovered the opportunities of new communications techniques to arrange violent battles. Racist and extremist right-wing political propaganda is spread over websites in many countries and pornographic pictures of very young children are distributed in simple ways on electronic highways. Besides, prominent political theorists like Benjamin Barber unambiguously reject the use of 'innovative technologies' such as interactive television as a panacea for the problems of modern democracies. In his view, these technologies are detrimental to democratic decision-making, because they '. . . could further privatise politics and replace deliberative debate in public with the unconsidered instant expression of private prejudices'. It is this tension between the enormous opportunities of new information and communication technologies and the dangers of anti-democratic, fragmented and privatised public opinion that forces us to reconsider the ways we have been thinking about representative democracy and democratic citizenship.

Jan W. van Deth
Series Editor
Mannheim, June 2003

Preface and acknowledgements

This book has a long history with the ideas behind it emerging first at an ECPR research session in Uppsala, 1999 and being continued in a workshop on 'electronic democracy' held as part of the ECPR Joint Sessions in Grenoble, France 2001. The build-up to the workshop in Grenoble served to confirm the growing academic interest in this topic since we received a large number of proposals on a wide range of topics. While we faced a hard job in selecting the workshop papers, in turn, the number of papers we could actually include in this volume was even fewer. A number of them, not published in this volume, have since been published in a 2003 special issue of Party Politics.

Although not all workshop participants are represented in this edited volume, the book clearly represents a joint effort by all those who contributed in Grenoble, and we want to express our deep thanks to them. The paper presentations and the lively discussion were invaluable in helping stimulate and shape our thinking about the structure and content of the book. The participants included: Joachim Åström, Christine Bellamy, Kees Brants, Andrew Chadwick, Rod Hague, Stuart Hodkinson, Natalya Krasnoboka, Christopher May, Catherine Needham, Jim Newell, Pippa Norris, Oren Perez, Charles D. Raab, Holli A. Semetko, Seung-Yong Uhm, Eric Uslaner and Thomas Zittel. Jan van Deth also attended an early session to present a very thought provoking 'key note' paper on the evolution of the studies of democratic participation in the representative context.

We also want to thank the contributors for their patience in dealing with our numerous requests for revision, and the Routledge team, Heidi Bagtanzo and Grace McInnes, for their guidance, patience and support throughout. Our special thanks are directed to Series Editor, Jan van Deth, and the two referees of the proposals for their helpful comments and advice.

Proposal preparation and early stages of manuscript production were facilitated by the TMR 'Political Representation in Europe' scheme, directed by Hermann Schmitt, which brought Rachel Gibson to the Mannheim Centre for European Social Research (MZES) during 2002. The final stages of editing the chapters and writing the conclusion was also made possible due to the support of the MZES and the Volkswagenstiftung, which hosted Rachel Gibson for a visit in Spring 2003. Finally, Rachel Gibson and Stephen Ward acknowledge the support of the ESRC's Democracy and Participation programme in funding their

'Internet, Political Organisations and Participation' project (L215252036), which provided much of the theoretical background and ideas informing the book. Andrea Römmele acknowledges the support of the Volkswagenstiftung.

Rachel K. Gibson, Andrea Römmele and Stephen J. Ward

1   Introduction

Representative democracy and the Internet

Rachel K. Gibson, Wainer Lusoli, Andrea Römmele and Stephen J. Ward

Introduction

The Internet is now firmly established in the realm of mass communication for many advanced industrial societies. In the course of less than ten years its use has expanded dramatically from being a specialist tool of computer programmers and academics to an everyday means for ordinary citizens to conduct a wide range of daily activities such as sending messages to one another from home and/or work, checking news headlines or movie times and buying and selling products. Paralleling the rapidly increasing diffusion of the technology at the mass level has been the use made by political actors at the organisational and institutional levels. From the more embedded legislative and executive structures of representative democracy to the more fluid forms of political parties, pressure groups and more recently single-issue campaign networks, there has been an increasing enthusiasm for using Internet technology to communicate and coordinate activities. Despite these developments, micro- or individual-level analysis has tended to predominate over studies of innovation at the macro and particularly, meso levels. Such an oversight is due to a number of factors not least of which is the difficulty in collecting data, relying as one does on the openness of the organisations and institutions to divulging details of the changes and innovation they are undergoing. The neglect has a more substantive basis, however, in that the first wave of theorising about the role of the Internet in democracy focused very much on its capacity to promote direct democracy. In such models political mediation was largely dispensed with as the new technology allowed for more frequent in-depth communication between individuals. The Internet forms a global network, free from centralised control with intrinsically empowering characteristics – costless, space-less, timeless. As the barriers to mass communication were eroded citizens could participate more fully in decision-making. Indeed, many observers applauded such moves, seeing them as removing the need for the creaking and increasingly underperforming units of representation such as parliaments, parties and other political organisations.

These early theories, it would seem, have failed to predict the direction and momentum of change. The first wave of Internet adaptation has taken place and the machinery of representative democracy is still standing, indeed on a surface level, very little seems to have really changed. Parties still campaign, politicians are elected and governments are formed, although their governing credentials are coming under increasingly critical scrutiny. This book seeks to shift the lens back towards these intermediaries of government and provide an understanding of how they are functioning using the new information and communication technologies (ICTs) in a variety of democratic contexts. Rather than continuing with radical hypothesising on the disappearance of the state and its ancillary organisations, therefore, we argue a shift in focus is needed to a more explicitly empirical and institutionally determined understanding of the nature of change induced by new ICTs. One that consciously contains the debate to questions about adaptation rather than wholesale reform and that begins with an awareness of the limitations faced by established political actors in opening up via new ICTs, rather than an extolling of the range of technological possibilities.

To that end we have assembled a range of perspectives on the use of new ICTs by the key bodies of representative government, each of which brings to bear knowledge of their pre-existing practices or current *modus operandi*. Some are explicitly comparative, such as Chapters 3 and 4 by Needham and Zittel, others cover a particular level of government or type of political actor in a specific national context. Overall, we seek to build a picture of adaptation across democratic systems and also an understanding of the pace of change across representative structures. How much change is it realistic to expect within such entities? Are the more formalised units of government, such as bureaucracies and parliaments, slower and more inflexible in their approach to using the new media than pressure groups or individual parliamentarians? Given the range of national experiences presented, what can we deduce about the importance of contextual factors at the systemic level as levers of reform? The answers to these questions do of course lend themselves to more normative speculation about the process of adaptation and whether the new ICTs could lead to the improved performance of our representative system. However, the focus of this volume is on description and explanation rather than prescription. This introduction begins that process of analysis by identifying the main actors within the representative system within two broad categories: (1) micro-level individual online engagement and (2) meso/macro-level online mobilising by different institutions/ organisations, and then assessing the research to date on their adaptation to new ICTs.

The micro level: individual engagement and the Internet

The idea of the media acting as a mobilising force, as opposed to being seen as a malign or enervating influence on public interest in politics has long since proved to be intriguing. Television in particular has been seen to simplify and personalise politics to voters, focusing on the horserace aspect of who was winning and the moral failings of the candidates while contributing little to individuals' knowledge base (Crotty and Jacobson 1980; Graber 1988; Putnam 2000; Eveland and Scheufele 2000). In addition, the rise of more depersonalised strategies of direct communication by parties such as telephone banks and mass mailing in place of grass roots campaigning have been seen as heightening this disconnection between voters and the political system (Bimber 2001; Römmele 2002). Even social movements – the eleventh-hour saviours of late-twentieth-century democracy – stood accused of not just failing to challenge public apathy but actively fuelling it by leaving little room for members' participation beyond dues paying. As Jordan and Maloney described it, the environmental movement has become little more than a 'protest business' (1997) for the vast bulk of members, meeting citizen/consumer needs for a quick 'feel good' return on a limited financial investment. The Internet, however, with its interactivity, opportunities for user control and independent publishing was regarded as a new and radical force that could help to counter and possibly reverse these negative trends.

Some of the earliest evidence on individual users was compiled by the Pew Research Center for People and the Press in 1996. Their study of the US population revealed that there was indeed a social and economic divide between those who did and did not have access to the Internet. The former were far more likely to be male, highly educated, wealthy and white than their non-wired counterparts. Not surprisingly, given this demographic split, the so-called 'digital divide' meant that those who were online were more active and interested in politics than the average voter. Crucially, however, further studies found that after controlling for the higher socio-economic status of users, Internet use was not associated with any marked improvement in political activity (Bimber 1998).

This story was confirmed by updates from Bimber using data from 1996 to 1999, collected in random digit dial (RDD) telephone surveys that found no significant increases in a range of behaviours such as donating money and attempting to influence others vote decision among those accessing the Internet (Bimber 2001). This was seen as particularly disappointing by advocates of what was now termed 'e-democracy' since the demographics of Internet users had begun to broaden quite markedly, particularly in terms of gender and income. Schuefele and Nisbet (2002) offered similarly uninspiring conclusions from their telephone survey of New York residents, which examined the effects of different types of Internet use on a range of political behaviours and levels of factual knowledge. None of the modes of Internet use, including political information-seeking was found to have any significant effect on individuals' proclivity to engage in politics, either in a conventional sense (i.e. voting, contacting) or in more participatory forums.

Positive effects were not entirely dismissed, however. Norris (2001), following her analysis of survey data from the United States and Europe up until 2000 argued that Internet use was linked to higher levels of mobilisation but that this was largely confined to those who were already active, pulling them further into an upward spiral or 'virtuous' circle of participation. She concluded:

> the rise of the virtual political system seems most likely to facilitate further knowledge, interest, and activism of those who are already most predisposed toward civic engagement, reinforcing patterns of political participation.
>
> (p. 228)

Although, politically the story of the net seemed to be lacking much of a punchline, more pessimistic pronouncements emerged regarding its social effects. A number of studies began to emerge highlighting the damaging effects of the online life for social relationships and the underlying fabric of civil society. Studies of Internet effects on various measures of social capital revealed a reinforcement of existing trends towards disengagement among voters, producing isolation and alienation. Nie and Ebring (2000) reported negative effects of Internet use on individuals, levels of sociability and increasing feelings of alienation and connection to society. Kraut *et al.* (2000) echoed these findings, with the latter characterising the heavier users of the Internet as a 'newer lonelier crowd' in cyberspace. Other studies, however, such as those by Putnam (2000) and Uslaner (2001) reported a more negligible picture. Putnam, reporting on data from the DDB Needham Lifestyle survey, said that after demographic controls were applied Internet users and non-users did not differ significantly in their levels of civic engagement. Uslaner (2001) in his analysis of data from 1998 and 2000 Pew Center survey and the 1996 American NES has argued for a largely 'nil' effect of Internet use on social capital. 'The Internet ... is not a reservoir of social capital' nor does it deplete the amount already in existence (p. 22). While there appear to be some positive associations in that the heaviest users of the Internet have wider social circles, those engaging in online chat appear to be more distrustful of others. Overall, he argues, 'there is little evidence that the Internet will create new communities to make up for the decline in civic engagement that has occurred over the past four decades in the United States ...' (p. 22). Using data from the 1998 National Geographic Web Survey, Wellman and his colleagues arrive at similar conclusions (Wellman *et al.* 2001). Notably, a positive association is found to exist between online and offline participatory behaviour with higher rates of participation in voluntary organisations and politics being associated with heavier use of the Internet. However, they also found that people's interaction online supplements their face-to-face and telephone communication, without increasing or decreasing it.

Overall, therefore, the verdict that emerged from the initial analyses of the Internet and individual engagement in public life was at best, ambiguous. Basically, it was not possible to specify any one universal type of Internet effect on participation. One thing was clear, however, Internet use by itself was clearly not transforming inactive people into participators with regard to 'real world politics'.

More recently, attention has shifted towards investigating specifically online forms of participation, both in terms of those engaging in it and attitudes towards it among non-users. Significantly, here there has been a more uniformly positive story uncovered. A 2001 Hansard Society/MORI survey shows that almost four in five UK non-Internet users would engage in online interaction with their MP and online surgery to raise problems with MPs via the Internet as well as via an email address, so that constituents can contact him/her through a consultation forum where he/she can read constituents' views. Equally promising, the study found that younger respondents were more enthusiastic for these features to be introduced (Coleman 2001). Data from the Pew Internet Survey of online communities (2001) shows equally interesting results as regards youth, traditionally a non-political group. Youngsters are indeed slightly more likely to be in contact with political groups or organisations online than other age groups, which assumes more relevance given that only one in three respondents reported being in contact with the group before contacting them online, vis-à-vis two in three for the oldest reference group.[1] Such findings have also been confirmed from national opinion data gathered in the United Kingdom during 2002, which revealed that young people were significantly more likely to engaged in online participation than offline forms, including voting and more active types of participation (Gibson *et al.* 2002). A more recent Hansard survey confirms this point, finding that younger voters (18–24-year-olds) were significantly more likely to have visited the Westminster website (34 percent) and were much more likely to do this than writing to their MP (Coleman 2001). Broader reports on youth participation following the 2001 UK election from the Electoral Commission (2002), Demos (2002) and the Government's Children and Young Peoples Unit (2002) have also indicated the usefulness of technology in engaging younger voters. Of course, these positive findings do raise the prospect of the disadvantages faced by older voters if participation moves more into the online environment. In addition, one needs to be careful not to ascribe too much power to the technology itself as the solution to what are underlying problems of motivation. Finally, while young people may be more susceptible to Internet-based invitations to participate they are also likely to be quite scathing of technological gimmicks. Thus, parties and political organisations need to be careful that they don't actually lose supporters in their efforts to promote themselves in cyberspace. However, one can also argue for the greater validity of these findings than those from the offline environment. The Internet presents a wholly new environment for participation with its emphasis on user control and immediacy. These studies capture these context-based effects more fully by examining political activities that are embedded in it.

Thus, the micro-level data on the Internet's impact on participation while it is abundant and growing, is at present, somewhat inconclusive. This is no doubt due partly to the fact that it is still too early to assess the long-term effects of the new technology. At the individual level, ICTs should be viewed as a tool for political socialisation, particularly of younger citizens. As the Internet becomes part of life for increasing numbers of people, it enters various domains of the domestic, the personal, the social and the political. As a result, ICTs shape, and are shaped by, the forces of societal modernisation that underpin the latest evolution of participation patterns, at least in advanced democracies (Norris 2002). Certainly, we should not rule out the Internet as a means of politicisation for individuals. Given its strong appeal among the younger age group it clearly has mileage as a useful means to target apathy and cynicism among our newer citizens. However, in the short term, before accepting the null hypothesis of nil effects, more direct study would seem to be required of online political activities. As Wellman and his colleagues have noted, 'it is time for more differentiated analyses of the Internet, and analyses, which embeds it in everyday life, offline as well as online' (2001: 22). Certainly if current practice is any guide then as participation moves more into cyberspace then it would appear that there may be a more positive story yet to emerge. One obvious development in individual-level uses of the new technology that could have widespread effects on participation patterns and theory is the introduction of Internet voting. With task forces established in the United States and the United Kingdom to assess the possibilities for online general elections and a number of pilot schemes at the local and state levels taking place across Europe, North America and Australia (Solop 2000; Gibson 2002a,b) there is clearly mounting interest in the prospects for Internet voting. However, with the security concerns and problems of lower turnout among minorities and older citizens (Alvarez and Nagler 2000) the idea of Internet voting from home look to be some way off. Beyond voting, however, it is clear that patterns of participation are undergoing change worldwide.

The meso and macro levels: new ICTs and representative structures

Much of the work that has been done on the adaptation of institutions and organisations to the new technology has been generated from the political communication perspective rather than from institutional specialists. Thus, there has been a tendency for focusing on websites and email communication, and on discussions of the varying styles of communication taking place, such as interactivity versus information dissemination. As we have indicated elsewhere (Gibson *et al.* 2003) this literature has spawned varying claims about the potential use and value of new ICTs to political institutions and we group these into four basic scenarios: full-scale erosion; limited erosion; modernisation and reform; and radical regeneration.

- Erosion.   Much of the early literature on e-democracy or cyberdemocracy has focused on the possibilities for direct democracy and closer connection of individuals to government and policy-making. Work by Rheingold (1993) and Grossman (1995), for example, extolled the possibilities of the Internet for forging new and stronger forms of political engagement by citizens. One consequence of this focus on the nexus between citizen and government was to question the continuing relevance of representative institutions and organisations. Among the more radical commentators of the time there was a tendency to regard them as antiquated structures and regarded the interactive capabilities of the new ICTs as paving the way to more direct forms of mass rule (Becker 1981; Grossman 1995; Negroponte 1995; Rheingold 1993; Morris 2000). Self-governing would supersede state machinery as Internet based systems of voting, referenda and discussion were set up. Details of how such systems were to work remained sketchy, however, and as the empirical evidence of a lack of interest in politics online accumulated (Norris 2001; Bimber 1998), the dreams of a return to the Athenian agora appeared to have faded.
- Limited erosion.   In place of full-scale erosion, a more limited usurping of government institutions was envisaged. Electronic communication channels would provide for more direct communication between executives and

citizens. Online consultation and polls by government would streamline the political process, reducing the reliance on unwieldy intermediary bodies such as legislatures and parties (Bellamy and Raab 1999). Single-issue groups and direct-action politics would increasingly dominate society as the role of aggregative structures declined (Bimber 1998).

- Modernisation.　Taking a rather more positive view of the impact of the new technologies on our representative structures, some accounts saw them as offering the possibility for reform and modernisation (Gibson and Ward 2000). New ICTs could improve the image of representative institutions particularly with younger people who are the least likely to vote or to see the relevance of the representative system. The website could act as a modern marketing tool for all parts of our representative system. Furthermore, efficiency gains should also be possible with websites serving as rapid, 24-hour, 7 days a week, service delivery points and information archives for the public replacing some of the need for expensive and slower personal, telephone or postal transactions.

- Reinvigoration.　Finally, some commentators have adopted a more radical view of the restructuring possibilities surrounding the introduction of new ICTs. If properly developed, the communication technologies could sit at the core of a reinvigorated representative institution that could truly listen and thus re-engage the public (Coleman 1999a,b). Rather than just modernising internal practices, this would provide more opportunities for the public to participate in the political system and would reconnect representative organisations with the public. ICTs provide institutions and organisations opportunities for engagement through their own websites and email, such as live question and answer sessions, and discussion fora and could seek feedback on particular issues via email or electronic polls. Legislatures, parties, trade unions and the like, could all employ e-consultation and discussion allowing citizens to feed in more formally their experiences and knowledge to policy debates. All of this could potentially open up representative organisations to new audiences, since it has been argued that use of ICTs could lower the costs of participating and act as more attractive channels of communication for some groups in society such as the housebound or those with childcare responsibilities.

The systematic empirical testing of these various development paths has thus far been rather limited. Very few comprehensive and/or comparative studies of various government/political structures in terms of their presence and styles of communication on the Internet have been undertaken.[2] In the following we consider some of the main trends from the empirical evidence collated so far in relation to the different parts of the representative political system from the formal governmental through to informal parts of civil society.

Executive branch: e-government

The idea of e-government has spread rapidly across the globe, even countries that lack basic infrastructure often profess an attachment to goals of e-government

(Norris 2001). In the main, governments, e-government strategies have tended to concentrate on e-commerce, Internet regulation and in particular, making government services available online. Underlying the provision of e-services is the notion of modernisation (see earlier) creating a leaner more efficient state (see the modernisation scenario) where services actually meet citizen demand and citizens can actively shape those services through online feedback mechanisms. Such a viewpoint is summarised by one advocate who claims:

> Public organizations are rapidly becoming networked, and they are using these networks to produce and deliver services. This will ultimately lead to efficiency improvements much as happened in the private sector. Government bureaucracies will gradually become flatter, faster, and more customer friendly. Services will become better integrated and customized, with rich self service options.
>
> (Mechling 2002: 155)

Whether e-government or e-service provision has much to do with participation or democracy is, however, questionable. Advocates argue that through e-government citizens will gain additional rights and additional chances to input into the policy process (akin to the idea of consumer democracy; see Chapter 2 by Bellamy and Raab), which should eventually increase their trust in the political system. However, critics suggest that e-government represents little more than modernisation without any necessary democratic improvements (Bellamy and Taylor 1998).

Certainly, so far, we can see rapid progress in meeting headline targets of placing services online. A recent report issued by the office of the e-envoy in the United Kingdom on the readiness of governments around the world to develop the e-economy provides extensive information on a range of related topics including regulatory frameworks and roll-out of broadband.[3] Overall, the study concludes that United States, Sweden and Canada lead the world in the extent to which they have moved services online and further, established mechanisms for gauging the effects of such policies. Yet, as a number of recent studies indicate, deep-rooted problems remain in some government structures, which limit any democratic potential (Margetts and Dunleavy 2002). The inflexible, hierarchical and closed nature of large government bureaucracies mean they are often ill-suited to a more open networked style of government. Similarly, government concerns about security of public records has slowed the pace of experimentation with electronic provision.

Legislatures and legislators

The spread of legislative websites whilst less universal than government sites has nevertheless also been rapid. Norris (2001) found that over half the countries in her global survey had some form of legislative website. Whilst in the United States, congressional sites for legislators have become virtually universal (see Chapter 4 by Zittel) by contrast, in the United Kingdom, less than a third of MPs have their own personal websites (Jackson 2002). Again the political context, broad systemic rules and institutional history and resources have all been cited as important factors in the uptake and use of the technology by the legislative branch of government. It has been commonly argued, for example, that new purpose built parliaments have an advantage over those with longer historic traditions and buildings, since they can more easily incorporate ICTs into their agendas and infrastructure. For example, the newly established Scottish Parliament (Smith and Gray 1999) sought to define itself as a new and more participatory parliament appropriate to the New Millennium and (at least rhetorically) made Internet technology a key feature of its communications strategy, allowing for submission of online petitions and running e-consultation. Overall, in terms of participatory usage, the series of case studies presented in a special issue of *Parliamentary Affairs* (Coleman *et al.* 1999) revealed that whilst legislative experimentation is taking place with regard to new ICTs, participatory uses are still quite rare. Where e-consultation has taken place it has met with mixed results. The Westminster Parliament has undertaken ten e-consultations between 1998 and 2002. The Hansard Society has thus far released in-depth analysis of two of these experiments. On the whole the findings are generally positive – new voices were heard in parliamentary process, the quality of evidence and debate was relatively high and MPs found the process valuable. However, on the down side participants were disappointed with the lack of response from MPs and perhaps crucially it did not appear to improve participants, opinion of the parliamentary system (Coleman *et al.* 2002).

Whilst there has been a number of studies of parliamentary activity and also public response to it there has been limited study of the views of representatives. Peter Chen presents the most comprehensive survey when he examines the opinions of Australian elected officials at four levels of government – members of parliament of the Commonwealth, States, Territories and local government councillors and aldermen (2002). Compared to the average Australian citizen, representatives are 'high users of new media technologies, and have very positive outlooks as to the future importance of this media form' (p. 61). There are three more specific findings, as to the impact of new media on the democratic process. First, representatives do not consider new media as important as traditional media for their information distribution and electioneering activities. Second, new media has replaced traditional media for a number of functions related to the representative office, only for the more ICT skilled, urban representatives. Furthermore, three in four members of this category do not rule out the idea of e-voting, and around 65 percent consider new media important or very important for consulting with citizens. Finally, there are still a number of barriers to the use of ICTs, 'especially for rural representatives, ATSIC and local government councillors, and councillors with relatively low skill levels' (p. 61).

Disparities in the perception and adoption of ICTs between different branches of the legislative and executive are also reported in the United States (Ault and Gleason 2003). Results from interviews and focus groups show that Members of the House and their support staff are not very concerned about ICTs and their implications.[4] On the other hand, senators, their office staff and staff of Senate committees 'seem to be more aware of both the potential and the hazards of information technologies' (p. 72). Finally, government administrators have already been through an ICT 'reality check'. They routinely use information technologies within their agencies, ICTs being included in plans for future development. These different adoption dynamics, it is argued, respond directly to organisational logics related to the aims, routines and function of specific legislative and executive bodies.

Political parties

Parties have increasingly merited a degree of attention. Early work on the US and UK parties (Margolis *et al.* 1997; Gibson and Ward 1998) has been followed by studies in other countries such as the Netherlands (Voerman 1999), Italy (Newell 2001), Russia and Ukraine (Semetko and Krasnoboka 2003) and Japan (Tkach 2003). From such studies a general consensus has emerged regardless of country. First, that parties like other formal institutions have moved online in large numbers between 1994 and 1998. Second, that parties' public websites tend not to exploit the participatory elements of new ICTs. Much of the information provided is one-way, top-down, party to voter rather than two-way interactive communication. Third, that the sites are often aimed at either an elite audience of opinion-formers (journalists/researchers) and/or at the converted party members. Consequently, the value of party sites as a mobilising force for the non-partisan voter has been questioned (Norris 2003). Fourth, that although parties are beginning to use technology for internal party debate (via closed intranets, bulletin boards, email lists) these rarely widen participation extensively (Gibson and Ward 1999; Voerman and Ward 2000; Löfgren 2001; Pederson 2001), nor do these electronic channels necessarily empower ordinary members since such channels rarely play a formal role in decision-making and for a large part are controlled by central party HQ. Nevertheless, recently conducted research suggests that parties may gain at least two benefits from using ICTs: technology can help parties reach a younger audience than otherwise would be the case through traditional media (Gibson *et al.* 2002, 2003) and also ICTs can be useful in deepening the participatory activities of activists, that is, allowing them to conduct additional party activities more often (Gibson *et al.* 2003). Both these factors could be crucial in maintaining parties as participatory vehicles over the coming decade.

New social movements and protest networks

Less formalised political organisations such as protest networks or flash campaigns whilst attracting considerable media coverage have gained less coverage from academic surveys. In part, this reflects a methodological problem of how to study rather amorphous, often anonymous and rapidly changing protest campaigns. Nevertheless, a number of studies have indicated that the most likely beneficiaries of the new media are loosely organised ad hoc protest campaigns

(Bonchek 1995; Bimber 1998; Hill and Hughes 1998). In part, this is because of the relative low cost of the net and the lack of editorial control, which means that fringe campaigns have greater opportunities to voice their concerns and get their message across than they do via the traditional media. Moreover, email and hypertext links make it easier than before to mobilise protest quickly and link together previously unconnected individuals even breaking down traditional barriers of time and space. The potency of email and the net as a mobilising tool has been seen in a number of recent mass demonstrations and rallies, not least the anti-globalisation protests in Seattle in 1999 and the Stop the War rallies in 2003 (Cisler 1999; Doherty 2002).[5] Arguably, it is these decentralised formalised types of networks that offer greater flexibility to experiment with the technology and exploit its interactive potential, since they are not held back by formal organisational rules or hierarchical chains of command. Thus some of the more novel uses of the technology such as political hacking, virtual sit-ins and blockades have come from informal protest networks, particularly in environmental and human rights and social justice fields (Wray 1998; Pickerill 2000).

Whilst it is relatively easy to provide examples of novel practice amongst protest campaigners, it is more difficult to generalise or assess the wider impact. Critics have argued that far from levelling the playing field for such organisations, a process of normalisation is at work in cyberspace where creeping corporate ownership of the Net and surveillance of online users' habits have become important (Guidi 1998). The entry points to the Internet offered by big media corporations such as AOL, Time Warner and Microsoft in terms of portals can be seen as 'walled gardens' – controlled environments where subscribers' choices as to what they see and do online are predetermined and also tracked (Wilhelm 2000). Such developments mean that it becomes increasingly difficult for alternative and independent organisations and sources of news to gain a mainstream audience. The idea that the WWW is actually simply replicating the offline dominance of the major political and economic organisations has gained considerable support from some studies (Margolis and Resnick 2000).

Overview of the chapters

The aim of the book, therefore, is to examine a range of key actors within representative democracy – political parties, pressure groups and new social movements, plus executive and legislative government bodies at the national and local levels – within different national contexts and assess how they are using the technology to fulfil their traditional roles. By doing so, we aim at connecting to the debate on new institutionalism, which appears with growing frequency in political science. We argue that the use of new ICTs, experimentation and innovation will take place within the existing institutional frameworks and any study of parliaments, executive agencies or political parties will need to take that into account. Put simply, context matters. Of course, such institutionalism does not preclude these bodies from making bold advances in using the new tools available to them and exploiting the possibilities offered by the new media (March and Olson 1989;

Hall and Taylor 1996). While some of these structures have been the subject of increasing empirical investigation such as political parties and local government, others such as interest groups, international organisations and new social movements have not attracted significant scholarly attention. Second, they assess the extent to which they are seeking to expand on that role in any way, that is in a more participatory direction due to the new interactive communication possibilities offered by the net.

Chapter 1 by Charles Raab and Christine Bellamy opens up the volume by discussing the problems as well as opportunities that new ICTs present for today's centralised but increasingly strained 'post-parliamentary' governments. Raab and Bellamy theoretically lay out the possible consequences new ICTs can have on political institutions, on intermediary organisations, on policy networks and finally, on the state in general by focusing on the use of new ICTs by individual citizens. Chapter 2 by Catherine Needham presents an empirical content analysis of government websites and web-based consultation in the context of government policy commitments in the United States and Britain. Through surveying the contents of government websites, evaluating previous web-based consultations and analysing government policy commitments on their own Internet presence, an assessment can be made of the government's commitment to net-based consultation. These findings are then compared with an evaluation of the extent to which these governments are using the Internet to facilitate state–citizen interaction through other channels – such as online service provision and information dissemination. In Chapter 4, 'Electronic Democracy and Electronic Parliaments', Thomas Zittel considers the importance of technological developments versus the institutional setting by looking at the US House, the Swedish Riksdag and the German Bundestag. Zittel defines the term electronic democracy as an (ideal) three-layered concept that encompasses three different levels of political analysis: a general conception of democracy, an institutional/structural dimension (democratic design) and a behavioural dimension (participatory behaviour). This concept enables thorough empirical analysis by drawing from a quantitative content analysis of all websites in the three parliaments and from numerous background interviews with members, parliamentary staffers and outside experts.

This first section concludes with Chapter 5 by Joachim Åström, examining the relationship between ideas, intentions and initiatives in the process of wiring Swedish local governments. Do local politicians in Sweden believe in the use of the Internet in the political process? How far do local government websites provide comprehensive information and opportunities for interactive communication? Åström analyses the ideas and experiments of Swedish local government through an attitudinal survey of local politicians towards ICTs and then compares the responses with the actual content of municipal websites.

The second part of the volume examines the use of new ICTs at the meso level, focusing on the adaptations taking place among more formal political organisations such as parties and trade unions to the more fluid and loosely organised pressure groups. Chapter 7 by Oren Perez examines the globalisation process and emergence of largely autonomous, global institutions (WTO, International

Organisations for Standardisation and ICANN). It puts forward the argument that there is a need for innovative institutional structures that would enable the public to scrutinise such global organisations and their organisational norms. It has been suggested that the Internet offers one such potential vehicle for transnational public debate. The author reveals how the Internet while not eliminating the traditional problem of collective public action can contribute to the creation of transnational communities. Greer and LaPointe (Chapter 6) bring the focus down to the national level and examine the changing use made by candidates of the web during the 2000 and 2002 US senate and gubernatorial elections. Candidates as current and future leaders provide a particularly relevant insight into how well the representative system is adapting to the challenges and opportunities presented by the new ICTs. While the questions posed focus on the influence of party on the uses made of the web, attention is directed towards the impact of broader external factors such as the closeness of the election race, as well as individual factors such as candidates' gender and age or status as an incumbent. Chapter 8 by Stuart Hodkinson focuses on non-governmental actors and discusses the role of new ICTs in reviving trade unionism. The essay profiles the decline of unionism in the face of globalisation and the potential benefits of the Internet to bring about a new internationalism among organised labour. Finally, Jenny Pickerill, in Chapter 9, compares the response of two different forms of environmental organisation: the well-established pressure group Friends of the Earth UK and the protest network Woomera2002 in Australia. The chapter assesses the differences that organisational structure, participatory culture and political context make in terms of the deployment of ICTs. In short, Pickerill analyses whether loose, non-hierarchical networks are better able to exploit the technology for mobilisation purposes than more established formalised pressure groups.

In combining macro- and meso-level data from different contexts we aim to provide a snapshot, albeit a non-systematic one, of how well the organs of representative democracy are utilising the new communication tools, as well as raising the question of how far context matters. Specifically, the chapters investigate how far these intermediaries are encouraging participation with the new ICTs, versus opting for the more static information provision model. While it is hoped that signs of proactive participatory uses for the technology emerge, the amount of interactive communication taking place is not presented as a yardstick for giving the thumbs up or down to certain bodies. The point that is returned to in each of the chapters is that context matters. Depending on their size, age and function there will be differing systemic and technological opportunity structures within which democratic organisations and institutions operate. We need to adjust our expectations for innovation and change accordingly. A long-established legislative chamber would inevitably be slower to incorporate the Internet into its operations compared with a newly started environmental movement filled with young computer-literate individuals. Now that representative democracy has withstood the predicted erosion, it is the existing organisational and institutional capacity and incentives we argue that provide the best guide to predicting the implications of the new ICTs for democracy.

Notes

1 The figures presented here were elaborated from the 2001 Pew Internet and Community Survey. The questionnaire, data set and basic cross-tabs are publicly available for academic research at <http://www.pewinternet.org> from 8 February 2002.
2 One exception is Pippa Norris's global survey *Digital Divide* (2001), which explores some of these issues in terms of both individual-level participation and institutional and organisational mobilisation.
3 'International E-economy Benchmarking: The Worlds Most Effective Policies for the e-Economy,' Booz Allen Hamilton, November 2002. Available at <http://www.e-envoy.gov.uk/oee/oee.nsf/sections/esummit-benchmarking/$file/whole_report.pdf>, accessed on 26 November 2002.
4 The results are based on a restricted *n*, and should be taken as exploratory only.
5 For a good account of Stop the War campaign's use of the technology see Alistair Alexander 'A Revolution for Revolt,' *The Guardian*, 20 February 2003.

References

Alvarez, R. M. and Nagler, J. (2000) 'The Likely Consequences of Internet Voting for Political Representation', paper prepared for presentation at the Internet Voting and Democracy Symposium, Loyola Law School, Los Angeles, CA.

Ault, J. T. and Gleason, J. M. (2003) 'U.S. Government Decision Makers' Expectations and Patterns of Use of Emerging and Existing Information Technologies', *Government Information Quarterly*, 20 (1), 63–76.

Becker, T. (1981) 'Teledemocracy. Bringing Power Back to the People', *The Futurist*, December, 6–9.

Bellamy, C. and Taylor, J. (1998) *Governing in the Information Age*, Buckingham: Open University Press.

Bennett, W. L. (1998) 'The Uncivic Culture', *PS*, December, 741–61.

Bimber, B. (1998) 'The Internet and Political Transformation', *Polity*, 31 (1), 133–60.

Bimber, B. (2001) 'Information and Political Engagement in America', *Political Research Quarterly*, 54 (1), 53–68.

Bonchek, M. (1995) 'Grassroots in Cyberspace', paper presented at 53rd Annual Meeting of the Midwest Political Science Association, 6 April, Chicago.

Chen, P. (2002) *Australian Elected Representatives' Use of New Media Technologies*, Centre for Public Policy, University of Melbourne.

Cisler, S. (1999) 'Showdown in Seattle', *First Monday*, 4 (2), <www.firstmonday.dk/issues/issue4 12/cisler/index.html>, first accessed 4 January 2002.

Coleman, S. (2001) *Democracy Online*, London: Hansard Society.

Coleman, S., Taylor, J. and van de Donk, W. (eds) (1999) *Parliament in the Age of the Internet*, Oxford: Oxford University Press.

Coleman, S., Hall, N. and Howell, M. (2002) *Hearing Voices*, London: Hansard Society.

Crotty, W. J. and Jacobson, G. C. (1980) *American Parties in Decline*, Boston: Little, Brown and Co.

Doherty, B. (2002) *Ideas and Actions in the Green Movement*, London: Routledge.

Eveland, W. P. and Scheufele, D. A. (2000) 'Connecting News Media Use with Gaps in Knowledge and Participation', *Political Communication*, 17 (3), 215–37.

Gibson, R. K. (2002a) 'Elections Online: Assessing', *Political Studies Quarterly*, Winter 2001–2002, 116 (4), 561–83.

Gibson, R. K. (2002b) 'Internet-Voting and the European Parliamentary Elections of 2004', E-voting and the European Parliamentary Elections Conference, The Robert Schuman Centre for Advanced Studies, Florence, Italy.

Gibson, R. K. and Ward, S. J. (1998) 'UK Political Parties and the Internet', *Harvard International Journal of Press Politics*, 3, 14–38.

Gibson, R. K. and Ward, S. J. (1999) 'Party Democracy Online', *Information Communication and Society*, 2 (3), 340–67.

Gibson, R. K. and Ward, S. J. (2000) 'Conclusions: Modernising without Democratising?', in Gibson, R. K. and Ward, S. J. (eds), *Reinvigorating Democracy? British Politics and the Internet*, Aldershot: Ashgate, 205–12.

Gibson, R.K., Lusoli, W. and Ward, S.J. (2002) 'Online Campaigning in the UK', American Political Science Association Annual Meetings, Boston, Mass, September 2002.

Gibson, R. K., Nixon, P. G. and Ward, S. J. (eds) (2003a) *Political Parties and the Internet*, London: Routledge.

Gibson, R. K., Lusoli, W. and Ward, S. J. (2003b) 'Virtually Participating: A Survey of Party Members Online', *Information Polity*, 7 (4), 199–215.

Graber, D. (1988) *Processing the News*, New York: Longman.

Grossman, L. K. (1995) *The Electronic Republic*, New York, NY: Viking.

Guidi, L. (1998) *Bologna 'Civic Network'*. Web Document, G8 Government Online <http://www.statskontoret.se/gol-democracy/italy.htm>, first accessed 9 February 2000.

Hall, Peter A. and Taylor, R. C. R. (1996) *Political Science and the Three New Institutionalisms*, MPIFG Discussion Paper 6.

Hill, J. and Hughes, K.(1998) *Cyberpolitics*, Lanham: Rowman & Littlefield.

Jackson, N. (2002) 'MPs and Web Technologies – An Untapped Opportunity?', paper presented to the UK Political Studies Association Conference, University of Aberdeen.

Jordan, G. and Maloney, W. (1997) *The Protest Business*, Manchester: Manchester University Press.

Kraut, R. *et al.* (2000) 'Information and Communication', *Information Systems Research*, 10, 287–303.

Löfgren, K. (2000) 'Danish Political Parties and New Technology', in Hoff, J, Horrocks, I. and Tops, P. (eds), *Democratic Governance and New Technology*, London: Routledge, 57–70.

March, J. and Olson, J. (1989) *Rediscovering Institutions*, London/New York: Simon & Schuster.

Margetts, H. and Dunleavy, P. (2002) *Better Public Services Through E-Government*, London: National Audit Office.

Margolis, M., Resnick, D. and Tu, C. C. (1997) 'Campaigning on the Internet: Parties and Candidates on the World Wide Web in the 1996 Primary Season', *Harvard International Journal of Press Politics*, 2 (1), 59–78.

Marlin, A. S. (1999) 'Politics on the Web, Why and Where?', *Campaigns and Elections*, 20 (3), 11–12.

Mechling, J. (2002) 'Information Age Government: Just the Start of Something Big?' in Kamarck, E. and Nye, J. S. (eds), *Governance.Com*, Washington, DC: Brookings Institution Press, 141–60.

Morris, D. (2000) *Vote.Com*, Los Angeles: Renaissance Books.

Negroponte, N. (1995) *Being Digital*, London: Coronet.

Newell, J. L. (2001) 'Italian Political Parties on the Web', *Harvard International Journal of Press Politics*, 6 (4), 60–87.

Nie, N. H. and Ebring, L. (2000) 'Internet and Society: A Preliminary Report', Stanford Institute for the Study of Quantative Society <www.stanford.edu/group/siqss>

Norris, P. (2001) *Digital Divide*, Cambridge: Cambridge University Press.

Norris, P. (2002) *Democratic Phoenix*, Cambridge: Cambridge University Press.

Norris, P. (2003) 'Preaching to the Converted', *Party Politics*, 9 (1), 21–46.

Pedersen, K. (2001) 'Ballots and Technology in the Danish Parties', paper presented to the ECPR Joint Session Workshops, 6–11 April, University of Grenoble.

Pickerill, J. (2000) 'Environmentalists and the Net,' in Gibson, R. K. and Ward, S. J. (eds), *Reinvigorating Democracy?* Aldershot: Ashgate, 129–50.

Putnam, R. (2000) *Bowling Alone*, Simon Schuster: New York.

Rheingold, H. (1993) *The Virtual Community*, New York, NY: HarperPerennial.

Römmele, A. (2002) *Direkte Kommunikation zwischen Parteien und Wählern*, Opladen: Westdeutscher Verlag.

Schuefele, D. and Nisbet, M. (2002) 'Being a Citizen Online', *Harvard Journal of Press/Politics*, 7 (3), 55–75.

SDA (2001) *World Internet Project Italy*, Milan: SDA Bocconi <http://www.economiaemanagement.it/Universita/Allegati/wip8english.pdf>

Semetko, H. and Krasnoboka, N. (2003) 'The Political Role of the Internet in Societies in Transition: Russia and Ukraine Compared', *Party Politics*, 9 (1), 77–104.

Smith, C. F. and Gray, P. (1999), 'The Scottish Parliament in the Information Age' in Coleman, S., Taylor, J. and van de Donk, W. (eds), *Parliament in the Age of the Internet*, Oxford: Oxford University Press, 67–79.

Solop, F. I. (2000) 'Internet Voting and the 2000 Election, A Case Study of the Arizona Democratic Party Primary Election', Paper presented at the 55th annual conference of American Association for Public Opinion Research, Portland, Oregon, USA, 18–21 May.

Tkach, L (2003) 'Politics @ Japan: Party Competition on the Internet in Japan', *Party Politics*, 9 (1), 105–23.

Uslaner, E. (2001) 'Trust Civic Engagement and the Internet', paper presented to the ECPR Joint Session Workshops, 6–11 April, University of Grenoble.

Verba, S., and Nie, N. H. (1972) *Participation in America*, Chicago: The University of Chicago Press.

Voerman, G. (1999) 'Distributing Electronic Folders: The Digital Electoral Campaign of 1998 in the Netherlands', Documentatie-centrum Nederlandse Politieke Partijen, University of Groningen.

Voerman, G. and Ward, S. J. (2000) 'New Media and New Politics', in Voerman, G. and Lucardie, P. (eds), *Jaerboek Documentatiecentrum Nederlandse Politieke Partijen 1999*, Groningen: University of Groningen, 192–215.

Wellman, B., Quan Haase, A., Witte, J. and Hampton, K. (2001) 'Does the Internet Increase, Decrease, or Supplement Social capital?', *American Behavioral Scientist*, 45 (3), 49–64.

Wilhelm, A. G. (2000) *Democracy in the Digital Age*, New York and London: Routledge.

Wray, S. (1998) 'Electronic Civil Disobedience and the World Wide Web of Hactivism', <http://www.nyu.edu/projects/wray/wwwhack.html>, New York University.

2 Electronic democracy and the 'mixed polity'

Symbiosis or conflict?

Charles D. Raab and Christine Bellamy

I have a fantasy in which a modern Constitutional Convention assembles a group of fifty-five men or thereabouts whose commitment to democracy and whose wisdom are not in doubt. Their task is to design democratic institutions suitable for this small planet in the year 2000. And so they come to the problem of the unit (Dahl 1967: 957–8).

Introduction: the problem of democracy in the 'mixed polity'

Dahl's wise men disagreed about which unit was the most suitable for democracy, on a scale ranging from the very local to the global. Yet, because politics occurs at all these different territorial levels, Dahl argued that we ought to consider different democratic models for units of different size and kind. The arguments for democracy at the local end of his scale turned, as they have always done, on the prospect for direct citizen participation in collective decision-making, while the necessity for representative institutions was plain at any level beyond the very small.

Here we are, past the year 2000. The implications of ICTs did not enter into Dahl's thinking, nor did – or could – the prospect of a postmodern, post-parliamentary politics. Nevertheless, the central thesis of this chapter is that 'the problem of the unit' remains with us still. Indeed, it has been made much more complex by enhanced possibilities for direct participation through ICTs, and by the postmodern vista that brings into view a wider variety of collectivities. In postmodern thinking about the networked society, moreover, these collectivities are increasingly defined not simply in terms of territory, but in terms of interests, affinities or identities of all sorts. Some collectivities are 'real', while others are 'virtual', existing only in cyberspace, and some might be very short-lived. Some aspire to some degree of autonomy, to the right to decide matters for themselves. Certain of these matters are internal, relating to deliberation and implementation of rules, policies and issues relating only to the collectivity in question, while others are concerned with their relations to other polities, including states. For some groups, it is difficult or impossible to estimate the size of membership, or to establish clear criteria for joining or exclusion. For some, too, it is impossible to identify a leader or leadership group, because such roles are eschewed, rather like student movements in the late 1960s.

In this kind of thinking, cyberspace subverts spatial boundaries, including those of territorial political communities at all levels. It empowers affinity groups that cut across jurisdictions, and vastly increases the possibilities of forming temporary or longer-lasting collectivities. This notion of a partly connected, partly disconnected, interweaving and shifting constellation of political forums and arenas makes Dahl's problem look simple, grappling as he did with a set of less inclusive, more stable, more territorially defined political arrangements than would be possible in the postmodern scenarios. It also makes the design and reform of democratic processes – especially considering how they might be experienced by persons who are involved in more than one of these collectivities – far more interesting, but much less tractable.

Our purpose here is to cast light on the issues that are involved, by exploring the relationship between the 'modern' politics that Dahl took for granted – especially its characteristic orientation to representative democracy – and an ICT-powered, postmodern politics characterised by more diffuse structures and less commensurable political norms. In order to explore this relationship, we conceive of politics as increasingly taking place in a 'mixed polity'; that is, a polity composed of a mixture of different, and not obviously compatible, political forms, some that bear obvious affinities with postmodern politics and others that continue to be shaped by the legacies of the modern period. In the history of Western constitutional ideas, 'mixed government' was usually conceived as a mixture of (pre-modern) monarchical and aristocratic elements with (modern) democratic elements, but we borrow the term to denote a polity composed at once of modern *and* postmodern elements. *If* postmodern practices are emerging – and we think that this is probably the case – then they must be taking root amidst an institutional framework that has been shaped in modern times. Their juxtaposition thus creates a mixed polity of considerable complexity.

We conceive of the mixed polity, then, as a welter of jurisdictions, networks and domains, some defined in terms of recognised territories, some defined in formal institutional terms, some based on interests and affinities, some constituted online, but many defined in hybrid terms. We argue, too, that the study of the mixed polity cannot for long evade or ignore classical questions to do with membership, accountability, representation and the legitimacy of decisions. In political structures of traditional, territorial units that have persisted from the modern into the postmodern era, there is a continuing pressure to maintain processes that make possible some kind of aggregative and integrative functions in and among the different networks and sectors in which politics takes place. We assume, however, that these processes are not likely to enjoy the kind of centrality and primacy that classical constitutional theory, at least, accords institutions in the 'electoral chain of command' that connects citizens to central institutions of decision-making.[1] Instead, democratic processes focused on electoral politics, representative government and parliamentary debates will have to fight for a place amidst a growing array of competing, cross-cutting forums and countervailing ideas. How, and indeed whether they can be expected to do so successfully, is a question we begin to address here.

Various scenarios are taking shape in contemporary thinking about the fluid politics of the mixed polity. They involve ICTs to different degrees. Some democratic forums – such as established policy communities – are strongly institutionalised and provide the means of participation for insider groups in policy-making within conventionally defined, territorially referenced units, albeit often in ways that are both closed and opaque. Other groups operate in the well-established structures of civil society, at different levels, including the grass roots. Their political influence upon the wider polity is probably best described as limited and sporadic: it is certainly far from non-existent but tends to be issue-specific and contingent, although it is also oriented towards formal political processes. Beyond these well-recognised scenarios is a postmodern one in which still other groups function at the margins of civil society, with almost no connection to conventional public decision-making arenas and almost no awareness of, or contact with, the machinery of parties or parliaments. Some of these may constitute themselves solely as virtual, cyberspace 'communities' detached from place and from the political issues and processes of territorially based politics.

The (as yet empirically unproven) premise behind much postmodern writing (e.g. Holmes 1997) is that, in principle at least, it will be easier for groups – however transient and ephemeral – to flourish in the 'virtual society' formed in cyberspace. By this reading, the virtual society can support a much more inclusive politics, one that is capable of sustaining large numbers of such groups and involving individuals in multiple memberships, defined by their particular mix of special interests. At the very least, 'real-world society' in general may become more aware of their existence and demands, so that they are enabled more easily and confidently to assert and negotiate their claims. For this postmodern scenario to come to pass, however, it is necessary to assume some kind of connectivity between the politics that takes place in these different groups – virtual, territorial, affinity-based or whatever. Will this really be the case, or will postmodern politics simply grow in the interstices of the modern constitutional state, with no more heed to its health or demands than that paid by postmodern critics who have simply written it off? If territorial boundaries give way in cyberspace, does it follow that what must give way as well is the idea that politics has essentially to do with decision-making within, and on behalf of, a discrete and bounded collectivity? If it does so follow, does it mean, first, that postmodern politics undermines the possibility of holding any institutions or persons to account for the consequences of decisions, or for the probity and technical quality of governmental processes. Second, does it mean, too, that, if decision-making is a matter only for each of these polities in and for itself, then the need for debate, discussion, argument – in short, the aggregation or reconciliation of the views or interests of any wider collectivity – is obviated?

ICTs: reinvigorating or marginalising formal political institutions?

These questions arise from the disjuncture between the significance ascribed to formal political institutions in modern and postmodern writings, a disjuncture that lies in their intrinsically opposed views about the significance and desirability of social complexity and political order, and in the implications of these views for the ways in which they relate to evolving concepts of representation, aggregation and accountability. At some danger of oversimplification, it may be said that, as it developed in western Europe in the late eighteenth and nineteenth centuries, representative and responsible government promoted a concept of order that placed a premium on hierarchical, top-down control of the demands made by civil society on the political world. The practice of representation (better understood perhaps as 're-presentation') emerged as a device for simplifying the way the political elite conceived of society as well as for classifying the sets of views that came to be expressed. In other words, constitutional models such as mixed government and then representative democracy held an emergent pluralisation at bay by structuring and legitimating the kinds of interests that were given a voice and the channels through which they were able legitimately to express their demands. They served, therefore, to reduce the volume and scope of issues that the political system was obliged to process and resolve, as well to restrict the range of acceptable solutions. It can therefore be argued that representative democracy emerged as a particularly orderly and mostly successful device for reducing political complexity in an era when the growth of the electorate, the growth of the mass media, and the growth in the range and scope of the administrative state could be expected to increase massively the range of demands on the political system. To a significant but – as we argue later – decreasingly successful extent, representative democracy has served to channel, and therefore to restrict, these demands while providing a legitimate democratic front. Above all, representative democracy has secured for governments a degree of freedom and space to deal with social problems by negotiating in sometimes relatively closed networks with powerful interests on which, however, they have therefore become increasingly dependent. In other words, representative democracy buttresses the primacy of central political institutions and protects them by providing legitimate mechanisms for managing complexity (Easton 1965).

This is a solution to the problem of order that has also carried a high political price, not least in increasing exclusion, public disillusionment and apathy. It is also one that has become increasingly less convincing as representative bodies and elected governments have become less able to monopolise and control processes of public decision-making. In previous writing (Bellamy and Raab 1999a,b; Bellamy 2000), we analysed the problems faced by representative democracy at the end of the twentieth century and examined how far ICTs offer scope for its reform and renewal, with particular reference to its British parliamentary form. In particular, we were concerned to probe the significance of ICTs for the management of complexity. Two key questions arose. First, will ICTs serve, for example, to encourage the emergence of a wider range of more open, less easily manipulated interactions between parliamentary elites and members of the public, thus reinvigorating representative democracy? Second, will they provide governments with the means of re-centring public decision-making on the 'electoral chain of command' or will they simply reinforce existing problems and trends?

To examine the first of these questions, we surveyed the possible uses of such devices as telephony, digital TV, personal computers and networked terminals in public or commercial spaces, and analysed the democratic significance of ICTs, using a four-rung 'ladder of informatisation' of a politics based on parliamentary institutions (Bellamy and Raab 1999a,b). This 'ladder' is reproduced in the Appendix. We concluded that the application of ICTs *could* well improve parliamentary procedures and bring representative institutions closer to the public. But we also found that there are few signs that representative institutions are, as yet, much interested in innovations on the higher rungs. This is not surprising, for a number of reasons. Not least of these is the severe challenge that the development of new information and communication flows pose to what are often deeply entrenched infrastructures and processes for handling information and communications, and for controlling the uses to which they are put. The 'reinforcement' thesis (Danziger *et al.* 1982) holds that existing institutions tend to tame new technologies and shape them to their own purposes: technology thus becomes a tool for the reinforcement of existing power structures. Democratic institutions find it easier and less threatening to innovate – and particularly to embed innovation into their day-to-day routines – in ways that are commensurate with existing communication paradigms, established structures of political control and well-established organisational roles.

It follows that we should expect parliaments, too, to focus more effort on 'informatising' their own internal business arrangements and on the delivery of information to the public, with much less interest being shown in stimulating and incorporating more open democratic interaction. We therefore believe that, especially in the longer term, the significance of ICTs is more likely to lie in the service of direct, non-representative forms in which citizens interact with each other in ways that do not presuppose the existence, or even the primacy of, central political institutions. In such a context, attempts to 'wire up' parliaments might be better seen as futile, rearguard actions by deeply conservative institutions jealous of their prerogatives and legitimacy. For these reasons, our overall thesis was that informatisation can go only so far in adapting conventional political institutions to the politics of a diffused, pluralist, postmodern society.

This conclusion is reinforced by a broad-brush assessment of the implications of ICTs in relation to five trends that are commonly perceived to be undermining the primacy and legitimacy of the 'electoral chain of command' in Western representative democracies. These trends are:

- the overtaking of conventional politics by electronic media;
- the power of party discipline over representative institutions;
- the control of representative institutions by political executives;

- the displacement of decision-making into policy networks;
- the 'hollowing-out' of the state.

We next examine each in turn.

The overtaking of conventional politics by electronic media

The Internet is often regarded as a *pluralising* medium, facilitating the creation of more diverse sources of information as well as new, independent channels of political communication and debate. Far from reinforcing trends to more highly managed forms of democracy, cybersociety, it is widely believed, could subvert or supplant the power of politicians, bureaucrats and media tycoons. There has been considerable excitement, therefore, about the burgeoning of community networks, electronic public squares and online bulletin boards (Tsagarousianou *et al.* 1998). Petitions are organised electronically; electoral campaigns are revitalised by online access to candidates' information and electronic hustings; and electronic channels are used to disseminate dissident information and views from within repressive, closed regimes.

The potential significance of such opportunities for democratic participation may be inestimable, for many of them bear directly upon the core processes of accountability and representation. However, practice is lagging, especially insofar as it bears on the quality of interaction among citizens, elected representatives and governments. For many years to come, most people will continue to receive a significant proportion of their political communication from old-style broadcast media. Moreover, the increasing convergence of communications and entertainment media, together with the growing competition between their service providers, could seriously challenge traditional public service broadcasting. Unless they can convey the view that politics matters and is interesting to citizens, ICTs will have failed to overcome the apathy that corrodes the current system of representative democracy. But, beyond this consciousness-raising effect, the new technologies must provide the means for greater participation, on the one hand, and accountability on the other. Supporting these functions might well be within the scope of ICTs, depending upon how they permeate society and are designed with political accessibility in mind, not just as 'consumer' tools for fun, shopping, receipt of state benefits and the like, and certainly not as instruments for top-down surveillance and control.

The power of party discipline over representative institutions

In principle, ICTs could easily support a variety of new channels of communication *within* political organisations, through which the patterns of information flows might be changed and powerful resources made available to ordinary members to help them challenge party machines. On the other hand, party elites might be equipped with a more extensive and effective armoury of electronic tools that might reinforce their communicative supremacy; history attests to the difficulty of reforming party organisations. There is evidence that party bureaucracies are alert to the possibilities of ICTs for strengthening central control, improving the efficiency of electoral campaigning and reaching supporters and voters. Whether they are using ICTs for creating party structures that are more open to influence from below is less certain (Ward and Gibson 1998). Moreover, as we will discuss in the following, in the information age traditional parties are as likely to be side-stepped by new political processes, or 'hollowed out', as they are to reinvent themselves with new ICTs.

The control of parliaments by political executives

The executive's control of parliament is built into the bones of Cabinet systems such as that of the United Kingdom, where it is a consequence of the development of party-political discipline over a century or more. This control is not likely to be easily loosened simply by the informatisation of representative institutions, especially if this means little more than enhancing government's ability to give information to parliament, MPs' ability to communicate with individual citizens or parliament's ability to broadcast to the public. Recent and cautious reforms of parliamentary procedures within the United Kingdom, although not without important effects on the scrutiny of the executive and on the ability of some citizens to affect decision agendas more effectively, have so far failed to bring about fundamental change in the relationship between parliament and government. To the extent that ICTs have been involved in these changes – for example, the televising of proceedings (utilising the technologies of the 'first media age'), the greater availability of documents and reports on the Internet (utilising the technologies of the 'second media age') and procedures for petitioning legislatures – they offer only modest comfort to the 'optimistic' school. Reports from other countries – for example, the United States, Denmark, Slovenia and others (Coleman *et al.* 1999; Margolis and Resnick 2000) – point to a similar conclusion. Improving the ability of representative institutions to hold executives to account depends more on structural and procedural changes, perhaps assisted by ICTs, than on ICTs themselves.

The displacement of decision-making into policy networks

The fragmentation of the governmental system into specialist policy communities or 'subgovernments' embracing both public and private interests has long been recognised, for example, in the seminal work of Richardson and Jordan (1979) who coined the term 'post-parliamentary politics' to underline its significance for the 'electoral chain of command'. There has been rather less comment on the de-centring of democracy that may result from this trend, as opposed to tacit acceptance of it as an inevitable way of managing complexity and interdependence in the modern world (but see Kooiman 1993; Kickert *et al.* 1997). The question arises, then, as to how ICTs could help to reverse, or at least help to manage, the trend towards decision-making in what are often closed, non-transparent networks outside the main arenas of parliamentary democracy. This question directs us to consider the extent to which the policy elites that have become integrated into these networks are themselves subject to democratic control and renewal.

This issue resonates, therefore, with the growing preoccupation in recent democratic theory with strategies for democratising the multiple centres of power and decision-making in the complex, interdependent structures of modern governance (Etzioni-Halévy 1993). Insofar as new kinds of electronically supported information flows and resources, including those generated by new kinds of civic networks and bulletin boards, could help to support such strategies, then informatisation could mitigate counter-democratic tendencies associated with policy networks.

There are, however, two important qualifications to be made about such optimistic scenarios. The first is that by enabling speedier communication and sharing of information in and around networks, ICTs may themselves be implicated in the proliferation of networking as a form of governance, masking complexity and fragmentation by reducing the costs and inconvenience in managing relationships across boundaries. In facilitating the trend towards networks, ICTs also conspire in producing its political consequences. It is likely that some players will develop better ICT infrastructures than others and – other things being equal – that they will be able to win more often in the political games played in networks. The growing dependence on ICTs means that these tools will play an important part in modifying power balances amongst participants: ICTs, like money or votes before them, are becoming a powerful resource for political competition. There are likely to be new sets of 'haves' and new sets of 'have-nots' in the networked polity. What Schattschneider (1960) called the 'mobilisation of bias' – in which some issues, and the interests associated with them, are organised into politics whilst others are organised out – might well persist in the networked polity, even taking new forms, as ICTs rewrite the rules of the game. That would hardly be a democratic outcome.

Second, even if networked technologies could increase the inclusiveness of at least some kinds of decision-making processes, we need to consider what kind of democratic politics would ensue. Democratising the internal processes of political parties, strengthening and democratising civil institutions (some perhaps in a virtual sense) and enhancing the accountability and circulation of elites within networks all speak to the *aggregative* as well as the *expressive* functions of representation and accountability. But they would do so mainly in relation to each of the many dispersed centres of power in a complex world. What is largely unanswered is whether and how such scenarios could map onto, or help to reinvent, the processes of electoral politics and political debate in traditional political units, especially the core processes of representation and accountability.

The 'hollowing-out' of the state

The preceding discussion provides specific illustrations of a more general point, that governing may be too complex and societies too diffuse to be steered effectively, at least through the traditional structures of the Weberian state. One version of this argument is that the state is being 'hollowed out' both from without and within (Rhodes 1996). In this view, power shifts away from centralised state institutions in downward, outward and upward directions, although there are serious doubts that central governments are quite so rapidly and extensively losing their grip over policies and their implementation in many fields (Pierre and Peters 2000). What is the case, however, is that the constraints on states' autonomous power over strategic and economic decision-making have become more apparent as governments become increasingly entwined in the management of international interdependencies. Internally, too, governments are confronted by policy networks, as discussed earlier, in which the role they play ranges from uncertain leadership to deep dependence (Weller *et al.* 1997).

In addition to these problems, governments operate within multi-centric societies, with shifting modes of influence and multiple sources of power. Moreover, diversity and complexity go beyond the structural to the cultural: society is not only multi-centric but multicultural and varied in its values. The processes of representative democracy cannot be unaffected by such changes, and attention must therefore be directed to the cultural provenance of the accounts and stories that are brokered in representative institutions. How are they negotiated, and by whom? Whose narratives do they represent? Even to pose these questions is to doubt whether all voices can be equally represented, heard and reconciled through the restricted and highly managed channels of representative democracy. They might be more faithfully articulated through new, more direct, more pluralised modes of democratic politics.

The argument here is that democratic practices must change to accommodate a socially diverse society, just as they must also respond to the emergence of more diffuse and complex governing arrangements. Flexible ICT networks appear to offer the technical means for acknowledging and coping with such complexity. But for this very reason, they raise important normative issues. Without new forms of coordination and aggregation, there is a real danger that ICTs will simply amplify the fragmentation of public space, balkanising politics into multifarious and shifting constituencies that cannot be aggregated by any obvious means into collective decision and action. Moreover, cybersociety transcends national boundaries as the parameters of political activity, reinforcing trends towards the globalisation of politics. It is far from clear that the representative institutions of individual states can find an adequate response. Representatives may, for example, wish to consider the extent to which, and the means through which, they should take notice of the outcomes of political debates conducted in the public squares and bulletin boards of cyberspace. However, such efforts at incorporation may – rightly perhaps – be seen as forlorn attempts to tame new technologies and resist the possibility of legitimising new democratic forms.

The conclusion to be drawn from this brief survey of the declining health of representative democracy is that there are few reasons to suppose that informatisation will either greatly disturb or accommodate the main lines indicated by these five trends. If anything, it is people operating outside the context of representative institutions who are the most enthusiastic about ICTs, and they appear to see more exciting possibilities for a politics without representative democracy (e.g. Holmes 1997; Poster 1993, 1997). They are therefore bent either on replacing it or paralleling it with what they deem to be more authentic, or direct, democratic forms that are better suited to a post-parliamentary politics.

But what kind of 'politics' can that be? Politics as a process concerned with the making and implementation of decisions by governmental institutions figures only vaguely in images of postmodern politics, in which the emphasis is far more on discourse and communication than on deliberation, decision and execution. Where parliamentary decision-making aggregates and condenses, political discourse about a postmodern world disaggregates and expands, celebrating variety and the rich pluralism of opinion. That discourse, in itself, aims at no terminal point of aggregative decision. It therefore aims at no action for which anybody can be held accountable under any code of accountability. It is also, therefore, of course, a politics in which 'representation' seems to have little real meaning or resonance as part of a legitimising theory of democracy, and in which 'accountability' is hard to locate, either conceptually or empirically. This implies serious consequences for the aggregative and accountability functions that lie at the heart of representative democracy in large-scale societies – at least, as that form of democracy has been traditionally understood.

Does this matter and, if so, why? Answering these questions needs to start with confronting a set of underlying issues to do with the nature and locus of power and decision-making in the virtual polity, the continuing role and nature of the modern 'state' and how we should think about the relationship of one to the other. To go back to Dahl (1967): what are the political units in which the practice of participation and accountability in the mixed polity could and should be articulated? Before we open up these issues, let us revisit the discussion of a prior question: what are representative political institutions *for*?

Integration, plurality and collectivity

The traditional answer to this question is that democracy is not simply about providing opportunities for individual citizens to express their personal opinions, to promote their private interests or to seek redress for individual grievances – or indeed to join together with other citizens to mobilise the power to do these things – though it must certainly embrace all these possibilities. Individuals also hold interests in common as a *collectivity*, a 'public', that shares goods and values in common, makes rules for collective life, and establishes widely accepted principles for promoting mutual well-being. This recognition of the importance of the 'public domain' has certain crucial implications for assessing the claim that a political system is 'democratic'.

First, a democracy must establish open, inclusive processes by which public issues can be not only *aired* but also *resolved*, and through which the value system underpinning them can be constantly tested and renewed. Second, the decisions that are made, and the actions that are undertaken, on behalf of the public must be open to public display, scrutiny, challenge and revision. Third, the damage that those decisions and actions might do to individuals and groups must be preventable or at least remediable. Thus, representative democracy involves an inclusive process, in which participants display certain moral qualities, especially tolerance of each other's perspectives and interests and a willingness to mediate them with reasoned argument. The ideal that is often put forward is a form of *deliberative democracy*, involving a search for the best outcome for the collectivity as a whole, one that is acceptable to, or at least not harmful for, all participants (Fishkin 1991). 'Deliberative democracy', of course, can mean different things, as recent discussions show (Elster 1998), but most theorists adhere to a core definition, which:

> includes collective decision-making with the participation of all who will be affected by the decision or their representatives: this is the democratic part. Also...it includes decision-making by means of arguments offered *by* and *to* participants who are committed to the values of rationality and impartiality: this is the deliberative part.
>
> (Elster 1998: 8; emphasis in original)

Our understanding of aggregation *includes* deliberation (or discussion, or debate) as the means for arriving at a (perhaps voted) conclusion of decision- and policy-making. In using this term, we wish to avoid the connotation of 'mere' aggregation through voting, though we part company with any notion of deliberative democracy that suggests that all can be resolved simply by maximising opportunities for rational discussion.

All this means that there is a necessary duality – and therefore an important and inescapable tension – at the very heart of the notion of the 'public'. Ranson and Stewart (1994: 60) observe that '[p]ublic means not only "the public as a collectivity" (the whole) but also "the public as plurality" (the many)'. Thus a 'citizen' is, at once, both a member of a society with collective interests and an individual within an aggregation of individuals all of whom have private and partial interests. The exercise of citizenship therefore implies not only the power to influence decision-making and to hold decision-makers to account, but to engage in both of these processes in ways that acknowledge and accommodate the interrelationships between public purposes and private concerns. Viewed from the 'top', private interests are not only those held by individuals, but also include sectoral interests formed by, and defining, groups below the level of the collectivity as a whole, as in most accounts of 'pluralist' politics. Viewed from below, however, the issue is not so simple. Faced with a multitude of arenas, interests and roles, how can individuals handle their relationships with the diverse and diffuse communities and networks to which they potentially belong?

As we have seen, Dahl (1967) discussed the problem of recognising and accommodating a range of territorially defined collectivities within a single state. Most 'modern' democratic theory assumes that the collectivities in question are coterminous with fixed, constitutionally recognised, political units, such as those bounded by a nation, a province or a local authority area. Such theory is usually couched, therefore, in terms of a simple, one-dimensional relationship between individual citizens and the unit(s) in question, a relationship that is mediated primarily if not exclusively through processes of representation and accountability, channelled through representative bodies. Thus, as we have seen, the political significance of the representative democracy project lies in the way it reinforced the ideal of a highly integrated, geographically defined polity, even as the world became a more complex place. Representative democracy assumes both the possibility and desirability of a single political sovereign ('parliamentary sovereignty') conceived usually in centralised and hierarchical terms. It therefore assumes a unified and unitary structure of command, such as the 'electoral chain of command'. Above all, it assumes a single and inclusive forum of the political nation, reflected, for example, in the primacy of the House of Commons in the UK political system. This arrangement is constitutionally compatible with the existence of lesser territorial political entities, which nest within the overall national polity, although in practice there may be unresolved tensions among levels. In the UK, once again, where local governments are creatures of Acts of Parliament rather than having entrenched constitutional status, relationships have been highly conflictual over long stretches of time, and many issues concerning the relationship between Westminster and the devolved systems of Scotland, Wales and Northern Ireland remain unresolved.

Assumptions about the primacy of the overarching polity have been institutionalised through long-standing practices. They emphasize the role of elected representatives as gatekeepers as well as conduits of democratic opinion, filtering both the number and range of opinions and issues that come into political account. They also assert the desirability of simplifying and aggregating opinions and issues to the point where they are capable of being re-presented and resolved in a single forum, and they establish administrative arrangements capable of guaranteeing the primacy, inclusiveness and effectiveness of feedback. These institutional assumptions are also reflected in how we think about the polities nesting within the state. In these ways, the rhetoric and practices associated with representative democracy may be seen as important techniques for *controlling* and making more manageable the political effects of social complexity and diversity at each level of a territorially defined state.

In contrast, however, political theorists have recently become much more conscious of the growing mismatch between the confinement of democratic politics within the restricted channels of representative politics, and the multiple nodes of power to be found in complex systems of governance. These nodes include many that transcend the increasingly blurred and shifting boundaries between state and society, and between one state and another. At the same time, what has become more apparent is the plurality of connections experienced by individuals to the multifaceted social and governmental worlds they inhabit. The 'collectivities' through which individuals seek to pursue their interests are plural, contingent, overlapping and often transient: they are neither simply defined nor fixed, and they are not circumscribed by geography alone. They are constituted by a variety of criteria, of which the territorial is only one. They are also far from being uniformly dominated by formal state institutions or by conventional political channels.

Parliaments and postmodernisation

Most accounts of postmodern society and politics dwell upon the transformation of the state, and upon the shift of public decision-making away from the primacy of central institutions in a more fragmented, diffuse polity. Here there are plural nodes of decision-making, as networks and markets supplant or coexist with bureaucracies and hierarchies (Maidment and Thompson 1993). In some versions, there are no normatively privileged ruling institutions and no central core of agreed public purposes or moral values. For some writers, this shift is inevitable and is viewed dispassionately: because collective goals cannot be pursued in the postmodern polity, it is meaningless, and *merely* nostalgic, to give them much further thought. It is futile, moreover, to fret about the design of institutional forms that might give them effect (see, e.g. Frissen 1999: chapter 5, commenting on recent Dutch parliamentary reform commissions). Indeed, for theorists such as Poster (1997), it is useless to try to imagine a postmodern 'democracy': even to employ this term is to imprison the future in the worn out categories of modernism. For writers such as these, the stance has to be one of *letting go*. For others, however, these trends are to be regretted not least because they empty politics of collective content, meaning and morality. The danger is not so much that politics will transmute into a war of all against all, but that:

> it will not be about anything in particular. There is no inquiry, no debate, no agreed-upon grounds for asserting truth-claims, no propositions to be tested, no persuasion, no refutation, and no requirement that words connote the same phenomena for everyone.
>
> (Fox and Miller 1995: 69)

The postmodernisation of politics would cut society adrift from the prospect of improvement guided by generally agreed aims, including the pursuit of egalitarian ends (van Stokkom 1992, cited in Frissen 1999: 107). Furthermore, postmodernists view ICTs as the handmaiden of these accelerating trends. 'Cyberspace' is virtual, and cannot be tied to or mapped onto the formal institutions of the Weberian state. 'Cyberdemocracy' can be developed in all kinds of ways that owe nothing to the territorial collectivities that their members may inhabit. The very concepts of 'membership' or 'citizenship' are unclear and elusive; so too, in consequence, are 'decision' and 'policy'. The very notions of 'representation' and 'accountability' appear, then, to be irrelevant, embarrassingly outmoded and of little value in these postmodernising political scenarios.

If this scenario does accurately describe an emergent future, then, as we have speculated before, the application of ICTs to reinvigorating representative democracy amounts to 'wiring-up the deck-chairs' on a ship of state that is doomed to sink below the waves (Bellamy and Raab 1999a). But what, then, are we to make of democratic innovations such as the historic re-creation of a devolved Scottish government – one, moreover, that is replete with plans for the extensive use of ICTs in its parliamentary and governmental organisations, as well as facilitating communication between these organisations, citizens and social groups? Is this simply to provide the deckchairs with tartan cushions? The very centrepiece of the new devolved arrangements is the establishment of a representative body – a parliament – one that is related to an accountable executive, and one of a type that, we are increasingly told by postmodernists, is fast being consigned to redundancy or oblivion.

This question brings us back to the issues at the heart of this chapter. What role can there be for central political institutions in the mixed polity, and how (and how effectively) could the performance of this role be subjected to democratic involvement and accountability? A scan of contemporary political theory suggests that it is possible, in principle, to adopt one of four broad responses to these questions in the literatures on postmodernism and pluralisation. The *first* – associated with certain post-Marxist literature (see variously, Miller 1989; Mouffe 1992; Hirst 1994) – finds it impossible, in the end, to let go of the concept of the Weberian state, however hollowed out it becomes. This writing continues to see the state as a special kind of association that can and should control the terms on which all other associations exist and act. The talk in this literature is of a continuing process of pluralisation, in which the state itself fosters a more diverse, participative, inclusive society as a continuous act of political will. It devolves more of its own functions, for example, to voluntary associations in civil society, and takes positive steps to nurture a wider range of communities. It may thereby come to recognise a much wider range of identities and demands, including those from hitherto excluded groups. However, the overriding claims of social justice mean that it must ultimately retain both the right and capacity for regulating civil society and mediating among the different constituencies that compose the polity. In other words, there is a powerful if residual notion that the state, and therefore democratic institutions within the state, should continue to provide a forum for deciding what is good and just for the collectivity as a whole. The assumption is that democratic debate can continue to take place on the basis of common values, bringing, for example, equality and justice to the fore. It follows that parliaments, however limited their powers, should and could still aspire to serve as symbols of political integration and as important sources of coherent policy.

The *second* response is more commonly associated with post-communitarian and liberal theorists further to the Right (e.g. MacInytre 1988; Rawls 1972). It acknowledges – not always with complacency – the multiplicity and diversity of identities and values in contemporary society and, in consequence, denies that there is a common platform of values capable of supporting a widely accepted notion of what is socially just. Indeed, the assertion of such a notion is bound to be oppressive to those who do not share in the dominant value system. However, they believe that it might, nevertheless, be possible to agree on a set of procedures that could permit different groups to compete in the political arena on terms that could be generally acknowledged as 'fair'. In this formulation, central institutions take overarching responsibility for mediating and supervising relations of competition and exchange that exist among groups and networks. Aggregation is important, but it amounts to no more than an agreement about procedure. Voting, for example, is good enough.

The *third* response – which, as we have seen earlier, is mainly associated with postmodernism as a theoretical perspective (Connolly 1991; Poster 1993; Fox and Miller 1995; Frissen 1999) – is the belief that aggregation in either of these senses is neither a feasible ambition nor normatively desirable. Formal governing institutions may survive, but have no generally accepted prior claim to regulate or mediate among other associations, groups or networks. Postmodern society is seen, rather, as a web of affinities and affiliations, often shifting and never permanently fixed. Social bonds are formed from webs of meaning that are constantly renegotiated and always contingent. From this perspective, any attempt to re-centre politics on the state, to impose an overarching set of values or procedures, is therefore bound to be partial and oppressive: aggregation is an inherently dangerous aspiration. What, however, is there to prevent this ambition being realized? What, too, is there to ensure that webs are open, or to prevent the emergence of new forms of exclusion? At this point, postmodern theory tends to fall back on the assertion that postmodern politics are likely to be associated with new dispositions and attitudes, ones that are capable of fostering new connectivities and more open, more welcoming political discourses and communicative orientations. It therefore fosters a hope that postmodern society can engender greater mutual respect. Whether this hope is based on anything more solid than unfounded optimism is as yet far from clear.

The *fourth* response – one to which our own analysis tends – acknowledges postmodern tendencies to fragmentation and balkanisation, and agrees that they cast important doubts on the practical competence of the modern state. But, at the same time, it is much more sceptical about the possibility of an unproblematic, universal shift to a new postmodern political style. It seems more likely that the emerging polity will be a hybrid or mixed social form, in which the contradictions between modernity and postmodernity set up tensions that will prove to be impossible to resolve. On the one hand, the mediative, aggregative, aspirations of the state and its central machinery will never finally wither (though the capacity to fulfil them may well become severely attenuated), and the traditional functions of representative bodies – aggregation, representation and ensuring accountability – will never become entirely redundant. On the other hand, the pluralisation of society, the growing complexity of decision-making, the diffusion of governance and the growing popularity of anti-foundationalist discourses will make it increasingly difficult to sustain the legitimacy and the effectiveness of the 'electoral chain of command'.

The end of parliamentary institutions?

It might seem, on the one hand, that the effort and money spent on reinventing representative institutions amounts to little more than a sentimental clinging to an outdated tradition, to a much-loved political teddy bear. Who *really* believes in them any more? No need to pension them off, however: time will take its toll, despite all the effort devoted to modernising and informatising these bodies. Political and governmental institutions correspond to the societies they inhabit and lead. When – even in Scotland or other places seized with a new-found sense of political identity – we can no longer be certain what constitutes the 'collectivity'; when its manifestation is no longer uniquely tied to an identifiable territory coterminous with a contemporary 'state'; when interests can be aggregated at global and sub-state levels; when deliberation and decision-making can take place in multiple arenas at many levels or at no 'level' at all; then the claims of the parliamentary-democracy project look increasingly threadbare.

On the other hand, it is possible to assert that, though in practice representative bodies may be of small relevance to the making of decisions and to the exercise of power, they nevertheless play an essential part in bestowing meaning and legitimacy on governance, however dispersed and diffused. Indeed, it may be argued that this role will become more, not less, important in conditions of political change, fragmentation and unpredictability. In the proper sense of Bagehot's (1867/1963) famous term, parliaments, and the party politicians who strut across their floors, have become 'dignified' parts of the political system, exercising few direct powers but playing an equally important role in focusing interest and fixing popular attention. Their most significant function is to act as the front offices of politics, displaying the issues of the day, and influencing and reflecting the changing political climate which is, at bottom, the only effective restriction on the powers of back-office networks. For example, it is not necessary to believe that the Scottish people fell victim to a delusion that a self-governing nation collectively required an 'efficient' deliberative body in order to argue the case for the establishment of the Scottish Parliament. Rather, by this view, the Scottish Parliament is a symbolically necessary institution, acting both as a powerful source of legitimation of, and a lodestone for, Scottish aspirations both inside and outside the Scottish political world. It is also, obviously, a working legislature, but it would be to underestimate its full significance to see this as its sole function.

This argument assumes, then, that representative institutions are still perceived as a special source of democratic legitimacy, capable of establishing the democratic credentials of a regime in a way that no other institutions can. It assumes, too, that postmodern politics has not yet established its own claims to legitimacy or transcended what is still, largely, a modern or even pre-modern political culture. Elements of postmodern politics must coexist with the modern consciousness of a past in which the achievement of the representative franchise was the distinctive mark of political belonging, and in which the attrition or abolition of parliamentary institutions signalled important dangers. It is true, of course, that, in the recent past, these dangers were more often associated with the assertion of centralised, authoritarian regimes rather than the splintering of power in an array of disparate networks and groups. But can we face a postmodern future without the blessing of representative institutions? On what objects should political legitimacy now come to rest? A diffuse agglomeration of self-governing, sometimes transitory, fragments?

Parliaments in the mixed polity: still an efficient part of the political system?

This discussion gives force to our view that the most salient feature of contemporary government is that *we are situated between parliamentary and post-parliamentary forms of governance in a mixed polity that uncomfortably embraces elements of both.* The future, indeed, is just as likely to consist of diverse combinations of these forms, as it is to witness either the replacement of modern politics by postmodern politics or the successful resistance of the postmodern by the modern. Elements of modernity will persist into a postmodernising world, which will exhibit varying kinds and degrees of accommodation and tension. In this mixed polity, networks may proliferate but will not have entirely supplanted older, bureaucratic structures of policy-making and implementation. Central administrative machines may continue – altering in shape and scope, reinventing their modes of steering or rowing, hiving off some functions, decentralising others and devolving still more – but they will neither wither away nor become irreversibly hollowed out. In practice, networks tend to adjust to and incorporate these machines, rather than entirely displace them. Markets may be playing a more prominent role in the allocation of values, but they do not normally stand alone and are entwined with other arrangements (Thompson *et al.* 1991). Indeed, one interesting manifestation of the mixed polity is that 'co-production' between the state and society is coming to be seen as a favoured way of making and implementing policy (Kooiman 1993; Kickert *et al.* 1997) even though, from a democratic point of view, many commentators are concerned with their democratic legitimacy (e.g. Rhodes 1997). The main point we make here is that governments are far from irrelevant or invisible in both the literature on and the practice of governance, although their role, influence and accountability are often unclear.[2]

The scenario of postmodern governance is of a *kaleidoscope* of many forms, including those that reflect older concepts of policy-making, representation and deliberation. Its elements are sometimes conflicting, often tailored to the influences of different domains and often inappropriately applied. But it is always variegated rather than uniform, and *that is what is 'postmodern' about it.* Above all, the postmodern polity *celebrates* complexity. As we saw earlier, the modern polity recoils from it, denying it or trying to reduce it, and representative democracy has offered important techniques for bringing this about. The mixed polity, on the other hand, must search for ways of accommodating complexity while also coming to terms with the far from unspent legacies of representative democracy.

It may be, too, that parliaments will still have, and *should* have, a substantive, as well as a legitimating, role to play, in helping to provide for representational, aggregative and accountability functions in the mixed polity. Or perhaps a better way of expressing this is that the performance of a 'dignified' role (in Bagehot's terms) necessarily involves the possibility that representative institutions will continue to have a powerful, if not always easily and directly measurable, influence on public policy and governmental decision-making. As Judge

(1999: 140; emphasis in original) writes, citing a host of supportive literature:

> To conclude that parliament's substantive contribution to law-making is limited, even peripheral in the case of detailed formulation and implementation, does not mean that parliament is peripheral to the process of policy making itself. Often the contribution of parliaments are [*sic*] indirect..., or perform a 'climate setting' role, or, through oversight of policy implementation, contribute to the 'next round' of policy development...But, even if it is conceded that, despite all of this, parliament's practical contribution to policy making is relatively restricted, the crucial point remains that parliamentary representation is still of *paramount importance* in the legitimation of public policy outputs.

The functions of representation and accountability

This argument points to the conclusion that representative bodies will continue to remain (however peripherally) part of the 'efficient' element of the polity, relevant to the direct exercise of whatever effective power still accrues to the Weberian state. We assess this assertion, by exploring what the concepts of representation and accountability might mean, why they might still be important and how they might be operationalised, in the mixed polity. Perhaps unsurprisingly, our tentative conclusion will be that the tensions and contradictions in such a polity make it much more problematic to see how representative institutions can help to make them work but – more contentiously perhaps – we nevertheless assert the continuing importance of these concepts to the democratic health of the contemporary polity. This then, is a conceptual and practical problem that needs to be more thoroughly addressed in relation to the postmodernisation and virtualisation of democracy.

As we have seen already, representation can be seen as a way of coping with overload by simplifying and aggregating demands made upon decision-making bodies, as systems models such as Easton's (1965) show. Structures outside or at the boundary of the 'black box' do not transmit raw pressures or messages; instead, they filter, combine, restate and select them in ways that can then be processed by the government machine. Although systems approaches oversimplify and thereby distort the nature of politics and policy-making, they nevertheless serve a useful purpose by pointing up the role of gatekeeping institutions in the political system. In particular, they set out the rationale for aggregative functions that help to keep the system's fuse from blowing. Representative institutions play a significant gatekeeping role, but elected representatives transform what they 'represent'. The degree to which they distort (misrepresent) the views, interests and demands that they 'stand for', and the reasons why they take-up some while rejecting others, is an important evaluative question, one that exposes the extent to which the frustration of unalloyed popular demands is legitimate in a democratic polity. Representative government is government in which no one person or section can get all they want. Compromise is not only functionally crucial but is thereby cloaked in legitimacy to the point where it is seen as a positive virtue.

In such a system, no one wins outright but some potential issues lose outright by not even getting past the gatekeepers. Depending on the electoral importance of different mixes of interests, the skill of the gatekeeper lies in convincing losers that they have at least had their interests taken into account – a problem that is best pointed up in the Burkean notion of virtual representation. As has been well understood for many years, the success of gatekeeping skills depends upon there being a substantial degree of popular deference to, or trust in, the system – in its processes and incumbents – in order to reconcile as many groups as possible to a process in which they can never entirely win and may sometimes badly lose.

More recently, the crucial, complexity-reducing function of trust has been examined by Luhmann (1979), and its importance is now being rediscovered in the proliferating literatures on co-production, power-dependency, and networks. In the networks of the mixed polity, the mutual negotiation of roles and the critical role played by the exchange of resources, involves trust in the willingness and ability of partners to work to mutual advantage (Raab 1992). In its further development of these relationships into 'contingent interdependency' (Frissen 1999: 227), postmodern governance does not obviate, but may even extend, the need for trust. Frissen writes:

> Administration . . . should primarily rest on a trust in autonomy. Not because autonomy self-evidently produces what is good but because confidence in autonomy is both intelligent and pleasant. It is intelligent because the administration links up with processes of social fragmentation in a flexible fashion . . . It is pleasant because it avoids the administrative perversions . . . of totalising intervention and the destruction of variety. It thereby eliminates the need for fraud, deceit and calculation on the part of autonomous actors and domains towards the central planners . . . But this is not a trust in some ideal of basic democracy or in some naive anarchism. It is a trust based on a respect for contingency, an appreciation of fragmentation and the hope for connections.
> (Frissen 1999: 226)

What has changed in the concept of 'trust' is that its use and meaning has shifted over time. No longer are we so concerned as were Burke, Bagehot or Almond and Verba, for example, with the trust of the people in the 'system' as a whole – vertical, bottom-up, generalized trust, if you like. Instead, we have become much more interested in how trust is created in the context of specific relationships for particular purposes. Some examples are the establishment of popular trust relations within a pervasive but specific functional regime (e.g. governments' current concern with establishing popular trust in e-commerce (Raab 1998); the establishment of trust between partners in a public/private partnership; and, as in the quotation above, the establishment of trust between tiers within devolved political or managerial arrangements. What all these examples illustrate well is that this growing interest in trust reflects the more diffused, flexible and contingent nature of contemporary governance, and this must include the exquisite difficulties of establishing trust relationships in the virtual world of cyberspace.

At first sight, at least, it seems obvious that while postmodern life may create an increasing need for trust, it may, at the same time, place decreasing emphasis on the effectiveness of – or indeed, the need for – gatekeeping. In contrast to hierarchical conceptions of order that were embedded in the model of representative democracy, complexity is not a problem for postmodern politics; indeed it may even be positively welcomed as reflecting more accurately the complexity of postmodern societies. The problem that has preoccupied theorists as diverse as Hobbes, Burke, Crick and Easton – that of reconciling diversity and order – seems to disappear. The idea that politics has to do with the difficult task of making authoritative decisions within, on behalf of and with the acceptance of the members of a collectivity fades away. Whereas gatekeeping inevitably frustrates desires, the plural segments and arenas of the postmodern polity hold out the prospect of gratifying and indulging them. There is no gatekeeping because there is no certain place to erect the gates; by the same token, there can also be no 'black box'. But this means, too, that postmodern politics undermines the possibility of, and indeed ceases to nurture the ambition for, holding anyone to account for the probity, quality or consequences of public acts. If no one is in charge, the concept of 'stewardship', a concept that is inherent in the liberal emphasis on accountability (Gray and Jenkins 1985), is also extinguished.

None of this can be shrugged off as of little or no consequence for the quality of governance and the health of democracy. For all its faults, the system of representative democracy classically recognises the need to provide political authority for making and implementing binding decisions at the 'macro' level, whatever or wherever that level may be for the decision in question. It provides, for example, a well-recognised means for establishing and renewing an overarching legal framework, for the democratic control or regulation of public goods. Above all, perhaps, it supplies a legitimate technique for extracting and allocating money and other resources for purposes that exceed the scope and capacities of smaller or less inclusive domains. It also provides authoritative constitutional and political arrangements for mediating relations between these collectivities.

But if social action or public decision-making is simply a matter for each one of a plethora of social fragments, the possibility of collective deliberation or even transparency about transcendent issues is thrown into doubt. If the public sphere is splintered into a pluralistic array of transient groups, the wider repercussions of actions in one domain on other domains will be difficult to recognise and control. Perhaps this could be done simply by *ad hoc* connection and local negotiation and exchange. If so, it is not clear how these processes could be made to involve the most appropriate stakeholders, or how outcomes could be implemented and enforced, whatever the material, organisational and political resources available to the unit in question. It may be that central institutions carry residual responsibilities for seeing that questions such as these are addressed, and that the implementation of outcomes is adequately supported and resourced. But what would give them the legitimacy and – just as important – the political capability to do so, is problematic.

Conclusion

Such issues serve to point up the true importance of ICTs for the emerging mixed polity, and for our understanding of post-parliamentary democracy. The significance of electronic means for political participation is often seen to lie in the circumvention of the need for representation or mediation. But such a shift towards direct democracy does not *by itself* necessarily pose a threat to the public realm or its central institutions. Participatory democracy (Pateman 1970; Budge 1996) still involves decision-making by and for the collectivity as a whole, and therefore still involves the ideals of representation and accountability. It is rather the *de-centring* of those institutions in postmodernity that challenges the centrality of these concepts, whether democratic processes are supported by ICTs or not.

If a representative institution is a *centripetal* force, the *centrifugal* force of cyberspace is its antagonist. In the mixed polity, we can expect that the processes of mutual adjustment between sectors, groups or interests will increasingly take place outside the central arenas of representative democracy. This shift inevitably obscures both the locus and processes of decision-making, making it impossible for members outside these forums to fix responsibility or influence outcomes, though in practice much might depend on what constitutes domains or fragments within the mixed polity and the extent to which their memberships overlap. Thus it might depend on which categories or groups are involved; whether they are mutually exclusive or cross-cutting; whether the sectors are horizontally or hierarchically aligned or nested; what the criteria are for membership and who, in the end, determines and enforces them; and what kinds of internal processes and leadership are extant in various domains. But these contingent approaches to participation and representation are silent on a central question: whether the interest of the wider polity in the affairs of each domain can and should be recognised. Is anyone responsible, for example, for ensuring that the interaction of the parts adds up to something approaching fairness, equity and coherent policy?

As we have seen, our working assumption is that we will be faced with a mixed polity in which postmodern novelty will coexist with the political legacies of modernity. In particular, the political machinery associated with the modern state will continue to exist, even if many of its functions are devolved or dispersed. Governments will continue to raise taxes and allocate expenditures, representative bodies will continue to legislate, nation states will continue to conduct diplomacy, maintain armies and go occasionally to war, and territorially defined collectivities will still function and assert their authority. However attenuated, it is the machinery of government – as that term has been customarily understood – that will probably bear the brunt of mediating, cohering and regulating the diffuse, overlapping networks of governance. The paradox is that, far from withering away, central institutions, including parliaments and the like, may be faced with *intensified* problems of managing political complexity. These problems are born of the assumption – which we share – that there may be circumstances in which it is desirable to hold some rings, at least, between disparate elements, and that it will be important to do so in ways that are recognised to be democratic and legitimate. Whether in the end, politics in the mixed polity *can* be centred in these ways, remains, of course, to be seen.

Appendix: applying a 'ladder of informatisation' to parliamentary democracy

---

Online participation in proceedings of parliamentary committees
Online participation in citizen juries and deliberative panels
Online participation in focus groups
Participation in political forums in civil society, such as electronic public squares and village halls
Mobilisation of opinion through online petitions and political campaigns
Online participation in election hustings

Online advice bureaux held by MPs
E mail correspondence between MPs, citizens and the Executive

---

Publication of MPs' voting records and position papers
Information about the availability of MPs
Parties' election manifestos and candidates' position papers
Broadcasting of parliamentary proceedings
Publication of records of parliamentary proceedings and votes
Publication of official and parliamentary reports, policy documents and draft bills

---

Expert-systems support for legislation
Electronic voting for MPs in parliamentary votes
Online access for MPs to draft bills, minutes of debates, committee agendas, etc.
Online access for MPs to library and information services
Electronic voting in parliamentary elections

Source: Bellamy and Raab, 1999b.

This ladder is designed to illustrate the broad distinction between the use of ICTs to strengthen the efficiency and effectiveness of the state in controlling and serving citizens, and the use of ICTs as 'citizen technologies'. On the lowest rung are proposals for strengthening parliamentary democracy by enhancing the efficiency and effectiveness of elected representatives, thus enhancing the influence and prestige of parliaments. Such innovations respond to the claim that a major source of parliaments' failure to deliberate wisely and to scrutinise government effectively lies in the low quality and independence of information possessed by elected representatives. ICTs could redress such problems by, for example, providing online access to significantly enhanced library and research services. However, whilst these measures may be valuable improvements in the way in which representatives work, they do not necessarily widen citizen participation or significantly improve the processes of parliamentary democracy.

On the second rung, better provision of information to the public is available through networked technologies, such as the Internet or digital TV, which offer fast, cheap and effective ways of disseminating a wide variety of information. This might include records of parliamentary debates; draft legislation and committee papers; information about MPs, including their availability to constituents, voting records or position statements; information from Ministers, such as answers to parliamentary questions; and information about elections, including party manifestos and campaign materials. Potentially, at least, the wider and greater availability of such material could enable citizens to undertake their roles as electors and constituents more competently and intelligently, but it also increases their reliance on point-to-mass, 'broadcast' channels of information dissemination and thus on those who control those modes.

These two rungs, and the categories of technology-mediated innovation associated with them, involve the use of technologies as accessible sources of richer, more comprehensive, more flexibly organised information resources. However, they take relatively little advantage of the interactive capabilities of ICTs for supporting qualitatively different kinds of interaction and participation in the democratic process. Our third level therefore denotes a range of proposals for exploiting, for example, the interactive possibilities of telephone helplines or email in creating new bonds between representatives and the public. The third rung, however, remains more or less within the realm of communications involving citizens as individuals who largely interact with representatives over their private concerns.

The fourth and top rung, on the other hand, involves proposals for using ICTs to offer members of the public opportunities to participate more directly and, at least as important, more collectively, in the policy 'input' processes of parliamentary democracy. These opportunities may also enable more direct and collective approaches to holding representatives and governments to account, as we will explore here. The early history of electronic democracy is littered with experiments, often termed 'electronic town meetings' or 'city forums', to use cable TV to involve voters actively in election hustings, in discussions with elected representatives or in confrontations with officials (Abramson *et al.* 1988). The Internet provides even richer, more widely available, opportunities for democratic interaction on the issues of the day, particularly in the formative stages of making policies or laws. It is not difficult, for example, to conceive of arrangements that could permit members of the public or spokespersons of pressure groups to present online evidence to parliamentary committees.

These 'higher rung' applications of ICTs appear to present unambiguously positive opportunities for strengthening the involvement, competence and power of citizens in the processes of parliamentary democracy. We enter, however, a couple of important caveats. The first is that it is by no means obvious that dissemination will necessarily be either universally rapid or egalitarian. The foregoing analysis indicates that those facilities capable of supporting the richest information services and the most convenient interactive communications media will be disseminated most quickly and intensively amongst young, educated people in the higher social classes, especially those who currently enjoy continuous, personal access to PCs and who will continue to form a significant *tranche* of the market for cellular phones. For this reason, indeed, many governments and commercial companies assume that, for several years to come, call centres – accessed, in the main, by customers using touch-pad phones connected to land-lines – will continue to provide important channels for high-volume, low-value transactions, such as claiming welfare benefits. In other words, although facilities for e-commerce and e-government will almost certainly spread rapidly in the next few years, it does not automatically follow that all sections of the public will thereby enjoy equal access to those technologies and services that are best suited to supporting more sophisticated democratising inputs.

The second caveat is that it is by no means self-evident that investment in ICTs will necessarily favour the rapid emergence of higher-level applications, so far as electronic democracy is concerned.

Notes

1 We use the term 'electoral chain of command' to capture the relationship between electorate, parliament and government in European constitutional democracies in conformity with the model offered, e.g. in Hoff *et al.* (2000: 4).
2 The following extract is taken from a recent Dutch policy document (Dutch Parliament, 2000: para. 2.1) and captures well the tensions apparent in a system caught uneasily between Weberian, social democratic and postmodernist assumptions:

> Government and citizens are increasingly operating in a network society in which they are becoming more and more equal and in which the strength of government is determined by the delivery of quality and by the joint creation and sharing of policy information. Indeed, policy can in some cases even be said to be a co-production. Yet at the same time justice must also be done to the more traditional function of government, for example maintaining law and order and exercising the monopoly on protecting safety and security, although government is also having to take on new roles such as interactive and communicative leadership. Government has, however, traditionally been a referee too, and has as such been responsible for the public interest, taking account of minority interests. A new balance must be struck in the network society between government, the market sector and civil society. With the advent of the network society, government must invest in newly shaped information relationships.

References

Abramson, J., Arterton, F. and Orren, G. (1988) *The Electronic Commonwealth*, New York: Basic Books.

Bagehot, W. (1867, reprinted 1963 with introduction by Crossman, R.) *The English Constitution*, London: Fontana.

Bellamy, C. (2000) 'Modelling Electronic Democracy', in Hoff, J., Horrocks, I. and Tops, P. (eds), *Democratic Governance and New Technology*, London: Routledge.

Bellamy, C. and Raab, C. (1999a) 'Wiring-Up the Deck-Chairs?', *Parliamentary Affairs*, 52 (3), 518–34.

Bellamy, C. and Raab, C. (1999b) 'Parliamentary Democracy and New Technology', paper prepared for the Colloque Internationale, *Les Parlements dans la Société de l'Information*, organised by the Sénat and CEVIPOF, Paris, 18–19 November 1999.

Budge, I. (1996) *The New Challenge of Direct Democracy*, Cambridge: Polity Press.

Coleman, S., Taylor, J. and van de Donk, W. (eds) (1999) *Parliament in the Age of the Internet*, Oxford: Oxford University Press.

Connolly, W. (1991) *Identity and Difference*, Ithaca, NY: Cornell University Press.

Dahl, R. (1967) 'The City in the Future of Democracies', *American Political Science Review*, 61 (4), 953–70.

Danziger, J., Dutton, W., Kling, R. and Kraemer, K. (1982) *Computers and Politics*, New York: Columbia University Press.

Dutch Parliament (2000) *Contract with the Future*, Memorandum Lower Chamber, session year 1999–2000, 26387, nr. 8, 19 May.

Easton, D. (1965) *A Systems Analysis of Political Life*, New York: John Wiley & Sons.

Elster, J. (ed.) (1998) *Deliberative Democracy*, Cambridge: Cambridge University Press.

Etzioni-Halévy, E. (1993) *The Elite Connection*, Cambridge: Polity Press.

Fishkin, J. (1991) *Democracy and Deliberation*, New Haven: Yale University Press.

Fox, C. and Miller, H. (1995) *Postmodern Public Administration*, Thousand Oaks, Calif.: Sage.

Frissen, P. (1999) *Politics, Governance and Technology*, Cheltenham: Edward Elgar.

Gray, A. and Jenkins, W. (1985) *Administrative Politics in British Government*, Brighton: Wheatsheaf Books.

Hirst, P. (1994) *Associative Democracy*, Amherst: University of Massachusetts Press.

Hoff, J., Horrocks, I. and Tops, P. (eds) (2000) *Democratic Governance and New Technology*, London: Routledge.

Holmes, D. (ed.) (1997) *Virtual Politics*, London: Sage.

Judge, D. (1999) *Representation*, London: Routledge.

Kickert, W., Klijn, E-H. and Koppenjan, J. (eds) (1997) *Managing Complex Networks*, London: Sage.

Kooiman, J. (ed.) (1993) *Modern Governance*, London: Sage.

Luhmann, N. (1979) *Trust and Power*, London: John Wiley & Sons.

MacIntyre, A. (1988) *Whose Justice? Which Rationality?* London: Duckworth.

Maidment, R. and Thompson, G. (eds) (1993) *Managing the United Kingdom*, London: Sage.

Margolis, M. and Resnick, D. (2000) *Politics as Usual*, Thousand Oaks, Calif.: Sage.

Miller, D. (1989) *Market, State and Community*, Oxford: Oxford University Press.

Mouffe, C. (ed.) (1992) *Dimensions of Radical Democracy*, London: Verso.

Pateman, C. (1970) *Participation and Democratic Theory*, Cambridge: Cambridge University Press.

Pierre, J. and Peters, B. (2000) *Governance, Politics and the State*. Basingstoke: Macmillan.

Poster, M. (1993) *The Second Media Age*, Cambridge: Polity Press.

Poster, M. (1997) 'Cyberdemocracy: The Internet and the Public Sphere', in Holmes, D. (ed.), *Virtual Politics*, London: Sage.

Raab, C. (1992) 'Taking Networks Seriously', *European Journal of Political Research*, 21 (1–2), 69–90.

Raab, C. (1998) 'Electronic Confidence', in Snellen, I. and van de Donk, W. (eds), *Public Administration in an Information Age*, Amsterdam: IOS Press, 113–33.

Ranson, S. and Stewart, J. (1994) *Management for the Public Domain*, Basingstoke: Macmillan.

Rawls, J. (1972) *A Theory of Justice*, Oxford: Clarendon Press.

Rhodes, R. (1996) *Understanding Governance*, Milton Keynes: Open University Press.

Rhodes, R. (1997) 'Foreword', in Kickert, W., Klijn, E-H. and Koppenjan, J. (eds), *Managing Complex Networks*, London: Sage.

Richardson, J. and Jordan, A. (1979) *Governing Under Pressure*, Oxford: Martin Robertson.

Schattschneider, E. (1960) *The Semisovereign People*, New York: Holt, Rinehart and Winston.

van Stokkom, B. (1992) *De Republiek der Weerbaren*, Houten: Bohn Stafleu Van Loghem.

Thompson, G., Frances, J., Levacic, R. and Mitchell, J. (eds) (1991) *Markets, Hierarchies and Networks*, London: Sage.

Tsagarousianou, R., Tambini, D. and Bryan, C. (eds) (1998) *Cyberdemocracy*, London: Routledge.

Ward, S. and Gibson, R. (1998) 'UK Political Parties on the Net', *Harvard International Journal of Press/Politics*, 3 (1), 14–38.

Weller, P., Bakvis, H. and Rhodes, R. (1997) *The Hollow Crowns*, Basingstoke: Macmillan.

3   The citizen as consumer

E-government in the United Kingdom and the United States

Catherine Needham

Introduction

New information and communication technologies (ICTs) have the potential to radically reconfigure the state–citizen relationship. The Internet, in particular, has the scope to have an enormous impact on state–citizen dialogue, given its capacity to surmount geographical barriers and allow interactive and simultaneous mass transmission. Forms of state–citizen interaction that have been dominant for over a century, such as constituent surgeries, public meetings and face-to-face consultative hearings can be replaced by email and online discussion forums. Such developments have led Grossman to argue, 'Interactive telecommunications technology makes it possible to revive, in a sophisticated modern form, some of the essential characteristics of the ancient world's first democratic polities' (Grossman 1995: 48).

The extent to which this transformative potential is being realised depends to a large extent on how established institutions are responding to the opportunities being provided by the new ICTs. As the introductory chapter to this volume has highlighted, context matters, and the adaptability of conventional actors in the political system is expected to be shaped in large part by their existing internal norms and patterns of behaviour. This chapter addresses this issue through an evaluation of the 'electronic government' programmes of the United Kingdom and United States. The term electronic government here refers to all forms of government–citizen interaction online but excludes participation on election or party websites, or citizen-to-citizen interaction.[1] The goal is to assess how extensively central governing institutions have integrated new technologies into their patterns of working. In order to do this the online activity of the executive and legislative branches of government are analysed to identify the priorities that the two governments have set in establishing their online presence, and then assessed against the empirical evidence. The first section of the chapter discusses the theoretical debates surrounding electronic government, outlining the implications of different forms of online operability for democracy and citizenship. The model of the active citizen, providing input into policy-making via online feedback channels, is contrasted with the citizen-consumer, a passive recipient of electronically delivered outputs from the state.

The chapter then goes on to examine the design and implementation of e-government strategies in the United Kingdom and the United States, to see how far individuals are encouraged to be citizens or citizen-consumers in their electronic interactions with government. Policy documents on electronic government are analysed alongside a review of current online provision to measure the extent to which priority is given to service and information provision, or to consultation and feedback. On the basis of this, the two governments' online presence is evaluated against both their own stated policy objectives and against normative standards regarding democratic engagement with citizens. Finally, conclusions are drawn about the extent to which the moves towards e-government in these two countries conform to the models of adaptation outlined in the introductory chapter. How far does the evidence support the idea of a decline and erosion of the familiar aggregative structures of executives and legislatures in society, as opposed to the prospect of renewed relevance and revitalisation?

New ICTs, democracy and the citizen

Predictions about the impact of new ICTs on democracy range from the sceptical to the optimistic. Some, such as Barber (1999) and Hague and Loader (1999) have highlighted the scope for ICTs to be used to nurture 'strong democracy', enabling citizens to become active participants in the political community. Others, such as Elshtain (1982), reject the democratising potential of such technologies, arguing, 'interactive systems encourage social atomisation and...foster the impression that an electronic transaction is an authentic democratic choice' (Elshtain 1982: 109). Some, including Margolis and Resnick (2000) and Davis (1999) highlight the potential for the new technologies to be co-opted by governments and used to consolidate existing political power structures. Across these different perspectives there is agreement that technology is not deterministic in its effects; the impact of technological change is mediated by the political and cultural context. As Noveck puts it:

> It is not technology per se which either fosters or denigrates the connection between communications media and participatory democratic culture. Technology exists within a framework of values and ideals both inherent to it and imposed by the external legal and institutional structures.
>
> (Noveck 2000: 20)

The impact of new ICTs on democracy and citizenship depends to a large extent on how governmental institutions choose to develop their online presence and set their priorities for web-based interaction. Whilst citizenship can flourish outside the institutional context, it is through institutions that government–citizen interactions are controlled and mediated by government. Governmental actors both initiate interactions and configure the channels through which citizens can contact government. As governments develop publicly available websites they must make a choice about which aspects of these interactions to move online, and decide how far the opportunities presented by technology should reshape the *content* of these interactions as well as their form. The extent to which technology will be democratising in its potential will depend in large part on the willingness of governments to act as leader and facilitator of expanded democratic participation.

In developing an online presence, governments choose whether to move their offline functions online, or to transform those functions to take full advantage of the opportunities presented by new technologies. Such a choice must take into account the three primary mechanisms through which governments interact with citizens: the provision of public services, the provision of information and consultation on policy. Government must decide how to move these three processes online and which of them to prioritise in developing online operability. This choice has implications for citizenship and democracy because these processes impact differently on the experience of citizenship. Service provision involves a bilateral transaction between government and user, often with little user-control over the process. The citizen as service recipient acts as a citizen-consumer, and the role is passive in the sense that service users have little scope to influence the set of choices on offer. As Gyford puts it, 'consumption is an act of receipt rather than creation' (Gyford 1991: 169). Through posting information online a government tells citizens about what it is doing, allowing users to make more informed choices about the services they use and expanding accountability. Again, however, there may be little scope for citizens to control the content and comprehensiveness of this information. Consultation is a more expansive role, in which the citizen becomes an active participant in government rather than a passive consumer. If consultation is used extensively it can mark a shift towards more participatory forms of democracy.

The range of options facing governments is shown in Table 3.1. At its least expansive, the Internet can be used as a tool to deliver government services and to process transactions, without offering any scope for enhanced participation. At this extreme lies pure representative democracy, a Schumpeterian model in which citizens are asked only to vote in periodic relations and are expected to be passive recipients of government services (Schumpeter 1965). At the other end of the scale, governments can use the interactive potential of the Internet to bring in innovative forms of deliberative democracy, allowing the citizen to participate fully in policy-making processes. This could involve a shift towards direct democracy, with representative institutions supplemented or replaced by mechanisms that allow ongoing consultation of the citizenry. In between these extremes of transactional efficiency and radical institutional transformation, lie opportunities to deepen citizen participation within the boundaries of representative democracy, through the expansion of consultation opportunities.

The sections that follow investigate where executive and legislative institutions at central level in the United States and the United Kingdom lie on this continuum and whether their position is static or moving. The chapter surveys policy statements on e-government and the content of central government websites. It discusses the extent to which governments have developed online sites with

Table 3.1 Impact of electronic government on institutions and democracy

Form of electronic government	Institutional impact	Model of democracy
		Representative
Service delivery	Executive branch coordinates online service delivery	Citizen acts as citizen-consumer; no active role between elections
Information provision	Executive and legislative branches post information online	Citizen can become more informed about government and its functions
Offline consultation moved online	Executive and legislature use Internet to facilitate and open up existing consultation mechanisms	Citizens have new channels to communicate with government, which shadow offline equivalents
Advisory online forums of citizens and policy-makers	New consultative institutions set up to advise on policy	Citizens can participate in new institutions; government controls range and impact of consultation
Decisions taken by online forums	Deliberative institutions established to supplement or replace representative institutions	Direct citizen control replaces representative democracy on some or all policy questions
		Direct

a consolidating rather than transformative effect, using technology to move their offline functions online rather than embracing a more deliberative model of democracy. It also looks at how far such outcomes conform to or conflict with governments' own policy statements on e-government.

Policy objectives

It was in the mid-1990s that central governments in the United States and the United Kingdom began to issue strategy documents as a basis for developing their online presence. Prior to this, government policies in the area of new telecommunications had focused on establishing a regulatory framework and widening access to the Internet, rather than on how the new technologies might impact upon the role of government itself. As these governments began to develop their online strategies, three trends were discernible in both countries:

- Electronic government was detached from wider telecommunications strategies and sited in an executive agency or department with a managerial rather than a business focus.
- The domain of electronic government was conceived of in functional or service delivery terms rather than in the participatory terms.
- Users of electronic government services were designated as consumers or customers, terms that were used interchangeably with that of citizen.

The movement of electronic government from the broader telecommunications arena to a managerially focused executive agency or department has been prominent in both countries. In the United Kingdom, responsibility shifted from the Department of Trade and Industry to the Cabinet Office. The first major policy statement on electronic government in the United Kingdom, the 1996 green paper *Government Direct: The Electronic Delivery of Government Services*, was issued through the Office of Public Service in the Cabinet Office. In 1998, the government established an e-Envoy's office, also within the Cabinet Office, with the remit of 'leading the drive to get the UK online'. The office now employs approximately 200 people, working on different aspects of e-government under the 'UK Online' initiative. In the United States, electronic government was positioned within the Reinventing Government agenda established by the incoming Clinton administration in 1993, and overseen by the vice president's office. Since the 2000 election, the coordination of electronic government has shifted to the Office of Management and Budget, which appointed an interagency task force in August 2001, led by an associate director for Information Technology and e-Government.

The second prominent feature to emerge regarding electronic government was an emphasis on service delivery or information provision rather than consultation or interaction. In the United Kingdom, the 1996 green paper *Government Direct: The Electronic Delivery of Government Services*, made its orientation towards service delivery evident in the title. Opportunities for citizens to use the new technologies to offer feedback to government receive scant attention. In the foreword to the document, Roger Freeman, the minister for Public Services in the Cabinet Office wrote, 'I believe that it will help to bring government closer to the individual and give citizens . . . more control over their dealings with government' (Cabinet Office 1996). Yet, as Chadwick and May point out:

> Only one sentence in the whole document (which runs to some thirty-eight pages in the downloadable version) makes direct mention of how ICTs might provide for greater citizen influence on policy-making: 'E-mail will also make it easier for people to contribute views to the policy-making process.'
>
> (Chadwick and May 2001a: 20)

In the *Modernising Government* white paper, published in March 1999, the Labour administration, newly elected in 1997, outlined its broad e-government strategy. It called for an improvement in government service delivery, and highlighted online provision as the best way to achieve this. The document emphasised the potential for information technology to 'enable government to offer services and information through new media like the Internet or interactive TV' (Cabinet Office 1999). The deadline of 2002 was set for a list of transactions that would be available online, including booking driving tests, submitting self-assessment tax returns and getting information and advice about benefits. Full electronic service provision was promised by 2008, a deadline that was later reduced to 2005. Opportunities to use the interactive potential of the new technologies to bring citizens more directly into policy-making were not covered by the document. Citizen input was limited to 'market research and user feedback', in order to 'improve the design and organisation of services and other processes, and focus them more firmly on citizens and businesses' (Cabinet Office 1999).

A more detailed strategy for 'Information Age Government' in the United Kingdom was published in spring 2000, entitled *E-Government: A Strategic Framework for Public Services in the Information Age*. It emphasised the potential of new technologies to bring about a 'transformation of the way government and citizens interact' (Cabinet Office 2000a). Again, as the title implies, the focus was on service delivery. In the foreword to the report, Cabinet Office Minister Ian McCartney said, 'We are at the start of an information revolution which is changing the way companies do business and the way citizens get many of the services and goods they need' (Cabinet Office 2000a). References to expanding consultation of citizens within the document are limited to loosely framed calls for 'greater democratic participation and openness' and a 'better informed and more participatory democracy through electronic consultation and better responses to feedback' (Cabinet Office 2000a). Strategies for achieving these goals are not discussed.

The e-Envoy's office published the UK Online's first annual report in the autumn of 2000. The document listed twenty-five aims of the UK Online strategy. Of these, fifteen related to e-commerce, aimed at facilitating business transactions online; five related to service delivery (such as moving services and procurement online); four were oriented towards improving access and skills training for net users. Only one could be categorised as relating to greater citizen involvement. This called for the government to: 'Drive forward citizen participation in democracy as part of the UK Online citizen portal' (Office of the e-Envoy 2000). Again, no details were given about how this forward momentum would be achieved.

In the United States, the service orientation has also been explicit as the government has developed its online strategy. The administration committed itself to establishing a strong online presence for government as part of the National Performance Review (NPR), set up by the new Clinton administration in March 1993. Vice President Al Gore pledged that knowledge received from the information superhighway would 'spread participatory democracy' (Davis 1999: 21). As the opportunities to harness the Internet to deliver services became apparent in the mid-1990s, online delivery became a goal of the NPR and the subsequent Reinventing Government initiative. The *Access America* report published in 1997 spoke of creating a government, 'where all Americans have the opportunity to get services electronically and where, aided by technology, the productivity of government operations will be soaring' (National Partnership for Reinventing Government 1997). Sally Katzen, the deputy director at the Office for Management and Budget – with oversight of the electronic government agenda – gave a speech in October 2000, in which she defined e-government as involving 'access to government information and services 24 hours a day, 7 days a week' (Katzen 2000).

The service orientation has continued under the Bush administration. Bush's budget proposals for 2001–2002, published in February 2001 in a document entitled, 'A Blueprint for New Beginnings', include a section on Government Reform, which outlines the next phase of e-government. The document states, 'The

President believes that providing access to information and services is only the first step in e-Government'. It goes on to discuss the need to establish 'citizen-centered' government, but the primary route through which this is to be achieved is via better user control of online services. According to the document, 'By enabling individuals to penetrate the Federal bureaucracy to access information and transact business, the Internet promises to shift power from a handful of leaders in Washington to individual citizens' (Bush 2001: section ix). The document does stress the importance of allowing citizens 'to go online and interact with their Government' (Bush 2001: section ix). However, there is no indication given of what form this interaction will take and how it will be achieved. When Bush's budget proposals were being discussed in front of the Senate Committee on Governmental Affairs, Sean O'Keefe, deputy director of the Office of Management and Budget gave the Committee more detail about the impact of e-government proposals on individual citizens, saying, 'We are focused on building easy to find one-stop-shops for citizens – creating single points of easy entry to access high quality government services' (O'Keefe 2001). The US government like its UK counterpart, envisages interaction in terms of better access to services rather than enhanced opportunities to participate in decision-making.

The third common feature of the development of government websites in the United States and the United Kingdom has been the increasing identification of users of the sites as consumers and customers, alongside, or even instead of, 'citizen'. The 1996 UK *Government Direct* green paper, states that the aim of the government's electronic strategy should be 'to make electronic direct delivery of services the preferred option for the majority of government's customers (both citizens and businesses)' (Cabinet Office 1996). In the 1999 *Modernising Government* white paper, the minister for the Cabinet Office, Jack Cunningham, calls for government to recognise that people are 'consumers as well as citizens' (Cabinet Office 1999). In the foreword to the *Information Age* strategy paper, Cabinet Office Minister Ian McCartney states, 'Information Technology is a powerful enabler but the starting point should always be to identify what the customer wants and then to look at how we use IT to identify this' (Cabinet Office 2000a).

Policy statements in the United States have also favoured consumerist language. One of the goals of the National Performance Review was to make the federal government 'customer driven', according to an executive order issued by Clinton in September 1993. The order stated, 'The standard of quality for services provided to the public shall be: "Customer service equal to the best in business"'. In the Introduction to the *Access America* report, Al Gore argued, 'Information technology (IT) was and is the great enabler for reinvention. It allows us to rethink, in fundamental ways, how people work and how we serve customers' (National Partnership for Reinventing Government 1997).

On the basis of the policy documents, it appears that governments have sought to harness the consolidating opportunities of the Internet rather than its transformative potential. Government websites are primarily expected to be mechanisms through which governments can perform their existing service-based functions rather than as an alternative channel through which government and citizen can communicate. Although consultation and participation are mentioned in several reports they receive scant attention, with little detail provided about how the Internet can be used as a medium to expand citizen consultation. In both countries there appears to be some rhetorical support for expanding consultation online, but no clear strategy or timetable outlining how this is to be achieved. There is a tension between the consumerist language of the policy documents and the accompanying claims that the Internet can be a tool for the expansion of citizenship.

Overall, therefore, these patterns of development suggest a commitment to the overall project of e-democracy on the part of the US and UK governments that is functional, at best. The orientation of the policy-makers and bureaucrats has been largely utilitarian, driven by an understanding of the technology as offering a means to do more of the same, in a quicker fashion, rather than on unleashing its inherently interactive and democratic potential.

Delivering e-government

Service delivery

Governments have invested substantial resources and political capital in expanding online service delivery. In the United Kingdom, in March 2001, the government announced that, with the aid of Microsoft, it had set up a new server designed to ensure that the 2005 target of full online service delivery would be met (Martinson 2001). Douglas Alexander, the e-commerce minister, announced in June 2001:

> The most recent survey of departments shows that for the whole of central government there are 521 services provided to the citizen or to business. Of those 218 services are enabled [online] now, 384 services will be enabled by 2002, and 517 services will be enabled by 2005.
>
> (Alexander 2001a)

The UK Online portal was launched in February 2001, allowing citizens to conduct a range of transactions online. It is now possible for citizens to apply for a passport, notify government of a change of address, fill in self-assessment tax forms, buy a TV licence and even report certain crimes to the police (Office of the e-Envoy 2001a).

In the United States, an early priority of the Clinton administration was online delivery of benefits (via the Electronic Benefits Transfer System), including social security, Medicare and Medicaid. In 1996, Clinton and Gore launched a 'Commonly Requested Services' feature on the White House home page, allowing users to access an electronic form and transmit it directly to the Social Security Administration (National Partnership for Reinventing Government 1997). In a 1999 memorandum, Clinton required that 'the heads of executive departments and agencies shall, to the maximum extent possible, make available online, by December 2000, the forms needed for the top 500 Government service used by the public' (Clinton 1999). This medium-term guarantee reinforces the commitment to full online service delivery by 2003. In January 2001, the *Access America's* e-Gov site published a statement on Electronic Government, asserting, 'Today e-gov is putting people "online, not in line" '. It claimed, 'By the end of 2000, nearly forty million Americans were doing business with government electronically. On a regular basis, people are accessing information to solve problems themselves through the Internet, via telephones, and through neighbourhood kiosks' (National Partnership for Reinventing Government 2001). A survey for Brown University published in September 2001 found that 34 per cent of federal sites offered some form of online service transaction. The most heavily used services were online tax filing and vehicle registration (West 2001). In August 2001, President Bush signalled his support for the expansion of e-government with the creation of the e-Government Task Force within the Office of Management and Budget (OMB). The associate director is charged with distributing the president's proposed $100 million e-government fund for interagency initiatives over the next three years (Office of Management and Budget 2001).

In developing their online service capabilities, central governments in the United Kingdom and the United States have sought to organise services around user need, rather than mirroring the organisational structures of government. UK Online, for example, aims to 'pull together packages of information and services focused around those experiences from the citizen's point of view'. For people moving house, for example, 'there's a life event that leads to sites with information about house prices, to local schools and transport and the government's pilot change of address service which streamlines the process of telling key departments when you've moved' (Cabinet Office 2000b). According to Cabinet Office Minister Ian McCartney, 'In time the portal will help revolutionise the relationship between government and citizens by turning public services inside out. Instead of being organised around government bureaucracy, they'll be organised for the citizen's convenience' (Cabinet Office 2000b). In the United States, the *Access America* report called for the integration of services across different federal agencies so citizens can 'custom-tailor' government to their specific need, developing websites such as 'Access America for Students' and 'Access America for Seniors' (National Partnership for Reinventing Government 2001).

In the area of service delivery, both governments have made substantial progress in moving their capabilities online. Future plans include greater customisation of sites and the extension of online transactions. The drive to customise services is attributed, in both countries, to a claim that users will expect government sites to match the scope for customisation and responsiveness that is delivered by non-governmental sites. In launching the Electronic Government Act 2001, for example, US Senator Joe Lieberman stated, 'The people are demanding the same 24-7 access to government information and services now available to them from the private sector online' (Lieberman 2001). Jack Cunningham, minister for the Cabinet Office in the United Kingdom, in the introduction to the *Modernising Government* white paper, argued, 'We need to make sure that government services are brought forward using the best and most modern techniques, to match the best of the private sector . . . especially electronic information-age services' (Cabinet Office 1999: 5). People's experiences as consumers are assumed to shape their expectations as citizens.

Information provision

Service delivery is the responsibility of the executive branch of government, and hence its online expansion has been spearheaded by the executive, whereas the provision of information online has been shared between executive and legislative branches.

Executive branch

It is now possible to find an extremely wide range of information on departmental and agency sites – ranging from the full text of government bills to local road traffic information. In the United Kingdom in 1994, as government departments began to establish their own websites, the 'open.gov' portal was established, which aimed to create a single point of entry for people who wanted access to government information. By December 1994 open.gov was receiving 35,000 hits a week; by August 1999 this had increased to over 14 million per week. The site has been criticised for its non-intuitive name, and an unwieldy search engine, but it does provide an organisational index of all public bodies on the Internet, a topic index, a list of what's new on government sites and links to other government portals. In summer 2001 open.gov was consolidated with the UK Online site to create one central portal.

The National Audit Office's *Government on the Web* report, published in December 1999, surveyed the information facilities provided by UK government websites. It found that almost 90 per cent included a statement of current activities; 67 per cent included a 'what's new' section; 60 per cent contained a mission statement; and 56 per cent included a list of basic responsibilities (National Audit Office 1999). Three-fifths of sites included a designated contact route, but often this was by fax or telephone rather than email. Over a fifth of sites included details of how citizens could complain or appeal against decisions. The report found, however, that 'Features that allow more extended interactive communication of information with citizens are still weakly developed in public agency sites. Only one in six sites allowed any forms to be downloaded by users, and only one in eight allowed users to submit forms to the agency online. Chat rooms or forums for outsiders to discuss issues were provided by less than a tenth of sites' (National Audit Office 1999).

Beyond the provision of departmental information, the UK Online site operates a daily news service. The *Sunday Times* likened this news component to the government printing its own newspaper – something last done during the general strike of 1926 – and alleged that civil servants have dubbed UK Online 'Pravda.com' (Carr-Brown 2001). Applicants for editorial positions on the site were told that they will 'work with No 10 on developing the presentation strategy of cross-government news' (Carr-Brown 2001). The news service presents information in a format very similar to that used on the BBC website, creating an impression of impartiality, although the site does little more than reproduce departmental press releases.

Like its UK equivalent, the US government's portal provides access to a high volume of information. Via the 'Firstgov.gov' portal it becomes possible to navigate through the fragmented federal bureaucracy, with organisational charts providing an indication of the structure of the government, including the proliferation of agencies attached to it (Firstgov 2001). The site links to 30 million pages of information, services and online transactions. Most divisions within agencies and departments maintain their own website; the Department of Defence alone has 3,000 websites with about 1.5 million pages (National Audit Office 1999). There are links to Congress, the judiciary and state and local governments. A link entitled 'Doing Business with Government' takes the browser to a list of the online transactions for citizens, including filing a tax return and reserving campsites at a national park. The Brown University study found that 80 per cent of federal sites incorporated a search engine and 41 per cent allowed interested browsers to register for email updates about changes to the site (West 2001).

Agency sites in the United States provide a range of information, which Davis categorises under four headings: mission description (i.e. general statement of what the agency does); mission activity (ongoing updated information about activities of the agency); consumer information (details of specific services agency provides); and interactivity (links allowing citizens to interact with agency staff). Davis points out that it is the last element – the interactivity – that is usually missing:

> Nearly every site volunteers agency e-mail addresses or, in many cases, even displays forms that users can complete to transmit e-mail messages... Citizens are given the impression that they are important to the agency's mission. But that interactivity has not been used to affect the agency's decision-making process.
>
> (Davis 1999: 138)

These findings closely match those of the National Audit Office's content analysis of UK websites, discussed earlier. Davis is highly critical of the quality and content of information carried online in the United States. He argues,

> Each level or branch of government, or individual agency or member office, is using the Internet to fulfil the same functions carried on offline – primarily touting the accomplishments of the office or individual, and/or soliciting public support for policies. All of these activities are carried out at the taxpayer's expense. The Internet thus is a public relations rather than a public participation tool.
>
> (Davis 1999: 146–7)

Legislative branch

Government information in the United States and the United Kingdom is also provided on sites managed by the legislative branch of government. The parliamentary website in the United Kingdom includes the full text of parliamentary proceedings, with an online version of Hansard. The site also publishes parliamentary bills and votes, details of issues under investigation by select committees and their reports and library research papers. The search engine is cumbersome, however, and the site is difficult to navigate for those who are not familiar with parliamentary structures and procedures. These shortcomings have been recognised by site designers and a redesign to make it more user-friendly began in summer 2002.

Congressional sites offer much the same information, but it is presented in a more user-friendly format. As in the United Kingdom, full transcripts of floor proceedings are available, along with roll call votes and the text of committee hearings. Via the 'Thomas' search facility, operated by the Library of Congress, browsers are able to view online versions of the *Congressional Record*, read historical documents such as *The Federalist Papers* and get a tutorial on how Congress works. The extensive search facilities ensure, as Owen *et al.* point out, that, 'Today, any user can check the status of any bill or amendment – a capability formerly held only by lobbying firms and interest groups' (Owen *et al.* 1999: 13).

Consultation

Executive branch

In both the United States and the United Kingdom, consultation on policy questions is routinely practiced by executive agencies and departments, allowing experts and interested parties to give detailed feedback on proposals between elections. Governments are usually keen to involve those groups whose compliance is required for policy enforcement, and to take the temperature of public responses to proposed legislation. In moving their consultation functions online, governments have been faced with a choice between maintaining offline consultation, moving existing forms of consultation online or developing new forms of consultation.

In the United Kindom, the first e-envoy Alex Allan, appeared to show a keen awareness of the consultative potential of the Internet, arguing:

> It is in the promotion of online consultations and forums that the Internet offers truly novel means of communication. A means of communication where messages and themes can emerge in ways that may not be expected, as the participants bounce ideas off each other.
>
> (Allan 2000)

In developing web-based consultation processes, the executive branch of government in the United Kingdom has, however, tended to move existing procedures online, rather than to use the interactive potential of the Internet to design innovative consultation. In 1996 government departments began to post consultative information on the web, supplementing offline information provision. Early in 1996, a joint Department of Health/Welsh Office consultation on the Mental Health Act 1983 Revised Code of Practice was uploaded onto the web in a zipped file. The site was not highly publicised, however, and the information was accessible only to those who were capable of unzipping a file. Submissions to the consulting department could only be done by conventional mail (Finney 1999: 363).

More interactive forms of consultation began to be introduced towards the end of 1996. In November of that year the government's Advisory Committee on Genetic Testing (ACGT) posted its draft code of practice on over-the-counter devices for genetic testing (such as commercially available tests for cystic fibrosis) on the web along with a discussion forum. Interested parties could participate either by joining the discussion forum or by making a written submission. Participation rates were low, which probably reflects the narrow and specialised subject matter and the limited publicity given to the consultation. Only twenty responses were posted on the discussion forum (Finney 1999). The interactive features of the Internet were utilised more fully in December 1997, when the Home Office in association with the independent, non-partisan public online forum UK Citizens Online Democracy, consulted over the government's *Right to Know* (Freedom of Information) white paper. The online consultation was well publicised in offline media and ran in parallel with a traditional printed consultation. Background resources were provided on the site, and respondents were given a range of ways to submit their views. One hundred and sixty nine submissions were made online (Finney 1999: 371).

In both consultations, the sponsoring agency or department had agreed to include submissions made via the electronic discussion forum in its analysis of the consultation results. Yet, in the case of the ACGT, when the Committee Secretariat published its summary of consultation responses in January 1997, submissions made within the discussion forum were not included. Finney concludes: 'there was no indication that submissions made solely on the website ... were ever formally considered in the final code of practice' (Finney 1999: 370). The outcome of the Freedom of Information consultation was also disappointing. Stephen Coleman, director of the e-democracy programme at the Hansard Society, describes his frustration with the outcomes of what he describes as a 'model consultation':

> This was exactly how a consultation should work. Lots of people came on ... something like 80 per cent of people who came on to the site had never submitted anything previously to government before. What happened at the end of the consultation? The white paper was withdrawn, the legislation didn't go through. And when the freedom of information bill came back it was in a spirit completely opposed to anything the consultation had suggested.
>
> (Coleman 2000)

In both these cases there was no discernible impact on the outcome of the consultation. It is unclear, however, whether this arose from a lack of commitment to the online consultation exercise within the sponsoring department/committee, or whether it reflected hostility to the findings of the consultation.

The next stage in the development of online consultation came in 1998, when departments began to make consultation materials available on their websites and to provide email addresses to enable respondents to give electronic feedback. This process became standardised when the UK Online site went live in December 2000. The site includes a 'Citizen Space' portal, which offers users the opportunity to participate in online policy discussion forums and to view ongoing departmental consultations. The discussion forums are well used, containing over 30,000 postings on issues from sport to food safety. A commitment is given by administrators of the forum that a summary of the discussions will be sent to the prime minister, although one interviewee described this – off the record – as 'nonsense'.[2]

In addition to the more generalised discussion forum, visitors to the Citizen's Space portal are provided with a register of all ongoing departmental consultations, with hyperlinks to relevant consultation documents and an email feedback procedure. The register shows whether the consultation is currently open, pending or closed, whether consultation results are posted and whether a discussion forum is linked to the consultation.[3] Of the consultations, less than 1 per cent provided a discussion forum, where citizens could browse the submissions made by other visitors to the site, and contribute to the discussion. In all other cases the only opportunity to participate was through sending an email to the consulting department. Of the closed consultations, approximately one-quarter provided results, but in most cases these results only summarised the submissions to the consultation process rather than explaining how submissions fitted into the decision-making process. This is despite a promise made on the site that, 'you will be able to read a summary of the views expressed and the reasons for the decisions taken' (UK Online 2001).

The UK Online register offers an efficient gateway into e-consultation through the provision of a central portal. By limiting responses to email submissions, however, it fails to develop the full interactive potential of the net. There is little scope for respondents to exchange views between themselves or with public officials. The absence of feedback about the impact of email submissions on departmental decision-making makes it difficult to estimate the effect on legislative outcomes. These findings run counter to the pledges given in the government's new code of practice for written consultation in November 2000 (including Internet-based consultations), which emphasised the need for accessibility, adequately lengthy consultation processes and feedback on consultation responses (Cabinet Office 2000c). All departments were expected to work to these standards from January 2001. An insight into the government's view of online consultation was given during the pilot stage of UK Online where it was stated, 'The responses are weighted according to who has sent them in. This means that the views of the organisations and experts, who have been invited to respond, count for more than the view of other organisations and people'.[4] This revealing paragraph appears not to share the faith in public participation expressed by the 6th Report of the Neill Committee on Standards in Public Life, which emphasised that 'Without the consultation of a wide cross-section of the public the openness and accountability of Government can be impaired' (Neill Committee on Standards in Public Life 2000). The paragraph was removed from the UK Online site when it was officially launched two months later in mid-February.

There are some suggestions that the UK Online site will be developed to allow greater interactivity in the future. Early in 2001, a Policy and Best Practice team was established within the office of the e-Envoy, which refers to itself as the 'e-Democracy team' although not formally designated as such. Ways to expand and redevelop the Citizen Space element of UK Online are being explored within that brief. The e-Commerce minister, Douglas Alexander, gave a speech in October 2001 in which he called for the Internet to be used to broaden and deepen democratic participation, and stressed the potential for new technology to establish a new relationship between government and citizens. He said:

> We must open up new democratic channels, through which government and representatives can relate to citizens. We must make citizens feel democratically empowered beyond their few seconds in the polling booth. I believe that it is now time to set all this activity into a clear policy framework and put e-democracy on the information age agenda. Government should set out what it means by e-democracy and how it intends to use the power of technology to strengthen democracy.
>
> (Alexander 2001b)

The speech coincided with a new campaign to publicise the UK Online initiative. Yet, the campaign itself offers no new ways to interact with government, and indeed is designed to offer 'an integrated consumer focused publicity campaign' (Department for Trade and Industry 2001). Alexander's speech was, however, heralded by Steven Clift as 'a completely new phase in the evolution of thought about government's democratic role in the information age' (Clift 2001a).[5] It was supplemented by the appointment of a ministerial committee, chaired by the leader of the House of Commons, Robin Cook, which has been asked to 'consider ways of strengthening the democratic process by engaging the public and their elected representatives through the use of the internet and other electronic means'. Alongside a study of the viability of e-voting, the committee will look at 'the use of new technologies to give citizens enhanced opportunities to participate in the democratic process between elections' (Leslie 2001). This is the first time that a national government has established a Cabinet-level committee on e-democracy. Until ministers earmark funds and set a timetable for developing the consultative aspects of the Internet, however, their level of commitment will remain unclear.

The US central government currently lags behind the United Kingdom in its use of net-based consultations, perhaps surprisingly given the advanced broadband technology and the high penetration rates of the Internet in the United States. As yet, however, there has been little evidence of a centrally coordinated strategy to mobilise citizens through online consultation. The Brown University survey found that 86 per cent of federal sites offered email links, and 19 per cent allowed browsers to post comments on message boards or discussion forums. However, actual interactivity was limited (West 2001). The Firstgov portal does not offer the register of consultations that is provided by UK Online. Feedback is limited to comments on service provision; links to consultations are absent. A survey of the 131 feedback links offered by agencies listed on the Firstgov site on 7 December 2001 found that 82 per cent of the links offered only contact information, allowing users to communicate with the relevant agency by email, telephone or post. The remaining 18 per cent invited feedback on specific issues (such as the experience of visiting a national park), provided a complaint form, invited the reporting of problems or crimes or asked for responses to an online survey (Firstgov 2001). None of the links connected the user to legislative consultation. According to Steven Clift of the Minnesota-based Democracies Online website, 'When you compare the availability of online interactivity from the US government with the UK, the lack of US government interest stands out. There is no real chance to be an e-citizen on the government's online turf here, for now we can only participate in commercial and non-profit online spaces' (Clift 2001c).

In part the absence of interactivity may reflect the structure of US government. Government departments do not have the jurisdictions of their UK counterparts, and most legislative initiatives are drafted at state level or in Congress. Agencies or departments are more likely to consult on a new regulation than a major piece of legislation. Despite these limitations, Americans utilise national government websites more heavily than state or local websites, signalling that such sites represent an important point of contact. A survey for the Council for Excellence in Government found that 54 per cent of Internet users had visited federal government websites, whereas 45 per cent and 36 per cent had visited state and local government websites respectively (Council for Excellence in Government 2001: 9).[6] If people are going to be brought into consultation exercises, particularly where the issues are of national significance, federal government sites can reach a wide sample of the American population.

An indication of the potential public interest in online consultation can be seen in the first such exercise undertaken by a federal agency, which attracted widespread public participation. In 1997, the US Department of Agriculture (USDA) initiated an electronic consultation process following the publication of a proposed standard on the marketing of organic agricultural products. The government's online journal *Govexec.com* described it as, 'the first fully electronic rule-making for a major regulation in federal history' (Shulman 2000). It attracted considerable media attention. According to Shulman, 'Following publication of the proposed rule over the Internet, the USDA received over 275,000 public comments by e-mail, www, fax and postal mail'. Indications are that it did lead to a change of policy on the part of the Department of Agriculture. At the end of the initial consultation process in May 1998, Agriculture Secretary Dan Glickman announced that 'fundamental' changes would be made in the proposed rule, promising, 'If organic farmers and consumers reject our national standards we have failed' (Shulman 2000: 4). The revised code of practice that emerged in March 2000 was very different in tone from the original draft consultation, which had been heavily weighted towards the interests of food producers rather than consumers. Dr Margaret Mellon of the Union of Concerned Scientists, a persistent critic of the USDA's original proposal, expressed her support for the new rule, arguing that it 'could turn out to be the most important rule the USDA has issued in 20 years' (Shulman 2000: 4).

Following the USDA experiment in electronic consultation in December 1999, the Clinton administration issued a memorandum that underscored the importance of upgrading 'the capacity of regulatory agencies for using the Internet to become more open, efficient and responsive' (Clinton 1999). Each agency head was required to 'permit greater access to its officials by creating a public electronic mail address through which citizens can contact the agency with questions, comments or concerns' (Clinton 1999). However, there was no requirement that agencies use the Internet to extend their formal offline consultation procedures.

Since that date a number of agencies have held online discussions. The Environmental Protection Agency (EPA), for example, held a consultation on how to improve public involvement in EPA decision-making. This process involved over 500 individuals, including citizens, representatives of industry, environmental groups, small business, states, local governments, tribes and other groups. Participants could discuss the draft Public Involvement Policy and offer suggestions on how EPA should implement it (Environmental Protection Agency 2001). The Welfare to Work agency within the Department of Labour published a new regulation in March 2001, and allowed browsers to submit comments online using a standard form. However, neither of these consultations is clearly linked from the Firstgov portal; neither are they signposted on the home page of their respective departments. This suggests that people have to know what they are looking for and be familiar with the site design if they are able to participate in online consultation, making it hard to engage the wider, non-expert community in the process. The lack of a central register of consultation on the US federal government site means that consultation exercises must get media attention if they are to ensure high levels of participation. The USDA participation on organic food was successful in securing this level of publicity, probably due to the wider media debate on organic and genetically modified food. Less media-friendly subjects are not likely to be adequately publicised without strong government backing.

As in the UK, there have been recent moves in the US to emphasise the democratising potential of new technologies. Mark Forman, the associate director of the Office of Management and Budget for information technology and e-government, speaking at the Council for Excellence in Government's Imagine E-Government Awards ceremony in July 2001 said:

> The next step in electronic government will be to transform it into an 'e-democracy,' in which the public uses the Web to get direct access to the government ... The Internet allows communication between communities and

the government on a larger scale than has ever been possible. Communication is really the heart of e-government – communication between citizens and the government.

(Vasishtha 2001)

As in the United Kingdom, however, tangible policy commitments on defining and expanding 'e-democracy' have not thus far been forthcoming.

Legislative branch

Legislatures in both the United States and the United Kingdom act as arenas for public consultation over legislation, supplementing the consultation undertaken by the executive branch. In both countries, web-based interaction between citizens and their representatives is possible both through members' own Internet sites and through initiatives undertaken by legislative committees. In the United Kingdom, around one-fifth of MPs have their own websites, although a survey rated those that did exist very poorly – branding them 'inept', 'flaccid' and 'bland' (Steinberg 2000). All MPs now have publicly available email addresses, but the fear of overload has made most MPs very circumspect in their usage, and until constituency screening processes are in place they will probably continue to be so (Coleman 2001: 8).

The expansion of consultation at parliamentary level has been spearheaded by parliamentary select committees, a number of which have piloted e-consultation projects in collaboration with the Hansard Society on issues ranging from domestic violence to data protection.[7] Unlike executive-based consultations, which are formally open to all, the Society-run consultations have followed the 'expert witness' tradition of select committee hearings. A data protection consultation, for example, was held in 1998 in collaboration with the Parliamentary Office of Science and Technology (POST), and was limited to invited participants from the data protection field, including lawyers, IT specialists and people involved in privacy legislation in other countries. Similarly, in October 1999, the Hansard Society again worked with POST to coordinate a consultation with scientists and engineers as part of the House of Lords Science and Technology Committee Inquiry into Women in Science. According to Coleman:

> When we started talking to parliamentary committees about running consultation over the internet, the assumption that we had was that if the consultations are going to result in real evidence for committees the only way we can produce that evidence is by thinking very carefully about how we get people to deliberate and who we invite to do that. So the first thing we did was rule out opening a website and say to everyone and anyone come on and speak, because you can extend democracy without opening things up to everyone. And if you can extend democracy in this way the question is who needs to be involved, who currently is not being heard, how do you help them have their say in a useful way.
>
> (Coleman 2000)

Sometimes the closed aspect of the online consultation proved a necessity given the sensitive nature of the material discussed. The initiative on domestic violence in spring 2000 run by the Hansard Society on behalf of the All Party Parliamentary Group on Domestic Violence was limited to female victims of domestic violence. Participants were identified via the Women's Aid organisation, and then provided with a special password and PC access. Security and anonymity were essential given that most participants were living in refuges and needed to protect their identity and location. MPs from the Domestic Violence Group logged onto the website periodically to follow the online debate, a factor Coleman believes encouraged participation: 'We asked people why they participated and whether they felt more motivated to participate in the domestic violence consultation because they were speaking to parliamentarians. And they said yes, no doubt whatsoever' (Coleman 2000). The Hansard Society has also run a consultation in conjunction with the Social Security Select Committee on tax credits, and assisted the House of Lords Select Committee on Stem Cell Research with an online consultation forum. Stephen Coleman, project director, predicts that such consultations will in the near future become a standard part of committee hearings (Coleman 2000).

The extent to which these legislative consultations have an impact on outcomes is difficult to assess given that select committees and parliamentary groups are charged with making recommendations and scrutinising departmental actions, rather than making policy. Coleman acknowledges that the findings of the Women in Science consultation did not match the needs of the sponsoring committee, and so was not effective. The data protection consultation took place at a late stage in the policy process, with respondents being asked to comment on an existing code of practice rather than being brought in at the design stage, which led to criticisms from some participants about the consultation's effectiveness (Parliamentary Office of Science and Technology 1998). Following the domestic violence consultation, Margaret Moran (chair of the All-Party Group) requested government action to improve the protection of children in situations of domestic violence in a Commons statement in June 2000 (Moran 2000). The Children Act sub-committee of the Lord Chancellor's advisory board on family law agreed to take into account the findings of the consultation when looking at proposed change to the act (Kennedy 2000). The findings of the tax credits and stem cell consultations were formally presented to the select committees involved, but appeared designed to enhance the committee members' understanding of the issues rather than to feed directly into legal changes.

In the United States, in contrast to the UK experience, all members of Congress have their own professionally designed site, with biographical details and links to committee and floor activity. From each member's website, a centrally administered link generates a form through which browsers can send an email to a chosen Senator or Congressman. Both Congress and Parliament face the common problem of how to process the number of emails received by members. In the United States, this was estimated by the Congress Online Project to be 48 million in 2000, and growing by an average of 1 million messages per month (Congress Online Project 2001).

As in the United Kingdom, it is at the level of committee hearings that online consultation has been introduced into the legislative process in the United States. Given the size and dispersion of the US population and the traditionally open nature of the committee system to outside interests, one might expect the idea of Internet-based submissions and discussion to be well advanced. However, as is the case with the executive branch of government, the US legislature has not shown the willingness of its British counterpart to experiment with online consultation procedures. The first Congressional online consultation was launched in May 2001 by Senators Fred Thompson and Joseph Lieberman, respectively the chairman and ranking member of the Senate Governmental Affairs Committee, which aimed to 'improve the access of the American people to their government'. The website invites comment on 'ways to advance the cause of digital government, to promote innovative uses of information technology and to expand citizen participation in government' (Lieberman 2000). Browsers can view fifty-nine proposals for the expansion of e-government, and offer comments on linked discussion forums. In a survey of the site on 7 December 2001, it was found that 445 comments had been posted. The most popular topic, accounting for almost a quarter (23 per cent) of total responses, was that of 'citizen's access', in which respondents were asked whether there should be more citizen access to government officials and activities. The vast majority – perhaps unsurprisingly – called for greater citizen involvement in decision-making.

All proposals on the site are exploratory rather than tied into specific legislation so it is not possible to review the impact of the site on legislative reform at this stage. At the same time as the site was launched, an Electronic Government bill was introduced into the Senate. Its expressed aims are 'To establish measures that require using Internet-based information technology to enhance citizen access to Government information and services, improve Government efficiency and reduce Government operating costs, and increase opportunities for citizen participation in Government' (Electronic Government Act 2001). The participative element of the bill refers to expanded access to information, which is a narrow interpretation of participation. The launch of the website on Electronic Government *after* the bill had been drafted is, perhaps, an indication of the extent to which consultation is as yet peripheral to the policy-making process.

Conclusion

The experience of electronic government in the United Kingdom and the United States is one of limited ambition and mixed achievement. The policy documents issued by both governments display a pronounced lack of radicalism. In both countries, electronic government has primarily been conceived as a way to expand the provision of services and information. Consultation and participation are discussed as general goals but little detail is provided about how the Internet can be used as a medium to expand citizen consultation. Where greater interactivity is proposed it often refers to better access to services rather than enhanced opportunities to participate in decision-making. Policy-framers reserve their detailed commitments for service delivery, whilst the expansion of citizen involvement remains a vague aspiration. Policy documents juxtapose the language of the service consumer with that of the participatory citizen, but indicate that it is the consumer's demand for online services that will be satisfied before any participatory yearnings of the citizen.

The practice of e-government largely reflects these policy objectives. In developing their websites, governments have shown a focused approach to online service provision and a more tentative attitude to online consultation. In the area of service delivery, both US and UK governments have made substantial progress in moving their capabilities online and have established deadlines for full online service provision – although it may be that as the deadlines approach the definition of 'full' starts to be refined.

The provision of online information is also an area where governments have made substantial progress. It is possible for citizens to become much better informed about government, its organisation and outputs, than was the case before the development of the Internet. Documents that previously were available only in public libraries, if at all, can now be downloaded directly to the user's PC. The provision of information is a key tool in ensuring government transparency and equipping interested citizens to challenge decision-makers, and its expansion constitutes an important step towards improving government accountability.

Progress in the development of online consultation has been tangible, if slow. In both the United States and the United Kingdom, offline consultation exercises now have an online component, with interested parties able to read and respond to policy documents online. Legislators in both countries have established mechanisms to allow online submissions to committee hearings. The appointment of a ministerial committee on electronic democracy in the United Kingdom, and signals from the US Office of Management and Budget that 'e-democracy' represents the next step in electronic government, may signal a new interest in using the Internet as a tool for consultation and interaction.

If the records of these governments are judged on their own terms they can be declared a cautious success. There are some areas in which the government has failed to match its own commitments, however. The information provided has tended to be promotional rather than discursive, and has been oriented towards enhancing service usage rather than consultation. For online information to be useful to the citizens it has to be logically organised and available via an effective search engine, and this is not yet the case across government. Many sites expect browsers to have extensive knowledge of internal government organisation to access relevant data.

The expansion of online consultation has been limited by inadequate feedback mechanisms. Interactive sites where users can discuss documents with other browsers or government officials are less common than those that simply post information in a downloadable format. Often the only response a citizen can give is via an email link, which disappears into the ether leaving the citizen unclear about how far their views will be taken into account by policy-makers. The UK Online site has expressed a commitment to improving feedback mechanisms but more efforts need to be made to uphold and widen this commitment.

There are clear similarities but also important differences between the countries in their implementation of e-government. The US government, especially at congressional level, offers a wider range of information online with more user-friendly portals and search engines than its UK counterpart. The more extensive Freedom of Information laws in the United States create a legal presumption in favour of disclosure, which may support a different attitude towards information provision than in the United Kingdom. The incoming Freedom of Information law in the United Kingdom may create pressures to expand the information provided online, although the law equips ministers with a range of tools to block exposure. Online consultation is better developed in the United Kingdom than in the United States, with the UK Online's consultation register providing an entry point into consultative processes, which is missing in the United States.

From the normative perspective, neither the policy nor the practice of e-government has matched the radical transformative effects envisaged by the technological utopians. In both countries, central governments have failed to develop any really extensive and influential mechanism of citizen input via the Internet. Online interactivity is not yet a standard element of consultation exercises at executive or legislative level. The provision of email addresses has made one-way communication easier, but has served as a complement to traditional written submissions rather than signifying a shift to a quicker and more interactive style of operation. Very few consultation exercises offer interactivity between citizen and state, in which MPs, bureaucrats or government ministers provide feedback to consultation respondents. Neither has there been any evident terminal erosion of governmental bodies as a result of harnessing the new technology. From the perspective of the models of adaptation outlined in the introduction to this volume, therefore, it would not seem that any one has been followed religiously. The basic fabric of the state is very much intact and it does not appear that the arrival of new ICTs has raised any serious questions about its continuing relevance. Neither has there been a vigorous embracing of the possibilities presented for deepening and widening citizen participation, in any practical sense. At best one can say that a strategy of limited utilitarian reforms has been engaged in, with parliament and the executive branch focusing on accessibility to information and service provision.

The lack of radical transformation should not come as too much of a surprise, however. As the social shaping logic would dictate, existing institutions have little incentive to render themselves obsolete, and are much more likely to adapt new technologies to existing practices than to allow technology to shape practice. It is clear that in neither the United States nor the United Kingdom has the government moved to the extreme of direct democracy highlighted in Table 3.1. The findings discussed in this chapter suggest that governments are positioned midway along the scale. They have made a commitment to full online service delivery; a large amount of information is now online; many of the offline consultation processes have some online component. Electronic government has not moved beyond this point, however, to stimulate institutional innovation or democratic transformation. In this sense, governments' online presence mirrors its offline role in maintaining a form of representative democracy that provides limited opportunities for citizens to make representations to government. It has not propelled governments in the direction of more direct forms of democracy.

There are some indications that governments in both countries may now be giving greater consideration to the democratising potential of the Internet, and repositioning their e-government strategies to encourage greater citizen participation. If online consultation does develop it could have important consequences not only for the government–citizen relationship, but also for the balance of power between institutions. Direct consultation of citizens can be a resource for the executive branch of government, used to sideline the representative claims of the legislature by giving the executive an independent channel to public opinion. In this scenario, consultation could contribute to existing trends for the executive to accrue power at the expense of the legislature. Alternatively, if legislative bodies are innovative in their use of consultation at committee stage this may strengthen pre-legislative scrutiny of bills and be a tool in the armoury of legislators. In Britain, particularly, where parliamentary scrutiny of bills has tended to be a formality in the past, the willingness of committees to be experimental in the use of online consultation may signal a new assertiveness.

If governments do move in this direction, it will be a slow and incremental shift. Surrendering their own control over policy-making is unlikely to be a priority for politicians. Recent interest in expanding citizen involvement may reflect a desire to maintain governments' relevance, in an age when declining turnout and new forms of Internet-based campaigning are threatening to sideline mainstream politics. If governments feel that they must harness new forms of participation to maintain their own legitimacy, the emphasis of electronic government may shift slightly towards consultation and involvement. Without these incentives, it is likely that the government will engage in dialogue with the citizen-consumer, but leave the active citizen silenced.

Notes

1 'Electronic' (or 'e-') is used in preference to the many alternative prefixes – digital, virtual, cyber – as this term has become the most widely used by governments themselves and in analyses of online activity. The term government, as used here, refers to both executive and legislative institutions, except where otherwise specified.

2 Interview conducted 21 November 2000.

3 On a visit to the site on 6 November 2001, there were 451 consultations listed, 61 of which were open.

4 This was downloaded from <http://www.ukonline.gov.uk/online/citizenspace/consultation/default.asp> on 14 February 2001, but has now been removed from the site.

5 Clift was a founder of the Minnesota E-democracy programme in 1994. The programme aimed to provide political information and online discussion forums for local users. It is now widely held to be one of the most successful local electronic democracy initiatives. See <http://www.e-democracy.org>

6 The Council for Excellence in Government is a non-partisan, non-profit organisation undertaking research to further the goal of better government performance. The fieldwork for the survey was done during 14–16 August 2000 by the research firms of

Peter D. Hart and Robert M. Teeter. It was a three-part study that included surveys of: 150 government officials; 155 business and non-profit leaders; and 1,003 members of the general public. The margin of error for the survey is +/− 4 per cent.

7 The Hansard Society for Parliamentary Government is an independent non-partisan educational charity, whose president is the Speaker of the House of Commons. See <http://www.hansard-society.org.uk>

Bibliography

Alexander, C. and Pal, L. (eds) (1998) *Digital Democracy*, Oxford: Oxford University Press.

Alexander, D. (2001a) Interview, *Guardian Unlimited*, 22 June <http://www.guardian.co.uk/Archive/Article/0,4273,4208681,00.html>, accessed on 8 October 2001.

Alexander, D. (2001b) Speech to Conference on Democracy in the Information Age, 25 October <http://www.dti.gov.uk/ministers/speeches/alexander251001.html>, first accessed 11 November 2001.

Allan, A. (2000) 'E-democracy', Lecture to the Hansard Society, 22 May.

Barber, B. (1999) 'Three Scenarios for the Future of Technology and Strong Democracy', *Political Science Quarterly*, 113, 573–90.

Blair, T. (2000) 'Foreword: Draft Code on Written Consultation', London: Cabinet Office, 12 April.

Bush, G. (2001) *A Blueprint for New Beginnings* <http://www.whitehouse.gov/news/usbudget/blueprint/budix.html>, first accessed 7 December 2001.

Cabinet Office (1996) *Government Direct: The Electronic Delivery of Government Services*, London: HMSO, <http://www.citu.gov.uk/greenpaper.htm>, first accessed 12 January 2001.

Cabinet Office (1999) *Modernising Government*, Cm 4310, London: HMSO <http://citu.gov.uk/moderngov/whitepaper/4310.htm>, first accessed 10 November 2000.

Cabinet Office (2000a) *E-Government* <http://www.iagchampions.gov.uk/iagc/strategy.htm>, first accessed 12 January 2001.

Cabinet Office (2000b) 'UK Online Citizen Portal Goes Live', Press Release, 4 December.

Cabinet Office (2000c) 'New Approach to Public Consultation Will Give People Bigger Say in Government – Mowlam', Press Release, 27 November.

Cabinet Office (2000d) 'Code of Practice on Written Consultation', 27 November <http://www.cabinet-office.gov.uk/servicefirst/index/consultation.htm>, first accessed 12 February 2001.

Carr-Brown, J. (2001) 'No 10 Spins Its Own News on "Pravda.com"', *Sunday Times*, 18 February.

Chadwick, A. and May, C. (2001a) 'Interaction Between States and Citizens in the Age of the Internet', paper presented to the American Political Science Association, San Francisco, August, <http://pro.harvard.edu/abstracts/040/040004ChadwickAn.htm>, first accessed 16 September 2001.

Chadwick, A. and May, C. (2001b) 'Interaction Between States and Citizens in the Age of the Internet', paper presented to the European Consortium of Political Research Joint Workshops, Grenoble, April, <www.essex.ac.uk/ecpr/jointsessions/grenoble/papers/ws3/chadwick_may.pdf>, first accessed 21 March 2001.

Clift, S. (2001a) 'UK Government's Major E-Democracy Push', Online. Email: clift@ publicus.net (26 October).

Clift, S. (2001b) 'UK Gov E-Democracy Efforts – Ministerial Committee on E-Democracy', Online. Email: clift@publicus.net (5 December).

Clift, S. (2001c) 'Engaging Citizens in Policy-Making', Online. Email: clift@publicus.net (19 February).

Clinton, W. (1999) 'Memorandum for the Heads of Executive Departments and Agencies', 17 December <http://ec.fed.gov/wh_egov.htm>, first accessed 12 February 2001.

Coleman, S. (1999) 'Cutting Out the Middle-Man: From Virtual Representation to Direct Deliberation', in Hague, B. and Loader, B. (eds), *Digital Democracy*, London: Routledge.

Coleman, S. (2000) Director of Studies, Hansard Society, Interview with the author, 21 November.

Coleman, S. (2001) *Democracy Online*, London: Hansard Society, <http://www.hansard-society.org.uk/MPWEB.pdf>, first accessed 30 October 2001.

Coleman, S. and Normann, E. (2000) *New Media and Social Inclusion*, London: Hansard Society.

Congress Online Project (2001) 'E-mail overload in Congress' <http://www.congressonlineproject.org/email.html>, first accessed 6 November 2001.

Council for Excellence in Government (2001) *E-Government: The Next American Revolution* <http://www.excelgov.org/>, first accessed 16 March 2001.

Cunningham, J. (1999) 'Introduction', *Modernising Government*, London: HMSO.

Davis, R. (1999) *The Web of Politics*, New York: Oxford University Press.

Deloitte Consulting and Deloitte & Touche (2000) *At the Dawn of E-Government* <http://www.us.deloitte.com/PUB/egovt/egovt.htm>, first accessed 12 February 2001.

Department for Trade and Industry (2001) 'Alexander: Opportunities for Democracy in the Information Age', News Release, 25 October <http://www.nds.coi.gov.uk/coi/coipress.nsf/2b45e1e3ffe090ac802567350059d840/eca70dbb4d8645f380256af00037cba1?OpenDocument>, first accessed 7 December 2001.

Electronic Government Act 2001 (2001) <http://lieberman.senate.gov/newsite/egov.pdf>, first accessed 6 November 2001.

Elshtain, J. (1982) 'Democracy and the QUBE Tube', *The Nation*, 7–14 August.

Environmental Protection Agency (2001) 'Public Involvement in EPA decisions' <http://www.network-democracy.org/epa-pip/>, first accessed 6 November 2001.

Finney, C. (1999) 'Extending Public Consultation via the Internet', *Science and Public Policy*, 26(5), 361–73.

Firstgov (2001) 'Firstgov: Your First Click to the US Government' <http://www.firstgov.gov/>, first accessed 7 December 2001.

Grossman, L. (1995) *The Electronic Republic*, New York: Viking.

Gyford, J. (1991) *Citizens, Consumers and Councils*, London: Macmillan.

Hagen, M. (1997) 'A Typology of Electronic Democracy' <www.uni-giessen.de/fb03/vinci/labore/netz/hag_en.htm>, first accessed 8 October 2001.

Hague, B. and Loader, B. (eds) (1999) *Digital Democracy*, London: Routledge.

Hill, K. and Hughes, J. (1998) *Cyberpolitics*, Lanham, Md: Rowman and Littlefield.

Katzen, S. (2000) Testimony to the Committee on Government Reform, Subcommittee on Government Management, Information and Technology, US House of Representatives, 11 October, <http://www.whitehouse.gov/omb/legislative/testimony/october_2_2000.html>, first accessed 7 December 2001.

Kennedy, Jane (2000) Parliamentary Secretary – Lord Chancellor's Department, *Hansard*, 7 June: Column 113WH, <http://www.parliament.the-stationery-office.co.uk/>, first accessed 15 March 2001.

Leslie, C. (2001) *Hansard*, 29 November: Column 353WH, <http://www.publications.parliament.uk/pa/cm200102/cmhansrd/cm011129/halltext/11129h01.htm#11129h01_spmin0>, first accessed 12 December 2001.

Lieberman, J. (2000) 'E-Government Project Launched to Improve Citizen Access to Government', News Release, 18 May, <http://www.senate.gov/~lieberman/press/00/05/051800a.html>, first accessed 16 August 2001.

Lieberman, J. (2001) 'Electronic Government Act of 2001', News Release, 1 May, <http://www.senate.gov/~lieberman/press/01/05/2001501810.html>, first accessed 16 August 2001.

Lieberman, J. and Thompson, F. (2000) 'E-Government' <http://www.senate.gov/~gov_affairs/egov/index.cfm>, first accessed 16 August 2001.

Livesey, P. (2001) Assistant Director, E-Government Policy & Best Practice Team, Interview with the author, 23 February.

Malina, A. (1999) 'Perspectives on Citizen Democratisation and Alienation in the Virtual Public Sphere', in Hague, B. and Loader, B. (eds), *Digital Democracy*, London: Routledge.

Margolis, M. and Resnick, D. (2000) *Politics as Usual*, Thousand Oaks, CA: Sage.

Martinson, J. (2001) 'Microsoft Comes to Aid of e-Envoy', *Guardian*, 27 March.

Moran, Margaret (2000) *Hansard*, 7 June: Column 112WH, <http://www.parliament.the-stationery-office.co.uk/>, first accessed 15 March 2001.

National Audit Office (1999) *Government on the Web*, London: HMSO.

National Partnership for Reinventing Government (1997) 'Introduction by Al Gore', *Access America Initiatives* <http://www.accessamerica.gov/docs/intro.html>, first accessed 12 February 2001.

National Partnership for Reinventing Government (2001) 'Electronic Government' <http://govinfo.library.unt.edu/npr/initiati/it/>, first accessed 12 February 2001.

Neill Committee on Standards in Public Life (2000) *Sixth Report* <http://www.official-documents.co.uk/document/cm45/4557/4557.htm>, first accessed 15 March 2001.

Norris, P. and Jones, D. (1998) 'Virtual Democracy', *The Harvard International Journal of Press and Politics*, 3(3), 1–4.

Noveck, B. (2000) 'Paradoxical partners', *Democratization*, Spring, 7(1), 18–35.

O'Keefe, S. (2001) Testimony to the Senate Committee on Governmental Affairs, 11 July <http://www.whitehouse.gov/omb/legislative/testimony/20010710-1.html>, first accessed 7 December 2001.

Office of the e-Envoy, Cabinet Office (2000) *UK Online Annual Report*, London: HMSO, <http://www.e-envoy.gov.uk/2000/progress/anrep1/text/default.htm>, first accessed 6 April 2001.

Office of the e-Envoy, Cabinet Office (2001a) 'Things You Can Now Do Online' <http://www.e-envoy.gov.uk/online_now.htm>, first accessed 7 December 2001.

Office of the e-Envoy, Cabinet Office (2001b) 'E-Communications Group' <http://www.e-envoy.gov.uk/ecomms_index.htm>, first accessed 14 October 2001.

Office of Management and Budget (2001) 'Mark Forman Named Associate Director for Information Technology and E-Government', News Release, 14 June, <http://www.whitehouse.gov/omb/pubpress/2001-13.html>, first accessed 7 December 2001.

Owen, D., Davis, R. and Strickler, V. (1999) 'Congress and the Internet', *Harvard International Journal of Press and Politics*, 4(2), 10–29.

Parliamentary Office of Science and Technology (1998) 'E-1, December 1998, Data Protection – On-line Discussion', December <http://www.parliament.uk/post/report.htm>, 12 February 2001.

Schumpeter, J. (1965) *Capitalism, Socialism and Democracy*, London: Allen & Unwin.

Scobbie, Moira (2000) 'Responses to Digital Scotland Task Force Report', June <www.scotland.gov.uk/digitalscotland/responses/moiras.pdf>, first accessed 12 February 2001.

Shulman, S. (2000) 'Citizen Agenda-Setting, Digital Government and the National Organic Program', paper presented to the American Political Science Association, Washington, DC, August.

Silcock, R. (2001) 'What is E-Government?', *Parliamentary Affairs*, 54, 88–101.

Smart, V. (2001) 'The Shambles of E-Whitehall', *Guardian*, 16 August.

Steinberg, T. (2000) 'Parliamentary IT briefing', *Institute for Economic Affairs*, November.

Stringer, G. (2001) 'Putting Government Online, Bring Citizens Online', Speech to the Global Forum conference, Naples, Italy, 15 March.

Ten Downing Street Press Office (2001) 'Opportunities for Democracy in the Information Age', Press Release, 25 October, <http://www.number-10.gov.uk/news.asp?NewsId=2840&SectionId=30>, first accessed 6 November 2001.

UK Online (2000) 'Future Plans' <http://www.ukonline.gov.uk/futureplans/>, first accessed 15 February 2001.

UK Online (2001) 'How Government Consults' <http://www.ukonline.gov.uk/online/citizenspace/default.asp?url=/online/citizenspace/consultation/how_govt_consults.asp>, first accessed 14 October 2001.

Vasishtha, P. (2001) 'Citizen Communication Will Nourish e-gov', *Government Computer News*, 30 July 2001, 20, 21 <http://www.gcn.com/vol20_no21/news/4755-1.html>, first accessed 7 December 2001.

Waller, P., Livesey, P. and Edin, K. (2001) 'E-Government in the Service of Democracy', *International Council for Information Technology in Government Administration*, 74, June <www.ieg.ibm.com/thought_leadership/issue74-waller.pdf>, first accessed 10 October 2001.

West, D. (2001) 'E-Government and the Transformation of Public Service Delivery', paper presented to the American Political Science Association, San Francisco, August, <http://pro.harvard.edu/papers/024/024007WestDarrel.pdf>, first accessed 16 September 2001.

White, M. (2000) 'Blair Sets Earlier Target Date for Online Whitehall', *Guardian*, 31 March.

4 Digital parliaments and electronic democracy

A comparison between the US House,
the Swedish Riksdag and
the German Bundestag[1]

Thomas Zittel

Parliaments on the net

As in many areas of social life, computer networks along with other kinds of new digital information and communication technology have entered the parliamentary sphere. This is the conclusion of a volume edited by Stephen Coleman, John Taylor and Wim van de Donk, which collects in-depth case studies on the digitalization of modern parliaments such as the British House of Commons, the Danish Folketinget and the Australian Parliament (Coleman *et al.* 1999). A comparative survey on new information technology among members of eleven legislative assemblies provides further comparative evidence on this trend towards digital parliaments. The respondents to this survey report the general availability of personal computers as well as widespread access to the Internet across all cases.[2] Intranets, videoconferencing technology, mobile phones and notebooks belong to the standard equipment of most of the respondents to this survey. These kinds of empirical data stress the efforts that have been made on the part of legislative assemblies to catch up with the most recent developments in telecommunication technology.

To many students of media and political communication the proliferation of computer networks heralds the coming of an electronic democracy, which opens up new avenues for political participation. According to former chairman of NBC Lawrence Grossman, a new political system is already taking shape in the United States. He argues that new digital media are turning America into an electronic republic, which vastly increases the people's day-to-day influence on political decisions (Grossman 1995: 3). Journalist Wayne Rash concludes his empirical study on digital politics in the United States with the observation that the Net is already giving voters a voice that reaches directly to the highest levels of government (Rash 1997: 181).

From a theoretical point of view, these so called 'cyberoptimists' point towards the vast technological potential of the Internet for decentralized and interactive mass communication. They subscribe to the notion of technological determinism that assumes a causal relationship between major technological breakthroughs such as computer networks on the one hand and social structure on the other.

According to this perspective, the social diffusion of new digital media will trigger far-reaching social change in almost automatic ways (Toffler 1980; Naisbitt 1982; Street 1992: chapter 2; Hoff 2000). From an empirical point of view, cyberoptimists emphasize new strategies of digitalized political communication in the parliamentary realm to argue their case.

Parliamentary websites are one of the most visible indicators for these changing strategies in political communication. In her book, Pippa Norris reviews on the Digital Divide the whole universe of parliamentary websites around the world. Her numbers indicate that legislative Websites have become a universal trend throughout Scandinavia, North America and western Europe with the exception of Cyprus (Norris 2001: 132–3). A count by the Inter-Parliamentary Union found out that 87 per cent of all national parliaments in Europe have established a presence on the web by April 2000 (Inter-Parliamentary Union 2000). A variety of case studies offer more in-depth analyses on the history and the content of particular parliamentary websites. Some of these studies emphasize the fact that these digital publications have been launched during the mid-1990s in an attempt to increase the transparency of the parliamentary process and to exploit new opportunities for interactive communication. To achieve this goal, legislative websites allow among others easy access to the full text of plenary transcripts and to information on the progress of legislation. Interactive elements such as email addresses or discussion fora are designed to foster interactive communication with citizens (Casey 1996; Coleman *et al.* 1999; Fühles-Ubach and Neumann 1999; Mambrey *et al.* 1999; Coleman 2000).

In contrast to cyberoptimism, some students of electronic democracy are sceptical regarding the significance of digital parliaments for democratic government and political participation. These so called 'cybersceptics' claim that digitalized political institutions do not live up to the standard of electronic democracy and thus represent examples of technological modernization rather than political transformation. A substantial number of students of digital parliaments, for example, voices concern about the suboptimal uses of the Internet in many parliaments that have been subject to research (Coleman *et al.* 1999: 369–70). According to Michael Margolis and David Resnick, legislative websites can be expected to reinforce support for the dominant political attitudes and established political parties rather than to transform current systems of interest representation (Margolis and Resnick 2000: 93–4). While cyberscepticism should be applauded to reintroduce a more realistic tone to the debate on electronic democracy, it nevertheless shares two important shortcomings with its counterpart.

First, many empirical studies on electronic democracy raise the question of relevance. They suffer from a lack of political theory in failing to define and explain a standard or a theoretical frame that could be used to identify relevant empirical phenomena from the perspective of democratic theory. Most of these studies take conceptual shortcuts by drawing far-reaching conclusions on democracy that are based upon the analysis of political communication. These analyses take strategies of political communication and the implementation of interactive mass communication on the Net as a vantage point to evaluate progress towards electronic democracy. However, while the use of new technological opportunities for the purpose of political communication is an important prerequisite of political impact, it is not a sufficient one. In this chapter we argue that we have to take the procedural and structural implications of a specific act of political communication into account in order to be able to draw conclusions regarding its larger impact on democracy. We thus need a standard that identifies relevant acts of digital communication from the perspective of democratic theory. This standard has to be based upon technology as well as upon structural and procedural considerations.

A second shortcoming concerns the lack of general evidence regarding the impact of new digital media such as computer networks on democracy. Most of the available empirical analyses are impressionistic or in a case study format. The explorative nature of most of these case studies and the lack of a common relevant theoretical focus does not allow for cumulative knowledge and for general conclusions regarding the impact of new digital media on democracy (Lijphart 1971; Peters 1998: chapter 6). In order to produce more general conclusions on this question, we need more case studies based upon a relevant common theoretical frame. A second strategy of empirical research on electronic democracy should be based upon the comparative method in order to unveil the current political ramifications of new digital media in general and to understand the impact of digital parliaments in particular.

This chapter touches upon both problems to shed light on the political ramifications of digital parliaments. It will proceed in three distinct steps: In a first step, it will sketch an ideal model of electronic democracy. The aim is to define a meaningful standard that takes into account the procedural and structural dimension of politics in order to assess the relevance of digital parliaments for democracy. In a second empirical section, we will analyze different digital parliaments on the basis of this model in order to test the two hypotheses sketched here. In this empirical section we compare the US House, the German Bundestag and the Swedish Riksdag. This empirical analysis draws from a quantitative content analysis of personal websites in these three parliaments and from qualitative case studies on institutional reform in digital parliaments. A third section takes the result of this analysis as a vantage point to reconsider the link between technological change in telecommunications and political change and to speculate about prerequisites of electronic democracy beyond technological change in telecommunication.

The rational for the selection of our cases is based upon the magnitude of technological change in telecommunication. Each of the three parliaments in our sample experienced change in telecommunication infrastructure at a similar level. The German Bundestag, for example, started in the mid-1980s to equip its members with personal computers (Lange 1988; Einemann 1991; Mambrey *et al.* 1991). By 1989, forty-seven German MPs had access to this new technology either directly in their own office or indirectly via committees or parliamentary party organization (Einemann 1991: 11–14). Today, almost every single workplace in the German parliament is equipped with state-of-the-art desktops, which run on the basis of the most recent software. Along with this proliferation of personal computers, the Bundestag built up a powerful network infrastructure. In 1995, when the World Wide Web (WWW) took off, only very few members had access via modems and commercial online-providers, sometimes at their own expenses. With the move to Berlin, the Bundestag implemented a Local Area Network that connects all computers internally as well as externally.

A quite similar development took place in the Swedish Riksdag. According to a Swedish MP, thirty years ago, his predecessors were restricted to only two telephone booths in the lobby to enter into contact with the media or their constituents (Gylling 2000). Today, there are mobile phones, fax machines and personal computers all around the place. The number of personal computers in parliamentary buildings increased, for example, from 10 in 1987 to 1,800 in October 2000.[3] Moreover, an increasing number of Swedish members use portable notebook computers to connect via a 128 Kbit line to a Local Area Network with a 100 Mbit Backbone and a 2 Mbit connection to the Internet. A mobile videoconferencing system with cameras, screens and a sound system that can be used at various studios within the buildings of the Riksdag supplements this new communication infrastructure in the Swedish Riksdag (Ulfhielm 1998).

Similar developments in the US House are summarized by a story published in the *Washington Times* in 1999. This story reported the tremendous investments made over a time span of five years to equip the US House with the most recent communications technology. In the course of these efforts, the US House provided congressmen and their staffers with new personal computers and software, renovated congressional office buildings with new fibre optic cables and provided at least one T1 Internet connection line to each office with an access rate of 1.5 million bits per second (Archibald 1999; see also Casey 1996). Apart from internal technological change, each of the three parliaments we selected experienced far-reaching external technological change in telecommunication as well. In Sweden, Germany and the United States significant numbers of the population own personal computers and have access to the Internet. According to survey research, by early 2000, almost half of the population in the United States and Sweden was online while in Germany, about 20 per cent of the population had access to the Internet at this point in time (NUA 2001).

In this chapter we ask whether our three digital parliaments use the Internet along the lines of our model of electronic democracy or rather whether these three digitalized legislative assemblies are falling behind this standard. While the first observation would support the claim of cyberoptimists, the second finding would stress the cybersceptics point of view. Our comparative design furthermore allows testing for differences between the three cases under study regarding the implementation of electronic democracy in the process of technological change. This outcome would point towards the impact of intervening contextual variables.

What is electronic democracy?

The term democracy has been linked to many adjectives during the course of its history: direct democracy, representative democracy or parliamentary democracy are some of the most widely known combinations. The term electronic democracy marks a more recent version. Adjectives are analytical tools to empirical theorists of democracy to specify and clarify this very broad concept. They are a means to characterize specific forms of democracy and to distinguish between different basic types of this form of government (Collier and Levitsky 1997). This observation raises questions regarding the meaning of electronic democracy and the specific form of democracy it signifies.

In the debate on electronic democracy this term is frequently used as a catchall concept. It combines different empirical phenomena such as the websites of political parties or parliaments, electronically mediated debates on political topics, community networks, electronic voting or even the provision of administrative services via new digital media (Leggewie and Maar 1998; Kamps 1999). We argue that this type of usage is too unspecific and not suited to foster a clear understanding of electronic democracy. More important, its most serious shortcoming lies in the tendency to take conceptual shortcuts by drawing conclusions on democracy on the basis of the study of political communication and communication technology. This general usage of the term ignores the fact that democracy cannot be reduced to communication but rather that it is also about institutions. A definition of electronic democracy has to take these defining elements of democracy into account.

There have been some efforts to conceptualize electronic democracy in a more explicit and comprehensive manner (see e.g. Arterton 1987; Hagen 1997; Bellamy 2000). These mainly theoretical undertakings chose to model this concept in terms of a real type on the basis of empirical developments and discourses regarding the use of new digital media in the political realm. While these analyses give way to a more sophisticated understanding of the phenomenon at hand, they still suffer from major shortcomings. We argue that at this early stage of technological developments one cannot assume to capture relevant phenomena with this kind of method. Real types simply do not provide analytical lenses that are sharp enough to distinguish the relevant from the irrelevant and to detect small and so far hardly visible trends in the transformation of democracy. As a consequence, most of the available models of electronic democracy are somewhat fuzzy and hardly able to give us a clear idea what electronic democracy is all about and how to distinguish it from other types of democracy. They also do not put their finger on the general problem of conceptual shortcuts in the debate on electronic democracy. Most theoretical models of electronic democracy are therefore ill-suited to guide systematic empirical research on the political impact of new digital media.

In contrast to these earlier theoretical analyses we model electronic democracy as an ideal type that is based upon basic ideas of democracy and is structured along three different levels of political analysis. By using this method, we aim to forego the problem of conceptual shortcuts and to sharpen our analytical lenses in the study of electronic democracy. We define electronic democracy, as outlined in Figure 4.1, as a three-layered concept that emphasizes political participation as a core value in the process of decision-making (conception of democracy),

	Participatory democracy		Liberal democracy
Conception of democracy	• Individual as part of the political community		• Antagonism between individual and political community
Democratic design	• Direct democracy via electronic means • Direct, participatory system of representation via electronic means • Foster civil society via new media	⟺	• Strictly representative system • Indirect system of representation • Protect private sphere
Participatory behaviour	• Taking decisions via electronic means • Deliberate via electronic means to prepare political decisions • Getting political information via electronic means to learn about political decisions and decision-making process		• Voting

Figure 4.1 Electronic democracy: a three-layered concept.

sketches three different strategies for institutional/structural reform to make democracy more participatory via new digital media (democratic design) and aims at influencing individual behaviour by increasing all types of political participation via the use of new digital media (participatory behaviour).

This definition marks a sharp distinction between political communication on the one hand and electronic democracy on the other. At the level of participatory behaviour, it excludes individual acts of digital communication that are not aimed at influencing political decision-making such as exchanging ideas in a USENET group or retrieving information on community services (see e.g. Barnes *et al.* 1979: 42). At the level of democratic design our model emphasizes the need for digitalized communication and interaction to be integrated into the decision-making process in order to count as an element of electronic democracy. We do not consider acts of digitalized public relations such as discussion fora run by the parliamentary bureaucracy as an element of electronic democracy per se.

Our definition of electronic democracy also makes a strong statement regarding our third level, which focuses on different conceptions of democracy. At this level, we do not consider electronic democracy as a distinct type of democracy. We argue instead that most of the discourse on electronic democracy closely resembles the debate on participatory democracy and that electronic democracy rather becomes a distinct phenomenon at the other two levels of our model.

Conceptions of democracy focus on the level of ideas and primarily ask about the nature of citizenship (Rawls 1971). At this most general level, we distinguish between two basic ideas (conceptions) of democracy: participatory and liberal democracy. Participatory democracy perceives the self as part of the political community. It therefore strives to involve individuals as much as possible into the political process. From this point of view, democracy becomes a way of life (Pateman 1970; Barber 1984; Fishkin 1991; Habermas 1992). This perspective is in stark contrast to a liberal conception of democracy, which perceives individuals as autonomous entities independent from the political community and which assumes a basic antagonism between individuals and their social environment. Individuals are perceived as consumers and private beings who do not care much about political involvement, who develop interests apart from the political community and who are sometimes in conflict with the political community. Liberal theory emphasizes the legitimacy of these interests and aims at protecting the private lives of citizens. From this point of view, democracy merely becomes a process of collective decision-making (Schumpeter 1950; Sartori 1987).

The liberal conception of democracy is considered the dominant paradigm of modern democracy. It owes part of this dominance to the problems of its counterpart to design a participatory scheme of democracy under conditions of the modern nation state. Theorists of participatory democracy are ardent critics of the liberal model. They perceive liberal democracy as 'thin democracy' that threatens the stability of democracy, creates negative policies and leads individuals to live isolated and estranged lives. But a community of millions of citizens and an area of hundreds of thousands of square miles silenced many protagonists of participatory democracy when it came to questions of designing participatory democracy in terms of specific political institutions (Schmidt 2000: 175).

This is where electronic democracy comes in. Electronic democracy shares with the participatory model its general conception of democracy. Its goal is to make democracy more participatory, to involve citizens more into the political process and to strengthen political community (Hagen 1997; Kleinsteuber and Hagen 1998). Theorists of electronic democracy perceive new digital media as means to implement their ideal under the conditions of the nation state and to overcome most of the technical obstacles to participatory democracy (Krauch 1971; Etzioni *et al.* 1975; Becker 1981; Slaton 1992). This definition provides a standard at the level of ideas and motivations to evaluate current developments regarding the use of new digital media in general and regarding digital parliaments in particular. We should assume that digital parliaments matter to democracy in cases where this kind of motivation prevails among political actors.

Apart from this macro-analytical perspective, most critics of participatory democracy focus on the micro-analytical level while arguing against this conception of democracy. They emphasize low rates of political participation and the lack of political interest among ordinary citizens as an indicator that speaks against the feasibility of participatory democracy (Berelson *et al.* 1954; Campbell *et al.* 1960). According to these critics, individuals have more important things in their mind than politics, and voting should be considered the only type of political participation citizens might be able to squeeze into their busy schedules. As a reaction to these claims, early theorists of electronic democracy stressed digital media as a tool to foster various types of individual participation beyond voting such as retrieving political information to learn about political decisions, entering into political debates to deliberate political decisions and registering political opinions on policy issues (Krauch 1971; Etzioni *et al.* 1975; Becker 1981; Slaton 1992).

These theorists used the vehicle of experiments in order to demonstrate that citizens are ready to take advantage of new digital means of political participation. This was the conclusion German teledemocrat Helmut Krauch drew from an early project he organized in cooperation with German TV in 1971. In this experiment on teledemocracy, a representative panel of citizens was given the opportunity to follow a televised debate on problems of environmental protection and to register opinions on several questions that were raised in the course of this debate via a digital phone system. The votes were registered by a mainframe computer, electronically processed and turned into graphs, which were immediately displayed to the discussants (Krauch 1971). American teledemocrats Ted Becker and Christa Slaton used digital phone lines in 1981 to poll citizens in New Zealand in order to involve the public in long-range strategic political planning (Becker 1981; Ryan and Becker 1983). According to Becker, New Zealanders were excited about the new participatory tools and took to teledemocracy like birds to trees. As a consequence, Becker perceives advances in interactive cable TV and in home computer systems as prerequisites for a bright future in political participation (Becker 1981: 8).

Political Philosopher Amitai Etzioni took a different path towards electronic democracy by emphasizing deliberation in his experiments with telecommunications media. In the mid-1970s he and his collaborators organized a series of telephone conferences to study this medium as a means to foster political dialogue. The purpose of this experiment was to demonstrate that '[…] the technological means exist through which millions of people can enter into dialogue with one another and with their representatives and can form the authentic consensus essential for democracy'. Etzioni concluded his studies with the observation that phone conferences are well suited to increase the quantity as well as the quality of political participation (Etzioni *et al.* 1975).

These kinds of experiments were designed to demonstrate the interest of ordinary citizens in digital political participation beyond voting. They suggest another standard to evaluate the impact of new digital media in general and digital parliaments in particular. On the basis of this standard we have to ask whether citizens are using parliamentary websites to retrieve information on the parliamentary process or whether they take advantage of interactive features to communicate with the parliamentary sphere. This understanding of electronic democracy is focused on the behavioural level of political analysis.

Original theorists of participatory democracy argue for a close link between participatory behaviour and participatory institutions or designs. Unfortunately, students of electronic democracy have been much less specific regarding this third element of electronic democracy. There has been little interest to link the idea of participatory democracy via digital means to specific institutional designs. Having reviewed the literature on electronic democracy we have to conclude that current concepts of electronic democracy are under-complex in institutional terms – to say the least. However, the discourse on electronic democracy as well as available models of electronic democracy include general considerations that are pointing towards three broad strategies of democratic design via new digital media.

The first two strategies are only of passing interest in the context of our argument. The first argues that new electronic media should be used to implement measures of direct democracy such as electronic referenda or initiatives (Budge 1996). This perspective does not advocate to completely abolish representative types of democracy and to shift from a representative mode towards a direct mode of decision-making. It only proposes to take some decisions by means of direct democracy while others should be taken by elected representatives. In recent years there have been several experiments and pilot projects that aim to solve not only technological problems related to electronic referenda but which also aim to answer questions regarding necessary procedural and structural problems in the process of implementation (Muralt Müller 2000; Buchstein 2001; Mutter 2002).

The second strategy of democratic design via new digital media highlights cyberspace as a new type of public space, which could be organized as an autonomous self-regulatory social sphere. Theorists of cyberdemocracy assume that this new type of social sphere will strengthen civic engagement and social cooperation (Rheingold 1993; Schuler 1996; Katz 1997). There are no elaborate institutional designs available so far to put more flesh on this general concept of cyberdemocracy as a means for democratic decision-making. However, some students of the Internet point towards the history and the organization of the Internet as an example for a self-regulatory and decentralized political sphere based upon new digital media (Hofmann 1998). From this perspective, the Internet ought to be free from any type of state intervention and state regulation in order to be able to emerge as a new type of civil space.

A third strategy of institutional reform is most consequential for our initial question regarding the relevance of digital parliaments for democracy. It stresses the function of political representation as the main target of political reform. It advocates a shift from an indirect system of interest representation towards a direct and participatory system of political representation. The current system of political representation stresses intermediate organizations such as political parties, interest groups or mass media as major linkages between citizens and the state. Political parties are of crucial importance in this current system of interest representation. Modern democratic theory perceives political parties as mass organizations that mobilize citizens, aggregate and articulate political interests and link these interests to the decision-making process. Elections are in the core of this process. Parties compete in political elections on the basis of manifestos, the party who wins a majority forms a government and implements its manifesto. It is crucial to this system that parties impose a rigid discipline on the MPs to secure the implementation of their manifesto (Katz 1987; Weber 1990; Gallagher *et al.* 2001).

This current system of interest representation has been criticized for its trend towards oligarchy (Michels 1911), for being systematically selective regarding the type of social interest that could gain representation (Schattschneider 1975) and for being biased towards a certain type of information that is being communicated particularly via the mass media (Sarcinelli 1998). According to these critics, this system of indirect representation establishes weak links between citizens and the state. Citizens remain in the role of voters who have the opportunity to decide upon government policies during subsequent elections, while many cannot gain access to crucial information, cannot take the political initiative to voice their interests or cannot influence policy-making according to their interests.

The alternative system of direct, participatory political representation is structured in very different ways. In this system, intermediary organizations such as political parties are weak and direct communication and interaction function as the main linkage between the public and the state. Theorists of electronic democracy assume that new digital media such as the Internet can be used to redesign prevailing indirect systems of interest representation and to close the gap between citizens and parliaments in twofold ways.

The first approach perceives new digital media as a way to link individual representatives closer to particular constituents (Arterton 1987; see e.g. McLean 1987; Snider 1994). According to this approach, the bandwidth and the decentralized structure of computer networks allow each individual member easy and efficient access to mass communication in order to enter into a constant dialogue with his constituents, to disseminate information on his policy views and to learn about the policy views of the constituents. Moreover, the merging of communications technology with data processing technology allows even individual MPs to constantly poll citizens on specific policy issues. The Internet thereby functions as a direct link between individual members and citizens and enables MPs to bypass traditional linkage structures such as mass media, political parties or interest groups. With this infrastructure in place, single representatives can become delegates of particular constituents (Pitkin 1967).

Another type of participatory representative system by electronic means stresses the possibility to draw citizens closer to the parliamentary process. Electronic consultations, for example, allow a more representative sample of citizens to voice their opinions on pending legislation and to deliberate with each other as well as with policy-makers in the wake of political decisions (Coleman 1999, 2000; Needham 2001). Parliaments could also decide to adjust established principles of public access to the technological potential of the Internet to open up the parliamentary process to public scrutiny and to use new digital media to publicize public information in far-reaching ways.

While both schemes of participatory political representation presuppose the implementation of new digital media technology as well as new patterns of political communication, they also stress the need for institutional and structural adjustments. The first scheme of participatory political representation presupposes a decentralized pattern of digital communication and interaction between citizens and legislative assemblies rather than a centralized one. It thus suggests strengthening the autonomy of individual MPs in relation to their party. The second scheme of interest representation via digital media suggests a close link between digital communication and the parliamentary process in institutional terms. In the context of this scheme the integration of digital communication in the decision-making process becomes a crucial question.

The following empirical analysis focuses on the US House, the German Bundestag and the Swedish Riksdag. It asks whether the technological developments in telecommunication within these digital parliaments are in line with the models of participatory representative design sketched here. In our analysis we focus on the structural level in order to evaluate the technological developments in modern parliaments and to determine whether digital parliaments matter to democracy. We neither ask about the motivation and ideas that drive the digitalization of parliaments nor do we ask whether citizens are using the new opportunities to communicate and interact with parliaments. In a first section, we focus on the media strategies of individual representatives. We ask whether individual representatives are using the Internet and whether they are using this medium in ways to enter into closer relationships with constituents. Next we focus on institutional policies and ask whether digital parliaments trigger institutional reforms that are designed to open up the parliamentary process and to allow for direct citizen participation. Due to restrictions in space, we will only be able to sketch some preliminary findings from a more comprehensive study on political representation in the networked society.

Digital parliaments and individual representatives on the net

Each of the three parliaments established a presence on the WWW between 1995 and 1996 by introducing an official parliamentary website. However, there are striking differences between these parliaments regarding the degree to which parliamentary subunits are using the WWW for external communication. This finding results from a count of all links at the main website of these three parliaments on a specific day in January 2000. This count displays a clear difference between the US House on the one hand and the German Bundestag and the Swedish Riksdag on the other hand. Figure 4.2 demonstrates that in the US House, websites are used at all parliamentary levels to almost 100 percent. Contrary to this, in the German Bundestag and the Swedish Riksdag, committees are not using websites at all and MPs are still a minority on the net. In the Swedish Riksdag, even the parliamentary party organization does not have a presence on the web. Therefore, in both European national parliaments, digital communication is much less decentralized than it is in the US House of Representatives.

Unfortunately, we do not have quantitative data on the development of personal websites in the US House, the Riksdag and the Bundestag. A comparison between the US House and the German Bundestag, which is displayed in Figure 4.3, demonstrates individual initiatives within a similar time frame in mid-1995. But while in the US House members rapidly started to use websites as a means of communication, there was much less enthusiasm in the German Bundestag until mid-1998. It was only after mid-1998 that more and more

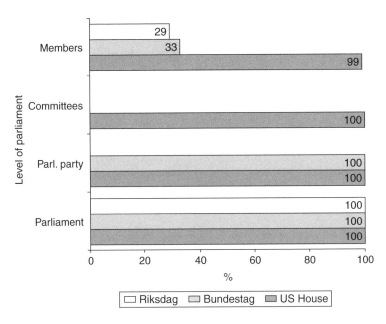

Figure 4.2 Websites per parliamentary unit in the US House, German Bundestag and Swedish Riksdag, January 2000.

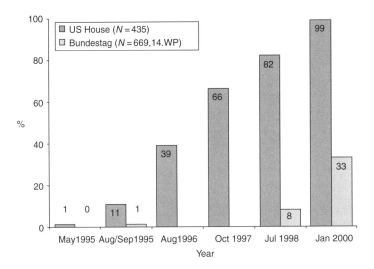

Figure 4.3 Personal websites in the US House and the German Bundestag, 1995–2000.

members of the German Bundestag were starting to use this medium. But still, in January 2000, there were considerable differences between the German Bundestag on the one hand and the US House on the other.

Apart from the act of using personal websites, the decentralization of political representation is also dependent upon the way that personal websites are being used: Do these Websites foster access to crucial information on the parliamentary process? Do they stimulate direct dialogue between MPs and citizens? Do they increase members' knowledge about the policy views of their constituents? To answer these questions, we downloaded the personal websites we have identified and performed a quantitative content analysis.

This analysis produces two main findings. First, in all three parliaments, personal websites are not used in a way to consequently implement the model of a direct, participatory system of political representation. Only a minority of members uses their websites to increase public dialogue and to learn more about the policy positions of their constituents. Furthermore, only a minority of members increases access to crucial information on the parliamentary process via their websites; second, there are important differences between the three cases under study. Members in the US House provide more access to crucial parliamentary information via their websites as well as more opportunities to register opinions than their European counterparts. Contrary to this, Swedish and German websites are aiming more towards public dialogue than the American websites. We will illustrate these general findings in greater detail in the remainder of this section.

Almost all of the websites we analyzed provide basic interactive elements such as email addresses or webmail forms. However, this kind of interactivity is of a private nature and means little progress compared to traditional forms of one-to-one communication such as constituency letters or phone calls. Discussion fora or public guestbooks are more progressive forms of public communication on the WWW because they involve representatives in public dialogues. Our analysis demonstrates that in all three parliaments, only a very small minority of members uses these kinds of applications on their websites. Apart from these similarities, there are obvious differences regarding the dominant type of interactivity between the US House on the one hand and the Swedish Riksdag as well as the German Bundestag on the other. Figure 4.4 demonstrates that compared to the US House more members use sophisticated interactive applications in the Riksdag and the Bundestag. We also observe a slightly greater interest in the use of email and webmail forms among Swedish and German MPs.

Another characteristic of a participatory and individualized scheme of representation is the congruence between the policy views of constituents and the decisions taken by their representative. This presupposes a clear understanding of the constituents' positions on specific policies on the part of the individual representative. So far, national opinion polls did not provide individual representatives with information of that nature. At best, they gave guidance to national parties and the party leadership on how their followers feel regarding crucial issues of national importance. They did not inform single representatives on how

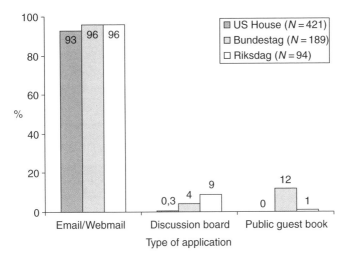

Figure 4.4 Interactivity of personal websites in the US House, German Bundestag and Swedish Riksdag, January 2000.

particular constituents think of issues they care most about. Online surveys offer an easy and very cost-efficient means to change this situation. This Internet application allows constituents to register their opinions on political issues with a single mouse click and thus enables representatives to learn about their policy views. As Figure 4.5 demonstrates, in all three parliaments only tiny minorities were using this application in January 2000 on their personal websites. But again, Figure 4.5 also demonstrates differences between these different cases. While 6 per cent of the US representatives with websites use online surveys, basically none in the two European parliaments use the surveys.

In-depth information on the parliamentary agenda and the policies that are up for decision is a crucial prerequisite for the formation of policy views. In a next step of our analysis, we asked whether personal websites in the US House, the German Bundestag and the Swedish Riksdag foster access to this type of information. A first indicator for this is the quantity of textual content on personal websites. A website with little or no textual information can hardly be regarded as a means to more relevant political information. Although a website with a lot of textual content does not guarantee access to crucial information, it increases the probability that it is serving exactly this kind of function. We calculated the quantity of textual information per single website in standard letter size to compare the member websites in the three parliaments regarding the quantity of textual information they provide. Figure 4.6 demonstrates that across all three parliaments only a minority of personal websites exploit the opportunity to provide large amounts of text. However, there are considerable differences between the US House on the one hand and the two European national parliaments on the other.

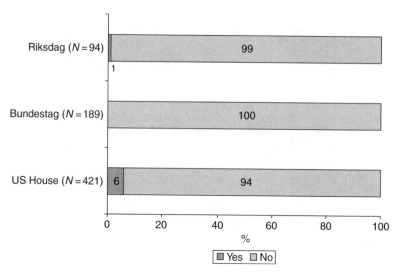

Figure 4.5 Online surveys on personal websites in the US House, German Bundestag and Swedish Riksdag, January 2000.

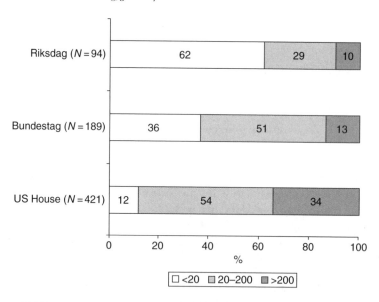

Figure 4.6 The quantity of textual information on personal websites in the US House, German Bundestag and Swedish Riksdag, January 2000.

A large majority of personal websites in the Swedish Riksdag and a significant minority in the German Bundestag fall below twenty pages of textual information. This type of digital brochure contains only a welcome page with the picture of the member, a biography and some basic information such as a postal address or his committee assignments. Contrary to this, digital brochures are less widespread in the US House of Representatives. The median is even more illuminating in this respect: it is 133 for the US House compared to 24 for the German Bundestag and 1 for the Swedish Riksdag.

A high quantity of textual information is not an equivalent for the availability of relevant political information, which helps constituents to understand the policy position of their representative and to screen his legislative behaviour. To study the quality of content, we analyzed the type of information that could be found on personal websites in the three parliaments. Figure 4.7 demonstrates again similarities and differences between the US House, the German Bundestag and the Swedish Riksdag.

Across these three parliaments, many personal websites lack crucial information on the parliamentary process. As Figure 4.7 demonstrates, press releases are the kind of information that is most likely to be found on the websites of individual representatives. The function of press releases is to provide news to the mass media in a suitable format that is short and to the point. Press releases do not aim at the ordinary citizen and do not provide comprehensive access to information on the parliamentary process. Therefore, they do not increase the transparency of the parliamentary process. This function could be performed, for example, by a comprehensive selection of issue-position papers of a member, an in-depth analysis of the issues a member cares about most and a comprehensive documentation of his legislative behaviour. As we can see in Figure 4.7, across the three parliaments under study, many personal websites lack these types of information.

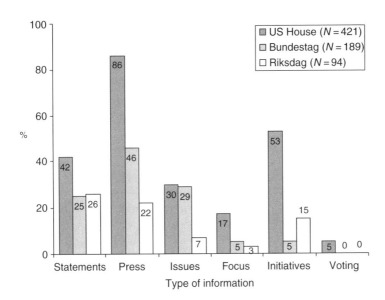

Figure 4.7 The type of information at personal websites in the US House, German Bundestag and Swedish Riksdag, January 2000.

However, besides this similarity, again there are stark differences between the US House of Representatives on the one hand and the German Bundestag and the Swedish Riksdag on the other. In each of the categories displayed in Figure 4.7, the US House is in the lead regarding the number of personal websites in line with our model of direct, participatory representation. The differences are particularly striking with regard to information on the parliamentary initiatives of single MPs.

Digital parliaments and institutional reform

Another scheme of direct, participatory representation presupposes the integration of digital communication into the decision-making process. Parliaments might decide to reconsider their policies regarding public access to parliamentary information because of new technological opportunity structures. They might also take decisions to use the Internet as a means to increase public participation in the parliamentary process. In this section we ask about debates regarding institutional reforms that aim towards this direction. The subsequent remarks will provide a very brief summary of three case studies on this topic, which cover the period until January 2000.

In the German and the Swedish cases, there has been little open debate on whether to use the Internet to make legislative assemblies more participatory. One of the main arenas regarding debates on the institutional ramifications of the Internet in the German Bundestag has been the special commission (Enquete), 'Zukunft der Medien in der Informationsgesellschaft'. This commission dealt among others with the issue of public participation via the Internet. Yet, the public hearing the commission held in September 1997 mainly focused on the local level and on administrative reform while only a few questions to the witnesses touched upon the national level and the issue of participation via electronic media. Member of the Bundestag, Michael Meister, asked a representative of the administration about the government's concept for providing legislative information on the Net (Deutscher Bundestag 1997: 50), and Social Democrat Jörg Tauss questioned Claus Leggewie, professor of political science at the University of Gießen, about the necessity of legislative initiatives (Deutscher Bundestag 1997: 63). Neither of these questions stimulated any debate on specific institutional reforms towards participatory democracy. This stresses the general point, made by one of the witnesses during the hearing, that in the German case the relationship between models of electronic democracy and existing democratic institutions is unresolved (Deutscher Bundestag 1997: 49). Models of electronic democracy have not yet been translated into specific programmes of institutional reform. At the same time, the political use of the Internet within the Bundestag has not raised open controversies on institutional issues as well.

The final report of the special commission on 'Zukunft der Medien in der Informationsgesellschaft' underscores the perception of an unresolved relationship between models of electronic democracy and existing democratic institutions. It contains a chapter on 'citizens and government' including sections on access to information and new types of participation. The latter section sketches new opportunities for political participation via the Internet such as electronic dialogues and electronic voting without relating these new technological options to existing political institutions and without raising questions regarding necessary institutional adjustments. The section on access to information simply points to existing legislative information on the Internet without raising the issue of the information's quality and quantity and without debating the types of information that could and should be published on the Internet (Deutscher Bundestag 1998: 78–9).

In the Swedish Riksdag, the new digital communications infrastructure triggered administrative policies to increase staff for parties and members. According to one high-level administrative official, the administration of the parliament assumes that the Internet will increase communication between members and citizens and that the members need help in dealing with this new situation. Apart from this, there have been two main institutional arenas where members of the Swedish Riksdag debated the institutional ramifications of the Internet. The IT group in the Swedish Riksdag consisted of one representative of each party as well as representatives of the administration of the Riksdag. Its purpose was to link parties and the administration regarding questions of communication technology. According to several participants, this group was mainly focused on the development of the technical infrastructure of the parliament and did not take up the issue of possible institutional ramifications of the new communication infrastructure. The IT group was dissolved in 2000 in the course of an administrative reform in the Riksdag.

The commission on democracy was a parliamentary commission that assembled an unusually large number of MPs under the chairmanship of a former minister of education. It was created in 1998 for a period of two years to study the current state of democracy in Sweden, to discuss means to revitalize Swedish democracy and to make proposals in this respect. In early 2000, the commission submitted a final report that emphasized the need for more public dialogue and deliberation in Swedish politics. It did acknowledge the potential of new information technology for 'widening the opportunities for citizens to participate in and influence problem formulations and discussions before decisions are made by elected assemblies' (Swedish Ministry of Justice 2000: 7). However, the commissions' report has not produced specific policy recommendations. It has been under review ('remis') during the course of the year 2000 and it will now be the task of the newly established department of democracy to come forward with specific policy recommendations. According to an official of this department, this process is in a very early stage so far. Therefore, we can conclude, that, as in the German case, there have been no specific open policy debates on more participatory schemes of representation via new digital media.

This is different in the case of the US House of Representatives. We identified several controversies indicating that House rules regulating access are in a state of flux because of the proliferation of Internet technology. These controversies touch upon two specific questions: first, should the US House change existing rules to make public documents more accessible via the Net and to increase the publicity of the process; second, should the US House change existing rules to make public information that has not been public before.

The first question touches upon the difference between the notions of 'to make public' and 'to publicize'. Many important proceedings in the US House, such as committee hearings, are public in the sense that one can attend. But they are not heavily publicized. In this case as in any other cases concerning information on the committee process, the decision on publication in printed format rests solely with each committee chair. Yet, even in cases of publication, the number of copies is limited, publication in hard copy takes up to a year and copies are not free of charge. Thus, timely and easy access, even to public documents, is heavily restricted. Parliamentary television has brought about some changes since its introduction in 1979 but the carrying capacity of C-SPAN I, which broadcasts proceedings of the US House, is limited and thus C-SPAN has to be selective, though to a lesser degree than commercial news outlets.

Then designated Speaker of the House, Newt Gingrich, touched upon this issue when he promised in November 1994 to require that 'all documents and all conference reports be filed electronically as well as in writing [...] so that information is available to every citizen in the country at the same moment that it is available to the highest paid Washington lobbyist' (Gillespie and Schellhas 1994: 188). The issue of public access to congressional documents was put on the agenda of a Task Force on Committee Review, established by the House Republican organizing conference in December 1994 with a mandate to review the committee structure of the House and make recommendations. In July 1996, the Task Force recommended changes in House Rules that would force House committees to facilitate access to a variety of specified committee documents via the Internet (US House of Representatives 1996a). Representative Rick White, a member of the Task Force, subsequently introduced legislation aimed at implementing these recommendations.[4]

These efforts went nowhere in the 104th Congress. The Resolution introduced by Representative White was referred to the House committees on Rules and Oversight. Neither committee took action, and the legislation was never brought to the floor. Subsequently, a much weaker provision was inserted in the Rules of the House at the beginning of the 105th Congress. This provision required that each committee 'shall to the maximum extent feasible, make its publication available in electronic form' (US House of Representatives 1997: 12), which still leaves much discretion to committee chairs.

The House floor became the arena where members debated the second question, whether previously non-public documents should be made public via the Internet. The focus of this debate was on material prepared by the Congressional Research Service (CRS), a congressional support agency that is part of the Library of Congress and whose mission is to provide non-partisan policy advice to members. Up to then, CRS material was only available in hard copy and in electronic form via the House Intranet to congressional staffers. Citizens could obtain material via their representative, but would not know what material was available, would have to depend on the willingness of their representative to release material on a specific question and would have to bear costs in terms of time and effort to get hold of this material. In 1998, Representative Christopher Shays and Senator John McCain simultaneously introduced a bill in the House of Representatives and the US Senate to make CRS material publicly available over the Internet on a CRS website[5] (Fasman 1998: 16; Friedly 1998; *Washington Post* 1998: A12). Both bills did not receive a necessary majority in a final floor vote.

Apart from these debates on public access, some slight attention was given to possible reforms to foster dialogue between members and their constituents. When the Subcommittee on Rules and Organization conducted a hearing in May 1996 on the possible legislative impact of new communications technologies, one of the committee's members, participated via videoconference. The option to allow MPs to participate in parliamentary proceedings via the Internet became an important subject to debate in the course of this hearing (US House of Representatives 1996b). Since then, committees have extensively used this infrastructure to ensure the participation of witnesses who could not be present or to cut down on travel costs to save the taxpayers' money. But the participation of a member via the Internet remained unique.

This technological option would allow members to spend more time in their district and to be closer to their constituents while conducting parliamentary business via the Internet. Technologically, this form of participation need not be restricted to fact-finding hearings as it was the case in the hearing on May 1996. One could also imagine representatives conducting mark up sessions or other kinds of official business via the Internet while being closer to their constituents in the district. However, this presupposes changes in House rules that demand representatives to be physically present while conducting official business. According to several staffers, these kinds of institutional changes are subject to informal considerations but they have not stimulated serious and open policy debates so far. Figure 4.8 provides a comparative summary of debates on institutional reform, which aim at a more participatory system of political representation via new digital media and which were visible in the three parliaments until early 2000.

Do digital parliaments enhance electronic democracy?

The preceding analysis reveals trends towards more participatory schemes of political representation in the process of putting parliaments on the Net. However, these trends are of a very moderate nature and hardly revolutionary in scope. While many MPs already take advantage of the Internet, their way of using personal websites is not suited to strengthen schemes of direct, individualized representation. And while we were able to identify some visible debates aimed at using the Internet to make the parliamentary process more transparent and participatory, the outcome is far from revolutionary as well.

At first glance, this conclusion supports a cybersceptic point of view that decries visions of electronic democracy as utopian driven by the enthusiasm and

	US House	Bundestag	Riksdag
	Debates in parliamentary groups	Official hearings	Floor
Poll citizens on policy issues			
Deliberate with citizens		Participation of MPs in parliamentary procedures via the Internet	
Access to parliamentary debates and information	Increase publicity of committee documents (change of house rules); make more legislative information public (debate on floor)		

Figure 4.8 Digital parliaments and institutional reform in the US House, German Bundestag and Swedish Riksdag, January 2000.

the excitement about new technologies in telecommunication. From this perspective, electronic democracy is in line with a multitude of promises and visions that were related to past technological changes in telecommunication and which never materialized in the end (Kubicek *et al.* 1997; Jarren 1998). Cybersceptics perceive digital parliaments as indicators for technological modernization rather than political transformation. However, a more cautious interpretation of our analysis suggests two important reservations regarding this line of reasoning.

First, we have to remember that the findings of our analysis are nothing more than a snapshot taken at a very early stage of a dynamic technological development. As a consequence we lower our expectations and acknowledge the significance of small effects, which might be first traces of a larger trend towards political transformation. Future progress in telecommunication technology will foster theses early initiatives during the decades to come. With universal access to the Internet, increasing bandwidth, more reliable systems of data-security and new types of hardware such as Web-TV the available digital opportunity-structure will increase in sophistication and will constantly put pressure on systems of political representation to develop into direct and participatory systems of representation. Apart from this general note of caution in response to cyber-scepticism, our analysis suggests a second important objection to both contenders in the debate on electronic democracy.

The preceding analysis emphasizes the fact that trends towards electronic democracy vary with political context. While in some circumstances, the future of electronic democracy appears to be bleak, it obviously is much brighter in other circumstances. This finding contradicts the universalism that characterizes cyberoptimism as well as cyberscepticism. It rather points towards the importance of political context in the process of political change in the networked society. Given the existence of a multitude of political environments we assume that electronic democracy will eventually flourish in many versions, different in scope and design. The crucial research question concerns the existence of systematic relationships between political context, technological change in telecommunication and electronic democracy. The variance in our comparative analysis provides the basis for *ad hoc* explanations, which could give guidance to further more systematic research on this core question in the debate on electronic democracy.

Differences between the Riksdag and the German Bundestag on the one hand and the US House on the other regarding the implementation of electronic democracy are the most visible finding of our comparative analysis. Regarding these differences we have to ask why parliaments that experience technological change at a similar level, implement this technology in different ways. *Ad hoc* speculations on this question point towards a variety of structural factors such as differences in the type of government. The Riksdag and the Bundestag are situated within a parliamentary system that does not provide many incentives and institutional capacities to individual representatives to focus on particular constituents and to structure the representative process in a participatory mode. This is due to the fact that legislative assemblies in parliamentary democracies possess the power to make and break governments. This function imposes a rigid discipline on parliamentary majorities and pushes individual representatives to focus on their party, to concentrate on internal bargaining and to structure the parliamentary process accordingly. Contrary to this, parliaments in presidential systems such as the US House do not possess this function and therefore leave individual representatives much more room to establish a closer relationship to particular constituents. The systematic difference between the US House on the one hand and the Riksdag and the Bundestag on the other could be explained along this line of reasoning. Due to the existing incentive structure, MPs within parliamentary systems should thus not be interested in direct, decentralized schemes of representation no matter what the technological opportunities are. Contrary to this, representatives within presidential systems should be much more open to direct schemes of political representation and thus to technologies that foster the implementation of such schemes.

The preceding analysis stresses that it would be a gross simplification to overemphasize a unicausal relationship between a specific institutional feature such as the type of government on the one hand and the prospects for electronic democracy on the other. The lack of interactivity on the personal websites of American MPs might indicate the impact of additional contextual features. The hesitancy of US Representatives in using discussion fora, which does not fit with the general pattern of our analysis, could reflect the strong first amendment tradition of the United States. While in Germany and Sweden, the principle of freedom of speech is balanced with the principle of fair speech, in the United States we have a clear hierarchy of values that prevents any kind of censorship, regardless of content. The rulings of the Supreme Court demonstrate this tradition in a very obvious manner. The risks of using public discussion fora can only be controlled in the American case by not using them at all. Contrary to this, in Sweden and Germany, improper contributions to public discussion fora can be censored on the basis of the principle of fair speech.

The differences between Swedish and German MPs serve as another example against the assumption of a clear unicausal relationship between a specific institutional feature on the one hand and electronic democracy on the other. German MPs are more eager to utilize the new digital opportunity structure compared to their Swedish colleagues despite the fact that Swedish as well as German MPs operate in the context of a parliamentary system. This variance might be based upon differences regarding the electoral connection. The German electoral system allows for a higher degree of personalization compared to the Swedish electoral system. Half of the German MPs are elected in single-member districts by a majority vote while the other half is elected via a party list in a proportional vote. Many of the latter were also candidates in one of the district races. Contrary to this, the Swedish electoral system is characterized by a much lower degree of personalization. It has been reformed in 1998 to give voters the opportunity to either elect a party list or a single candidate and thus increased the systems, potential for a personal vote. But according to students of Swedish electoral law, these new opportunities are not well established in the hearts and minds of Swedish voters so far (Möller 1999). In general, the Swedish electoral system is still a list-based system that emphasizes parties rather than individual candidates. On the basis of this observation one might argue that the degree of personalization of electoral systems affects the incentives among individual representatives to take advantage of the new digital opportunity structure in order to cultivate a decentralized and direct system of political representation.

By way of conclusion, we have to stress that technological modernization in general and digital parliaments in particular will not automatically push towards new forms of democracy. We rather have to emphasize the impact of political context on the future of political representation in the networked society. Contrary to cyberscepticism we perceive the glass as half full rather than half empty in this respect. While some contextual environments act as an obstacle to electronic democracy, others might also work to its advantage. It remains a crucial task to future theoretical as well as empirical research to study this interrelationship between political context, technological change and electronic democracy (Zittel 2002a,b). This type of research should be seen as a prerequisite in the attempt to understand the political significance of digital parliaments and technological modernization.

Notes

1 This essay is part of a larger study on the relationship between new digital communications media and representative government. I am indebted to many staffers and members in

the US House, the German Bundestag and the Swedish Riksdag who gave large portions of their time to support my research. I am particularly grateful to representative Johnny Gylling. I am also grateful to the Fritz-Thyssen-Foundation, which has supported, my research with a generous grant, and to the Department of Government of the University of Uppsala, which provided a hospitable research environment during my field research in Sweden.

2 This survey was taken during a two-day European conference of Members of National Parliaments on Communication Technologies, which took place in Helsinki and Tallinn on 11–12 September 2001 <www.epri.org/main/static_main_1_131_ENG.htm> June 2002.

3 Numbers compiled by the Swedish Riksdag.

4 See H.Res. 478, July 1996; Congressional Record H 7658.

5 See US House of Representatives, 105th Congress, 2nd Session, H.R. 3131; US Senate, 105th Congress, 2nd Session, S. 1578.

Bibliography

Archibald, G. (1999) 'Congress spends $ 1billion on Computers', *Washington Times*, 12 September 1999, C 1.

Arterton, C. F. (1987) *Teledemocracy*, Newbury Park: Sage.

Barber, B. (1984) *Strong Democracy*, Berkeley, Calif.: University of California Press.

Barnes, S., Kaase, M. *et al.* (1979) *Political Action*, Beverly Hills: Sage.

Becker, T. L. (1981) 'Teledemocracy', *The Futurist*, 15, 6–9.

Bellamy, C. (2000) 'Modeling Electronic Democracy', in Hoff, J., Horrocks I. and Tops, P. (eds), *Democratic Governance and New Technology*, London/New York: Routledge.

Berelson, B., Lazarsfeld, P. and McPhee, W. (1954) *Voting*, Chicago: University of Chicago Press.

Buchstein, H. (2001) 'Modernisierung der Demokratie durch E-Voting', *Leviathan*, 29 (2), 147–55.

Budge, I. (1996) *The New Challenge of Direct Democracy*, Cambridge: Polity Press.

Campbell, A., Converse, P. E., Miller, W. E. and Stokes, D. E. (1960) *The American Voter*, Chicago: University of Chicago Press.

Casey, C. (1996) *The Hill on the Net*, Boston: AP Professional.

Coleman, S. (1999) 'Cutting out the Middle Man', in Hague, B. N. and Loader, B. D. (eds), *Digital Democracy*, London/New York: Routledge.

Coleman, S. (2000) 'Parliament in the Information Age', in Gibson, R. K. and Ward, S. (eds), *Reinvigorating Democracy?* Aldershot: Ashgate.

Coleman, S., Taylor, J. and van de Donk, W. (eds) (1999) *Parliament in the Age of the Internet*, Oxford: Oxford University Press.

Collier, D. and Levitsky, S. (1997) 'Democracy with Adjectives', in *World Politics*, April, 430–51.

Deutscher Bundestag (1997) Enquete – Kommission Zukunft der Medien in Wirtschaft und Gesellschaft, Öffentliche Anhörung zum Thema 'Nutzung von Informations- und Kommunikationstechniken in der öffentlichen Verwaltung. Auswirkungen auf die staatliche Souveränität und das politische System', Wortprotokoll, 22 September 1997.

Deutscher Bundestag (1998) Enquete-Kommission 'Zukunft der Medien in Wirtschaft und Gesellschaft', *Drucksache* 13/11004, Schlussbericht, Bonn.

Einemann, E. (1991) *Computer für die Volksvertreter*, Marburg: Schüren.

Etzioni, A., Laudon, K. and Lipson, S. (1975) 'Participatory Technology', *Journal of Communication*, 25, 64–74.

Fasman, J. E. (1998) 'States Find Little Difficulty with On-Line Research', *The Hill*, 18 March, 16.

Fishkin, J. S. (1991) *Democracy and Deliberation*, New Haven/London: Yale University Press.

Friedly, J. (1998) 'Members Introduce Bills to Publicize CRS Research', *The Hill*, 4 February.

Fühles-Ubach, S. and Neumann, H.-P. (1998) 'Zwei Jahre Deutscher Bundestag im Internet', *Nachrichten für Dokumentation (NfD): Information – Wissenschaft und Praxis*, 4.

Gallagher, M., Laver, M. and Mair, P. (2001) *Representative Government in Modern Europe*, Boston, MA: McGraw Hill.

Gillespie, E. and Schellhas, B. (eds) (1994) *Contract With America*, New York, 188 (Newt Gingrich, Remarks before the Washington Research Group Symposium).

Grossman, L. K. (1995) *The Electronic Republic*, New York: Viking.

Gylling, J. (2000) 'A Swedish Perspective', in *Hansard Society E-Guide for Parliamentarians*, London: Hansard-Society.

Habermas, J. (1992) 'Drei normative Modelle der Demokratie', in Münkler, H. (ed.), *Die Chancen der Freiheit*, München: Piper.

Hagen, M. (1997) *Elektronische Demokratie*, Hamburg: Lit Verlag.

Hoff, J. (2000) 'Technology and Social Change', in Hoff, J., Horrocks, I. and Tops, P. (eds), *Democratic Governance and New Technology*, London: Routledge.

Hofmann, J. (1998) 'Am Herz der Dinge – Regierungsmacht im Internet', in Gellner, W. and von Korff, F. (eds), *Demokratie und Internet*, Baden-Baden: Nomos.

Inter-Parliamentary Union (2000) 'Guidelines for the Content and Structure of Parliamentary Websites', approved by the *Inter-Parliamentary Council at the 166th Session*, Amman, 6 May.

Jarren, O. (1998) 'Demokratie durch Internet?' in Eisel, S. and Scholl, M. (eds), *Internet und Politik*, Konrad-Adenauer-Stiftung, Interne Studie 164/1998.

Kamps, K. (ed.) (1999) *Elektronische Demokratie?* Opladen/Wiesbaden: Westdeutscher Verlag.

Katz, J. (1997) Birth of a Digital Nation, *WIRED*, 5 April.

Katz, R. S. (1987) *Party Governments*, Berlin: de Gruyter.

Kleinsteuber, H. J. and Hagen, M. (1998) 'Was bedeutet "elektronische Demokratie"?' *Zeitschrift für Parlamentsfragen*, 1, 128–43.

Krauch, H. (1972) *Computer Demokratie*, Düsseldorf: VDI-Verlag.

Kubicek, H., Schmid, U. and Wagner, H. (1997) *Bürgerinformation durch 'neue' Medien?*, Opladen: Westdeutscher Verlag.

Lange, H.-J. (1988) *Bonn am Draht*, Marburg: SP-Verlag.

Leggewie, K. and Maar, C. (eds) (1998) *Internet Politik*, Köln: Bollmann.

Lijphart, A. (1971) 'Comparative Politics and the Comparative Method', *American Political Science Review*, 65, 682–93.

Mambrey, P., Vorwerk, E. and Wurch, G. (1991) *Computer im Deutschen Bundestag*, Opladen: Westdeutscher Verlag.

Mambrey, P., Neumann, H.-P. and Sieverdingbeck, K. (1999) 'Bridging the Gap Between Parliament and Citizens – The Internet Services of the German Bundestag', in Coleman, S., Taylor, J. and van de Donk, W. (eds), *Parliament in the Age of the Internet*, Oxford: Oxford University Press.

Marschall, S. (1999) *Öffentlichkeit und Volksvertretung*, Opladen/Wiesbaden: Westdeutscher Verlag.

McLean, I. (1987) *Democracy and New Technology*, Cambridge: Polity Press.

Michels, R. (1911) *Zur Soziologie des Parteiwesens in der modernen Demokratie*, Leipzig: Klinkharot.

Möller, T. (1999) 'The Swedish Election 1998', *Scandinavian Political Studies*, 22, 261–76.

Muralt Müller, H. (2000) 'E-Government – Herausforderung für Behörden', *Neue Züricher Zeitung*, 14 April <http://www.parlament.ch/E/Egovernment/nzz14042000_e. htm?servlet_get_content>, first accessed 5 January 2001.

Mutter, C. (2002) 'Das Rubbelfeld auf dem Stimmzettel', *Die Weltwoche*, 3 January, 1, 15.

Naisbitt, J. (1982) *Megatrends*, New York: Warner Books.

Needham, C. (2001) 'Electronic Consultation in the UK and the USA', paper for presentation at the 2001 Joint Workshops session, Grenoble, 6–11 April.

Norris, P. (2001) *Digital Divide*, Cambridge, MA: Cambridge University Press.

NUA (2001) 'How Many Online ?' <www.nua.ie/surveys/how_many_online>, first accessed 7 January 2002.

Pateman, C. (1970) *Participation and Democratic Theory*, Cambridge, MA: Cambridge University Press.

Peters, G. (1998) *Comparative Politics*, New York: New York University Press.

Pitkin, H. F. (1967) *The Concept of Representation*, Berkeley, CA: University of California Press.

Rash Jr. W. (1997) *Politics on the Nets*, New York: Freeman.

Rawls, J. (1971) *A Theory of Justice*, Cambridge, MA: Cambridge University Press.

Rheingold, H. (1993) *The Virtual Community*, Reading, MA: Addison-Wesley.

Ryan, D. and Becker, T. (1983) 'The Commission for the Future and the New Zealand Televote', *World Futures*, 18, 309–15.

Sarcinelli, U. (ed.) (1998) *Politikvermittlung und Demokratie in der Mediengesellschaft*, Opladen: Westdeutscher Verlag.

Sartori, G. (1987) *The Theory of Democracy Revisited*, Vols 1 and 2, Chatham, NJ: Chatham House.

Schattschneider, E. E. (1975) *The Semisovereign People*, Hinsdale, Ill: Dryden Press.

Schmidt, M. G. (2000) *Demokratietheorien*, Opladen: Leske & Budrich.

Schuler, D. (1996) *New Community Networks*, Reading, MA: Addison-Wesley.

Schumpeter, J. A. (1950), *Kapitalismus, Sozialismus und Demokratie*, Bern: Francke.

Slaton, C. D. (1992) *Televote*, New York: Praeger.

Snider, J. H. (1994) 'Democracy On-Line', *The Futurist*, September/October.

Street, J. (1992) *Politics and Technology*, Basingstoke: Macmillan.

Swedish Ministry of Justice (2000) Sustainable Democracy. English Translation of the Recommendations made by the Government Commission on Swedish Democracy in their Final Report, 12 September, Stockholm.

Toffler, A. (1980) *The Third Wave*, New York: Bantam Books.

Ulfhielm, C. G. (1998) *Information Technology in the Swedish Parliament*, unpublished manuscript, Stockholm.

US House of Representatives (1996a) 'Task Force on Committee Review', *Report of Reforming Committee Operations, Procedures and Staffing*, Washington, DC, 16 July.

US House of Representatives (1996b) *Committee on Rules, Public Hearing on Legislating in the 21st Century*, Washington, DC, May.

US House of Representatives (1997) *Rules of the U.S. House of Representatives. Effective for 105th Congress*, Washington, DC

The Washington Post (1998) 'Whose Research is it?' 7 July, A 12.

Weber, M. (1990) 'The Advent of Plebiscitarian Democracy', in Mair, P. (ed.), *The West European Party System*, Oxford: Oxford University Press.

Zittel, T. (2002a) 'Wither Responsible Party Government?' Revised paper presented to the *Joint Sessions of Workshops of the European Consortium of Political Research*, Turin, 22–27 March.

Zittel, T. (2002b) 'Political Representation in the Network Society', paper presented to the Workshop on the Cross-National Study of Legislatures at the 2002 Annual Meeting of the American Political Science Association, Boston, 29 August–1 September.

5 Digital democracy

Ideas, intentions and initiatives in Swedish local governments

Joachim Åström

Introduction

It has commonly been suggested that the public in post-industrial societies has become increasingly disenchanted with the traditional institutions of representative government, detached from political parties and disillusioned with older forms of participatory activity. The political parties – the most important intermediary link between the people and the centre of government – seem to have lost their hold on the voters. Fewer voters are able to identify with a single party, the voting behaviour becomes more and more flexible and the number of party members decreases (Gidlund and Möller 1999). In addition to this, there is an increase in the general distrust felt towards parties and politicians. Field surveys indicate that confidence in politicians and parties during the last decades has been undermined in almost all countries where time series surveys have been conducted (Norris 1999a). In Sweden, formal studies are available since the 1960s, and they all indicate that confidence in politicians has been undermined, slowly but constantly (Holmberg 1999). Due to this evidence, there is a 'crisis of democracy' debate running.

While the trends are evident, the explanation for, and interpretations of, these phenomena have proved more controversial. Among other things, the interpretation depends on how one judges citizens' dissatisfaction with the possibilities for political participation and with the outcomes of political decision-making. According to one line of argument the problems are output related, rather than input related. Decline in identification of citizens with political parties does not necessarily mean that the legitimacy of the central institutions of representative democracy is eroding. Citizens can use other non-institutional forms of action for attaining political goals. Instead, low trust is considered as being due to weakened government performance. People who are critical of the various services they receive tend to be less trusting than people who are satisfied. Following this line of reasoning, the policy prescription should be to enhance the effectiveness of problem-solving rather than democratic responsiveness to the demands of citizens (Klingemann and Fuchs 1995).

The opposite line of argument implies that we are facing a crisis of political communication. The diagnoses claim a challenge to representative democracies has arisen, which can be met only by decisive reform. Declining voter turnout and lack of attendance at public meetings are heralded as evidence of citizen apathy and a fundamental disconnection between citizens and their government. Citizen apathy and a general culture of indifference to politics calls into question both the extent to which councils can claim to represent their communities and their broader legitimacy to govern. Social science literature has advanced numerous hypotheses to explain citizen apathy. Political economists, for example, argue that citizen non-action is actually the result of a rational calculus comparing the costs and benefits of participation. Given that any single individual's effort is unlikely to make a difference and that the costs of participation are high, most citizens will choose not to take part in political activities (Downs 1957). The policy prescriptions for reducing citizen apathy usually involve a set of proposals to simplify public participation in government by encouraging authorities to become more transparent and to develop a range of consultation and participation techniques.

More recently, new information and communication technologies (ICTs) have been put forward as one possible solution to the perceived problems of communication. According to Gibson and Ward (1998), the Internet has the potential to increase internal party democracy and intensify interparty competition. Hague and Loader (1999) suggest that ICTs could potentially promote government accountability, create a better-informed citizenry and facilitate public deliberation and participation in the decision-making process in state and civil society. Budge (1996) believes that the development of the Internet makes direct democracy feasible in a mass society for the first time. In many different ways then, the Internet offers opportunities to reconnect people to the political process.

Will hopes for a digital democracy be realized? In Sweden, prospects for a digital democracy might be considered better than in many other countries. The rapid expansion of the Internet, combined with the ongoing broadband expansion, imply that a technological platform now exists in order to develop applications that in different ways are considered to strengthen democracy. According to statistics during the second half of the year 2000, 76 per cent of the Swedish population between 16 and 79 years of age had access to a computer at home, and 65 per cent had access to the Internet at home (SCB 2001). As use of the Internet and World Wide Web by citizens has increased, many have touted the web as a means to increase citizens' political involvement. According to several state-backed studies in later years, the Internet should be used to promote government accountability and to increase public participation in politics (SOU 2000: 1; 2001: 48).

Still, changes in political behaviour are far from certain. Technological change must be translated into political change through decisions made by the members affected. They must decide whether they want to adapt to a new communications environment, and if so, in what ways (Zittel 1999). This chapter examines the relationship among ideas, intentions and initiatives in the process of wiring Swedish local governments. The first part reviews the normative theoretical argument in favour of digital democracy, while the second draws on evidence from a survey examining how local politicians in Sweden relate to these new ideas.

Do they believe in the use of the Internet in the political process? Are some opportunities via the Net more supported than others? The third part of the chapter, moving from formal norms to active norms, focuses on the role and function of local government websites. How far do these sites provide comprehensive information and opportunities for interactive communication? What factors help to explain the patterns that we find? The conclusion summarizes the core findings and considers some implications for understanding the role of the Internet in a Swedish context.

Theories of digital democracy

In many countries there are programmes for 'democratic renewal' these days. Renewal does not, however, take the same form everywhere, and the direction of development is frequently being contested. 'Digital democracy' is often used as a title for programmes of democratic renewal based on new ICTs. As such it captures both the perceived problems with the existing institutions of local government and the ambitions of the current reform process. It suggests that local democracy is failing and that new ICTs can help to address these failings in order to revitalize democratic practice. In this way digital democracy has a precise meaning: it is about adjusting the institutions of local government to make them more democratic. On the other hand, the concept of democracy, and equally its digital manifestations, is inherently ambiguous (Held 1987). Programmes of digital democracy are grounded in different notions of democracy and connect different democratic values to technological change. In this respect it might be fruitful to distinguish between different models of digital democracy. In this part of the chapter three different models will be presented: direct, interactive and indirect. The direct model is basically about providing more effective means for direct registrations of citizens' opinions on current issues. The essence of the interactive model is to strengthen civic engagement and political activism through online discussion and deliberation. The indirect model of democracy refers to opportunities to strengthen the core institutions of representative democracy through dissemination of information and transparency. By sketching these models, it is possible to see in what direction digital technologies are pulling local democracy. Are intentions and initiatives in local governments in line with the indirect model of democracy, or are they part of a move towards a more direct or interactive democracy?

Direct democracy

One common point of view in the debate on digital democracy is the recommendation of citizens' direct participation in political decision-making. In this argument, citizens are, or at least can be, adequately informed in most issues and they know their interests better than anyone else. If each person is the best judge of his/her best interests and the object of policy is as far as possible to advance these, this makes a strong case for every citizen to participate in the making of public choices.

It is of utmost importance that the will of the majority is allowed to directly influence decisions in all areas of society. Accordingly, representation can be seen as a practical necessity in some situations, but must generally be regarded as a necessary evil that could and should be avoided in different ways (Premfors 2000).

Use of ICTs is seen as one such way. The core of the direct democratic claim rests on the idea that communication capacity is a kind of rate-limiting factor in political engagement and influence. At present, political professionals, interest groups and other elites dominate the comparatively limited resources for effective political communication. The Net can decentralize access to communication and information, increasing citizens' political resources. As a consequence individuals' engagement in politics will increase, as will their influence. In this vision not only will a mass audience be able to follow politics and express its views to government, but it will also be fundamentally less dependent on linkage organizations and group politics (Bimber 1998).

The more radical proponents of this model see ICTs as the decisive means by which direct democracy Athenian style can be implemented in today's society. In their proposed model professional politicians and political parties become more or less redundant. Instead a new kind of public rule will emerge. Through computer networks, individuals' views and opinions can be solicited, registered, stored and communicated, enabling direct democracy to be implemented not only at a local level but nationally and even internationally. With ICTs, effective political participation does not have to diminish with scale (Dahl and Tufte 1973). At all levels, representation can be substituted by independent cyber citizens who act in a responsible manner at the electronic agora, without any professional politician acting as an intermediary and guardian (Ilshammar 1997).

Less radical proponents do not want to abolish the representative system altogether, but combine it – 'revitalize it' – with direct elements. In Budge's (1996) vision there would still be an elected party-based government. This government would put important bills and other political decisions to popular votes, just as it does with legislative votes under representative democracy. The function of the Net is to facilitate this running public referenda. Another possibility often referred to is a more frequent use of advisory opinion polls, by way of new technology, making sure that the parliament really knows what the people want. McLean (1989), for example, argues that the new media can do much to make governments more responsive to the wishes of the public by linking members more closely to their constituents.

Interactive democracy

While the most important participatory activity in the direct model of democracy is tied to the moment of casting a vote into the ballot box, interactive democracy pays more attention to public debate as a political tool. An interactive democracy can be described as a group of citizens whose matters of common concern are dealt with through ongoing discussions, debates and deliberations.

The great value of the discussion is due to the fact that one believes that people let themselves be convinced by rational argumentation. The primary driving force of humans is personal autonomy, that is, a strife to realize the projects they rate the highest, however the individuals' perceived interests and wishes are decided in the dialectic process of social interaction. The source of legitimacy is, consequently, not the predetermined will of individuals, but rather the process of its formation, that is, deliberation (Barber 1984; Bohman 1996; Elster 1998).

Similar to direct democracy, interactive democracy wants and indeed requires active citizens. Real democracy is realized only to the extent that ordinary people are given opportunities to carry on a dialogue and act on matters of common interest. Unlike direct democracy that trusts that people would learn if we only bring power to them, interactive democracy emphasizes the need to involve people in discussion and deliberation processes. Following the proponents of this model, it is an illusion to believe that qualified standpoints in complex societal issues are 'out there' automatically and can be caught easily in polls or referendums in accordance with the principle of majority (Fishkin 1991). Participation is seen not only as a means to give people power, but also to provide education and an opportunity to develop an opinion among fellow citizens. Whereas previously the role of participation was mainly to make the representative system more representative by active dialogue between politicians and citizens, today much attention is paid to the benefits of horizontal communication among citizens: when people discuss societal issues, a platform is created for respect, confidence, tolerance and openness, crucial ingredients of an interactive democracy (Friedland 1996). Following this line of reasoning, Barber (1984) recommends that the capabilities of the new technology should be used to strengthen civic education, guarantee equal access to information and tie individuals and institutions into networks that will make real participatory discussion and debate possible.

In practice, this kind of interactivity could be facilitated in many different ways. Schuler (1996) stresses in particular the possibility to create interactive information systems that support information exchange and communication within a geographically defined area, known as community networks. Others emphasize the possibility for communication within groups that need to bridge geographical distances, for example, parties and interest organizations (Gibson and Ward 1998). A third group of authors stress the possibility to use ICTs in deliberative processes among a representative sample of citizens (Etzioni 1972; Dahl 1989).

Indirect democracy

In the model of indirect democracy it is only the members of the political elite who fully participate in the political process. This is because the ordinary citizen is considered as being not that interested in politics or for that matter qualified to participate. Instead, the basic idea is having several elites competing for citizens' votes. Elections are about choosing leaders based on a general account of the programmes they represent. The elites must then have sufficient room to manoeuvre, to revise and detail their political programmes. The ground for legitimacy is the

Table 5.1 Three models of digital democracy

	Direct democracy	*Interactive democracy*	*Indirect democracy*
Aim	Sovereignty/equality	Autonomy	Individual freedom
Ground for legitimacy	Principle of majority	Public debate	Accountability
Citizens' role	Decision-maker	Opinion former	Voter
Mandate of the elected	Bound	Interactive	Open
ICT-use focusing	Decisions	Discussion	Information

accountability of the elites – the public in free elections should be able to decide whom they want to govern their common affairs (Schumpeter 1976).

The new technology is not seriously considered to be able to have an influence on the characteristics that make the representative system the best solution; citizens will not be any wiser, nor less partial or more willing to really get into political issues (Sartori 1987). Instead, the democratizing potential of the new technology is regarded as being related to politicians' possibilities to spread information and gather support. The display of politics in the media is sometimes said to have caused a crisis in political communication (Blumler and Gurevitch 1995) and is often stated as the main reason for the growing distrust towards politicians (Möller 2000). Today, politicians are given an opportunity to communicate directly with citizens without interference from the media. In this way, the Internet might make it easier for the representatives to justify their policy with restored confidence.

When it comes to technical development, there are also hopes that citizens will be able to make their electoral choices and predict the consequences of casting their ballot more easily. Government websites can provide particularly effective mechanisms for providing the public with detailed and comprehensive information about the legislative procedures and activities, allowing public scrutiny of the policy process and promoting the accountability of elected members to their constituents (Norris 2000a). Moreover, the new technology is believed to have an equalizing effect on parties, and intensify interparty competition. Since the cost of starting a home page is quite low, small as well as large parties can be given the opportunity to spread their messages and introduce themselves to the voters (Gibson and Ward 1998). Competition strengthens indirect democracy since it forces the parties to produce products that citizens really want. Table 5.1 summarizes the underlying concepts of the three models of digital democracy.

Attitudes towards digital democracy

Many scholars have devoted attention to ICTs, and the literature provides a broad range of ideas on how the Internet may revive democracy. But how do local policy-makers relate and respond to these ideas? To influence policy choices, ideas must reach and convince decision-makers whose roles include evaluating the overall goals and tools of policy, initiating policy change and overseeing implementations of new policies. We now examine (1) whether Swedish politicians in general are optimistic or pessimistic about the democratic potential of the Internet, and (2) which opportunities via the Internet they find attractive. The data is based upon a survey questionnaire sent to the Swedish chairmen of the municipal executive boards. The survey, conducted during the spring of 2000, was returned by 80 per cent of the 289 chairmen.

Cyberoptimism or pessimism?

The debate on digital democracy has been a lively one, altering between ominous pessimism and exuberant optimism. Cyberoptimists, as we have seen, express hopes that the Internet may provide new opportunities for democracy as governments go online, facilitating communications between citizens and the state. Cyberpessimists are more sceptical, suggesting that new technology cannot be expected to transform existing power structures, make political decision-making more transparent or revive public participation. The first question aims at positioning the Swedish politicians along this optimism–pessimism continuum. How do they view the democratic potential of the Internet and other computer networks? (See Table 5.2.)

The conclusion to be drawn from Table 5.2, is that there is a general positive opinion about the democratic potential of ICTs among the Swedish chairmen of municipal executive boards. More than 80 per cent of the respondents agree that the technology has the potential to enhance the quality of democracy today or in the future. But even if the majority of politicians seems to be optimistic about the possibilities of the new technology, this does not necessarily mean that they are prepared to experiment with digital democracy. Concerns are often expressed about the gap between technology haves and have-nots (the so-called 'digital divide'), and that digital democracy will exacerbate inequalities among citizens. Tambini (1998) distinguishes two fundamentally different attitudes towards this problem: conservative and radical. The conservative attitude implies that key functions in the democratic process are kept offline in order not to treat unfairly persons with no access to the new technology. Following this line of reasoning the

Table 5.2 The politicians' views on the democratic potential of ICTs

	Percentage	*No. of politicians*
New ICTs have the potential to enhance the quality of local democracy even at this time	28	62
New ICTs are important new mediums that can enhance the quality of local democracy in the long run	53	124
New ICTs can enhance the quality of local democracy to some extent, but its alleged significance is exaggerated	16	35
New ICTs will not have any real significance for the quality of local democracy	2	4
Total	99	225

Internet will not be allowed any greater importance until it is made available for everyone on the same conditions. The alternative, the radical solution, implies that you try to keep everything online regardless of whether everybody has access to the medium or not. Democratization for a few is considered better than no democratization at all. What are the Swedish politicians' attitudes towards this dilemma – are they radical or conservative? (See Table 5.3.)

In previous studies it has been shown that there is a strong awareness of the limited nature of the audience among politicians. Many politicians interviewed refer directly to the unrepresentative nature of the socio-economic profiles of Internet users, frequently noting the inequalities involved in giving undue weight to the information haves, at the expense of those without the means to access technology (Åström 1999; Magarey 1999; Gidlund and Möller 1999). In the light of these studies, the figures in Table 5.3 are quite surprising. Table 5.3 says that almost 50 per cent of the Swedish chairmen of the municipal executive boards do not think that unequal access among citizens give cause for a limited use of ICTs in the democratic process. Of course, this radical view might be a reflection of the rapid diffusion of computers and the Internet among citizens; as the electorates constituents are relying more heavily on Internet communications, it becomes more and more difficult for politicians not to use the Internet themselves. But the result also indicates that we are brought up against different interpretations of the potential of the Net to create political equality. For those who consider the activity on the Net to be a complementary addition to other political activities and that gives former peripheral groups access to information and political arenas, the technology does not need to be generally available for the political landscape to be levelled out. For those who believe that the activities on the Net threaten to further widen the existing gaps in society, the technology should be available to everyone in order to experiment with digital democracy.

Following this line of reasoning, we can distinguish between politicians who affiliate with the *mobilization perspective* within the literature and those who affiliate with the *reinforcement perspective* (see Bellamy and Taylor 1998; Norris 2000b). The concept of mobilization is based upon the assumption that the activity on the Net represents a distinct form of political participation, which in several ways differs from conventional activities, such as working in political parties or lobbying against elected representatives. By facilitating participation and increasing the availability of political information, the Net is considered to be able to reduce

Table 5.3 Does unequal access among citizens give cause for just a limited use of ICTs in the democratic process?

	Percentage	*No. of politicians*
Agree completely	11	25
Basically agree	40	89
Basically disagree	33	74
Disagree completely	15	33
Total	99	221

the imbalance of public social life. From the more sceptical reinforcement perspective, technology is considered to be shaped by the already influential and it also becomes a tool in the process by which power structures are reinforced. This means that the social imbalance one can find in traditional political activities will be found on the Net as well.

So far the empirical studies of the social and political characteristics of net activities tend to support the reinforcement theses. Those who are politically active also use the Internet, and those who do not engage in politics, also do not use the Internet (Norris 1999b; Martinsson 2001). However, politicians' interpretations of the democratic potential and ability of the technology to create political equality can be assumed to be of importance when it comes to their will to experiment with new methods and techniques based on ICTs. A pessimistic interpretation of the technology in combination with a reinforcement perspective would, if we are right, result in a lack of interest and a limited use of it, while a general optimism combined with a mobilization perspective would result in commitment and active initiatives. If we put these two issues in relation to one another, we can thus create four categories of politicians: radical optimists, conservative optimists, radical pessimists and conservative pessimists. The pessimists, as we can see in Table 5.4, clearly belong in the reinforcement camp, while the optimists are split in two relatively equal groups. Also, it becomes evident that the radical optimists constitute the largest category.

Direct, interactive or indirect democracy?

In order to get an idea of the political representatives' course of ambition, they were asked to show their attitudes towards five proposals that occur in the debate on how to use ICTs in the democratic process. Could it be that some proposals to use the new technology, more than others, are attractive to Swedish politicians?

For citizens to be able to make their choices at general elections, they need the information that makes it possible to form an opinion of the parties and candidates competing for their votes. Only if they can study political programmes and form an opinion of how those in authority have been acting, will they be able to make choices reflecting their political preferences. This kind of reasoning constitutes the core of the indirect model of democracy. Information is a determining factor when it comes to citizens being able to scrutinize those in authority and hold them responsible for their actions, collectively as well as individually. This

Table 5.4 Four categories of politicians (in percentage)

	Mobilization	Reinforcement	Total percentage
Cyberoptimism	Radical optimists 46	Conservative optimists 36	82
Cyberpessimism	Radical pessimists 3	Conservative pessimists 15	18
Total percentage	49	51	100

kind of information may come, and most often does come, from several different sources. Usually, information is provided through media, but sometimes also through political campaigns and discussions with individual politicians. The local government websites may be a complementary addition to these sources, not just by providing the same information, but also by providing a more detailed and easily accessible information, such as records from various meetings. The first question aims at reflecting this accountability-enhancing aspect of Internet usage: how do politicians view the proposal to publish online political records of the city council and committees?

A further kind of information is that which may underlie political standpoints and decisions. In order to make democracy more participatory, citizens must get the chance to study the political issues before the decisions are made. This argument constitutes an important part of the direct as well as the interactive model of democracy. Access to decision data is not just considered a determining factor when it comes to informed participants but for political commitment as well. Earlier, the access to decision data was very limited. Today, an effective website may offer extensive and detailed policy-relevant information and a chance to study the most obscure and difficult propositions and reports. Our second question is whether the Swedish politicians are willing to invite citizens to the political process by publishing decision data on the Internet before city council and committee meetings take place.

The third question deals with the possibility of creating new public arenas where citizens can participate in political discussions. The occurrence of such arenas is particularly important in interactive democracy, which above all gains legitimacy and stability out of active public dialogue: horizontally, so that citizens can decide on their preferences, and vertically, so that citizens can express their wishes "upwards" to parties and representatives. From this perspective, it is a public concern to create these arenas, and they should be supported by public means (Cohen 1997). The municipalities can, for instance, offer online discussion forums and chat pages on their websites, and thereby try to encourage an active citizenship, stimulate public debate and provide new channels to citizens in order to make them more influential. What are the local politicians' views on using online discussion forums that include the public?

In the direct model of democracy it is not just considered important that citizens get the opportunity of keeping up with politics and expressing their wishes to those in authority, it is also considered important that they can do this without being dependent on intermediate links. The Net can, from this point of view, enable continuous online polls and create immediate electronic feedback from voters to the elected (Bimber 1998). The use of opinion polls enables the representatives to get an idea of the preferences of their voters in a way that makes citizens less dependent on media, interest groups, parties and other intermediate organizations for their participation. The question is whether politicians consider it good or bad to conduct online polls in local issues of current interest?

Internet voting can be seen as a way of making the election procedure simpler, more flexible and cheaper from the perspective of increasing participation in general elections and thereby strengthening the legitimacy of the representative system. The disabled, the elderly, travellers and people under stress would not have to go to a voting place to cast their votes. But Internet voting is also an important part of the direct model of democracy, since this method, together with a more well-informed and competent electorate, offers a chance of making direct participation more frequent (Solop 2000). Finally, we query politicians' attitudes towards conducting online referendums.

Table 5.5 summarizes politicians' views on the different proposals for changing democracy by using ICTs. The proposals are placed in order of preference; the most favoured proposals are found on top of the table, and the least favoured at the bottom. The results reveal that there is a majority of positive attitudes towards four out of five proposals. Thus, the majority of the proposals for change seem to appeal to most politicians. However, the number of positive opinions becomes fewer when moving from proposals that concern dissemination of information to proposals that concern two-way communication. It is also worth noting that politicians' opinions on the democratic potential of the Internet, and its chance to create political equality, have an impact on the very issues that deal with communication. When it comes to the proposals that concern the dissemination of information, there are no big differences between the various categories of politicians. They have, however, relatively different attitudes towards the proposals that concern the discussion forums, public opinion surveys and Internet voting.

The most attractive proposal when it comes to communication concerns the possibility to create a discussion forum on the Internet, which indicates that politicians

Table 5.5 Attitudes towards a number of proposals for using ICTs in the democratic process

Proposals	Percentage of politicians favourably disposed to the proposal				
	Radical optimists	Conservative optimists	Radical pessimists	Conservative pessimists	All
Publish political records online	91	91	83	88	91
	(99)	(79)	(6)	(33)	(226)
Publish documents before meetings online	89	82	67	79	85
	(102)	(79)	(6)	(33)	(228)
Use online discussion forums	89	75	50	39	76
	(102)	(77)	(6)	(31)	(224)
Conduct online polls	78	57	50	38	65
	(102)	(76)	(6)	(32)	(223)
Conduct online referendums	44	19	17	9	29
	(99)	(78)	(6)	(33)	(222)

Note
The politicians could choose between the following alternatives when answering the questions: 'a very good proposal', 'a fairly good proposal', 'a neither good nor bad proposal', 'a rather bad proposal', 'a very bad proposal' and 'no opinion'. The percentage favourably disposed refers to those whose answers were 'very good proposal' or 'a fairly good proposal'.

are more positive to proposals that lean towards interactive democracy, rather than direct democracy. This impression is confirmed by the fact that the only proposal that receives more negative votes than positive ones, is the proposal to conduct popular votes on the Internet. To be sure, the issue of Internet voting has been racing up the political agenda in Sweden, due to, among other things, the declining participation in general elections. A parliamentary assembled commission has proposed that Internet voting should be given a trial run (SOU 2000: 1), the majority of the political parties has claimed to be positive towards Internet voting (Vision 01-02-04), and according to a recent public opinion survey, 55 per cent of the voters would prefer the Internet to the traditional voting place if there was a choice (SCB 2001). But the proposal for more frequent elections by conducting popular votes in specific factual issues, implies a more pronounced ideological dimension, which is also suggested by the answers in Table 5.5. A common view is that having more frequent voting between elections runs the risk of making politics too populist. Numerous politicians might then not risk making unpopular though important decisions with an election always at hand. The fact that twice as many radical optimists as conservative optimists have a positive attitude towards this, also suggests that the view on equality is particularly important when it comes to electronic voting. This is not surprising, since one of the most serious charges against Internet voting involves the question about the discriminatory impact it may have for specific groups in the population. According to Davis (1999), electronic voting, as a supplement to traditional voting, would not disenfranchise others, but it would still disadvantage them vis-á-vis the more active. And exclusive Internet voting certainly shifts the bias toward the middle and upper classes: the already politically active.

To sum up, it seems as if the ideas to develop democracy by using the Internet have reached and convinced the Swedish chairmen of the municipal executive boards. They are not just optimistic about the potential of the technology in order to strengthen democracy, many of them are also positive towards the more participatory orientated reform proposals. Only the proposal for conducting popular votes on the Internet receives more negative votes than positive ones. It is now time to study if politicians' positive opinions about ICT are being put into action on the local political arena. Is there a connection between word and deed, between formal and active norms?

Assessing the online conditions

The most direct method of studying how local governments are using the Internet, is a systematic examination of their Internet products, that is, their websites. A content analysis of 289 Swedish local government websites was conducted during January and February in the year 2001. Of course, this examination can only provide a snapshot of websites at one point in time. The exercise needs to be repeated in future years to monitor how far local government websites adapt to the new technological developments. Also, we need to do more in-depth analysis of sites. Still, this study can provide a first indication of how far the municipalities have gone when it comes to offering citizens information and possibilities for interactive communication on their websites.

Today, all Swedish municipalities are represented on the Internet, but there are wide variations in quality and activity. The first thing we examined was the various information features that local government websites have online. More precisely, we studied citizens' possibilities to receive information in connection with the meetings of the municipal council and the municipal executive board. It was demanded that the municipality provide all information, and not only selected parts thereof, both when it comes to minutes or other documents from meetings. A greater insight presupposes that both parties in the communications process are equal, that is, that the citizen has the possibility to get hold of the document he or she wants from the municipal machinery.

From Figure 5.1 it becomes apparent that many local governments have put online accountability-enhancing material such as minutes. Also, the vast majority of sites provide the meeting schedules for municipal council (75 per cent) and municipal executive board (65 per cent). Considerably fewer municipalities present the issues that will be discussed during the next meeting on the Internet. One can also note that it is more common to publish the agendas before the open municipal council meetings (45 per cent) than before the closed municipal executive board meetings (32 per cent). In order to really give citizens a possibility to study the issues on the agenda and encourage participation on equal conditions, one has to climb further up on 'the ladder of information' (Bellamy and Raab 1999), by letting them study the documents that underlie decisions before the decisions are made. Figure 5.2 shows that, today, only 4 per cent of the municipalities do this before the municipal council meetings, and 3 per cent do it before municipal executive board meetings.

In our examination of the websites, we also looked for several key features within each site that would facilitate the interactive connection between government and citizens. The first of these features was email capability. Here we studied, among

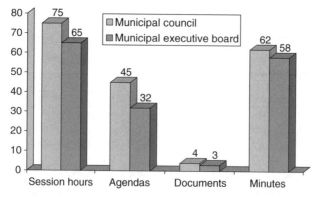

Figure 5.1 Online provision of information (in percentage).

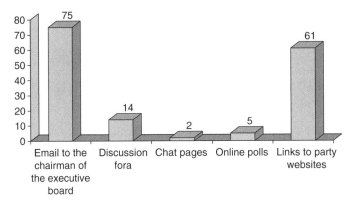

Figure 5.2 Opportunities for interactive communication (in percentage).

other things, whether a website visitor could email the chairman of the municipal executive board. If a person can merely look at information on a government
website without being able to contact at least one politician, the potential for two-
way interaction is thwarted. On the majority of the websites this technology was
available; 75 per cent had the email address to the chairman of the municipal
executive board.

While email certainly is the easiest method of contact, there are other methods
that government websites can employ to facilitate democratic conversation. These
include opportunities for public participation in online polls, regular online discussion forums and chat pages. These technologies were nowhere near as prevalent
as email; only 14 per cent of the websites offered discussion forums, 2 per cent
offered regular chat pages or recurrent chats with politicians and 5 per cent used
online polls. The access offered to the parties was somewhat limited as well. The
parties or their representatives were very seldom given the opportunity to comment on the pursued policy or to present their own policy on the local
government websites, and only six out of ten municipalities facilitated citizens'
contacts with the parties by providing links to their own websites. Even if this, to
some extent, has to do with the fact that local parties do not have working websites, these findings also suggest that local governments are not trying very hard
to use the Internet to promote interparty competition.

Although politicians have a positive attitude towards the opportunities offered
by the Internet, it is easy to conclude that they fail to exploit these opportunities
on their websites. For instance, 85 per cent of politicians claim to be positive
towards publishing documents on the Internet before meetings and 75 per cent
claim to be positive towards using discussion forums, as against only 4 and
14 per cent respectively of the municipalities. This means that there is an interesting discrepancy between what politicians say they want and what they really
do. To analyze further this relationship we need to compare municipalities more
systematically. Experience shows that some organizations are not as open to new

ideas as others. While some municipalities always tend to adopt them, others allow themselves to be influenced only on rare occasions. There are wide variations in openness, and there seems to be a pattern. This has been described in terms of some municipalities being pioneers while others are followers or standbys (Schmidt 1986), or that some municipalities are active while others are passive (Henning 1996). The innovation research is, however, characterized by considerable disagreement about the factors that have an influence on the tendency to innovate. Factors found to be important for innovation in one study are found to be considerably less important, not important at all or even inversely important in another study (Downs and Mohr 1976: 700).

In the following step, we examine the relationship between the leading politicians' attitudes and the municipalities' tendency to innovate. This is done with the help of three indexes. The Information Index and the Communication Index were each produced by summing the separate indicators in Figures 5.1 and 5.2, and by standardizing the results to 100-point scales. The indicators of the two indexes were then added together into an overall Total Score (see Table 5.6).

Earlier we made the assumption that politicians' interpretations of the democratic potential and ability of technology to create political equality should be of importance when it comes to their will to experiment with new methods and techniques based on ICTs. We said that a pessimistic interpretation of the technology in combination with a reinforcement perspective, probably would result in a lack of interest and a limited use of it, while a general optimism combined with a mobilization perspective probably would result in commitment and active initiatives. The results in Table 5.6 show that politicians' attitudes towards new ICTs hardly have any significance at all on the information provided and the opportunities for interactive communication offered by the local governments. Local governments in which the chairman of the executive board is a 'conservative pessimist' provide websites that are almost as rich in information, and give almost as many opportunities for interactive communication, as those that have a 'radical optimist' as chairman. While we are not controlling for any municipal-specific factors, the result must be treated with some caution, but the result undeniably confirms the impression that there is a great difference between what politicians claim they are aiming at, and what they actually do.

Table 5.6 Local government websites and attitudes towards digital democracy

	Mean information index	*Mean communication index*	*Mean total score*	*Number of municipalities*
All	46	31	38	289
Radical optimists	49	34	40	97
Conservative optimists	45	30	37	79
Radical pessimists	42	33	37	6
Conservative pessimists	47	30	37	32

Conclusions

In this chapter we have examined the relationship among ideas, intentions and initiatives in the process of wiring Swedish local governments. We started off by reviewing some of the normative theoretical arguments in favour of digital democracy, and by examining how the Swedish chairmen of municipal executive boards relate to these new ideas. We found, on the whole, optimistic views and positive attitudes not only to the proposals supporting the indirect model of democracy, but also to proposals aiming at developing more participatory forms of democracy. The most significant finding, however, came up in the third part of the chapter and concerns the lack of causality between politicians' expressed intentions and the local government initiatives.

In light of the four basic scenarios listed in the introduction of this volume, only a few local governments have tried to develop a new mode of democracy in which different components of indirect, direct and interactive democracy are combined to create a more open, participative and responsive polity at the local level. Two good examples of this is the use of online referendums in the cities of Kalix and Nyköping as the basis of local decision-making on some important issues. Other examples include more interactive, or deliberative, forms of participation as in Bollnäs and Älvsjö. Digital democracy activities in these cities contain a number of innovations in the democratic procedures, for example, open dialogue forums, citizen panels, video broadcasting from the council and opportunities for citizen proposals. As the analysis shows, most local governments do, however, use the Internet for modernization rather than radical regeneration. Although politicians have a positive attitude towards the interactive opportunities offered by the Internet, it is easy to conclude that they fail to exploit these opportunities on their websites. Instead the websites serve as information archives for the press and public, and email may sometimes function as a replacement for telephone or postal queries.

The stability of political forms demonstrates the importance of an institutional perspective in a terrain that remains dominated by the assumption that information technology determines structure. At the core of the so-called new institutionalism is the notion that institutions do not necessarily change due to a changing technological environment, or that preferences alone shape politics. Institutional theories provide accounts of the constraints that institutions impose on action. Following the institutionalist line of reasoning, the effects of the Internet on government will be played out in unexpected ways, profoundly influenced by organizational, political and institutional logic. Technologies themselves influence choice, but the relationship is indirect, sometimes subtle, and exercised in combination with other economic, cultural, political and social influences. This is why the Internet does not always lead to institutional transformation but sometimes is enacted to strengthen the status quo (Fountain 2001). Even if this chapter is not the place to discuss the whole range of factors that might influence how local governments shape new ICTs it is possible to outline a few characteristic features of the Swedish local ICT policy that might be of importance for the discrepancy between politicians' expressed intentions and local government initiatives.

First, it seems like the municipalities have entered the world of new technology almost without any predefined, explicit strategies. The most manifest evidence of this is that only 20 per cent of the municipalities have agreed on a policy on ICT and democracy (Kommunaktuellt 2000: no. 16). This, and claims from spokesmen of the municipalities that there has been some resistance within the organizations towards the implementation of the new ICTs, imply that new technology is still not a very well-integrated part of the municipalities' activities. In many cases, the initiative to adopt new ICTs comes from individuals without any prior discussions within the organization, mainly as a result of other municipalities' adoption of websites as well as the general public rhetoric on the information society. Consequently, decision-making proceeds by successive limited comparison and learning by trial-and-error. This achieves simplification through limiting the number of alternatives considered to those that differ in small degrees from existing policies.

Second, it is evident that politicians' access to and knowledge of the Internet have received scant attention. It is rather common that politicians themselves, and laymen politicians in particular, do not have access to the basic requirement (computer, email and the Internet) that are necessary in order to take an active part in the political activities on the Net (Ranerup 1999). If ICT is to be used to a greater extent in the democratic processes, it is, however, necessary that politicians generally have the ICT easily accessible in their political work. This means that politicians need to not only decide upon communication strategies, but also to decide whether to give themselves hardware and software, as well as the expertise to connect to and use the Internet in the ways suggested by these strategies (Zittel 1999). So far, few municipalities seem to have accepted this challenge; only 10 per cent of the municipalities offer home computers to their politicians, and usually this offer only applies to members of the municipal executive board and its working committee (Kommunaktuellt 2000: no. 16).

A third distinctive trait of the local ICT policies is that the power of social production lies within the bureaucracy. Instead of moving the development forward, politicians have relied on ICT experts to create solutions. This means that the municipalities' Internet usage, to a great extent, is dependent on the fact that there are motivated actors within the organization, who have the will and ability to organize ideas and activities so that the process can be driven forward (Wihlborg 2000). Municipal officers often have an active interest in using the advantages of the new media, but at the same time they also find it difficult to develop new democracy functions if they do not have politicians' active consent; with the result that the same functions as earlier are conveyed, but on the Net, and that ICTs in themselves become the solution to the problems of democracy.

On the basis of these characteristic features of the Swedish local ICT policy, it is possible to argue that the loose connection between politicians' attitudes and the municipalities' web activities, at least partly, might be due to the fact that (a) politicians have not yet set up a distinct policy on how to use the new technology within the municipality; (b) that there is still no working ICT support for elected politicians and (c) that the development of digital democracy is driven more by municipal officers than by politicians. This does not, however, mean that it should be only a matter of time for digital democracy to arrive. It is also possible that local ICT policies rest on symbolic or image-reasons rather than rational decision-making. The current interest in reforming democracy in Sweden as well as the general Internet hype indicates that there is certain pressure by the institutional environment to incorporate modern and legitimate ideas about digital democracy. Local governments are more or less forced to adapt to the new technological environment with regard to its profile, legitimacy and identity in relation to other organizations and their citizens. This does not, however, mean that there is always a true desire to bring in citizens and give them opportunities to participate in decision-making processes. If local governments use ICTs for image-reasons and not in the first place to expand and make easier communication between citizens and politicians, ideas will stay 'disengaged' and not have any real impact on the organizations' activities (Brunsson 1989; Rövik 1998).

The discrepancy between what politicians claim they are aiming at and what they actually do certainly leaves questions to be dealt with in future research: What are the mechanisms translating technological change into political change? How do media and media changes relate to political change and different concepts of democracy? How does the Internet affect culture and practices? To answer these questions we need to examine in-depth why the technology is translated, how it is translated and by whom. Above all, it seems important to link ideas more closely to institutions for political innovations are often blocked or hampered by the present political institutions, which are orientated towards and structured according to a different political public. There is a time lag between the new developing public, which tries to reorganize institutions, and the present public that has formed the present institutions. This tension between stability and change makes the future role of ICTs with regard to democracy an open question.

References

Åström, Joachim (1999) 'Digital demokrati?' in *IT i demokratins tjänst*, SOU 1999: 117, Stockholm: Fritzes.

Barber, B. (1984) *Strong Democracy*, Berkeley: University of California Press.

Bellamy, C. and Taylor, J. A. (1998) *Governing in the Information Age*, Buckingham: Open University Press.

Bellamy, C. and Raab, C. D. (1999) 'Wiring-up the Deck-Chairs?' in Coleman, S., Taylor, J. and van de Donk, W. (eds), *Parliament in the Age of the Internet*, Oxford: Oxford University Press.

Bimber, B. (1998) 'The Internet and Political Transformation', *Polity*, XXXI (1): 133–60.

Blumler, J. G. and Gurevitch, M. (1995) *The Crisis of Public Communication*, London: Routledge.

Bohman, J. (1996) *Public Deliberation. Pluralism*, Cambridge/London: MIT Press.

Brunsson, N. (1989) *The Organization of Hypocracy*, New York: John Wiley.

Budge, I. (1996) *The New Challenge of Direct Democracy*, Cambridge: Polity Press.

Cohen, J. (1997) 'Deliberation and Democratic Legitimacy', in Hamlin, A. and Petit, P. (eds), *The Good Polity*, New York: Basil Blackwell.

Dahl, R. A. (1989) *Democracy and Its Critics*, New Haven/London: Yale University Press.

Dahl, R. A. and Tufte, E. (1973) *Size and Democracy*, Stanford: Stanford University Press.

Davis, R. (1999) *The Web of Politics*, Oxford: Oxford University Press.

Downs, A. (1957) *An Economic Theory of Democracy*, New York: Harper & Row.

Downs, G. W. and Mohr, L. B. (1976) 'Conceptual Issues in the Study of Innovation', *Administrative Science Quarterly*, 21, 700–14.

Elster, J. (1998) *Deliberative Democracy*, Cambridge: Cambridge University Press.

Etzioni, A. (1972) 'Minerva', *Policy Sciences*, 3, 457–74.

Fishkin, J. S. (1991) *Democracy and Deliberation*, New Haven/London: Yale University Press.

Fountain, J. E. (2001) *Building the Virtual State*, Washington, DC: Brookings Institution Press.

Friedland, L. A. (1996) 'Electronic Democracy and the New Citizenship', *Media, Culture & Society*, 18 (2), 4–16.

Gibson, R. K. and Ward, S. J. (1998) 'U.K. Political Parties and the Internet', *Harvard International Journal of Press/Politics*, 3 (3).

Gidlund, G. and Möller, T. (1999) *Demokratins trotjänare*, SOU 1999: 130, Stockholm: Fritzes.

Hague, B. N. and Loader, B. D. (1999) *Digital Democracy*, London: Routledge.

Held, D. (1987) *Models of Democracy*, Cambridge: Polity Press.

Henning, R. (1996) *Att följa trenden – aktiva och passiva kommuner*, Stockholm: Nerenius & Santérus förlag.

Holmberg, S. (1999) *Representativ demokrati*. SOU 1999: 64, Stockholm: Fritzes.

Ilshammar, L. (1997) *Demokr@i. Det elektroniska folkstyrets möjligheter och problem*, SOU 1997: 56, Stockholm: Fritzes.

Klingemann, H.-D. and Fuchs, D. (1995) *Citizens and the State*, Oxford: Oxford University Press.

Kommunaktuellt 2000, no. 16, *Snigelfart när demokratin ska ut på nätet.*

Magarey, K. (1999) 'The Internet and Australian Parliamentary Democracy', in Coleman, S., Taylor, J. and van de Donk, W. (eds), *Parliament in the Age of the Internet*, Oxford: Oxford University Press.

Martinsson, J. (2001) 'Den svenska nätopinionen', in Holmberg, S. and Weibull, L. (eds), *Land, du välsignade?* Göteborg: SOM-institutet.

McLean, I. (1989) *Democracy and New Technology*, Cambridge: Polity Press.

Möller, T. (2000) *Politikens meningslöshet*, Malmö: Lieber.

Norris, P. (1999a) *Critical Citizens*, Oxford: Oxford University Press.

Norris, P. (1999b) *Who Surfs Café Europa?* paper presented at the Annual Meeting of the American Political Science Association, Atlanta, 1–5 September 1999.

Norris, P. (2000a) *Democratic Divide?* paper presented at the American Political Science Association annual meeting in Washington, DC

Norris, P. (2000b) *A Virtuous Circle*, Cambridge: Cambridge University Press.

Petersson, O. (2000) *Demokrati utan partier?* Stockholm: SNS förlag.

Premfors, R. (2000) *Den starka demokratin*, Stockholm: Atlas.

Ranerup, A. (1999) 'Elektronisk debatt i kommunal politik', in *IT i demokratins tjänst*, SOU 1999: 117, Stockholm: Fritzes.

Rövik, K. A. (1998) *Moderne organisasjoner*, Bergen-Sandviken: Fagboksforlaget.

Sartori, G. (1987) *The Theory of Democracy Revisited*, New Jersey: Chatham House Publishers.

SCB (2001) *IT i hem och företag*, Örebro: SCB.

Schmidt, S. (1986) *Pionjärer, efterföljare och avaktare*, Lund: Kommunfakta förlag.

Schuler, D. (1996) *New Community Networks*, New York: ACM Press.

Schumpeter, J. A. (1976) *Capitalism, Socialism and Democracy*, London: Allen and Unwin.

Solop, F. I (2000) *Digital Democracy Comes of Age in Arizona*, paper presented at the American Political Science Association national conference, Washington, DC.

SOU 2000: 1, *En uthållig demokrati*, Stockholm: Fritzes.

SOU 2001: 48, *Att vara med på riktigt*, Stockholm: Fritzes.

Tambini, D. (1998) 'Civic Networking and Universal Rights to Connectivity: Bologna', in Tsagarousianou, R., Tambini, D. and Bryan, C. (eds), *Cyberdemocracy*, London/New York: Routledge.

Vision 01-02-04, *Politikerna vill ha e-val 2006*.

Wihlborg, E. (2000) *En lösning som söker problem*, Linköping: Linköping Studies in Arts and Science.

Zittel, T. (1999) *The Internet and U.S. Representatives*, paper presented at the International Conference on Parliaments in the Information Age, Paris, 18–20 November 1999.

6 Cyber-campaigning grows up

A comparative content analysis of websites for US Senate and gubernatorial races, 1998–2000

Jennifer D. Greer and Mark E. LaPointe

Introduction

This chapter focuses on one of the key supports of representative democracy – current and prospective elected representatives. Specifically, we examine individual candidates' use of the new information and communication technologies (ICTs) in the race for state executive and national legislative office in the United States. While politicians are vital parts of the representative institutions they serve, during their battles for voter sympathy one might expect them to opt for more individualistic and direct channels of communication with the electorate. This may especially be the case in the United States with its more candidate-centered form of election campaigning and governance. Such a system offers a more flexible and diverse platform for candidates to experiment and innovate in how to engage voters. The goal of this chapter is to assess how far candidates' use of web communication during the 1998 and 2000 US Senate and gubernatorial elections actually reflected these more direct and experimental possibilities. Specifically, did candidates tend to follow offline campaign trends and adopt a largely symbolic and image-based message that took an attacking stance toward opponents? Or, did they opt for more participatory features and seek to present policy-rich information in positive and inviting ways? We also ask whether the communication style on the sites changed very much between the two election cycles. And finally, we assess the role of various structural factors, such as the level of office sought, and individual characteristics of the candidate, such as gender or incumbency status, in influencing candidates' online communication style. In addressing these questions, the chapter presents an alternative perspective on the response of executive and legislative institutions to the challenge of new ICTs from that offered by Catherine Needham and Thomas Zittel in Chapters 3 and 4 in this volume. While their work revealed these bodies as a whole to be cautious in increasing their openness and public access via new ICTs, it might be that the elected individuals comprising them take a somewhat bolder stance.

The Internet was first used by US presidential candidates in 1992 (Davis and Owen 1998), although according to most accounts, 1996 marked the real beginnings of cyberpolitics with most major and minor party presidential candidates establishing sites in that year. Two years later, media observers were calling the

1998 election "the most wired in history" (Miller and Schrader 1998: A1). Indeed, D'Alessio (2000) found that 43 percent of the 1,296 US Senate, House of Representatives, and gubernatorial candidates had established websites in 1998, up from 18.7 percent in 1996. The website put up by former wrestler Jesse Ventura in his bid for the governorship of Minnesota in particular, gained head-lines for its simple text-based approach. The site was credited with generating a strong surge of support from younger voters and securing his surprise victory (Fineman 1999). Overall, however, cyber-campaigning was not expected to make a widespread impact on real-world politics until at least the 2000 electoral cycle, when people were predicted to become more familiar with the Internet as a mass medium (Corrado 1996). Some rather less-optimistic verdicts on the impact of cyber-campaigning were also delivered during this period. One congressional campaign manager, for instance, lamented in 1996 that his site had been visited just 26 times, and that half of those visits were by the candidate checking on the number of hits (Dulio *et al.* 1999). During the 1990s, therefore, the web was generally seen as having exhibited more potential than impact as a campaign tool (Just 1997: 100).

By 2000, almost every contender for a major office in the United States had a campaign-specific website, as did contenders for most minor offices. Anecdotes at all levels of politics suggested that sites were becoming an integral part of cam-paigns. The day after Republican presidential candidate John McCain's decisive win in the New Hampshire primary, $415,000 reportedly poured into his cam-paign via his site, up sharply from the $10,000 daily trickle into the site prior to the victory (Kornblut and Abraham 2000). Within a week, it was estimated that the site had raised 2 million dollars and recruited 22,000 new volunteers (Birnbaum 2000). Signs of the Internet's significance also emerged at the local level in the race for mayor in Snellville, Georgia in 2000. Challenger Brett Harrell credited his site with bringing in 500 votes, a yield that allowed him to unseat the 26-year incumbent. Harrell commented afterward, "I think there will not be another election – local to the White House – that won't be affected by the Internet" (Shelton 2000: 1JJ). The popular press noted a distinct change in candi-dates' orientation toward the Internet as news media prepared for elections in 2000. "E-campaigning has gone from a novelty to a necessity in less than a year… The Internet is fast becoming a Virtual New Hampshire: a quirky but pivotal place where campaigns are launched or scuttled" (Fineman 1999: 50). Evidence of this growing commitment can be seen in terms of the financial resources being channeled toward online campaigning. In the lead-up to the 2000 presidential election, contenders from the major parties had full-time web teams and consult-ants, and at least 16 percent of the sites for all congressional and gubernatorial campaigns in 1998 were run by professional consultants (McManus 1999a). By late 1999, *Campaigns & Elections* magazine listed about thirty companies specializ-ing in online politics and political websites were estimated to be a $2.5 billion a year industry (McManus 1999b: 76).

US Internet users, on the whole, treated candidates' sites with a modicum of interest. While almost one in five or 18 percent of Americans used the Internet for campaign news in 2000 (a dramatic rise from the 4 percent who did so in 1996) only 8 percent of online users visited a candidate or campaign site. This compares with just over half of online campaign-news users relying on the online versions of traditional news outlets (Pew Research Center 2000). In addition, when asked about the value of the experience, only a third of those who visited campaign sites rated them as "very useful," compared to the 57 percent of online news users who gave CNN.com this high rating (Pew Research Center 2000). This rather muted reception led one commentator to point out, "Despite considerable hype, perhaps the Internet has yet to become a player on par with TV" (Lynch 2001: 24). Certainly visitors to campaign sites may have been turned off by what some analysts have termed "cyber-fluff" (Greer and LaPointe 1999) and "brochureware" (Miller and Schrader 1998: A1) masquerading as content. Sites were generally seen as thin on content and interactivity and offering little more than glossy photographs and rosy biographies of candidates and their families (Kamarck 1998).

The question being investigated in this chapter is how far such impressions are justified. Are sites really stuck in existing and largely static forms of campaigning or have candidates begun to exploit the web's dynamic and interactive capabilities? In addition, if changes are taking place, how can we explain them? Is it simply a function of time, or a particular party taking the lead? To answer these questions we conduct a systematic content analysis of Senate and gubernatorial candidates' websites in 1998 and 2000. Specifically we focus on three main aspects of website content:

- To what extent are candidates infusing their sites with a wider variety of information graphics and interactivity as the web evolves?
- Do candidates offer positive or negative messages on their sites and how far they emphasize image-oriented messages versus issue-oriented politics?
- To what extent are those variables that play a role in traditional campaign communication, such as gender and party and candidate standing, also related to these features of online communication?

This study investigates these topics by examining the content and communication style of campaign sites in two recent US election cycles for two distinct levels of office: state gubernatorial and federal Senate races in 1998 and 2000. In doing so, this chapter moves forward the study of cyber-campaigning in a number of ways. First, it adds a longitudinal component to such analyses; to date, most analyses have examined sites for one type of candidate in one election cycle (Epstein 1996; Klotz 1998; Greer and LaPointe 1999). In addition, comparative analyses of candidates' and parties' campaign sites have focused on the content and overall design of the sites rather than their general tone or style of communication. In systematically examining the tone of the messages being delivered on the sites, we can more rigorously investigate the idea that the web serves as a less hostile and more positively oriented forum for political campaigning.

In examining these questions, the chapter can also address broader debates in the literature about the transformation taking place in political campaigning in what has been termed the postmodern (Norris 2000) or professionalized era (Gibson and Römmele 2001) that began to emerge in the United States in 1988 (Farrell and Webb 2000). As these authors have pointed out, previous shifts in campaign eras, namely from the premodern to the modern, have been intimately linked with changes in communication technology. While newspapers were tied to the premodern campaign era, television ushered in the modern era. The arrival of the Internet and other new digital means of communication are now leading to a fresh set of possibilities and challenges for political actors. These new technologies are producing a fragmentation, proliferation, and blurring of information and entertainment sources and a 24-hour news cycle. As such, campaign communications are increasingly marked by narrowcasting and adapting messages to the audience (Farrell and Webb 2000). "Such trends," as Norris points out, lead to a "postmodern conceptualization [that] sees politicians as essentially lagging behind technological and economic changes and running hard just to stay in place by adopting the techniques of political marketing in the struggle to cope with the more complex news environment" (Norris 2000: 149).

Inevitably, therefore, the postmodern era has seen an increasing role for professional media advisors, advertising, and polling, and a heightened emphasis on "spin" and image. Such trends are clearly observable in the American "candidate-centered" context, which has significantly fewer limitations on how to campaign than other countries (Farrell and Webb 2000: 108). However, as Norris (2000) has argued, the "new channels of communication also allow for greater interactivity between voters and politicians" akin to that which characterized the premodern era (p. 140). This is a point echoed by Wring and Horrocks (2001), who argue that while the new media may fragment and distil the political process into sound bites, it also presents the chance to encourage more interactive citizen practices (pp. 191–200). Thus, in examining the questions regarding candidates' emphasis on style versus substance and negative campaigning, we can address some of these broader questions about the direction that postmodern campaigning is taking under the influence of the Internet.

Campaigning online: the story so far

Empirical studies of campaign websites

Although virtually all parties across the world had established websites by 2002, they have probably been used most intensively for campaigning in the United States (Farrell and Webb 2000: 111). Such exploitation has no doubt followed from the fact that the US, along with the Scandinavian democracies have led the way in terms of public access and use of the net with rates of 59 percent and higher as of late 2002 (NUA 2002).

Early analysis of US election sites revealed that for the most part, candidates were content to simply migrate their offline publicity material to the online environment.

Websites were filled with speeches and position papers. Homepages for the 1996 US Senate elections typically included a photo of the candidate, biographical information, a position statement, and contact information – the traditional fare for campaign information (Meadow 1989; Bryant 1995; Johnson-Cartee and Copeland 1997). A few sites in 1996 featured virtual postcards, screen savers, video clips, and trivia, however, most were fairly unadventurous (Epstein 1996; Hall 1997; Klotz 1997). Presidential sites in 1996 were equally predictable (Reavy and Perlmutter 1996). McKeown and Plowman (1998) concluded that while the Dole and Clinton sites in 1996 allowed the candidates to provide more in-depth information than they were able to convey on television, neither candidate was effective in using the technology to increase interactivity with voters.

The picture did not appear much different in 1998. While Davis and Owen (1998) did note that a few sites used the interactive nature of the medium to solicit opinion, collect money, and identify supporters, most studies pointed to a less than aggressive use of the participatory features of the Net. LaPointe (1999) found that standard campaign information and photographs dominated Senate websites in the 1998 election. This pattern was replicated on gubernatorial candidates' sites in 1998 with interaction outside of E-mail being sporadic (Greer and LaPointe 1999). Kamarck's study of sites for US Senate, House, and governors' races in the 1998 elections underscored this picture of websites as static electronic brochures, where "pictures of the family, text of speeches and issue papers are all standard fare... Many campaign sites seek to get you to volunteer or contribute money – although few allow you to volunteer in cyberspace or make campaign contributions over the Web" (Kamarck 1998: B4). Dulio *et al.* (1999) found that while 73 percent of congressional candidates in 1998 solicited contributions on their sites, just less than one-third of that group allowed visitors to make contributions online. Others simply gave out a campaign address or asked for contributors to enter their addresses. Finally, questionnaire data collected by Faucheux from 270 candidates in local, state, and federal elections in 1998 revealed that while nearly all campaigns (97 percent) reported biographical information on their sites and 90 percent reported policy positions, just over half (52 percent) reported offering opportunities for any feedback. Faucheux remained hopeful, however, that "more creative Internet strategies will be hatched and more 'bells and whistles' will be explored and employed over time" (Faucheux 1998: 25).

Overall, in terms of the sheer volume of websites, more US candidates used the web in the 2000 elections. Kamarck (2002) found that although website use by gubernatorial candidates did not increase between the two election cycles, use by Senate candidates increased slightly and among House of Representatives' candidates, use of the web nearly doubled, from 35 to 66 percent. Kamarck also found that by 2000 more incumbents were using websites in their campaigns and candidates in very competitive races were more likely to use the Internet as a campaign tool. In 2000, a survey by Netelection.org found that 78 percent of incumbent congressional candidates in competitive districts established sites, compared with 50 percent in secure districts (Lynch 2001).

Analyses of US election sites after 1998 did suggest some areas of content improvement among presidential candidates. The Democratic nominee for president in 2000, Al Gore, developed an interactive children's area and live streaming of his Nashville headquarters via a webcam. The site also featured downloadable computer wallpaper with the Gore logo, an interactive information generator on states' voter registration rules, and a place where visitors could create their own issue-oriented web page (Fineman 1999; Tillett 2000). Online fundraising also attracted more attention in 2000. Kamarck (2002) reports that the majority of major party candidates were using their websites for fundraising. This was no doubt due to the fact that a year earlier the US Federal Elections Commission decided online credit-card donations were eligible for matching federal funds. This was a "very important symbol ... that legitimizes the Web as a real part of American politics" (von Sternberg 1999: 6A).

While some work has been done on tone or style of the political message being delivered by candidate sites in the United States, this aspect of online campaigning has not been investigated as frequently and in as much depth as the functional aspects discussed here. What evidence has been collected has concentrated on the use of negative campaigning and has shown the web to be something of a neutral to upbeat zone. Klotz (1997), for instance, found that only seventeen of fifty US Senate candidates mentioned their opponent in an unfavorable light on their sites in 1996. Other studies have shown that both Senate and gubernatorial candidates in 1998 had highly positive homepages and saved the rare attack for pages deep within the sites (Kamarck 1998; LaPointe 1999; Greer and LaPointe 1999).

Finally, as well as building a picture of what is being offered by candidates on the web, a very limited amount of work has been done to identify the individual and environmental factors that may determine the differences discovered in site content and communication style. Gender differences, for instance, have been observed as important for online campaign style. Women candidates in the US Senate races of 2000 were found to have used a greater percentage of the web's interactive capabilities than male candidates (Puopolo 2001). Incumbency has been found to be an important factor in shaping website content. LaPointe (1999) found that Senate incumbents had significantly more interactive sites and were significantly more positive in their message than challengers. This is not too surprising since as Fenno has pointed out, office holders need to establish a positive reputation for their on-the-job performance (Fenno 1996). However, research has shown also that congressional and gubernatorial incumbents were also more likely to rely on official government sites instead of putting up their own campaign sites (Klotz 1998; D'Alessio 2000). Incumbents in jeopardy, however, proved to be more likely to establish an independent website (Kamarck 1998).

Party has also been argued to influence online campaign communication since minor parties and independents may see the web as a way to combat the "freezing out" they receive from the traditional media (Gibson and Ward 1998). Recent research by Gibson *et al.* (2003) on the German party system has also lent support to the idea that parties' primary goals (i.e. vote maximization, office seeking, etc.) may play a role in determining how far they emphasize the participatory features of the web as opposed to its electioneering and information-provision capabilities. In the United States, Republican sites were found to outperform Democrats in 1996, in terms of the information offered on candidate's policy stances, and facilities for making financial contributions as well as signing up for mailing lists (Tedesco *et al.* 1999). D'Alessio (2000) later found Democrats to be slower adopters than Republicans in US House, Senate, and gubernatorial contests. Analysis of the 2000 Senate races in the United States, however, showed that 61 percent of Democrats' sites had a mission statement, compared to 47 percent of Republican sites. Democrats were also found to be more likely to discuss education than Republicans, but Republicans were more "web savvy," because they were more likely to include volunteer options, voter registration information, a market place, audio, video, motion graphics, links, pop-up features, and several other features (Puopolo 2001). Major party candidates were also found to be more likely than minor party candidates to use the Internet as a campaign tool. Most minor party candidates' sites are basic and tend to be associated with the Reform Party, Libertarian Party, or the Green Party (Kamarck 2002).

This review makes it clear that cyber-campaigning and our understanding of it is evolving. There is evidence of innovation but also of a bias toward controlled dissemination of information, rather than more radical strategies to promote participation. The primary goal of this chapter is to investigate these impressions through systematic empirical analysis of Senate and gubernatorial candidates' websites in the 1998 and 2000 elections. The sites are content analyzed with regard to the information, graphics, and interactivity that they contain as well as their overall tone in terms of attacks on opponents. The differences that emerge are then explored with a range of variables that have been associated with variance in offline campaigning such as candidates' gender, outsider status, and party affiliation, in addition to election year (1998 versus 2000) and type of office sought. The findings are then discussed in terms of what they reveal about the overall direction in which candidates' sites are moving, and finally what those changes say about the move toward a more postmodern style of campaigning.

Data and methods

The population studied in this research is gubernatorial and Senate candidates' websites in the 1998 and 2000 US elections. In 1998, gubernatorial races were ongoing in thirty-five states, and Senate races were being fought in thirty-four states. In 2000, thirteen states were choosing a governor, and thirty-four Senate seats were up for grabs. The campaign websites were found from state-by-state listings published online by Politics One (www.politics1.com) and Election Net (www.electnet.org). In addition, the Yahoo Internet directory (www.yahoo.com), the Excite search engine (www.excite.com), and, in 2000, the Google search engine (www.google.com) were used to find any other campaign sites the directories might not have included. Any candidate having a homepage on the web, whether sponsored by the campaign or the candidate's party, was included in this study. Candidates who had web pages but had lost their party primary were excluded unless they continued to run as an independent for another party after the primary. Incumbents that had only a government-sponsored site as their web presence were also included. The web sources consulted proved very comprehensive with only four sites added to the dataset that were not found using the directories.

In terms of research design, Senate and gubernatorial candidates' sites were examined for several reasons. First, there are relatively few studies of them, with most US analysts tending to look mainly at presidential sites. Second, Senate and gubernatorial contests provide a large number of sites for analysis but not so many that the entire population cannot be studied. Finally, because these contests are alike in a number of key ways – both have statewide constituencies, require large budgets, and attract candidates at about the same stage in their political careers – it is possible, following the most similar systems design logic, to pool the data and create a larger sample, from which the impact of the varying political and demographic influences can be more readily detected.

Methodologically, following the practice of previous studies of parties online, coders collected basic website data on the presence or absence of certain types of information items (i.e. candidate biography, stand on issues, constituent help), types of visual elements (pictures, video, animation), and interactive features (i.e. E-mail address, guestbook, bulletin board). If the items were present, the website scored one and if absent zero was assigned. The number of items present within each category was then summed to create total information, graphical element, and interactivity scores for each candidate (further information on the items scored can be seen in Tables 6.1–6.4 in the results section). Higher numbers on each score indicated that more of the types of information, graphical elements, and interactivity were present.

In addition to types of content available, researchers examined the focus and tone of the sites. Only the first page of the site was examined for these variables because homepages mark the entry to the sites. Also, examining the entire content of the site for focus and tone would have proven prohibitive. Focus was measured by a seven-point scale whereby "1" indicated a homepage devoted solely to candidate image and "7" was selected for a homepage devoted solely to campaign issues. A score of "4" represented a mixed image/issue focus. Tone of the site was measured by a five-point scale whereby "1" indicated a homepage that was 100 percent positive and "5", one that was 100 percent negative. A score of "3" represented an even mix of positive and negative. A neutral option was included (e.g. for sites that only had a directory on the homepage), however, no sites were found to be neutral in tone. Attacking was measured on a seven-point scale with '1' indicating no attacking present on the homepage and "7" indicating the entire homepage was devoted to attacking. The attacking measure was designed to measure a narrow subset of negative communication beyond that measure by the tone variable. Specifically, negative communication referred to content that was directly aimed at attacking another candidate or party. Unlike the content measures, therefore, these measures of style and tone were assigned according to coders overall judgment of a site, rather than counts of items present or absent. In order to ensure coder consistency, two different sets of trained coders examined the sites in each election. Their scores were fairly consistent on the tone measures, with intercoder reliability averaging 84.7 percent. This was slightly lower than the overall reliability for the entire instrument (see later).

Finally, data was collected about candidates including gender, party affiliation, and candidate standing (challenger or incumbent). Type of site used by the candidate also was noted. Some candidates were incumbents and only used their official governmental site. Others, typically minor party candidates, had only a page or a brief mention on a party site, while other candidates' only web presence was on a business, citizens group, or other type of site. Sites specifically focused on one candidate's bid for a given office were coded as candidate-specific election sites.

Data was collected from the Monday to the Sunday immediately preceding the Tuesday general elections in each election cycle (from October 26 until November 1 in 1998 and from October 30 to November 5 in 2000). This time frame was chosen because, as Election Day nears, candidates and campaign communicators are most engaged in trying to win votes (Fenno 1996). Candidates establishing sites, therefore, would have to have done so by this time. Sites not accessible during the first check were rechecked up to the Sunday before the election. If still not accessible on that day, demographic information on the candidates was collected using the Politics One site but site information was recorded as missing data. In 1998, 129 sites were identified for active gubernatorial candidates and 93 for Senate candidates (222 sites analyzed in total). In 2000, 46 sites for gubernatorial candidates were identified and 125 for Senate races were found (171 in all). In total, 393 sites were analyzed. In both years, two coders collected data, with 10 percent of the sites coded by both coders. Intercoder reliability for the entire coding instrument (i.e. both content and tone measures) on the 40 sites ranged from 74.3 to 98.1 percent for an average of 91.3 percent.

Findings

First, descriptive statistics are presented about the sites across the two time periods being studied, based on the characteristics of the candidates running them in terms of office sought, gender, party, and incumbency status. Then, the content and tone of the 393 sites are discussed and compared by election year and finally, we present a more rigorous statistical analysis that examines the impact of election year on site content and tone, along with other important candidate and election variables.

Overall profile of websites

The distribution of sites according to individual candidate characteristics is reported in Table 6.1, according to year. Overall, there were more senatorial sites than gubernatorial, reflecting the fact that the former outnumbered the latter in total number of races during the period studied. In terms of demographics, websites were much more likely to be run by male candidates than female in both election years. Again this was reflective of the overall campaign environment,

Table 6.1 Distribution of Senate and gubernatorial sites in the 1998 and 2000 elections according to selected election and candidate-specific variables

Background variable	1998	2000	Total
Office sought			
Senator	93 (41.9)	125 (73.1)	218
Governor	129 (58.1)	46 (29.9)	175
Gender			
Male	189 (85.1)	149 (87.1)	338
Female	33 (14.9)	22 (12.9)	55
Type of site			
Govt.	20 (9.0)	9 (5.3)	29
Party	31 (14.0)	7 (4.1)	38
Candidate	155 (70.1)	151 (88.8)	306
Other	15 (6.8)	3 (1.3)	18
Party			
Republican	67 (30.2)	49 (28.1)	115
Democrat	68 (30.6)	43 (25.1)	111
Minor/independent	87 (39.2)	80 (46.8)	167
Standing			
Insider	118 (53.2)	85 (49.7)	203
Outsider	104 (46.8)	86 (50.3)	190
Race type			
Open	56 (25.2)	49 (28.7)	105
Incumbent running	166 (74.8)	122 (71.3)	288
Total for election cycle	222	171	393

Notes
Figures are raw 'n' followed by percentages in parentheses. Percentages are calculated from the column totals for each variable by year. For example, in 1998, 41.9 percent of the sites analyzed were those of Senate candidates and 58.1 percent those of gubernatorial candidates.

rather than any inherent bias in the technology since major parties put forward only eleven female nominees in the races for Senate or governor in 2000. Indeed, our findings show that ten of those eleven nominees ran websites indicating that women candidates actually had a highly proactive stance toward cyber-campaigning. Most sites were candidate-specific campaign sites, rather than official government sites or party sites, particularly by 2000. In terms of party, Republicans and Democrats operated most sites, but a significant number of minor party and independent candidates also ran sites in both election years. In addition, almost half of the sites that were put up belonged to candidates who had never held any elective office, indicating outsiders were keen to use the medium. Finally, websites were more common in those races where an incumbent was running compared with those vying for an open seat. This distribution can also be seen to reflect offline campaign dynamics to a large degree in that Senate and gubernatorial races with incumbents outweighed open races by a factor of about four to one in 1998 and 2000.

After examining the distribution of the sites in terms of their "background" features, the sites were then scrutinized in terms of their content and overall style.

Table 6.2 Mean scores for content, style, and tone of
candidates homepage by year

Style and tone measures	1998	2000
Information	4.18	6.33***
Graphics	1.49	1.88***
Interactivity	1.97	3.96***
Focus	3.77	4.20*
Tone	1.70	1.76
Attacking	1.50	2.36***

Notes
Independent sample *t*-tests for significant increases or
decreases in scores between 1998 and 2000. A p value <0.05
is indicated by *; *** indicates $p<0.001$.

Information dissemination, graphics, and interactivity

Information was measured using a 0–11 scale, in which candidates scored one point for each information item present on their sites. While every site scored at least 1, no site scored maximum points, and only two sites scored 10. On average, candidates scored 5. The range of information presented increased significantly from 1998, when candidates scored an average of 4.2, to 2000, when this rose to 6.3, a statistically significant increase ($t=11.74$, df $=384$, $p<0.001$).

As Table 6.2 also shows, the emphasis on graphics rose between the two election cycles. Within a range of 0–3, the average graphical element score increased from 1.5 in 1998 to 1.9 in 2000, a jump that proved statistically significant ($t=4.89$, df $=386$, $p<0.001$). Finally, for interactivity, sites were awarded 1 point for each of 12 elements coded. As many as 36 sites scored 0 points on this index, offering no interactivity at all, not even an E-mail address. The two most interactive sites scored 10, while the average score was a low 2.8. As with the previous content areas, interactivity showed a significant increase between 1998, when sites had an average score of 2.0, and 2000, when sites averaged 4.0 ($t=9.99$, df $=3.84$, $p<0.001$).

Focus and tone of homepages

Complementing the analysis of content were our measures of the focus and tone of the site's homepage. As Table 6.2 shows, sites were evenly balanced between complete focus on image (1) and on issue (7) with a mean score of 4.0 for all 383 sites. Overall, 73 sites (18.6 percent) were considered entirely image-oriented and 17 (4.3 percent) entirely issue-oriented. Interestingly, sites did become significantly more issue-focused between the election cycles, scoring 3.7 in 1998 and 4.2 in 2000 ($t=2.09$, df $=382$, $p<0.04$).

In terms of tone, the results show that overall the sites were very positive, scoring 1.7 on average (where 1 = all positive and 5 = all negative). In fact, 51.4 percent

(202) of the 385 valid homepages were entirely positive. Another 28 percent (111) were mostly positive, and 12 percent (48) had an even mix of positive and negative communication. Only 6 percent (24) were mostly or entirely negative. As Table 6.3 reports no marked differences were observed in the overall tone of the sites according to election cycle. After overall tone was analyzed, a more specific type of negative communication was examined. Attacking indicated the extent of negative communication directed specifically at opponents or their parties (measured on a scale where 1 equaled no attacking and 7 equals all attack). The results confirm that attacking was rare, with an average attack score of 1.9 (indicating that less than 10 percent of the site was devoted to attacking)

Table 6.3 Website content for Senate and gubernatorial candidates by year

Content item	1998	2000
Information		
Candidate biography	194(89.4)	159 (93.5)
Stand on issues	186 (85.7)	162 (95.9)***
Highlighting achievements	103 (47.5)	114 (85.2)***
News, press releases	139 (64.1)	128 (75.7)*
Voting information	79 (36.4)-	154 (91.1)**
Separate links page	56 (25.7)	48 (28.2)
Constituent help information	38 (29.2)	14 (8.3)**
Information about opponent	40 (18.4)	71 (48.6)***
"Other" – novel information	33 (15.2)	70 (41.4)***
General government information	22 (10.1)	29 (17.2)*
Information about family	18 (8.3)	81 (55.0)***
Graphical elements		
Photo/graphic	199 (90.9)	169 (99.4)***
Animation	82 (37.6)	91 (75.8)***
Video/audio	44 (20.2)	60 (35.3)***
Interactivity		
E-mail address	158 (72.8)	154 (91.1)***
"Get involved" CGI form	85 (39.2)	101 (59.8)***
Online contributions accepted	43 (19.8)	104 (61.5)***
Other interactivity	38 (17.5)	43 (25.4)
Subscription service	30 (13.8)	88 (51.7)***
Downloadable content	20 (9.2)	58 (34.3)***
Search capacity	11 (5.1)	17 (10.1)
Guestbook	11 (5.1)	6 (3.6)
Cyber bumper stickers	10 (4.6)	14 (8.3)
Data collection of visitors	8 (3.7)	39 (23.1)***
Voter survey	6 (2.8)	27 (14.4)***
Bulletin board	7 (3.2)	19 (11.2)**

Notes
Figures are raw '*n*' followed by percentages in parentheses. Percentages refer to the overall number of sites containing the specified item in a given year. Chi-square statistics test for significant increases or decreases in numbers of sites containing content items between 1998 and 2000. A *p* value < 0.05 is indicated by *; ** indicates *p* < 0.01; and *** *p* < 0.001.

and 63 percent of homepages were entirely void of attacks. However, as Table 6.3 shows, sites in 2000 were significantly more attack-oriented than in 1998 (2.4 versus 1.5, $t = 6.25$, df $= 384$, $p < 0.001$). Therefore, while sites were quite positive overall, negative campaigning in the form of attacking opponents did creep into campaign sites in 2000.

By way of expanding on the changes in the mean scores of the content variables reported in Table 6.2, Table 6.3 presents a breakdown of the frequencies for individual items across the two years.

From Table 6.3 it is apparent that although there was an overall increase in information provision over time, some items did appear less frequently in 2000, notably, candidate biographies, links pages, and help to constituents. While the fall in biographical and linkage information is rather puzzling, the drop in the constituent help might be explained by the fact that fewer candidates were relying on government sites by 2000, which arguably, would be more likely to focus on serving constituent needs. In 1998, fifty-one of the sites analyzed were classified as official government and party sites and by 2000 this had dropped to sixteen. Graphical elements featured more heavily on all sites by 2000, with all but one site containing a photo and more than a third carrying audio or video. As Table 6.4 shows, however, it was animation that proved to be the most popular new addition, with almost three-quarters of sites featuring it in 2000 as opposed to just over a third in 1998. In-depth probing of interactivity between the election years reveals that while several types increased significantly over time, the biggest jumps were in tools that allowed visitors to register their support through volunteer forms or online contributions. Opportunities to sign up for news bulletins also increased substantially, as did forms for data collection about users. As Table 6.3 shows, the most commonly available feature, however, remained E-mail contact across both years.

Regression analysis

From these results it would appear that election year or time plays a key role in determining the nature of web campaigning among US candidates. However, these differences might also simply be a function of the larger number of gubernatorial sites analyzed in 1998 compared with 2000. In order to identify the independent impact of these factors, along with a range of other potential influences on candidates' website usage we employ ordinary least squares regression. Thus, the scores for content and tone (as dependent variables) were regressed on a series of dummy variables created to capture the effects of election year and office sought, along with candidate's gender, party affiliation, and status as a political insider, and whether the race was open or included an incumbent. The results are reported in Table 6.4.

The findings, reported in Table 6.4, confirm that election year is indeed the key variable influencing candidates' website production. Senatorial and gubernatorial sites in 2000 were basically far more functional yet also rather more aggressive and negative than had been the case in 1998. In short, the sites were richer and more sophisticated in the three content categories of information, graphics, and interactivity, and overall slightly less image focused, but also more negative in tone.

Table 6.4 Results of regression analyses of content and style measures of candidates' websites

Independent variables	Information	Graphics	Interactivity	Focus	Tone	Attack
Office sought 0 = Sen., 1 = Gov.	−0.004 (0.172)	−0.255** (0.144)	−0.458* (0.199)	0.708** (0.209)	−0.004 (0.098)	−0.449** (0.146)
Standing 0 = insider, 1 = outsider	−0.562* (0.238)	−0.165 (0.118)	−0.316 (0.275)	0.539 (0.290)	0.427** (0.135)	0.449* (0.202)
Party 0 = major, 1 = minor	−1.42*** (0.241)	−0.261* (0.119)	−1.34*** (0.279)	0.779** (0.294)	0.117 (0.137)	0.002 (0.205)
Race type 0 = open, 1 = incumb.	−0.289 (0.181)	−0.127 (0.090)	−0.484* (0.210)	−0.003 (0.219)	0.245* (0.103)	0.267 (0.154)
Year 0 = 1998, 1 = 2000	2.25*** (0.168)	0.335*** (0.083)	1.95*** (0.194)	0.579** (0.204)	0.002 (0.096)	0.701*** (0.143)
Gender 0 = male, 1 = female	0.107 (0.223)	−0.008 (0.111)	0.411 (0.259)	0.168 (0.272)	−0.002 (0.127)	−0.274 (0.190)
Model Adjusted R^2	0.458	0.126	0.343	0.125	0.085	0.149

Notes
Each column indicates a separate regression. Unstandardized betas are reported first, followed by their standard error in parentheses below. A p value <0.05 indicated by *; $p<0.01$ by **; and $p<0.001$ by ***.

After election year, however, the most important influence on websites was type of office being sought and also the party affiliation of the candidate. Specifically, while Senate and gubernatorial candidates offered similar amounts of information on their sites, the former offered significantly more interactivity and graphics and tended to focus more on image rather than issues. Major party candidates offered more of everything in terms of content on their site, although minor party candidates did tend to be less personalized and focus more on the issues. In terms of the impact of other factors, it seems having held office before (being a political insider) led one to provide more information and take a more positive stance. Outsiders were significantly more likely to adopt a more negative tone and attack other candidates. Those races where incumbents were running also tended to see more negativity but also were more focused on interactivity. Gender was notably not important as a predictor of any of the features of campaign websites measured here.

Discussion

So do these findings reveal the new media to be an arena for innovation and change? At first glance one might argue they tell a largely unimpressive story. Sites for major party candidates had more of everything than did those of the minor parties in terms of information, graphics, and interactivity although they did tend to be less focused on policy issues than minor party sites. Political insiders (incumbents and other past or current office holders) also made more information available and tended to be more positive in tone than political outsiders. Although this study didn't examine candidates' financial commitments to the sites, these results support the idea that established political forces are reinforcing their offline dominance (Margolis *et al.* 1997; Norris 2000). One interesting caveat to note here, however, is that while women ran fewer sites than men in both election years, those that did, displayed no significant differences in content and style to their male counterparts, according to the measures used here. While this finding should be treated with some caution given the small number of female candidates included in the analysis, it does raise the interesting possibility of the web as a gender-neutral communications terrain. As such it would clearly differ from previous forms of media advertising where distinct differences have been observed (Trent and Friedenberg 1983; Johnson-Cartee and Copeland 1997).

Despite evidence of a resurfacing of preexisting patterns of political influence, however, these findings also indicative that candidates are becoming more functional and experimental in their approach to the web. Specifically, it seems candidates are becoming savvier in using the web to disseminate news to voters and the media. Certainly journalists are becoming keener to incorporate campaign sites into their election coverage, linking to them directly or telling their audience to visit their sites for more information. In addition, the interactivity of the Internet is clearly being exploited more in elections, with 2000 seeing the proliferation of voter surveys and volunteer forms on offer from candidates. Such initiatives, however, do not necessarily signal the move toward a more participatory democracy. More options for citizen input need to be met by a symmetrical response from elites in order to empower both parties. Indeed, as McKeown and Plowman (1999) have pointed out, much of the political elites' use of new ICTs has tended to take an asymmetrical form, involving voters in ways that are largely beneficial to the campaign.

In terms of how far the Internet is promoting the shift toward a postmodern style of campaigning, these results certainly show that the new technologies are producing a bifurcation in campaign strategy. Campaign websites are becoming both more informative and interactive, but are also using more sophisticated graphics and taking a more negative stance toward opponents. Thus, while websites may be allowing candidates to open up deeper and more direct channels of communication with voters than they had in the "modern" era, they are also being utilized in a flashier, attack-oriented manner. The fact that these changes are related most strongly to election year rather than type of office sought, type of party, or candidate gender, suggests that cyber-campaigning is evolving, to a certain extent on its own steam or according to its own logic, not as a result of a particular type of candidate or party approach.

Any nod to technological determinism here, however, is fleeting. The findings of this chapter essentially return us to the central theme of this volume – the importance of representative democracy as a context for political actors' use of the web. While candidates are showing signs of greater interest in the interactive capabilities of new ICTs, such deployment is generally oriented toward extracting resources from the citizen to aid the campaign, rather than for introducing new forms of direct democracy. Certainly, the reemergence of old habits in the form of negative advertising in the websites of 2000 suggests that candidates' approach to campaigning in the new media is not departing radically from existing practice. The extent to which these emergent trends continue over time, however, is of course a key issue for researchers to explore and one that we shall return to in the US presidential elections of 2004.

Bibliography

Bryant, J. (1995) "Paid Media Advertising," in Thurber, J. A. and Nelson, C. J. (eds), *Campaigns and Elections American Style*, Boulder, Colo.: Westview Press.
Birnbaum, J. (2000) "Politicking on the internet," *Fortune*, March, 84–6.
Corrado, A. (1996) "Elections in Cyberspace," in Corrado, A. and Firestone, C. (eds), *Elections in Cyberspace*, Washington, DC: The Aspen Institute.
D'Alessio, D. (2000) "Adoption of the World Wide Web by American Political Candidates, 1996–1998," *Journal of Broadcasting and Electronic Media*, 44, 556–68.
Davis, R. and Owen, D. (1998) *New Media and American Politics*, New York: Oxford University Press.
Dulio, D. A., Goff, D. L. and Thurber, J. A. (1999) "Untangled web," *PS: Political Science & Politics*, 32 (1), 53–9.
Epstein, E. (1996) "Election '96 Internet Style," *PC World*, May, 174–80.
Faucheux, R. (1998) "How Campaigns Are Using the Internet," *Campaigns & Elections*, September, 22–6.
Fenno, R. F. (1996) *Senators on the Campaign Trail*, Norman, Okla.: University of Oklahoma.
Farrell, D. and Webb, P. (2000) "Political Parties as Campaign Organizations," in Dalton, R. and Wattenberg, M. (eds), *Parties Without Partisans*, Oxford: Oxford University Press, 102–28.
Fineman, H. (1999) "Pressing the Flesh Online," *Newsweek*, September 20, 50–3.
Gibson, R. and Ward, S. (1998) "U.K. Political Parties and the Internet," *Press/Politics*, 3 (3), 14–38.
Gibson, R. and Römmele, A. (2001) "A Party Centered Theory of Professionalized Campaigning," *International Journal of Press Politics*, 6 (4), 31–44.
Gibson, R., Römmele, A. and Ward, S. (2003) "German Parties and Internet Campaigning in the 2002 Federal Election," *German Politics*, 12 (1), 79–104
Greer, J. and LaPointe, M. E. (1999) "Meaningful Discourse or Cyber-Fluff? paper presented at the annual meeting of the International Communication Association, San Francisco, May 1999.
Hall, M. (1997) "One to One Politics in Cyberspace," *Media Studies Journal*, 2, 97–103.
Johnson-Cartee, K. S. and Copeland, G. A. (1997) *Inside Political Campaigns*, Westport, Conn.: Praeger.
Just, M. R. (1997) "Candidate Strategies and the Media Campaign," in Pomper G. M. *et al.* (eds), *The Election of 1996*, Chatham, NJ: Chatham House Publishers.
Kamarck, E. C. (1998) "Stalking the Wild Netizen," *Newsday*, October 25, B4.

Kamarck, E. C. (2002) "Political Campaigning on the Internet" in Kamarck, E. C. and Nye, J. S., Jr (eds), *Governance.com*, Washington, DC: Brookings, 81–103.

Klotz, R. (1997) "Positive Spin," *PS: Political Science & Politics*, 30 (3), 482–6.

Klotz, R. (1998) "Virtual criticism," *Political Communication*, 15, 347–65.

Kornblut, A. E. and Abraham, Y. (2000) "Campaign 2000 / Republicans Touting Conservative Themes, Bush Shifts Tone in SC," *The Boston Globe*, February 3, A28.

LaPointe, M. (1999) "Cyberpolitics and the U.S. Senate," unpublished thesis, University of Nevada-Reno.

Leiter, L. (1995) "Goodbye BBQ and Buttons, Hello Web and Home Page," *Insight on the News*, September 25, 46–8.

Lynch, M. (2001) "E-lection Wrap-Up," *Chief Executive Magazine*, January, 24–8.

Margolis, M., Resnick, D., and Tu, C. (1997) "Campaigning on the Internet," paper presented at the annual meeting of the American Political Science Association, Washington, DC, September 1997.

McKeown, C. A. and Plowman, K. D. (1998) "Reaching Publics on the Web During the 1996 Presidential Campaign," paper presented at the annual meeting of the Association for Education in Journalism and Mass Communication, Baltimore, Md., August 1998.

McManus, T. (1999a) "A Democratic Medium Plays Big 2000 Role," *Advertising Age*, October 11, 62–4.

McManus, T. (1999b) "Political Campaigns Pivot on Web," *Advertising Age*, December 13, 76.

Meadow, R. G. (1989) "Political Campaigns," in Rice, R. and Atkin, C. (eds), *Public Communication Campaigns*, Newbury Park, CA: Sage.

Miller, G. and Schrader, E. (1998) "Internet's Role in Campaigns Still Limited," *Los Angeles Times*, October, 28, A1.

Norris, P. (2000) *A Virtuous Circle*, Cambridge, UK: Cambridge University Press.

NUA (2002) *How Many Online* <http://www.nua.com/surveys/how_many_online/index.html>, first accessed December 12, 2002.

Pew Research Center (2000) *Youth Vote Influenced by Online Information* <http://people-press.org/reports/display.php3?ReportID = 21>, first accessed December 12, 2002.

Puopolo, S. (2001) "The Web and U.S. Senatorial Campaigns 2000," *The American Behavioral Scientist*, 44 (12), 2030–47.

Reavy, M. M. and Perlmutter, D. (1996) "Presidential Websites as Sources of Information," paper presented at the annual meeting of the Association for Education in Journalism and Mass Communication in Los Angeles, June 1996.

Shelton, S. (2000) "Candidates Warming Up to Internet; Plugged In," *The Atlanta Journal and Constitution*, June 4, 1JJ.

Sternberg, B. von (1999) "Cyber Campaign is Getting Crowded," *Star Tribune*, June 3, A6.

Tedesco, J. C. *et al.* (1999) "Presidential Campaigning on the Information Superhighway," in Kaid, L. L. and Bystrom, D. G. (eds), *The Electronic Election: Perspectives on the 1996 Campaign Communication*, Mahwah, NJ: Lawrence Erlbaum Associates.

Tillett, S. (2000) "Getting personal – Campaigns Deliver E-Business Lessons," *Internetweek*, September 25, 128.

Trent, J. S. and Friedenberg, R. V. (1983) *Political Campaign Communication*, New York, NY: Praeger.

Wring, D. and Horrocks, I. (2001) "The Transformation of Political Parties?" in Axford, B. and Huggins, R. (eds), *New Media and Politics*, London: Sage.

7 Global legal pluralism and electronic democracy

Oren Perez

> ...the age of photography corresponds precisely to the explosion of the private into the public, or rather into the creation of a new social value, which is the publicity of the private: the private is consumed as such, publicly.
>
> (Roland Barthes, *Camera Lucida: Reflections on Photography*, 1993: 98)

The emergence of the Internet has transformed the way in which we experience the private and public spheres. On the one hand the Internet has opened new ways for projecting private experiences into the public sphere using various webcast technologies. On the other hand, the Internet promises to reshape the boundaries of the public space. Political communication no longer needs to be centred on face-to-face interactions undertaken in uniquely designed spaces, but can be accessed from the private domain through atomized computer screens and electronically mediated interchanges. What does this blurring of old boundaries mean for the body politic? This chapter seeks to address this broad question with reference to one particular facet of the public sphere: the broadening realm of transnational law.

The increasing encroachment of international legal norms into the previously secluded boundaries of the nation state has raised questions about the legitimacy of this emergent system of governance. This chapter explores how the Internet might be used to address some of these concerns. In doing so, the chapter moves us beyond questions about the Internet's impact on established domestic institutions to examine its role as creator of wholly new representative structures, outside the national context. It is argued that new information and communication technologies (ICTs) do offer significant potential for the development of more inclusive transnational governing structures, but that the realization of such structures depends on focused intervention by civil society and the support of existing national and international bureaucracies. Any theorizing about the possibility of Net-induced democratization at the international level, therefore, must be situated within familiar analytical frameworks about 'collective action' and 'interest mobilization'. Thus, while the focus is on these new, extra-national legal actors, the chapter returns us to a central theme of the book – the understanding that technology alone cannot engineer change. The adoption of new ICTs, even among newly forming representative bodies without a long history or large constituencies, is subject to broader environmental constraints.

The emergence of new forms of global law that operate beyond the traditional geopolitical boundaries of the state system is a key component of the globalization process (Teubner 1997; Perez 2002). This expanding network of global laws is highly diverse, both in terms of its thematic interest and organizational structure. It includes new types of state-oriented systems such as the World Trade Organization (WTO), as well as private regimes covering areas such as technical standardization, governance of the Internet, and transnational commerce.

While many of these systems of transnational law have evolved in the shadow of the new global economy, their impact is not confined to the economic realm. International governance now extends to civic territories such as free speech, art, and the protection of the environment. The legal system of the WTO, for example, has dealt with disputes relating to the risks of synthetic growth hormones in cattle, the industrial use of asbestos, and damage caused to sea turtles from shrimp trawling.[1] International standards setting organizations such as the International Organization for Standardization (ISO) and the Codex Alimentarius Commission have been involved in the production of controversial standards for environmental management (the ISO 14000 series) and foods derived from biotechnology.[2]

The expanding geographic and normative framework of these international organizations has, not surprisingly, led to calls for increasing the openness and transparency of their operations. Coming in for particular scrutiny are the Bretton Woods triad of the WTO, the World Bank and the International Monetary Fund (IMF). The large-scale protests that took place in Seattle in 1998, and Québec, Gothenburg and Genoa in 2001 bear strong testimony to the growing public demand for greater accountability on the part of these organizations and increased awareness of the social and humanitarian consequences of their actions (Ecologist 2000).

The central impetus mobilizing these challenges, one can argue, is a procedural understanding of democratic legitimacy. The right of the transnational regime to govern is established by it allowing the affected community some say in the design and implementation of the ruling norms. In order to be legitimate, some measures need to be in place to ensure that public consent and control is provided.[3] The key issue, therefore, facing these new global legal and political entities, in the light of these challenges, is whether they can devise processes through which these ideals can be realized. Properly responding to this democratic deficit requires the development of inclusive and non-hierarchical decision-making structures, which could break the confines of the current nationalistic order, and offer the public direct access to processes of global norm-production.

This chapter focuses on the possible contribution that the Internet can make, and is making, to the development of these novel decision-making structures. In particular, it examines whether the Internet can offer ways to incorporate the public more meaningfully into the infrastructure of global legal regimes. The capacity of the Internet to short-cut barriers of space and time, make it, at least prima facie, the ideal medium for transnational deliberation. Indeed, this has been shown, somewhat ironically by the fact that the Internet has played a major role in facilitating the protests against these new global regimes. Protestors have used the Internet extensively, both to publicize their critique and, more instrumentally, to coordinate their actions. Websites such as Protest.Net, www.indymedia.org, www.WebActive.com and www.corpwatch.org have turned into 'hubs' of political communication. All of these websites include details of upcoming protests, action alerts and links to other protest websites. This extensive political usage of the Net has even led some commentators to assert that the Internet could revolutionize the face of global politics.[4] However, despite the impressive growth of civic protest over the Internet, the use of the Internet to incorporate the public in transnational governance processes appears to be very limited. The question remains, therefore, whether the Internet has indeed the capacity to foster more inclusive structures of global law-making.

The chapter addresses this question in three stages. First, the traditional conception of transnational governance is reviewed and its weaknesses for understanding and addressing the issues raised by the emerging system of global law are identified. A more contemporary interpretation of international regime formation is then presented that requires a democratic and truly global decision-making forum. Second, the role of the Internet as a means of realizing such ambitions is explored, using the idea of politics as a problem of 'collective action'. The discussion presents a simple game-theoretic model to illustrate the capacity of the Internet to facilitate the emergence of viable transnational communities. In the third and final section, three case studies are presented to show how some international regimes are currently attempting to utilize the Internet to facilitate a more democratic mode of operating. The focus here is on the WTO, the ISO and Internet Corporation for Assigned Names and Numbers (ICANN).

The problem of legitimacy and the Westphalian paradigm

According to the Westphalian, or intergovernmental paradigm of international regime formation, legitimacy rests with state consent – either to a specific set of norms (treaties) or to the establishment of a body with norm-producing powers such as the WTO (Caldwell 1996: 146). The consent of the state is secured through the actions of its authorized agents (state officials), and thus is only indirectly related to the wishes of the state citizenry (Petersmann 1999). This view of the creation and monitoring of international regimes is problematic on a number of grounds. First, from a procedural point of view, the idea that state officials represent and are bound by the preferences of the people is, at best, questionable. The constitutional framework of most states does not provide for any regular, or even sporadic opportunities for public consultation and discussion over transnational issues.

Even if the paradigm could be tweaked to provide for more direct democratic state-based supervision of transnational negotiations, however, it faces a more crucial problem of practical relevance. Essentially, this model has been overtaken by the new realities of norm creation at the international level. According to the Westphalian paradigm, the international organization is a highly controllable entity, which is wholly dependent on the states that created it. This vision of organizational obedience, however, fails to appreciate the increasingly autonomous nature of transnational organizations, as well as the fact that many systems of transnational law rely on bases of support that are located outside the state system. This kind of deep independence characterizes both state-oriented regimes such as the WTO, and global private regimes such as the *lex mercatoria*. To a large extent these legal systems operate as autonomous decision-making structures that are sheltered from the influence of interstate politics. In this sense the Westphalian model of detached polities and fragmented deliberation is wholly inappropriate as the basis for any new model of global cooperation. Indeed one can argue that it forms a barrier to the development of the more internationally oriented communicative processes that are needed by these regimes to enhance their legitimacy.

The legitimacy of these new forms of a-national law, therefore, requires the development of new, cross-border structures of decision-making, which will provide the public with more meaningful forms of participation. The argument of this chapter is that the Internet can provide such novel participatory structures through its ability to deliver 'direct deliberation' on a global scale. Direct deliberation interprets the democratic process as a 'collective decision-making that proceeds through direct participation by and reason-giving between and among free and equal citizens' (Cohen and Sabel 1997: 314). It defines the 'public arena' in which such deliberation takes place as a product of common aims or concerns, and not as a reflection of national identities. This interpretation of democracy as a legitimate way of 'living together' does not rely on the capacity of all-embracing deliberation to produce consensus (and hence, consent). Rather, the legitimizing force of democratic deliberation is postulated to rise from a culturally shared belief in the moral legitimacy of decisions, which were made through a fair and open dialogue. It is the openness of the deliberation process to all those concerned, and its relative fairness, which gives the democratic process its legitimizing power.

A model of electronic participation

This section seeks to assess whether the Internet can be used to construct more inclusive governance structures in the transnational domain. It considers in that context the differences between electronic and non-electronic participatory schemes. These questions are considered through a simple game-theoretic model, which is based on the understanding of politics as a problem of 'collective action'. The goal of using game theory here is to expose the strategic dilemmas that can arise from the introduction of a transnational scheme of e-participation. This exposition brings out more clearly both the various advantages of the Internet as a participatory medium, and its basic limitations.

Constructing a model of e-participation requires a clear definition of 'electronic democracy' or 'electronic participation'. It is possible to distinguish in this context between three different ways in which the Internet can be harnessed to the democratic process. First, the Internet constitutes an efficient means for achieving transparency. Indeed, as one author has put it 'The Internet can make genuinely public what has only been nominally public' (Starr 2000). Transparency is a necessary condition for the evolution of meaningful delibera- tion. Second, the Internet can be used by the international organization to elicit public comments on its normative output. Here, the Internet is used to facilitate unidirectional communication: the international organization – placed at the receiving end – is responsible for collecting, interpreting and judging the com- ments of the public. The deliberation process is controlled by the international organization. The Internet is not used here as a medium for conversation but only as a cost-effective delivery service, which carries messages between disassociated individuals and the relevant institution. Finally, the Internet can be used also to facilitate wide-ranging dialogue between the institution and the public and within the public itself. Under this multidirectional model none of the communicators has exclusive control over the timing and content of communications. Only this last option comes near the ideal picture of 'directly-deliberative democracy'.

The model developed in this section is based on a unidirectional participation scheme. This scheme was favoured for several reasons. First, from a pragmatic perspective it is probably a more realistic assessment of the scope of ambition among international institutions for new forms of public dialogue. Second, it is a simpler model but retains the basic collective-action dilemma that participation on an international level encounters, and that the Internet can purportedly help resolve. Thus, heuristically it is preferable. The model, following Olsonian logic, envisages participation as a game whereby 'public (or normative) goods' are secured as benefits that accrue to the (transnational) community as a whole, leav- ing costs to be borne (exclusively) by the individual participators. I leave the exact nature of the public good undefined. In our context it will usually reflect the possibility of bringing about a change in the content of a proposed transnational norm (hence the term 'normative good').

The structure of the model is as follows.[5] The relevant community (defined as the set of people who could be influenced by a particular transnational norm) consists of N people. Each member of the community faces a binary choice: they can either participate, with a cost of C_i, or not participate, in which C_i is saved (C_i reflects the direct costs of participation). It is assumed that the public good would be provided with probability α only if K people or more participate.[6] This assumption portrays the international organization in largely cynical terms, as responding only to the level of public pressure (modelled here as a function of the number of individual 'reactions'), rather than to the substantive quality of the arguments presented.[7] A successful participatory process yields for each of the N members an expected utility of $V_i(Pg)$. V_i is a function of predetermined individual political/ideological preferences.[8]

From an individual perspective there are two major impediments to collective action. First, because the public good (Pg) could be provided (with probability α) only if the threshold K is achieved, any individual effort that would be made without the presence of additional $K-1$ contributions will be wasted (with probability 1). Thus, a player who believes that there will be, overall, only $K-1$ contributions (including his), will not find it in his interest to participate. Second, a player who believes that there are K participants (beside himself) will have little incentive to participate as his voice will not add to the probability of the public good being provided.[9] This means that – for an individual to contribute – it is not enough that the (expected) value of the public good should be greater than the cost of participation. Rather, a rational individual will make an effort to participate only if he believes that he is the Kth participant, that is, that he has a pivotal role in generating the public good. Before investing resources in the political game the individual would need, then, some assurance that his contribution is indeed critical. This turns the game of transnational deliberation into an 'assurance game'.

A preliminary condition for the emergence of a 'participatory community' is the existence of at least K individuals for whom the participation cost is smaller or equal to the expected value of the public good. The individual rationality condition requires, then, that:

$$\text{Ci} \leq \text{Vi (Pg)}^{10} \tag{1}$$

where Ci is the cost of participation and Vi(Pg) measures the expected utility of i from the public good. Assume that N' people (of the total community N) satisfy this basic condition. Under these assumptions the model anticipates two types of Nash equilibrium:[11]

(a) $N'!/(K!(N'-K)!$ that is all the possible combinations of K contributors out of the set N' of potential contributors.[12] We can interpret this number as representing the number of potential coalitions. I will denote the set of these coalitions as B_k (with $X_j \in B_k$ denoting a particular coalition).
(b) Another possible solution is one in which no one contributes.

It is possible to gain some insight into the question of individual criticality by comparing the number of potential solutions at N' and at $N'-1$. This comparison is based on the assumption that each individual evaluates his criticality by considering the influence of his withdrawal from the N' community in terms of the decrease in the number of potential coalitions. The effect of such withdrawal can be appreciated by expressing the number of potential solutions at $N'-1$ contributors (denoted B) in terms of the number at N' (denoted A):

$$B = A \times [(N'-K)/N']^{13} \tag{2}$$

Equation (2) points out two important features of the criticality question. First, when the value of N' (the group of potential contributors) is relatively large compared to K (the threshold community) the importance of each individual contribution decreases (since B approaches A). Second, because the value of A is likely to rise quickly with N', the value of B is likely to remain high even in small ratios of $(N' - K)/N'$; this will contribute again to a diminishing sense of criticality by an individual participant.[14]

It should be noted that the model outlined here does not purport to explain the process by which a particular equilibrium or coalition (out of these multifarious equilibria) is eventually selected. Extensive research on this so-called emergence puzzle, however, has revealed that larger groups exhibit lower levels of cooperation than smaller ones. The main reasons for this are thought to be the decline in perceived efficacy among individuals in a group as it expands. Basically those in larger groups are less likely to believe that their contribution is essential for the provision of the public good. This is consistent with the interpretation offered to equation (2).[15] In addition, the decreasing opportunities for communication in large groups are also seen to adversely influence the sense of solidarity and mutual commitment in these groups (Colman 1995: 218–21).[16] Overall, however, this research has still not resolved the problem of equilibria selection; it has only identified the kind of conditions in which the prospects for cooperation increase – the exact profile of this emerging cooperation remained uncertain (Ostrom 2000).[17]

The results of this research put a pessimistic note on the possibility of a transnational electronic community emerging *spontaneously*. A large and scattered collection of individuals provides a poor basis for the emergence of spontaneous cooperation. To incorporate these difficulties into the model, I have chosen to construct the selection puzzle as a problem of transaction cost, treating the lack of perceived efficacy and appropriate communication opportunities as barriers to the emergence of a threshold community. These costs are denoted C_T.[18] C_T reflects the costs of generating more opportunities for communication (within the relevant community), or of providing the potential participants with some kind of assurance that their 'voice' is critical.[19] C_T could be modelled as a function whose value increases (in a constant or decreasing rate) with the number of participants. It should probably contain also some fixed-cost element. The investment of C_T is treated, then, as a necessary condition for the emergence of a threshold community.

The introduction of the notion of transaction cost adds an additional constraint to the set of feasible equilibria.[20] To be viable any potential coalition should be able to fund the coordination costs; that is, the aggregate (net) value of the public good, within any viable coalition, should be higher than C_T. Formally, this idea could be represented in the following way:

$$\forall X_j \in B_k, \, X_j: \sum_{i=1,k}(\text{Vi}(\text{Pg}) - \text{Ci}) \geq C_T \tag{3}$$

This condition could be interpreted in two different ways. A first interpretation assumes that this 'hidden' value will be extracted and utilized by a group leader in order ·to finance the coordination effort. A second (and less literal) interpretation views this condition as an indicator of social concern rather than a fiscal attribute. This interpretation recognizes the possibility that some (but not all) of the coordination services will be provided and/or funded by external sources (e.g. public agency), without the presence of actual 'extraction' from the community. However, it assumes that for such external intervention to materialize, the external agency should be convinced that there is strong public interest in the provision of the public good.[21]

How will the introduction of electronic participation influence the results of this model? The first influence would be to reduce C_i. The term C_i consists of two main factors: the costs of gathering information on the subject of the political process (e.g. the details of a proposed international standard) and the participation costs (making your voice heard).[22] The introduction of the Internet reduces these costs. Getting information is now much easier, especially as more and more international institutions take seriously the demand for greater transparency (see the discussion in the third section). Further, the costs of responding to the information should decrease since the Internet opens up new and cheaper ways for submission of views. While the introduction of the Internet can also generate new types of costs such as information overload, these costs should be outweighed by the new efficiencies of retrieval and response, especially when users are focused on extracting particular information about a given normative dilemma.

A second, and even more crucial influence, concerns the coordination costs (C_T). The introduction of the Internet should reduce, substantially, the transaction costs associated with organizing a threshold community. In particular, the Internet opens up new and cheaper ways for institutional entrepreneurs to take the lead and organize a particular coalition.[23] Coordinating a threshold community requires the group leader to communicate with each of the group members. Such communication will usually contain information on the issue at hand, and a signal ensuring the criticality of the addressee. The Internet should reduce substantially the costs of this communication, by allowing the leader to use various automated tools for communication. Assuming that the introduction of the Internet has reduced the individual communication costs by a factor of λ, it is reasonable to assume that the coordination costs will be reduced by a factor of $K\lambda$.[24] This reflects the simple intuition that the group leader can use the Internet to interact simultaneously with all the members of the group. In the pre-Net era both C_i and C_T have been (in the transnational context) prohibitively high – blocking, in effect, the evolvement of transnational participatory schemes.

The introduction of Internet could thus turn the project of transnational participation into a truly practical option. The impact of the Net is not limited, however, to the issue of participation/coordination costs. The introduction of the Net could also influence the long-term dynamics of the transnational interaction. So far the participatory process was described as a single-shot process.[25] It was assumed that the participation would take place in the context of a particular discussion (e.g. around a specific transnational norm), and would not form an integral part of the law-making process. The political community would have to be formed anew in each round of participation (with repeated investments of the 'fixed-cost' element of C_T). With the Internet, the transforming of this 'scattered' process into a continuous one becomes much easier (and cheaper).[26] The Internet provides various cost-efficient means, through which an emerging transnational community could be kept alive through time. These include tools such as group lists, e-newsletters, chat-rooms, instant messaging and electronic archives. These different mechanisms enable both the facilitation of continuous conversation and the creation of (enduring) group memory. This kind of time-persistency is an essential element of a true polity.[27] In the pre-Net era, the cost of constructing such infrastructure on a global scale would have made it impossible to implement.

The Internet, then, is more than a cheap participation mechanism. Its extensive global reach and rich repertoire of community-sustaining techniques turn it into an essential tool in the effort to develop meaningful transnational democracy. Shifting the participation process into the electronic domain does not resolve, however, the basic collective-action dilemma that characterizes political action. Indeed, the model that was presented in this section makes clear that the emergence of e-participation cannot be taken for granted, and is strongly dependent on the availability of central direction. By emphasizing the 'enabling' and anarchistic character of the Net, many writers have tended to overlook this dependency (e.g. Hammond and Lash 2000), and its potential implications – in particular, the susceptibility of e-participation to hierarchical manipulation. Thus, one of the challenges facing those seeking to institutionalize mechanisms of e-participation is to find ways to promote coordinated activity yet keep the sponsors of such activity accountable.

Use of the Internet by international institutions

Having outlined, in theory, the usefulness of the Internet for facilitating wider involvement by civic actors in the creation and operation of international regimes, this section examines how far international organizations are meeting these expectations in practice. Three major global regulatory bodies are held up for scrutiny – the WTO, which replaced the General Agreement on Tariffs and Trade (GATT) in 1995; the ISO, which deals with issues of technical standardization; and the ICANN, which regulates the system of domain names on the Internet. These organizations present an interesting mix for analysis in terms of their overall Internet experience and embeddedness in the state system. The WTO and the ISO are both from the pre-Net era. The WTO, as a traditional treaty-based system, is rooted strongly in the Westphalian tradition, while the ISO is more of a hybrid organization in that its members are not governments, but national standardization bodies from some 140 countries. The ISO remains closely linked to the state system, however, in that some members are private bodies, for example, the British Standards Institution, whereas some are governmental agencies, for example, the French Standards Agency, AFNOR (Association française de normalisation).

ICANN, by contrast, is a new, Internet-spawned phenomenon that relies extensively on new technology to carry out its functions. While it relies to a certain degree on the backing of the state system, its jurisdiction and legitimacy are highly dependent on the non-governmental sector. Given its more intimate connection to the Internet, and greater detachment from established national actors, ICANN is anticipated to be more adept in exploiting the innovative and participatory uses of the technology than either the WTO or the ISO.

The chapter turns first to the case of the WTO. The establishment of the WTO was a triumphant culmination of a long institutionalization process that began in 1947 with the establishment of the GATT (Jackson 1997: 31–78). The WTO is concerned, primarily, with the facilitation of transnational commerce and the abolition of trade barriers. The WTO differs from its predecessor, the GATT, in two key respects. First, unlike the weak dispute settlement (DS) system of the GATT, the WTO DS system is highly independent, and is much more immune to political pressures. Its establishment has marked the creation of a new and independent source of normative power in the global arena (Perez 2001: 73–103). Second, the normative setting of the WTO is far more ambitious than that of the GATT. It is not limited to a single trade-sector or to one type of regulatory barrier, but reflects a broad attempt to integrate the global economy. This jurisdictional expansion has resulted in an increased incidence of conflicts between trade and other societal objectives such as environmental protection, and a growing public critique of its legitimacy and accountability (Charnovitz 1996; Esty 1999).

One way in which the WTO has sought to respond to this perception of a democratic deficit has been to increase the transparency of its operations, and to do so it has turned to the web. Almost all of the WTO documents, including secretariat reports, committee protocols and judicial decisions are accessible online – no mean feat especially when one considers the cloak of secrecy that characterized GATT proceedings. In addition, the WTO sought to promote wider public 'engagement' in its affairs, and again the Internet was seen as a crucial part of this strategy. A dedicated community forums section was created on the website that was designed to serve the interests of the media, NGOs and the general public. The goal being to 'provide an opportunity for the public to comment on the WTO, its activities, and the trading system'.[28] In this section participants could post messages, converse with one another in chat rooms and occasionally in WTO-initiated question and answer sessions, with WTO personnel and outside experts.[29] Particular emphasis has been placed on NGOs on the WTO website with special pages set up to brief and interact with NGOs in the months leading up to the fourth Ministerial Conference that took place in Doha, Qatar in November 2001.[30]

While these initiatives are laudable they do not appear to be leading to any great leaps forward in terms of public engagement. As of mid-July 2001 there were less than 250 messages posted on the WTO Forum, a low number by any account and particularly so if one takes into account its growing public profile, especially among the Internet-using segment of the population. While the low level of interest may be due to lack of awareness of the participatory opportunities offered on the website, it may also be due to the lack of formal standing for the community forum within the WTO decision-making structure. The site does not indicate how any feedback will be used by the organization. The opening paragraph to the 'NGO room', for instance states that the WTO 'recognizes the role NGOs can play to increase the awareness of the public in respect of WTO activities' but does not provide details about how NGOs can contribute more meaningfully to the substantive work of the WTO.[31] Overall, therefore, the WTO is linking new communication technologies to an emerging recognition of the legitimate political role of NGOs in its deliberations. However, for practical purposes such groups remain largely outside the decision-making process.

The global push towards standardization has become encapsulated in a wide variety of international organizations governing areas such as electronic engineering and telecommunication, the International Electromechanical Commission (IEC); food standards, the Codex Alimentarius Commission; and technical standards, the ISO. While the products of these organizations are to a large extent voluntary, the globalization process and the new regime of the WTO has in effect upgraded their status, making it much more difficult for both private players and states to disregard them (Perez 1998). Further, despite the apparently specialized and remote nature of their work, such bodies do have far-reaching social implications that merit deeper public scrutiny. Perhaps the strongest example of such societal importance is the ISO and its work in developing a new set of environmental standards – the ISO 14000 series – covering a range of practices relating to management systems, auditing, performance evaluation, labelling and life cycle assessment (Murray 1999: 40–9). Unlike some of ISO's other products, the ISO 14000 series is not really 'technical' – in the sense that it is not composed of detailed technological or emissions protocols. The ISO 14000 series has a broader agenda, which is to teach organizations, in a general and abstract fashion, 'how to think about environmental problems'. Furthermore, this normative agenda is not limited to the corporate realm. The ISO 14000 series seeks, in effect, to provide a comprehensive discourse, which would be used by society as a whole, for judging the environmental behaviour of organizations.

Despite the broad normative implications of this series, however, the project was not subjected to a wide deliberative process (UNCTAD 1996). The standard-making process in the ISO provides overall few opportunities for public participation.[32] The main 'legislative' work is carried out by ISO technical committees and subcommittees; only ISO members have the right to participate in the work of the various committees, that is, to receive drafts, make comments and approve ISO standards.[33] The ISO online presence does little to break the 'closure' of its norm-production process. The ISO website (www.iso.ch) does not offer real opportunities for public involvement. External observers cannot consult existing standards or drafts of future standards but are required to purchase them from the ISO, which retains intellectual property rights to them.

Such practices certainly cast considerable doubt over the ISO claim that 'it shall strive at all times to perfect the application of consensus and transparency principles in standardization, and in this way promote the values of rationality, utility, safety and environmental protection for the benefit of all peoples' (ISO 1999: 3). Internally, however, uses of new communication technologies have been more successfully directed towards opening up decision-making processes. During 2001 a sophisticated system of electronic balloting was introduced, which was designed to speed up the process of voting and securing feedback on ISO draft standards.[34]

The Net – one of the key social domains of the modern society – is also subject to extensive regulation by a-national sources. With the growing importance of the Net as a medium for communication, the question of its control has become an issue of deep social concern. Since its early years of popular use the net has changed from a space of absolute freedom to a more regulated environment (Lessig 2000). One of the key organizations to emerge in this regard has been the ICANN – a non-profit corporation formed in 1999 with far-reaching powers to manage the Internet.[35] Specifically, ICANN bears responsibility for managing the Internet protocol (IP) address space allocation and the domain name system. Domain names are addresses of websites and comprise two levels: the generic top-level domain name space (i.e. 'com', 'net', 'org', etc.) and the unique country-code top-level domains such as 'uk' for United Kingdom and 'il' for Israel. One of the main concerns that accompanied its creation was how to ensure that this new body would respect the egalitarian and free spirit of the Internet. To achieve this ICANN was founded on the principles of an inclusive governance structure that would utilize the unique advantages of the Internet. It was seen as a novel alternative to the traditional, pre-Internet model of a multinational governmental treaty organization.

The regulation of the ownership of domain names provides a good example to ICANN's vast powers. The registration of domain names is based on a simple registration rule of first-come, first-served. The openness of this system, however, enabled people to register a domain name with an offline counterpart that they did not hold the moral or legal rights to, such as trademarks and personal and organizational names (a practice that became known as cyber-piracy or cyber-squatting). ICANN, together with the World Intellectual Property Organisation (WIPO) developed a global, web-based, dispute settlement system for resolving trademark domain name disputes.[36] The rules became effective in October 1999 and have been employed since then in disputes involving a wide range of 'names', from Julia Roberts, to Dior, Penguin Books, and Nandos.[37] While the establishment of this system was seen as necessary to further development of the Internet, it raises difficult questions with respect to the proper balance between corporate interests (trademark holders) and the interests of the ordinary Net users.

ICANN's inclusive strategy was based on three key elements. First, it sought to provide maximum transparency by offering accurate and timely descriptions of its regulatory agenda via its website. Second, it attempted to secure public feedback, again through its website, by offering opportunities for comment on its regulatory and policy-development work.[38] Finally, ICANN sought to incorporate the public directly into its governing apparatus through its universal representative scheme, called the 'at-large membership' programme. According to ICANN's by-laws its board should consist of nine public directors from a total of eighteen.

The 'at large' programme developed and implemented an electronically mediated voting process that enabled the Internet community to elect at-large directors to ICANN's board. The global election took place in 2000.

ICANN's strategy represented a bold attempt to build a new type of global governance. However, over the last two years, its inclusive structure, and in particular the at-large programme, have been subject to increasing internal criticism. The view within ICANN was that a system of electronic voting that is based on email addresses to identify individuals – the system that was used in the 2000 election – cannot reliably represent public interest. It was argued that this mechanism is 'administratively and financially unworkable on a global scale for a sizeable electorate, and fraught with potential dangers ranging from capture to outright fraud' (ICANN-At-Large-Study-Committee 2001). The dual qualification system, which was used in the 2000 elections and required each voter to have an email and postal address as physical proof of existence, was seen as cumbersome and highly impractical (ICANN-At-Large-Study-Committee 2001). In view of these difficulties ICANN is currently considering alternative participatory mechanisms that will be less ambitious in terms of their democratic profile, but, arguably, will allow it to serve more efficiently the interests of the Internet community (Lynn 2002). Such reforms, however, were strongly criticized by external observers (Klein 2001).

Despite the scaling back of some of its participatory ambitions, these efforts by ICANN to incorporate the public in the management of the Net represents a radical departure from the notion of 'indirect supervision' contained within the state-centred model of international regime formation, as outlined earlier. As expected, the WTO and the ISO have made rather less-strident efforts to harness the technology in the service of direct democracy. It would be wrong to dismiss their efforts as merely cosmetic gestures, however. The fact that both of these pre-Net organizations have made a deliberate effort to use the Internet to open up new opportunities for participation signals a significant shift towards greater openness. Indeed, what is common to ICANN, the WTO and the ISO (albeit to varying degrees), is that they all used the new ICTs to cut the transaction barriers that have impeded the development of meaningful participatory processes in the pre-Net era. The websites of the WTO and ICANN (and to a less degree the ISO) include some of the features discussed in the second section as necessary for the emergence of viable transnational communities, such as easily available information and chat-rooms. Thus, while none of these organizations' use of new ICTs comes close to the ideals of the anti-globalization movement or of democratic purists, their activities, particularly those of ICANN, indicate a firm commitment to finding a model of e-politics that can serve as a basis for a more inclusive transnational politics in the future.

Conclusions

The chapter began with the question of whether the Internet opens the way for meaningful participation in the production of transnational norms. The answer to this question was provided in two ways. First, I explored theoretically whether the Internet could provide conditions that were supportive of participatory communities at the international level by reducing both the costs of individual participation and the transaction costs associated with the construction of a threshold community. The capacity of the Internet to reduce barriers of time and space along with its ability to sustain a high volume of multi-directional communications (connectivity), and to provide efficient archive services (memory) were seen as providing very strong potential for the efficient organization of transnational political action. I then turned to a series of 'real-world' examples of international organizations that were applying the Internet to their operating practices for some insight into how far these theoretical expectations could be realized. The evidence from our three examples of the WTO, the ISO and ICANN revealed that while not fully realizing Internet-based participatory democracy, these organizations were making notable strides towards utilizing the medium to render themselves more participatory and accountable.

One of the key lessons to have emerged from the game-theory model, however, was that despite its various advantages, the Internet does not eliminate the collective-action problem that permeates any political endeavour. The emergence of spontaneous cooperation over the Net cannot be taken for granted. This was certainly demonstrated in the three case studies analyzed, since all revealed a reliance on some form of central coordination to facilitate online participation. Such dependency on centralized direction of course introduces additional tensions in terms of the risks to free expression and the emergence of technocratic elite. The challenge here, therefore, is to devise mechanisms that could ensure the meaningfulness of the deliberation process, despite the existence of such 'residual' authority. Take, for example, the transnational process of standard setting. It is possible to imagine several mechanisms by which the integrity of the deliberative process could be guaranteed. First, the constitution of the international organization should ensure that the public is given a meaningful role in decision-making structures. The organization could be obliged, for example, to collect a certain threshold number of public comments before submitting a standard for approval, and to incorporate a specified number of these comments into the final rule. There could also be a requirement for making public the reasons for rejecting any civic proposals. Electronically available archives of public comments should allow readers to check these institutional commitments. Such obligations could counter the current tendency of public officials to discount electronic mail, which is perceived as 'cheap talk', and give more credence to traditional modes of communication (Bimber 2001: 3).

Aside from these more generic barriers to developing meaningful forms of Internet-based participation, one should not disregard the additional 'technological' challenges that international organizations face in setting up Net-based participation. One obvious challenge comes in the shape of the electronic global divide. A fair and equitable scheme of electronic participation cannot be implemented without the support of a highly accessible computer network. This is certainly not the case for many countries in the world today. There are big gaps in the percentage of Internet usage between the developed and developing regions. The 2001 UNDP annual report notes that while in high-income OECD countries (excluding the United States) 28 per cent of the population are connected to the Net (54 per cent in the United States), the percentage in developing regions ranges from 3.9 per cent in Eastern Europe to 0.4 per cent in Sub-Saharan Africa and South Asia (UNDP 2001: 13). A further threat to the project of electronic participation in the transnational realm is the potential it holds for identity fraud. The greater anonymity and remoteness of cyberspace makes authentication of individuals problematic in general, but when one moves to the global level this problem is compounded, as ICANN discovered when trying to implement its 'at-large' elections.

E-democracy, therefore, does not resolve some of the chief dilemmas of democratic political action. However, it does offer one of the most promising paths by which the public can be incorporated into the 'making' of global law. As was indicated in the third section this process has already begun. The experiences of the WTO, the ISO and ICANN provide useful lessons for utilizing the new ICTs to support new participatory schemes. The challenge society is facing today is to continue this experimentation process and extend it to other transnational domains.

Notes

1 See: *EC – Measures Concerning Meat and Meat Products (Hormones)*, Report of the Appellate Body, WT/DS26/AB/R, WT/DS48/AB/R, 16 January 1998; *United States – Import Prohibition of Certain Shrimp and Shrimp Products*, Report of the Appellate Body, WT/DS58/AB/R, 12 October 1998; *European Communities – Measures Affecting Asbestos and Asbestos-Containing Products*, Report of the Appellate Body, WT/DS135/AB/R, 12 March 2001.

2 The ISO 14000 series is a wide-ranging collection of international, voluntary environmental standards, which deals with a variety of corporate-management issues. For details on the Codex Commission see <http://www.codexalimentarius.net/>.

3 This view of legitimacy stands in contrast to non-procedural accounts that are based on the compatibility of a regime with a particular understanding of the common good. Such accounts are problematic since they presuppose an agreed-upon definition of the common good, and leave unresolved the question of the criteria for determining compatibility. For more extensive discussions of these issues see Bodansky (1999), and Weiler (1997).

4 See 'The Changing Face of Protest', *The Financial Times*, 31 July/1 August 1999: 12; Guy de Jonquie 'Network Guerrillas', The Financial Times, 30 April 1998 (commenting on the successful campaign against the OECD failed Multilateral Agreement on Investment).

5 The model builds on a long tradition of threshold public-goods models, which started with Olson's 'The Logic of Collective Action'. See, for example: McLean (2000: 655), Palfrey and Rosenthal (1994), and Rapoport (1985).

6 It is assumed here that the public protest has a discrete effect: that is, the political good would be provided with some probability (e.g. α) in K, but not in $K-1$. α does not increase in K. It is possible to relax this assumption and to build a model that links between the numbers of participants and the probability of the political good being provided. I do not pursue this path here.

7 In real life, public reactions are likely, of course, to differ in their content and effect. This could reflect the lack of a clear consensus in the public, and various other factors (e.g. the fact that the identity of the commentator might influence the response of the international organization). On the assumptions of our model the debated norm will not be changed unless there are at least K people, which agree that this change is worthwhile.

8 In my model Vi is constructed as a purely instrumental variable. I thus do not assume that the act of participation holds some intrinsic value for the participator, which is independent of the instrumental value of his political action. This assumption is somewhat contrary to Downs (1957) famous calculus of voting. Downs argued that voting holds an intrinsic value for voters, which reflects a citizen's sense of duty towards the community in which he lives and his desire to preserve the institution of 'democracy'. I believe, however, that this assumption is inappropriate to the transnational game discussed here. Downs's argument takes place within a well-established community, with shared values, tradition and history. None of these exists, a priori, in the transnational context. A citizen's duty is something that evolves parallel to the emergence of a community; it is not something that could be presumed independently of such emergence. The notion of civic duty cannot provide, then, an exclusive and independent explanation to the individual decision to participate. It becomes part of the strategic calculus that characterizes the participation process, and thus cannot resolve the puzzle of its original emergence.

9 This is a reflection of my earlier assumption that raising the number of participants from N to $N + 1$ does not increase the probability of the good being provided. Relaxing this assumption could change the reasoning profile of a potential contributor. In such a case, an individual might still decide to contribute, even though he believes there are K contributors (without himself), if he believes that the increase in the probability of the political good being provided (caused by his participation) would be higher than his participatory costs. This, of course, could change the game equilibria.

10 Another implicit condition is that the net value of the political action – (Vi(Pg) − Ci) – is larger than the (net) value of any alternative action – the outside option – that the individual could have pursued instead (in or outside the Net). Otherwise, even if condition (1) is satisfied, the individual will not take this path.

11 I assume that $k \neq 1$ and $k \neq N$. It is assumed also that the rules of the game, as well as the values of all the relevant factors (e.g. of K, N', α) are common knowledge.

12 Each of these combinations represents a stable Nash Equilibrium because none of the players has an incentive to deviate from it unilaterally. None of the $N - N'$ players will have an incentive to participate because for them Ci > Vi(Pg). None of the $N' - K$ players will have an incentive to participate because, although for them Ci ≤ Vi(Pg), by not participating they can save Ci but still get Vi(Pg). As to the K participants – because each of them believes (by assumption) that he is 'pivotal', he would not defect because this would mean losing Vi(Pg) − Ci.

13 Since $B/A = [(N' - c)!/(K!(N' - 1 - K)!]/[N'!/(K!(N' - K)!] = (N' - K)/N'$.

14 A numerical example could help in illustrating the dilemma facing an individual participant (i), in deciding whether to participate in a political game. Imagine that there are thirty potential participants (N') and that the size of the threshold community (K) is 10. The first solution that was noted above means that there are 30!/(10!(30 − 10)!), that is 30045015 possible equilibria (or coalitions). If the individual would rule himself out of the potential contributors there would still be 29!/(29!(29 − 10)!) or 20030010 potential equilibria. While the number of potential coalitions was reduced by one-third it remained high enough to discount any sense of individual criticality, making 'free-riding' an appealing option. Note, however, that if all the members of the community would follow this line of reasoning none would contribute. Thus, i is facing two plausible, but contradictory predictions, in which his investment is portrayed as both critical and redundant.

15 For studies that examined the extent to which the perception of 'individual efficacy' plays a role in the decision of individuals to contribute to the provision of public goods, see Colman (1995: 215–21), and Yamagishi and Cook (1993).

16 Ostrom *et al.* (1994) conducted a thorough investigation of the problem of public-good provision under various laboratory settings. Their findings indicate that adding opportunities for communication in the game yields, in a very consistent fashion, higher levels of cooperation. See, Ostrom *et al.* (1994: 145–69, 195–9).

17 The profile of any selected equilibrium (or coalition) should be treated probably as a random phenomenon, caused by accidental fluctuations and unplanned perturbations in the border between society and consciousness. A similar uncertainty exists in the case of physical systems. See Kelso (1995 10).

18 For this broad interpretation of the idea of transaction cost, see Calabresi (1991).

19 To the critical role of 'assurance' in the emergence of cooperation in prisoner-dilemma type games, see, for example, Hayashi *et al.* (1999).

20 Going beyond this image of 'transaction costs' as a constraint on the number of viable coalitions requires a very detailed description of the mechanism that will be used to counter any transaction barriers. The features of this mechanism (e.g. the intervention of a group leader seeking to construct a threshold community) will determine a new game. As it is impossible to provide a complete catalogue of these potential mechanisms, the structure of this unfolding game and the strategic dilemmas it generates, cannot be specified in advance. However, what is important in our context is that there are convincing empirical studies, which show that offering more opportunities for communication and assurance signals raises the prospects of cooperation. For an example of a concrete analysis, which explores the effect of a particular coordination mechanism (recommended contributions) on the voluntary provision of public goods, see Croson and Marks (2001).

21 Assuming some kind of institutional intervention does not mean that we should rule out the potential role of private group-leaders. Even if the public agency agrees to fund (or provide directly) some of the coordination services (e.g. website facilities) it could still leave the stage open for external leaders.

22 The introduction of the Internet should also reduce the opportunity costs of participation by reducing the time needed for participation.

23 This term is from Canan and Reichman, which gives a detailed account of the role of institutional entrepreneurs in the development of the Ozone regime (2002: 188–9).

24 As was noted earlier C_T is comprised of two elements: variable and fixed. Here I refer only to the variable element.

25 This single-shot image is also consistent with the national experience – for example, in the context of environmental impact assessment regimes – which are also geared towards single-shot rounds of participation (Biswas 1992: 240–1; Dipper *et al.* 1998: 735).

26 Assuming that the political game is a repeated game (with infinite horizon) rather than a single-shot game increases substantially the number of potential equilibria. For our needs it would suffice to say that any solution of the single-shot game is also a solution of the infinite game. Thus, any viable coalition of the base game will constitute a solution to the repeated game. Furthermore, any combination of these coalitions could also serve as a solution of the repeated game (to operationalize such a solution we would need some randomizing device that would 'pick' a different coalition at each stage-game; because any such coalition is a Nash solution to the stage game such solution would be incentive compatible). See, Ostrom *et al.* (1994: 71–2).

27 An additional advantage of this time persistency is that it provides some immunity from fluctuations in the saliency of a particular transnational domain.

28 See <www.wto.org/english/forums_e/forums_e.htm>, accessed 17 July 2001.

29 A recent WTO-initiated discussion focused on 'Trade and Sustainable Development' <http://www.itd.org/forums/tsdfor.htm>. Message postings have focused on issues

such as 'Protest and WTO', 'Environment and WTO' and 'Is the WTO inherently evil?' (WTO Forum; accessed 17 July 2001).

30 See <www.wto.org/english/forums_e/ngo_e/ngo_e.htm> also, 'WTO Secretariat activities with NGOs', WT/INF/30, 12 April 2001, and the NGO information page for the fourth Ministerial Conference, available at <http://www-chil.wto-ministerial.org/english/thewto_e/minist_e/min01_e/min01_ngo_e.htm>, accessed 16 December 2001.

31 Ibid.

32 A thorough discussion of ISO 'constitutional' framework is beyond the scope of this chapter. For a more detailed discussion, see UNCTAD Report (UNCTAD 1996: 21–40). It is particularly enlightening in this context to compare the ISO to a recent global initiative – the 'Global Reporting Initiative' (GRI) – which, through a much more open and inclusive process, seeks to develop standards of sustainability reporting. For further details see the GRI website <www.globalreporting.org>

33 The details of the standard-setting process are set in *ISO/IEC Directive (Part 1): Procedures for the Technical Work* (a copy of which is available from the ISO website). A brief description can be found in the document *Stages of the Development of International Standards* <www.ISO.ch/infoe/proc.html>, accessed 1 March 2001. The ISO constitution distinguishes between three forms of membership: full members have the right to participate as P-members in Technical Committees, which gives them the right and obligation to vote on all questions submitted for voting within the technical committee, including enquiry drafts and Final Draft International Standards. Correspondent Members can only participate in the standard-setting work as Observing-Members (O-Members), which allows them to attend meetings, receive documents and submit comments. A third category – subscriber membership – usually for countries with very small economies, establishes only a very limited contact with the ISO. See, *Introduction to ISO*, available at <www.iso.ch>, and paras. 1.7 – 1.7.5 of ISO/IEC Directive (part 1). NGOs can only gain access to the ISO standard-setting process as 'Liaison' organizations, a status that enable them to observe the standard-setting process, but does not give them formal voting rights. Furthermore, to gain this limited access, NGOs have to get the approval of the ISO Chief Executive Officer. See paras. 1.15 – 1.15.5 of ISO/IEC Directive (part 1).

34 See, Weissinger (2001), and <www.iso.ch/e-balloting>. The new balloting scheme maintains the system of voting rights that was established by ISO/IEC Directive (part 1). See, *User Guide to the Electronic Balloting Application*, Version 1.1 (December 2000), available at <www.iso.ch/e-balloting>

35 ICANN was incorporated under California law as a 'public benefit corporation', for a more detailed description of ICANN and its history see <www.icann.org> and Weinberg (2000: 192–213).

36 WIPO is an intergovernmental organization (by 17 July 2001 it had 177 member-states), which is responsible for the creation of a worldwide framework for the protection of intellectual property rights; for further details see the WIPO website at <www.wipo.org>. For further details about the dispute settlement rules see *ICANN Uniform Domain Name Dispute Resolution Policy*, available at <www.icann.org/udrp/udrp-policy-24oct99.htm>. For the consultative history of this policy – known as the 'First WIPO Internet Domain Name Process' – see <ecommerce.wipo.int/domains>. It should be noted that ICANN and WIPO are not the only players in the game of 'controlling the Net'. Probably the most important co-players are governments (especially the United. States and the EU) and big private players such as Microsoft, Adobe, AOL, AT&T and IBM.

37 These disputes were dealt with by WIPO Arbitration and Mediation Center. The full text of the decisions can be accessed at <arbiter.wipo.int/domains/decisions/html>. See *Julia Fiona Roberts* v. *Russell Boyd*, Case No. D2000–0210; *Parfums Christian Dior* v. *QTR Corporation*, Case No. D2000–0023; *Penguin Books Ltd.* v. *the Katz Family*, Case No. D2000 – 0204; *Nandos International Limited* v. *M. Fareed Farukhi*, Case No. D2000–0225.

38 See <www.icann.org/participate and forum.icann.org>

Bibliography

Bimber, B. (2001) 'Information Technology and the "New" Politics,' unpublished paper <http://www.polsci.ucsb.edu/faculty/bimber/research/index.html>, first accessed 2 November 2002.

Biswas, A. K. (1992) 'Summary and Recommendations', in Biswas, A. K. and Agarwal, S. B. C. (eds), *Environmental Impact Assessment for Developing Countries*, Oxford: Butterworth-Heinemann.

Bodansky, D. (1999) 'The Legitimacy of International Governance', *American Journal of International Law*, 93, 596–624.

Calabresi, G. (1991) 'The Pointless of Pareto', *Yale Law Journal*, 100, 1211.

Caldwell, L. K. (1996) *International Environmental Policy*, Durham: Duke University Press.

Canan, P. and Reichman, N. (2002) *Ozone Connections*, Sheffield: Greenleaf Publishing.

Charnovitz, S. (1996) 'Participation of Nongovernmental Organizations in the World Trade Organization', *University of Pennsylvania Journal of International Economic Law*, 17, 331–59.

Cohen, J. and Sabel, C. (1997) 'Directly-Deliberative Polyarchy', *European Law Journal*, 3, 313–42.

Colman, A. M. (1995) *Game Theory and Its Applications in the Social and Biological Sciences*, Oxford: Butterworth/Heinemann.

Croson, R. and Marks, M. (2001) 'The Effect of Recommended Contributions in the Voluntary Provision of Public Goods', *Economic Inquiry*, 39, 238–49.

Dipper, B., Jones, C. and Wood, C. (1998) 'Monitoring and Post-auditing in Environmental Impact Assessment: A Review,' *Journal of Environmental Planning and Management* 41 (6), 731–48.

Downs, A. (1957) *An Economic Theory of Democracy*, New York: Harper and Row.

The Ecologist (2000) 'Special Report: Globalizing Poverty', *The Ecologist*, 30, 6.

Esty, D. (1999) 'Why the World Trade Organization Needs Environmental NGOs', International Centre for Trade and Sustainable Development Working Paper, <http://www.cid.harvard.edu/cidtrade/issues/environmentpaper.html>, first accessed 2 November 2000.

Hammond, A. and Lash, J. (2000) 'Cyber-Activism: The Rise of Civil Accountability and Its Consequences for Governance', *iMP Magazine*, May 2000, <http://www.cisp.org/imp/may_2000/05_00hammond.htm>, first accessed 2 November 2000.

Hayashi, N., Ostrom, E., Walker, J. and Yamagishi, T. (1999) 'Reciprocity, Trust, and the Sense of Control', *Rationality and Society*, 11 (1), 27–46.

ICANN (1999) 'The Membership Advisory Committee Commentary on the Principles of the At-large Membership' <http://www.icann.org>, first accessed 29 November 2000.

ICANN-At-Large-Study-Committee (2001) 'Final Report on ICANN At-Large Membership', <http://www.icann.org>, first accessed 27 June 2002.

ICANN-Committee-on-Evolution-and-Reform (2002) 'ICANN: A Blueprint for Reform', <http://www.icann.org>, first accessed 27 June 2002.

ISO (1999) 'ISO in Brief', <http://www.iso.ch/presse/longrang.pdf>, first accessed 1 March 2001.

ISO (2001) 'The ISO Survey of ISO 9000 and ISO 14000 Certificates – Tenth cycle' <http://www.iso.ch>, first accessed 26 July 2001.

Jackson, J. H. (1997) *The World Trading System*, Cambridge, MA: The MIT Press.

Kelso, J. A. Scott (1995) *Dynamic Patterns*, Cambridge, MA: The MIT Press.

Klein, H. (2001) 'The Future of Democracy in ICANN', *CYBER-FEDERALIST*, 11, <http://www.cyber-federalist.org>, first accessed 27 June 2001.

Lessig, L. (2000) 'Architecting for Control', Keynote address given at the Internet Political Economy Forum, *Cambridge Review of International Affairs*, Cambridge, UK, 29 May.

Lynn, M. S. (2002) 'President's Report: ICANN – The Case for Reform', <http://www.icann.org>, first accessed 27 June 2002.

McLean, I. (2000) 'Review Article: The Divided Legacy of Mancur Olson', *British Journal of Political Science*, 30, 651–68.

Murray, P. C. (1999) 'Inching Toward Environmental Regulatory Reform – ISO 14000', *American Business Law Journal*, 37, 35–71.

Ostrom, E. (2000) 'The Danger of Self-Evident Truths', *Political Science*, 33 (1), 33–44.

Ostrom, E., Gardner, R. and Walker, J. (1994) *Rules, Games, & Common-Pool Resources*, Ann Arbor: The University of Michigan Press.

Palfrey, T. R. and Rosenthal, H. (1994) 'Repeated Play, Cooperation and Coordination', *Review of Economic Studies*, 61, 545–65.

Perez, O. (1998) 'Reconstructing Science', *European Foreign Affairs Review*, 3 (4), 563–82.

Perez, O. (2001) 'Ecological Sensitivity and Global Legal Pluralism', unpublished PhD thesis, London School of Economics and Political Science.

Perez, O. (2002) 'Using Private-Public Linkages to Regulate Environmental Conflicts', *Journal of Law & Society*, 29, 77–110.

Petersmann, E. U. (1999) 'Dispute Settlement in International Economic Law', *Journal of International Economic Law*, 2, 189–248.

Rapoport, A. (1985) 'Provision of Public Goods and the MCS Experimental Paradigm', *American Political Science Review*, 79, 148–55.

Starr, P. (2000) 'The Electronic Commons', *The American Prospect*, 11.

Teubner, G. (1997) '"Global Bukowina": Legal Pluralism in the World Society', in Teubner, G. (ed.), *Global Law Without a State*, Aldershot: Dartmouth.

UNCTAD (1996) *ISO 14001: International Environmental Management Systems Standards*, Geneva: United Nations Conference on Trade and Development.

UNDP (2001) *Partnerships to Fight Poverty: UNDP Annual Report 2001*, New York: United Nations Development Programme.

Weiler, J. H. H. (1997) 'Does Europe Need a Constitution?' in Gowan, P. and Anderson, P. (eds), *The Question of Europe*, London: Verso.

Weinberg, J. (2000) 'ICANN and the Problem of Legitimacy', *Duke Law Journal* 50, 187–260.

Weissinger, R. (2001) 'Electronic Balloting', *ISO Bulletin*, 32 (April), 3–6.

WTO (2002) 'WTO Website User Survey', <http://www.wto.org>, first accessed 24 June 2002.

Yamagishi, T. and Cook, K. S. (1993) 'Generalized Exchange and Social Dilemmas', *Social Psychology Quarterly*, 56 (4), 235–48.

8 Problems@labour

Towards a net-internationalism?

Stuart Hodkinson

Introduction

This chapter takes as its context the widely recognised global crisis of *national* trade unionism in a 'globalised/networked/informatised capitalist era' (Waterman 2001), and argues that although this crisis requires a revival of union *internationalism*, the history of past labour internationalisms reveals possible 'inherent' barriers to such cross-border solidarity. This is where the Internet may come in. Some thinkers and activists in and around the international labour movement argue that while new information and communication technologies (ICTs) have been integrally responsible for national union decline, they have also provided workers for the first time with 'the means to coordinate globally in the age of the multi-national corporation' (Davison 2000: 1). The aim of this chapter is to come to some preliminary conclusions about the potential of the Internet to overcome past and present obstacles to union internationalism through a critical review of what I call the 'net-internationalism' perspective. The first part of the chapter sets out the crisis of trade unionism under globalisation and examines the problematic case for a new 'union' internationalism. Part two sets out the claims of 'net-internationalism', which are then critically discussed in part three. The conclusion argues that while the Internet has provided new and important tools for labour internationalism, it is not the virtual solution to real-world solidarity building.

Globalisation, trade union decline and the dilemmas of internationalism

Perhaps one of the defining features of contemporary global capitalism is the decline of trade unionism to the extent that it 'now faces in large parts of the world almost total elimination as a significant social institution' (Thomas 1995: 4). While there is sharp disagreement in academic and trade union circles as to the long-term implications of this crisis, few contest the present malaise in a climate of mass unemployment, stagnant average real wage growth, chronic employment insecurity, dwindling union membership and the global trend towards the curtailment of trade union rights and political influence. This represents a dramatic turnaround from what is considered the height of trade union power – the post-1945 era or so-called 'Golden Age' of capitalism (Marglin and Schor 1990). Despite the deep variation that existed between different national industrial relations systems, union power was generally reflected at the level of the labour market, the labour process, public policy and civil society. Unions were particularly powerful in western Europe where they 'reached a degree of influence in the economy and a level of social protection for workers, which had never existed before' (Visser 2000: 426).

Unprecedented postwar economic expansion driven by state-led reconstruction helped create full employment conditions and thus strong bargaining power for organised labour. Collective bargaining took wages and workers 'out of competition' with each other, curtailing employers' ability to divide and rule over their workforces and enabling large real wage gains and improved working and living conditions (Visser 2000: 426). Unions' market and industrial strength translated into significant political influence with their participation in 'neo-corporatist' government macroeconomic and industrial management systems (Crouch 1992). Employers and public institutions recognised unions as their 'indispensable partners in the industrial order' and integrated them into policy-making circles (Regini 1992: 2–3, 6). Welfare states effectively removed wage-determination from competitive labour markets while the underlying Fordist mass-production manufacturing model was conducive to unionisation and collective bargaining. Crucially, the domestic capacity of states to pursue union-friendly demand-management and full employment policies was supported at the international level by the postwar international monetary system, which restricted short-term capital flows and speculation (Cox 1994; Drache 1996).[1] This political and economic power also made unions key social actors in community and class struggle.

By the 1990s, this 'Golden Age' of organised labour had evaporated and '[t]he prolonged pattern of divergence had been replaced by the convergent trajectories of union decline' (Western 1997: 21). Explanations of these trends are inevitably much disputed and while most approaches point to the impact of mass unemployment and deindustrialisation, their significance is contested. For example, business-cycle approaches emphasise the changing elasticity of demand for labour effects on union bargaining power and unionisation (Hirsch and Addison 1986); sociological approaches focus on the changing nature of work and workers, and in particular the erosion of working-class consciousness (Meiksins 1998); and Marxian political economy approaches variously highlight the crisis of Fordism, the role of class conflict and the intervention of the state (Boyer and Drache 1996; Kelly 1998; Panitch 1998). However, while all of these explanations are relevant, it would appear impossible not to conclude that a crisis of unionism that literally spans the entire global economy must have its root cause in a universal or global set of processes and dynamics. The argument adopted here is that the central material and ideological factor in trade union decline is *globalisation*.

Globalisation is a highly contested term and many even dispute its existence, but there is little doubt that something quite unprecedented has happened to the world economy in the last thirty years. In its simplest sense, globalisation refers to 'the increasing economic integration of the world' towards a *global* as opposed to an *inter*national economy characterised by growing interconnectedness and interdependence between countries, cultures and economies (Brown and Hogendorn 2000). The most important aspect of globalisation is the transformation of the production process, which is increasingly globally organised and technologically networked, incorporating 'components produced in many different locations by different firms, and assembled for specific purposes and specific markets in a new form of production and commercialisation: high-volume, flexible, customized production' (Castells 1996: 96). This deterritorialisation of production has enabled Transnational Corporations (TNCs) to quickly transfer many parts of their production line virtually anywhere in the world and thus create a 'world market for both labor and industrial sites' (Mittelman 1996a: 4). This has enabled companies to pursue a range of strategies towards decimating labour's collective power such as subcontracting work offshore (Castells 1996; Klein 2000) or by making 'plant survival and new investment dependent upon unions accepting certain new demands such as restricting wage claims or industrial activity' as well as the intensification of the work effort (Bacon and Blyton 1999). Governments too have become 'increasingly constrained in their freedom of manoeuvre by the economic policies of other states as by the investment decisions of internationally mobile capital' (Gill and Law 1988: 92). This has reduced the state's capacity to pursue policies favourable to trade union influence. Overall, the result is that capital can now 'divide and rule' over governments and workers by threatening to source from or transfer production and jobs to other countries, or to curtail future investments.

In this context, labour organising on a national scale appears increasingly at odds with a new globalising economy, and it would seem axiomatic that if they are to at least survive, unions must engage in international cooperation and solidarity with fellow workers in other countries and continents to protect global wages, employment and labour standards and confront and constrain the power of capital mobility by increasing the power and efficacy of the democratic welfare state. Indeed, the rationale of labour internationalism is contained within the very structural logic of a networked global capitalism. Global campaigns against TNCs could have a major impact because TNCs dominate many 'nominally independent employers' and set 'world-wide trends in working conditions' (Moody 1997: 62). Successful action is feasible because TNCs are vulnerable at many points of their cross-border chains and thus 'the entire production network can be brought to a standstill' through local strikes in key locations (Breitenfellner 1997: 547). And as we shall shortly discuss, the use of new ICTs by global firms in their strategies against labour can be turned to labour's advantage through cross-border union communication networks of information-sharing on corporate economic data, pay-bargaining and management strategies (Lee 1997).

However, the prospects for a new labour internationalism appear deeply uncertain. Despite the *praxis* of worker internationalism since at least 1864 with the founding of Marx's International Working Men's Association (*aka* the First International), the actual history of international worker solidarity has been dominated by failure, continually undermined by nationalism, economism, ideological divisions, organisational problems and resource weaknesses. For example, during the

Cold War, the international union movement split into two rival factions when anti-Communist unions withdrew from the World Federation of Trade Unions (WFTU) to create the International Confederation of Free Trade Unions (ICFTU) in 1949. This not only isolated Eastern unions from West, but it also 'sharpened divisions between communist and non-communist unions in Western countries' (O'Brien 2000: 537). The ICFTU and WFTU essentially became 'transmission belts for the priorities of the interests of US and USSR labor-state alliances' while domestic labour politics of developing countries were increasingly penetrated by Cold War politics through 'divisive interventions rather than assistance towards the creation of autonomous unions' (Thomson and Larson 1978; Spalding 1988; Stevis 1998: 9). Cold War divisions also scuppered the attempt to create World Company Councils (WCCs) and achieve global contract and multinational bargaining during the 1960s and 1970s (Stevis 1998: 13). Meanwhile, efforts to overcome these obstacles were continually frustrated by the poor means of communication between trade unions of different industries, countries, continents and the cost of flying officials from around the world to conferences and meetings (Lee 1997: 13).

Recent optimistic voices have argued that the end of the Cold War has removed the major 'ideological cleavage' that had previously split workers' organisations (O'Brien 2000: 536). Yet its legacy remains undoubtedly disruptive. The past 'divisive interventions' of the ICFTU and the American Federation of Labor-Congress of Industrial Organization (AFL-CIO) in particular have not been expunged from the collective memories of developing countries and the domination of international trade union structures by Cold War politics has left them weak 'with limited powers and resources' (Stevis 1998: 12). Yet even if one accepts that the geopolitical climate has become more conducive to a renewed internationalism, there exist strong theoretical arguments that the pursuit of cross-national cooperation among workers is inherently compromised. For example, when Levinson (1972) argued that the internationalisation of capital would inevitably overcome the objective and subjective barriers to full-scale international trade unionism, he was decisively countered by a sustained outpouring of writings which argued that building international solidarity would always be confronted by the natural 'disunity of labour' in contrast to the intrinsic 'organic unity of capital' (Olle and Schoeller 1977; Haworth and Ramsay 1988; Ramsay 1997: 510). In other words, while all workers share the same structural relationship to capital as wage-labour in the *abstract*, in the *concrete* they do not share the same circumstances, realities and relations 'among themselves and with actually existing employers' (Hyman 1999: 95). Hence, globalisation may erode such differentiation by compressing the global and local experience, but under acute internationally competitive conditions with the threat to jobs and livelihoods of possible capital flight, it could just as easily divide labour along national lines. Olle and Schoeller (1977) argued that internationalism could therefore only be *politically* constructed, but conceded that such a task was always threatened by states and firms appealing to nationalist and protectionist sentiments.

It is almost certainly as a result of these factors, as well as many others, that as capitalist relations have gone global, the scope of union organisation, strategy and ethos has remained nationally embedded. Indeed, virtually all union strategies aim to adapt union members to competitive business considerations and engage in 'enterprise egoism', that is, making the survival of the firm the union's top priority to ensure that *their* members maintain *their* jobs (Hyman 1999). This nationalistic approach serves only to accelerate and deepen the power of TNCs and harm the overall position of labour in the global economy – as unions compete with each other for investment and world market shares, their competitive offers on wage levels, working conditions and productivity are not one-off adjustments but form part of a constant blackmailing process that hits the poorest workers and countries hardest first and keeps going to workers *everywhere*. By accepting and engaging themselves in the globalisation process, unions are being reconstituted from both inside/outside into mere agencies of global capital.

Nevertheless, the last decade has seen signs of an upsurge in international trade union activity and cross-border solidarity and a growing number of activists and academics argue that the qualitative form of this resurgence contains one important and potentially significant difference from the past – the Internet. It is to these claims that we now turn.

Cyberspace and solidarity: the emergence of net-internationalism

Since the end of the Cold War, a pronounced escalation has occurred in the international activities of trade unions and labour movements. Most writing focuses on the 'vertical' activities of 'official' structures of international trade unionism such as the ICFTU, the International Trade Secretariats (ITSs) and the European Trade Union Confederation (ETUC) to whom national trade unions are affiliated and use to represent and coordinate their international efforts. Taylor (1999: 4) argues that through these institutions, '[t]he international trade union movement has established a common agenda for collective action at the international level in recent years'. Recent research has also documented more 'horizontal' cross-border cooperation between national unions. Lambert and Webster (2001: 337, 349) focus on the emergence of SIGTUR 'a new network/organization of southern unions...from Latin America, Southern Africa, Asia and Australasia' whose aim is 'to build a strong Southern unionism focused on global action campaigns' in alliance with other social movements. There is also significant work on the activities of internationally minded NGOs such as Women Working WorldWide involved in grassroots cross-border labour networking, bypassing official union structures and working directly with unorganised workers or independent labour movements (Hale and Shaw 2001).

This revival of labour internationalism's' is rooted in both *necessity* with the crisis of national labour organising in the era of globalisation, and *possibility* with the technological, ideational and structural processes of globalisation helping to breaking down previous obstacles and opening up new opportunities for transnational labour activism. The focus here is on the technological aspect with the role played by new ICTs and particularly the *Internet*. As Bailey (1999: 1) argues, '[c]omputer technology has created the conditions for a global communication network that is essential to the operation of capitalism today'. Yet while the Internet has been integral to the 'electronic reconstitution' of class relations, there has also been a simultaneous upsurge in computer-mediated local, national, regional and crucially *global* protest demonstrated in the now classic example of the Zapatistas in 1994, which precipitated a number of highly public uses of the Internet by different groups. It is in this context that many unions, grassroots activists and labour academics have begun purring about the possibilities and activities of the Internet for both trade union revival, and specifically, labour internationalism.

In his groundbreaking book, *The Labour Movement and the Internet: The New Internationalism*, Lee (1997) sets out the bones of what I call 'net-internationalism'. In short, he argues that the very instrument of TNC power can be turned against global capital through its adoption and adaptation by the trade union movement in its pursuit of international solidarity. His central proposition, mirroring other contributions in this area, is that while the Internet is not a panacea, computer-mediated communications (CMC) are actively (re)-internationalising the labour movement by solving some of the problems that beset previous internationalism through the annihilation of time/space/cost, in the communication of *information, organisation* and *solidarity culture*. The following analysis provides a synthesis of these arguments.

The most important aspect of the Internet for internationalism is its ability to store, process and enable additional and alternative hyper-rapid 24-hour cross-border information-sharing between trade unions all over the world. Through email, electronic messages containing anything from simple text to computer programs, databases and pictures can be sent to potentially unlimited numbers of other trade unionists in seconds and at very low cost. Websites can store text, pictures, sounds and even videos, which can be used by trade unions to publish information on virtually everything, and is accessible to anyone and anywhere when connected to the Internet. This has a number of important benefits. Members can be immediately alerted to changes in national collective agreements, negotiations, macroeconomic data, employer strategies and production techniques as well as labour disputes, strikes and employer/state assaults. By linking every national trade union website home page to the other, and to official and independent international websites, members can just as easily find out international union news as local and national news, effectively joining up all the trade union and labour movements around the world in what he calls a 'global labour information highway'. Through online strike newspapers, websites can be used to refute management or government propaganda and explain workers' actions, gain media coverage and international support by helping to 'speed up the availability of counter-information which can be used to contradict false (or the absence of) reporting in mainstream news services' (Pollack 2000: 2). Moreover, email and websites can help to by-pass the 'elite-controlled mass media in terms of both obtaining information and getting it out' (Cleaver 2000: 16). So, workers from different countries get a sense of similar struggles in other regions and countries, regardless of time, place and race through an informational flow that they would not otherwise have received and thus a struggle or series of struggles they would ordinarily not have known about.

This communication tool will also overcome many past *organisational* obstacles to coordinating international solidarity efforts. For example, by combining global interactive databases with email, online chat and videoconferencing, trade unions can hold 'virtual' international conferences and meetings for the purposes of *multinational collective bargaining* with TNC employers (Thorpe 1999: 219–20). Lee (1997: 13) argues that this 'virtual' medium for international meetings is the 'solution to the budgetary problems' faced by the WCCs in 1970s. The increasing availability of Internet translation programs, although imperfect, also enable such information to be shared to all trade unionists of whatever nationality and language. Moreover, by turning trade unions into 'e-unions' or 'cyberunions', not only can they achieve an optimum level of organisational efficiency releasing scarce resources, they can also become what Bill Gates calls in business circles 'digital nervous systems' (Darlington 2000b: 2). Lee (1997: 184) argues that as every trade union gradually comes online, it will eventually be possible to have what he calls a 'global early warning network' on trade union rights whereby through email (or phone or fax if necessary), any news story of a worker or union involved in a sudden and serious violation of their human and labour rights could be posted to every trade unionist in the world instantly asking for their support. Finally, organisation *through* cyberspace can also become militancy *in* cyberspace by using the Internet to directly target employers and states through 'hactivism' or international action sending mass emails of protest often by simply clicking on a specific link on a trade union website that has a specially designed web engine to launch 'ping' or mail bomb attacks against websites that overtax its 'reload' function or load memory banks with emails (Cleaver 1999: 17).

Reinforcing the instrumental global information and communication flows facilitating international action, the Internet is also seen as creating a new, more conducive place for reinforcing and building a shared 'global solidarity culture' of labour everywhere (Waterman 2001). Cyberspace helps forge these cross-border cultural affinities in two main ways. First, the use of hypertext and hyper-linking on the World Wide Web and its ability to instantly pick up foreign workers' news, culture and struggles '*contributes by its very nature* to internationalism and the ideals of global solidarity' (Waterman 2001: 39) and thus helps trade unionists to 'transcend their own local and national limitations' and feel 'part of a global community based not on language or skin colour, but social class – and a vision of a new society' Lee (1997: 179). Second, constructing what Hyman (1999: 107) calls an 'organic solidarity' for a new global workforce requires a continuous dialogue at every level and cyberspace provides this discursive arena. Waterman (2001: 16) argues that the very 'logic of the computer is one of feedback', thus helping unions and workers move away from a unidirectional, one-to-many, top-down instrumental flow of information towards a multidirectional, reciprocal, dialogical exchange that could take place through e-conferences, mailing and discussion lists, a dialectical process 'in which initial positions are transformed and a new synthesis reached' between workers of different countries.

Of course, the literature is still in its infancy and lacks critical theoretical and empirical investigation, and the deliberate synthesis presented here hides considerable differences in conceptual frameworks, arguments, visions, expectations and examples employed. In the space allowed, it is not possible to engage in a detailed theoretical analysis of these perspectives, but it is worth briefly mapping out a preliminary framework for future research. Generally speaking, there are three interrelated but distinct categories of net-internationalism: instrumental-organisational, organisational-solidaristic and solidaristic-communicative. Instrumental-organisational approaches fall under Waterman's (2001: 16) conceptualisation of the dominant union approach/use of the Internet as primarily a tool for 'faster, cheaper, further-reaching' communication, presenting new opportunities for organisational efficiency and mobilising trade union action and would best describe the work of Darlington (2000a,b) and Shostak (1999). Organisational-solidaristic perspectives focus on the informational and organisational benefits of the Internet for subjective solidarity-building through building a global worker-culture within the existing international trade union movement and would best describe the position of Lee's (1997) and Bailey's (1997) position. The solidaristic-communicative approach might be associated with the work of Waterman (2001: 16) and takes this theme one step further, seeing the Internet primarily as 'cyberspace' and cyberspace as a kind of Habermasian 'ideal speech situation', a place with 'unlimited possibilities for international dialogue, creativity and the invention/discovery/development of new values, new attitudes, new dialogues'. Within these three approaches, a range of expectations exist on what contribution the Internet can make to internationalism depending on both the respective analysis of the problems confronting internationalism and the relative efficacy of the Internet in solving these.

Discussion: problems@labour or problems@internet?

There is little doubt that the informational, organisational and solidaristic qualities of the Internet are being increasingly employed by national and international trade union organisations. First, of an estimated 391 million people online (www.euroktg.com/globalstats), Lee estimates that well over 60 million are probably trade unionists (Lee 2000a: 14–16) and whereas in 1999 around 1,500 labour websites existed, today there are 2,700 trade union websites alone (Lee 2001 citing Freeman), albeit dominated by North American and western European unions. In Britain, nearly all TUC-affiliated unions are online (Ward and Lusoli 2003) and there are now around 300 union websites, a substantial growth from the 211 in late 2000 (<http.dmoz.org> Lee 2000b). In the United States, fifty-six out of sixty-six AFL-CIO-affiliated unions are online with dozens more local branches networked (AFL-CIO 2001). Importantly, nearly all international union organisations are online such as the ICFTU, ILO and ITSs with multilingual website access to their press releases, campaign information, resource tools and latest international trade union news.

Second, many regional and international union organisations have been using new ICTs to develop interactive databases of information on multinational corporations, economic trends and management strategies for the purposes of national and international *collective bargaining* as well as more proactive strategies. For example, the Public Services International (PSI) has a multilingual database on privatisation and associated multinationals, with files on over 2,000 companies monitoring takeover and merger activities, financial and political developments and issues of performance, pricing, financing, employment and political relations, including corruption. The database is used to answer enquiries from trade unions affiliated to PSI, and others, on the companies and other information contained in the database. It also allows online access to information on companies, recent news and PSI-related reports and publications. The PSI is trying to develop electronic links between databases and information on privatisation between trade union and universities from Brazil, Canada, India, South Africa and Spain (www.psiru.org).

Third, the interaction between the infinite sources of corporate information located on the World Wide Web, the creation of union websites and databases and the growth of independent labour movement websites, mailing and discussion lists and web forums, has created an embryonic form of what Lee (1997) envisages as an 'online international labour press' with a built-in 'global labour early warning network'. For example, embodying and indeed forming much of this is Lee's own *LabourStart* website (www.labourstart.org) – the most comprehensive, multilingual and up-to-date global labour news service in all forms of media. The main website contains links to global labour news stories (national, regional and internationalist) usually taken from official online media and directly added to a database by 127 volunteer correspondents from around thirty different countries. The database then updates the website every 15 minutes. *LabourStart*'s home page has a summary of the latest world's major union headlines of that and previous recent days. The main site contains important features such as requests for urgent international solidarity action, discussion forums, a 'Labour News Network' to which contributors add/delete modify their own labour-related stories, directories of trade union websites and labour media, a 'Global Labour Calendar' with a day-by-week-by-month events guide for unions and software to both place a 'Labour NewsWire' on any other labour website – a live news feed of *LabourStart*'s latest five or ten headlines from either own country or globally in your own language – and a trade union web browser dedicated to unions. LabourStart is in 10 languages – Dutch, English, Esperanto, French, Italian, Norwegian, Portuguese, Spanish, Swedish and Turkish, and aims to add one more language every month through volunteers.

Fourth and perhaps most important has been the ability to rapidly mobilise international acts of solidarity through the Internet. By posting requests for solidarity on mailing lists and/or union and labour websites, campaigns such as the 1995–1998 Liverpool Dockers lockout received international prominence and saw dockers in the United States, Australia, Spain and Israel take solidarity action in their support. In 1997, the Bridgestone/Firestone dispute with the United Steelworkers of America came to an end when the International Federation of Chemical, Energy, Mine and General Workers' Unions (ICEM) helped the US union launch an international 'cyberstrike' against the tyre corporation: unionists and other web surfers were shown how to bombard the company with protests during a global 'day of outrage' by 'providing a list of addresses on its website to facilitate the unauthorised occupation of the sites and electronic mailboxes of the company's management, as well as of those of car makers and distributors, tyre retailers and other bodies with a stake in Bridgestone' (Breitenfellner 1997: 547). The Internet was vital to the success of the 1998 Australian dockers' dispute with their government in 1998. Lee (2000c: 5) argues that within days of the dispute starting, 'the threat of a boycott of Australian shipping emerged . . . largely thanks to the web and email' creating international solidarity. Finally, in early 2000, the South Korean union KCTU won the release of seventeen workers arrested and brutalised during a non-violent trade union sit-in by sending urgent appeals by email to international contacts, publishing the president's email address and urging protest messages to be sent (Lee: 2000c 7).

Yet, while these achievements appear impressive, we need to be critically aware of their actual and potential significance for 'union internationalism' itself, and this is a far more contested terrain of debate. Objectively, the Internet is providing workers and their organisations with revolutionary new organisational and communicational tools to engage in internationalism. Plenty of evidence supports the idea that the Internet is facilitating internationalism through transnational business networks, international discussion/mailing lists, cross-border political appeals for solidarity support and cross-border protest organisation. The Internet enables for the first time, in theory, a qualitative and quantitative shift in inclusivity, representativeness and internationalism. National trade union and labour groups from different countries can now meet, discuss, debate, dialogue, swap information and stories in cyberspace and in real time without having to set foot outside their offices and countries when previous means of communication were almost non-existent in relation to this. A top-down process can now become a two-way process. This is not necessarily a shift from verticalism to horizontalism, but it does enable feedback mechanisms that can transform, radically, initial positions and reach consensus.

For example, the Internet allows top-level position papers, which will eventually form the expression of the 'international labour movement's' position, to actually be downloaded from the ICFTU or ITS website anywhere in the world, disseminated to first previously marginalised national labour organisations in the South, and then, given the nature of the position being proposed, to the membership, analysed in detail and consulted upon with drafted additions and amendments. This should allow for a more representative position to be created and if it is not, then national unions and movements can produce alternative position papers or critiques, again circulating them among their membership, but also to sympathetic supporters in other countries, to build up a counter-consensus which may not only dramatically internationalise the debate, but may also lead to the 'official' body changing its position and thus gaining the support of a much larger group of the world's workers. This happened, for example, at the women's Fourth World Conference in Beijing in 1995, when the Internet was used by women's NGOs to facilitate the participation of thousands of women from around the world. As Gittler (1999: 95) argues:

> [t]he public electronic spaces for discussion and information sharing also helped demystify UN proceedings. Discussions previously reserved for a few governmental delegates and observers at the United Nations were now open to anyone able to access the medium.

However, there is much more to overcoming the obstacles to internationalism than the Internet can solve on its own, due to both the nature of these obstacles and some of the shortcomings of the Internet, which are focused on here. It is essential to reiterate that as we start to move away from the richest countries with predominantly white service and industrial workforces towards the poorest, predominantly black, Arab and oriental agricultural proletariats, computer access falls from being insufficient to almost non-existent. Only about 5 per cent of the global population are actually online and therefore the vast majority of trade unionists, actual and potential, do not and cannot use the Internet. While it is possible to use other technologies in conjunction with the Internet as the global women's movement has through 'connected' women acting as bridges to 'unconnected' groups 'by repackaging on-line information and sharing it through other communication channels such as print, fax, telephone, radio and theatre' (Farwell *et al.* 1999: 106), most of the developing world has no real telecommunications infrastructure to do even this. Moreover, both the Internet and international trade unionism remain dominated by the English language and while translation software may solve the technical side, it does not create political will. For example, contrast the resource-poor LabourStart and its volunteer system in nine different languages, growing month by month, to the relatively resource-rich ICFTU and its paltry three languages (English, French, Spanish).

Problems are also faced through the increasing employer and state offensive on Internet use and privacy. Employers in the United States, Britain and Germany have recently been given powers to legally monitor and sack workers browsing websites and using email for personal use and even union work. This highlights the weakness of email itself, which Lee (2000b) compares to 'sending a postcard... open to reading by all the computers that pass it along the internet to its destination'. Consequently, employers are actively challenging and prohibiting employee use of corporate computer networks for union activity (see Miller 2000 on the recent dispute between the *Washington Post* and its employees). Moreover, as recent research by Lee (2000a) reveals, the institutions created by the US government to manage, govern and decide the future of the Internet, primarily ICANN, are 'completely unrepresentative, undemocratic, and unaccountable... all completely dominated by transnational corporate capital'. While the implications of this control require more research, we have already seen corporations turning the tables on cyber-solidarity actions. In December 2000, the *Narco News Bulletin* – a US-based publication highlighting the role of US corporations in Narcotics production and trade – suffered a six-day shutdown after its email account and website suffered major technical problems from an alleged mail-bomb attack by the US lawyer-lobbyist firm Akin Gump who allegedly represent the Colombian government and drugs traffickers (Giordano 2000). This has been compounded more recently by the confirmed existence of ECHELON – a global satellite system for intercepting private and commercial communications including email (European Parliament 2001).

Many of these problems are openly acknowledged by cyber-enthusiasts and it is true that some are being overcome all the time through technological and software development. However, where net-internationalism is perhaps at its weakest is in its most important and radical claims concerning the solidaristic and cultural potential of cyberspace. It is not just memories of the Cold War and the divisive interventions of the ICFTU and AFL-CIO in developing countries that present fundamental barriers to internationalism. The everyday experiences of workers in a globalising economy remain nationalistic, parochial, highly localised and differentiated and are continually shaped by capitalist ideology, in particular the ideology and practice of economic nationalism. So, while a radical and effective internationalism will not be achieved without the development of what Waterman (2001) calls a 'global solidarity culture', the problem is how to get to this state and whether the Internet, or cyberspace, can help achieve this. Waterman certainly believes so, arguing that through the Internet, a 'global solidarity dialogue' can construct the kind of organic solidarity required for it to be internationally felt and adhered to.

However, Waterman and others are regrettably, if understandably, vague about the details. In practical terms, how and when is this dialogue going to take place and who will it take place between? Are we talking about the leaders and elites of the world's various trade unions, including the official international organisations, getting cosy in cyberspace? Is it a dialogue between elite and grassroots? Or is this just a grassroots thing? Given that the Internet is still only, and likely to remain so for the considerable future, largely a plaything of North America, Europe and sporadic elements in the developing world, how 'global' do we envisage this dialogue being? Waterman is right that the logic of the computer is 'feedback' – but who will be sending and who will be feeding back? If dialogue is problematic then how difficult will it be to create a solidarity culture both globally and between workers?

Tarrow (2000: 11, 13) reminds us that solidarity culture comes from social networks that provide the 'interpersonal trust, the collective identities and the social communication of opportunities that galvanise individuals into collective action'. Such identities are 'negotiated among people who know one another, meet frequently, and work together on common projects...identities are dependent on networks'. These vital social networks have, therefore, only been hitherto accessible to local and national people. Can they be accessible to an international community? Does the Internet recreate the necessary conditions for such global social networks to evolve into solidarity activity itself? Waterman would seem to believe so, but it his reference to the work of Escobar (1999) as his inspiration that betrays his own doubts. Escobar (1999: 32) talks of a 'cultural politics of cyberspace' best achieved and most effective if there is 'an ongoing tacking back and forth between cyberpolitics...political activism in the physical locations at which the networker sits and lives'. The power of the Internet to create a political community of feeling in this way is undeniable and can be witnessed during the unsuccessful 1996–1997 Citizens for Local Democracy (C4LD) campaign in Ontario, Canada, in the preliminary organisation of global civic movement that shut down the WTO at Seattle in 1999. Through browsing the website and becoming involved in the online cyberpolitical community, C4LD saw local people actually inspired to go to physical meetings and participate in the campaign. Just as Escobar argues, solidarity was built by what C4LD's principal web activist Liz Rykert called 'breathing in and breathing out' with members from both real and virtual worlds continually moving back and forth between the two realms, creating a community of feelings and shared values (O'Malley 1998: 22). The same is true of Seattle.

So clearly the Internet can create solidarity cultures, but can Escobar's model and those of C4LD and Seattle be applied to labour internationalism? It would appear not. Their strength lies both in the ability of activists to move in and out of real and virtual activist communities due to their proximity, and the fact that these two supposedly different worlds are actually the same because it is the *same* people doing the 'tacking in and out'. In contrast, workers engaging in internationalism cannot move as easily back and forth from cyber- to real-world activism because they do not live in the same locality nor work in the same conditions. The solidarity cultures and networks created on the Internet are unlikely to be cemented by real-world contact between say Canadian and Japanese workers, but it is this very interface between cyberspace and real place of everyday, face-to-face relations that is the key to the most important part of solidarity – building trust.

Moreover, C4LD and Seattle were essentially single-issue campaigns working towards a definite end goal in a fixed real-world location and dominated by pre-existing, and in the case of Seattle *internationally* organised, social movements and NGOs – perhaps symbolically, organised labour played a very small part in these cyber-communities. So the Internet didn't so much create a global solidarity culture as link different solidarities together globally. Groups such as the environmental movement were already coherent activist movements with an inherently global ethic and outlook and a long history of internationalism and even pioneering cyberactivism. So when Seattle activists left their cyber-communities, they re-entered their actual communities and their existing coherent activist groups and engaged in local workshops, meetings and events. Again, these ingredients do not correlate to union internationalism because the world's unions do not have a specific target, goal or project, nor do they have a pre-existing global solidarity culture. To compound this, global solidarity must form on the basis of workers and trade unions who are already suffering from a crisis of national solidarity, who are arguably inherently non-internationalist and many of whom harbour deep suspicions of the Internet as a threat to jobs and their way of life. This makes international networks, especially between trade unionists, extremely ephemeral and fragmentary, and whereas this might be a strength for horizontal social movement networks, it might be a weakness for labour internationalism.

This is supported empirically by the fact that not only is the overwhelming use of the Internet by trade unions for *non*-international solidarity purposes such as recruiting new members (customers) and providing members with legal advice (competitive service provision), but when net-internationalism does take place, it tends to take the form of a commercial 'e-greeting' card – the unidirectional sending of solidarity messages to striking or struggling workers to let them know that other people support their struggle, know about it and are behind its continuation. So, in sophisticating the medium of internationalism, the Internet is not changing the message itself.

Conclusions

This chapter has argued that although the dynamics of the global crisis of organised labour necessitate a revival of union internationalism to confront and reverse globalisation, the history of labour internationalism demonstrates that achieving effective cross-border worker solidarity is highly problematic, being continually jeopardised by subjective (nationalism, economism, ideology, history) and objective barriers (organisation, communication, resources). The Internet is actively overcoming many of these past obstacles to labour internationalism by enabling unions to mutually inform, organise and construct solidarity across national borders with unprecedented speed and reach. However, when adding together the continuing obstacles posed by Internet access, ownership and control with its shortcomings for building a global solidarity culture in a movement defined by its national outlook, it is important that the Internet does become fetishised as the virtual solution to real-world solidarity building. Navigating through this impasse may not so much mean changes to the Internet but changes within the international labour movement itself.

Note

1 Such a portrayal of the postwar 'European industrial-relations model, however, is highly abstract and many contributions have argued against this romanticised view of the Golden Age on two counts. First, comparativist approaches tend to emphasise the deep variation that existed in the levels of collective bargaining, the degree of centralisation of unions' and employers' own internal administration and the role of unions in economic and social policy, typically contrasting the virtually impotent labour movements of countries like France, Italy, Switzerland and Holland with Scandinavian countries where union federations were 'involved with the government in the *administration* of much public policy, not just consultation' (Crouch 1992: 171). Second and more fundamentally, some Marxist writers have argued that union movements' involvement in state institutions and corporatist bargaining arrangements were unsustainable ticking time-bombs that have contributed to today's crisis of organised labour. Corporatism simply enabled state and capital to co-opt powerful union

movements and reconstitute them from class organisations for the expression of workers demands to state-subservient institutions administering wage restraint through incomes policies.

References

AFL-CIO (2001) <www.aflcio.org/unionand/unions.html>

Bacon, N. and Blyton, P. (1999) *Meeting the Challenge of Globalisation*, Nottingham and Cardiff University.

Bailey, C. (1997) *Towards a Global Labournet*, paper presented to the LaborMedia'97 Conference, Seoul, South Korea, 10–12 November.

Bailey, C. (1999) *The Labour Movement and the Internet*, 2nd Seoul International LaborMedia'99 <www.amrc.org.uk.hk/Arch?3401.htm>, first accessed December 2000.

Boyer, R. and Drache, D. (eds) (1996), *States Against Markets*, London and New York: Routledge.

Breitenfellner, A. (1997) 'Global Unionism', *International Labour Review*, 136 (4), 531–55.

Brown, W. B. and Hogendorn, J. S. (2000) *International Economics in the Age of Globalization*, Ontario, New York, Hertfordshire, Rozelle: Broadview Press Ltd.

Castells, M. (1996) *The Information Age. Volume I: The Network Society*, Oxford: Blackwell.

Cleaver, H. (2000) *Computer-Linked Social Movements and the Global Threat to Capitalism*, Department of Economics, University of Texas, USA.

Cox, R. (1994) 'Global Restructuring', in Stubbs, R. and Underhill, G. R. D. (eds), *Political Economy and the Changing Global Order*, London: Macmillan, 45–59.

Crouch, C. (1992) 'The Fate of Articulated Industrial Relations Systems', in Regini, M. (ed.), *Future of Labour Movements*, London, California, New Delhi: Sage, 169–87.

Darlington, R. (2000a) *The Creation of the E-Union*, text of presentation made to an Internet Economy Conference, London School of Economics, 7 November.

Darlington, R. (2000b) *Books On Business* <http://members.tripod.co.uk/rogerdarlington/>, first accessed October 2000.

Davison, C. (2000) 'Unions Get Connected', *The Standard.com Europe*, 7 November.

Drache, D. (1996) 'From Keynes to K-Mart', in Boyer, R. and Drache, D. (eds), *States Against Markets*, London: Routledge, 31–61.

Escobar, A. (1999) 'Gender, Place and Networks', in Harcourt, W. (ed.), *Women@Internet*, London: Zed.

European Parliament (2001) *Temporary Committee on the Echelon System*, Meeting 29 May.

Farwell, E., Wood, P., James, M. and Banks, K. (1999) 'Global Networking for Change', in Harcourt, W. (ed.), *Women@Internet*, London: Zed, 102–113.

George, S. (2000) 'Seattle Turning Point', *Le Monde Diplomatique*, January.

Gill, S. and Law, D. (1988) *The Global Political Economy*, New York and London: Harvester Wheatsheaf.

Giordano, A. (2000) *About the Cyber Attack on Narco News*, December <www.narconews.com>

Gittler, A. (1999) 'Mapping Women's Global Communications and Networking', in Harcourt, W. (ed.), *Women@Internet*, London: Zed, 91–101.

Hale, A. and Shaw, L. (2001) 'Women Workers and the Promise of Ethical Trade in the Globalised Garment Industry', *Antipode*, 33 (3), 484–509.

Haworth, N. and Ramsay, H. (1988) 'Workers of the World Untied', in Southall, R. (ed.), *Trade Unions and the New Industrialization of the Third World*, London: Zed Books.

Hirsch, B. T. and Addison, J. T. (1986) *The Economic Analysis of Unions*, London: Allen & Unwin.

Hyman, R. (1999) 'Imagined Solidarities', in Leisink, P. (ed.), *Globalization and Labour Relations*, Cheltenham: Edward Elgar, 94–115.

Kelly, J. (1998) *Rethinking Industrial Relations*, London and New York: Routledge.

Klein, N. (2000) *No Logo*, London: Flamingo.

Lambert, R. and Webster, E. (2001) 'Southern Unionism and the New Labour Internationalism', *Antipode*, 33 (3), 337–62.

Lee, E. (1997) *The Labour Movement and the Internet*, London and Chicago: Pluto Press.

Lee, E. (2000a) *The Internet Belongs to Everyone*, Labour and Society International.

Lee, E. (2000b) 'How the Internet is Changing Unions', *Working USA*.

Lee, E. (2000c) 'Email Privacy is a Trade Union Issue' <www.labourstart.org/nettips1/>, first accessed January 2001.

Lee, E. (2001) 'Beyond the Website', *LabourStart*.

Levinson, C. (1972) *International Trade Unionism*, London: Allen & Unwin.

Marglin, S. and Schor, J. (eds) (1990) *The Golden Age of Capitalism*, Oxford: Clarendon.

Meiksins, P. (1998) 'Same As It Ever Was', in Meiksins-Wood, E. *et al.* (eds), *Rising From the Ashes*, New York: Monthly Review Press, 28–40.

Miller, G. (2000) 'Guild Pushes to Use Paper's E-Mail System to Reach Workers Labor', *Los Angeles Times*, December 25.

Mittelman, J. H. (1996a) 'The Dynamics of Globalization', in Mittelman, J. H. (ed.), *Globalisation*, International Political Economy Yearbook Vol. 9, Boulder: Rienner, 1–19.

Mittelman, J. H. (ed.) (1996b) *Globalisation*, International Political Economy Yearbook Vol. 9, Boulder: Rienner.

Moody, K. (1997) 'Towards an International Social-Movement Unionism', *New Left Review*, 225, 52–72.

O'Brien, R. (2000) 'Workers and World Order', *Review of International Studies*, 26, 533–55.

O'Malley, K. (1998) 'Grassroots in Cyberspace', *Canadian Forum*, January/February.

Olle, W. and Schoeller, W. (1977) 'World Market Competition and Restrictions upon International Trade Union Policies', *Capital and Class*, 2.

Panitch, L. (1998) 'The State in a Changing World', in *Monthly Review*, 50, 11–22.

Pollack, A. (2000) *Cross-Borders, Cross-Movement Alliances in the Late 1990s*, Global Solidarity Dialogue <www.antenna.nl/~waterman/pollack.html>, first accessed January 2001.

Ramsay, H. (1997) 'Solidarity at Last?' *Economic & Industrial Democracy*, 18, 503–37.

Regini, M. (ed.) (1992) *The Future of Labour Movements*, London, California, New Delhi: Sage.

Shostak, A. (1999) *CyberUnion*, Armonk, NY: M. E. Sharpe.

Spalding Jr, H. A. (1988) 'US Labour Intervention in Latin America', in Southall, R. (ed.), *Trade Unions and the New Industrialization*, London: Zed Books, 259–86.

Stevis, D. (1998) 'International Labor Organizations, 1864–1997', *Journal of World-Systems Research*, 4 (1), 52–75.

Tarrow, S. (2000) *Beyond Globalisation*, Departments of Government and Sociology, Cornell University.

Taylor, R. (1999) *Trade Unions and Transnational Industrial Relations*, Geneva: International Institute for Labour Studies.

Thomas, H. (ed.) (1995) *Globalization and Third World Trade Unions*, London: Zed.

Thomson, D. and Larson, R. (1978) *Where Were You Brother*, London: War on Want.

Thorpe, V. (1999) 'Global Unionism: The Challenge', in Waterman, P. and Munck, R. (eds), *Labour Worldwide in the Era of Globalisation*, London: Macmillan, 216–22.

Visser, J. (2000) 'From Keynesianism to the Third Way', *Economic and Industrial Democracy*, 21 (4), 421–56.

Ward, S. and Lusoli, W. (2003) 'Dinosaurs in Cyberspace?' *European Journal of Communication*, 18 (2), 147–179.

Waterman, P. (2001) 'Trade Union Internationalism in the Age of Seattle', *Antipode*, 33 (3), 312–36.

Western, B. (1997) *Between Class and Market*, Princeton, NJ: Princeton University Press.

9 Rethinking political participation

Experiments in Internet activism in Australia and Britain

Jenny Pickerill

Introduction

> We've got a desert indymedia set up in the back of a truck, trying to keep stuff away from the dust which is ... flying around everywhere ... it is participatory media so anyone can come and write a story ... giving people here an unmediated voice for their perspective.
>
> (Andrew, desert.indymedia)

Camped in the inhospitable Australian desert outside the Woomera refugee detention centre 500 km north of Adelaide, over 1,000 activists collaborated in an action against Australia's policy of mandatory detention of asylum seekers and its use of the inner desert as a dumping ground. The Woomera2002 auto-nomadic festival of freedom attracted international media attention as they physically pulled down the fences of the centre and helped several dozen refugees escape (Williams and Plane 2002). Internet and email were used extensively in both the organisation of the action(s), and in sharing the protests with the world direct through their own media.

Environmental and social justice activists[1] began using email and newsgroups in the late 1980s and by the mid-1990s several websites appeared publicising groups' campaigns (Young 1993). The use of new information and communication technologies (ICTs) by activists has since facilitated participation mobilisation, the coordination of actions and has been used as a tactical tool in itself (Lubbers 2002). While activists face constraints in their use of ICTs – such as access problems, threats from online surveillance, corporate control and the tensions of using environmentally damaging technology – many have been able to appropriate and subvert the technology to their advantage.

In addition to identifying the particular ways in which activists have benefited or struggled with the technology (Pickerill 2001b), examination of activists' ICT use can be used to explore the extent to which ICTs facilitates groups who employ different organisational forms. Crucially, are some forms of activist networks or groups better able to benefit from ICT use than others? Such questions require an examination of organisational form. Within environmental and social justice movements there is often an emphasis upon participatory democracy. Thus analyses of components of these movements serve as an important comparison to some of the more institutionalised political structures explored in this book.

The core premise of this chapter is that the use of ICTs has disproportionately benefited small grassroots groups and individual activists linked only into fluid networks using cellular structures. It is these groups who often suffer from a lack of resources but were able to be more inventive in using the technology because of their ideology and free-flowing organisational structure. Consequently, they gained a temporary advantage over some other less-inventive established organisations and helped create a degree of equality within the environmental and social justice movements.

Case studies and context: Woomera2002 and Friends of the Earth UK

In this chapter two case studies representing different forms of activism in Britain and Australia[2] are employed to investigate the questions outlined here. The Woomera2002 actions were a temporary demonstration of a diffuse and fluid network that took place in the desert in Australia in March 2002, whilst Friends of the Earth (FoE) UK is a well-established formal environmental lobbying organisation with its headquarters in London. For the purposes of this chapter the desert.indymedia network will be the main focus of analysis for the Woomera2002 case study. Composed largely of independent media activists in Melbourne and Brisbane with a grounding in autonomous (and for some anarchist) principles, the indymedia[3] group were the main employers of ICTs and were the focus for the distribution of activist media during and after the actions through the Melbourne indymedia website.[4] Furthermore, many of those involved in the desert.indymedia network had had core roles in the coordination and promotion of the Woomera2002 convergence.

Although both are located in similar environmental and social justice movements and are aware of each other's existence,[5] they operate within different organisational and national contexts. Both Britain and Australia have vibrant and diverse environmental movements. Participants range from radical green activists who engage in direct action to strong professional lobby groups who are able to work closely with sectors of government (Rawcliffe 1998; Hutton and Connors 1999; Doyle 2000). The traditions of these two countries also overlap, most obviously through the British colonialism of Australia from the eighteenth century that is reflected in Australian contemporary legislative structures, social and cultural practices and continued role of the British monarchy in Australia. Furthermore, Australian and British environmental and social justice activists have shared a direct-action repertoire, such as the use of lock-ons, tree-sits and tunnels and the use of 'manufactured vulnerability' (Wall 1999; Doherty 2000: 62).

There are of course key differences too. Australia is governed under a federal system, which gives the eight states independent governments[6] (Lovell *et al.* 1995). In comparison to Britain it is a relatively new federation that has yet to understand the needs and ways of its indigenous aboriginal population (Valadian 1990; Neill 2002). Furthermore, the Australian Green Party has been successful in gaining a foothold in parliamentary politics. This is in stark contrast to the lack of formal representation in the Westminster Parliament of the British Green Party. These differences are reflected in the ways activist groups choose to operate but as we shall see there are also strong similarities between ICT utilisation irrespective of national context.

This chapter begins by appraising the current debates surrounding the impact of ICTs on political power struggles and then goes on to delineate the divergent organisational forms of activism. The two case studies are then examined in relation to the implications of ICT use for altering the processes of political leverage, with particular emphasis upon the influence of organisational form on the use of technology.

The Internet organisations and campaigning: politics as usual?

Initially, ICTs were presented by utopians such as Rheingold (1994) as providing new spaces for social interaction free from the hierarchical and bureaucratic pressures of existing society. These democratic properties could also facilitate public participation in political processes, through the bypassing of traditional government hierarchies, and aid the development of social cohesion (Frederick 1997; Tsagarousianou 1998). Bonchek (1995) argues that the formation of collective political action is facilitated by ICTs because the use of computer networks reduces transaction costs associated with organising collective action. He also notes, however, that current dynamics lead to unequal Internet access across social strata, which result in a domination of affluent, young, male and often highly educated individuals using the technology and consequently only some groups benefit from its use. Indeed, ICTs can also contribute to an increase in marginalisation of sectors of society through the creation of intolerant 'purified communities' in online culture (Belt 1998). ICT users bring with them their existing intolerances, such as racism or homophobia. The Internet therefore remains a social space and cultural product that is as prone to antagonisms as any other media (Froehling 1997; Warf and Grimes 1997; Cleaver 1998).

Such unequal access and increasing infusion of existing social values and prejudices into cyberspace, led Margolis and Resnick (2000) to argue that over time existing political practices, leverage and power would be mirrored on the Internet as cyberspace becomes 'normalised'. Resnick (1998: 65) goes so far as to suggest that, 'for all their commitment to radical change, the presence of activists on the Net is part of the process of political normalisation...they represent a familiar element of democratic pluralism'. There is, however, an alternative interpretation of what this 'pluralism' of political interests on the Internet represents. Rather than simply being a reflection of existing political practice, Bimber (1998) argues that ICTs enable a plethora of issue groups to operate without institutional support or structures and to mobilise quickly at low cost. This 'accelerated pluralism' is fashioned by 'more rapid and more intense citizen responses to mobilization efforts by linkage groups' and 'the possibility of decreasing coherence and stability in interest group politics, as the group process loses some of its dependence on stable public and private institutions' (Bimber 1998: 144). According to this understanding, activism via ICTs would remain centred around groups and networks (rather than lone individuals), but these linkages would be more diffuse, fluid and short term, and the cycle of mobilisation would move more quickly. Moreover, some forms of organisation, especially traditionally resource-weak informal groups may find the use of ICTs particularly beneficial. Although the provision of more information and ability to increase communication does not lead to greater political participation in itself[7] (Bimber 2001).

In terms of participant mobilisation, most research has underlined the importance of existing inclusion in social movement networks and that this integration is dependent on face-to-face interaction (McAdam 1988; Wall 1999). Only occasionally can 'strangers' be mobilised through 'moral shocks' (Jasper and Poulson 1995). Consequently, Diani (2001) argues that ICTs will aid different types of movements in different ways. Accordingly, organisations mobilising mainly professional resources using ICTs, such as FoE, are able to create virtual communities,[8] but this does not affect their overall mobilisation potential. In contrast, organisations mobilising mainly participatory resources requiring direct participation, such as those at Woomera2002, rely more upon face-to-face interaction and hence, ICTs result in virtual extensions that maintain the importance of the existing networks. Nevertheless, most groups can at a minimum benefit from ICT use by enhancing their ability to communicate effectively with increased speed, reduced costs and ease of interaction between an internationally dispersed network (Pickerill 2001a).

Participation and the impact of organisational-structure culture and context

Organisational form is often a reflection of the ideological, cultural or economic goals of its participants. There is no particular model of organisation, or unidirectional organisational evolution, which can be applied to social movements. There tends to be heterogeneity and plurality in the forms of organisation, a constant process of 'adopting, adapting, and inventing' (McCarthy 1996). Social movement organisations tend to favour decentralisation, participatory democracy, internal solidarity and *ad hoc* short-lived leadership. Organisational models have been differentiated by Doyle and McEachern (1998) according to the degree of organisation, distribution of power and the degree of commitment required from participants. These potential differences have resulted in a panoply of organisational forms, such as: local nuclei, umbrella organisations, party models, public interest groups, movement associations and supportive organisations (Della Porta and Diani 1999).

Integral to the choice of organisational form for a group is an understanding of the strategy by which environmental protection or social justice can be achieved. There are multiple strategies for environmental change espoused by different ecological groups. These strategies can reflect contrasting approaches to the value of democratic processes (Doherty and de Geus 1996). Some appear to advocate authoritarianism in order to ensure comprehensive environmental protection and Goodin (1992: 120) suggests that 'it is more important that the right things be done than that they be done in any particular way or through any particular agency'. There are, however, many links between environmentalism and a desire for a 'particular sort of decentralised face-to-face democracy' (Dobson 2000: 120), a form of participatory democracy and commitment to local politics that seeks involvement from as many individuals as possible in societal decisions (Seel and Plows 2000). Furthermore, many environmentalists have deliberately emphasised the importance of openness, participation, decentralisation and inclusion within their campaigning (Paehlke 1988). In practice, this has taken the form of 'informal and non-hierarchical forms of organisation' (Doherty *et al.* 2000: 11). This is often evident in radical direct-action networks such as Earth First! or associated groups whose principles included being 'non-authoritarian, non-coercive and non-hierarchical' and providing a 'democratic space' for participants (Anon 1999a). One increasingly popular structure amongst environmental networks is the use of affinity groups for coordination and actions:

> The affinity group is not a form of organization that treats everyone the same, or a mode of action where people are required to make the same commitments.... The groups act as a group, it has a task, but the basis of action lies in personal relationships and the recognition of the individuality of each person.
>
> (McDonald 2001)

In this way, different roles are taken on by participants of the affinity group, such as media spokesperson or first aider, but crucially there is a sense of trust and often a buddy system to ensure that everyone works together on a task and the goals of the group are achieved[9] (Starr 2000). As such, an affinity group is a mechanism through which participatory democracy can more closely be practised through self-organisation, with spokescouncils[10] being used to coordinate between affinity groups.[11] Alternatively, the more traditional model is via a branch structure based on geographical areas. Such local groups can run autonomously but are commonly linked, guided and influenced by a central headquarters. This structure is more popular amongst large-scale membership, non-governmental organisations (NGOs) (Rawcliffe 1998).

FoE, Woomera2002 and participatory democracy

Despite sharing a theoretical commitment to the ideals of participatory democracy, FoE UK and Woomera2002 practised it in disparate forms. Woomera2002 auto-nomadic festival of freedom[12] was a temporary manifestation of activists' networks to protest about refugees, anti-nuclear issues and the dispossession of indigenous lands. It has also been described as being 'an internet-assisted campaign' (Williams 2002: 4). It was an alliance of a variety of affinity groups[13] that met in the desert and coordinated actions through spokescouncils. Consensus was not always reached because of the variety of affinity groups involved and in particular a clash with 'old left' centred forms of organising (x-trot 2002).[14]

Predominantly, however, many affinity groups reflected the Do-It-Yourself (DIY) culture and networks of radical autonomous activists common in the non-violent direct-action campaigns of forest and anti-globalisation activism in Australia[15] (Burgmann 1993; Cohen 1997; Hutton and Connors 1999; Doyle 2000). Such grassroots activism often operated in contention with more centralised forms of organisation typified by Greenpeace Australia and the Australian Conservation Foundation. Overall, there was an emphasis upon a non-hierarchical organisational structure that encouraged individual autonomy, expression and experimentation. There was no formal membership and the convergence was financed through personal commitment and donations.

In contrast to Woomera2002, FoE UK employs a hierarchical organisational structure, while still advocating staff participation in informing the strategic direction of the organisation. Launched in London in 1971, FoE has become a particularly influential NGO in British politics (McCormick 1991; Lamb 1996). Although FoE UK's perspective is rooted in an ideology that radical political and social changes are required in order to avert further environmental destruction, its choice of aims and tactics[16] prevent it from being a radical environmental group[17] (Wapner 1995; Rawcliffe 1998). It is composed of regional campaign coordinators and 250 local groups with a national office overseeing campaigns, but not determining local group activities (Doyle and McEachern 1998). However, it is still criticised by more radical groups for being too centralised, hierarchical and bureaucratic. FoE's leadership is 'authoritative rather than representational' (Lowe and Goyder 1983: 53) and Jordan and Maloney (1997) suggest that FoE members are mainly passive *supporter*s of the group, rather than active *members*. In this sense, they argue, FoE's internal structure is not democratic or participatory but is more akin to a 'protest business' and local groups and individual activists have little influence upon decisions at the centre.

Organisational use of ICTs: altering the processes of political leverage?

The ways in which ICTs are adopted and utilised within activist groups and networks reflect their existing organisational forms and ideologies (Slevin 2000: 136). Moreover, the context in which ICTs are adopted is crucial in determining how it will be utilised, how quickly it is adopted and how innovatively it is employed. Available resources for use of ICTs are obviously a key stumbling block. Activists face a variety of access restraints: financial difficulties, differing skills attainment and hardware and software problems are experienced by many. Such factors result in an uneven utilisation of the technology. However, both in FoE and Woomera2002 there were efforts to overcome these access problems by fundraising, (re)using old equipment and limiting time online. Furthermore, at Woomera2002 access to ICTs was provided through a temporary indymedia centre[18] – computers rigged up in a truck at the protest camp – and there were attempts to share technical skills through informal exchanges.[19] Activists also had to overcome the paradox of using advanced technology whose production and use has extensive environmental and social consequences.

The level of leverage that activist groups have in politics can be influenced by ICTs in several ways; *internally to the organisation* – through rapid interaction, convergence of communications, innovation through freedom to experiment and challenging internal hierarchies, and *externally of the organisation* – through cohesion and swarming, and reducing containability. Each of these is now explored through the case studies.

Rapid interaction

Activists are able to use ICTs for increasing the speed and regularity of their communication, thus reducing the onus of distance. Furthermore, such rapidity can facilitate networking, improve response times and aid the gathering of information. The ability to generate support and mobilisation were also possible within a shorter timeframe by providing an easy conduit through which to notify activists about events. Activists were able to interact at an international level quickly using ICTs during campaigns at FoE, especially on actions that involved regular communication with other chapters of FoE.

The value of speed was further illustrated in the distribution of activist media reports from Woomera2002. News about the events was published quickly and such information contributed towards the construction of a rapidly evolving storyline, which was a collection of first-hand accounts, links to mainstream news, transcripts of audio links, analysis and contributions from people who were not present:

> It was unmediated . . . the article went up and it was instantaneous, you didn't have to wait for the 7 o'clock news and wait for it to go through all the corporate filters.
>
> (Barry, Brisbane indymedia[20])

In effect, the actions and its consequences unfolded on the website in only a short lag from real time and posting continued throughout the night after the main actions.

Convergence of communications

ICTs have the potential to ease some of the stresses and strains that organisations and groups face during internal communication and coordination. By using ICTs to overcome organisational communication difficulties, the technology may contribute to improving the flow of information within a group and thus, potentially, aid its effectiveness in achieving its objectives.

FoE appeared to benefit from the convergence of communications. For example, Bell, a former FoE regional coordinator, identified time savings as a result of having a website that

> cuts out a lot of wasted time and misconceptions about what we do and certainly if you see the campaigns that we are involved with it avoids the general impression that FoE can help on everything.

FoE's Intranet aided information coordination and discussion within the core of FoE (the head and regional offices). ICTs also facilitated an informality in forms of communication between departments, as email tends to be used without the associated social graces that occur with face-to-face meetings, which in turn quickened the rate of exchanges. Despite this, and an increasing number of email public enquires, most requested information was only available as hardcopy, so post had to be used in response. Furthermore, FoE's size and the large amount of information that it produced slowed its ability to update electronic information quickly and renders FoE unable to benefit fully from the speed and interactivity ICTs offers. As one former FoE official noted:

> it takes us so long to get stuff on our own web pages internally simply because there's a big queue'. Like other FoE publications, in order for new informa- tion to go on the website the information must be cleared through a proce- dure and a set of channels. This involves checks for content, booking time with web managers and then getting it out on-line. This can take time.
>
> (Festing, former FoE housing campaigner)

FoE's use of ICTs to converge its communications has been further limited by the sceptics within their ranks. As one local organiser commented: 'I would see the Internet as a necessary evil if you like. It's there so you've got to use it, but if there are other ways of getting the information I would use those alternative methods' (Packham, Newcastle FoE).

For the Woomera2002 convergence, ICTs were used significantly prior to the protest festival in coordinating various affinity groups' participation. ICTs were particularly useful in communicating across the large distances of Australia and across the various time zones. ICTs facilitated the linking of participants of a dis- parate network without the cost of individual phone calls. Not only were emails used to coordinate amongst or between specific groups (while maintaining the importance of face-to-face meetings in mobilising participation)[21] but there was a large central and regularly updated website. This outlined the issues, contacts and affinity groups and provided logistical information about campsites, health and legal support. There was also a 'rideboard', that linked together people looking for lifts and a countdown that helped build a sense of momentum towards the commencement of the protest.

Innovation through freedom to experiment

A lack of rigid organisational structure has enabled many activists to feel free to experiment with different uses of ICTs. In comparison, more formally hierarchically structured environmental organisations have a greater number of stages through which to gain approval of the use of a technology that may slow down or restrict its adoption of ICTs. Although FoE developed their website and email system as early as December 1994 and in the process were the 'first environmental campaigning organisation with a presence on the Internet' (Pipes 1996: 63), this was due to the commitment and enthusiasm of a few individuals who did not seek formal permission and constructed the website in their spare time. Had they done so, Weatherley (former FoE IT manager) suggests 'I would have been chewed out by several management team members', stalling FoE's use of ICTs as a result of senior staff 'techno-innocence' (Burt 1999). The subsequent request for official funding was hindered by the need to appeal to those in the chain of command, which caused resentment by those wanting to develop ICTs use further:

> I think FoE should have grabbed it by the reins a lot sooner...we lost a hell of a lot of ground that we'd got because FoE just would not invest in the internet, and it's almost not until almost everyone else has that they see the need.
>
> (Pipes, former FoE GIS coordinator)

FoE decided to outline boundaries on ICT use, such as suggested email etiquette and protocol, thus constraining use within policy guidelines. This is not to say that FoE have not used the technology in innovative and novel ways but that the ambitions of some if its staff were constrained by the organisational structure. FoE were also constrained in that ICT adoption required significant financial investment for an organisation of their size. Moreover, formal groups such as FoE need to retain a control over their image and the activities of their staff and might not have felt as comfortable with ICTs because they were not able to control their use as much as they would have liked and consequently felt threatened by it (cf. Mobbs 2000).

In contrast, more loosely structured groups, such as Woomera2002, with significantly less funding have to rely upon using what resources they had available and for those with access to experiment. Activists were able to utilise a small amount of technology to make a big impact, without having to worry about organisational policy. In networks such as Woomera 2002, consensus was not required before people took action. Those groups whose structure has enabled rapid and experimental adoption of ICTs have often used the technology in particularly innovative ways.

The indymedia format itself is innovative, indymedia 'software represents a confluence of interests, influences and experiences which makes it, in many ways, the state of the art in Internet activism' (Meikle 2002: 89). The site is organised using an open publishing model[22] that enables any user to upload their story or viewpoint onto the website with minimal editorial interference (Arnison 2001). The website format also enabled an easy melding of publication types – text, audio, photographs and cartoons – to be posted alongside each other. A particularly innovative aspect of ICT use at Woomera2002 was the development of the PIMP system – the Phone indymedia Patch System:

> PIMP is basically like an answering machine for indymedia. You dial the PIMP number, then go through the voice menu, selecting the appropriate options, and then leaving a message after the tone. This message is then turned into an MP3 file, automatically uploaded to indymedia
>
> (Nik, desert.indymedia)[23]

This meant that reports could be uploaded to indymedia without accessing a computer. Consequently, there were several MP3 audio reports recording as the actions took place, which were then available online within minutes. It also enabled detainees within the centre to communicate and contribute to the debates, 'there were actually a couple of phone calls from people inside Curtin [detention centre] who were doing solidarity actions' (Barry, Brisbane indymedia).[24] Systems such as PIMP are groundbreaking and all the more so for being developed with little money by volunteers.

This freedom is especially relevant to the use of ICTs because its use has spread so rapidly. In order to use the technology to their advantage, activists have had to utilise the opportunities quickly, and what was deemed as innovative and novel (and thus attention grabbing) quickly becomes standard.

Hierarchies: nuclei, formalisation and subversion

Many activist groups face a continuous pressure to formalise and to evolve into more rigid (often hierarchical) organisational forms. This is often due to the need to solve resource issues, overcome communication problems, provide a more united image and attempt to reach a larger audience. Traditionally grassroots direct-action campaigns have been viewed as temporary. Over time they either dissipate or develop into a more formal organisation fighting for their original or broader cause. In the latter case, this formalisation tends to result in oligarchy and the associated problems of added bureaucracy and hierarchical decision-making structures (Doyle 2000). How far ICTs enable activists to subvert the development of such hierarchies or merely create new ones is discussed in the following.

Woomera2002: ICTs creating hierarchies?

For Woomera2002 many strove to operate using non-hierarchical methods such as affinity groups and spokescouncils to prevent oligarchies developing and enabling decisions to be made collectively with all participants having an equal influence. However, even in groups that appear to have few organisational structures, informal or latent hierarchies develop around some tasks, often as a result of skill differentials or because some members had been involved for longer than others (Freeman 1970).

Prior to the desert camp being established at Woomera, there were only a few people directly involved in Melbourne indymedia, 'there is no real indymedia collective, there's a couple of individuals...no-one really wanted to form a group' (Sam, Melbourne media activist). The desert.indymedia collective formed with three people and grew to ten once at Woomera. It involved a collaboration of activists from a variety of Australian indymedia groups. There were no designated leaders or management chains of responsibility. Rather the collective developed around who wanted to be involved, 'there's no hierarchy, there's no news team, there's just a space for everyone to do their own thing' (Barry, Brisbane indymedia).

Due to access problems the indymedia site was uploaded via a hotel room and a local ISP, but for security reasons only a few people knew of this process, 'no one outside of a small collective knew about the location for the uploads – we wanted to keep it as secure as possible' (Nik, desert.indymedia). The decision to restrict knowledge of this space was made by the smaller collective and enforced on later participants, 'as more people came on board it was explained why we did things this way, not everyone was happy, but about six people uploaded from the space' (Nik, desert.indymedia).

Despite being a non-hierarchical group, the use of ICTs triggered the development of a cluster of those individuals who were most involved in the use of the technology.[25] An informal nucleus surrounded the use of ICTs and subsequently largely controlled its implementation. Such clusters do not represent a hierarchy, as there were no chains of command, but still serve a similar purpose to an oligarchy. In part, this reflected the limited number of participants with the necessary technical skill, 'there's a lot of pressure on those people, for one thing, and we're totally reliant on them...It all makes it quite fragile' (Adam Data, Dorks Advocating Total Anarchy).[26] There were attempts to share knowledge of how to use indymedia, but technical-skill sharing was still relatively limited.[27]

In an action such as Woomera2002, hierarchies can develop around several issues: who maintains and understands the online linkup of the indymedia centre; who gains access to the limited number of computers; whether any editorial control is operated and thus some posts get removed; and what posts get linked to through the features section of the website. In particular, hierarchies can also develop around the process of editorial control. Although the Melbourne indymedia site utilised an open publishing broadcast model, a few posts have in the past been hidden:

> The only times that we have hidden a story is when someone's published someone's personal address or when someone's published something that has impersonated someone else and it's obvious that it's an impersonation.
>
> (Sam, Melbourne media activist)

> Posts are occasionally removed...I've used my discretion and taken down two sentences of...swearing...but only very occasionally.
>
> (Adam Data, Dorks Advocating Total Anarchy)

Even this limited editorial interference caused debates about 'where's the line, how do you define who can take it down and then who are they accountable to... how do you define what is not the right content for the website?' (Alex, Melbourne indymedia). Consequently, Melbourne indymedia have developed decision-making processes and outlined how the editorial collective operate using modified consensus[28] with the aim of providing 'an unmoderated, open-publishing newswire' (Anon 2002e), which helps prevent the development of hierarchies of access to knowledge, debate and contributions.

At Woomera2002 the radicalness of the actions meant that some information (such as the locations of escaped refugees) was sensitive and thus did not get published online. Most activists were aware of this precaution, but in addition the people 'who were uploading media were aware of those issues and if something was incriminating they wouldn't publish it, and go back to that person ... and just discuss with them the issues' (Barry, Brisbane indymedia).

Despite the existence of these nuclei, ICTs have helped groups maintain their non-hierarchical networks. By easing the processes of communication, the need for formal structures or centralised offices are reduced. Individuals are able to communicate cheaply and regularly through ICTs without necessarily meeting face to face, or by formalising the contact. ICTs enabled the networks to remain fluid and loose, and to adapt to the changing involvement of different participants. It also provided a cheap medium through which to attract participants and coordinate their contributions. ICTs provide a medium through which the group can remain visible even if there are few participants, little activity is taking place or they are low on funds. Their web presence can continue to evolve at whatever pace participants choose, but does not fade when not attended to. Hence, ICTs are a medium where activists can move onto other projects and yet still maintain their initial campaign, such as the indymedia site. This fluidity enables campaigns to be dynamic for longer as they do not become constrained by the resource issues that so many activists face.

A test for the exclusivity of the nuclei is the extent to which non-collective members take part in projects such as desert.indymedia. With open access through the indymedia truck 'there were a lot of people who used it who aren't actively involved in infrastructure in indymedia' (Barry, Brisbane indymedia), and there were a large number of postings to indymedia during and after the actions. The desert.indymedia collective were also making a conscious effort to break down hierarchies by eroding the distinction between activists and journalists: 'for melb.indy there is no distinction, we don't 'cover' events, we set up the conditions for people to cover them themselves. We also upload to indymedia, but we do so as activists, not journalists' (Nik, desert.indymedia). Other participants did not perceive this cluster of individuals around the technology as intentional or exclusive, and there was a feeling that people were free to become involved. This was aided by the reflexivity of collective members who tried to resolve their privileged positioning:

> power is something that we don't think and talk about enough in any sphere, just power of access and knowledge and confidence ... if I have power and

access then my responsibility is to help someone else gain that space as well or use that space to create more spaces and it's not necessarily squashing anyone else if I'm trying to create more space.

(Alex, Melbourne indymedia)

One of the ways in which hierarchies can be subverted is through impermanency. The Woomera2002 group was 'only going to exist up until we go out to Woomera and then it's not going to exist anymore' (Alex, Melbourne indymedia). While the Melbourne and Brisbane indymedia collectives were longer standing there was an emphasis upon fluidity, 'there's always that feel to formalise what you're doing... I think amateurism's really important' (Nik, desert.indymedia).

In addition to ICTs being used by non-hierarchical groups to retain their forms of organisation, the technology has been accredited with flattening existing hierarchical structures (Walch 1999). FoE's hierarchy was challenged by the use of ICTs at the same time as being maintained and reinforced by it. The use of ICTs by FoE facilitated greater flows of communication between those in head office, regional offices and London. This streamlining of communications was also facilitated by the development of the Intranet and enabled a campaign to be based in (and coordinated from) Leeds,[29] which further challenged the dominance of London. ICTs eased previous communication problems between local groups:

it has never been feasible to ring round all these groups...this is so much easier because I just write one message and it goes out to about twenty different groups round the country.

(Welch, Newcastle FoE coordinator)

Although ICTs could have helped FoE improve local-group networking amongst themselves and for such groups to become 'information hubs' this did not happen (Burt 1999). There has always been a concerted effort by national FoE to encourage local networking – particularly through the funding of regional campaign coordinators. ICTs may aid this process but did not trigger it (Washbourne 2001). ICTs have been used to share information, especially through the campaign-specific email discussion lists, but barriers remain to intergroup communication and especially to sustained dialogue. The information networks still flow primarily via the head office, rather than between local groups. Thus the possibility of a non-hierarchical national network between local FoE groups seems limited. The use of ICTs actually maintains the central London head office as the hub of all information flows. Furthermore, the official stages through which information has to pass in order to be published on the national FoE website reinforces the hierarchical structure of the organisation onto any use of ICTs. The differing levels of access to ICTs available to staff also maintained the hierarchical structure by reinforcing the present division of resources. Mobbs (2000) suggests that with ICTs, decentralisation of centralised organisations becomes inevitable. At FoE, however, there remained many barriers to changing their hierarchical structures.

The traditional need to centralise (to benefit from economies of scale) was reduced by ICTs that enabled cheap, fast, decentralised communication between participants. Although ICTs increased and eased communication flows around the FoE UK network (incorporating head office, regional offices and local groups), the importance of the hierarchical network was maintained. Not only do the stages through which website content is decided preserve the traditional hierarchies, but email has predominantly been used to exchange information between central office, regional office and local groups in a linear fashion, rather than to subvert the hierarchy by using ICTs for intergroup dialogue. Thus, ICTs have not been proven to promote the circumvention of existing formal hierarchies.

Working together: strengthening the cohesion of networks and swarming

One of the main advantages of utilising ICTs are their ability to aid networking with other activist groups, aid mobilisation and generate collective and cohesive campaigns. This can also help strengthen cohesion between those involved in environmental and social justice struggles and extend links to other political activists. Furthermore, ICTs can be utilised as a component in multiple tactics that can be swarmed upon a target simultaneously.

Although many groups attempt to use ICTs to mobilise participation in their campaigns, the value of ICTs is hard to discern because of the use of multiple methods to attract participants, and the importance of non-ICTs methods is often retained. Hence, the use of ICTs did not particularly increase the ability to mobilise participation in protest events within existing environmental groups or like-minded cliques (because there are already adequate networks). Rather, ICTs served to reinforce the *strength* of existing network ties and enable quick and cheap communication within them.

A specific example of the use of ICTs by FoE to communicate with other organisations was the development of the URGENT (the Urban Regeneration and Greenfield Environment NeTwork) website. It was a separate site autonomous from FoE and has information from a variety of different organisations, including FoE, CPRE and direct-action groups. Its aim was to provide a comprehensive overview of the housing debate in the United Kingdom and links to different groups:

> it's basically about a spirit of co-operation because one of the lessons we learned from the anti-road movement was…Friends of the Earth…needs to co-operate with other groups, and it needs to be seen to be doing that in a way which is not pushing our weight around.
>
> (Festing, FoE)

For Woomera2002 the main website served as a focal point for coordinating a disparate collection of groups prior to the convergence. Furthermore, by channelling activists' news reports to the Melbourne indymedia website, part of a global independent news network with a recognisable and easy to find URL, activists were contributing to the general cohesion of online media activism. The connections made through ICTs gave the comfort of solidarity to activists (Cleaver 1998). This increases the ability of activists to network on a global scale and for wider social movements to emerge out of such coalitions. Other links outside the movement facilitate the cross-fertilisation of alternative ideas and the sharing of skills.[30] ICTs have also strengthened existing networks as they offer another media for communication. This is especially useful for radical activists who lead slightly transitory lives and do not have a permanent base for mail or phone.

Hacktivism (hacking with a political motive) and other forms of online activism such as virtual sit-ins have also been used in addition to existing forms of lobbying (Wray 1998). However, the most effective tactics combine online activism with existing forms of protest – to *swarm* targets with several techniques being used simultaneously. This was evident at Woomera2002 through physical action occurring at the same time as people posted reports and analysis to the indymedia site, and virtual interaction through the Virtual People Smuggler.[31] The indymedia centre enabled activists to have directorship over the representation of their cause and actions, to distribute their media quickly and to an international audience. This helps activists add to opponents' woes by not only conducting an action, but being able to advertise their success afterwards. Online participation was encouraged through the Virtual People Smuggler:

> a space for people who were unable to physically attend to partake in someway. So people sort of wrote pieces, messages of solidarity, that sort of thing, I think it was just an outlet for people who couldn't come.
>
> (Barry, Brisbane indymedia)

Although the virtual presence did not actually involve a targeted action, participants were able to join an online tactical bloc, express their views about the physical actions occurring and communicate with each other. The freedom of ICTs to exist beyond the barriers of national borders, 'confined neither by geopolitical limits nor the standard aesthetics of protests, the Virtual People Smuggler pays tribute to the chatrooms, spoof sites, weblogs, online gaming, independent media as virtual, vital and, therefore, actual moments in the crossing of borders' (Lovink 2002).

Containability

The ability to contain activists' concerns and publicity of their protests is reduced through the use of ICTs. Activists' views can be disseminated more freely and to a wide audience partly because of the current inability to regulate or curtail ICT use. There was a constant stream of diffuse and disparate updates of news and discussion from Woomera2002 via the indymedia website. This was especially significant given the location of the festival, near a remote town in the desert, it would have been relatively easy for news of the action to be contained. With multiple authors and opinions, the activists were able to represent the complexity of the action and its participants. This was in contrast to the mainstream media's language using terms such as 'riot', 'stormed', 'wild clashes' and depicting many of the participants as extremists[32] (Anon 2002c,d; Williams and Plane 2002). Moreover, many of the PIMP audio reports were with refugees who had escaped and were being harboured by the activists. These not only provided credence to the claims of success by the activists, but served to further humanise the reports of refugees plight, and reduce the ability of the government to manipulate the stories about refugees' motivations and conditions in the detention centres. This immediacy of the activist news might have helped influence the interpretations given by mainstream media. The use of PIMP could also bypass any attempts at preventing access to the internet or indymedia, 'we actually had the facility to do emergency uploads via mobile phone...but at the same time the PIMP system would have been just as good' (Barry, Brisbane indymedia).[33]

Despite this variety of online publication, however, most information was distributed through the one indymedia website. Although the indymedia brand is global and has received coverage from mainstream media sources, there remain issues over how wide the audience might be and whether users are able to see beyond the 'walled gardens' of choices created by ISP portals (Malina 1999). As 'a constructive space where you're actually trying to communicate to audiences that aren't necessarily familiar with the issues of activism I think open publishing needs to be questioned a little bit' (Sam, Melbourne media activist). Furthermore, not all news could be reported, because communication could have jeopardised the freedom of the escaped refugees.

Groups are also able to maintain their non-hierarchical forms of organising, sustaining a nomadic form of power and centre-less organisation, which are hard to target by the centred state authorities and hierarchical multinational organisations, thus further reducing containability. This is particularly important when opponents have tried to exercise power over some NGOs by attempting to seize assets. FoE had to withdraw from the Twyford Down actions in 1992 because such a court injunction was imposed on them (Lamb 1996). In contrast, it is virtually impossible to identify individuals or assets of loosely defined horizontal networks.

Leveling the playing field

Activists who are able to gain access to ICTs have been able to increase the speed of their interaction, integrate a variety of media in innovative ways, strengthen the cohesion of their contacts and develop novel online tactics. Although it is difficult to measure the before and after effects of ICT use, more political leverage is gained by non-hierarchical grassroot groups (such as Woomera2002) than formalised NGOs (such as FoE UK). This is because ICTs help reduce the importance of resources for smaller groups. ICTs enable cohesion of disparate networks through the ease and speed of communication – which corresponds to the loose affinity model structure of direct-action movement. By facilitating the internal and external cohesion, the operating and organisational ability to collectively organise large-scale protests is improved.

Moreover, ICTs aid groups' ability to resist formalisation, therefore maintaining the participatory democracy project and leaving power with the individuals making consensus decision-making. Furthermore, convergences such as Woomera2002 have illustrated that participatory democracy models of organisation can work.[34] There were many successful elements of the Woomera2002 actions and the use of ICTs played an important role in many crucial aspects – in aiding the coordination of the convergence and in quickly disseminating news and discussion of the actions (Pickerill 2002). The Woomera2002 network was able to remain fluid, loose and dynamic and retain a web presence even when participation or resources were low. Using the desert.indymedia case study it has been illustrated that although resources are necessary for ICT utilisation, it is inventiveness, enthusiasm and adaptability that are vital and it is these attributes that are encouraged in non-hierarchical grassroot networks.

Previously, established NGOs formed in order to benefit from economies of scale by harnessing the resources necessary to coordinate large-scale actions or lobbying campaigns. Using ICTs, however, groups are able to subvert the need for centralisation (in office space, for newsletter production, etc.) and physical manifestation (as in the physical presence of activists) (Kellner 1999). Thus they are also able to bypass the bureaucratic implications of formalisation. The larger NGOs are actually less able to benefit from the spontaneity offered by the new technology because of the tradition of centralisation and top-down control over decision-making and operations. The consequence of this trend is the increased political leverage gained by small activist-groups.

The importance of national context is hard to delineate using these case studies. However, in these cases the most influential factors were not institutional, political or social structures, but the activists' ideology of participatory democracy that shaped the ways in which they sought to utilise ICTs. As such, there appear to be similar enduring trends even in different national contexts.

There are, however, certainly threats to the political leverage gained by activist networks. ICT use is increasingly being normalised by large-scale mass utilisation and the influx of corporate ownership (Margolis and Resnick 2000: 208). This commercial commodification not only restricts the free spaces available to activists but increases the possibility of surveillance by both the state and those wishing to profit from ICTs. Activists have attempted to subvert such interference by using encryption, foreign hosts and being aware that what they post online may be under surveillance. In addition, activists are using ICTs in a similar way to their radical appropriation of some physical spaces (e.g. the Reclaim the Streets practice of occupying roads and holding parties in the middle of motorways). By claiming their own virtual spaces and developing their own brands of media (such as indymedia) activists can seek to simply maintain parallel spaces to those of corporates and continue in their experiments of participatory democracy.

Conclusions

The cases examined in this chapter have made conscious efforts to employ ICTs in a certain way, which reflects and is reflected in their organisational form. Slevin (2000: 139) suggests several strategies of using ICTs to facilitate organisations' ability to succeed in the uncertain complexity of modern society. Of these, he supports the idea of 'opening out' organisations and making them more inclusive using 'the Internet to facilitate and incorporate active bottom-up alliances'. Thus, in effect, moving closer towards models of participatory democracy advocated by the more radical activist groups. While he argues against total inclusion[35] there is an acknowledgement that moving away from hierarchical models is necessary for organisational survival, and perhaps survival for political structures too.

When examining the possibility of participatory democracy through Internet activism the context of this chapter has been very specific. The particular context of environmental campaigning (and social justice to a lesser extent) tends to be dominated by individuals who although may be resource weak in terms of capital investment, are not necessarily marginalised in society but can come from privileged social locations – often being white, middle class and tertiary educated. Therefore, while direct democracy for *all* citizens is unlikely to be achieved, certain networks are able to move towards practices of participatory democracy using ICTs. Manifestations such as Woomera2002 contributed to the refugee debate within Australia (and internationally), enabled several hundred of its citizens to make their opinions clearly heard and ICTs significantly contributed to their ability to achieve this. In contrast, FoE UK were less successful at encouraging participatory networks to develop, but have still used ICTs in innovative and advantageous ways. Whilst not all small activist-groups can benefit in similar ways from such ICT use, in certain contexts where access, skills and knowledge are present, activists organising in small-scale autonomous groups can use ICTs more effectively than more established lobbying organisations. This has implications not just for the way political partici-pation is examined, but for the value that is placed on hierarchically structured organisations when faced with the rise of fluid, grassroot mobilisations.

Acknowledgements

This research was undertaken through funding provided by an ESRC PhD Studentship (1997–1999) and a Leverhulme Trust Post Doctoral Research Fellowship (2001–2003). This chapter advances some assertions proposed in my contribution to the Fibreculture Reader (2001, Melbourne), and I would like to thank the editors for permission to continue that theme. I would also like to thank all the research participants for their time, energy and reflections, and Stephen Ward and Michele Willson for valuable comments on this chapter.

Notes

1 The definition of an 'environmentalist' is diffuse, with an increasing number of social justice issues being taken onboard by what were traditionally explicitly environmental

organisations. Friends of the Earth UK are a case in point. One of their main campaign priorities in May 2002 was 'challenging corporate power', which clearly has
environmental implications but is also concerned with issues of equality, fair trade and
community.

2 The data for these case studies was collated through in-depth face-to-face interviews
undertaken with participants in Britain and Australia, and from secondary sources
such as group literature, publications and media reports. British fieldwork was performed between June 1997 and June 1999. Australian fieldwork was undertaken
between March 2001 and March 2003.

3 The indymedia network is a global network of alternative media websites. The global
website is <www.indymedia.org> with over 70 regional centres across the world, each
with their own websites fashioned from the original model (Hyde 2002; Meikle 2002;
Scalmer 2002). The Melbourne indymedia website was set up during the protests against
the World Economic Forum in Melbourne, September 2000 (Gibson and Kelly, 2000).

4 Footage and stories from Woomera2002 were posted onto the Melbourne indymedia site –
<www.melbourne.indymedia.org>. Additional footage and discussion was also posted
onto the Brisbane indymedia site – <www.brisbane.indymedia.org>

5 Friends of the Earth Australia is a radically different organisation from its British counterpart, operating using a non-hierarchical grassroot participation model, its volunteers
are often involved in the organisation of radical protest such as Woomera2002.

6 Federalism means that activists can attempt to assert their influence on both their state
and federal governments. In certain key campaigns, such as the Franklin Dam protests
in 1983 and efforts to prevent the logging of the South West forests of Western
Australia in 2001, activists were able to mobilise state voting power around the specific
campaigns to lead pro-environmental parties to power, the Australian Labor Party
(ALP) in each case (Doyle 2000; The Wilderness Society 2001).

7 Bimber argues 'the only form of participation which is demonstrably connected to
Internet use is donating money' (2001: 53).

8 'Virtual communities' refers to networks that are not based on any face-to-face interaction and have been formulated entirely through ICTs.

9 'An affinity group is a group of people who have an affinity for each other, know each
others strengths and weaknesses, support each other, and do (or intend to do) political/
campaign work together' (Anon 2002a).

10 A spokescouncil is a forum for delegates from affinity groups to 'discuss actions, enable
cooperation and share information between lots of different groups. Decisions made at
the spokescouncil are not binding – which means that any decisions of the meeting as
a whole are only given effect if there is consensus' (Anon 2002b).

11 For example, during the anti-WTO Seattle protests in 1999, Starr (2000: 116) observes,
'groups with different messages, tactics and skills coexisted without attempting centralized organising . . . the anarchist alternative to bureaucratic top-down systems'.

12 More information is available at <www.woomera2002.com>

13 Some of the affinity groups present included: Boatpeople, desert.indymedia, No One
is Illegal, Pt'Chang, Refugee Rights Action Network and xborder.

14 How to work in the presence of Socialists (such as the Socialist Worker Party and
Democratic Socialist Party) is one of the main internal conflicts of recent global protest
events in Britain and Australia (Anon 1999b; Anon 2001).

15 However, Woomera2002 was essentially a mix of environmental and social justice
campaigning. The debate about refugees has become much more than a social justice
issue in Australia – debates have raged over what population Australia can support and
its environmental limitations.

16 FoE's strategy has been five pronged: (1) the use of political lobbying and legislative
activity, (2) scientific research and information provision, (3) employing the media,
(4) the mobilisation of the public through local groups and (5) coordination and
co-operation with other groups (Pickerill 2001b).

17 Its aversion to the use of illegal direct action and its emphasis upon political lobbying and legislative activity contrasts with more radical environmental groups such as Earth First! FoE UK has also been criticised for not having a strong green philosophy (Lamb 1996).

18 Though this temporary centre itself raised logistical issues – dealing with the heavy police presence (the activists were trespassing by establishing their camp near the detention centre), generating power, finding a landline – all on a low budget.

19 Adam Data (Dorks Advocating Total Anarchy) noted 'we've had a few people contact us with technical questions and wanting to learn some programming or set up their server. So we're going to organise a Linux workshop'.

20 Barry is speaking as a participant of the Brisbane indymedia collective but not as a representative.

21 Nik (desert.indymedia) noted 'it's better not to organise a group via email, but better to…network over email, that's like a networking of the groups…you need to ground email. It's like info sharing, it's no good having the info sharing unless you print it off and give it to other people. So I think you need to ground the inspiration and ground the information…it's a networking device and I think in a lot of ways it's no substitute'.

22 'Open publishing means that the process of creating news is transparent to the readers. They can contribute a story and see it instantly appear in the pool of stories publicly available…Readers can see editorial decisions being made by others. They can see how to get involved and help make editorial decisions' (Anon 2002e).

23 Nik is speaking as a participant of the desert.indymedia collective but not as a representative.

24 The involvement of detainees in participatory media is set to be further improved through a project of Melbourne indymedia: 'one of the projects that has come into being since Woomera2002 is a mobile phone project – a project that aims at supplying phones (with media and other numbers pre-programmed in) to detainees…to let them speak in their own voices for themselves (which is what indymedia is all about)' (Nik, desert.indymedia).

25 Similar clusters of control develop around other tasks or technology due to skill differentials or access, such as the mobile phone, CB radio, camcorder, or activities such as climbing, tunnel building or media relations. However, few have the potential of ICTs to shape the campaign or protest. The consequences of such nuclei also depend upon whether other participants approve of the way in which the ICTs are being used, or whether they disagree with the way the campaign has been portrayed on, for example, a website.

26 Adam Data is a code name for an activist; he speaks as a participant of the Dorks Advocating Total Anarchy collective but not as a representative.

27 Alex (Melbourne indymedia) commented, 'I think whatever form of activism you're involved in, skill sharing is really, really difficult, but there are always, always bottlenecks of information. Like so many groups that I've been involved with get to a certain point where one or two people are carrying the whole group on their shoulders, based on their experience and knowledge and confidence and power and history with that particular organisation…because of the urgency that drives activism people don't often think that there's space for new people to do things because we don't have time for people to make mistakes or learn…I guess the other thing is that people's identity is so bound up with their activism that sometimes you don't necessarily want to skill-share…I don't think people like letting go of their identity that much'.

28 A process where if consensus does not occur initially, there is further discussion and if there is still no consensus then a 75 per cent vote can pass a proposal (Anon 2002e).

29 The Real Food campaign is coordinated from the Leeds regional office and staff use the ISDN line to connect to the Intranet and access all the files that staff in London were able to.

30 Prior to ICT use activists have still sought to learn from how other movements operated, however, ICTs have quickened and cheapened the process of communicating between often distinct identities (Rucht 1993).

31 See <http://noborder.org/peoplesmuggler> for more information.

32 However, unlike many other significant and radical actions, Woomera2002 was covered internationally by mainstream media (including the BBC in England (see Mercer 2002) and CNN in America), which facilitated the publicity of the activists' concerns. This coverage was probably influenced by the sensitivity of the refugee debate at the time, and the nature and uniqueness of the actions.

33 There were limitations even with the PIMP system however, David (posting to Fibreculture email list, 16 April 2002) noted 'problem was for the rest of us that the protesters' camp...was serviced by exactly one telephone, which was obviously quickly jammed with coins. People I knew with wireless said the mobile coverage was shocking'.

34 Starr (2000: 116) also argued that participatory democracy worked during the organisation of the anti-WTO Seattle protests, 'groups with different messages, tactics and skills coexisted without attempting centralized organising. That coexistence was the material of the blockade's success. Everyone who participated has now experienced the anarchists alternative to bureaucratic top-down systems. We saw self-organisation at work and it worked'.

35 Slevin (2000: 134) suggests that 'organisational activities would soon come to a grinding halt if the views of all those who are part of an organisation would have to be actively canvassed and balanced with respect to every decision made'.

References

Alex (2002) '3CR Talks to Alex Kelly of Indymedia at Woomera', transcript of radio interview posted to Melbourne Indymedia, 30 March.

Anon (1999a) 'The First Year of Tyneside Action for People and Planet', *Do or Die*, no. 7, Brighton.

Anon (1999b) *Vampire Alert!* Leeds Earth First! <www.leedsef.org.uk/swp.htm>, first accessed March 2000.

Anon (2001) *Monopolise Resistance?* SchNEWS: Brighton.

Anon (2002a) *What Is an Affinity Group?* Woomera2002 convergence <www.woomera2002.com/affinity.php3>, first accessed July 2002.

Anon (2002b) *What Is a Spokescouncil?* Woomera2002 convergence <www.woomera2002.com/spokes.php3>, first accessed July 2002.

Anon (2002c) 'Ruddock Critical of Lack of Police Action at Woomera', *The Age*, Melbourne, 30 March.

Anon (2002d) 'Woomera Protesters "Wasting Their Time": Ellison', *ABC News*, 30 March.

Anon (2002e) 'Melbourne Independent Media Centre Editorial and Decision Making Policies and Processes', <http://melbourne.indymedia.org/decpol.php3>, first accessed July 2002.

Arnison, M. (2001) *Open Publishing Is the Same as Free Software* <www.cat.org.au/maffew/cat/openpub.html>, first accessed March 2002.

Belt, V. (1998) 'Technological Change and Urban Change', *CURDS Working Paper*, University of Newcastle upon Tyne: Newcastle upon Tyne.

Bimber, B. (1998) 'The Internet and Political Transformation', *Polity*, 31 (1), 133–49.

Bimber, B. (2001) 'Information and Political Engagement in America', *Political Research Quarterly*, 54 (1), 53–67.

Bonchek, M. (1995) 'Grassroots in Cyberspace', presented at the 53rd Annual Meeting of the Midwest Political Science, Chicago, 6 April.

Burgmann, V. (1993) *Power and Protest*, New South Wales: Allen and Unwin.

Burt, E. (1999) 'Information and Communication Technologies' presented at research seminar ICTs: Reshaping Voluntary Organisations? at London Voluntary Section Resource Centre, 18 November.

Cleaver, H. (1998) 'The Zapatistas and the International Circulation of Struggle: Lessons Suggested and Problems Raised' <http://www.eco.utexas.edu/Homepages/Faculty/Cleaver/lessons.html>, first accessed November 2000.

Cohen, I. (1997). *Green Fire*. Sydney: HarperCollins Publishers.

Della Porta, D. and Diani, M. (1999) *Social Movements*, Oxford: Blackwell Publishers.

Diani, M. (2001) 'Social Movement Networks', in Webster, F. (ed.), *Culture and Politics in the Information Age*, London: Routledge, 117–28.

Dobson, A. (2000) *Green Political Thought*, London: Routledge, third edition.

Doherty, B. and de Geus, M. (1996) 'Introduction', in Doherty, B. and de Geus, M. (eds), *Democracy and Green Political Thought: Sustainability, Rights and Citizenship*, London: Routledge, 3–17.

Doherty, B., Paterson, M. and Seel, B. (2000) 'Direct Action in British Environmentalism', in Seel, B., Paterson, M. and Doherty, B. (eds), *Direct Action in British Environmentalism*, London: Routledge, 1–24.

Doherty, B. (2000) 'Manufactured Vulnerability', in Seel, B., Paterson, M. and Doherty, B. (eds), *Direct Action in British Environmentalism*, London: Routledge, 62–78.

Doyle, T. (2000) *Green Power: The Environment Movement in Australia*, Sydney: University of New South Wales Press.

Doyle, T. and McEachern, D. (1998) *Environment and Politics*, London: Routledge.

Frederick, H. (1997) 'Mexican NGO Computer Networking Cross-Border Coalition Building', in Bailie, M. and Winseck, D. (eds), *Democratizing Communication*, Cresskill, New Jersey: Hampton Press, 255–85.

Freeman, J. (1970) 'The Tyranny of Structurelessness', *Berkeley Journal of Sociology*, <http://flag.blackened.net/revolt/hist_texts/structurelessness.html>.

Froehling, O. (1997) 'The Cyberspace "War of Ink and Internet" in Chiapas, Mexico', *The Geographical Review*, 87 (2), 291–307.

Gibson, J. and Kelly, A. (2000) 'S11 – Become the Media', *Arena*, 49, 10–11.

Goodin, R. (1992) *Green Political Theory*, Cambridge: Polity Press.

Hutton, D. and Connors, L. (1999) *A History of the Australian Environment Movement*, Cambridge: Cambridge University Press.

Hyde, G. (2002) 'Independent Media Centers: Cyber-Subversion and the Alternative Press', *First Monday*, 7 (4) <www.firstmonday.org/issues/issue7_4/hyde/index.html>, first accessed May 2002.

Jasper, J. M. and Poulson, J. D. (1995) 'Recruiting Strangers and Friends', *Social Problems*, 42 (4), 493–512.

Jordan, G. and Maloney, W. (1997) *The Protest Business?* Manchester: Manchester University Press.

Kellner, D. (1999) 'Globalisation From Below? Toward a Radical Democratic Technopolitics', *Angelaki*, 4 (2), 101–13.

Lamb, R. (1996) *Promising the Earth*, London: Routledge.

Lovell, D., McAllister, I., Maley, W. and Kukathas, C. (1995) *The Australian Political System*, Melbourne: Longman.

Lovink, G. (2002) The Virtual People Smuggler, post to Fibreculture discussion list, 25 March.

Lowe, P. and Goyder, J. (1983) *Environmental Groups in Politics*, London: George Allen and Unwin.

Lubbers, E. (2002) 'Net.activism', in Lubbers, E. (ed.), *Battling Big Business*, Greenbooks: Devon.

Malina, A. (1999) 'Perspectives on citizen Democratization and Alienation in the Virtual Public Sphere' in Hague, B. N. and Loader, B. (eds), *Digital Democracy*, London: Routledge, 23–38.

Margolis, M. and Resnick, D. (2000) *Politics as Usual*, Thousand Oaks, CA: Sage Publications.

McAdam, D. (1988) *Freedom Summer*, Oxford: Oxford University Press.

McCarthy, J. D. (1996) 'Constraints and Opportunities in Adopting, Adapting and Inventing', in McAdam, D., McCarthy, J. and Zald, M. N. (eds), *Comparative Perspective on Social Movements*, Cambridge: Cambridge University Press, 141–51.

McCormick, J. (1991) *British Politics and the Environment*, London: Earthscan Publications.

Meikle, G. (2002) *Future Active*, Sydney: Pluto Press.

Mercer, P. (2002) 'Activists Outwit Australia's Asylum Policy', *BBC Online*, 31 March.

Mobbs, P. (2000) 'The Internet, Disintermediation and Campaign Groups', *ECOS*, 21.

Neill, R, (2002) 'Black Lives White Lies', *The Weekend Australian*, 29–30 June, 19 and 22.

Paehlke, R. (1988) 'Democracy, Bureaucracy and Environmentalism', *Environmental Ethics*, 10.

Pickerill, J. (2001a) 'Weaving a Green Web', in Webster, F. (ed.), *Culture and Politics in the Information Age*, London: Routledge, 142–66.

Pickerill, J. (2001b) *Weaving a Green Web?* Unpublished PhD thesis, Department of Geography, University of Newcastle-upon-Tyne, UK.

Pickerill, J. (2002) 'Positive outcomes of Woomera2002 actions' posted to Melbourne Indymedia, 31 March, <www.melbourne.indymedia.org/front.php3?article_id= 24633& group=webcast>.

Pipes, S. (1996) 'Environmental Information on the Internet', *ECOS*, 17 (2), 63–6.

Rawcliffe, P. (1998) *Environmental Pressure Groups in Transition*, Manchester: Manchester University Press.

Resnick, D. (1998) 'Politics on the Internet', in Toulouse, C. and Luke, T. W. (eds), *The Politics of Cyberspace*, London: Routledge, 48–68.

Rheingold, H. (1994) *The Virtual Community*, London: Secker and Warburg.

Rucht, D. (1993) 'Think Globally, Act Locally?' in Liefferink, J. D., Lowe, P. D. and Mol, A. P. J. (eds), *European Intergration and Environmental Policy*, London: Belhaven Press, 75–95.

Scalmer, S. (2002) *Dissent Events*, Sydney: University of New South Wales Press.

Seel, B. and Plows, A. (2000) 'Coming Live and Direct: Strategies of Earth First!' in Seel, B., Paterson, M. and Doherty, B. (eds), *Direct Action in British Environmentalism*, London: Routledge, 112–32.

Slevin, J. (2000) *The Internet and Society*, Cambridge: Polity Press.

Starr, A. (2000) *Naming the Enemy*, Annandale: Pluto Press.

Tsagarousianou, R. (1998) 'Electronic Democracy and the Public Sphere', in Tsagarousianou, R., Tambini, D. and Bryan, C. (eds), *Cyberdemocracy: Technology, Cities and Civic networks*, London: Routledge, 167–78.

Valadian, M. (1990) 'Australian Aborigines in the 1990s', *Sydney Papers*, 2 (1), 29–36.

Walch, J. (1999) *In the Net: An Internet Guide for Activists*, London: Zed Books.

Wall, D. (1999) *Earth First! and the Anti-Roads Movement*, London: Routledge.

Wapner, P. (1995) 'Politics Beyond the State', *World Politics*, 47, 311–40.

Warf, B. and Grimes, J. (1997) 'Counterhegemonic Discourses and the Internet', *The Geographical Review*, 87 (2), 259–74.

Washbourne, N. (2001) 'Information Technology and New Forms of Organising?' in Webster, F. (ed.), *Culture and Politics in the Information Age*, London: Routledge, 129–41.

The Wilderness Society (2001) *A Fringe of Green; Protecting Australia's Forests and Woodlands*, The Wilderness Society, Australia.

Williams, T. (2002) 'Woomera Democracy Fails Consensus Test', *The Australian*, 2 April, 4.

Williams, T. and Plane, T. (2002) 'Protesters Storm Woomera', *The Australian*, 30 March.

Wray, S. (1998) 'Electronic Civil Disobedience and the World Wide Web of Hacktivism' <http://www.nyu.edu/projects/wray/wwwhack.html>, first accessed May 2001.

x-trot (2002) 'Lessons from Woomera: A Libertarian Marxist Perspective', posted to Melbourne Indymedia, 2 April.

Young, J. E. (1993) *Global Network*, Washington, DC: World Watch.

10 Conclusion

The future of representative democracy in the digital era

Rachel K. Gibson, Andrea Römmele and Stephen J. Ward

This book began with a number of hypothesised scenarios for the future of representative democracy in the era of the new digital communication technologies. From full-scale erosion to radical reform and renewal. The question remains, therefore, what the chapters in this volume can tell us about where liberal democracies stand, in general, on this spectrum of change. In addition, what do cross-institutional comparisons reveal about the relative openness towards new technologies among these structural supports for the representative system? Are the more porous and flexible actors, such as parties and pressure groups, exhibiting a rapidity of change that stands in marked contrast to their more fixed and institutionalised counterparts? This conclusion, therefore, works first to draw some insights into the general systemic picture drawn from a variety of national contexts, and then complements that by peering beneath to compare the relative adeptness of key representative bodies in using the new technologies for participatory purposes.

Certainly, the guiding assumption for the book was that representative democracy appeared to have successfully withstood the first predicted onslaught from the new communications media, such that while some attrition might be taking place, systemic collapse was not a realistic alternative. The chapters presented clearly confirm this premise. However, in addition, they reveal that the slightly less apocalyptic but still gloomy prognosis of limited usurpation appears also to be inaccurate. Indeed of the four scenarios presented in our introduction, it is the third alternative – limited but effective reform and modernisation – that appears to be the most valid descriptor for the changes observed.

In a theoretical piece, Charles Raab and Christine Bellamy (Chapter 2) take Dahl's 'problem of the unit' as their point of departure. What relationships do we find in a polity made up of different units, the mixed polity? What role do ICTs play in a polity composed of a mixture of different, and not obviously compatible, political forms? Are new ICTs reinvigorating or marginalising formal political institutions, especially parliament? Two scenarios are pointed out by the authors: First, would ICTs serve to encourage the emergence of a wider range of more open, less easily manipulated interactions between parliamentary elites and members of the public, thus reinvigorating representative democracy? Or will it be 'politics as usual' and simply reinforce existing problems and trends?

The central finding of their work is that although we might see signs of more direct democracy through ICTs, we will most likely be faced with a mixed polity in which postmodern novelty will coexist with institutions from modernity. And it will most likely be government regulating the diffuse, overlapping networks of governance and by doing so may be faced with intensified problems of managing political complexity. Thus, far from withering away, central political institutions will continue to play a central role.

Catherine Needham (Chapter 3) outlines trends at work in the executive and legislative branches of government in the United States and the United Kingdom towards e-government and the more elusive citizen-oriented e-democracy. At minimum, it is clear from her work that MPs and public servants clearly understand the increasing importance of using the technologies to improve their image with voters. The chapter is overwhelming in terms of its cataloguing of the numerous policy documents commissioned by politicians to investigate the possibilities offered by new ICTs for improving government performance. Such a flurry of activity, however, more importantly, has not just simply taken the form of words. Commitments to extensive entry portals to government services and experimentation with e-consultation show a willingness to deploy new ICTs in a meaningful and innovative public way. Such initiatives are indeed particularly notable within the UK parliament. Overall, however, between the two stories of effective e-democracy reform and modernisation, her chapter does plump for the latter as being the main headline. Governments have clearly devoted more resources to improving service delivery and meeting 'consumer' demands than enriching citizens' participatory lives.

Thomas Zittel (Chapter 4) looks more specifically at the challenges of e-democracy for parliaments from a comparative perspective, both in terms of external relations with voters and for internal organisation and communication. His examination of the Swedish Riksdag, the US House of Representatives and the German Bundestag reveals that the process of putting all three parliaments on the Net has opened up some new channels for voter participation, although they are very moderate in ambition and scope. Certainly the notion that the floodgates of direct democracy have been opened is soundly rejected, particularly by the German and Swedish cases. The comparative approach adopted by Zittel, however, allows him to temper criticism of such the slow pace of change by reference to the political context. His analysis reveals that there are crucial differences between the structure of representation underlying the Swedish Riksdag and the German Bundestag on the one hand, and the US House of Representatives on the other that need to be taken into account when assessing their openness to using new ICTs in these participatory ways. Parliamentary systems like Sweden and Germany, provide little incentive to their representatives to focus on particular constituents and to structure the representative process in a more participatory way. The point of reference of an individual representative in parliamentary democracies is on the party more than on the voter. Parliaments in presidential democracies, however, show less party discipline and individual representatives have closer links to their constituencies and to voters.

Joachim Åström's essay on the Swedish local government (Chapter 5) further confirms the idea of institutionalised logic driving, or perhaps more accurately, slowly prodding the process of new ICT adaptation. Given Sweden's very high rates of Internet access, the prospects for digital democracy might be considered better than in many other countries. However, while the attitudes of elites, in this instance, the chairmen of municipal executive boards, may be optimistic towards using the Internet to develop more participatory forms of democracy, very few local governments are found to have actually attempted to implement such ideas. Of those local governments that have sought to use the Internet more extensively, the analysis reveals an emphasis on modernisation and efficiency rather than e-democracy reforms. Such conservatism, as Åström points out, while it is founded on a variety of factors, also reveals a basic institutional inertia among Swedish local governments. Government leaders clearly do place a high priority on online participation but the concrete political and technological changes necessary to realising these ambitions escape them.

Turning to look at the response of the more porous and flexible aspects of the representative system to the challenge of the new ICTs, the findings are, in certain respects, rather surprising. Adaptation among the more institutionally linked actors, namely the individual representatives and those seeking office, as described by Greer and LaPointe (Chapter 6), is arguably less adventurous than the efforts made by legislative institutions more generally (as described by Needham). While on the one hand, the developments in website content across the 1998 and 2000 US elections revealed an increasing boldness among candidates for using the media to campaign, these initiatives are not necessarily geared towards developing the participatory potential of technology. Very few candidates undertook to develop dialogue with voters, or to make themselves accountable through their sites, and in fact the figures showed a decline among incumbent candidate sites in providing constituent help in 2000. Information became more plentiful but sites also became glitzier and perhaps, most significantly, more negative. Thus, despite the new media presenting a plethora of novel communication tools and offering a basis for a new style of political campaigning, the movement towards 'politics as usual' seems to be one of the more discernable and pronounced trends among candidates for office, at least in the United States.

Chapter 7 by Perez turns our attention to organisations at the international level and how they are adapting to new ICTs as a way of creating greater openness and accountability. The chapter covers a range of organisations that exhibit differing levels of institutionalisation Thus, in addition to the highly state-centric and formalised regime of the World Trade Organisation (WTO) we also learn about the efforts being made by the less government-oriented International Organisation for Standardisation (ISO), as well as the more recently created virtual entity, the Internet Corporation for Assigned Names and Numbers (ICANN). Overall, a similar story of modernisation and limited reform emerges with the WTO and ISO revealed as having taken some small and halting steps towards using the new technology to open themselves up to greater scrutiny from the public. More constructive uses, however, have been made in regard to making their internal processes more transparent. Somewhat surprisingly, ICANN, despite being an internet-formed and focused entity, is not revealed as a trail blazer in terms of incorporating more participation from its global constituents via the new media. Indeed, if anything it seems to be retreating from its earlier commitments to canvass Internet users for decision-making purposes. Of course, as Perez's analysis also points out, the more restrained efforts by international regimes in terms of mobilising popular opinion and input, should be placed in context of their more pronounced collective-action dilemma. With a global constituency, an individual's return on their participation to achieve a public or even private good is more diluted than at the national level, inevitably lowering their incentive to contribute. However, in what is perhaps one of the most instructive parts of the book, Perez also demonstrates how the Internet actually forms one of the most effective tools for reducing the transaction and coordination costs for international political actors. Thus, ultimately, the chapter places the responsibility with these regimes, rather than the technology or the public, to ensure more participatory uses are made of the new ICTs.

One of the increasing challenges for representative institutions and organisations and indeed representative democracy more generally is the growing internationalisation and globalisation of politics and economic markets. Many policy issues now have an international dimension and supranational structures, such as the EU and the WTO, have become increasingly important. Yet, for the most part, representative organisations, such as parties and trade unions, remain rooted in the nation state. However, one of greatest areas of participatory potential of the Internet is its ability to provide a tool for creating transnational links and internationalising protest. As Hodkinson notes (Chapter 8), there are an increasing number of examples of international action facilitated by new ICTs. Yet, Hodkinson also reminds us strongly that protest in cyberspace should not be seen in a vacuum. Organisational/institutional culture, history and context are crucial to understanding the dynamics of net-based protest. In the case of the labour movement, it would appear that inherent long-term barriers to international cooperation cannot be overcome altogether by use of the technology. Indeed, in the case of the labour movement, ICTs may create new barriers to international solidarity and mobilisation – not least because of the global digital divide but also because some workers view the technology as a threat to their livelihoods.

Overall, the official labour movement and national trade unions have been relatively conservative in their use of the technology largely concentrating on providing basic information or trying to modernise their appeal via e-service provision. The innovation that has emerged from Labour movement has tended to come from activist networks or even individual campaigners. Whilst much has been made of the ability of technology to create new ties and links, Hodkinson suggests that in the case of trade unions, technology has so far rarely created brand new international ties and even when it has, it has been difficult to sustain them. Face to face activism remains crucially important in building long-term trust and solidarity.

Pickerill (Chapter 9) similarly underlines the importance of issue-context and organisational structure as catalysts for net mobilisation but paints a more positive picture of the value of ICTs in this case for environmental activists. Whilst noting overall that environmental movements have been some of most active users of the Internet-based technology, Pickerill outlines marked differences between different types of environmental organisation. In part, it should come as no surprise that the environmental movement has used the technology creatively, since it has a long-established record of expanding the repertoire of protest activities. Nevertheless, Pickerill suggests that the Internet is likely to be of particular benefit to more loosely organised, direct-action focused, protest networks. As with the labour movement, this is not to suggest that the technology creates protest. For the most part, core activist networks are already in place, but where there is a focused issue and shared goals, Internet technology makes it easier for such networks to punch above their weight and generate greater awareness of their campaigns than would otherwise be the case. The fluid structures of protest networks mean that they are free to experiment with new ICTs, and unlike representative institutions and organisations they have less to lose. In part, this is because they are not formally answerable to anyone except themselves. They are not spending public money, if they make mistakes they are under less scrutiny from the traditional media than formal organisations and they lack hierarchies of control.

Clearly the growth of direct-action protest and so-called dis(organisations) pre-dates the emergence of Internet technology. However, what this study suggests is that such technology may accelerate some of the broad pre-existing trends within representative politics – in this case the facilitation of issue-based protest politics. This does not necessarily mean the usurpation of representative organisations or the promotion of particular models of protest activity. As Pickerill illustrates, ICTs can assist most organisations, (from formal pressure groups to protest networks), to achieve their aims more efficiently but she argues that the latter have the most gain from deploying the technology effectively.

Thus, based on the evidence presented in this volume, it would appear that modernisation and reform are the watchwords that best characterise the impact of the new ICTs on representative democracy as a whole. From the more formal structures of executive and legislative power to the looser intermediaries of environmental movements, there is evidence of genuine enthusiasm for deploying the technologies towards more democratic and reformist ends. What we do not see as yet, however, is much evidence that this adaptation is producing any fundamental change in how these units operate or the ends that they pursue. From the descriptions offered here, it seems that our democratic intermediaries are mostly interested in the technology as a means to continue performing their existing functions, only to a better level. This seems to be the case whether they are the older and more embedded institutional structures or more fluid and flexible organisational actors. Thus, our initial propositions about the different aptitude displayed by macro- and meso-level representative bodies towards making innovative use of the interactive properties of the new ICTs do not appear to be supported.

Whether these patterns will continue into the future is an open question. Hopefully, however, this book has provided something of a benchmark for studying the pace and direction of those future developments across a broad range of political actors, as representative democracies move further into the digital age.

Index

eBooks – at www.eBookstore.tandf.co.uk

A library at your fingertips!

eBooks are electronic versions of printed books. You can store them on your PC/laptop or browse them online.

They have advantages for anyone needing rapid access to a wide variety of published, copyright information.

eBooks can help your research by enabling you to bookmark chapters, annotate text and use instant searches to find specific words or phrases. Several eBook files would fit on even a small laptop or PDA.

NEW: Save money by eSubscribing: cheap, online access to any eBook for as long as you need it.

Annual subscription packages

We now offer special low-cost bulk subscriptions to packages of eBooks in certain subject areas. These are available to libraries or to individuals.

For more information please contact webmaster.ebooks@tandf.co.uk

We're continually developing the eBook concept, so keep up to date by visiting the website.

www.eBookstore.tandf.co.uk

ORIGINS
OF MOLECULAR BIOLOGY
A Tribute to Jacques Monod

edited by

André Lwoff   and   **Agnes Ullmann**

Institut Pasteur
Paris, France

ACADEMIC PRESS   New York   San Francisco   London   1979
A Subsidiary of Harcourt Brace Jovanovich, Publishers

ACADEMIC PRESS, INC.
111 Fifth Avenue, New York, New York 10003

United Kingdom Edition published by
ACADEMIC PRESS, INC. (LONDON) LTD.
24/28 Oval Road, London NW1 7DX

Library of Congress Catalogue Card Number: 79-50407

ISBN 0-12-460480-3

PRINTED IN THE UNITED STATES OF AMERICA
79 80 81 82   9 8 7 6 5 4 3 2 1

CONTENTS

v

CONTRIBUTORS

Numbers in parentheses indicate the pages on which authors' contributions begin.

ROBERT L. BALDWIN (203), *Department of Biochemistry, Stanford Medical Center, Stanford, California 94305*

HENRI BUC (213), *Institut Pasteur, 28 rue du Dr. Roux, 75015 Paris, France*

MARIE-HÉLÈNE BUC (179), *Institut Pasteur, 28 rue du Dr. Roux, 75015, Paris, France*

GÉRARD BUTTIN (125), *Institut de Recherche en Biologie Moléculaire, Faculté des Sciences, Université de Paris VII, 2, Place Jussieu, 75221 Paris Cedex 05, France*

MADELEINE BRUNERIE (37), *Institut Pasteur, 28 rue du Dr. Roux, 75015 Paris, France*

JEAN-PIERRE CHANGEUX (191), *Institut Pasteur, 28 rue du Dr. Roux, 75015 Paris, France*

GEORGES N. COHEN (89), *Institut Pasteur, 28 rue du Dr. Roux, 75015 Paris, France*

GERMAINE COHEN-BAZIRE (49), *Institut Pasteur, 28 rue du Dr. Roux, 75015 Paris, France*

MELVIN COHN (75), *Salk Institute, San Diego, California 92112*

FRANCIS CRICK (225), *Medical Research Council, Laboratory of Molecular Biology, Hills Road, Cambridge CB2 2QH, England*

ANTOINE DANCHIN (243), *Institut de Biologie Physico-Chimique, 13 rue Pierre et Marie Curie, 75005 Paris, France*

MICHEL GOLDBERG (183), *Institut Pasteur, 28 rue du Dr. Roux, 75015 Paris, France*

FRANÇOIS GROS (117), *Institut Pasteur, 28 rue du Dr. Roux, 75015 Paris, France*

BERNARD L. HORECKER (143), *Roche Institute of Molecular Biology, Nutley, New Jersey 07110*

FRANÇOIS JACOB (95), *Institut Pasteur, 28 rue du Dr. Roux, 75015 Paris, France*

MADELEINE JOLIT (31), *Institut Pasteur, 28 rue du Dr. Roux, 75015 Paris, France*

ADAM KEPES (149), *Institut de Recherche en Biologie Moléculaire, Faculté des Sciences, Université de Paris VII, 2, Place Jussieu, 75221 Paris Cedex 05, France*

DANIEL E. KOSHLAND, JR. (209), *Department of Biochemistry, University of California, Berkeley, California 94720*

SALVADOR E. LURIA (239), *Massachusetts Institute of Technology, Cambridge, Massachusetts 02139*

ANDRÉ LWOFF (1), *Institut Pasteur, 28 rue du Dr. Roux, 75015 Paris, France*

BORIS MAGASANIK (137), *Massachusetts Institute of Technology, Cambridge, Massachusetts 02139*

A. M. PAPPENHEIMER, (55), *Biological Laboratories, Harvard University, 16 Divinity Avenue, Cambridge, Massachusetts 02138*

ARTHUR B. PARDEE (109), *Sidney Farber Cancer Institute, Charles A. Dana Cancer Center, 44 Zinney Street, Boston, Massachusetts 02115*

DAVID PERRIN (133), *Institut Pasteur, 28 rue du Dr. Roux, 75015 Paris, France*

MARTIN POLLOCK (61), *Marsh Farm House, Margaret Marsh, Shaftesbury, Dorset SP7 0AZ, England*

MAXIME SCHWARTZ (171), *Institut Pasteur, 28 rue du Dr. Roux, 75015 Paris, France*

ROGER Y. STANIER (25), *Institut Pasteur, 28 rue du Dr. Roux, 75015 Paris, France*

GUNTHER STENT (231), *Department of Molecular Biology, University of California, Berkeley, California 94720*

ANNAMARIA TORRIANI (43), *Massachusetts Institute of Technology, Cambridge, Massachusetts 02139*

AGNES ULLMANN (165), *Institut Pasteur, 28 rue du Dr. Roux, 75015 Paris, France*

JEFFRIES WYMAN (221), *Centro di Biologia Molecolare, Consiglio Nationale delle Ricerche, Città Universitaria—00185, Rome, Italy*

IRVING ZABIN (157), *University of California at Los Angeles, School of Medicine, Los Angeles, California 90024*

PREFACE

Occasionally the career of a scientist is marked by an important discovery. It is most unusual that it be illuminated by an uninterrupted series of great discoveries, and still more unusual when each discovery gives rise to new concepts and opens new vistas.

Sometimes a scientist by his work or personality influences his contemporaries. It is rare that he establishes a school. The founder of a school must dominate a field. He must have enought insight to foresee the direction research has to assume in order to achieve his goal. He should be able to judge the potential of young scientists and to assess the manifold aspects of their personalities so that he can provide them with projects in harmony with their interests and talents. He should be able to propose projects that can be solved or be channeled in a productive manner. He should love his students and collaborators, and be generous. Jacques Monod possessed all these qualities, therefore he was not only a brilliant scientists, but the founder of a renowned school as well.

During the first phase of his career, Jacques Monod worked alone. In the Institut Pasteur, he attracted a number of scientists. Some were students at various phases of their scientific careers, often at onset, others were mature, accomplished scientists. They worked with him a few months or a few years; some stayed at the Institut Pasteur. They had different personalities.

These scientists were asked to narrate their adventure; to relate their experiences with Jacques Monod. Almost all responded with enthusiasm; and most provided the contributions they promised. The result is fascinating. One sees Jacques Monod through the eyes of his technician, his secretary, his peers, his friends, and also of his enemies—love, friendship, and hate. The portraits of Jacques Monod—or, better still, images of the manifold aspects of his personality—are often painted with talent. Necessarily, the personality of the contributor appears as a watermark.

More important, the history of various discoveries is unfolded. This unique document illustrates the birth and development of concepts. It also shows the importance of a close, friendly, confident cooperation between different types of minds, the importance of interactions. One learns how a great scientist receives, discusses, rejects, accepts, assimilates, and creates ideas; how ideas are turned into experiments; how experimental results are interpreted and how concepts are born; in short, how science is constructed. The reader participates in the formulation of problems, in the conquest of knowledge, and in the building of a discipline—a unique contribution to the life of a laboratory and to the dynamic history of science.

It will be noted that the depiction of the same discovery may be told differently by different scientists who worked at the same time in the same laboratory. Obviously, the personality of the narrator has sometimes influenced the narration. Certainly each one perceives the importance of his own contribution better than that of others. Where is truth? Does truth exist? The métier of detective, or coroner, is difficult.

Some aspects of Jacques Monod's activities have been omitted: mountain climbing, music, the underground, human rights, philosophy. Our goal was to depict the scientist. An intense light has been projected on one of the founders of molecular biology. Light engenders shades, and the contrast contributes to the relief. The image of Jacques Monod has been shaped step by step, and a portrait has emerged. "One becomes and one remains as others have seen you."

The royalties of this book will be deposited in a Jacques Monod Memorial Fund, which will be administrated by the Institut Pasteur. We wish to express our gratitude to the staff of Academic Press for their friendly cooperation.

ANDRE LWOFF
AGNES ULLMANN

A Tribute to Jacques Monod
1910–1976

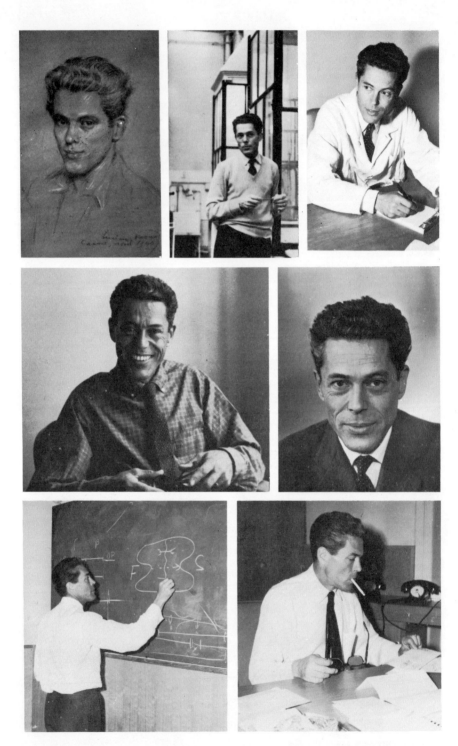

Jacques Monod: 1910–1976. The first picture is a drawing made by his father in 1927.

Photographs were taken by Madeleine Brunerie, Ralph Alberto, Rene Saint-Paul, Jean Hardy, and others.

JACQUES LUCIEN MONOD*
1910–1976

A. M. Lwoff, For. Mem. R. S.

CHILDHOOD

Jacques Lucien Monod was born in Paris on 9 February 1910. When he was seven, his family moved to Cannes. Jacques always felt himself more Provencal than Parisian.

The Monod family originated from a Swiss pastor who came from Geneva to France in 1808 and whose descendents now number several hundreds. Professors, civil servants, pastors, and doctors have been the dominant products of this Huguenot family. Monod's paternal grandfather was a general practitioner and his wife belonged to a Protestant family from the Dauphiné. His father, Lucien Monod—born in 1867—was a painter, engraver, and art historian. Lucien Monod's watercolours, flowers, landscapes, and portraits reveal great sensitivity and talent. At the same time, he was a scholar with a lifelong and passionate interest in the work of the intellect. His admiration for Darwin was transmitted to his son; it was thus that Jacques became interested in biology. Moreover, Lucien Monod was a free thinker, imbued with a positivist faith in the joined

*Reprinted with the kind permission of the Royal Society from the *Biographical Memoirs of Fellows of the Royal Society.*

1

progress of science and society. On the whole a remarkable exception in this puritan family.

Monod's maternal grandfather, Robert Todd MacGregor, the son of a Scottish minister, had emigrated to the States at the age of eighteen in 1852. His maternal grandmother was a New Englander, whose ancestor, Edward Elmore, had arrived in the colonies in 1632. Jacques Monod's mother Sharlie Todd MacGregor was born in Milwaukee in 1867. In Jacques Monod's writings one sometimes finds quotations attributed to MacGregor: they are from Jacques Monod himself.

Until 1928, Jacques Monod attended the College at Cannes—now a Lycée. One of his teachers, M. Dor de la Souchère, professor of Greek, was an excellent humanist. Jacques Monod freely acknowledged his debt to this highly cultured man, whom he admired and loved. M. Dor de la Souchère created the museum of Antibes, and is now—in 1977, at the age of 89—its curator. He loved Jacques and wrote me a moving letter after the death of his pupil.

In addition to his other gifts and interests, Jacques' father was a devotee of music. The musical as well as the intellectual life at the family home was intense, and Jacques himself learned to play the cello. Clos Saint Jacques, accordingly, provided an exceptionally favourable environment for the development of a sensitive and intellectually gifted child.

THE BEGINNING

Jacques Monod passed the baccalaureat in the summer of 1928 and came to Paris in October to study biology. He studied zoology, geology, general biology, and general chemistry, and in 1931 became *licencié ès sciences*. Only later, did he realize that the teaching in natural sciences in the Sorbonne was then twenty years or more behind the times. Only one professor, George Urbain, who taught thermodynamics, left a mark on him. Like many students in zoology, Jacques Monod came to the Station Biologique at Roscoff. There he met the four scientists to whom—as he said in an interview—he owed his true initiation in biology. "To Georges Teissier, the taste for quantitative descriptions; to André Lwoff, the initiation to the powers of microbiology; to Boris Ephrussi, the discovery of physiological genetics; to Louis Rapkine, the idea that only the chemical and molecular descriptions can give a complete interpretation of the functioning of living beings."

In October 1931, Jacques Monod received a fellowship to work with Edouard Chatton, professor of biology at the University of Strasbourg. Edouard Chatton was the great protistologist of his time. He had worked in the Institut Pasteur in Paris and in Tunis and was an accomplished microbiologist. Under his firm guidance, Jacques Monod became familiar with microbiological techniques and disciplines. Among other things, he learned to grow ciliates in bacteria-free cultures; the organisms were to provide the material for his first studies on growth. In Strasbourg, moreover, he was associated with the work on the stomatogenesis of ciliates: hence publications (1), (2), and (3). It is strange that in his autobiographies and interviews, Jacques Monod never mentioned the name of Edouard Chatton.

In October 1932, Jacques Monod obtained another fellowship and returned to Paris where he first spent two years in the Laboratoire d'Evolution des Etres organisés. He never mentioned the name of its director, Maurice Caullery, a good zoologist and a good teacher of modern biology—including genetics. Thereafter he became assistant in the Laboratoire de Zoologie.

From October 1932 he was thus free, that is, sentenced to discover for himself, painfully, the problem which would satisfy his exacting mind. The search lasted three years. Its course is marked by a few papers on axial gradients in ciliates, on galvanotropism, and on the role of symbiotic chlorellas (4—7).

In the summer of 1934, Jacques Monod had embarked on the *Pourquoi pas?* visited Greenland and published a preliminary account of his observations dealing with natural history (1935:8). This account remained preliminary.

INCURSION INTO GENETICS

In the spring of 1936, Monod was preparing to take part for the second time in an expedition to Greenland. Boris Ephrussi was going to spend a year with T. H. Morgan's group; he convinced Monod that genetics was interesting and important, and helped him to obtain a Rockefeller Fellowship; they went together to Pasadena. This very year, the *Pourquoi pas?* was lost with all hands on the coast of Greenland. Genetics had saved the life of Jacques Monod, a debt that he would later repay.

At the California Institute of Technology, with Morgan's group, Monod not only learned genetics but discovered a scientific world very different from the old Sorbonne: easy personal relations with scientists of all ages, free exchange of ideas, lively critical discussions, friendly cooperation.

Back in Paris, Monod spent a few months in Boris Ephrussi's laboratory at the Institut de Biologie Physico-chimique. There he attacked some problems of physiological genetics, implanting imaginal disc in drosophilas. However, this did not correspond at all to Monod's taste or tendencies, and he went back to the Laboratoire de Zoologie de la Sorbonne which he had entered in October 1934 as an assistant and where, under the influence of Georges Teissier, he started to work on growth.

GROWTH

The first paper on growth was published in 1935 (9). The growth rate of *Glaucoma* (later *Tetrahymena*) *piriformis* was measured as a function of the concentration of nutrient. I was then working on the nutrition of *Tetrahymena*—very little was known at that time—and Jacques came to discuss his work. I told him that ciliates were the worst material to attack the problems of growth, and advised him to use a bacterium able to grow in a synthetic medium, for example *Escherichia coli*. "Is it pathogenic?" asked Jacques. The answer being satisfactory, Monod began, in 1937, to play with *E. coli* and this was the origin of everything. For it is the systematic analysis of the various parameters of growth of *E. coli* which led to the study of induced enzyme synthesis—at the time enzymatic adaption—a study which developed into the physiology of the gene and the laws of molecular biology.

Monod first showed that the growth yield as a function of the amount of the energy source provided is independent of growth rate. This means that the fraction of metabolic energy utilized for the maintenance of cellular structures is negligible compared to the fraction utilized for biosynthesis. The growth yield was measured with numerous sugars, as well as the growth rate as a function of the concentration of the limiting carbon source. The results suggested that, at low concentration, the growth rate is controlled by an enzymatic reaction. It turned out later that the controlling factor is, at least under certain conditions, specific permeation. The measurements of growth rate as a function of temperature permitted a determination of the activation energy of the limiting reaction(s).

After having considered growth in the presence of one sugar, it seemed of interest to study the interaction of two carbon sources. In some mixture of two sugars one observes two distinct growth cycles, separated by a lag phase. This he called diauxy. Jacques Monod has told how, in December 1940, at the Institut Pasteur, he came and showed me the diauxic curve and asked, "What could that mean?" I said it could have something to do with enzymatic adaptation. The answer was, "Enzymatic adaptation, what is that?" I told Monod what was known—what I knew—and he objected that the diauxic curve showed an inhibition of growth rather than an adaption. We know today that repression and induction are complementary, but I simply repeated that diauxy should be related to adaptation. Anyhow I gave him Emile Duclaux's *Traité de microbiologie,* Marjory Stephenson's *Bacterial metabolism* and a few reprints I had secured, among them the precious Ph.D. thesis of Karström—which I never saw again.

It turned out that the glucose was inhibiting the synthesis of a few enzymes responsible for the metabolism of other sugars—catabolic repression—but the enzymes involved in diauxy were nevertheless adaptative. Induced enzyme synthesis was the key to diauxy.

In 1941, Monod was awarded his Ph.D. for his thesis, "Recherches sur la croissance des cultures bactériennes" (16). The importance and originality of this fundamental and now classical work were not perceived by the members of the jury. After the ceremony, the director of the laboratory where Monod was working told me, "What Monod is doing does not interest the Sorbonne." This was alas true.

THE TRANSITION

"From this very day of December 1940, wrote Jacques Monod, "all my scientific activity has been devoted to the study of enzymatic adaption." Yet during the dark years, he had joined the underground. He had even been arrested by the Gestapo, but cleverly managed to escape. However, he could no longer work in the Sorbonne and came clandestinely to the Institut Pasteur where he could perform a few experiments. Among other things, he showed that the enzymatic adaptation coupled with biosynthesis was—and probably reflected—synthesis of the specific protein involved.

After the liberation of Paris, Monod joined the army and played a determining role in the integration of the resistance force. As a member of the staff of General de Lattre de Tassigny, he met American officers and had an opportunity to read some American scientific journals. In this way, he came across the Luria—Delbrück paper on the spontaneous character of some bacterial mutations and the epoch-making publication of Avery, McLeod and McCarthy which identified the transforming principles as deoxyribonucleic acid.

The war ended and Monod returned to Paris. At the Sorbonne, he worked in a small room which opened on a corridor lined with glass cabinets containing skeletons and stuffed animals. He was doing everything himself: washing glassware, preparing culture media, autoclaving. No one in the Laboratoire de Zoologie took any interest in enzymes and Monod was rather unhappy.

I invited him to join the Service de Physiologie Microbienne as Chef de Laboratoire. He was no longer obliged to wash his glassware and to autoclave. Moreover, the Centre National de la Recherche Scientifique provided him with a technician. He selected Madelein Jolit who, until 1971, participated efficiently in his researches. Moreover, a few microbiologists were active in the attic. They knew how to isolate bacterial strains and to select mutants. They were aware of the existence of lactose positive (L+) mutants, in L− strains of *E. coli*, and of the work of Massini and his followers.

Jacques Monod and Alice Audureau selected an L+ mutant from an L-*mutabile* strain of *E. coli* isolated from my digestive tract (hence *E. coli m.l.*). They showed that the β-galactosidase is an adaptive enzyme. The hypothesis had been earlier proposed that the L− → L+ mutation is an alteration of an enzyme precursor common to the different specific enzymes metabolizing sugars. A gene mutation was not—at the time—considered as the basis of the phenomenon.

Yet Monod, who had also studied the bacterial ability to synthesize methionine, concluded that it was controlled by a gene mutation (1946:29). The gene had entered the scene. However, it would take some time before the idea developed that the mutation controlling the utilization of lactose is a virtual genetic property revealed only in the presence of lactose; before the link between genetic and biochemical determinants was established and finally, before the problem of genetic regulation was posed.

PRELIMINARY GAMES

The problem of the relations between gene and enzyme, and more generally of regulation, was not ripe for an attack. So for a few years, Monod played with various problems. The role of CO_2 in bacterial growth was analysed with André Lwoff (1947:31, 37, 43). It was shown that aspartic and glutamic acid could partially replace the requirement of CO_2 for the development of *E. coli*: a certain number of essential metabolites could be synthesized only by carboxylation. Then with Elie Wollman, Jacques Monod discovered (1947:32) that infection by a bacteriophage would prevent the adaptive synthesis of β-galactosidase, whereas the activity of the enzyme present at the time of infection is not affected.

This very same year, Monod was invited to discuss enzymatic adaptation at the Growth Symposium. This was the stimulus for reviewing the data concerning the induced synthesis of enzymes and their possible interpretations. In section IV "Adaptive enzymes and genes" the fundamental problem of relation between gene and enzyme is posed. "The problems consists of evaluating the respective role of hereditary factors (i.e. genes or other self-duplicating units) and environmental factors (substrate) in the synthesis of an enzyme" (1947:36).

While writing this remarkable review, Monod realized that the phenomenon of enzyme induction was mysterious, that almost nothing was known about it. However, owing to its specificity, its regularity, its dependence, on a mutation and on the environment, it necessarily involved an interaction between a genetic and a chemical determinant; and it appeared of such interest, of such profound significance, that Monod decided to go ahead. The respective role of the gene and of the inductive substrate in enzyme formation was posed. The enzyme, of course, was β-galactosidase.

BY-PRODUCTS

The goal had been defined, but the way toward the solution of the problem was far from being straight. It was necessary to learn as much as possible about the physiology of *E. coli*, and a few discoveries not directly relevant to the main problem emerged from these explorations.

The first was the discovery with Anne-Marie Torriani of a new enzyme, amylomaltase (1949:40, 41; 1950:46). It catalyses a reversible synthesis of amylose from maltose. The length of the amylose chain is controlled by glucose. Very long amylose chains are formed in the absence of glucose, for the degradation of the polysaccharide does not take place in the absence of the monosaccharide.

The second was an important experimental and theoretical contribution to the methodology of continuous bacterial growth, the bacteria being maintained indefinitely in a chemical and physiological stable state (1958:48). The method consists in creating conditions such that a limiting substrate is provided at a rate inferior to the total metabolic capacity of the organism. A stable state is thus automatically reached, characterized by a constancy of all the significant elements. The experimental potentialities of the method are wide. It provides a means of changing instantaneously the growth rate without modifying either the composition of the medium or the temperature. It also offers the possibility to select specific mutants—and this remarkable tool has been, and still is, widely used. It should be stated that a similar method has been devised independently and simultaneously by Aron Novick and Leo Szilard.

The third was the effect of irradiation with ultraviolet light on enzyme synthesis. François Jacob had arrived in the attic in 1950. A year later, he began to be interested in β-galactosidase. J. Monod, A. M. Torriani, and F. Jacob showed (1951:52) that bacteria irradiated with a heavy dose of u.v. rays are unable to synthesize β-galactosidase, but can still produce bacteriophage after infection. The effect of the irradiation cannot be attributed to a general effect on metabolism; it is a specific alteration of the bacterial component responsible for the synthesis of the enzyme which accounts for the u.v. effect.

These discoveries were on side-roads, but nevertheless played a determining role in the solution of the problem.

THE VERY NATURE OF ENZYME INDUCTION

Soon after the war, Alvin Pappenheimer visited the Institut Pasteur. He was deeply interested in the induced synthesis of enzymes and thought that immunological methods might be helpful for the analysis of the phenomenon. This led to the suggestion that one of his students should come and work with Jacques Monod. So, during the winter of 1948, Melvin Cohn arrived in Paris, a good immunologist and biochemist, a remarkable experimenter, hard working, enthusiastic , lively, and friendly . He mastered not only the problem of induction but also the art of living on fellowships, and so managed to spend seven years in the attic. He played a major role in the characterization of the enzyme, in the study of substrate and inducer specifically and, more generally, in the life of the laboratory.

The β-galactosidase extracted from *E. coli* (with A. M. Torriani and J. Gribetz 1948:39) was purified and its properties studied with Melvin Cohn (1951-50). Monovalent ions are all activators, but differ in their effectiveness. The displacement of a strongly active ion by a less active one results in a decrease of enzyme activity. Moreover, the relative activating power of different ions is not fixed but varies with the substrate employed, (with Germaine Cohen-Bazire 1951:49).

Then Melvin Cohn and A. M. Torriani started the immunochemical study of β-galactosidase and of related proteins. The preparation of a specific antiserum made it possible to estimate the enzyme as an antigen and thus to attack the kinetics of enzyme formation. The experiments suggested that, in the presence of the inducer, a total biosynthesis from amino acids took place (with A. M. Pappenheimer and G. Cohen-Bazire 1952:57). Later on, with David Hogness and Melvin Cohn (1955:65) it was proved that the enzyme is formed from amino acids synthesized after the addition of the inducer. Moreover, the molecule of β-galactosidase is fully stable *in vivo,* as are, under normal conditions of growth, the other protein molecules of the bacterium. The romantic dogma of "the dynamic state of living matter" was seriously shaken. Fierce counter-attacks were launched, but they were unsuccessful and the dead god went down to the grave.

Thus the induced production of an enzyme was the total biosynthesis of a protein from newly formed amino acids. Therefore the increase of enzymatic activity during induction was a true measure of the synthesis of the specific protein.

INDUCERS AND INHIBITORS

Until 1952, only the substrates of enzymes were known to serve as inducers of those enzymes. Three theories had been proposed to account for the inducing activity of the substrates: (a) the synthesis of an enzyme is determined by its activity; (b) the synthesis of an enzyme is limited by a dynamic equilibrium controlled by the specific substrate—inducer complex (whatever this could mean); (c) the substrate—inducer complex plays an organizing role by combining with the precusor of the enzyme. These were purely hypothetical and rather metaphysical notions.

A systematic study of many galactosides was undertaken by Jacques Monod, Germaine Cohen-Bazire, and Melvin Cohn (1951:51) and continued with Melvin Cohn (1952:55).

A number of unexpected—at the time strange—data emerged from these studies:

(a) Some substrates are inducers.
(b) Some substrates are devoid of inducing power.
(c) Some galactosides devoid of any affinity for the enzyme are powerful inducers.
(d) Some galactosides exhibiting a high affinity for the enzyme are not hydrolysed.
(e) Some compounds are substrates and anti-inducers.
(f) Some inducing compounds are not attacked by the enzyme and inhibit competitively its activity.

It turned out that only β-galactosides are substrates, whereas the inducing activity is associated with the presence of an intact galactoside residue either in α or in β linkage.

The interpretation of these data was complicated by the fact that the inducing activity of some substances could be modified by mutations of the bacterium, and also that permeability effects might be involved. Whatever the case, these observations led to the conclusion that the activity of the inducer could not be due to a reaction with the enzyme, but rather to a "catalytic" effect on the enzyme-forming system. The new data concerning induction were analysed in connection with those relative to repressors.

Negative Control of Anabolic Pathways: Repression

Vogel and Davis had shown that in *E. coli* strains which require arginine or acetylornithine, acetylornithase was produced in the presence of acetylornithine but not in the presence of arginine. They had concluded that synthesis of the enzyme was induced by its substrate. Monod suggested that this could be interpreted as an inhibitory effect of arginine, rather than an inducing effect of acetylornithine. This was the origin of the concept of repression, and led to the discovery that the constitutive synthesis of β-galactosidase is inhibited by β-galactosides (with G. Cohen-Bazire 1953:58). It also led to the study of the regulation of enzymes operative in two anabolic pathways: the tryptophan pathway with G. Cohen-Bazire (1953:59), and the methionine pathway with Melvin Cohn and Georges Cohen (1953:61).

It turned out that the synthesis of tryptophan synthetase is inhibited by tryptophan, and the hypothesis was proposed that specific inhibition could be a general property of enzyme-forming systems. In agreement with this hypothesis, synthesis of methionine synthetase proved to be inhibited by methionine.

Thus the synthesis of two enzymes operative in the biosynthesis of essential metabolites was shown to be under negative control. It was difficult to conceive that induction and repression were the expression of two different mechanisms.

The inducer could be an antagonist of an endogenous repressor. A digression is necessary here.

Another By-Product: The Permease

Among the numerous mutants isolated from the original *m.l.* strain were the so-called "cryptics." They are able to synthesize β-galactosidase but unable to metabolize β-galactosides. The mystery was solved by Monod, Rickenberg, Cohen, and Buttin (1956:68). Labelled thiogalactosides accumulate rapidly in induced wild-type bacteria, but not in uninduced ones. Nor do they accumulate either in cryptic mutants. The ability to accumulate galactosides is under inducible control. The various parameters of induction were analysed: kinetics, specificity, etc. The conclusion was clear: the factor responsible for thiogalactoside accumulation could only be a specific protein, controlled by a gene *y* distinct from the galactosidase gene *z*. The synthesis of this protein was induced by β-galactosides together with that of β-galactosidase. The protein was christened galactoside permease. A novel category of enzymes which mediate the penetration of small molecules into the bacterium had appeared on the scene; a new chapter of cell physiology was open.

The existence of permeases was the unavoidable logical conclusion of a series of rigorous experiments. It was immediately objected that their existence rested on *in vivo* experiments. It was also objected that one should not give a name to a protein before it has been isolated. The same objection was made later to the "repressor." Many enzymes have been named before anything was known about their nature; also genes, and all viruses. A few years after the discovery of "permease," galactoside transacetylase was isolated by Zabin, Kepes, and Monod (1959:79; 1962: 94). The permease, discovered in 1956, was isolated only in 1965 by Fox and Kennedy.

The study of the permease and the transacetylase had revealed an unexpected situation. A number of mutants constitutive for β-galactosidase synthesis had been isolated, and it turned out that the mutation was pleitropic. Not only was the β-galactosidase constitutive, but also permease and trans-acetylase. This was strange because each of the three enzymes was, of course, controlled by a distinct gene.

Once the physiological relation between β-galactoside and β-galactoside permease was understood, once it was known that they are controlled by two distinct genetic elements but nevertheless subject to the same determination of induction, the problem of the expression of these genes was posed.

BIRTH OF THE REPRESSOR

François Jacob and Elie Wollman had discovered the mechanism of the sexual process in bacteria. Following conjugation the + "male" bacterium injects its chromosome into the − "female" partner. The process can be interrupted at will. Thus the kinetics of the entry of a given gene could be followed and the gene sequence determined as a function of the time of entry. A new method was available for the study of gene physiology. The problem of regulation could be attacked thanks to a new and powerful tool.

The work of Monod and his disciples had shown that in $E.$ $coli,$ the synthesis of β-galactosidase depends (a) on a gene z governing the capacity/incapacity to produce the enzyme, (b) on a genetic factor known to exist under the forms $i+$, wild type, corresponding to inductibility and i −, mutant, corresponding to constitutivity. Genetic analysis revealed that the z and i genes are closely linked.

The synthesis of β-galactosidase was followed in zygotes resulting from the conjugation of male bacteria with females carrying respectively "opposite" z and i genes. The $z + i +$ and $z - i −$ parents are mated in the absence of inducer. Both parents are unable to synthesize the enzyme, one because of the absence of inducer, the other because of the deficiency of gene z. It is necessary to add that the male is streptomycin sensitive whereas the female is resistant. This allows the male to be killed selectively at any time.

The results differ with the direction of the cross. With the system $\male z - i − \times \female z + i +$ no enzyme is synthesized. With the system $\male z + i + \female z - i −$ enzyme synthesis starts 3−4 minutes after entry of the $z +$ gene into the female. This means that the factors z and i, despite their linkage, belong to two functionally different units able to cooperate through the cytoplasm. The $z +$ gene is immediately expressed in an i − cytoplasm, whereas the constitutive gene i − is not expressed in an $i +$ cytoplasm. Contrary to expectation, the $i +$ gene is dominant. This dominance is manifested in the zygote: the synthesis of enzyme stops after 2 hours because the zygote has become phenotypically inducible. Such is the epoch-making classical Pardee−Jacob−Monod (PaJaMa) experiment (1958:72; 1959:74), which led to the hypothesis that the $i +$ gene produces a repressing substance which was called "repressor" and which blocks the expression of the $z +$ gene.

One problem was solved; many more were posed. A systematic genetic and biochemical offensive was launched. About a thousand mutants differing in their capacity to produce β-galactosidase, galactoside permease, and galactoside transacetylase were isolated and used to construct a detailed genetic map. It turned out that the synthesis of the protein of the β-galactosidase system is controlled by one gene, distinct from the structual ones. This controlling gene, expressed in the cytoplasm, is responsible for the production of the specific repressor.

The problem of enzyme biosynthesis thus appeared in a new light: the two known regulatory effects, induction and repression, should be two aspects of the same fundamental mechanism. F. Jacob and G. Cohen studied various mutants in which the synthesis of tryptophan synthetase was altered: the sensitivity to the repressive action of tryptophan is controlled by one specific gene and the "repressed" allele is dominant over the "derepressed" one. Repression is determined by a gene producing a specific cytoplasmic repressor activated by a specific metabolite which is the end-product of a biosynthetic chain of reactions: tryptophan.

Monod and Jacob discussed the problems of regulation in a series of critical reviews which are now classics (1961:96; 1963:97, 98, 99). The tendency was to consider induction as the result of the expression or neutralization of an anti-inducer. It turned out that it was an antirepressor effect. In fact the hypothesis had been proposed by Leo Szilard during a seminar given at the Institut Pasteur. As will be seen later, Leo Szilard's intuition was correct.

THE MESSENGER

During conjugation structural genes of the male are introduced in the female: this allowed an attack on the problem of gene expression. It was generally believed at the time that genes produce stable structures which accumulated in the cytoplasm. Since ribosomal RNA was the only known RNA, it was presumed to act as a template for protein synthesis. A number of experimental findings were not in accord with this presumption and a new hypothesis was proposed: the structural gene produces a metabolically unstable RNA (1960:86). This RNA was christened *messenger* (1961:87). The messenger soon ceased to be an *etre de raison* and became a molecule.

OPERON AND OPERATOR

The concept of operon stemmed from the study of lysogeny. In a lysogenic bacterium the structural genes of the prophage are not expressed. Moreover, a lysogenic bacterium is "immune" against superinfecting homologous bacteriophages. The specificity of immunity is determined by a "C" region which obviously controls the activity of the rest of the prophage genome. Immunity is a dominant character and has a cytoplasmic expression. When a prophage is introduced by a male chromosone into the cytoplasm of a non-lysogenic female, its development is induced: all the structural genes are derepressed: this is the phenomenon of zygotic induction, discovered by F. Jacob and E. Wollman. The analogy with the Pardee–Jacob–Monod experiment is obvious. Moreover, the genes involved in the production of enzymes that mediate a particular bio-chemical sequence are frequently adjacent. The hypothesis that the phage DNA molecule is not only a unit or replication but also a unit of activity was proposed by F. Jacob in his September 1958 Harvey Lecture; it led to a series of experiments which established the operon as a respectable citizen (1960:80, 86; 1961: 87, 90; 1962: 93; 1963: 97). Again, new mutants of *E. coli* were isolated and analysed. A new specific structure became necessary to account for the specificity of action of the repressor, a new structure subject to mutation. It was the operator gene or "operator." A single operator controls the expression of β-galactosidase, permease, and acetylase structural genes. The operator acts only on the adjacent gene located on the same chromosome. Certain mutations "inactivate" the operator, thus preventing the expression of the structural genes. A detailed analysis showed that the operator is the terminal part of the last structural genes—that of the galactosidase.

Thus, units of coordinate transcription exist in the chromosome: these units are the operons. An operon is composed of structural genes connected by an operator, subject to the action of a repressor produced by a regulator gene.

NATURE OF THE REPRESSOR

The coordinated regulation of enzyme synthesis is controlled by two genes: the regulator gene, responsible for the formation of the repressor, and the operator gene, responsible for the expression of the operon. The problem of the nature of the repressor was posed. The repressor has to recognize both the inducer and the operator. It is a privilege of proteins to form steriospecific complexes with small molecules. The repressor could only be a protein. The conclusion remained hypothetical until the repressor was isolated and proved to be a protein. In the meantime, the systematic study of numerous mutants of regulation led to the identification of the types predicted by the theory. The repressors produced by some mutants were either unable to recognize the inducer or unable to recognize the operator. And, necessarily, of course, some of the mutants of the operator gene were unable to recognize the wild-type repressor.

The regulator gene could only be a structural gene coding for the repressor. In the operon, only the operator is a pure receptor and transmitter of signals. A general scheme of the mechanism of regulation was proposed (1961:87, 88, 91).

Within ten years, the problems posed by the induced synthesis of β-galactosidase in *E. coli* had been solved. The new ideas were applied to a large number of catabolic and anabolic pathways, to viral development as well as to differentiation. Everything was clear. A coherent scheme accounted for the interplay

of regulator gene, operator, structural gene, messenger, and repressor. It accounted also for the nature of various types of mutations affecting regulation.
Out of the monotonous succession of nucleotides there emerged the concept of
operon as a coordinated unit of integrated structures and functions.

These discoveries can be considered from another viewpoint. The nature of
molecular communications had, for a long time, been a complete mystery. Nothing was known about the way messages coming from the outer world or ema-
nating from metabolic systems could affect the genetic material. The problem
was solved: the inducer, its reactions with the repressor, the reaction of the repressor with the operator gene, the effect of the operator gene on the structural
genes of the operon, were clarified.

ALLOSTERY–SYMMETRY

In a biosynthetic pathway, the activity of the first enzyme is inhibited by the
product of the last enzyme. The Novick–Szilard–Umbarger effect had not received an interpretation. J. P. Changeux, a student of Jacques Monod, had
shown that the activity of threonine deaminase is inhibited by L-isoleucine and
that the enzyme can lose its sensitivity to the inhibitor while remaining active.
The kinetics suggested a bimolecular reaction, and it seemed that threonine and
isoleucine were bound to different sites.

The interaction between the inducer and the—at the time hypothetical—repressor was extremely rapid and entirely reversible. Probably, only a very small
number of molecules were involved, which nevertheless triggered first the complex mechanism of the repeated transcription of the operon, and secondarily,
the repeated translation of the messenger, that is the repeated formation of
thousands of peptide bonds. The inducer seemed to act as a chemical signal
recognized by the repressor, but did not participate in any of the reactions
for which it was responsible.

During the winter of 1961, David Perrin and Agnes Ullmann were working
late one evening, in the laboratory, when Jacques Monod, pale and tired, entered
the room and said: "Mes enfants, j'ai découvert le deuxième secret de la vie"
(I have discovered the second secret of life). "Please sit down, rest and have a
drink," said Agnes. Yet the secret had not vanished after the rest and Monod
explained what it was. The activity of enzymes depended on their conformation
which was controlled by the attachment—or detachment—of an effector. The
observed actions of effectors were due to indirect interactions between distinct
stereospecific receptors. The interpretation was applicable to the repressor which
would have two binding sites, one for the inducer, the other for the operator
gene. *Allostery* was born, the name as well as the concept. However, the theory
was not at first accepted by the enzymologists of the laboratory who were

worried rather than excited by the "non-classical" aspect of the curves they observed.

In 1961, in Cold Spring Harbor, Monod and Jacob (91) gave the general conclusion of the symposium. The fact was stressed that the inhibition of an enzyme may be caused by substances which are not steric analogues of the substrate. The expression *allosteric inhibition* was coined to describe the phenomenon. The discussion led to the conclusion that two distinct, albeit interacting, binding sites exist on *allosteric enzymes*. The effector acts by altering the conformation of an enzyme; the alteration is stabilized by the formation of a complex. It is interesting to recall that in the discussion which had followed the presentation of Changeux's paper, during the 1961 Cold Spring Harbor Symposium, B. Davis called attention to the effect of oxygen which modifies the affinity of haemoglobin for oxygen.

The concept of allostery was further discussed by Jacob and Monod (1962: 98) and applied to the "induced-fit" theory of Koshland, the mutual effect of substrate and enzyme on molecular configuration. The following year (1963: 100), Monod, Changeux, and Jacob extended the concept and insisted on the fact that allosteric effects are entirely due to reversible conformational alterations induced in the protein when it binds to the specific effector.

From the symmetry of the curve of saturation of haemoglobin by oxygen, Jeffries Wyman had been led to suggest that a structural symmetry of the molecule was involved. This was the origin of the classical Monod–Wyman–Changeux paper (1965:106). The general properties of allosteric systems are stated. (1) Most allosteric proteins are oligomers made of several identical units. (2) Allosteric interactions are correlated with alteration of the quaternary structure of the proteins. (3) Heterotropic effects, involving interactions of different ligands, may be either positive or negative; homotropic effects, involving identical ligands, are always cooperative. (4) The individual isolated units, the monomers, when associated to form the allosteric protein, are called protomers. (5) Protomers are linked in such a way that they all occupy equivalent positions. (6) Each allomeric molecule possesses at least one axis of symmetry. (7) One protomer possesses only one binding site for each ligand. (8) The conformation of each protomer is constrained by its association with the other protomers. (9) The association between monomers is specific—and most oligomeric proteins are stable—despite the fact that no covalent bonds are involved. (10) The protomers are probably linked by a multiplicity of noncovalent bonds. It is this multiplicity which confers stability on the association.

In an isologous association of monomers, when the domain of binding involves two identical binding sites, there is a twofold axis of rotational symmetry. The problem of symmetry was extensively discussed, as also the fact that each protomer is somewhat "constrained" and should adopt the same quaternary conformation. Lastly, the finality of size and structure of proteins is evoked. The authors conclude their classical paper by stating that they "have tried to develop and justify the concept that a general and initially simple relationship between symmetry and function may explain the emergence, evolution and properties of oligomeric proteins as 'molecular amplifiers,' of both random structural accidents and of highly specific, organized, metabolic interactions." The pinnacle of the theory of allostery was Monod's discussion on symmetry and functions in biological systems (1968:122). Allostery made it possible to interpret and to integrate a great number of isolated observations into a coherent unifying concept. In almost all papers attention had been called to the danger of inconvenience of a concept endowed with such explanatory power that it did not exclude anything. It is why Boris Magasanik called it "the most decadent theory in biology." A decadence which must have triggered in Jacques Monod a secret feeling of deep satisfaction.

REGULATORY SYSTEMS AND EVOLUTION

To understand the regulation of cellular functions at the molecular level, mutants were widely used, and proved to be a most powerful tool. The genetic control of regulatory mechanisms was also essential for the understanding of the mechanism of evolution. It is easy to demonstrate that efficient regulatory systems confer selective advantages. In a medium devoid of β-galactosidase, the production by a constitutive bacterium of some 6000 molecules of β-galactosidase represent a waste of amino acids and of energy. When constitutive and adaptive strains are placed together in a medium devoid of the substrate, the adaptive strain is selected: it multiplies more rapidly than the constitutive one.

This conclusion is also valid for anabolic systems. A dual regulation is at work in the machinery responsible for the biosynthesis of essential metabolites. The end-product, through a repressor, controls the activity of the structural genes of the system. The end-product also controls the activity of the enzymatic machinery. Here again, the regulatory mechanism confers a selective advantage.

Regulation is performed by small molecules; and a prerequisite for their action is the existence of a receptor site on the protein—whether enzyme or repressor. The properties of a protein—whether enzyme or repressor—are controlled by its tertiary and quaternary structure, in turn determined by the primary structure. Since the primary structure is determined by the genetic information, it follows that the evolution of regulatory systems is the consequence of mutations, necessarily random, of the genetic material: regulatory, operator, and structural genes. ural genes.

The problem of regulation led to the problem of evolution. Jacques Monod's essay on the philosophy of modern biology, "Le hasard et la nécessité" (Chance and necessity), is the by-product, or better the unavoidable consequence, of the work on regulation. It is in essence a modern version—accessible to the layman—of Darwin's ideas concerning evolution and selection, Francis Crick's comments on the book (*Nature, Lond.* 1976, **262**, 429–430) are the following: "Written with force and clarity, in an unmistakable personal style, it presented a view of the universe that to many lay readers appeared strange, sombre, arid, and austere. This is all the more surprising since the central vision of life that it projected is shared by the great majority of working scientists of any distinction." This very successful book was translated into many languages and provoked much discussion. Due to the limited space at my disposal, a critical examination of Monod's philosophical views is unfortunately not possible.

HEAD OF A DEPARTMENT

The enzyme β-galactosidase, how beloved it has been, was only a tool for the understanding of the relation between genes and enzymes; how often have I heard Monod complaining that he was far away from the gene. When the work on the induced synthesis of enzymes was started in 1941, nothing was known except the phenomenon; the concepts developed essentially from 1948 on. In the first phase, biochemical, Melvin Cohn played a determining role. In the second, genetical and regulatory, François Jacob's intervention had been essential, and this was—Francis Crick *dixit*—the "grand collaboration." Between 1948 and 1963, the main problems posed by the induced synthesis of enzymes (that is regulation) were solved, and molecular biology was created *ex nihilo*.

From 1945 on, Monod had worked in the service of Physiologie microbienne, in the attic laboratories. In 1953, he was made head of the Department of Cellular Biochemistry and moved into new quarters at the end of 1955. Both in the attic or in his new laboratory, Monod showed remarkable gifts as a leader. He received a very large number of students and postdoctoral workers, and oriented them in conformity with their tastes and aptitudes. As noted by Francis Crick, he "treated his students with affection and candour, as if they were members of his family." He proferred ideas generously and enjoyed discussions. The weekly seminars were exciting shows.

DIRECTOR OF THE INSTITUT PASTEUR

In April 1971, Monod was appointed Director General of the Institut Pasteur. He was 61. It may seem strange that a dedicated passionate scientist could, in full activity, abandon the laboratory. Perhaps he sensed that with allostery and symmetry he had reached the peak of his scientific achievements. Possibly he did not fully realize that the directorship would destroy almost entirely his scientific activity—and most of his freedom. Monod liked to plan, to organize, to decide, to command. The directorship of the Institut Pasteur was an extraordinary challenge for a man of great energy, endowed with a clear vision of what the evolution of an institute of biochemical research should be. The most likely hypothesis is that his sense of duty played a determining role in his decision. Be that as it may, the Institut Pasteur deserved to be loved, and the encounter between Jacques Monod and the prestigious institute could not fail to be a great event.

All Pasteurians had suffered from the many errors in the organization and management of the institute, not to speak of the scientific planning—or absence of planning. The development of research, as well as the financial balance, was compromised; and Monod was well aware of the extent of the disorder. He abandoned the direction of the Service de Biochimie Moléculaire, where he was replaced by Georges Cohen, and he was soon obliged to abandon also his professorship at the Collège de France. He nevertheless continued to discuss the planning and results of research with his disciples, as evidenced by his last two publications of 1974 and 1976 (130, 131).

The Institut Pasteur is a research institute. But it has an industrial wing which provides about half the budget. The other half comes from various sources. These include such governmental agencies as the Centre National de la Recherche Scientifique, the Institut National de la Santé et de la Recherche Médicale, the Délégation Générale à la Recherche Scientifique et Technique, and private organizations like the Fondation pour la Recherche Medicale, and private donors. In April 1971, the financial situation was catastophic.

Jacques Monod had first to learn how to run a business. Within a few months he had become an expert in management, to the point that he was asked by François Dalle, an industrialist, to write a foreword to his book *Quand l'entreprise s'éveille a la conscience totale.* He had analysed the situation of the institute, built and set in action the industry, defined the main axes of the offensive of renovation. The industrial sector had to be restructured, priority given to new products, foreign markets sought. In addition, a rigorous administrative and financial structure had to be put in place. Impressed by the seriousness of these measures, the government decided to increase its financial aid.

This was only one part of the director's responsibility. Emile Duclaux had succeeded Louis Pasteur in 1895 as head of the Institute. Since his death in 1904, there had been a succession of directors and deputy directors, some of them eminent scientists, such as Emile Roux, Elie Metchnikoff, Albert Calmette, and Gaston Ramon. Yet the Institute had to be entirely rethought and reorganized as a consequence of the evolution of biomedical sciences. Moreoover, the golden age of tropical medicine, microbiology, and parasitology had passed, and, as a result of decolonization, the status of the numerous extraterritorial branches of the Institut Pasteur had changed. Jacques Monod was not an M.D., and yet he very rapidly dominated the problems posed by the evolution of medical microbiology, virology, immunology, and experimental pathology. A reorganization of research was necessary. Some departments had to be suppressed, others expanded or created. A number of difficult problems were solved with energy, sometimes in the face of fierce opposition.

Between April 1971 and June 1976, the scientific and industrial policy had been defined and put into effect. A most remarkable achievement, particularly in view of the fact that Jacques Monod was handicapped for six months, in 1972, by viral hepatitis, and after October 1975, by the disease which was responsible for his death. Yet illness never stopped him from assuming his responsibilities. He showed in his role as an administrator the rigour, eagerness, logic, and intelligence that had been evident in the direction of his laboratory.

OUTSIDE SCIENCE

Science has been the dominant activity of Monod's life, the field where he expressed his creativity and originality. Yet, science, inhuman science, could not by itself satisfy the aspirations of a man of rich diversity and tremendous energy, endowed with an intense curiosity, a great artistic sensitivity and a deep humanity, conscious of his duties as an intellectual and as a citizen.

Monod was a lover of music and for years played the cello in a quartet. He had also created a Bach choir, "La Cantate," which he directed until 1948. With his friend François Morin, he had translated Sir James Jeans's book *Science and Music*.

He had been seriously tempted to make a career as a conductor. Certainly the direction—and domination—of an orchestra could have given him great satisfaction. In 1936, he was offered a position as a conductor in the United States and the temptation was great. Three events determined his choice. First, a conversation with Louis Rapkine, who, as he told me, convinced Monod that he lacked the basic musical knowledge necessary to conduct an orchestra; second, the fact that with the study of bacterial growth, Monod had found his scientific way; third, his marriage, in 1938, with Odette Bruhl, an archaeologist and orientalist, specialist in Tibetan painting, who became curator of the Musée Guimet. His wife, who died in 1972, was a person of great charm, sensitive and discreet, who brought to Jacques both stability and the enrichment of a complementary culture. They had twin sons. One is a physicist, the other a geologist.

So music was sacrificed on the altar of science. Science had won, but the love for music persisted throughout his life as a constant temptation and, perhaps, a regret. The radio station "France Musique" gives every week a two-hour *concert égoïste.* The programme is scheduled by laymen and lively discussions take place. Jacques Monod had been twice on the stage during the year 1975. These two concerts were revealing of Monod's taste; by the way, it was while listening to them that I learned that Monod's godmother had been the first wife of Claude Debussy.

The passion for music went hand in hand with intellectual interests. Monod was a great reader and possessed a good knowledge of classical as well as modern literature. He used to read books with the same critical rigour that he would put into the analysis of an experiment. In this connection, the interview he gave to *Lire* in 1975 is characteristic. Monod liked not only to read, but to write. His style is clear and incisive. The forewords to Ernst Mayr's *Populations, espèces et evolution,* Karl Popper's *Logique de la découverte scientifique,* and Medvedev's *La grandeur et la chute de Lyssenko* are revealing of the various aspects of Monod's intellectual gifts and talents. By the way, he was perfectly bilingual: his English—spoken or written—was as excellent as his French.

Monod was conscious of his responsibilities and duties as a citizen. During the war, he took an active part in the underground. This action expressed his will to resist oppression and slavery. He had been very active in the "army of shadows" and exerted important responsibilities. In the position he occupied last, his three predecessors had disappeared. After the liberation of Paris, Monod played a determining role in the integration of the free French forces into the regular army, and was a member of the staff of General de Lattre de Tassigny.

The underground group to which Monod belonged was a communist one, and Monod felt he had to join the communist party. He left it soon after the war: he could not accept the rigid dogmatic attitude of the party, particularly the stand in the tragedy of Russian genetics. He could not accept an ideology which was a negation of truth, science, and rationalism, a negation also of human dignity (not speaking of the mass murders which have dishonoured so many communist states). He never stopped fighting for his conception of justice and for the respect of human values.

He soon found another battlefield. Contraception was unlawful in France. He supported the action of the "Mouvement français pour le planning familial" and became one of its honorary presidents. Later, he actively supported "Choisir," a movement which was fighting for the legalization of abortion.

A scientist who has been a professor at the Sorbonne was necessarily aware of the problems posed by the university. With Pierre Aigrain, Monod was responsible for the two "Caen Symposia" at which the university was reorganized, at least on paper.

Finally, Monod had participated in the creation of the "Centre Royaumont pour une Science de l'Homme" which tried to develop a scientific and synthetic approach to the problems which face mankind.

His intense intellectual activity was balanced by physical activity. Despite a handicap which was the sequel of poliomyelitis, Jacques Monod became a good rock climber, practising on Sundays at Fontainebleau. During the summer he performed difficult ascents in the Alps. Later, he abandoned the mountains for the sea and became an accomplished yachtsman. Those who have cruised with him on the *Tara* have told me that he was not only an excellent skipper, but also a kind one, which seems to be relatively rare.

Monod had decided not to ask for the renewal of his six-year term as director. He wanted to live his own life and to write *L'Homme et le temps,* a book which will never see the light.

In October 1975, an inexorable disease was diagnosed. He knew the prognosis but continued to assume his directorship. From time to time, he went to Cannes for a "rest," The last rest, at the end of May 1976, was active as usual: walking and sailing. The picture illustrating this biography was taken on 29 May by Jean Hardy. A day later, he realized that the end was approaching. He died quietly. His last words were "Je cherche à comprendre." All his life, he had tried to understand.

THE MAN AND THE MONUMENT

"Good looking, though small of stature, he commanded attention by his intelligence, his clarity, his incisiveness, and by the obvious breadth and depth of his interests. Never lacking in courage, he combined a debonair manner and an impish sense of humour with a deep moral commitment to any issue he regarded as fundamental." This is the portrait sketched by Francis Crick. Many of those who have known Jacques Monod will agree with this picture. But there is something more to be said and it would be dishonest to mask the shadows. Martin Pollock, in an obituary, wrote the following: "I have often wondered how many scientists there were from all over the world who struggled to get accepted as visiting workers under his stimulating guidance at the Pasteur and now carry with them the fruits of a contact, however brief, with a real master of enlightment. Perhaps the light that emanated was too dazzling sometimes. It was just this tendency to dazzle, and to exercise—indeed to demand—intellectual predominance over his fellow scientists which one might legitimately criticize. It was often very difficult to think independently in his presence when others were around. In open conference, he could be a tough and uncompromising opponent rather too ready to condemn without proper consideration. At times he could be exasperating and many found him arrogant, elitist or condescending. But it was quite a different matter in private discussions: there one was listened to attentively, with courtesy, if not always with respect. The polemics were no longer necessary."

The two facets of Jacques Monod's dual personality are well illustrated by these comments. On the one hand, a man of extreme courteousness and charm, showing great warmth to his friends. On the other, a man who could not accept public opposition to his views, who liked to impose his ideas and decisions, to dominate, conscious of his intelligence and his gifts and eager to manifest his authority. One should bear in mind that the construction of a scientific monument through forty years of uninterrupted effort implied a considerable amount of experimental work and a constant intellectual tension; it could be achieved only thanks to a certain hardness, a corollary of rigour and exactness. This may in part account for the negative traits which, by the way, were already apparent when Monod was a student.

Yet the defects were minor when compared to Monod's work which, from the growth of populations to molecular language, is marked by an uninterrupted series of discoveries. The impressive monument crowned by the most elegant spire of allostery bears witness to a great talent. The success was due to a conjunction of eminent gifts and to a pre-established harmony between the nature of the gifts and the nature of the task to which Monod devoted his activity. He was an excellent experimentalist. Rigor and precision were served by an implacable deductive logic. Critical sense never hindered imagination nor audacity.

The development of the work from diauxy to allostery is wholly admirable. It started with the interpretation of growth curves, and ended with the solution of the problem of regulation at the molecular level. The molecular language was deciphered: how molecules receive and transmit messages, obey, and command. New classes of structures and phenomena were brought to light; new concepts were built. Each step generated new questions until the central problem was solved. A scientist has to give birth to his own problems, step by step, in pain—and enlightment.

In addition to the gifts and talents of Jacques Monod, a number of factors played in his success. The right problem was posed at the right time in the right environment. The right bacterium was selected and the right enzyme. For an outsider, the success appears to be the highly improbably combination of improbably events. Yet, one should not forget the numerous trials and errors and the fact that selection intervenes constantly, at each step of the phylogeny of a scientific construction. The unfit is eliminated. Finally, one should also bear in mind that preadaptation plays a role in the choice of the working place; that cooperative effects exist, here as elsewhere; and the whole process becomes autocatalytic. That the name of Jacques Monod is so intimately associated with the birth, development, and triumph of molecular biology is not a matter of chance but of necessity. The necessity was Jacques Monod.

The work of a creative genius sometimes outsteps the man. The scientist—or the artist—may dread this transcendence which would destroy the *persona* he tries to shape; neither scientist nor artist is aware of the secret of his genius. However, any powerful construction of the mind or spirit engenders through its resonances the image of its creator, at one its reflection and its symbol. Such will perhaps be the fate—or privilege—of Jacques Monod, architect of molecular biology.

THE OUTER AND THE INNER MAN

Roger Y. Stanier

The prize of the general is not a bigger tent, but command.
Oliver Wendell Holmes, Jr.

In April 1971 Monod became Director of the Pasteur Institute. A previous attempt to put him in this post had been blocked at the highest level by President Pompidou who had not forgotten some disobliging public criticisms offered by Monod a few years earlier. It is rumoured that Pompidou, who had modest literary pretensions and even more modest literary talents, relented as a result of the success of *Chance and Necessity*. Why did Monod accept this onerous and unrewarding task, which consumed the last years of his life? A profound sense of indebtedness was probably the key factor. Since 1945, the Pasteur Institute had given him the freedom to pursue his own work, without making other demands on his time. Now its very existence was menaced; and Monod believed that nobody else had the drive, ability, and prestige to save it. As we shall see, he accomplished a great deal in five years; whether these reforms were sufficient to preserve the historical structure of the Institute still remains to be decided.

Monod's years as Director were shadowed by bereavement, sacrifice, and ill-

*Reprinted with permission of the editors of the journal from an obituary published by *Journal of General Microbiology*.

25

ness. His wife, the former Odette Bruhl, an orientalist and the curator of the Musée Guimet, was gravely ill in 1971, and died early the following year. The projected sequel to *Chance and Necessity* had to be put aside, and work on it was never resumed. Experience soon convinced him that even the light duties of a professor at the Collège de France were incompatible with the directorship, and he resigned from his chair. He suffered a severe attack of viral hepatitis in 1972, and became ill again in October 1975. This time, the disease was terminal. He had developed an aplastic anaemia, but continued working to the end, kept alive (as he casually remarked one day) by the blood of others.

A brief historical introduction is necessary to explain the multiple problems which confronted Monod in 1971. The Pasteur Institute had been created by subscription, the result of a wave of public enthusiasm, following Pasteur's development of a rabies vaccine; the original building is still called. "le Batiment de la Rage." A special law gave it the status of a private foundation recognized to be of public utility, making it one of the very rare scientific institutes in France largely independent of governmental control. Despite this, the Institute has always played a national role of fundamental importance: it is the central microbiological reference laboratory of France, the repository of nearly all national culture collections, and a major teaching centre for microbiology and immunology. Since its foundation, the Institute has engaged in the production of serums, vaccines and other biological products, on the sale of which its financial independence was originally based. Only after 1945 did this source of revenue begin to be supplemented to a significant degree by state support, which thereafter took an increasingly important place. The sources of state support were multiple and, in part, indirect; for example, many of the scientists and technicians who work at the Institute are employed by governmental organizations, such as the Centre National de la Recherche Scientifique.

The infusion of funds from external sources for some time prevented recognition that the Institute's industrial operations had been going downhill for many decades, as a result of antiquated production methods, failure to develop new products and improve old ones, and the absence of cost accounting; in short, a complete lack of sound business practice. Competition from private industry had made serious inroads into the traditional markets, both domestic and foreign. The gravity of the situation was further concealed by the absence of any overall control of the Institute's finances: nobody seemed to know where the money came from or where it went, and deficits were met by the dissipation of endowment funds. By 1971, however, it had become clear that bankruptcy could not be far away. The state would at that point intervene, to maintain those activities which it deemed essential; but the independence of the Institute would be lost. Monod assumed the directorship to try and avoid this outcome.

He had no previous administrative or business experience, and it took him some months to grasp the parameters of the problem. He then acted with energy and firmness. Since it was evident that the Director could not simultaneously head a research institute and run a business, a subsidary company—Institut Pasteur Production—was created, and its key officers were recruited from private industry. Monod's success in staffing the new company with men who were able, devoted, and loyal says much for his powers of persuasion; objectively, he had very little to offer them. The slow and painful task of revitalizing the industrial activities of the Institute was thus begun. However, financial projections revealed that even under the most optimistic assumptions, the Institute could not hope to attain financial equilibrium from this source; increased state support was indispensable. Monod therefore appealed to the government. A special commission was created to study the situation, and shortly before his death, the government agreed to help out.

Needless to say, the building up of the scientific activities of the Institute was also on Monod's agenda when he became Director. But when the financial preconditions were on the way to fulfilment, his time had run out. By an irony of fate, Monod will be remembered among the directors of the Pasteur Institute for his financial and administrative reforms, not for his role in determining its research programme.

The Outer and the Inner Man

The attempt to sketch a likeness of Jacques Monod is perhaps foolhardy; it would tax the powers of an observer as subtle and perceptive as Henry James. For this, there are several reasons. First, his many-sidedness; scientist, teacher, musician, writer, sportsman, administrator, and public figure. Second, his deeply ingrained sense of privacy; he kept his associations well compartmentalized, and few (if any) of his friends had more than a partial knowledge of the various facets of his life. The greatest difficulty of all stems from the complexity of his character, with its seeming contradictions: he could be considerate or brutal; courteous or rude; contemptuous of authority, or eager to exercise it.

In the personality of Monod, it is possible to perceive three superimposed and often incompatible elements. The most obvious personage was the liberal cosmopolitan, cultivated, urbane, and ironical, equally at ease in two languages and three cultures. His familiarity with Anglo-American speech and folkways trapped many English-speaking acquaintances and friends into imagining that he was, at heart, one of them. Nothing could be further from the truth. Under the cosmopolitan facade, Monod was quintessentially French: a patriot and a conscious representative of a very distinctive sub-culture, the Protestant *grande bourgeoisie*. Failure to recognize this led to misunderstandings, made easier by Monod's overt behaviour, notably his oft-expressed admiration for some Anglo-

Saxon attitudes, and his trenchant criticisms of the defects, as he saw them, of French society. This behaviour did not reflect a sense of estrangement from his own country and culture, but a passionate desire, almost Gaullian in its intensity and arrogance, to improve that country and culture.

Underlying the cosmopolitan and the Frenchman was a third persona, recognition of which is essential to an understanding of the man. Although separated by at least one generation from Protestant religion, Monod was imbued with the sternest and most pitiless version of the Protestant ethos: at heart, he remained a Calvinist. The novels of André Gide, another distinguished and wayward product of French Calvinism, provide a useful literary guide to this aspect of his character. Since France is still largely permeated by the Catholic ethos, Monod's Protestant conscience, important in determining both his own destiny and his relations with others, was not clearly recognized by many of his compatriots, who remained perplexed by its manifestations. This component of Monod's character was without question a fertile source of conflicts, internal and external, sometimes painfully overcome, sometimes unresolved.

An anecdote permits a glimpse of one internal conflict, which was overcome. Shortly after his arrival in Lwoff's attic, Monod had collaborated with Elie Wollman in a study of the effect of phage infection on β-galactosidase synthesis. Some time later, when the work on β-galactosidase has run into temporary difficulties, he confessed to one of his co-workers that he had been strongly tempted to work on phage, but had resisted the temptation "parce que j'en avais trop envie" ("I wanted too much to do it"). It would be difficult to find a better illustration of Samuel Butler's aphorism about the Protestant ethos, that virtue is the condition in which the pain precedes the pleasure!

Pitiless with himself, Monod could also act harshly towards others, particularly during his years as Director. For example, having decided to retrench by abolishing some small research units, mostly of mediocre quality and peripheral to the main interests of the Institute, he arbitrarily forced their heads into premature retirement, when half an hour of sympathetic discussion would in many cases have elicited a voluntary retirement. One of the individuals so affected had accompanied Monod to Greenland on the *Pourquoi Pas* in 1934, and had watched Monod's subsequent rise to fame with admiration and affection. He had served the Institute well in the past, but he was permitted to leave the scene of his life's work without a word of thanks from the Director.

Although Monod could be authoritarian and inflexible, he could also act with great generosity and kindness. The scientists, technicians, and secretaries who worked with him could always count on his sympathy, advice, and support; in return, he received an unreserved loyalty and devotion from nearly all of them. His time, his prestige, and his personal fortune were freely used to aid humanitarian causes and individuals. Although the fact never became public knowledge, several victims of both fascist and communist tyranny owe their escape and opportunity to make a new life in the free world to him. As a leader of the movement (finally successful) to legalize abortion in France, Monod often received anguished private letters appealing for his help. He always responded in the only way possible before the law had been changed: by sending money.

One common French quality which Monod did not share was the Latin brand of sentimentality. It differs from the English one in being lavished not on animals, but on national shibboleths and (in lesser measure) on fellow humans. Desperately searching as Director for solutions to the problems of the Institute, he hit on the notion of rebuilding it on the suburban campus at Garches, financing the operation by the sale of the very valuable land which it occupies in Paris. One day while he was expatiating on the virtues of this solution (never, of course, put into effect), the author of this memoir asked him what he proposed to do about the tombs of Pasteur and Roux, both on the Paris campus. "No problem," he replied, "We'll dig them up and take them along with us." Fortunately, no French colleagues were present to hear him utter this blasphemy!

If Jacques Monod's faults have been evoked here, that is because one cannot write other than honestly about such a man. At the risk of eliciting sniggers from readers for whom the very notion of the hero is a medieval anachronism, it must be said that he was of heroic stature. I hope this is evident from the preceding account of his life.

A BIT OF LUCK

Madeleine Jolit

In June 1945, I graduated in chemistry from the E. N. P., a vocational school in Bourges, and went back home to the Jura. A friend of my family, who lived in Paris, had just heard, from Parisian friends of hers, that a scientist, who was then teaching at the Sorbonne, was looking for a technician. In fact, a visit to Paris just after the war was the main attraction for me when I made the journey to the Institut Pasteur to present myself to Monsieur Monod.

I waited sitting on a stool in a tiny laboratory located at the top of the building under a mansard roof, when a very young man, to whom I first did not pay much attention, came in whistling. He was wearing canvas trousers and a sports shirt with an open collar. Still whistling he put aside a vial that he was holding in his hand and gathered a few papers that were scattered on the desk. Then he noticed me and introduced himself. Where had I gotten the idea that scientists were strict and severe looking old gentlemen?

I only knew a little of mineral chemistry and had some vague notions of organic chemistry; my school year had ended by a period of training in a foundry. What was I doing in this service of "Microbial Physiology" whose obscure name did not mean anything to me? He looked at my notebooks, asked me a few questions, and then said, "At any rate, I prefer that you know nothing, because no school could teach you what we are going to need: I am in search of the secret of life." Astounded, I accepted the position . . . just for a try.

"It is not he, it is not he," that's all I could think of and kept repeating to myself during that endless morning when members of his family and a few friends were waiting in the garden of his home in Cannes to accompany him to the Grand Jas (Cannes cemetery). No, it could not be Monsieur Monod, whom I had just seen lying motionless, absent. It was not possible. I could not realize it altogether, nor did I want to understand it, and yet I was already feeling deep in myself that is was all over—that never again would I find this extraordinary presence.

It is his silhouette in the lab that comes first to my mind, in the days when we were working in the "attic," when he used to stride into the lab, a smile on his lips, whistling, happy, just as he would do later into his "service"; whether leaning over the bench explaining the work to me, or sitting, and dictating the numbers he was reading on the Warburg manometer . . . the first numbers only, for, as soon as he had understood the result, he would leave the rest of the experiment to me. We were working on the first assays of amylomaltase.

I can also remember his laughs mixing with those of Melvin Cohn as they happened to meet in the small cluttered corridor on which the labs opened, and the doors were rarely closed. Mel Cohn was always carrying out several experiments at the same time, so that, whether working beside the centrifuge, the incubator, or in the cold room, he kept moving about a lot. And he always had a minute to tell a story, start a conversation, or speak of his "last finding." Ideas were exchanged, but scientific matters were not the only subjects that caused the joyful explosions that made the lab resound with roars of laughter.

Lunches in the lab were also great moments, although savoring the food did not matter much to Monsieur Monod. It was a time when discussions started again, ideas were continuously arising, matters of everyday life were not excluded. Simone de Beauvoir and her book, *The Second Sex,* which had just been published, provided, among other things, the theme of joyous polemics. By contrast, he had a respectful and admiring friendship for Louis Rapkine who used to visit him quite often. They would enter into serious and calm conversations exchanged in a low voice.

I remember his arrival at the lab one Monday morning: "Madeleine, what is necessary is catalase! Yes it is catalase which partly reactivates the bacteria sterilized by UV. I thought of that yesterday while climbing rocks at Fontainebleau." It was indeed the answer to all the strange results we had recently obtained and to that series of experiments which he had made me carry out again and again. Everything seemed to yield to his will; that is why I told him once, "With you there is no fun. We always find what you have announced." And I can see again the grave and amused smile which showed on his face at hearing this.

He always gave me several experimental projects at the same time. "Like that," he used to say, "there is always something that comes out right. It keeps up our spirit and in that way we get several results every day." At that time we were isolating mutants and carrying out the first assays of amylomaltase and galactosidase.

And then he invented the "bactogène," an apparatus designed—following the description he himself wrote on the patent request—to maintain "a continuous process for the cultivation of microorganisms, involving continuous and simultaneous addition of nutrient medium into, and removal of culture liquid from a fermenter. A method characterized by the fact that the culture is kept homogeneous." How enthusiastic he was when he talked of his toy! Every preparation was a festival, and yet it was not a small affair. René Mazé, the laboratory assistant, was in charge of this impressive machine which occupied a place of honor in a large laboratory of a neighboring "service," in the midst of a maze of pipes. In a corner, a camp-bed was installed where Monsieur Monod would spend the night to keep watch on the growth of cultures, because the three of us had to take turns during the two days which were necessary for the process.

And the same man who was busying himself, for two days in a row, around the bactogene, was also capable of remaining completely silent for a long afternoon, laboriously isolating bacteria. I mostly remember him absorbed in his thoughts, absent-minded. His absence of mind was famous and made all of us smile. I often would knock at the door of his office, enter, wait, then go out after a few minutes, unnoticed; I would have to come back later. Sometimes I would again knock at the door, and he would immediately grasp the telephone, "Hello," and then, realizing his mistake, put down the receiver.

One day he came striding up the big stairs, as he did every morning, but laughing even more than the other mornings. Madame Odette Monod, who used to drive to work, had taken him in her car to the Institut Pasteur. When getting out he had held out some money to his wife . . . for the price of the fare! I do not know if she had accepted it, but I do hope she had, just for the fun of it.

Speaking of cars, there was a day when he could not find his own car. He had to declare to the police that it had been stolen; they soon found it exactly where he had parked it.

And yet, I remember what an attentive and passionate look he had when one day he entered the tiny lab where I was working holding the two bacterial strains which he had just received from Lederberg, one was a male strain, the other was a female. He began telling me about the sexuality of bacteria and got lost in dreams . . . he had already become a geneticist.

We were not very many in the group working in the attic; we were like a family. When I got married we had a celebration. For the Friday tea, Monsieur Monod asked Agnès Thébaut to cook two splendid strawberry pies in the sterilizing oven, and tea was replaced by Banyuls wine provided by Monsieur Lwoff.

Around that time, a professor of the Institut Pasteur, who was retiring, paid him a visit and took the opportunity to give him some advice about retirement pensions. It was with a fantastic laugh that he greeted this anxious kindness. "But I shall never retire, I shall never finish what I am doing!" "My young friend, you will see, time goes fast." To me it was perfectly obvious that Monsieur Monod could never be an old gentlemen and give up laboratory work.

Later, the atmosphere changed when he created the "service de Biochimie Cellulaire," located on the ground floor, whereas André Lwoff and Francois Jacob remained in the attic. We were then a larger group; the laboratories were clear and spacious, with high ceilings and modern equipment. He got his own laboratory and an office next to it, new impressive apparatuses, and students who came to crowd the "service."

For a while, when measuring the optical densities of our cultures, we kept referring to the "blue of the Meunier from upstairs" (the old photometer which we were no longer using); some nostalgia was still lingering. But, after some time, we spoke solely of galactosidase. How many assays we made! Later I heard someone say that the success of galactosidase was due to the fact that its assay was yellow, "otherwise Monod would have given up" since he pretended to be color-blind and maintained that he could only recognize one color, yellow. Many times he gave us opportunities to make fun of his mistakes in this respect, but I suspect him to have greatly taken advantage of this defect, for he could very well differentiate every single shade from white to purple, going through all the spectrum of pinks, of the bacterial strains on the EMB medium which was our daily bread. He nevertheless asked Madame Monod, whose good taste he trusted and admired, to come specially to choose the fabric of a curtain which was to hide some old cupboards in the library.

Monsieur Monod was busy setting up his new service, welcoming and taking care of his students both in the lab and at the University. Time was rapidly becoming short. He would work only occasionally at the bench now, participating in some permease assays, having a look at the Petri dishes. And yet he was still fascinated by the laboratory which attracted him from his office. I can still see him coming in with a cigarette in his hand, making a little round, reading the figures over my shoulder when I was installed at the Zeiss spectrophotometer or at the Geiger counter.

And then, as Monsieur Jacob says, came the time of the "i^-, o^c, i^s, y^- and z^+, and all that junk." Monsieur Jacob, anxious and ill at ease in his narrow lab, used to come down every morning with an "everything all right?" Then both he and Monsieur Monod, after glancing at the Petri dishes and reading the last results in my notebook, would resume their discussion. Monsieur Jacob would emphasize his remarks by making such funny faces that Monsieur Monod would burst out with laughter—at times, a break was necessary—but all of a sudden everything was beginning again. The same scene would repeat itself several times a day. In his office, comfortably seated in an armchair, I was taking notes for the pursuit of the work and Monsieur Jacob was pacing up and down the room. Monsieur Monod was writing on the blackboard. Next, it was Monsieur Jacob's turn to take the piece of chalk; after further information, everything was obvious and clear. Then Monsieur Monod would get up, erase the blackboard and say, "No François, we are going to demonstrate it differently, it will be more elegant: we shall start by showing that . . . " Completely lost, I was waiting.

Since that time, how often I have heard his colleagues, friends, and foes, pronounce the word "elegance" when speaking of his works! And each time, the vision of Monsieur Monod standing in front of the blackboard comes back to my mind.

I also remember him with his students, discussing, criticizing, giving advice, either standing next to them at their benches or meeting them in the corridor, or again at lunch time during the meals which were taken in common in the lab. At five o'clock he liked to have a cup of tea with us in the lab. I, thinking that some work was keeping him busy at his desk, we would bring him tea to his office. He then would come out, his cup in his hand, asking us whether we were punishing him; for it was time for a break and all would take this opportunity to talk of their own problems. I heard two of his disciples say, "What is wonderful with Monod is that he puts himself immediately in the mood; we can corner him at any moment." On the contrary, one of his most brilliant students reproached him for abandoning him in quandaries and leaving him alone entangled with problems. But much later that same student admitted that it had been much better for him and that he had benefited a lot more from this attitude. But there were others whom Monsieur Monod would lead more attentively, encouraging them frequently.

In May 1968, he told me, "It is always the same story. When I was their age we were told that we were impossible. What would our professors say now? At any rate these young people are not at all that much convinced. I keep telling them, 'Why don't you get rid of François [Jacob] and myself? You should do it.' But they are only making noise."

After this period conflicts often arose. The traditional paternalistic attitude had to be given up. One day when several young research workers were vehemently arguing, I made the remark that in Monsieur Monod's time they would not have had such ideas. One of them, probably the most obstinate, replied, "Monod is out of question, because *he* had an indisputable authority."

This authority was felt by all the personnel. We had a washing room where eight women were busy sterilizing the laboratory glassware and preparing culture media. He had placed me in charge of the organization of this "kitchen" and never used his authority to interfere in the quarrels that might arise. A tremendous work was actually done in the kitchen, which was nonetheless carried out with songs and laughter. He would smile at everyone, and welcome this cheerful agitation. I saw several of these women cry when we heard the news of his death, and one of them told me, "Why did we like him so much, Monsieur Monod? He did not spare us, how hard he used to work us!"

The news of the Nobel Prize had been a great festival for all of us. The lab looked like a huge work yard where everyone was looking for everyone. All the photographers wanted to take the snapshot of the day; seated near the Zeiss counter we were waiting for the picture of the laureate "hard at work" to be taken. I seized that opportunity to ask him, "Are you happy to have this award?" He did not answer me immediately, but after a while said, "Yes, for all the little things that flatter a man's vanity, I am pleased. But it will be heavy to bear; think of it, Madeleine, from now on I shall have to think very carefully and to pay great attention to what I shall say. It is a new responsibility; it will no longer be my personal opinion but that of a Nobel prize laureate." And he fell into deep thought. And then, just a little later, "Madeleine, I shall take you to Stockholm with me to receive the prize. It will be to celebrate our 20th anniversary in the lab." Of course I thought that he was out of his mind with excitement. But he did take me to Stockholm, together with the other Madeleine (Brunerie), his secretary, and we participated for ten days in all the ceremonies and feasts which usually take place on such occasions. He also gave me a part of his prize and wrote on the check "This is your share of the N. P." After the Royal ceremony it was snowing a lot and to return to our cars we had to go through a narrow passage and a small back staircase. At a curve of the passage Monsieur Monod was there holding Madame Monod's hand and exchanging with her the most happy and radiant look.

I have to make an effort if I want to remember him as the director of the Institut Pasteur. I paid him several visits in his huge, sad, empty office so different from the happy pandemonium of a lab. He always greeted me with warm and joyful friendship. After asking me news of my family, of Maxime Schwartz, his disciple with whom I am working now, of our work, he would soon go back to the "good old time," that is to say the time of the attic. Then memories would come back with the same images, the same anecdotes which did not age for us who had lived them, and each time they made us laugh just as much. And he would say, "You know, Madeleine, it has been an extraordinary time and we were all so happy. It is thanks to this unique atmosphere which we all had created. Such a group is very rare. I have known many labs in France and abroad, and I have never seen that. We have been very lucky."

ONCE UPON A TIME . . .

Madeleine Brunerie

Once upon a time, there was a teenage girl whose most beautiful dream was to meet a great scientist. I was that girl. And in late October 1946, when necessity made me look for a job, I wonder if it was only chance which led me to work at the Institut Pasteur, which I had once visited when I was studying in a high school in Paris.

Today, I shudder remembering how much I had wanted to leave the Institut Pasteur after the death of my first patron, Professor Michel Macheboeuf, in 1953. I owe it to his close family that I stayed on, and I anxiously waited almost a year for his successor.

On June 29, 1954, in the reserve room for laboratory material of the old *Service de Chimie biologique,* Jacques Monod appeared forever in my life as a charming and very courteous man. I first believed I would not be impressed by him as I had been by Professor Macheboeuf. It was true: he was much smaller in stature.

When I told him how much I wished to work as a technician, Jacques Monod answered quite frankly: "You can choose your job; I need a secretary as well as a technician." I then thought he had given me the chance of my life. A week later, letting him know I had chosen to work with him as a technician, he promptly argued that above all he needed a secretary. The dice was thrown . . .

37

I cannot remember for how long I had a grudge against him, if indeed I ever
had. A few days later, on vacation, I started learning English shorthand in order
to help him more efficiently as a secretary.

From then on, day after day, he impressed me more and more. I was discovering the scientist as well as the human being. I cannot say how many times I had
the opportunity to appreciate him as a great-hearted man. Competent people
will think of him as a scientist. But I would like to emphasize that even if I could
not understand very well the fundamental researches he was pursuing (which
was, in fact, molecular biology pioneering), it soon (1955) intuitively appeared
to me, from the reports he dictated, that Jacques Monod and his team were
doing very important scientific work. From that moment, he kept me enthusiastic about the researches he undertook, and I waited faithfully for the results he
expected.

Some time, in late October 1959, I understood that my secret hopes might
come true. A close friend of Jacques Monod wrote me confidentially, asking for
a curriculum vitae and reprints to support a proposal for a scientific prize to be
shared with André Lwoff (in fact the Nobel prize). I felt it was a confirmation
of my high opinion of him, and afterward, each fall, I waited hopefully for
Nobel news.

From his correspondence, I knew that Jacques Monod was an eager supporter
of human rights, and I even participated in one of his plans: the "extraction" of
Agnes Ullmann and her husband from Hungary. When Agnes left, after her second stay in the lab, in 1959, Jacques Monod entrusted me with the organizing
of secret communication with her; for instance, news from Budapest reached us,
hidden in a Bela Bartok record sleeve. As soon as the plan was ready, he left for
Hungary to try and make sure the operation would succeed. In fact, nothing was
certain until that morning of August, 1960, when I stood waiting for Agnes and
Tom at the Gare de l'Est, in Paris.

Work continued for everyone of the cellular biochemistry team. I loved the
life in our very active laboratory whose soul was Jacques Monod. Experimental work as well as new ideas or concepts were discussed at length not only in his
office, the labs, and the library, but more often just about anywhere else. I mean
in the dining room, during lunch, or afternoon tea, and in the corridor which
was called the pensotron (thinkotron). "Modesty befits the scientist, but not the
ideas that inhabit him," Jacques Monod used to say. Discussions were usually
very animated, and sometimes funny. They often were punctuated by jokes, and
I used to enjoy hearing, for instance, Mel Cohn and Jacques Monod bursting out
with laughter!

I was supposed to protect him from too many "undesirable" people from
outside, but he always wished to be approachable by any of his coworkers, collaborators, students, or scientists (even from the outside) who needed his advice,
or wanted to discuss scientific results or personal problems. Unfortunately, year

after year, with his increasing responsibilities, I know it was one of his deepest regrets not to be as available for this kind of contact as he would have wished to be.

To be his secretary was very exalting. It has been for me a source of both enrichment and modesty. Because of the nature of this job, I grew to know more about him and his close collaborators and friends, sometimes more than I would have liked to. But at the same time, it created a confident symbiosis between us and this was most precious to me.

As a secretary, I very much appreciated the fact that Jacques Monod was a fine writer in French as well as in English (his mother was born in Milwaukee of Scottish and New England parents). Publishing either a scientific work or a book (*Chance and Necessity*) usually took him a fairly long time as he would not hesitate to rewrite several times parts of the manuscript to make it as perfect as possible. He was as rigorous for himself as he was for others.

But I should also say that he often tried to spare me the retyping of some letter or report on which he had added some minor corrections: "Please, Madeleine, don't bother to retype it: it really does not matter."

While he wrote his publications and the chapters of his book in longhand, he preferred—in order to save time—dictating not only current letters, but also reports, grant applications, and sometimes lectures, either in French or in English. Endowed with a great readiness of mind, he had at the same time the capacity of isolating himself when necessary. I remember some entertaining moments when he paced my small office, dictating at length. He did not seem aware of anything happening around him, following only his thoughts. Several times, at tea time, not only did he finish his cup of tea and cakes, but also mine. If somebody knocked at the door, he frightened me by shouting, "Come in!" and went on with his dictation, either not seeing or forgetting the visitor who, after a while, just tiptoed out.

I will never forget another great moment when I was taking down in shorthand an application for a grant, when suddenly Jacques Monod stopped dictating and began writing some mysterious formulas and drawings on the blackboard. I was fascinated by this interlude. Suddenly, coming back to earth, he then exclaimed, "Look at this! I have it!" My pencil at rest, I felt fired with enthusiasm, not daring to move a finger for fear of dispelling his trend of thought. In fact, he soon went back to his lab to discuss the new idea or concept just born in his mind.

It was a pleasure to work with Jacques Monod. He was a very patient patron, and he always remained courteous and thankful. He knew I was doing my best for him, so when he saw me overwhelmed with urgent work, he told me: "Don't worry! When one has done everything one can do, one has done everything one was meant to do."

In August 1963, he was sailing around Spain for his vacation and could not reach Marseille in time to attend a symposium there. I knew the cable he sent from Gibraltar to excuse his absence was received with some irony by the participants, and it hurt me deeply. A few days after he returned to Paris, he accepted half-heartedly an invitation to participate in some summer school program the following year. I told him I disapproved of his reply, guessing he would cancel it later on, as he had done for the Marseille symposium. He did not like my remark at all. But finally, he declined the invitation. For some time after, in similar cases, he used to call me "Ma conscience."

On Tuesday October 12, 1965, owing to some leakages from Swedish sources, Jacques Monod revealed to me that the "Prize" had some chances to be given to André Lwoff, François Jacob, and himself. In the lab, only a few people shared the secret. Therefore, when the cable from Stockholm arrived the following Thursday, the suprise was great. Everybody, both in the lab and in the whole Institute, welcomed the news. For several days, the team of close collaborators lived in a kind of whirl. I thought I had imagined the perturbation such an event could raise, but I discovered how far I was from reality. Jacques Monod himself told me, four days later: "It's funny, since the Nobel was announced, my little inner dialogue has been cut off, and I felt rather sorry. Happily it came back this morning!"

This is where my fairy tale really starts.

A week or so after the official announcement and those terribly exciting days, Jacques Monod and I were filing the Nobel Foundation forms for the ceremonies in Stockholm, in December. He gave the name of each member of his close family and, looking at me affectionately, he said: "Please, add Madeleine Brunerie: I will need my secretary in Stockholm," leaving me no chance to believe he only did it to please me. That was one of the happiest days of my life. It sounded like a dream. I thought I knew him well, but I did not measure his generosity until that moment.

He, of course, invited Madeleine Jolit, his lifelong technician, to join us. What a happy and exciting period we both experienced, "the other" Madeleine and myself!

During ten days in Stockholm, we both shared every honor rendered to Jacques Monod who not only paid all the expenses of this unforgettable event, but gave each of us a large check on which he wrote "Your part of the Nobel."

Jacques Monod was generous with youth to whom he devoted most of his efforts and his time, and he never refused to receive young students interested in biology. To the best ones who wanted to become scientists, he first gave a very black picture of the career, especially to the girls. "If the future prospects of such a job do not frighten them, then they can try their luck," he used to conclude. How many owe him the choice of a scientific career?

He was also generous with people he did not even know. He never answered Christmas cards, but he never failed to reply to letters from troubled or ill people who asked him for moral help or medical advice. Not a physician himself, he always tried to give either the adequate information or the opinion from a specialist.

In the same way, this great man, sometimes terribly impressive, had the gift of being accessible to modest people who had a profound and sincere affection for him. When he sized someone up, he did not dissociate intellectual qualities from human ones. He told me several times that one finds exactly the same proportion of able and respectable people as well as stupid and worthless ones, in every class of society, whether among academicians or among street sweepers.

Jacques Monod was not only a good chief, he was also a warm friend to his close collaborators and fellow workers. I had the opportunity to realize this many times in rather sad circumstances. For instance, when one of our American postdoctoral fellows had a dramatic accident in which his young boy was killed; and in my own case, when I suddenly lost my father in 1963, and then during the long illness of my mother, as well as when she died in 1967. Everybody knew they could rely on him, and how precious his discreet and efficient help could be.

Very fond of literature, Jacques Monod also liked the theater, and often went to see plays even given by amateur companies (he came several times to the performances of the one I belonged to and encouraged us). In 1964 or so, he himself wrote a play entitled *"Le puits de Syène,"* a kind of antique allegory dealing with the relationship between science and society, and more specifically debating the question of the scientist's responsibilities and his connection with political power. After the Nobel was announced, he told me, half jokingly, he was happy to be a laureate, adding that he would have been happier still if his play had been produced!

I shared the best; I shared the worst too. I was near him in the office when he learned on the phone from Professor Jean Bernard in February 1971 the diagnosis of his wife's inexorable disease. He at once told me about it, and I admired him even more, if it was possible, for his courage. Eleven months later, Odette Monod passed away.

On April 15, 1971, Jacques Monod became general director of the Institut Pasteur. Accepting this leadership, he undertook it with the same passion he exerted in whatever he did. I kept his personal and scientific secretaryship, hoping I could go on working for him when he retired, after six years of directorship, in order to write his second book, *L'homme et le temps.* He only had time to put down a number of ideas for it on some scattered sheets of paper, found on his desk at home.

He often thought of his retirement, and discussed it several times with me. And because of this idea (or because he thought his illness was inexorable), Jacques Monod wanted me to become the assistant of Joël de Rosnay, a man he first met at the Institut Pasteur, and whom he had chosen long ago to help him give a new life to the prestigious Institute. How can I be thankful enough, now, for making it possible for me to be associated with the great enterprise he started for the salvation of the Institut Pasteur!

I keep in my heart two precious images of Jacques Monod when, in 1976, I went to his home, during his illness, to work with him.

The first one occurred some time in January. Among the mail I brought to him, was a letter from a very young boy called Bruno, who wanted to know what was the most important thread of his life. Jacques Monod dictated to me: "It is courage and love of truth, or rather, the hate of lies."

The second occurred on Thursday, May 10. We were working on his ultimate publication in the *Proceedings of the National Academy of Sciences** with Agnes Ullmann. He was seated at his desk, discussing with Agnes and then dictating to me some corrections, just as during our best moments at the Institut Pasteur. He looked much better. But did I inwardly feel he was near the end? I could not help staring at him, fascinated by the great man I knew. The manuscript being completed, the three of us went out for a walk through the *Champ de Mars* with Vicky, his young and impetuous dog. Then, we shared a delicious *paèlla* prepared for us by Rosario. During the meal, he told us he could not bear the idea of losing, because of illness, either the use of his brain, or of his limbs. . .

A few days later, on Monday, May 31, 1976, Jacques Monod died in Cannes where he had gone for a rest. It was a relaxed and happy holiday before the last attack of the inexorable disease which, in a few hours, carried him off, leaving without an answer his very last question: *Je cherche à comprendre.* Leaving behind his family, friends, and close collaborators facing an irreparable loss.

Can the thread which led me to the Pasteur Institute, and then to Jacques Monod, be called chance? Let us say it can. In fact, I encountered a double chance, not only by working with one of the world's most famous biologists, but also by living for almost a quarter of a century in close contact with a great man who enlightened, and still enlightens my life.

*"Catabolite modulator factor: a possible mediator of catabolite repression in bacteria," *Proc. Natl. Acad. Sci. U.S.A.* 73 (1976), 3476-3479.

LE LABO DE JACQUES

Annamaria Torriani

A mansard at the top floor of the main brick and stone building at the Pasteur Institute, comprised a wide wooden bench in the center, another long bench under the slanting ceiling, a small desk on the other side—my desk. Jacques, young and living as if on a tightrope, was exploiting his energies, his intelligence, his charm, to the maximum. He would move quickly along the corridor in short jumps (a way of disguising a small limp from polio in one leg), always whistling the same part of a Bach cantata. Arriving from Italy (February 1948) and leaving behind a profound desperate love and a most warm-hearted, serious companion, I found the charm and excitement of Jacques a bit obnoxious. Here is my first written account of him in a letter to Luigi.* "He was teaching me how to use the slide rule and took advantage of a good occasion to gently hold my hand in his (a beautiful, nervous, expressive hand with a golden ring and a green dark stone). It was a wrong approach, but it was gently done. For two hours he explained to me his work and our project. I have the impression of an intelligent man, with a vast, profound, and personal view of biology, but a bit fast in his mathematical deductions. As an enzymologist and chemist I don't think he is a genius. But . . . I may be totally wrong." For a while I was his only assistant and it was a real pleasure to see his mind at work. He had recently joined the Institut Pasteur as a member of André Lwoff's department. His thesis became my bible and was in fact the point of departure for our early research.

*When I went to Paris Luigi Gorini, who was to become my husband, was in Milano. After the antifascist underground, he had to start anew his interrupted scientific career which would then bring him to Paris (Laboratoire de Chimie Ciologique, Sorbonne) and to Boston (Dept. Microbiology, Harvard. Medical School). His achievements in science and in the advancement of human rights are well known to his friends and to the scientific community.

43

A very young woman (Madeleine Vuillet, now Mme Jolit), who had just finished her two years of school as a chemical technician was helping us. She knew all about "le labo" and was a great help. She had a very even, steady character and was an anchor for me in a new and stormy sea. Jacques had a small office just big enough for a desk, a bench, and a table, around which we usually had lunch. Food was still rationed and everyone cooked or warmed a small meal. Lunchtime was the most exciting time. With us were usually Pierre Schaeffer, tall, blond, and gentle, with a short trumpeting laugh; Elie Wollman, short, peppery, and always well informed; Ileane Jonesco, friendly and lonely. Bussard frequently joined us, as did Louis Rapkine for too short a time (since his short life was at the end). The talks were mainly about highly controversial subjects like politics, DeGaulle's past and present roles, and the daily editorials published by *Combat*. But music, art, America, "the atomic scientist," and Lysenko were also part of Jacques' interest and part of our arguments. Never in these spirited, lunchtime conversations did I hear anyone talking about families or everyday difficulties, personal problems or . . . solutions. Lunch was for intellectual pleasure—but sometimes the language or local jokes constituted a frustrating barrier for me. One day at lunch, shortly after my arrival, Jacques asked me if there were many atheists in Italy. I told him that the question was difficult to answer, since I thought that man is incapable of real atheism. To which Mme Lwoff (Marguerite) smilingly added; "That makes sense: Jacques has the cult of himself!"

It was in the laboratory, between one series of Warburgs and another, while thinking of the results, that Jacques would say to me (or to himself); "Mon petit, j'ai raté ma carriére, j'aurai du etre un grand couturier [he loved elegant women's dresses] ou bien chef d'orchestre [he was proud of having been one during his time in the USA]." Of course he would say that after an experiment in which his brilliant serendipity had been successfully challenged.

The laboratory was blessed by the efficient, industrious, and intelligent help of a technical factotum: Mazé, always serious in his work, yet smiling, friendly, and pleasant. He could do everything—bleed a rabbit or fix countless Warburg flasks, side-arms hooks and all in a magistral fashion. The smooth flow of research was supported by a group of hard working and competent women from Bretagne: Mme le Naour (the boss—I never knew her first name), her charming sister Agnès, and friendly Mimi. Day after day they boiled, rinsed, and sterilized heavy buckets of glass Petri dishes. They also cut glass tubing and pulled it through the flame to make hundreds of Pasteur pipettes. Who was Mr. Petri? No one ever asked, but Monsieur Pasteur . . . ! No one would have dreamed of writing Pasteur pipette without a capital "P," as I see it written now in the American catalogues!

In the laboratory population there was, every year, a substantial dose of English speaking scientists to whom André Lwoff would only speak French. He required them to answer the same, constantly (but not always patiently) correcting them. Jacques found it more comfortable to exchange opinions in English (which was his mother's tongue), never answering in French to their painfully constructed, often incomprehensible phrases. This made me furious: "I had come to a French speaking laboratory to understand science, not to learn English." But at the end, through all that hard listening, some English rubbed off and was of great use to me. Our guests were all pleasant, very friendly, and a bit lost. They frequently complained of diarrhea at first and then of the lack of friendliness toward foreigners in Paris. Seymour Cohen was the first American I met there when I arrived. He looked sort of lonesome, was very sweet, and danced very well. Then came Martin Pollock preceded by long discussions and hypotheses on his very special system: the mechanism of control of penicillinase. Jacques was excited by Martin's results, and liked his high class British accent and manners. With Martin we were constantly measuring penicillinase activity in Warburgs. Jacques would come in behind us and put a friendly hand on our shoulders, see the partial results in a glance and rush to the corridor to discuss them with "the others" (there were always two or three people ready to talk in the corridor). Martin, thus deprived of the best pleasure in science, was getting upset: "C'est le lab oratoir!" Later, came Mike Doudoroff. It made us all very happy since he was one of our scientific gods. Tall and bent with a smiling face and swollen hands which appeared clumsy, but were not, he was frequently inebriated, but always intelligent and warm hearted. We were purifying the amylomaltase and the "precipitate" had . . . precipitated on the floor! Mike was accustomed to misfortunes of that kind and quickly sucked it up by vacuum and used it! He also would open a Warburg flask every so often to add another substance he just thought of, which could modify the reaction. At the end I had no idea what was going on, but he did, and Jacques, who was a very neat and precise worker, nevertheless enjoyed the messy, bubbly way of Mike.

Mel Cohn, Seymour Benzer, Francis Ryan, Lane Barksdale, Alwin Pappenheimer, Dave Hogness, Aaron Novick, Cy Levinthal, and Howard Rickenberg, each brought a new personal input of experience, intelligence, and knowledge to the development of research. Each created life-long friendships. Jacques would tell me "they [the Americans] are the experts, I am a self-made man." In a way it was true. But his originality and spark was of continuous excitement and provided profitable discussions.

The core of the question in those days (1948-1950) was to understand why there was an increased rate of enzyme formation upon addition of the substrate (adaptation) or a diauxic inhibition. The working hypotheses in the lab were that "many different enzymes may stem from a common precursor or pool of precursor molecules"(Growth, 1947) and that the "master pattern configuration determining the specificity was not the enzyme itself but a pre-existing self-duplicating unit (the gene)" (*Ann. Rev. Microb.*). One day Monod suggested an experiment to demonstrate that enzyme and gene were two independent entities. The reasoning was the following: A mutation provoked by UV irradiation means a modification in one or more particles (or molecules of enzyme). Bacteria adapted to maltose, for instance, have a very large number of enzyme molecules, while the unadapted have very few. If a mutation required the inactivation of most of the enzyme molecules, it should be much easier to obtain such mutation in unadapted than in adapted cells. If, on the contrary, the gene hypothesis was correct, then the probability of mutation should be independent from the adaptation. But Wolman objected with the alternative hypothesis that the unadapted cells may contain a large number of inactive precursor molecules which would have to be eliminated to detect the mutation. Thus an equally low frequency of mutants would be expected in both adapted and unadapted cells. The experiment was never performed, like hundreds of other eliminated by active intellectual exchange: it was like a continuous game of checkers. Jacques dominated the scientific discussions particularly at seminars organized at Rue Pierre Curie (now Rue Pierre *et Marie* Curie) and jokingly called by friends "le Club des Monod-theist." The seminars were followed by dinners at the Brasserie Alsacienne where Nissman, Szulmajster, and Latarjet rivaled with Jacques, Cohen, and Bussard in the exchange of "contrepetries," i.e. scrambled words with hidden, mostly sexual, double meanings.

In the laboratory the exciting moments were many! With Jacques I learned that in science one gets excited every day: either by a new hypothesis or by the results supporting it, or by those which one day later will shake the hypothesis and require a new one. It was an exciting moment when, one day, at the end of an experiment, the addition of iodine to a Warburg flask unexpectedly produced a deep blue color (Monod and Torriani, 1948). We were studying the activity of the adaptive enzyme maltase on maltose (Gl α1, 4–D–glucose); no starch was expected to form, since we strongly believed in the recently described "Cori ester" (Gl–1–PO_4) as a requirement for starch synthesis (Cori, *Fed. Proc.* 4, 232, 1945). Why did we add iodine then? To measure the hydrolysis of lactose and of maltose, Jacques had the idea of using a glucose oxidase (or Notatine from *Penicillium notatum)* and measuring in Warburg the O_2 liberated by the following chain of reactions:

$$\text{maltose} \xrightarrow{\text{maltase}} \text{glucose} \xrightarrow[\text{oxidase}]{\text{glucose}} \text{gluconic acid} + H_2O_2 \xrightarrow{\text{catalase}} O_2$$

(Monod, Torriani, Gribetz, *Comptes Rendus*). It worked beautifully from lactose but from maltose it gave ½ of the expected glucose. Could it possibly be that one glucose from each maltose hydrolyzed by the enzyme was utilized to form a polysaccharide? It was, but we could not have seen it in the absence of Notatine because the accumulation of glucose inhibited the formation of starch-like material. We were very happy and Jacques wrote a nice note on the use of Notatine, only to find out, opening the *Biochem. J.* that day (42, 230, 1948), that Keilin and Hartree had just published the very same method! Disappointing, but "quoi qu'il en soit" (as Jacques frequently wrote in his papers); at any rate, the interesting fact was the synthesis of polysaccharides. To clearly convince ourselves that the starch-like substance was produced by a single enzyme and that it was produced in the absence of any phosphate, took us quite a few months, until we purified the enzyme in total absence of phosphates by using veronal or citrate buffer (Monod and Torriani, *Ann. Inst. Pasteur* **78**, 65, 1950; Torriani and Monod, *Comptes Rendus Acad. Sci.* **228**, 718, 1949). We had discovered a new enzyme in *E. coli* and Jacques, who was terrific at inventing new all-explanatory words, baptized it "amylo-maltase." This was probably the only time I felt stronger than Jacques! To do the balance of the reaction and to analyze the products we needed some chemistry; if mine was not great, Jacques' was worse. He did not pretend otherwise! For instance, to eliminate the iodine used for precipitating the polysaccharides we used alcohol. Jacques was boiling the mixture over an open flame to eliminate the alcohol; I suggested a reflux column which helped a lot! The biochemistry I knew, I learned it from Luigi.

Why were we studying amylomaltase and lactase? The working hypothesis was, as mentioned earlier, the existence of a pre-enzyme which was precursor to both lactase and maltase and possibly to other enzymes. We studied also a trehalase which was never worked out further. The approach was to study a number of inducible and constitutive enzymes. For each enzyme, mutants had to be isolated and Madeleine was doing this work directly with Jacques. The enzymes had to be extracted, purified, their molecular, and catalytic properties analyzed. Immunological analysis of wild type versus mutants would suggest if a precursor existed. The rate of synthesis would be compared for each enzyme when induced singularly or together. Jacques outlined this whole program for me the second day I was with him. And all of it was done by his group in the eight years I spent with him and . . . so much more!

Our experiments required a "system artificially set up by establishing a constant limited supply of an essential metabolite, while all other nutrients would be in excess" (*Ann. Rev. Microbiol.* **III** p. 371, 1949, see pp. 378 and 386). Furthermore H. Virtanen had just published a paper in which he suggested that in conditions of limiting N source, "the proteolytic enzyme of *E. coli* retains its activity [while] the dispensable enzymes, saccharase and lactase, decrease very sharply . . . The adaptive enzymes which are necessary only in definite nutritional conditions seem, as a rule, to decrease or disappear with the lowering of the nitrogen content of the cells" (A. I. Virtanen and U. Winkler; *Acta Chemica Scandinava* **3**, 272-278, 1949). Jacques thought that to keep a culture in continuous exponential phase would help to understand the kinetics of enzyme adaptation. Was it autocatalytic or not? And was Virtanen correct? On April 11, 1949, we spent the day at 37°C to give birth to the "bactogène!" Once the culture was in exponential phase on glycerol as C source, we started diluting ("rejuvenating")

by ½ with fresh medium and lactose every 30 minutes. The results were encouraging and Jacques wrote in my notebook the theory which was the basis of
the bactogène (Monod, *Annales Inst. Pasteur* **79**, 390-410, 1950). A few days
later we were repeating the experiment using a rotating flask with a simple
method of feeding and collecting. This method, or a very similar one, was also
devised by Novick and Szilard (*Science* **112**, 715-716, 1950) almost at the same
time and gave us and them and many others long years of pleasant work.

Life around Jacques was exciting, challenging, and not always easy. Those
whom he did not like or did not consider intelligent enough, Jacques looked
straight "through" as if they were transparant and did not exist. If they were
rude enough to ask a direct question repeatedly, he would wake up from a sort
of dream and snap a short phrase at them. He had a particular disdain for "les
sorbonnards" (the Sorbonne faculty): "Ils sont betes comme mes pieds!" So
they, the Fac Profs, chose not to have his arrogance among their ignorance!

Sometimes he would arrive at the lab by taxi, borrow from me some francs
for the fare . . . and never repay me, not knowing that I was in a sort of voluntary exile and very poor indeed. If I asked him, he would of course rush to give
the money back, but . . . he would forget about it between the time he put his
hand in the pocket, which was frequently empty, and the time he took out the
coins since something more interesting, such as a result or a telephone call,
would certainly intervene.

On Sundays Jacques would frequently go to the forest of Fontainebleu:
sneakers, rope, a little rug, and some pof-pof (a rosin powder) to climb rocks
that rose only a few feet high from the sand in the forest. It was all a ritual:
the rug and the pof-pof were necessary to clean the sneakers from the sand
which made the climbing very difficult. The same sand, properly washed, made
the extraction of enzymes so easy! I remember going there with him and Jean
Weigle, both well-trained climbers. The next day my arms were stiff since it
had been many years since I had climbed the Dolomites, and even the Warburg
flasks seemed very heavy!

Thirty years passed. Rapkine, Weigle, Ryan, Duodoroff, Mimi, are all gone.
Luigi left us shortly after Jacques. Luigi was my whole life and Jacques was
champagne to our intellectual pursuit.

REMEMBRANCE OF THINGS PAST

Germaine Stanier (Cohen-Bazire)

"L 'art du chercheur, c'est d 'abord de se trouver un bon patron."
A. M. Lwoff, cited by F. Jacob in
Of Microbes and Life, 1971.

During my university career at Toulouse, I had the exceptional luck to come under the influence of Monsieur Vandel, a man who offered a five-year course, continuously renewed, in general biology. It was then that I decided to become a research biologist, with the naive ambition to understand how a cell became two and how cells differentiate.

At that time, and indeed for several more years, no training in biochemistry (apart from the medical course) was offered in Toulouse to students in science. M. Vandel suggested that it would be desirable to learn this subject if I wanted to pursue a meaningful career in biological research. He accordingly wrote to Professor Javillier, who held the chair of biochemistry in Paris and asked him to take me as a graduate student in his laboratory. The episode lasted, all told, for eighteen months. Javillier, close to retirement, had delegated younger assistants to help out with research. The lectures, exclusively concerned with structural biochemistry, were held in overcrowded lecture halls. I was supposed to study the hypothetical relationships between lycopene and vitamin A_2; and provided

49

with a barrel of spoiled tomato juice from which to extract lycopene.

I shall always owe a profound debt of thanks to Professor Edgar Lederer, my godfather at the C. N. R. S., who listened to this sad tale and remarked; "You have a hopeless problem." He did not, however, suggest another one! Moreover, I was a long way from learning biochemistry.

When, in 1947, the late Professor Fromageot succeeded the chair of biochemistry in Paris, a general cleaning-up of Javillier's laboratory ensued. By that time, however, I had already renewed an acquaintance with an old friend, Georges Cohen, first encountered as a fellow student after the débacle in Toulouse. Following the completion of his doctorate in Monsieur Macheboeuf's laboratory at the Pasteur Institute, Georges was starting a new field of research: the analysis of fermentation products of clostridia, in Monsieur Prévot's laboratory at Garches. He generously offered to take me as an assistant, and in so doing, started my real education as a biochemist. There, we worked together in almost complete isolation, apart from rare visits to the Pasteur Institute in Paris and its library. The red letter days were the monthly meetings of the "Club de Physiologie cellulaire," which we faithfully attended. The reunions of the club were a unique educational experience. We had the opportunity to listen to and meet in an informal and congenial atmosphere, some of the leading contemporary biochemists and experimental biologists. The club was Jacques Monod's creation and reflected his generosity and devotion to the education of younger scientists. It was at one of these reunions that we first met.

After obtaining my doctorate in the spring of 1950, I plucked up the courage to approach Monsieur Lwoff to find out if it would be possible to work for a time in his laboratory. I explained that, although I was very happy to continue collaborating with George Cohen, a change of subject, even a temporary one, would be salutary.

I had attended the meeting "les unités douées de continuité génétique" at which André Lwoff and Jacques Monod had participated, and read with great fascination the recent review published in the *Growth Symposium* by Jacques Monod. By training and inclination, a biologist, I desired to become better acquainted with some aspects of research being pursued in his laboratory. André Lwoff very kindly listened and said; "Why don't you ask Boris Ephrussi?" My answer was "No, thank you." His amused smile did not ask for an explanation. Then quite seriously he said that there was no space in his laboratory, and he would be absent from Paris for several months, but I could work under Jacques Monod's supervision, if he agreed, for a month, starting the first of September.

On that first beautiful September day, Jacques Monod showed me how to measure the activity of β-galactosidase with orthonitrophenyl β-D-galactoside (ONPG) as substrate. He had just received from Melvin Cohn a sample of this new chromogenic substrate, discovered by Joshua Lederberg. I was then charged with the determination of the molar extinction coefficient of o-nitrophenol at neutral and alkaline pH in order to determine units of activity of the enzyme.

A few days later, Jacques Monod asked me to determine the Michaelis constant of β-galactosidase for ONPG. "Michaelis constant, what's that?" I said. "You find out" he answered laughing, while handing me his copy of Baldwin's *Dynamic Aspects of Biochemistry*. I spent the evening studying that particular chapter in Baldwin's book and at the end of the next day, brought him the answer. I must have passed the test! The following week Jacques Monod asked if I should like to remain in his laboratory. I was absolutely thrilled by a prospect which was beyond all my expectations. I thanked him profusely, said that I would like nothing more, but that it would mean leaving Georges without any collaborators. After a few sleepless nights, I opened my heart to Georges. With great generosity, he replied that I shouldn't think of him, but only of my scientific future. My conscience was somewhat salved by Jacques Monod's assurance that Georges would join his group as soon as space became available. This eventually happened in 1954; but by that time I had already left for the United States. Little did I know, at the time, that Georges had refused, on my behalf, a similar invitation a year previously because we could not both be accommodated in the crowded attic. Many years later, I also learned that before leaving Paris on his travels, André Lwoff had suggested to Jacques Monod that I might join his group, where, he thought, I could be a "valuable addition." (I leave the responsibility of these last two words to André Lwoff himself!)

If I have evoked at such length the roadblocks to the pursuit of a career in developmental biology, it is because—incredible as it now seems—it was the way it was in 1945-1950. I was indeed exceptionally fortunate to meet André Lwoff and Jacques Monod; but the matter rested on pure chance. In respectable French academic circles their names and work were completely ignored.

Thus began the most fruitful and exhilarating three years of my life. Others have described better than I can the atmosphere of friendship, gaiety, intellectual excitement, in short of "gai savoir" which pervaded the part of the attic occupied by the Service de Physiologie Microbienne. In the fall of 1950, Annamaria Torriani, Mel Cohn, and Madeleine Jolit were the only members of the group working closely with Jacques Monod. Annamaria was busily running Warburgs and cooking large quantities of rice for our lunches. Madeleine, cooped up in her tiny room, was searching for mutants and kept our cultures going. Mel Cohn was in England for a time, collecting and synthesizing all sorts of galactosides which we would try as inducers, substrates, or complexants of β-galactosidase.

At that time the challenging mystery was the role played by the inducer in the synthesis of the enzyme. Every day a theory was built and another buried. There was great excitement when we found that thiophenyl-β-D-galactoside, a very potent inhibitor of the enzyme was not an inducer and that meliboise, which was neither a substrate, nor a competitive inhibitor and not even metabolized in any detectable way by the cells (*E. coli* strain ML) was a very potent inducer: all theories involving the enzyme *per se* in its own induction were invalidated.

The study of the effect of cations on the activity of β-galactosidase and the affinity of its substrates was also part of my occupations. Jacques Monod thought that the first results on the competition between sodium and hydrogen ions on the activation of β-galactosidase should be published as a note to the Academy of Sciences. I must have rewritten that little paper at least five times before he was satisfied and finally agreed to present it to Monsieur Tréfouël for publication in the *Comptes Rendus*. On that occasion, Jacques Monod introduced me to Mr. Tréfouël, then director of the Pasteur Institute, who, after a desultory look at the manuscript, entertained us with an account of the qualities of his secretary's new electric typewriter.

It is not without nostalgia that I remember those times of close everyday collaboration with Jacques Monod. Looking back through my old notebooks I find protocols of experiments written either by myself or by him. Each day, the purpose of the experiment was noted and subsequently what we had learned from it. Sometimes, he could not refrain from writing his reflections on the day's results or simply what crossed his mind at the time. On the 5.II.51, I find: "O surprise! O beauté simple et naïve et intelligible, l'activité est proportionnelle à la concentration de l'inducteur"* (at low concentrations and in certain conditions). Another day (9.II.51): "Triste jour, j'entre dans ma 42ème année. Ce n'est pas que cet age me déplaise mais il me rapproche d'un age qui me plait moins. Pour célébrer ce jour . . . "† then comes the purpose of the experiment. He was always full of wonder about the beauty of the simple mathematical laws which biological systems obeyed: the beauty of a growth curve, for example.

In the fall of 1951, A. M. Pappenheimer, Jr.—"Pap"—appeared, on sabbatical leave, and shared my very small room in the laboratory. He wanted to improve his French and work on the induction of β-galactosidase; no doubt, that is the reason why Jacques Monod had put us together, since my spoken English was nonexistent.

Pap's imagination was challenged by Annamaria and Mel's recent discovery of the protein Pz present in uninduced cells, which crossreacted immunologically with β-galactosidase (Gz). Moreover the intracellular level of Pz decreased when Gz was synthesized. After a lengthy discussion, Pap and I decided to do a little simple experiment (secretly withheld from Jacques Monod) to test a possible relationship between Pz and Gz. We proposed to induce a culture in which

---

*"O surprise! O simple, naïve and intelligible beauty. The activity is proportional to the concentration of inducer."

†"Sad day, I enter my 42nd year. It is not this age that displeases me, but it brings me closer to an age I like less. To celebrate this day. . ."

growth had stopped from nitrogen limitation and to follow the kinetics of β-galactosidase synthesis after the addition of a nitrogen source.

Jacques Monod, who was always in and out of the lab, naturally wanted to know what we were doing. We did not want to tell him for the very good reason that we did not really know what to expect. If we found something interesting it would be a good surprise. He was a little annoyed with us, I could feel, but it did not take him long to guess. He was very sharp with me when I confessed that the reason for my secrecy was the lack of a precise hypothesis. "Always try to formulate one," he exclaimed. He then told us, "The way to do the experiment is to use amino acid auxotrophs." It became evident that the amount of enzyme synthesized was rigorously proportional to the amount of growth of the culture. From these experiments, Jacques Monod produced a conceptual masterpiece, a fine example of his extraordinary hypothetico-deductive acumen. The hypothesis of a dynamic equilibrium between Pz and Gz—or, for that matter, between any proteins—was given a serious blow. Thus was defined the differential rate of enzyme synthesis or what became known later (in the United States) as Monod's plot. The masterpiece was handed to me to be transmitted to Professor Fromageot, then editor of *Biochimica Biophysica Acta*. A few days later, Fromageot called and told Jacques Monod that he thought the paper far too theoretical. He answered "If you publish this as it stands, I promise that my next paper will contain only facts."

One of the most agreeable aspects of life in the attic was the ease with which one acquired the elements of adult education. Conversations at lunch time often dealt with politics or the most recent movies, but also with art, music, and literature. A typical product of the French pedagogical system and of life in a provincial town, my ignorance, particularly of literature, was profound. When I confessed one day to Jacques Monod that I had never read Camus, Stendhal, or even Anatole France, he laughed: "I envy you. You do not know how lucky you are to have all these pleasures in front of you!" Later on, when I was hospitalized for surgery, he brought me an armful of books.

After almost two years spent in Jacques Monod's laboratory, he began to cast about for a postdoctoral position in the United States. This eventually materialized in 1953, in the Department of Bacteriology of the University of California at Berkeley; and I sailed to apply my newly acquired biological insights to the problems of regulation of pigment synthesis of photosynthetic bacteria, little knowing that I should remain away from France, and my real home, the Pasteur Institute, until 1971.

By then, Jacques Monod had become the director of "la Maison," as old Pasteurians used to call it. Immersed in his worries and responsibilities, I didn't see him very often, sometimes in the hallways, where he would give me a kiss on both cheeks and ask if all was well. All was well as long as I knew he was there, somewhere.

WHATEVER HAPPENED TO Pz?

A. M. Pappenheimer, Jr.

I first met Jacques Monod at the 1946 Cold Spring Harbor Symposium. It was this symposium, I think, that finally convinced biologists everywhere that bacteria and even viruses, crystallizable as nucleoproteins, really did have mutable genes and chromosomes that could undergo sexual recombination and replication just as did the genes of animals and plants. At the meeting, André Lwoff gave a paper on "Biochemical Mutations in Bacteria" in which he reviewed Jacques' work on the new phenomenon of "diauxie" and its relation to adaptive enzyme formation. Lwoff discussed at some length a working hypothesis of Monod's which he summarized as follows: "Enzymes allowing attack of carbohydrates by bacteria are all derived from a *common precursor*. This precursor (preenzyme) has a slight general affinity for carbohydrates. Transformation of the precursor into an adapted, specific enzyme occurs as a result of the substrate-preenzyme combination (which would account for the specificity of enzymatic adaptation)" (1).

After the symposium, Jacques and André spend the weekend with us in Scotland, Connecticut, where, in addition to helping me select stones from an abandoned mill to build a terrace and stone wall, they agreed to save a place for me in André's Service de Physiologie Microbienne at the Pasteur Institute during my sabbatical leave from New York University in 1951-1952. It was fortunate indeed for me that I applied so early. By the time I arrived with my family in

Paris five years later, the "grenier" of André and Jacques was bursting at the seams and had already become the exciting and stimulating center of the emerging new field of molecular biology. Space was at a premium, and the atmosphere in the laboratory was incredibly exciting. At lunch, speculations and hypotheses on the mechanism of enzyme and temperate virus induction, how to test the theories and how to tear them apart, were feverishly debated in French and English simultaneously, in every kind of foreign accent and with everyone talking at once. The conversation was aided by a constant stream of visitors including my friend and former student, Mel Cohn, who had already been visiting for two years before my arrival. To the laboratory that year came Seymour Benzer, Max Delbruck, Luigi Gorini, Martin Pollock, Francis Ryan, Roger Stanier, Gunther Stent, Louis Siminovitch, and a great many others. It was an idyllic year both for me and my family. Weekdays, our three children went to the Ecole Alsacienne. On Sundays we would join Jacques, Odette, and their two boys to "faire les rochers" and picnic at Fontainebleau or one of the other "forets pres de Paris." One evening a week we would play chamber music at the Monod's apartment, 24 rue Monsieur le Prince. As I wrote for my chapter in André Lwoff's jubilee volume (2), I think the year our family spent in Paris was probably the happiest and most rewarding of my life.

On arriving at the Pasteur Institute, I told Jacques that I had come there to learn about adaptive enzymes and that I wished him to suggest a problem for me to work on. The idea that Lwoff had discussed at the 1946 symposium, namely that adaptive bacterial enzymes arose by transformation of a preexisting precursor was still the prevalent view five years later, but apparently Jacques was beginning to have some doubts about the hypothesis. At any rate, the question which he proposed I try to answer was the following: When an inducer such as a β-galactoside is added to a culture of *E. coli* (growing in the absence of glucose) does induction of β-galactosidase production involve modification of one or more preexisting precursor polypeptides, or is the enzyme a totally new protein synthesized from scratch? As a matter of fact, a strong candidate for a "preenzyme" had already been found in noninduced *E. coli* by Mel Cohn and Annamaria Torriani (3). Cohn and Torriani had shown that there was present in extracts from noninduced cells, an enzymatically inactive protein which they called Pz. This protein cross-reacted with antibodies raised in rabbits by immunization with purified β-galactosidase (Gz). The Pz protein was found in all strains of *Enterobacteriaceae* capable of fermenting lactose (4). Cohn and Torriani found that 80% or more of all the anti-enzyme in anti-Gz sera could be precipitated by Pz and that only 10-20% was truly specific for the enzyme itself. However, when mixtures of Pz and Gz were added together to their antisera, the enzyme was preferentially precipitated. Did the addition of an inducer to an uninduced culture of *E. coli* somehow bring about the modification of Pz so as to yield active Gz, analogous perhaps, to the conversion of trypsinogen to trypsin?

The experiment that Jacques proposed was indeed very simple. He had recently received a series of twenty auxotrophic mutants of *E. coli* from Bernard Davis, each requiring a different amino acid or accessory factor for growth. Would conversion of precursor to enzyme take place in the absence of an amino acid essential for growth? Jacques suggested that we test each mutant strain in turn by adding inducer (β-methylgalactoside) just after growth ceased due to having used up the required amino acid. I was assigned to a laboratory with Germaine Cohen-Bazire who taught me how to measure Gz by following the rate of hydrolysis of niphégal (*p*-nitrophenyl-β-galactoside) at 420 mμ.

I must confess that I did not really understand how all this was going to answer the question. I think what bothered me at the time about the suggested experiments with auxotrophic mutants, was that I could not see how an enzyme could be synthesized without cell growth, although my reasons for this (essentially erroneous) conviction were far from clear. I remember asking Jacques just what he was really driving at. He said that what he hoped to accomplish eventually, was the synthesis of β-galactosidase in a test tube using a cell-free system. I recall saying, "Jacques, if you succeed in doing that, you will be doing what God did. It will be equivalent to creating life." I little dreamed that within less than twenty years this would be a "fait accompli" not only for β-galactosidase and other proteins (5), but that Jack Murphy in my own laboratory would have produced diphtheria toxin *in vitro* using a system extracted from *E. coli* and DNA isolated from corynephage β (6).

Nevertheless, Germaine and I tested the auxotrophic strains. We soon found that no enzyme was produced if inducer was added to a nongrowing culture, no matter which amino acid had become limiting. Enzyme synthesis began almost immediately upon adding back the required amino acid or growth factor. At this time, the kinetics of enzyme production were being followed as a function of time. It seemed to me that if growth were indeed required, we should be measuring enzyme production with respect to the increase in bacterial mass. In fact, when Germaine and I plotted our results in this way we found that enzyme synthesis, after adding inducer, was directly proportional to the new growth from the earliest moment that an increase in bacterial mass could be detected. At first, I cannot say that I found our results particularly surprising or novel but when Germaine and I showed them to Jacques he became quite excited. Our results with the amino acid-requiring mutants had, of course, suggested that if P*z* were indeed a precursor, its activation required the synthesis of another polypeptide containing all the amino acids. Somehow, the inducer would have to trigger the synthesis of this polypeptide *de novo*. Jacques was struck by the fact that our method of plotting enzyme production suggested that *from the very outset*, enzyme was synthesized as a constant proportion of the total bacterial protein synthesis. He called this the "differential rate of protein synthesis." The fact that this rate was linear as soon as it could be measured after addition of inducer, would not have been predicted by the precursor theory. The maximum differential rate of β-galactosidase synthesis was found in the constitutive mutants (requiring no inducer) that Germaine had just succeeded in isolating, and amounted to a surprising 5% of the total protein synthesis! Obviously, under normal circumstances, organisms must have a way of regulating the synthesis of their own enzymes so that the synthesis of any given enzyme is only turned on in time of need (7).

But the question still remained: Why did uninduced *E. coli* contain the protein Pz which appeared to be so closely related to β-galactosidase both structurally and serologically? After a good deal of discussion, it was decided that the only way to eliminate the possibility that Pz might form part of the active enzyme would be by the use of radioactive isotopes. After discussions with Mel Cohn, the following experiment was proposed: *E. coli* would be grown in the absence of inducer on a medium containing $S^{35}O_4$[11] as sole source of sulfur until growth ceased. Inducer and unlabeled sulfate would then be added and samples would be withdrawn at short intervals, extracted and precipitated by a Pz-absorbed anti-β-galactosidase (anti-Z) serum. Since Pz is a sulfur-containing protein, if it formed part of the induced enzyme molecule, we would expect to find radioactivity in the specific precipitate from the Pz-absorbed serum. If it did not, then the newly synthesized enzyme should contain no labeled sulfur. Before leaving Paris, I performed the first such experiment. Although inconclusive, we did find that the radioactivity in the specific precipitate was a good deal less than would be expected if Pz were incorporated directly into the first enzyme formed. Our controls suggested that what radioactivity was precipitated with Gz was almost certainly due to contamination of the precipitate with other nonspecific sulfur compounds present in the crude bacterial extracts. It was obviously going to be necessary to purify the newly formed enzyme before its specific precipitation by anti-Z, to reduce the nonspecific precipitation of label, in order to obtain convincing results. This was accomplished in elegant fashion by Hogness, Cohn, and Monod (8). Thus if any part of Pz were present in the induced enzyme, it must be lacking in both its methionine and its cystine.

The final and complete elimination of the Pz protein as a precursor having anything to do with induction of β-galactosidase synthesis came a few years later when Cohn, Lennox, and Spiegelman (9) transduced the *lac* Z gene into an i^+z^- *Shigella dysenteriae* containing no Pz, and obtained *lac*$^+$ recombinant *Shigella*. Their finding demonstrated that the Pz locus was not linked to the *lac* operon and that synthesis of the gene product occurred *de novo* and was totally independent of Pz. That was in 1960. I have only found one paper referring to Pz since that time. In 1972 Erickson and Steers (10) reported on a cross reacting antigen present in a number of *Enterobacteriaciae* species which, like Pz, reacted with anti-β-galactosidase antisera. Of course, by 1961 there was no longer any reason to even think about precursors anymore, because the *lac* operator had been defined and it was recognized that the i-gene product was a repressor. Induction of enzyme synthesis resulted from derepression of the operator. Moreover, mRNA and DNA-dependent RNA polymerase had been discovered and the role of ribosomes in translation of mRNA was beginning to be appreciated. In *The Lactose Operon* (5) which appeared in 1970, the last entry in the index under "P," is "PyJaMa experiments." Pz is not mentioned.

So we return to where we started in 1951. What is Pz and whatever happened to it? I find it very difficult to believe that its close serological and structural similarity to the β-galactosidase protein, was the result of some purely fortuitous accident. Could Pz have evolved from a relocated stretch of DNA that arose by duplication of an ancestral Z-gene? If this were so, then according to Zipkas and Riley (11) we might expect to find the Pz-gene located approximately 90° or 180° away from the *lac* operon on the *E. coli* chromosome. Several laboratories (12-14) have recently described mutant strains of *E. coli* which carry a β-galactosidase gene that lies outside the *lac* operon. For instance, Campbell, Lengyel, and Langridge (13) demonstrated such a β-galactosidase in strains derived by successive mutations from an *E. coli* K12 strain that already contained a large deletion in its Z-gene. In this mutant strain, LC110-Ebg[+] (where Ebg stands for *evolved β-galactosidase activity*) the ebg-gene lies at 59 minutes on the *E. coli* map; almost exactly opposite the *lac* operon. One would like to know if the ebg-gene product bears any relation to Pz. According to Campbell *et al.*, extracts from the ebg[+] strain do not form a specific precipitate when mixed with anti-Z serum. However, it is not clear whether the anti-Z serum which they used would have given a precipitate with known Pz-containing extracts from uninduced bacteria. Perhaps the possibility of a relationship between Pz and the products of the ebg- and Z-genes should be explored further. For the present, however, the nature of the Pz protein and its function remain a mystery.

REFERENCES

1. Lwoff, A. (1946). *Cold Springs Harbor Symp. Quant. Biol.* **11**, 139.
2. Pappenheimer, A. M. Jr. 1971). In "Of Microbes and Life" (J. Monod and E. Borek, eds.), Columbia Univ. Press, New York.
3. Cohn, M. and Torriani, A. (1952). *J. Immunol.* **69**, 471.
4. Cohn, M. (1957). *Bact. Rev.* **31**, 140.
5. Zubay, C., Chambers, D. A., and Cheong, L. C. (1970). *In* "The Lactose Operon" (J. Beckwith and D. Zipser, eds.), Cold Spring Harb. Lab.
6. Murphy, J. R., Pappenheimer, A. M., Jr., and Tayard de Borms, S. (1974). *Proc. Natl. Acad. Sci. (USA)* **71**, 11.
7. Monod, J., Pappenheimer, A. M., Jr. and Cohen-Bazire, G. (1952). *Biochim. Biophys. Acta* **9**, 648.

8. Hogness, D. S., Cohn, M., and Monod, J. (1955). *Biochim. Biophys. Acta* **16**, 99.
9. Cohn, M., Lennox, E., and Spiegelman, S. (1960). *Biochim. Biophys. Acta* **39**, 255.
10. Erickson, R. P. and Steers, E., Jr. (1972). *Immunochem.* **9**, 29.
11. Zipkas, D. and Riley, H. (1975). *Proc. Natl. Acad. Sci. U. S. A.* **72**, 1354.
12. Warren, R. A. (1972). *Can. J. Microbiol.* **18**, 1439.
13. Campbell, J. H., Lengyel, J. A., and Langridge, J. (1973). *Proc. Natl. Acad. Sci. U. S. A.* **70**, 1841.
14. Hartl, D. L. and Hall, B. G. (1974). *Nature* **248**, 152.

AN EXCITING BUT EXASPERATING PERSONALITY

Martin Pollock

"L'univers n'est rempli que de bruits. L'homme, par choix, en
compose a son image une musique dont s'emerveille."*
MacGregor †

This book is not, I would suppose, intended to be a series of formal eulogies to
Jacques Monod; nor is it simply a "tribute" to a very remarkable person. I
imagine its aim, rather, is to provide a wide range of personal memoirs: the reactions, experiences, and subjective impressions of his friends and colleagues, compiled as a historical record of how Jacques appeared to those who knew him
well. That, in itself, is sufficient tribute to his memory. There is no need here for
facile expressions of adulation.

Anyway, this is how I look at it and I can do no more than describe as
honestly as possible how I felt about him in the light of my own experiences.
This must mean what some may take to be too deep an intrusion of my personality; but that cannot be helped. It also means that I have not attempted here to
view the grand sweep of his superb achievements in molecular biology; I have al-

*"The universe contains nothing but noises. Man chooses to create from them a music,
in his own image, which he then proceeds to marvel at."

† A pseudonym that Monod liked to use when he wished to quote himself.

61

ready done this elsewhere*; and anyway most people are already familiar with the story.

A picture of a personality drawn by a single individual is inevitably highly subjective and therefore to some extent tendentious. But to be real it must be honest and complete within that context. Moreover, in order to understand the deep structure that lies beneath the edifice of personal achievement, it is often the apparent trivia of every day life, the small things that go wrong, the reactions to difficulties and personal relationships that provide important clues. And these do not emerge in the published research reports or grand lecture reviews that claim public attention.

There are a few who, through ignorance or envy, have regarded Jacques mainly as a conceited and arrogant egoist. There are others, dazzled by his brilliance and charm, who could see nothing but genius and virtue. But most of us, I suspect, feel that he was a complex character who combined exceptional talents with great ambitions. Looking back now over the years, it still seems to me that his most outstanding characteristic—the key to understanding a number of otherwise puzzling and paradoxical features in his behavior towards others—was a supreme self-confidence in his own ability. I have never met anyone who had one-half such a high opinion of himself as had Jacques. And I could almost argue that it was justified in every sense except in the measure of the humility that is just as important as self-confidence. From this high sense of superiority came an egoism which was not, at first sight, any more marked than that from which we all suffer, but which penetrated more deeply into the structure of his behavior and could sometimes lead to the hurtful expression of an unfairly low opinion of others.

I began to sense his charm almost as soon as I first met him in André Lwoff's office in January 1947. But I only got to know him properly during my two visits to work in his laboratory: for three months in the spring and summer of 1948 and for a year or more over 1952/3, when I really fell under his spell.

I soon had reason to be extremely grateful to him for his help and encouragement. I was already thirty-two years old when we first met; but my career as a research worker (into which I had, so-to-speak, gate-crashed, through having a medical degree that facilitated acceptance into the British Medical Council's employ without the traditional Ph.D. training) was considerably delayed by my medical education and the war. I was really very inexperienced and unsophisticated and Jacques took on the role of a sort of Ph.D. supervisor-substitute (without the thesis or the degree) who guided and inspired me, and I revered his opinions with almost filial devotion. Not only was he working on *my* subject of "enzyme adaptation" and thought it was as crucially important to bio-

* "1965 Nobel Prize for Medicine" *Nature* (London) **208**, 1250. (1965); Obituary notice. Trends in Biochemical Sci. Sept. N 208 (1976).

logy as I did, but he shared my political orientation and general practical philosophical approach (in so far as I had one) and we had so many personal tastes in common.

It was superb to have found someone to admire and feel so much affection for in this way, especially in the exciting atmosphere of postwar France. I believed I had found a friend with whom I could identify myself and attempt to emulate.

It was Jacques who organized for me an invitation to my first International Congress (of Microbiology in Copenhagen in 1947) and it was Jacques more than anyone (with the possible exception of Marjorie Stephenson) who encouraged me in the work I was then doing on tetrathionate and nitrate reductase adaptation in coliform bacteria. He and André arranged for me to give lectures and seminars under the auspices of the Pasteur Institute and provided space in their laboratories where I could work in that wonderfully stimulating atmosphere of discussion and banter and challenge that was both nerve-racking and exhilarating.

Jacques would criticize my draft papers and discuss my sometimes rather naive ideas paternalistically (but not too obviously patronizingly) and on many occasions gave me opportunities to present my work under the aura of his blessing. He was sufficiently older and more obviously successful than me for it to be possible to accept his rather authoritarian manner—expressed with a sort of modest insistence that only someone who was supremely self-confident could afford to adopt—without irritation. But he was *almost* my contemporary and we were, for a time at least, in principle, rivals in the field of enzyme adaptation and I could not suppress a certain degree of envy of his superior intellect and the ease with which he could command attention in debate. It nearly always seemed I was trailing behind as, indeed, I was.

He was equally helpful in ordinary day-to-day affairs such as finding living accommodations for our family and advising about schools for the children and would put himself to some trouble in order to smooth over difficulties.

When I was living in Paris, Jacques, Odette, and their two sons were still occupying the rue M. le Prince apartment, a somewhat dilapidated place with a delightful atmosphere of the early nineteenth century. I still remember my deep regret when he finally left for a rather larger home near the Eiffel tower. Nothing ever seemed quite the same after he had moved to this new ("horribly bourgeois") abode on the avenue de la Bourdonnais which may have symbolized his worldly success but seemed to rob him of the romantic charm that emanated from "M. le Prince."

"It's terrible, Martin, when you have to stop being a 'bright and promising young scientist.' It happened quite a long time ago for me; but you yourself are just on the brink."

We often discussed our individual problems together at that time, mainly in a scientific context. We were both ambitious; that made us very egocentric (though I think Jacques concealed it better than I did). I had to admit that I found my own character very difficult to deal with. Nothing ever seemed easy: there were so many temptations. Yet there were some "innocents" who so rarely seemed to suffer from them.

"And you, Martin, have *all* the temptations. . . ." And so it seemed.

"And you, Jacques?"

"I'm *certainly* no innocent!" He spoke vehemently, without the slightest hesitation.

When I pressed him further about his ambitions and (rather wistfully) admitted that I envied him his successes, he emphatically pointed out that they were due to the tremendous effort he had put into his work; they had been achieved only at the expense of "great sacrifices" and immense struggles.

He would understand only too well how I suffered by feeling I was not successful or clever enough and he would rather condescendingly tell how in his childhood home persons were never judged by cleverness or success, but by their charm and character. I only once visited his home in Cannes and met his courteous and cultured parents; but even from so brief a contact I could well appreciate how his early background of gentle good taste could have played an important part in the expression of his artistic and somewhat indirect approach to scientific problems and the originality he introduced into the development of molecular biology. But it had not apparently curbed the appetite of his ambitions! One such ambition was certainly his desire to exert influence. . . When, very much later on, he was discussing the possibility of accepting the position of director of the Pasteur Institute, one of his main arguments in favor was his ability, so he explained to me, in committees, to persuade others toward his own point of view. He may have been attracted by the vision of power such an appointment would provide; but it was not perhaps so much just power for its own sake; it was more important for him to feel that he would have an opportunity to put his own ideas into practice because he believed so firmly that they were right.

Jacques was an *aristocrat*, in the original, literal meaning of the word. He had extremely high standards in many respects and on the whole lived up to them. I remember challenging him once, on the spur of the moment, when we were walking up some great broad stone steps on an island (I think Isola Bella) in Lago Maggiore during the Pallanza symposium of 1952.

"Do you feel, Jacques, that you are alone in the world? That the world consists in a way of *you* (on the one hand) and all the rest of humanity on the other?"

I meant to imply that basically he felt himself superior to, or at least better qualified than, most others. Looking (or pretending to be) rather self-consciously embarrassed, he agreed at once, with almost shattering candor. I was fascinated and even a trifle shocked.

I am sure he adored the idea of being a "Father to his People." Indeed, I believe this gave him a sense of responsibility which he took very seriously.

"Alors, mes enfants, comment ça va?" He would stroll in through the door of the laboratory where Annamaria Torriani and I were trying to interpret some recent results, beaming with a benevolent conviction that he would be able to make sense of the mess he half-liked to suppose we were creating. And, indeed, he would sometimes succeed. One of his favorite occupations was, in fact, the interpretation or re-interpretation of other people's research in a more significant fashion that he supposed they could do, or had done, themselves. And it must be admitted that he was rather good at it although it was not an offering that was always happily accepted by those concerned! I used to challenge him about this, too. He would accept a little gentle tease, but one had to be terribly careful. Although he certainly did not lack a sense of humor, I never attempted a real "leg-pull" because I did not believe he would have taken it. The cartoon I finally plucked up courage to pin up on his door at the laboratory (see paper 9) was an indication of what I was pretending to feel about him and his work at that time. He took no offense and, according to Mel Cohn, was actually quite pleased.

The immediate world for Jacques was Jacques and his "équipe": his circle of "pupils" and admirers. It applied mainly, of course, to science, but it extended in many directions: to groups he would take for climbing expeditions at Fontainebleau or to the crew on his yacht.

Warmly generous in so many ways to his friends and colleagues, he was often harsh in his assessment of their scientific abilities. So many of them were "charming," "delightful," or "attractive" but (alas!) "rather *stupid!*" But I soon discovered that his judgment was too frequently influenced by the extent to which their work and opinions conformed with, or supported, his own ideas. There were times when I began to think that the only person who constantly and consistently enjoyed Jacques' favor was Max Delbruck, in whom I am sure he recognized someone with talents *almost* as great as his own! By extrapolation from some of the remarks he made to me about some pretty able individuals, I shuddered to think what he thought of me'—at least as a scientist. One very upsetting incident will, indeed, indicate how he must have felt. It concerns the time when I was fortunate enough to be elected into the Royal Society and have the added pleasure of receiving the traditional polite letters of congratulation from friends and colleagues. I was under no illusion, even during the initial euphoria, that this could have been anything other than a pretty borderline case (if not quite unjustified). A word from Jacques would have been appreciated probably more than from anyone else. When nothing came I could pretend to myself for a while that there was no reason why he should have heard about it. But the truth was far worse. Later on in the same year (1962), during a small meeting of "Pasteuriens" I attended in Paris, someone asked Jacques if he knew about the election of his old friend and "pupil," to which Jacques answered quite openly to the group; "Oh, yes: it was a mistake. . ." I rapidly and emphatically endorsed his opinion before any possible embarrassment could permeate and everyone cooperated by changing the subject. Somehow or other I did not feel at the time so upset as I have been, on occasions, looking back of that rather shattering experience. It was shattering, however not so much because of what Jacques may have thought about my FRS. I really would not have been much put out if I had heard privately about his real opinion; I was becoming inured to his severe judgments and anyway I truly supposed that it *was* a mistake—at least in the sense that there were plenty of better people at that time who merited election more surely than myself. But expressing himself so openly in my presence seemed to indicate that he did not care for me enough to consider my feelings in the slightest degree. It was—and still is— a most puzzling affair because I cannot understand what conceivable purpose it was intended to serve. Did he truly wish to be so wounding? That is *not*, perhaps, entirely impossible.

There were other times when he could be atrociously insensitive to people's needs or feelings. There were several stories, often quoted. I myself remember noticing a curious habit he had of choosing French or English for conversation (he was completely bilingual) frequently according to what was the *least* convenient for the person he was talking to, even in a straight tete-à-tete discussion. Was this simply a blind lack of consideration or refusal to recognize what language he was using, or the other person's needs? Or was it some curious streak of perversity in his nature?

Somewhat analogous was the story (possibly apocryphal: I cannot relate it from first hand experience) of how Jacques, at the end of his day's work in the laboratory, would shut up the place, turn off the lights and apparatus that did not run through the night and go home, regardless of whether anyone else was still working there! For *him* the day had ended and that meant the end of the *day*.

Yet all through there was his gentle courtesy, his desire to enlighten and set people on the "right" path and his genuine concern for the welfare of those around him. He would take great pains to expound his ideas simply and clearly. Perhaps the most impressive of his qualities was his ability to *illuminate:* to interpret a puzzling situation so that everything seemed suddenly to fall into place and become comprehensible. This was due almost as much to the force of his personality as to his penetrating intellect. The same words from someone else would have had much less impact. Small wonder he inspired respect, admiration, and even devotion as well as exasperation.

I have dwelt previously on his intellectual domination and the way that his need to demonstrate this could weaken the self-confidence of those around him who could not easily face open confrontation. It can well be argued that this partial suffocation of lesser minds was a small price to pay for the great gifts that Jacques bestowed on the development of molecular biology and the clari-

fying vision he could offer to biologists generally. But why should it be necessary to pay such a price? It was certainly a personal problem for many of us who
worked under the glare of his exceptional mind. A genuine sense of the privilege
of being associated with him was sometimes tarnished by a feeling of being help-
lessly unappreciated—even in areas where there was some reason to believe a real
contribution had been made to a problem. And I suspect that this may have
been due partly because he could seriously underestimate the quality of work
done outside his "entourage." Like all scientists, however great, he must have
often drawn heavily, if unconsciously, from the work and ideas of others, but
he was not always perhaps fair in the manner or context in which he attributed his sources of inspiration.

I was myself so fearful of being intellectually swamped that I tended sometimes to become pettily unreasonable in my opposition to his ideas and stu-
pidly reluctant to benefit from his advice.

I remember, for instance, arguing fiercely against a "letter to Nature" on the
"Terminology of Enzyme Formation" that he drafted on behalf of the five
main workers on what was then called "Enzyme Adaptation." Jacques' and Mel
Cohn's work on β-galactosidase formation had shown that inducers need not be
enzyme substrates, and the teleological implications of the word "adaptation" so
irked Jacques that he could no longer bear the idea of it being used in this context. I argued against the dogmatic presentation of the opinions of a self-
appointed clique; I lamented the loss of the element of specificity (which
seemed critical) in the word "adaptation" and I cited the realm of immunology
where a teleogically useless or dangerous immune reaction did not seem necessarily to have implied that the phenomenon in general should not be regarded
as essentially *adaptive*. There is, here, incidentally, an interesting hint of Jacques'
philosophical distress engendered by the element of *purpose* supposedly contained in the concept of "adaptation," which emerged so powerfully in his
Chance and Necessity; but surely the idea of biological adaptation, in its evolutionary context, could be quite satisfactorily sustained without necessarily
implying any sort of grand design or purpose.

When I refused to sign, pointing out that the "edict" would be just as influential without my name to it, as long as it contained Jacques', Jacques resorted to
(subtly flattering) blackmail by threatening that in that case it would not be
sent for publication at all. I was thereupon told by another member of the
"Cabal" that I was being "purely obstructive" and I weakly submitted. Jacques
knew exactly how to get his own way!

It is rather ironic to note that (a) only five years later Jacques was putting
quotation marks around the word "inducibility" (the introduction of which had
been the essence of our letter) in the title of his famous paper, with Pardee and
Jacob, on β-galactosidase repression in inducible strains of *E. coli*, though I maintain that this was quite unnecessary even from his point of view; and (b) the

suggestion, in our letter, that what Stanier had previously referred to as "simultaneous" induction/adaptation was, after all, in some cases and with respect to the action of the inducer itself, truly simultaneous!

Another illustration of Jacques' need to dominate the whole field of enzyme induction (and *my* need to feel at least *slightly* independent!) concerned the first review I wrote on the subject (1958). I asked Jacques for, and was generously provided with, details of his recent unpublished findings and was also sent a copy of his (unpublished) Jessup lectures which I quoted where appropriate. But I did not send him a draft of my article until after it had been sent to press, i.e., too late for the major modifications which I feared he would insist upon and which it would have been difficult to refuse without offending him, or so I thought. However I did not succeed in escaping his annoyance for he wrote back protesting, perhaps understandably, in no uncertain terms and I had to explain frankly why I had not brought him in at an earlier stage. I was convinced that he needed to be involved more than just to check the few points where I had quoted his unpublished results; there would anyway have been no difficulty in correcting details of fact had I unwittingly misquoted any of his own findings.

It was mainly during 1952-1953, in close association with Jacques at the Pasteur Institute, that I was able to look behind the scenes and become involved in some of the scientific problems of enzyme induction as they were being studied in Jacques' group in the early days before the Great Enlightenment. It was the time of the Pz* red herring and the protein turnover controversy. I got into immediate trouble by not giving enough prominence to the Pz/Gz* relationship in my paper at a symposium organized by Jacques at the International Biochemistry Congress in Paris, 1952. Then again, Jacques had been mainly responsible for showing (in conflict with Schönheimer's principle of the dynamic flux of protein breakdown and resynthesis in living tissues) that in exponentially growing *E. coli* there was negligible protein breakdown. But he seemed to be far too rigid in assuming this must be true for all bacterial species, to the extent of almost discarding the work done by those who found otherwise, e.g. in *B. cereus* where protein breakdown does occur to a small, but significant extent even in logarithmically growing cultures.

Analogous again to this was his reluctance to appreciate the significance of the so-called "basal enzyme" (the level of specific enzyme activity found in uninduced inducible strains of microorganisms) as being a vital clue to the induction mechanism. Jacques had worked almost exclusively with *E. coli* β-galactosidase where basal enzyme was so low in the commonly used wild type that it *could,* in principle, have been explained (as he was always emphasizing) by the few constitutive mutants that were known to be present. My own ex-

---

*Pz was a protein in *E. coli* devoid of known enzymatic activity that was closely related to β-galactosidase (referred to then as "Gz") immunologically and (apparently) metabolically.

perience was founded on tetrathionate and nitrate reductase and penicillin β-lactamase where basal enzyme was far too high to be explained in this way. It was thus reasonable to suppose at the time that basal enzyme should be an important clue, whereas Jacques, somewhat fixed on β-galactosidase, remained relatively uninterested.

In 1953 there were two formal possibilities for explaining basal enzyme: the presence in small amounts of an endogenous inducer or the existence, before induction, of the necessary genetic information for producing the enzyme *without* an inducer. It seemed more difficult, especially in the penicillinase system, to postulate the formation of a penicillinlike substance spontaneously in *B. cereus* than to suppose that *E. coli* might be producing small quantities of a lactoselike molecule. I was thus naturally forced to consider seriously the hypothesis of preinduction information which directly implied that induction was due to the relief of some endogenous inhibition mechanism. I discussed the idea of looking for an inhibitor of enzyme formation that might be present in inducible strains. Jacques agreed at once that this was a formal possibility, but was obviously not very impressed with it. When I returned home I did a number of experiments using the *B. cereus* penicillinase system. These mainly consisted of preparing crushed cell extracts of the uninduced inducible strain 569 to see if they caused any inhibition of induction by penicillin in this strain, or of penicillinase formation in constitutive mutants. The results, of course, were totally negative and I soon lost heart. With hindsight it is easy to see why they failed. But of course their failure did not mean the hypothesis of relief from inhibition was incorrect, and I was finally led to conclude that it was the most probable explanation by more theoretical arguments. That, however, was not until 1957 when, ironically enough and unknown to me, Jacques and colleagues were hard at work with definitive experimental evidence.

So, in a way, I was right, but little credit is due because the idea at the time was only one of many possible hypotheses and I never pursued it with any determination. It is relatively easy to have a good idea; the real genius is to know how and when to follow it up with sufficient persistence to make something of it. Jacques and his group drove through with proper evidence to a final proof by using, with François Jacob, the genetics that he had long previously (in 1948) told me would be the way-in for solving the problem of "enzyme adaptation." But he never referred to our earlier discussions when he acknowledged Leo Szilard's suggestions on the repressor hypothesis later on; perhaps he had forgotten.

There is an obvious enough moral in that story which applies to most research workers!

Jacques had plenty of wrong ideas, like the rest of us, along with good ones. His talents lay particularly in his ability to feel his way through the intricate maze of encouraging/discouraging and indicative/misleading evidence to the right solution.

But there was powerful logic there too, as well as intuitive inspiration. For instance, it was during those 1952-1953 days of the "Belle Époque" at the Pasteur Institute which I am mainly writing about that Jacques conceived the absolute necessity—and feasibility (using Mel Cohn's immunological expertise)—of showing whether or not induced enzyme formation really corresponded to *de novo* biosynthesis of the enzyme protein itself. He argued, with inflexible logic and persistence, that all our molecular hypotheses about enzyme adaptation would continue to be a waste of time until we knew what molecular event we were measuring. This was strictly analogous to the need, ten years earlier, to know whether "enzyme adaptation" was a populational or cellular phenomenon. With hindsight, this seems obvious enough; but it was not so clear at the time. So, with Dave Hogness's and Mel Cohn's brilliant technology and excited enthusiasm, backed by the "Master's" encouragement and blessing, the famous piece of work on β-galactosidase was carried out with complete success and an unequivocal answer.

Against this background (with all its ups and downs, including a long frustrating period when it was not even possible to assay the enzyme properly because chromic acid from the cleaning fluid was unsuspectedly contaminating the pipettes) Annamaria Torriani and I were attempting to isolate the *B. cereus* induced penicillinase by "straight" biochemical methods. Being largely extracellular, this enzyme was "ahead" of β-galactosidase as a candidate for purification and we had Jacques' enthusiastic support, no doubt partly because he understandably enjoyed the idea of the work at least being *started* in his laboratory. When, finally, this work was completed to give a firm figure for the molecular activity of the enzyme, it was Jacques who argued that its main importance was to show that the inducer must act *catalytically,* since it could be calculated that there were at least 40 molecules of the enzyme formed on the average per cell for each molecule of penicillin fixed by the cells under conditions where no external inducer was present in the medium. This, he pointed out, formally disposed of the hypothesis that the inducer acted stoichiometrically by becoming itself part of the enzyme molecule. It was, I think, the only credit he ever bestowed on the *B. cereus* penicillinase system as an exclusive contribution to the understanding of enzyme induction. Ironically, pleased though I was with the "Master's" favor, I did not consider this to be of such critical importance because the "stoichiometric" hypothesis had never struck me as at all likely. But if Jacques was not directly responsible for the first purification of an inducible enzyme, he could at least be responsible for having interpreted its significance in the study of induction! But, alas, I do not think it *was* very important in that connection because it was off the main stream of evidence that finally led to a solution. The significance was really rather limited and I think also Jacques privately considered it so. The "bouquet" he bestowed was for a piece of work not important enough to worry him unduly. But perhaps it seems a little cynical to suggest that had it been of really crucial importance, he would have found it much more difficult to acknowledge its value.

We had Jacques' encouragement for that work but, to be fair, we really owed more—at least at the practical level—to Mel Cohn. It was Mel who finally spurred me on to undertake what I felt would be a very difficult task (there were no simple well-worked out techniques for protein purification available in those days) by actually starting to do some work on it himself, explaining that it was about time "to make that enzyme *talk*." That was enough to get me going, with the technical knowledge and infectious vigor of Mel behind me and with his ability to plunge into a practical problem in biochemistry and throw it about until it showed some response.

Other features of our meanderings during those early days—four or five years before the great clarifying discoveries of 1958 *et seq.*—were not so clear cut as the demonstration that enzyme induction was truly a *de novo* synthesis of specific protein from amino acids. The mechanisms by which this biosynthesis was switched on and off were as obscure to Jacques as to the rest of us. We talked about the "métabolisme des inducteurs" which was embodied in the hypothesis of an "organizer," formed as a result of inducer metabolism, that catalyzed enzyme production. Induction kinetics were not as simple as they seemed, even after Jacques' clarifying application of an "allometric plot" ($\Delta Z/\Delta B$) expressing increase in enzymatic activity against increase in cell mass instead of against time. This "trick" disclosed, in the case of β-galactosidase, a constant differential rate of enzyme production from the moment inducer was added, *provided that* induction conditions were "gratuitous" (i.e. not limited by metabolic dependence on the inducer itself). The apparent autocatalytic induction kinetics that supported the former "plasmagene" (self-replicating) hypothesis were thus shown to be totally misleading.

But *B. cereus* penicillinase induction kinetics were quite different from those of *E. coli* β-galactosidase. Their main feature was a prolonged lag phase of about 14 minutes after addition of penicillin before a steady rate of enzyme formation was established. And I fondly hoped that this lag would provide an important clue as to what was happening to the inducer (how the so-called "organizer" was formed or activated) in the cells before maximal induction was attained. To Jacques this lag was at variance with the $\Delta Z/\Delta B$ dogma and was considered rather "bizarre." This convenient word seemed to carry a slight implication of being more than just "odd": instead of the hope that it might be of positive value, it was rather something that had to be explained away. I looked at all those straight lines of the β-galactosidase $\Delta Z/\Delta B$ plot going through the origin so beautifully with mixed feelings. Then one day it was pointed out to me that they were just a *bit* selected. There were almost as many experiments giving plots showing a distinct lag corresponding to two or three minutes: small, but possibly significant. However, not much attention was paid to them; they did not conform. I was encouraged to think that perhaps after all the two systems did not differ so much; the lag might be universal and highly significant. But there was a double irony here because when, many years later, the mechanism of induction was more or less completely elucidated, the lag came into its own again as reflecting the short interval between initiation of transcription (corresponding to the onset of derepression) and termination of translation for the first molecule of β-galactosidase and its release from ribosomes. That allometric plot did not quite go through the origin after all and those curves showing a slight lag developed an enhanced prestige. But the penicillinase induction lag is still unsolved and it seems unlikely that it is due to the transcription–translation interval that apparently operates for β-galactosidase. It *is* perhaps a bizarre irrelevancy after all.

There is a third ironic curiosity arising from this problem: namely, the little known phase in Jacques' pilgrimage toward the true explanation of enzyme induction when, for a short period, he seemed to have abandoned the lesson of the allometric plot (at least in its simplest form) and began to believe that some sort of autocatalytic process contributed to induction after all. I do not believe these ideas of his were ever published and unfortunately I cannot remember the supposed evidence or his arguments; they were abandoned anyway soon afterward. But they had an unfortunate aftermath, of no general significance, but personally a little upsetting. Annamaria and I had set our hearts on exploiting the long lag phenomenon in pencillinase induction. We felt that it could provide some useful information and we started studying the differential effect of irradiation with ultraviolet light applied before, during, and after the lag period. Differences in sensitivity (as measured by rates of enzyme formation) were indeed found and we were hopeful of trying to interpret them in terms of nucleic acid metabolism. Perhaps rather lazily, I left my colleague with the task of finalizing some of the experiments and of preparing the first draft (which of course had to be in French) after I had left Paris. When the draft arrived, it worried me by the extent to which Annamaria had, in my opinion, been overinfluenced by Jacques' "autocatalytic" ideas to which I was very much opposed. So I decided, rather churlishly perhaps, that I could not add my name to hers on the paper; it would be better for her to go ahead and publish the work in her own way without me. However, when the final version eventually appeared it was very different. Jacques' "autocatalytic" phase was over, the paper had been considerably modified and became something altogether more acceptable. There were times when Jacques' opinions were almost whims; but they were always very influential!

Following the 1958 breakthrough I began to see less and less of Jacques. I think I must have become (for *him*) a bit of an irrelevancy, at least from the scientific point of view. He must have thought that the *B. cereus* induction system was no longer of any interest (if it ever had been) because the organism had no studiable genetics. It was difficult to persuade him to spend much time discussing these problems, let alone to come over to London (worse still, Edinburgh, where I had moved in 1965) to give a seminar; it would have been a waste of his time. But he was obviously delighted when Bill Hayes and I asked him to come over to inaugurate our new department of molecular biology in 1968. He loved the sort of "official importance" of such an occasion and the opportunity it gave him of bestowing his blessing on us all.

The last time I saw him was when he gave me a very private lunch at his home in Paris toward the end of 1974. I felt it truly an honor. He was as gently charming as ever and I longed to discuss everything under the sun with him as I always wanted to do—science, politics, philosophy, personal problems. But conversation did not run so smoothly; he was very preoccupied with his responsibilities as director of the Pasteur Institute which was in great difficulties. I had the sensation that what I said and how I felt were not of much interest to him. Indeed, why *should* they be?

Like so many others, I feel immensely privileged to have known Jacques Monod as I did, especially over a revolutionary period of absolutely fundamental developments in biology, to which he himself contributed so much. It could, at times, be painful, frequently personally disappointing, and occasionally it was quite exasperating. But I would not have missed it for anything.

IN MEMORIAM *

Melvin Cohn

"Did I take on that awesome gift when death parted my limp form
from his protective clasp?"

Mechkonin

The organizers of this symposium have asked me to trace in a personal way the
contributions of Jacques Monod to the origins of our present concept of induced
enzyme synthesis. I have chosen to deal with the Monod of the preoperon era of
induced enzymes because it is a largely unknown chapter which is particularly
illustrative of his creativity. This is appropriate because, in the last years of his
life, Monod was intensely preoccupied with the creative process. He set the
study of it as one of the goals of the Salk Institute which he helped found. In
Jacques Monod, this process was characterized by taste, elegance, and parsimony.

*The first part of this article is reprinted from the 1976 Cold Spring Harbor proceedings
on "Lactose."

75

Monod in writing his own rather personalized curriculum vitae begins by saying:

> I was born in 1910 in Paris but in 1917 my parents moved to the south of France where I spent my youth. Consequently I consider myself more of a southerner than a Parisian. My father was a painter, a vocation rare in a Hugenot family dominated by doctors, pastors, civil servants, and teachers. My mother was American, of Scotch descent, born in Milwaukee; another anomaly when one considers the mores of the French bourgeoisie at the end of the last century. I came to Paris in 1928 to begin my studies in the *Faculté des Sciences.*

Monod then recalls his debt to his teachers, André Lwoff, Boris Ephrussi, and Louis Rapkine. He tells us that in 1934 he was a Fellow of the Rockefeller Foundation at Caltech working with Thomas Hunt Morgan. In 1936 he returned to France soon to be faced with the Second World War—terrible years which he never mentions, leaving it as a blank in his curriculum vitae—during which time he was in the French underground. After the liberation, in 1945, Monod joined André Lwoff's laboratory at the Pasteur Institute.

I met Monod in 1947 at a Cold Spring Harbor Symposium. He presented a paper entitled "The Phenomenon of Enzymatic Adaptation and Its Bearings on Cellular Differentiation." He made the explicit point in his talk that we would have to understand enzymatic adaptation before we could understand differentiation, in particular antibody synthesis. This allusion plus the enthusiastic support of my teacher, Alvin Pappenheimer, Jr., is what sent me packing for Paris.

In the winter of 1948 I began my postdoctoral work at the Pasteur Institute in Paris. We were housed in an attic; at one end was André Lwoff's closed laboratory, on the door of which was a cartoon showing the Duke of Wellington addressing his officers after the battle of Waterloo under which was the caption "Tea cleared my head and left me with no misapprehensions." At the other end of the attic was the laboratory which Jacques Monod, Annamaria Torriani, and I occupied. That year the Paris winter without heat was merciless. The glacial acetic acid remained frozen on the shelf until noon at which time I had the distinct feeling that it was the heated discussion at the lunch table that thawed it out. Jacques was a choir master and during a good deal of that winter spent afternoons rehearsing the Bach Requiem he was to conduct that Christmas. Sundays we practiced rock climbing at Fontainebleau. There were many things to decide about the direction of the work but we simply could not settle down to any problem.

The most important preoccupation was that Monod who symbolized reactionary Mendel-Morgan genetics, came specifically under vitriolic attack by French Marxist biologists who looked upon the very existence of adaptive enzymes as proof that the substrate induced a directed mutation or a permanent hereditary modification in the cell. This position had a certain respectability since Sir Cyril Hinshelwood was defending the same point. Even J. B. S. Haldane felt constrained to write only apologetic essays in defense of genetics. We spent one Thursday evening of every month at the meeting of the Michurin-Lysenko Society, at the Sorbonne, superficially debating the facts of genetics but in reality what concerned us was the meaning of the scientific method. For Jacques Monod, who was *"engagé"* in the Sartre sense, the debates were ugly and degrading and they stomped on his sense of elegance and parsimony. He was moved to make his life's goal a crusade against antiscientific, religious metaphysics whether it be from Church or State. The last time we strolled together on the beach at Torrey Pines, in 1974, he was bitter. "The battle against such ignorance will never be won," he said. "All that one can do is die without calling a priest to the bedside."

In the spring of 1949, we settled down to work. I remember that I felt like "Alice in Wonderland" when Monod identified three key characteristics of adaptive enzymes for study.

1. The response to a given substrate was specific for that substrate, i.e., the phenomenon was adaptive. The consequences of the existence of systems which paradoxically seem to have a purpose yet arise blindly by variation and selection was a constant theme in his thinking culminating in his book *Chance and Necessity*.

2. The ability to metabolize a new substrate appeared as an autocatalytic function of time. This had led to the "plasmagene" hypothesis of Spiegelman in which a gene produced a cytoplasmic self-replicating unit which in turn synthesized the adaptive enzyme.

3. Substrates competed for each other in the induction of given enzymes. This was the striking "diauxie" phenomenon where an organism faced with two growth substrates metabolized one or the other preferentially. Today we call this *catabolite repression*. There was competition between substrates for the attention of the cell. For Monod, this implied competition for precursor subunit molecules.

Given what we now know, it seems remarkable that these three facts could have provided a solid basis for us to begin because they were so misleading. Yet Monod singled them out as he brought exquisite taste to bear on complexity. Today we know that of all the misleading truths at the time only these three could have led to the creation of the modern field of regulatory biology.

The Monod concept to explain these three facts was the following: A group of genes coded for a pool of precursor subunits could be complemented in various combinations to make different enzymes. It was the directive influence of the substrate which caused an aggregation of some of the subunits to make the corresponding enzyme. Once seeded, the crystallization process was autocatalytic. If two substrates were involved there was competition for subunits. In other words, a large number of induced enzymes could be constructed from combinations of a small number of subunits which preexisted the appearance of the substrate in the milieu.

The way to test this hypothesis was to show that all substrates as well as competitive inhibitors were inducers. The hypothesis limited the choice of systems for study. *Escherichia coli* had ideal growth properties, as well as an emerging genetics analyzable by mating and viral transduction. It expressed an adaptive enzyme, β-galactosidase which had a substrate, analogues of which were reasonably easy to synthesize. In 1950 I went to Bell's laboratory in Cambridge, England, and later to Helferich's laboratory in Bonn, Germany, to make the compounds which were sent back to Paris to test. By 1951, four findings changed our entire perspective.

1. Excellent substrates were *not* necessarily inducers, e.g. orthonitrophenyl-β-D-galactoside.
2. Excellent nonmetabolizable competitive inhibitors were *not* inducers, e.g. phenyl-β-D-thiogalactoside.
3. Poor nonmetabolizable competitive inhibitors could be excellent inducers, e.g. methyl- or isopropyl-β-D-thiogalactosides.
4. Noncompetitive inhibitors could be excellent inducers, e.g. the α-galactoside, melibiose.

The realization that his hypothesis was false had already crossed Monod's mind, when on Oct. 14, 1950 he sent a telegram to me in England (Fig. 1) concerning phenyl-β-D-thiogalactoside which I had last given him to test.

I include this telegram to illustrate the pleasure which Jacques Monod derived in proving that his favorite idea was wrong; "FANTASTIQUE" was the exact word. He was one of Karl Popper's greatest admirers and, like Popper, he insisted that scientific advance consisted in the falsification of hypotheses. I wish now that I would have realized that the Monod hypothesis on subunit complementation which proved wrong for induced enzymes was later to prove correct for induced antibodies.

The existence of nonsubstrate inducers had a profound philosophical impact for, like Ionesco, Monod had created a theatre of the absurd. A bacterium growing on succinate was producing a useless enzyme, β-galactosidase, in response to a substance it could not metabolize. Monod, with great humor, invented the renowned Scottish philosopher McGregor (his mother's maiden name), whom he quoted in all of his later writings. This time he attributed to McGregor the following quote: "Each of science's conquests is a victory of the absurd." The vitalist Hinshelwood-Michurin-Lysenko position which irked him had been answered with experimental vengence. For this reason he decided to

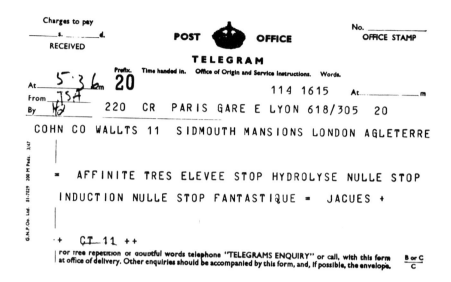

Fig. 1. Very high affinity stop hydrolysis negligible stop induction negligible stop fantastic = Jacques.

drop the term "enzymatic adaptation" and use instead "induced enzyme synthesis," a term which was adopted eventually in an encyclical (*Nature* 172, 1096-1098, 1953) issued by the Adaptive Enzyme's College of Cardinals, Monod, Pollock, Spiegelman, and Stanier.

These four findings provoked Monod to toy with an idea which was very daring for 1951. The inducer had to be recognized by a stereochemically specific molecule which was *not* the induced enzyme itself. However, this idea left unexplained the autocatalytic nature of the response to lactose, a fact which now pointed strongly to a self-replicating gene product, the "plasmagene," postulated by Spiegelman.

In 1951, Seymour Benzer, François Jacob, and Elie Wollman (returning from sabbatical leave) joined the laboratory. Jacob and Wollman viewed adaptive enzymes with great suspicion and by exploring elsewhere paved the way for the era of the operon. It was only in 1953 when Max Delbruck visited Paris and demanded accountability that the suspicion was diffused and our endeavors became respectable. Seymour Benzer on the other hand, nettled by Stanier's published statement that it could never be done, decided to tackle the question of the cause of the S-shaped autocatalytic induction curve. Using Monod and Wollman's finding that certain *E. coli* bacteriophages could block enzyme induced by lactose as the sole carbon source under conditions where only cells which contained enzyme could be lysed. It became obvious that the S-shaped curve was due to the heterogeneity of response of individuals in the population. A bacterium with one molecule of enzyme could metabolize lactose to make more enzyme and therefore had a great advantage. In other words, the postulated *E. coli* "plasmagene" turned out to be the bacterium itself. For Monod, the second paradox was resolved.

From these studies Monod now developed the concept of *gratutitous induction*. Under conditions where thè carbon source and the inducer were separated, the heterogeneity and the S-shaped induction kinetics disappeared.

At this point Monod was ready to face his third basic fact, the competition between substrates. This implied competition for precursors which had led him to the subunit hypothesis that preformed subunits were shared between different enzymes. It became inescapable that he know whether the enzyme was made *de novo* after induction, or from preformed precursor subunits.

The answer required an isotope experiment in a laboratory that had never seen even the shadow of a Geiger counter. Fortunately Monod captured the interest of a Canadian physicist, Lou Siminovitch, who had been working with Louis Rapkine and André Lwoff since 1947. Siminovitch had discovered ^{35}S and proposed its use as a general protein marker. Siminovitch scrounged through the physics laboratories of Paris collecting junked parts which he checked off on his scribbled wiring diagram. He handed the precious do-it-yourself kit to Monod who, like a child with a tinker toy, put it together and made it work. At the Christmas party that year I joshed Jacques in a skit which cast him as a bicycle repairman (*réparateur de vélos*).

David Hogness now in the laboratory began the experiment which required purification of very small amounts of β-galactosidase to greater than 95% purity. The only way to do this at the time was by immunologic methods. Six months later, Dave Hogness completed the definitive experiment nervously counting each point on the tinker toy through the night, while Monod played his cello and I uncorked André Lwoff's best properly chilled Sancerre wine which he had carefully hidden in the cold room.

The result was clear. The enzyme was made fron amino acids *de novo* after induction, at a maximum rate, virtually without lag.

This led Monod to formulate a new parameter which we christened as Monod's Law, symbolized by $\Delta Z/\Delta B$ (the differential rate of synthesis), the basic unit of which was physiological time.

With hindsight it is easy to appreciate taste in science. The three most important characteristics of induced enzyme synthesis formulated in 1949, misleading as they were, had led by 1953 to a clear definition of the problem and Monod was prepared to pursue it, virtually alone.

However, why we were so insufferably sure of ourselves is not clear to me.

Given what we know today one might say that we had not advanced very far. Justifiably annoyed by our arrogance, Martin Pollock produced a cartoon in 1953 (Fig. 2) which at the time was upsetting to me but brought pleasure to Monod.

Pollock's cartoon shows Monod standing over a starry eyed American (myself) symbolized by an outlandish tie, to whom he is saying "Bravo my fine fellow! You have made remarkable observations—naturally without having done or understood anything—but nevertheless spectacular. Bravo! Continue the good work."

In the wastepaper basket are the papers of Pollock on penicillinase; on the wall is a depiction of "Who killed cock robin (Sir Cyril Hinshelwood)?;" above that is Max Delbrück smiling approval; next to Max is plotted Monod's temperature as a function of Sol Spiegelman's publications (notice how normal it is after the Benzer experiment); Monod's law $\Delta Z/\Delta B$ is inscribed on the French tricolor behind us; and on the left was Pollock's evaluation of our accomplishments: we had destroyed all existing so-called facts, replacing them with nothing he was willing to believe (*faits confirmés*); and we had produced nothing but wild theories. This is how Pollock saw us in 1953. [He had a personal piece of advice to me which did not escape my notice, symbolized by the mouse in the left corner. Go back to the study of antibody synthesis in mice! In fact long before molecular biology could influence immunology Pollock proposed as the key, the study of the clonal distribution of antibodies (1 cell—1 antibody)].

Today, I understand Monod's reaction of pleasure because such understanding could only have been the consequence of profound friendship.

Just before the modern era of the operon, one striking fact which we had generated had been ignored. With George Cohen and Germaine Stanier, Monod had shown that the end product of a biosynthetic pathway, in this case, tryptophan and methionine, repressed the *synthesis* of the corresponding enzymes on that pathway. Not only was function inhibited as Novick and Szilard had shown, but constitutive enzyme synthesis itself was also repressed by its end product— a remarkable energy saving device.

In his Nobel lecture, Monod muses about this:

> I had learned like any schoolboy that two negatives are equivalent to a positive statement. Mel Cohn and I debated this logical possibility which we called the "theory of double bluff" recalling the subtle analysis of poker by Edgar Allan Poe. How blind I was not to take this hypothesis seriously sooner above all since several years earlier we had discovered that tryptophan inhibits the synthesis of tryptophan synthetase. I had always hoped that the regulation of constitutive and inducible systems would be explained by a similar mechanism. Why not suppose that induction could be effected by an anti-repressor rather than by repression of an anti-inducer? This was precisely the thesis which Leo Szilard proposed to us in a seminar. The preliminary results of the

Figure 2

injection experiment (PaJaMa experiment) confirmed Leo Szilard's penetrating intuition and my doubts about "the theory of double bluff" were removed.

In a parallel world next door to us were Elie Wollman and François Jacob creating the basis for genetic analyses which was soon to merge with induced enzymes to reveal what we know today as "operon theory."

I did not participate in the merger which began in 1956, after I left Paris. This period is modern operon history; the discovery of the permease and trans-acetylase; the PaJaMa experiment; operator constitutive and promoter muta- tions, coordinate induction, polarity, and that remarkable insight "messenger RNA," all part of the 1961 Jacob-Monod Cold Spring Harbor paper. It was another great classic written like Monod's 1947 Cold Spring Harbor paper in that simple and direct Anatole France style. It took only one more concept for- mulated in 1965, that of allosteric interactions, to round out the story of regula- tion at the physiological level.

The key to the power of these Monod theories, 1947, 1961, or 1965, was simply that they were physiological level theories capable of reductionism; that is to say they were capable of an analysis at the level of chemistry. They were truly theories of molecular biology. This was the basis of their elegance and their parsimony.

Monod and I never finished our 1974 discussion on the Torrey Pines Beach. What was the next problem of regulation to be? Monod was concerned with the universality of the elements used in the regulation of the *lac* operon. Was there a limited number of elements which required minor rearrangements or was the number going to be large? Did we have to search for new generalizing rules on how they had to be organized? Were there any new laws which would come from the wiring diagrams, the logic of the circuitry? Were both positive and negative regulation fundamental to the integrated organism or could indi- viduals have been constructed using only one or the other switch?

I believe that Jacques Monod had one of the most creative minds of our time not because he was a leader of righteous causes, not because he was a creator of molecular biology, not because he founded and directed institutes of learning. He had one of the most creative minds simply because he thought deeply, asce- tically, and in a Socratic way about how knowledge is acquired; and it is this process that he insisted should be the only basis for a system of ethical and es- thetic values.

ADDENDUM

André Lwoff asked me to write of "The Great Adventure in Lactose"; yet I have already accomplished that   and now wish to add small vignettes to that story in order to give another dimension to that adventure and to Jacques Monod.*

It was Dr. A. M. Pappenheimer, Jr. who steered me to Paris to work with Jacques Monod. It took one of the great teachers of our times and someone who cared deeply about me to have thought that move out so carefully. I am surprised, still today, at the way in which it turned out.

In 1949, my desk in the laboratory at the Pasteur Institute was too poorly lighted to work in the evenings. I soon learned that the tomb of Pasteur was well lit. Thanks to an understanding *concierge*, the gate to it was left unlocked in the evenings. I spread my papers out using the low tomb as a desk and blissfully studied into the wee hours, smiled upon by garish mosaics depicting Pasteur's great discoveries. Monod surprised me one late evening while he was showing visitors around and found the idea so congenial that we spent many evenings there chatting across the death mask of the Institute's Patron Saint. Imperceptibly we changed from English to French and from *vous* to *tu*. This is how we became friends with a love so deep that often without words we shared the many dramas of our lives.

From these earliest days, in spite of overriding problems, Jacques was preoccupied with the failure of French science and in particular the failure of the Pasteur Institute to have any credibility, much less, world leadership. He decried the mediocrity of the Sorbonne, *Académie des Sciences* and the *Collège de France*. Further, no improvement (as he jealously noted to be taking place in Germany and England) was in sight. His puritanical devotion to this theme throughout his life and his romantic dream about the Pasteur Institute not only was misunderstood and unappreciated, but it ruined much of the creativity he might have expressed in the later years of his life when he became director.

The political climate of the 1950s in the States and the bleakness of postwar Europe, sent many leading intellectuals, poets, writers, painters, sculptors, and scientists to work in Paris. At first it was the darkness of the hour rather than the renown of our laboratory that brought together in the "City of Light" so many outstanding minds. Paris was the world center of creativity. All of us lived in it: in the laboratory, at the lunch table, in the theater, at concerts, in art galleries, in book stores, at the *chansonnier, la cuisine, le salon metaphysique;* we were in the middle of history and politics; we were *les hommes engagés.*

So, Seymour Cohen, Bernard Davis, Michael Doudoroff, Stephen Fazekas, David Hogness, Niels Kjeldgaard, Margaret Lieb, Aaron Novick, A. M. Pappenheimer, Jr., Lou Siminovitch, Roger Stanier, Leo Szilard, and Annamaria

*In the first part of this article which was written for the 1976 Cold Spring Harbor Symposium of 1976 on "Lactose."

Torriani all came from afar, and along with one French student, Germaine Bazire, made up the preoperon era of our laboratory. This was unusual in France; at that time foreigners could not compete with the French for positions in other academic centers. Further, aside from maintenance support from the Pasteur Institute, both public and private American grants supported the laboratory—a "debt" Jacques never forgot.

Michael Doudoroff brought "heart" into our work. Experiments worked when he was around because he cared about experimenters, somehow making the goals and aspirations of others his own.

Together we worked a night shift starting early evening, then going to dinner and resuming in the laboratory toward midnight. Usually we were a bit high after a few bottles of beautiful French wine and our work seemed to sing.

It was late one night that we were carrying our preparation of amylomaltase through its last step of purification, a process that had taken two long months from the moment we grew a kilo of bacteria. We were distinctly drunk, happy, and loquacious.

As we were preparing to centrifuge the precipitate, I hit the beaker on the side of the lab bench and the preparation went all over the floor. I sobered up and became ill. Mike rushed to get a dust pan and large window wiper. He carefully gathered up the liquid, rinsed the floor with buffer, and gathered the rinsings. He reprecipitated the enzyme and recovered it from the floor in 70% yield. I watched in deep depression. He bragged often about the best preparation we had ever made. We never dared tell anyone.

During a short visit to the States, I attended by chance a seminar in New York by the famous Wisconsin biochemist, H. A. Lardy, who described his work on the cation activation of β-galactosidase. He pointed out that the enzyme was Na^+ activated, despite contrary reports by two unnamed French scientists that it was K^+ activated. As I already pointed out, the credibility of French science in the outside world was low. I was too neophyte and upset to dare defend our work.

On hearing my story, Jacques reacted by showing his great sense of proportion and led us to the discovery that both were right (but as he put it, only we had understood it!), for with lactose as a substrate β-galactosidase was K^+ activated, and with orthonitrophenyl-β-D-galactoside as a substrate it was Na^+ activated. This was my first lesson that science was an adversary system and it took Jacques' kind of internal security to cope with it. On numerous occasions, faced with similar situations, this incident has flashed across my mind.

In 1951, I had the theory that an inducible and constitutive enzyme differed only in that the latter was internally induced. So I decided to isolate the internal inducer (obviously a galactoside) from a constitutive β-galactosidase mutant. I

painstakingly grew a kilogram of bacteria, made extracts, and discovered immediately that they contained a potent internal inhibitor (not an inducer). Jacques
said immediately, "Drop it, the finding makes no sense given what we know of
physiology." Stubborn, six months later, I crystallized 10 mg of the inhibitor
and identified it as glucose. This was too embarrassing and I expected an "I told
you so." Instead, I received an admiring comment about my *tour de force* and
a bit of advice, "Once you have gone this far, find out how it works."

The experiments on memory in bacteria were devilishly long. Briefly, if glucose was added five minutes before inducer the enzyme never appeared; five
minutes after inducer and the enzyme was made forever. So, we had two stable
states of a given bacterium growing in a given medium depending on its memory
of the order of addition of glucose and inducer several eons ago.

These experiments required that we dilute the cultures every hour to keep
them growing continuously and Jacques and I took turns sleeping in the laboratory.

I decided one evening to simply set up an automatic system for feeding the
removal of culture. Since I had a liter of culture which I diluted with a liter of
medium every hour, I simply fed in a liter per hour of fresh medium and sy-
phoned off a liter of culture per hour continuously. To my surprise, the bacteria
could not keep up and the density of the culture fell. In fact, to maintain it I
could not feed more than 690 ml/hr. As I was wrestling with this paradox, obviously upset, Jacques sat down with me and asked if I had any idea why I could
not feed more than 690 ml/hr when I expected 1000 ml/hr. "It may sound wild
to you, Jacques, but I think I have discovered that bacteria, like men, have a
biological need for rest." He smiled patiently and said, "You have discovered
that the $\ln 2 = 0.69$. Think about that."

The next day, both he and I had the detailed theory of continuous culture.
However, I had been told the answer and it took the pleasure away.

We named the thing "The Bactogen."

Annamaria Torriani was central to our laboratory. We were an ensemble (at
first a trio) made possible by 'the aristocratic greatness of this woman. She had
been through years of underground activity during the period of Italian fascism,
and with Luigi Gorini was trying to build a new creative life. This extraordinary
duo greatly influenced my life and I loved them.

Annamaria was struck by the mutation lac^- to lac^+. When isopropyl-β-D-
thiogalactoside became available, we knew that both lac^- and lac^+ strains were inducible for β-galactosidase. Further, constitutive strains for β-galactosidase which
were lac^- had been isolated and Annamaria proposed that the mutation affected
a lactose transport system (today called permease) which had to be inducible.

Jacques' reaction surprised me. He insisted that the problem was hopeless if one had to assume that two enzymes were induced coordinately; all of the elegant indirect experiments which Annamaria did could not convince him that her hypothesis was worth considering. Only years later when direct experiments on this transport system became possible did Jacques change his mind in a way which led to the operon theory.

Almost two decades later, at a *sympatique* moment, Jacques slightly drunk, bragged that we had never been wrong. Today, I am wary when such a thought crosses my mind, for I can see how Jacques' memory was totally false. Almost no aspect of the operon theory was formulated correctly the first time: from the confusion of promoters and operators, and the postulate that the repressor was an RNA, to the denial that an operon ever existed.

This was not the important memory for Jacques to have had. What is important was the "the operon theory" came uniquely as a result of correction from within, not from without. It was this self-correction that made Jacques unique.

We strolled on the beach at La Jolla talking about Jacques' desire to become director of the Pasteur Institute. He knew that he could do it better than any other candidate. He felt that he was the only one who could get the loyal support of a scientific staff riddled with a sense of insecurity and inferiority. I tried to talk him out of it because, even successful, his creativity was more important than the revitalization of an institute. In the last year of his life, Jacques came to the realization that he had failed but so had the Pasteur Institute, for he left it as he found it—without leadership in the world.

Jacques tried to convert his failures at home into successes abroad. Everything he wanted for the Pasteur Institute he tried to achieve for the Salk Institute. He played the major role in writing an enlightened set of bylaws which with time and his absence have succumbed to the erosion of expediency. Often at our faculty meetings, he warned us to learn from the mistakes of the Pasteur Institute. Today, without his vigilance, we commit the very mistakes Jacques warned us to avoid. I wonder if such mistakes are inevitable (a sign of the times), or simply that only sages learn from history.

Jacques was far more gifted and creative than most of us who write about him today. His uniqueness came from the rare quality that his internal image of himself was accurate; he knew when he was derivative and when he was original, when he was honest and when he lied, when he used his heart and when he used his head.

To me he revealed, uninhibited, his puritanical accuracy in dealing with himself. He was in constant conflict between internal accuracy and external inaccuracy; and this drove him to leadership and tore him apart. One evening, he summed it up to me, "You can be rational and immoral, or irrational and moral. If I don't resolve this for myself, I will remain in pain either way." He came close in *Le Hasard et La Nécessite.*

PERMEABILITY AS AN EXCUSE TO WRITE
WHAT I FEEL

Georges N. Cohen

I met Jacques for the first time in September 1944. He was still wearing the uniform of a French Army major. We were just emerging from the hellish four years of Nazi occupation. I was totally ignorant of microbiology and, at the age of twenty-four I had but limited laboratory experience: six months at the Laboratory of Animal Physiology at the Sorbonne (1939-1940), a few months in the Laboratory of Pharmacology of the Pharmacy School in Montpellier (1941), about six months in the biochemistry department of the medical school in Marseille (1942), and a year in the Service de Chimie Biologique of the Institut Pasteur (1943-1944), then headed by Michel Macheboeuf—the whole thing interrupted by military service, some weeks of captivity, escape, underground life, marriage, birth of our first child. This, I should hope, conveys my lack of training and my profound need for guidance.

From the very first day, I was attracted by the radiating personality, and the scientific and human qualities of Jacques who rapidly became my mentor. Germaine Cohen-Bazire (the present Dr. Germaine Stanier), who had joined me at the Garches branch of the Institute to work on the mechanism of anaerobic fermentations, and I visited him every time we had a problem.

Very soon, Monod organized informal meetings at which we presented our work, subjecting it to the criticism of all the attendants. Later, I discovered that such seminars were common in the United States, but to my knowledge, this highly commendable habit had not yet been established in France. Germaine and I attended all of these seminars which were held either in a large laboratory of the Service des Fermentations, or in André Lwoff's office.

I had the ardent desire to join Jacques Monod's research team, but the space he was occupying in Lwoff's unit was too exiguous to allow my transfer. My purgatory at Garches lasted until the spring of 1954. However, I was enjoying Jacques' moral support and critical mind; his door was always open and he always listened with extraordinary patience to the report of our experimental results, subjecting them to benevolent but harsh censorship.

Following André Lwoff's suggestion, I spent a few months of 1948 at Oxford, in the Microbiology Unit headed by Donald D. Woods, where I learned the fundamentals of microbial nutrition. Returning to Garches, I became interested in the antagonisms between exogenous amino acids during the growth of *Escherichia coli*, in the hope of using this approach to elucidate certain biosynthetic pathways. During this period, Marie-Louise Hirsch and I observed that the growth of a leucine-requiring mutant of *E. coli* was inhibited by valine or isoleucine, whereas its growth on leucylglycine or glycylleucine was unaffected by the antagonists. I brought the manuscript to Jacques. In the discussion of the paper, one of the hypotheses put forward was the existence of a selective permeation system in *E. coli*, stereospecific for the three branched-chain amino acids. He struck out the corresponding paragraph with a choleric red pencil and told me, "Every time a microbiologist has no clear explanation for a nutritional puzzle, he calls upon permeability to conceal his ignorance." The paper appeared in 1953 with alternative explanations, which turned out to be entirely wrong (*Biochem. J.*, 1953, **53**, 25-29). The irony of fate was that in 1955, in Jacques' laboratory, Howard Rickenberg and I demonstrated the existence of a stereospecific permeation system for the three amino acids, not active on their peptides (*Comptes Rendus*, 1955, **240**, 2086-2088; *Ann. Inst. Pasteur,* 1956, **91**, 693-720). Jacques and I enjoyed telling this misadventure to younger people.

This brings me to my arrival in the Service de Physiologie Microbienne in 1954. Monod had been appointed Chef de Service in 1953, but was still working in Lwoff's laboratory, under the roof of the Institute—the famous attic. When I arrived there, the team consisted of Jacques, Melvin Cohn, David Hogness, Germaine Cohen-Bazire, and Annamaria Torriani. In Lwoff's group were Marguerite Lwoff, Elie Wollman, François Jacob, Dale Kaiser, Cyrus Levinthal, Julius Marmur, and Pierre Schaeffer. According to my recollections, the month of October witnessed the arrival of Bernard Davis, Aaron Novick, and Howard Rickenberg, and the departure of Cohn and Hogness to Saint-Louis, in the Department of Microbiology headed by Arthur Kornberg. It is during those few months between May and October that I discovered what was to be known as the β-galactoside permease.

I had decided to abandon for a while the study of amino acid biosynthetic pathways and to join the research actually done in my new environment. Mel Cohn and Jacques had just discovered the gratuitous induction of β-galactosidase by thiomethylgalactoside (TMG); Melvin had synthesized a small quantity of radioactive TMG. Jacques proposed that I see whether after addition of this labeled material to *E. coli* cultures, the radioactivity could be found linked to one of the cellular macromolecular components: DNA, RNA, or protein. In retrospect, this naive experiment had no chance of succeeding. It required the elaboration of the concept of a specific *lac* repressor by Pardee, Jacob, and Monod to enable Gilbert and Müller-Hill to succeed in answering the question asked by Jacques. However, the experiment brought interesting fringe benefits: the amount of radioactivity that could be found intracellularly was negligible in noninduced cultures, but very high in cultures that had been preinduced by growth in the presence of a galactoside.

In ten days time, I found that the induced "accumulation" of TMG was energy-dependent, reversible, and stereospecific. Internal radioactivity could be displaced by cold TMG and by other thiogalactosides but not by the corresponding glucosides. The material extracted from the cells behaved chromatographically as authentic TMG; if the exposure was prolonged, another spot became increasingly important. I called it TMG-X. A year later, Len Herzenberg (who was to become a renowned immunologist) identified it in our lab to be 6-acetylthiomethylgalactoside, the product of an enzyme also inducible and characterized by Zabin and Kepes as thiogalactoside transacetylase. When I returned from summer vacation, Howard Rickenberg had arrived and Jacques sent the two of us to Helferich's lab in Bonn to learn how to prepare thiogalactosides from 1-bromotetraacetylgalactose and mercaptans. After returning from Germany, we synthesized radioactive ^{35}S-thiomethylgalactoside from 50 millicuries of radioactive methylmercaptan. Since the latter boils at $6°C$, we had to take all sorts of precautions, but we did not contaminate Lwoff's laboratory. Once the ^{35}S-TMG was made, we resumed the work and found that strains constitutive for β-galactosidase were also constitutive for TMG "acceptors," the i^- mutation being pleiotropic. Some strains were devoid of acceptors but could make galactosidase, thus being cryptic. Others could not synthesize galactosidase, but the specific acceptors could be induced. Galactosidase and acceptors were thus independently genetically determined. Howard and I presented our preliminary results in 1955 (*Comptes Rendus. 1955. 240*, 466-68). Monod later joined us and he is responsible for the concept of a catalytic *permease*, as opposed to stoichiometric acceptor sites. Our results had been calculated so far in cpm/dry bacterial weight. Jacques made us recalculate the data in more sensible units; it appeared immediately that the molarity of the TMG incorporated into the cell was very high, reaching 2-4% of the bacterial dry weight. This excluded the hypothesis of a stoichiometric fixation on stereospecific receptors and led us to the concept of a catalytic permease, part of an "active pump" system. We developed this concept in two long papers in French and in a review in English, extending the concept to other small molecules, such as amino acids (*Ann. Inst. Pasteur,* 1956, **91**, 693-720 and 829-857; *Bacteriol. Revs.,* 1957, **21**, 168-194).

In retrospect, I am rather proud of this series of experiments which established the existence of a galactoside permease and laid the grounds for the discovery of thiogalactoside transacetylase. The fact that more than one activity is controlled by the same pleiotropic mutation did in an indirect manner help the development of the operon concept.

In 1955, Monod, Rickenberg, and I went down two stories when the untimely death of Michel Macheboeuf liberated the Service de Biochimie Cellulaire which was renovated thanks to the generosity of Madame Bethsabée de Rothschild, the baroness Edouard de Rothschild, and the Rockefeller Foundation of New York. During the renovation, Jacques was present every day, keeping an eye on the works, watching that all the details were according to his plans. The Service, which I head presently, looks pretty much today like what it became after this remodeling (the first to have taken place since the building construction in 1900). Jean-Marie Dubert, David Perrin, François Gros, Alain Bussard, and later Adam Kepes joined our group. The foreign visitors I remember very vividly in the period 1955-1957 were Leonard Herzenberg, Frederick Neidhardt, Dean Cowie, and Harlyn Halvorson. With the two latter, a strong personal friendship was established and I spent eighteen months in their laboratories during 1957 and 1958.

After that period, I went back to my studies on the regulation of amino acid biosynthesis in collaboration with François Jacob and Earl Stadtman. I earned the nickname of "Saint Georges l'Aminosaure," bestowed upon me by André Lwoff, for my insistence on working on something that was neither DNA, phages, colicins, or β-galactosides. The discoveries we made justified the creation of a small team of workers. In Monod's lab, I occupied 80 square feet. The laboratory was establishing the existence of messenger RNA, discovering operators and operons. I was at a loss with my problems among all this intellectual revolution. Although I had strong ties with the Institute and with Jacques, I decided to cut the umbilical cord (at the age of forty!) and emigrate to the United States where the National Institutes of Health was offering me ample space and facilities. I went to Bethesda in 1959 to make contacts with interested scientists and to examine the possibilities of sending my children to school. I accepted the position which was offered. I returned to France to prepare for our departure to find that Monod had obtained a promotion for me to Director of Research, and a new laboratory at Gif-sur-Yvette, near Paris. If I had thought for a while that Jacques had lost interest in me, I had been grossly mistaken. I stayed in France and, ten years later, I reentered the Institute, as the successor of André Lwoff. In 1972, when Monod became the director of the Institut Pasteur, he appointed me as his successor in the Service de Biochimie Cellulaire, where I am to this day, in the very laboratory where I started thirty-five years ago.

Others may relate in this book how Jacques' lab was associated with the discovery of the repression of biosynthetic enzymes by their end products and with the generalization of the negative regulation model in biosynthetic systems. Others may describe the rationale by which Jacques arrived at the concept of allosteric enzymes. I was physically present in his laboratory for a short period only (1954-1960), but very few have witnessed the birth of so many fundamental concepts in such a short period in a single place. This was due above all to the unusual intelligence of Jacques Monod.

As all human beings, he was not exempt from shortcomings, but the balance is overwhelmingly positive. His former students and colleagues occupy leading positions in France in the biological sciences, which Monod has greatly revolutionized not only in the Institute, but also in universities. He was a great scholar and a man of great charm, creating around him an atmosphere in which discoveries had to be made. His absence is and will continue for a long time to be severely felt.

THE SWITCH

François Jacob

One September afternoon in 1958, I walked into Jacques Monod's office. I was both extremely tired and extremely excited. Tired, because that night I had flown back from New York where I had delivered a Harvey Lecture. Excited, because while preparing this lecture at the end of July, I had found what seemed to me a new way of looking at both lysogeny and induced enzyme synthesis. During the summer there had been no opportunity to see Jacques. I was, therefore, especially eager to discuss these ideas with him and to examine their relevance to the lactose system. I spoke with the glib tongue that a mixture of fatigue and excitement often produces. Jacques barely listened to me. He began to smile and soon started to roar with laughter—that well-known laughter which almost filled the whole building and enabled one to locate him. He thought that the idea was simply childish, and he was ready to provide at least five arguments against it. My fatigue prevailed over my excitement, and I decided to postpone the discussion until the following day. I went to bed.

The collaboration between Jacques and myself had begun only in 1957. Until that time, like all members of the Pasteur group, we had frequent discussions, mainly at lunch time. But only occasionally did we perform experiments together. In fact we were working on what everybody then regarded as two completely different systems. In 1957, Jacques had at last brought order into a problem that had been long confused. The old phenomenon of "enzymatic adapta-

95

tion" became transformed into "induced enzyme synthesis," after Jacques and his group had shown that the increase in enzyme activity observed upon addition of inducer, resulted not from the conversion of a preexisting protein, as then frequently believed, but entirely from *de novo* protein synthesis. Furthermore, a remarkably ingenious analysis of the properties of lactose analogues had revealed the separate roles of β-galactosides as inducers and as substrates. *A posteriori*, these two points might have appeared sufficient to reject what Joshua Lederberg called the "instructive," as opposed to the "selective," mechanism of enzyme induction. Nevertheless, in a paper that Jacques wrote during the winter of 1957-1958 for a symposium in the Netherlands, a flavor of instructionism still persisted. In what he then considered *the* theory, the amino acids were assembled in the correct peptide sequence on a specific template, the ribosome, resulting in the formation of a precursor, the "preenzyme," which remained attached to the template. Specific and reversible combination of the preenzyme with β-galactosides then resulted in folding and detachment of the molecule to produce the active enzyme. Either spontaneously or under the inductive influence of another, endogeneous substance, the preenzyme could undergo a different type of folding to produce another protein configuration, endowed with another, unknown enzymatic activity. Jacques' main concern at that time was to explain by a unitary hypothesis two phenomena apparently worlds apart: enzyme induction and the inhibition of the synthesis of biosynthetic enzymes by an end product of the pathway. The latter phenomenon first detected by Jacques' group and by D. D. Woods, was subsequently further investigated in several laboratories and termed "repression" by Vogel. The necessary unity could be attained either by a "general induction" or by a "general repression" hypothesis; the former was favored by Jacques.

However, the most important aspects of the paper written by Jacques were not the theoretical underpinnings, but rather the clarity and the precision with which the questions raised by the lactose system were defined. It had become clear that a new methodology was required for further advances. The most promising approach to the study of the lactose system appeared to lie through genetic analysis.

It was just at this time that Elie Wollman and I had made bacterial conjugation a workable tool for such an analysis. In 1953, a very close collaboration with Elie had started on lysogeny. This field had been completely revived by André Lwoff. The main questions which then required analysis were of a genetic nature and could be approached through bacterial conjugation. As it turned out, conjugation did not simply help with the analysis of lysogeny; for lysogeny proved to be a major factor in understanding the mechanism of conjugation. One of the first experiments we did together revealed the phenomenon of "zygotic induction," i.e., the production of phage when a chromosome bearing λ prophage entered a nonlysogenic recipient cell, but not when the reciprocal cross was performed. This proved that the immunity of lysogenic bacteria is caused by a cytoplasmic factor preventing prophage expression; and it also showed that in conjugation, genes could be expressed without undergoing recombination. A second series of experiments involving separation of the happy couples in a Waring blender, a torture conceived by Elie, showed that the male chromosome was injected into the female at a constant rate, following a precise time schedule. Although Elie did not like the metaphor, this became known in the lab as the "spaghetti experiment" because the female appeared to swallow the male chromosome like spaghetti. It then became relatively easy to dissect the main events of bacterial conjugation; to construct a map of the bacterial chromosome; to demonstrate its circularity; and finally, to detect a class of genetic elements, the episomes, which moved back and forth between chromosome and cytoplasm. In short, conjugation had become a useful instrument for the analysis of any bacterial function.

In September 1957, the decision was reached with Jacques to use conjugation for a genetic analysis of the lactose system. Jacques had isolated a number of mutants affected in the production either of β-galactosidase or of permease, as well as constitutive mutants—the z, y, i trinity. It was easy to insert them in various combination in either male or female bacteria. Arthur Pardee, who had come to spend a sabbatical year with Jacques' group, was interested in the project. This led to the so-called PaJaMa (Pardee, Jacob, Monod) experiments. In brief, these experiments showed that β-galactosidase was synthesized at maximal rate within two to three minutes after entry of the gene in a cell; that the i gene determining the inducible vs. constitutive character of enzyme synthesis was distinct from the z and y genes, which controlled the synthesis of β-galactosidase and β-galactoside-permease, respectively; and finally, that inducibility was dominant over constitutivity. It was therefore the inducible i^+ allele, and not the constitutive i^- one, that was expressed in the cytoplasm by an active product. This finding did not support Jacques' earlier hypothesis, according to which constitutivity resulted from the synthesis of an endogenous inducer. However, it nicely fitted a proposal made by Szilard who happened to spend a few days in Paris at that time. Like Jacques, Szilard wanted to explain the induction and the repression of enzyme synthesis by a common mechanism. In contrast to Jacques' "general induction model," he preferred a "general repression model," for several reasons. The dominance of $i +$ over $i -$ was clearly in agreement with the latter model, which furthermore could easily accommodate the immunity of lysogenic bacteria. These new, abstract entities, the products of the $i+$ gene in the *lac* system and of the C_I+ gene in phage, were called "repressors."

The results of the PaJaMa experiments strongly influenced the thinking of the whole Pasteur group in two respects. One was, obviously, the nature of the regulatory mechanism involved in enzyme synthesis. The other was, somewhat less obviously, the nature of the "template" involved in protein synthesis. Proteins were known to be synthesized on ribosomes. Ribosomes were known to contain stable RNAs. And the central dogma then proposed by Francis Crick was epitomized as DNA → RNA → protein. At that time, it was tacitly admitted that the stable RNA components of ribosomes represented the specific templates for protein synthesis; in other words, a gene produced one or several specific ribosomes, which in turn manufactured the corresponding protein. However, the notion of stable intermediate RNAs was not in good agreement with the results of the PaJaMa experiments which had shown that, in a mutant bacterium unable to synthesize β-galactosidase, the transfer of the gene almost immediately led to a maximal rate of synthesis. During the long discussions with Arthur and Jacques, we examined some unorthodox ideas: perhaps there was no RNA intermediate and the protein was synthesized on the gene itself; or perhaps the RNA intermediate was very unstable. We did not like the former hypothesis; as for the latter one, there were very few arguments pro or con. We finally decided that the presumed instability of the intermediate RNA could be determined by transferring a ^{32}P-labeled lac^+ male chromosome into a lac^- female; allowing enzyme synthesis for a short time; and then destroying the gene by ^{32}P decay. The amount of residual enzyme synthesis following gene destruction would provide a measure for the stability of the template. In the fall of 1958, Arthur Pardee returned to Berkeley armed with the design of this difficult experiment, which he later very skillfully performed with his student Monica Riley.

During that year, 1957-1958, I came to work much more closely with Jacques and to know him better. At least twice a week there were long meetings in his office where various aspects of the work in progress were discussed. He had an unusual feeling for the interplay between theory and experiment, and was a virtuoso of the hypothetico-deductive method. Not only did he very rapidly perceive the experiment necessary to check a particular point; he also squeezed the results to the very limit of their significance. He had the gift, mainly possessed by poets, of seeing signs that others did not. At the same time, his attitude toward theories always amazed me. I have a certain taste for changing fixed ideas, for throwing old idols onto the garbage heap, even if I have contributed to setting them up. Jacques, in contrast, did not like to get rid of his theories. He had a strong tendency to stick to his model, sometimes slightly beyond the point of reason.

As is frequent with so rich and strong a personality, several different and sometimes contradictory individuals coexisted within Jacques Monod; two at least, if one considers only the scientist. Each took over in turn, depending on his mood and on the circumstances. The first of these individuals—let us call him Jacques—was a very warm and generous man of great charm; a man interested in people as well as in ideas, constantly available to his friends, ready to discuss their problems and find a solution; a man of great rigor and insight, always to the point, asking cogent questions, and sharply self-critical. The second individual—let us call him Monod—was incredibly dogmatic, self-confident, and domineering; a person unceasingly in quest of admiration and publicity, demanding to be the focus of attention; a person making definitive black-and-white value judgments on everything and everybody, fond of teaching fellow scientists the *real* meaning of their own work but sweeping away as nonsense any objection they might timidly offer. Jacques was able to bring all his personal activities to a halt and go out of his way to help a friend in a difficult situation. Monod could quite easily turn a friend into an enemy with a few words. In private, one dealt almost always with Jacques. In larger gatherings, one sometimes had to deal with Monod. Working with the former was an exceptional pleasure. Arguing with the latter could be a difficult experience. Fortunately, at that time, it was mainly Jacques who was in command.

The afternoon that I returned from New York, I was received by Monod. The next morning, however, when I again entered his office after an eighteen hour sleep I found Jacques. I started once more to tell my story, and the discussion between us went on until the end of the afternoon.

My main point was the following: We all had noticed the analogies between the results of zygotic induction with lysogenic bacteria and those of the PaJaMa experiments with the *lac* system. But only when trying to produce a reasonable picture of lysogeny for my Harvey Lecture on "Viral Functions" did I realize how far the parallel could be pushed. In both cases, a group of normally silent genes could be triggered and become expressed at will; in both cases, this silence was due to a single, distinct gene: C_I in phage λ, i in the *lac* system; in both cases, genetic analysis showed that the wild type allele of this gene was expressed by a cytoplasmic product, a repressor blocking in some way the expression of the other genes. These analogies appeared so great that the postulate of an identical mechanism seemed to me inescapable.

If so, each system with its particular advantages and disadvantages should aid in the analysis of the other. In lysogeny, genetic analysis was especially easy, while gene products were barely known and difficult to assay. Conversely, in the *lac* system, the proteins were easy to assay, but genetic analysis was not so precise. If one assumed an identical mechanism and a complementarity of the two systems, then lysogeny already set some constraints on possible models. In order to produce λ phage particles, some 50-100 different proteins had to be synthesized, all these syntheses being blocked by the C_I repressor. It seemed to me extremely unlikely that the phage did produce 50-100 different species of stable templates, of stable ribosomes, each one being blocked by the same repressor. Repression had to operate on one element common to all functions. It could prevent the synthesis of one peptide chain common to all proteins, an idea which I did not much like. Alternatively, it could work on a single lock, a master switch simultaneously controlling the production of several proteins at some level—then unknown—of the protein-synthesizing machinery. Since the only molecular species at that time known to contain the genetic information for the structure of several proteins appeared to be DNA, it seemed most likely that repression operated at the level of DNA. Starting from the viewpoint of the phage system, I therefore wanted Jacques' opinion about the implications for the *lac* system of two basic concepts: (1) Repression (or induction) operates not progressively, but like a switch, by a yes-or-no, an on-or-off mechanism that involves only two states. (2) Genetic units of an order higher than the gene must exist: "units of activity" that contain several genes subject to unitary expression, such expression probably being regulated at the level of DNA.

During my long presentation, Jacques offered only a few remarks designed to make me clarify certain points. I had the impression that he was interested, although somewhat reluctant to swallow the whole story. After a long silence, he began to argue carefully, point by point, attempting to explain as clearly as possible the implications of the model for the *lac* system. There were some aspects that he just didn't like; for instance the notion of repression acting at the genetic level. "However," he said, "this might simply reflect the bias of a scientist formed by classical genetic training." For him, the gene is a noble, intangible entity. "But bacterial geneticists," he added, "have shown that episomes can be introduced into or removed from a chromosome almost at will, a situation unthinkable ten years previously. Actually," Jacques concluded, "there is no direct evidence either for or against the idea of repression at the level of DNA, and we should keep this possibility in mind."

His objection to the switch, the on-or-off concept of protein synthesis appeared more serious to me. Differential β-galactosidase synthesis was always linear; but the rate of synthesis varied as a function of the nature and concentration of inducer. This, Jacques believed, could not be reconciled with an on-or-off system of synthesis. I myself have never been much of an expert in reaction kinetics. My main argument was the simplicity of a yes-or-no system for phage induction in lysogenic bacteria. A few weeks before, however, I had perceived that an on-or-off mechanism could in principle account satisfactorily for different rates of synthesis. This insight had come to me while I watched one of my sons playing with a small electric train. Although he didn't have a rheostat, he could make the train travel at different but constant speed, just by turning the switch on and off more or less rapidly. It seemed to me that a similar mechanism could govern protein synthesis, provided that the system had sufficient inertia. This argument did not appear very convincing to Jacques!

When considering the role played by polygenic units of activity in the *lac* system, Jacques immediately picked out an important implication of the model to which I had not paid attention. If both β-galactosidase and permease genes formed part of a single unit which could only be expressed as a whole, then the syntheses of the two proteins should be completely coordinated *under any con-*

dition; in other words, irrespective of the type of synthesis, the two activities should always occur in the same ratio. Indeed, if one knew more about the permease, the two proteins should even be always present in the same relative amounts. And Jacques firmly stated that this was not so. The glucose effect— i.e., the decrease in rate of synthesis in presence of glucose—did not affect β-galactosidase and permease to the same extent. Furthermore, several compounds, such as inositol-α-galactoside, induced β-galactoside-permease but not β-galactosidase.

For me this was a hard blow. In fact, it was exactly the type of argument I was both expecting and fearing to hear from Jacques. After a lag, it occurred to me that the glucose effect should not be perhaps taken too seriously since nobody knew what it meant, where it acted, or what the mechanism was. However, the uncoupling of induction by inositol-galactoside worried me since it could turn out to be fatal to the whole hypothesis, unless one wished to argue that the status of permeases, their nature and specificity, were not yet very clear.

It was late in the afternoon; I was completely exhausted while Jacques remained as fresh as in the morning. We stopped. We had drinks and started to talk with other members of the group. We soon began a new argument in which Monod replaced Jacques for a while. He always insisted on being purely logical. He decided that I was mainly intuitive. This was all right. I had no particular objection to being intuitive, until Monod claimed that intuition did not exist, and he never understood what it meant. Then I replied with the usual argument, the comparison between the computer and the human mind: while the former has to scan all possible situations before reaching a conclusion, the latter uses short cuts. The discussion soon cooled down and turned to the respective virtues of cognac and whisky.

From that day on, a particularly close and friendly cooperation began between Jacques and myself. The next few years remain in my mind as among the most active and exciting times of my scientific life. Very critical of the model to begin with, Jacques rapidly became more and more interested in it. His criticisms were more and more constructive. Some of his objections disappeared. Others, such as the uncoupling of induction by inositol-galactoside, remained as skeletons in the closet. We agreed, however, to leave them there for a while. Almost every day we had long working sessions, each bringing new results, each trying a new concept on the other, as if we were tennis players. As ever, Jacques continued to focus his attention on the *lac* system. I myself tried to consider both systems, fascinated as I was by the analogy between them. The detection of a mutant in one system immediately led to the description and the isolation of a symmetrical mutant in the other. If our collaboration became so close and our work so exciting, it was mainly because the more results we obtained, the greater the similarities became. In the course of our dialogue, each of us could proceed with his own internal monologue. I think that this may well be one of the keys to intellectual pleasure.

In the fall of 1958, during one of our sessions which I believe Georges Cohen attended, Jacques pointed out that if the switch considered as the acceptor site of the repressor did exist, it should be specific, therefore genetically controlled, and in turn liable to alteration by mutation. Immediately we began to discuss the properties expected from such a mutant, drawing arrows on the board to represent the elements of circuits. Such an acceptor mutant (called A^- at that time, later to become O^C) would no longer be sensitive to the repressor produced by the i gene; it should be constitutive. Furthermore in diploid cells, the chromosome carrying an A^- mutation should continue to be expressed in the presence of another chromosome carrying the wild A^+ allele. The hypothetical A^- mutation accordingly had very clear-cut properties. An A^- mutant should be constitutive; but in contrast to i^- constitutives, which are recessive to i^+ in diploids, A^- should be dominant over A^+. In addition, only β-galactosidase and permease genes located *cis* with respect to A^- should be expressed in A^-/A^+ diploids. During all this discussion, we had become very excited. Suddenly, I realized that a mutant presenting exactly these characteristics had been known in phage λ for several years. This was the so-called "virulent" (v) mutant that Elie Wollman and I had isolated and analyzed. It grew on bacteria lysogenic for λ. It was dominant, since it multiplied in lysogenic bacteria mixedly infected with v and v^+ phages. Finally the use of suitable genetic markers had shown that only those genes located in position *cis* to the v mutation were expressed. This mutant accordingly possessed every property anticipated for the acceptor of the repressor. How stupid I had been not to have thought of it before! From that day on, our joined confidence in the model increased by several orders of magnitude.

During the winter of 1958-1959, we were both busy testing experimentally different aspects of the model. Jacques wanted first to check the coordinated expression of β-galactosidase and β-galactoside-permease under the most varied possible conditions. This he did with Madeleine Jolit, Carmen Sanchez, and David Perrin. They showed that the ratio of the two activities was constant under all conditions, except when inositol-galactoside was the inducer. We were again forced to lock the closet. Two additional features in favor of the model also subsequently emerged from this work. Certain mutants in the β-galactosidase (z) gene turned out to produce permease in lower amounts than did wild type, while mutants in the permease (y) gene always produced a normal amount of β-galactosidase: polarity of expression soon became an additional argument for interpreting the *lac* region as a unit of activity. A new protein, β-galactoside-transacetylase, was discovered by Adam Kepes and Irving Zabin. This added a new gene to the *lac* region, a new activity to measure, and a new site of polarity. The induction of transacetylase was completely coordinated with that of β-galactosidase and permease, again except when inositol-galactoside served as inducer. Like β-galactosidase, transacetylase was not synthesized in response to inositol-galactoside which induced only the permease. This result began to weaken our belief in the strength of the inositol-galactoside argument.

As my contribution to the work, I wanted to isolate the dominant constitutive A⁻ mutant, homologous in the *lac* system to the v mutant of phage λ. This would have been easy, provided that stable diploids for the *lac* region had been available. Unfortunately, the zygotes obtained by conjugation and used in the PaJaMa experiment were only transient and did not allow mutant selection. However, a few months earlier, before Elie Wollman had left to spend a year in Berkeley with Gunther Stent, we had shown that in Hfr strains the sex factor F is transferred to females at the tail end of the chromosome. Furthermore, Edward Adelberg, who had spent a sabbatical year with us, had found upon his return to Berkeley a strange F⁺ derivative of an Hfr: the sex factor F had become autonomous, while retaining the memory of its former location in the Hfr chromosome. This property suggested that, when returning from the integrated to the autonomous state, the F factor had carried with it a small adjacent segment of the Hfr chromosome, just like transducing phage. If this were true, a way to obtain stable diploids for any chromosomal segment had been discovered, provided suitable Hfr strains were available. During the winter and spring of 1958-1959, Martine Tallec and I isolated a series of Hfr strains that ended close to the *lac* region, and we tried to derive F-*lac* from them. The first F-*lac* was obtained and characterized in June 1959. It covered the whole *lac* region, recombined with the chromosome, so that any *lac* mutation could be transferred to it, yielding stable diploids. From such a strain, it was easy to derive a constitutive dominant mutant. This was achieved three weeks later.

The cooperation with Jacques was closer than ever. In the large lab adjacent to his office on the first floor, people were adding inducers, assaying activities, and measuring syntheses. In my lab on the third floor, in André Lwoff's laboratory, mutants were being accumulated and mapped by conjugation. I spent a large part of my time going up and down the stairs. Almost invariably, every day ended in long discussions in Jacques' office, more and more arrows being drawn on the board. His logic, his imagination, and his tenacity were amazing. When a discussion was beginning to get off the track, he immediately stopped it, focusing the attention on what was the real point. He was always ready to invent some new experiment and to bet a bottle of whisky on its outcome.

During the fall of 1959, we were extremely busy checking the properties of dominant constitutive A⁻ mutants. The A⁻ mutation was first coupled with most other *lac* mutations on the chromosome and on the F-*lac* factor, to obtain all possible combinations of diploids in *cis* and *trans* positions. The properties of these strains were carefully determined and turned out to be exactly as predicted: the A⁻ mutation resulted in dominant constitutive expression of the three *lac* genes but only of those located in *cis* position. Furthermore, as expected of a structure that could switch the activity of the whole *lac* unit, the A⁻ mutation mapped at one end (z) of the unit. That part of the model which dealt with polygenic units of genetic activity had consequently received complete support. After a long debate on the respective virtues of Greek and Latin words, the *i* gene became a "regulator" gene, as opposed to "structural" genes which specify the amino acid sequence of proteins; the unit of activity was called an "operon" and the switch an "operator." The A⁻ mutation consequently became an "operator constitutive" (O^C). The general terminology applied of course, to phage λ as well as to the *lac* system.

There was another aspect of the model in which the symmetry between λ and *lac* proved to be important: the site of action of inducers. When the PaJaMa experiments had shown the existence of a cytoplasmic repressor, the site of inducer action had been transferred from the pre-enzyme to the repressor: β-galactosides were considered to inhibit the inhibiting effect of the repressor on β-galactosidase synthesis—what Jacques liked to call "double bluff"—thereby releasing enzyme synthesis. There was, however, no direct proof of that postulated interaction between repressor and inducer. During the winter of 1958-1959, while Alan Campbell was spending a sabbatical year with me, we isolated a new mutant of λ. This mutant was noninducible (ind⁻) by UV light or other inducers. In the λ version of the model, the regulator gene C_I was considered to produce a cytoplasmic repressor blocking the expression of one, or more probably, several operons. Ultraviolet irradiation was assumed to result in the production of some substance able to inactivate the repressor, thereby allowing expression of these operons and consequently phage multiplication. The ind⁻ mutation turned out to be located in the C_I gene, and to be dominant over the wild allele: in lysogenic cells multiply infected with ind⁻ and ind⁺ phages, the ind⁻ repressor prevented UV induced expression and multiplication of all λ chromosomes. The most likely interpretation of the ind⁻ mutation was a loss of sensitivity of the repressor to the unknown inducing substance produced by UV irradiation.

According to the rule of symmetry between the λ and *lac* systems, a homologous mutation had to be found in the *lac* system. This should be a mutation of the *i* gene that would be dominant over i^+ (or i^-) in diploids and resulting in noninducibility of the whole *lac* operon. At first, Jacques had some doubts about the possibility of obtaining such a mutation: were it to exist, he assumed that it would have already been isolated among the many *lac⁻* mutants he had produced. However, this mutant could conceivably be rare, and obtainable only from a diploid strain. Actually, it was with some difficulty that in the spring of 1960, I succeeded in isolating such mutants from a diploid i^+/i^+ strain. Located in the *i* gene, the mutations called i^S (for super-repressed) were dominant over both i^+ and i^- alleles. For an i^S mutant to produce the three Lac products in small amounts, inducer concentrations 100-1000 times higher than those required for wild type proved necessary. It seemed therefore that the mutated repressor was altered in such a way that it could scarcely be inactivated by inducers. The properties of such mutants were later worked out in greater detail by Clyde Willson and Mel Cohn in Paris.

Thus the pieces of the puzzle were being rapidly assembled. In the fall of 1959, Arthur Pardee sent us the first results of the experiment he had performed with Monica Riley: after destruction of the z gene by ^{32}P decay in zygotes which had already produced β-galactosidase, the enzyme was no longer synthesized. The conclusion that protein synthesis did not involve *stable* intermediate templates was thus inescapable. Since it was not possible to consider DNA itself as the template, an unstable intermediate RNA had to exist. Despite many discussions, in particular with François Gros who was the RNA specialist in the group, we did not get much further. At a meeting in Copenhagen attended by most molecular biologists during the fall of 1959, I discussed our ideas, in particular the idea of an unstable RNA as a template in protein synthesis: nobody paid the slightest attention. At Easter 1960, I went to a symposium on bacterial genetics in London and spent a few days in Cambridge. During a small meeting in Sydney Brenner's room at King's College, I described the latest results obtained in Paris and Berkeley on the regulation of protein synthesis and mentioned once again the unstable RNA hypothesis. Francis Crick and Sydney reacted immediately; they made the crucial connection between the unstable template hypothesis and RNA with a rapid turnover, which had been previously described by Hershey, and by Volkin and Astrachan in bacteria infected with T-even phages. This was a day of great excitement, which ended up in a party at the Cricks. In spite of the presence of many pretty girls, Sydney and I spent the whole evening planning the details of an experiment to be done at Caltech where we happened to be both invited at the same time. In June 1960, we thus met in Pasadena and performed this series of experiments with Matt Meselson in Max Delbruck's laboratory. Mainly thanks to Sydney's exceptional skill and quickness of mind, it could be shown that, upon infection with phage T4, the RNA with a rapid turnover—then called "tape" and later "messenger"—became associated with ribosomes formed prior to infection, and produced phage specific proteins. In Jim Watson's laboratory at Harvard, François Gros and Walter Gilbert simultaneously demonstrated the existence of a similar RNA with a rapid turnover in uninfected bacteria.

With the discovery of messenger RNA, the process of protein synthesis was shown to occur in two successive steps: transcription from DNA to messenger RNA, and translation of messenger into polypeptide chains on ribosomes. This gave a new impetus to the whole field. For the Pasteur group, it raised a number of specific questions, which were endlessly debated: Is there a unique messenger for the whole operon? Does repression act to prevent translation, or as it appeared more likely in view of messenger instability, does it act directly on DNA to prevent transcription? On the whole, however, the messenger concept gave strong support to our model. The repressor existed in two alternate states: active or inactive, resulting from interaction with the inducer. When active, it reacted with the operator, thus blocking the expression of the entire operon, either at the transcriptional or at the translational level. The whole system could be viewed as an on-or-off switch alternating between two states, just like the switch of the small electric train. The rate of protein synthesis was determined by the relative times spent in the on and off positions. A few years later, the notion of on-and-off regulation was used again by Jacques together with Jeffry Wyman and Jean-Pierre Changeux, when they explained the allosteric properties of proteins by their transitions between alternate conformations.

Our simple regulatory circuit—which an engineer could have easily designed —applied not only to *lac* and λ, but also to certain biosynthetic pathways. With Georges Cohen, we had shown the existence of a similar system acting in the regulation of the synthesis of enzymes involved in the production of trytophan. Even our old enemy, the uncoordinated induction of permease by inositol-galactoside, had vanished when it was realized that the permease thus induced was not β- but α-galactoside permease, whose structural gene was not located in the *lac* operon! This was the last skeleton to disappear. When the true role of inositol-galactoside as an inducer was discovered by Adam Kepes and Claude Burstein in June 1960, I was at Caltech with Sydney Brenner, hunting for the messenger. About half an hour before I was going to give a seminar, I received the following telegram: "Be careful. New compounds give uncoordinated induction galactosidase, permease, acetylase. Regards. Jacques." I took it as a practical joke, which it was, and sent back a telegram: "Model already destroyed. Proof inducer folds each protein. Regards."

At that time, we had both become convinced that the model gave a reasonably good description of the regulatory mechanism involved in the lactose, λ, and tryptophan systems. We usually called it *negative* regulation, meaning that in the absence of the regulatory gene product, the operon is expressed at high rate. We often discussed the possibility of the symmetrical situation, or *positive* regulation, where in the absence of the regulatory gene product, an operon would not be expressed at all. Our attitudes about positive regulation were opposed. I liked the idea of the existence of both positive and negative regulations, because it seemed to me that the combination of both types offered a much greater flexibility for complex systems and differentiation. Jacques, on the other hand, was not very fond of positive regulation, because he liked nature to provide unique solutions. Since a combination of two negatives were equivalent to one positive, he did not see the logical necessity of adding another, distinct mechanism. He made the clear-cut point that a decision could be reached experimentally only by deletions of regulatory genes: in negative systems such deletions should result in a constitutive expression of the structural genes, while in positive systems they should lead to a complete lack of expression of these genes. For a long time, however, Jacques remained refractory to positive regulation, even when, later in the 1960s, evidence in favor of it began to accumulate in several laboratories. It was shown, for instance, that regulatory genes N and Q of phage λ were likely to act in a positive way. Ellis Englesberg, then working on the arabinose system, gave several seminars at Pasteur. His results also required some positive effect of the regulatory gene product. After each seminar, however, he received a severe lesson in regulatory genetics from Monod, who always insisted on a notion "that even a schoolboy cannot ignore: $- \times - = +!$"

In the fall of 1960, Jacques and I decided to assemble the various pieces of information then available into a story, mainly written by Jacques. The paper was sent in December to the *Journal of Molecular Biology*. On the whole, the model described in this paper has withstood the test of time and of deeper biochemical analysis, with one major exception. For rather poor reasons, we had decided that the repressor should be RNA rather than protein. There were several arguments, the main one being that of specificity. We visualized the operator as a short string of DNA, a few nucleotides long. In the bacterial chromosome as a whole, the specificity of several hundred operators therefore had to be determined by short base sequences. The recognition of such sequences by proteins appeared to us to be difficult. On the other hand, recognition by RNA through base pairing would be easy. This notion had a major weakness: the interaction between a repressor RNA and a β-galactoside inducer required a protein, for which no mutation had ever been detected. During the winter of 1961-1962, however, together with Raquel Sussman, who was spending a year in Paris, I isolated a large series of new regulator C_I mutations in λ. Some of these mutations turned out to be thermosensitive; others were *amber*, i.e., corrected by suppressors known to act at translation level. This was unambiguous proof that the λ repressor was—or contained—a protein. It was then easy to look for and to isolate similar mutations of the *i* gene in the *lac* system. In both λ and *lac* systems, the time was thus ripe to hunt for repressors. They were captured at Harvard some years later.

However rigorous its planning, a piece of research always contains a good deal of sound and fury. Only *a posteriori,* as fixed by the flashes of memory, does it become organized into a story. By then, the story has lost much of the flavor of life. I am fully aware that the story I have told here is only one among many possible accounts that might be given of the same events. It does not reflect the random motion and background noise, the exaltation and boredom, the small pleasures and large disappointments which, in various combinations, make everyday life in a laboratory. Nor does it convey the richness of Jacques Monod's unusual personality and inimitable style. It is now more than one year since he has disappeared. It is still difficult to realize that he is no longer present in some room of Pasteur, ready to talk about anything and to bring you back to the real world: the lactose system.

THE PAJAMA EXPERIMENT

Arthur B. Pardee

In this memoir I recall what I can of my association with Jacques Monod during the sabbatical year I spent in his laboratory from 1957-1958. During this period we carried out the bacterial mating experiment, which was subsequently named the "PaJaMa Experiment" because it was done by Pardee, Jacob, and Monod (*J. Mol. Biol.* 1, 165, 1959). This experiment provided the fundamental basis for the regulatory phenomena of enzyme induction and repression.

Prior to 1957 I did not know Monod very well, having met him only briefly in 1952 when I gave a lecture on enzyme changes following bacteriophage infection, at the Pasteur Institute in Paris. Later that summer we both attended the Conference at Royaumont, at which many of the fundamental discoveries of molecular biology were discussed. During the next few years (1953-1957), work in my laboratory often was parallel to publications from Monod and Jacob's groups.

My interests in enzyme induction arose from several studies I had made: on enzyme changes following viral infection, on regulatory interactions between protein synthesis and nucleic acid synthesis, and from our discovery of feedback inhibition of enzyme activity, and of enzyme synthesis repression. All of these researches led me to questions regarding the means a cell used to regulate its metabolism. Evidently the regulation of enzyme *production* was at least as important as the regulation of enzyme *activity*, and these thoughts led me to study

109

enzyme induction and repression. During the mid-1950s both Monod's laboratory and mine came up with discoveries of inducible transport systems (permeases) and the repression and derepression.

During that period Gunther Stent, my colleague at Berkeley, visited the Pasteur Institute yearly and always came back with glowing reports of the progress in science there. I recall that I often told him about our most recent results and heard him respond that the Pasteur group had "done it already." It was a glorious day when I told him about something new that we had done and, after a long pause, he responded, "Well, they haven't done that, but they are thinking about it!"

The convergence of my research interests with Monod's led me to apply to spend my sabbatical leave at the Pasteur. At that time Monod and Jacob had been collaborating in studies on the transfer, between bacteria, of the genes for production of β-galactosidase and galactosidase permease. After these genes were transferred by conjugation from a galactosidase-positive (lac^+) donor to lac^- recipient, the mated cells were capable of forming colonies on lactose plates. These results demonstrated transfer of the genes for lactose utilization, as measured by their ability to permit growth. Monod suggested that I do the opposite experiment, i.e., to see if deletion of the transferred genetic material would arrest growth. His proposal for a method to delete the genes was based on some experiments done by Elizabeth McFall under guidance by Gunther Stent and myself. These studies showed that decay of ^{32}P that had been incorporated into bacterial DNA destroyed the capacity of the unmated cells to make β-galactosidase. So the initial project that I was to work on was to transfer ^{32}P-labeled genetic (lac^+) material by conjugation into lac^- cells, and then to ask whether decay of the ^{32}P would destroy the ability of the mated cells to grow on lactose plates. Although I did not do these experiments in Paris, they were later done by Monica Riley in my laboratory.

Upon arriving at the Pasteur Institute in the fall of 1957, Monod proposed that I first become acquainted with the mating system by asking whether transfer of the lac^+ genes into a lac^- cell would permit the mated cells to form β-galactosidase. This direct measurement of enzyme activity was a dramatic departure from the previous techniques for studying mating, which depended upon the appearance of colonies on selective plates a day or so after the mating event. The immediate or delayed appearance of an enzyme after conjugation could provide much more direct data than growth studies, as to the timing and mechanism of gene transfer and expression.

My first technical problem was to distinguish between production of the enzyme β-galactosidase by mated cells and the unmated donors. (The unmated recipient in a cross between a lac^+ donor and a lac^- recipient is genetically incapable of producing the enzyme.) Monod's suggestion was that I obtain chloramphenicol-resistant lac^+ donor cells; when mating was done in the presence of this drug the donors' protein-synthesizing ability would be blocked, but the mated cells might be resistant. Therefore only the mated cells would be capable of making the enzyme. But chloramphenicol-resistant *E. coli* are hard to produce. I suggested that we could use the streptomycin-resistance property of the recipients for our kinetic work; this marker had been used in all the previous mating and plating experiments to distinguish resistant mated cells from sensitive, unmated donors. Within a few days of my arrival (September 25, 1957) I had shown that streptomycin-resistant recipient cells provided a means for studying enzyme production as well as colony formation by mated bacteria. I think that this rapid initial success provided the mutual confidence that was essential for our later progress.

We soon demonstrated that the enzyme β-galactosidase appeared at maximal rate in mated cells within minutes of the time that the corresponding lac^+ genes were transferred, timing of transfer being measured by the interrupted mating technique of Jacob and Wollman. This result in itself was of great interest, since it demonstrated that the gene becomes active virtually as soon as it enters an appropriate environment. Also it showed that the techniques for mapping genes according to mating times were almost surely determining the time of entry of the gene into the cell. The discovery of messenger RNA had a major root in this experiment.

I recall noting with interest how technical approaches of our laboratories differed. It was a custom in the Pasteur Institute to make each measurement of β-galactosidase as a function of duration or reaction, with the result that each measurement was relatively laborious. Perhaps a dozen experimental values could be obtained in a day's work. I decided that a cruder approach would suffice, and that only one time point was needed for each measurement. In this way I could increase the acquisition of data by a factor of about 10 and yet have sufficient reliability to work out the main features of the mating system. I recall Monod coming into the laboratory and shaking his head in amazement at the way that I was setting up the experiments with a dozen cultures and a hundred or more sample tubes. This "rough-and-ready" approach was important in the rapid progress we made in the following months.

Following our success in demonstrating that enzyme production accompanies gene transfer, Jacques (as he preferred me to call him) suggested that I look at the transfer of the β-galactosidase (z^+) gene into a constitutive z^- recipient cell. It will be recalled that wild type *E. coli* need to be fed a low molecular weight inducer related to lactose to make them produce β-galactosidase. The Pasteur group had discovered constitutive mutants (*lac i^-*), which produce β-galactosidase at a high rate independent of the presence or absence of an inducing compound. Did the constitutive cells make the enzyme because an inducer is synthesized within them? We could transfer the z^+ gene into a cell that is z^- (and hence cannot itself make the enzyme) and that also has the constitutive property *lac i^-* as well. The proposed internal inducer would be expected to act upon the transferred gene; hence the mated cell should produce the enzyme in the absence of externally added inducer.

The first experiment of this kind was done on December 3, 1957. To our great pleasure, the enzyme appeared promptly upon gene transfer, in the absence of added inducer. Thus, conditions within the recipient cell were "constitutive" because the introduced genetic material found an environment that permitted its expression.

Although this result was qualitatively what we had hoped for, there were some problems. First, the rate of enzyme production in the absence of external inducer was lower than in the presence of the inducer at the end of an 80-minute period following mating. Second, transfer of the i^- gene into a z^+i^+ cell did not permit enzyme formation.

It was not until several months later that we worked out the kinetics of enzyme production in the original $z^+i^+ \rightarrow z^-i^-$ system. We showed that initial rates of β-galactosidase production were very similar with and without inducer. But within two hours the culture without inducer had stopped making β-galactosidase, while the culture with inducer continued to make the enzyme at an ever-increasing rate. The mated cells thus had switched from constitutivity to inducibility.

These results were considered in relation to the apparently converse phenomenon of repression, in which removal of a small molecule permits specific enzyme synthesis to occur. A common basis was sought by Monod, Jacob, myself, and Leo Szilard, who visited the Institute. Our thinking led to the now-familiar idea that the inducible cells contain an inhibitory substance, a protein named a "repressor," which prevents induction unless it is antagonized by the added low molecular-weight inducer. The constitutive cells have genetically lost ability to form the repressor (in some cases by deletion of genetic material), and hence their production of β-galactosidase is not blocked. Following mating, the gene (*lac i*$^+$) which codes for the repressor molecule is introduced along with the β-galactosidase gene (*lac z*$^+$). Expression of the repressor is delayed for an hour or more, in contrast to the almost immediate expression of β-galactosidase, a problem later studied further by Dr. Stephen Barbour in my laboratory. Immediately after mating, the cells do not contain the repressor, and the enzyme is formed; only after the repressor has accumulated during an hour's further growth does the requirement for inducer appear, to counteract the newly-formed repressor.

I think it is safe to say that this PaJaMa experiment provided the basis and frame of reference for further studies on the mechanism of enzyme regulation. It led to the isolation of the repressor protein by Walter Gilbert and Benno Müller-Hill, and their elaborate studies of repressor structure and action in their laboratory, and by Suzanne Bourgeois, Arthur Riggs, and others. The PaJaMa experiment is the basis of a historical-philosophical study of the nature of discovery by Kenneth Schaffner, who interviewed the individuals involved and reconstructed a composite of what happened (*Stud. Hist. Phil. Sci.* **4**, 349, 1974.

Contacts between Jacques and me did not end with my departure from the Pasteur Institute in the fall of 1958. We both studied induction and repression for a few years longer. Then we both became involved in determining the mechanism of control of enzyme activity (as distinct from enzyme formation). Prior to my sabbatical year (between 1953 and 1956), Richard Yates and I had discovered another major mechanism of metabolic control: feedback inhibition of enzyme activity as seen in the pyrimidine biosynthetic pathway (by cytidine triphosphate). This control mechanism was independently discovered by Edwin Umbarger, for the isoleucine pathway.

After my return to Berkeley in1958, I took up the question of how feedback inhibition works—how enzyme activity can be controlled (activated or inhibited) by compounds that do not at all structurally resemble the enzymes' substrates. I decided we needed a pure enzyme for these studies so Margaret Shepherdson and I completely purified the regulated enzyme, aspartate transcarbamylase, which Yates and I had previously shown to be under feedback control. My student John Gerhart and I during 1958-1962 then did some kinetic and physical chemical studies which led to our discovery toward the end of 1960 that an enzyme can have special regulatory sites designed for control. We showed by selective denaturation that regulatory sites are separate from the classical catalytic sites. We concluded that feedback-inhibitable enzymes are designed to be regulated, by possessing special regulatory sites to which effectors attach and modify catalytic activity.

From the PaJaMa studies on the molecular nature of induction—proposed to be the effects of interaction of a lactose-related inducer with the repressor protein, which initiates a quite different process of gene expression—Monod became interested in how a small molecule can modify a protein's function. He and I had discussed feedback inhibition during my sabbatical in 1957-1958. A little later he and Jean-Pierre Changeux started to study feedback inhibition of threonine deaminase by isoleucine, the system pioneered by Umbarger. We were in contact from time to time, and I gave a seminar about our results on the regulatory site of aspartate transcarbamylase at the Pasteur Institute in April of 1961. We recognized similarities between our two studies. Changeux's observations, closely similar to those of Gerhart and myself, and made independently and simultaneously, led them to conclude as we did, that regulatory sites exist in addition to catalytic sites.

Jacques coined the word "allostery" to signify the function of these other, regulatory sites (allosteric sites). He and François Jacob in 1961 made the far-reaching hypothesis that allostery applies beyond the control of enzyme activities and hemoglobin-binding of oxygen, and is perhaps the major mode for control and coordination of metabolism. Through allosteric interactions, a compound produced by one metabolic sequence can affect another chemically dissimilar, but functionally related process. In later papers, Monod, Changeux, and Jacob integrated the few solid pieces of data on allostery, principally our work and theirs on feedback inhibitable enzymes and classical studies on hemoglobin. Wyman, Monod, and Changeux developed an elegant mathematical model for the role of subunits in simple cases of allosteric regulation, based on a symmetry principle.

Gerhart and I proceeded with the molecular side of the problem during this time, aimed at providing definitive proof for the existence of allosteric sites. Our further kinetic, binding, and physical chemical studies on control of aspartate transcarbamylase culminated with Gerhart's beautiful experiments in which he separated allosteric sites physically from catalytic sites and showed that the enzyme consists of two sorts of protein subunits, one carrying catalytic and the other regulatory activity.

Jacques and I took different paths after the mid-1960s. We were invited to give the main lectures, on metabolic regulation, at the National Meeting of the Japanese Biochemical Society in October of 1966. I looked forward to our being together for a few days of leisure talk and sightseeing. But Jacques was awarded his Nobel Prize that month and remained in Europe. We saw little of each other after that.

A few personal footnotes might be amusing. I recall one experiment in which I intended to measure the appearance of β-galactosidase, while François Jacob was to determine the time of entry of the corresponding lac^+ genes by separating the mated cells with a Waring blender. I routinely did my mating experiments in 2-liter flasks using a very thin layer of liquid culture so as to give maximum aeration with minimum perturbation of the cells. When it came time for Jacob to take his samples, his pipet would not reach to the bottom of my flask; so there was a momentary crisis during which there was some rapid-fire French that never got published; the mated culture was rapidly poured into a smaller flask and the protocols of both laboratories became amalgamated.

My experimental results were discussed frequently and exhaustively whenever something novel happened. Many of our ideas were generated in these exciting discussions. I sometimes found myself at a disadvantage when both Jacob and Monod were in the conversation; as soon as the subject became really intense, they switched from English to French, and at a rate far too fast for me to follow. I had to interrupt and beg them to return to English, the laboratory's *lingua franca*. In fact, my French was so inadequate that I finally was assigned a French-speaking technician whom I'm sure was under orders not to use English; thus I was forced to expand my pitiful French vocabulary.

I close with a few more personal observations and memoirs of Jacques Monod.

He was a man of broad talents. One of our most pleasurable activities outside of the laboratory involved music. Jacques was an excellent cellist, and I, a much more humble student of the cello. I spent a fair amount of time visiting the luthiers in Paris looking for a cello; on a number of occasions he joined me in my search. I finally found an instrument to my liking (which I still possess and treasure). I recall taking it to his apartment and comparing it with his own instrument, a fine old cello, though dull brown and quite undistinguished in appearance. Mine, on the contrary, was a gleaming mahogany red and quite spectacular. Another scientist commented that we really should exchange cellos because the instruments, although both very fine, had just the opposite personalities from their owners!

Another interest of Jacques' was rock climbing. On one occasion he took us to the rocks in Fontainebleau, where he introduced me to the fine art of scaling the local boulders. He was an extremely skillful and agile climber, and he could get up vertical faces that looked impossible to climb, without hand or foothold. One of the few occasions on which he expressed strong emotion occurred when I stepped on his hand!

In science he expressed a number of fundamental approaches and ideas that remain with me. He frequently said that science is like art. He looked upon a finished piece of science like a finished painting. Perfection consists of doing just enough, not one stroke too many or one too few. His writings reflect this choice of a clean line over completeness.

He also had strong views on what should be accepted as evidence and what should be omitted. In particular, I recall a discussion of the operon idea, that a group of genes such as the ones for β-galactosidase and galactoside permease must be induced simultaneously, owing to the linkage of these structural genes to the same regulatory system.

I raised the objection that galactinol induces the permease but not β-galactosidase, in apparent contradiction with his hypothesis. He told me that in view of all the other facts, he was prepared to omit this one. I was horrified at his willingness to suppress valid data that did not fit his conceptions, to the extent that later I investigated this matter. He turned out to be right, since the permease that is induced by galactinol responds to the same assay but is different from the one linked to β-galactosidase. Hence the different permease can be induced by galactinol separately from β-galactosidase although the linked one cannot. Sometimes an ugly fact only seems to destroy a beautiful hypothesis. In initial stages of an investigation, where very little is known about a system, one should not expect every fact to fit perfectly.

Another facet of our conversations that remains with me concerns hypotheses. I was constantly suggesting hypotheses, some good and some less so, regarding the nature of our experimental results and their fundamental basis. Monod would reply that a hypothesis, no matter how clever, is only useful to the extent that can put it to a crucial experimental test. Nevertheless I feel one first needs a hypothesis, and then one tries to think of ways of testing it.

These recollections have a bearing on Jacques' ability to bring scientific ideas to general scientific notice. He had a tremendous talent for sifting and assembling information, for selecting the most important pieces, eliminating much that was logically secondary (including actual data), and constructing a logical edifice that was most compelling. He also had a remarkable ability to coin word-labels for major ideas: permease, operon, promoter, and allosteric come to mind at once. These traits were coupled with a forceful personality, striking appearance, and great clarity of speech and writing. His generalizations probably have had as much effect on science as have his discoveries.

His impact on an audience is beautifully illustrated by the following "appreciation," written just after having heard Monod's Harvey Lecture in New York (1961-1962), by a colleague who prefers to remain anonymous.

A Night at the Operon

Opening night at the Harvey Society featured an impeccable French scientist in one of the great performances of his career. Professor Jacques Monod captivated his colleagues by the eloquence and simplicity with which he pleaded his case. No other Harvey Lecture in our time has been characterized by such a brilliant exposition of a logical line uncluttered by experimental detail. One felt the great heritage of French literature and philosophy in every phrase. Descartes would have loved it. The audience sat breathless through the last extrapolation and at the end, the burst of wild applause surpassed any ovation heard in our town north of 57th street. Whatever the fate of the operon theory, Professor Monod has achieved a special kind of immortality tonight, in his creation of a new art form which transcends both science and literature.

Jacques had a remarkable combination of personal traits: brilliant, polished, self-possessed, dramatic when necessary, and always on display. He could be kind and thoughtful to his friends, but arrogant and distant to those in whom he was not interested. Once a colleague remarked that Jacques thought of himself as a Renaissance prince; indeed he acted like one. Truly he was a man to respect and in many ways, to admire.

My year in Monod's laboratory was certainly one of the most remarkable of my career. I learned there of the great power of genetics in combination with biochemistry. The day-to-day interaction with first-class minds, including Monod, Jacob, Lwoff, and Horecker, was enormously stimulating and it reinforced the high standard set by my associations with various previous mentors and colleagues. And far from least was my opportunity in that year to become acquainted with and to gain as a friend Jacques Monod, a man exceptional in both his intellectual ability and his strength of personality.

THE MESSENGER

François Gros

This book is meant to depict, by means of successive patches (as an impressionist painting), a man through the epoch he lived in, and this epoch through the man. The epoch, that of molecular biology, may in its turn be seen as a composition of various "scenes" as those which are threaded along a play by Bertolt Brecht, where a multitude of protagonists move about and spread their energy with passion. At first, we see no connection between their actions which even seem superficial and disorderly; but, as the play unrolls, we begin to perceive the paradigm, to recognize the hero who is the lordly inhabitant of the place, to understand the meaning and the logical organization which emerges from the confusion. Jacques Monod has been, and will be remembered as, one of those very great men around whom the main events of contemporary biology have synthesized and harmoniously gathered as the large tableaux around Brecht's hero. These events have indeed, most of the time, sprung from the powerful ideas which he, himself, conceived, or at times integrated with profit in the logical train of his thoughts.

The history of the messenger is particularly meaningful in that respect.

117

THE HEROIC PERIOD

If I try to remember the history of RNA through the prism of my memories, I can rediscover several images, warped by time, which are nonetheless of great emotional content, probably because they date back to the awkward beginning of my scientific research.

The history of RNA, such as I lived it before the great hypothesis of the messenger, is that of a mysterious substance which did not interest anybody except a few cytologists. It was the time of an inventory without passion or excitement when one observed in the cytoplasm, the pre-eminence of a molecule "whose properties were comparable to, although slightly different from those of the deoxyribonucleic acid (DNA)." For a time, the exclusive presence of the pentose nucleic acid in yeast cells—where it was first identified—was stressed, but the idea was soon given up (1947-1949). Actually, with the sophistication of cytochemical techniques, the "pentose rich compound" was soon shown to be present in all cells including bacteria which, for strange reasons, were for a long time not considered as normal cells! (The fact that they have no nucleus was at the origin of this way of thinking.) The time had not yet come to think of the special part played by RNA! I remember, retrospectively with extreme surprise, a theory according to which the "zymonucleic" acid was a reservoir of energy, yielding its phosphorus atoms to ADP, a sort of "phosphagen." It should be noted that until 1950, biochemistry was the science of degradation or energy-yielding processes, the archetypes of which were "muscular contraction" and "glycolysis." Many enzymes were known, which were able to "dissect" the pentose nucleic acid: pancreatic ribonuclease crystallized by Kunitz, nucleotidases on which Hermann Kalckar was so keen, various phosphatases. This RNA, progressively liquifying into its elements, was for all—including the apprentice biochemist that I was then—a cause of profound satisfaction, conscious as we were that the secret of life did reside in the covalent organization of nucleic acids.

I remember my exhilaration when, carrying out experiments that were highly significant at that time, I mixed bacterial suspensions, previously "washed" with ribonucleotides, and studied the oxidation of pentoses into acetic acid and CO_2 with a Warburg manometer, convinced that I was about to find the clue. (Warburg, how many holocausts were offered in thy name!) If I dare return to that maze of experiments it is because, in my opinion, they illustrate what I call the dynamism of "dead-end approaches." By considering the RNA as a mere *metabolic* substrate we by-passed the reality. This took place around 1950.

THE TEMPLATE HYPOTHESIS AND THE ROLE OF RNA IN PROTEIN SYNTHESIS

Three "groups" of concepts, which developed after the Second World War, have apparently allowed RNA to surge from limbo: these concepts ensued from several observations on the surprising size of this strange molecule as well as from the first results obtained by Brachet and Caspersson establishing a relationship between the protein-synthesizing capacity of the tissues and their RNA content. Last but not least, the "template hypothesis" also played its part in the understanding of RNA function.

The finding (Bawden and Pirie, Bonfenbrenner, *et al.*) that plant viruses contain, apart from proteins, ribonucleic acid, has not only led us to perceive the functional universality of the RNA in biological systems, but has also helped in the analysis of its physicochemical composition. Considered at the beginning as a tetranucleotide (Levenne model) composed of the four usual bases (adenine, guanine, cytosine, uracil), RNA was shown to be present in viruses as a large molecule, a *polymer*. As ultracentrifugation techniques developed, molecular parameters became more precise; but as molecular weights of one million or more were first reported, doubt began to hover. Could it be that the size of RNA was equal to or even exceeded that of the already known proteins? Possible artifacts, discontinuity, and the existence of repeated patterns united by linkers were imagined. And what else was not thought of! After some time, evidence had nonetheless prevailed: RNA proved to be very big—a macromolecule. We were still far from imagining that DNA could be yet larger, but a notion was diffusing of a molecule whose constituents are colinearly assembled according to a sort of *code* which might have a deep physiological significance to transmit genetic information. Indeed new ideas developed in a parallel direction concerning the biosynthesis of proteins, and models were imagined. Dounce, Lipmann, and Borsoock formulated their first template hypothesis: the colinear sequence of amino acids, which is the quasi-immutable mark of the species and predetermines the properties and functions of proteins, is not just the result of usual enzymatic catalysis. By analogy with what was known about the biosynthesis of polysaccharides, it was proposed that the protein sequence is, in some way, predetermined by some "primers" or "templates" whose chemical nature nonetheless still remained unknown.

But the works of Caspersson in Sweden and J. Brachet in Belgium operated as real trampolines in the study of the role played by RNA in the economy of the cell. Basing their judgments, first on microspectrophotometric measurements, and second on quantitative cytochemical analyses, these two biologists reached independently the conclusion that a direct relationship exists between the proteosynthetic activity of a tissue and the amount of RNA it contains.

It was to the merit of A. Claude and G. Pallade, then of Schachman, Pardee, and Stanier, to demonstrate that the RNA is mainly present in tiny cellular corpuscles, later named "ribosomes" by scientists of the Carnegie Institute in Washington. This finding of the particulate characteristic of RNA is at the origin of outstanding progress in molecular biology. It nonetheless led scientists to the wrong track.

At first, it was not difficult for the scientists of the Carnegie Institute (Bolton,

Cowie, Britten) to support with precise quantitative data the fact that *in vivo* the protein chains begin to appear on ribosomes before they accumulate in the soluble part of cytoplasm, the cytosol. In 1957-1958, the group of Zamenick and Hoagland, then that of Tissières and Watson, established (after Lipmann) the main stages of the biopolymerization of proteins by using cell-free systems. Thus the mechanism of what was then called the assembly of polypeptidic chains was progressively made clear. And yet the role of ribosomal RNA still remained ambiguous. Works by Graham and Siminovitch, and Koch and Levy had proved that this RNA was endowed with great metabolic stability both in bacteria and animal organisms. The template RNA would then have the stability of genes.

Surely, in 1949-1950, a decisive point in the evolution of concepts had been reached. But all the pieces of the puzzle had not yet been fitted into place. Little by little, without knowing exactly who was the first to formulate the proposition with exactitude, the idea arose that an RNA of great molecular weight, present in ribosomes, could operate as a template for the assembly of amino acids "activated" in a polypeptidic chain. It seemed that people were reaching their goal and yet there still remained a long way to go.

THE GENETIC CODE–THE HYPOTHESIS OF THE MESSENGER

Ideas on the genetic code and determinism had developed until then quite independently from the study of mechanisms of protein genesis. Along the same general lines, as a result of the template hypothesis, and because many examples tended to prove that genes played an active part in directing the assembly of amino acids for the formation of proteins (molecular diseases, enzymatic alterations connected with point mutations), several theories appeared concerning the *possible nature of the code*. Gamov and Crick argued brilliantly about the hypothesis of combinations of nucleotides (or bases) which might *determine* the order of amino acid chains, "calling," as it were, each amino acid to its right place in the sequence of polypeptides. F. Crick explained, with particular insight, why in his opinion, the combination used was a triplet code, without overlapping or "commas." But no experimental demonstration was available to support those beautiful ideas.

I think that it was about that time (1959-1960) that Jacques Monod began to get seriously interested in ribonucleic acids. Until then, in fact, he did not believe, or refused to consider, that these substances might be of some importance. The discovery of the polynucleotide-phosphorylase (Ochoa, Grunberg, Manago) had shaken him by making him realize that a biological system was able to fabricate polyribonucleotides in random sequences. Although he agreed with the ideas, then prevailing, of the template hypothesis, he could not understand how the RNA could fulfill its function of assembler or assembly line. The RNA came as an intruder in the organized world of his thoughts. I was about the only one in his group to deal with ribonucleic acids, and, upon my return from a period of training with S. Spiegelman, I had begun studying the effects that nucleic base analogues might have on enzymatic induction, first in yeast, then in *E. coli*. I have the feeling that Jacques recorded my results with great leniency and generosity but great skepticism. His reservation was based, in part, on rather indirect reasonings that would soon prove extraordinary fruitful.

In 1960, the famous experiment (Pardee, Jacob, Monod) of transferring a galactosidase gene from a male bacterium to a female one had done more than simply prove the existence of regulatory and repressor genes, it had opened the way to entirely unexpected data concerning the *kinetics* of the expression of the transferred gene. Everything happened as if during the minutes which followed the transfer gene Z started to function at a *maximum* rate and not in an autocatalytic way. We have to remember that, if we were to believe the most trustworthy authors, the genes, essentially composed of DNA, determined the specificity of proteins through the *mediation of ribosomes* whose RNA, an integral constituent, was metabolically stable. And yet nothing was observed in the kinetics of galactosidase synthesis which might look like a period of latency corresponding to the accumulation of new specific ribosomes. Such a difference between the metabolic stability of ribosomal RNA and the rapid induction or "deinduction" of bacterial populations in exponential growth did not fail to surprise J. Monod. He was even more puzzled when I let him know of an experiment I had just carried out using 5-fluorouracil, an analogue incorporable in RNA, which *immediately after addition* stopped the synthesis of active galactosidase molecules.

I also remember a seminar which took place in the great lecture room of the Institut Pasteur (1960). During that seminar on the biosynthesis of proteins, J. Monod drew a conclusion which emphasized the paradoxes which I mentioned above. For him there were two possibilities; either the ribosomal RNA was the famous template bearing the genetic information whose existence was now suspected by everybody, or—and this seemed less probable—proteins were assembled directly on the gene proper which then operated as a template. Unless, he thought, that a specific form of RNA, not yet identified, existed and was endowed with great metabolic instability, which would operate as a messenger between the gene of the protein. But, since no such thing was known, all was not yet well in the kingdom of Denmark.

Jacques Monod shared his doubts with F. Crick, S. Brenner, and F. Jacob during many passionate talks. It may be in the course of their conversations that their attention was drawn to the RNA of "Volkin and Astrachan." These authors had indeed already proved the existence of such a metabolicly unstable RNA by analyzing newly synthesized ribonucleic acids in bacteria infected with

T-even phages. The RNA, thus shown by ^{32}P labeling, had a very short life time but it also had a total base composition very close to that of the phage DNA. Little attention had been given to this extraordinary observation probably because the model system used in this experiment had, in a way, seemed "abnormal" and it was to be feared that metabolic deviation might be due to viral infection. Furthermore the authors themselves thought they might well be dealing with a precursor form of the DNA.

FINDING OF MESSENGER RNA

One day in June 1961, I met F. Jacob on the steps of the main building of the Institut Pasteur. Both of us were about to leave for the United States and we exchanged a few ideas on the experiments we were planning to carry out there, each one in a different laboratory. François meant to study thoroughly the nature of Volkin and Astrachan's RNA in Meselson's laboratory in Pasadena, where S. Brenner was to join him. As for me, J. Watson had invited me to carry out in his lab, work I had initiated some years before with F. Neidhardt on what was then called "the chloramphenicol particles."

What follows is well known. Jacob, Meselson, and Brenner brilliantly demonstrated that Volkin and Astrachan's RNA operated on *pre-existing* ribosomes as a template biopolymer, organizing as a real "viral messenger," the proteins newly synthesized by the phage.

For me it was more painstaking! When I arrived at Jim's lab, I was not yet thinking of working on messenger RNA. To study the RNA accumulated in the presence of chloramphenicol one had to examine the newly synthesized RNA in control cells, without antibiotic. C. Kurland, who had already acquired great practice in using sucrose gradients to fractionate macromolecules, was at the lab. He was extremely interested in the properties of ribosomal RNA. Our experimental projects included labeling with radiophosphorus during increasing periods of time, from two to three minutes to one hour. We were very much surprised when we found out that for very short labeling periods the distribution profiles did not coincide at all with those of ribosomal RNA. As labeling went on, we could notice a coincidence between the profile of newly synthesized RNAs and that of pre-existing RNAs. Jim was disappointed; the profiles were not regular; some heterodispersion could be observed. To cheer us up and forget experimental results, which should have filled us with joy but, for the time being, left us down-hearted, we used to take walks on the Harvard campus and talk about RNA and women (Jim was still single and extremely romantic). I don't remember how we came to talk of the effects of 5-fluorouracil and the Volkin and Astrachan's RNA and to make comparisons with our own results. It was then we ventured to think that the "pulse labeled" RNA might be worthy of interest.

After many control experiments, we reached the conclusion that an important fraction of "rapidly labeled" RNA had the properties of a messenger RNA; its reversible association to ribosomes and the study of its composition strengthened our conviction, but we hesitated a long time before drawing a conclusion for fear we might be in the presence of a metabolic precursor of ribosomes.

In Jim's laboratory, in the severe Harvard University building, adorned on both sides with two huge bronze rhinoceroses, we lived epic moments! The heat was suffocating, the laboratory glassware reduced to nil, the radioactivity counters old, enormous and noisy; many times experiments would trail along late into the night. Kurland and I would end our rapid labeling experiment at three o'clock in the morning. Immediately after, I would go to bed, fall asleep, then jump awake, and realize that, in order to make the tubes stand more evenly in the centrifuge, I had happily mixed the culture labeled for two hours with that labeled for two minutes—which did not seriously impair the results. We decided nonetheless that we had to get better organized: day shift; night shift. One day Jim introduced me to a Martian. I was supposed to give a briefing in chemistry to this eminent professor of physics. He used to follow me like my shadow and looked extremely intelligent (a ventured judgment, since I never heard him pronounce more than two words a day). This physicist with enormous glasses was W. Gilbert who rapidly made himself famous in biology.

Back in Paris, F. Jacob and myself had the pleasant surprise of finding out that the hydrodynamic and kinetic parameters of the RNAs which we had studied at 5000 kilometers from each other were closely related. The characteristics of a messenger were plainly established for the RNA formed after infection with a bacteriophage, and it also appeared from our own experiments that an RNA with similar properties did exist in normal bacterial cells but that it accumulated in such a small amount (23% of total RNA) that it had not been possible until then to identify it.

The birth, at times difficult, of messenger RNA was received with great acclaim. We must admit that it is only the laborious and gradual finding of the main chemical, metabolic, and particularly, template properties of the rapidly renewing RNA which succeeded in convincing everybody (1963). The finding of a strict complementarity in the sequences of the messenger and the homospecific DNA (Spiegelman) was also a major contribution. At the same time, the first experiments on the role of artificial messengers played by polymers also supported the hypothesis of Monod and Jacob as well as helped the study of the chemical nature of the code (Nirenberg, Ochoa).

During a symposium on molecular biology which took place in the Salle d'Iéna in Paris, upon my return from Watson's laboratory I introduced the first results I had obtained on messenger RNA. And I will always remember Jacques Monod saying to me, "This time, François, we have a beautiful story. We are going to have fun." (That was one of his favorite expressions.) I can see again his penetrating look and this sentence still resounds in my ears.

This is how the story of messenger RNA began. At least this was how I have lived its beginning. As in many other circumstances, Monod's genius made him doubt the reality of current ideas at given stages of the evolution of science, and made him clearly foresee transitory situations. He then supported the hypothesis with a network of facts, thus replacing doubt with certainty.

FROM LACTOSE TO GALACTOSE

Gérard Buttin

In 1954, the curriculum of a student in natural sciences, at the Ecole Normale, included a one year period during which he had to become acquainted with experimental work in a laboratory. I was such a student, more interested in knowing about the molecular mechanisms underlying cell physiology than hunting insects and flowers in their natural environment, convinced in addition that the most exciting field in which to tackle problems of cell physiology was the bacterial world. For biological students bacteria were part of the plant kingdom. This classification was perhaps based on more administrative than taxonomical considerations, but it led me to seek the advice of Roger Buvat, the head of the Department of Botany at the Ecole Normale. My good luck was that, in contrast to most biologists, he was interested in bacteria. He was somewhat disconcerted about helping me because the only place in Paris where such research topics were actively investigated was the Pasteur Institute, an institution which seemed to have had no interest at all in maintaining any connection with the University; yet, he managed to arrange an interview for me with Jacques Monod.

Hence, one morning in the summer of 1954, I went to "Pasteur" and met with Monsieur Monod. He asked me to explain precisely what I expected from a training period in his laboratory. I had to confess that I would not be free for research on a full-time basis. He expressed some concern but did not object. He

125

suggested a few reading references, which were all American journals. Due to my complete ignorance of the English language, I had to ask him to repeat the name of the magazines slowly. At this stage in our talk, I was almost prepared to forget about the idea. He looked a little surprised indeed that somebody should find this a problem but his only frightening comment was that I would have plenty of opportunity to "improve" my English. As I understood it better later on, his acceptance had some flavor of a challenge, which compensated for the difficulties to be expected.

I started working after the summer holidays, under the direct guidance of Germaine Cohen-Bazire and with a lot of advice from Annamaria Torriani. At that time, the *lactose* inducible system comprised only one enzyme: the β-galactosidase. Lactose analogs—the thiogalactosides—which were not substrates for the enzyme had recently been synthesized by Turk and Helferich. Some of them exhibited inducing properties, while others competitively inhibited the induction process. These "gratuitous" inducers—a term coined by Jacques Monod to express their property not to contribute to the overall cell metabolism—opened a new dimension in the quantitative analysis of induction kinetics. I undertook a systematic screening of the inducing capacity of all available thiogalactosides, of their affinity to the purified β-galactosidase and of their "apparent affinity" to the intracellular enzyme. Day by day, the complete lack of correlation between the values of these three parameters became more apparent. This further argued against the simple so-called "instructive" models of enzyme synthesis (viewing the active site of the β-galactosidase molecule as the target for the inducer) which a more restricted offensive, using the same weapons, had just started to put into question. Besides, constitutive strains, which synthesized β-galactosidase in media devoid of inducer, had been isolated. The prevailing hypothesis was that they accumulated an "internal" inducer. The availability of powerful inhibitors of induction prompted us to check their ability to block the constitutive synthesis, with entirely negative results. We were so disappointed that we shelved the constitutive strains, a fortunate decision because several years elapsed before it became clear that the inhibitors could not be more active in this system than a key trying to open a door which has no fitting lock. Germaine got over these frustrating results by concentrating attention on the cultures of photosynthetic bacteria, which together with *E. coli* monopolized her interest. I had no such refuge, but realize today how exceptional was this training period when Jacques Monod was free enough to devote the necessary time every evening to criticizing each experimental curve. When he left, it was customary that dinner service at the Ecole Normale was over.

A good deal of these talks in the "attic," where the laboratory was located, focused on possible interpretations of a simple observation: partially "preinduced" cultures synthesized almost immediately β-galactosidase at its maximal rate when exposed again to low inducer concentrations which, when supplied to uninduced cultures, triggered synthesis only progressively and after a marked lag. Obviously, the identification of the stable "factor," distinct from β-galactosidase, which accumulated during–and promoted–induction, would be a major clue to understanding the induction process.

The enlightenment came from the ground floor. There, George Cohen and Howard Rickenberg already occupied a room of the renewed Department of Biochemistry, of which Jacques Monod had been appointed head. Using radioactive thiogalactosides, they directly analyzed the uptake of these compounds by a variety of bacterial strains. It soon became clear that the inducible factor which puzzled us was a specific transport and accumulation system for β-galactosides: the "β-galactoside-permease." The properties of the permease accounted for most peculiarities observed in the determination of the "apparent affinity" of the galactosides for the intracellular enzyme. It was also clear, however, that the inhibition exerted by some thiogalactosides on the induction process could not be explained on the basis of a competition between inducer and inhibitor for the transport system. Besides the permease and the β-galactosidase active sites, a third intracellular structure which recognized the β-galactosides was unmasked, at the level of which these compounds had to exert their property to control induction.

I had no further chance to contribute to sketching out the target for the inducer. The school year was over. It had been rich with excitement; I had enjoyed the informal friendship of renowned scientists. I felt bitter when I thought of the near future: the preparation of the Agregation competitive examinations, and then military service!

Three years went by before I could return to the laboratory to prepare my Ph. D. thesis. Jacques Monod and his colleagues had all moved down from the attic to the Department of Biochemistry, which spread along both sides of a long corridor on the ground floor. This was now a busy avenue, channeling a flow of information which everyone could glean up from better informed colleagues. Some encounters were recurrent: every Monday morning Georges Cohen and Alain Bussard would exchange jokes and puns heard during the weekend. Some encounters were unpredicable; for example, literally bumping into David Perrin, who was always eager to sum up the content of the latest issue of P. N. A. S. as he simultaneously dissected the package or innards of a new laboratory apparatus.

Science had progressed. The analysis of the *lactose* system remained the research topic for most people in the department but the genetic approach had been fruitful enough to shift interest to a more precise understanding of the relationships between genetic material and inducible protein molecules. When I showed up, Jacques Monod was excited by the tremendous experimental possibilities offered along this line by the inducible enzymes of galactose metabolism. The Lederbergs had just shown that the chromosomal segment carrying the genetic information for these enzymes could be carried by the phage λ and thereby inserted in duplicate into the genome of a recipient bacterium. A manuscript by W. Arber described that more than one prophage genome could be integrated in this way. Obviously, the possibility was open in this system to carry out dominance and complementation studies for bacterial genes involved in the control of inducible enzyme synthesis; and piling up a variable number of galactose genes did not seem to be out of reach. This would allow a quantitative estimate of the influence of gene dosage on the rate of synthesis of a well-defined protein. I considered the transduction processes as the most amazing phenomenon in the microbial world and enthusiastically accepted tackling this problem.

Very little was known on the regulation of the three enzymes—galactokinase, transferase, and epimerase—which had been identified in this system, other than the fact that they were all induced by galactose. Well-informed of the advantages presented by "gratuitous inducers," I wished to characterize galactose analogs with properties mimicking those of the thiogalactosides in the lactose system. After we discussed this project, Jacques Monod came back holding a little pinebox full of odd tubes, each containing an uncommon sugar in trace amount. This treasure was a unique collection of rare chemicals, a gift from Gabriel Bertrand who despite his advanced age still frequently visited a laboratory piously preserved from the overall refurbishing of the department. The magic box did contain the key to the solution of my problem: a sample of pure D-fucose, which came to light as a nonmetabolized inducer devoid of any significant affinity to galactokinase. When it turned out that the lactose inducer TMG (thiomethylgalactoside) behaved in this system as a powerful specific inhibitor, my weapons were ready. With Agnes Ullmann's help, in one evening I synthesized enough TMG for several years of research work. The kinetics of galactokinase induction were analyzed; constitutitive strains were obtained by exploiting their property to grow on galactose in the presence of TMG; a set of galactose negative mutants was isolated, and the phage λ fulfilled its expected role in allowing the analysis of the complementation pattern between these mutants. Week after week, it became more obvious that the galactose genes expressed themselves as an integral unit, and obeyed a negative type of control. Genes governing induction were identified, with properties impressively similar to those of the so-called regulator (*i*) and operator (*o*) genes of the lactose system, to which "the model" attributed respectively the emitter and receiver function for a "repressor" signal. The galactose regulator mapped unambiguously on the bacterial chromosome at the antipodes of the supposedly "structural" genes of the three enzymes. This remote location was consistent with the properties expected from the emitter of a diffusible signal, and indeed it pleased everybody. The first attempts to map the operator gene were less successful. My data made it difficult to avoid the conclusion that it was located right in the middle of the enzyme genes, a result which then made it difficult to understand how at the molecular level the operator could control the expression of the whole structural sequence. Jacques Monod was skeptical. He could indeed suggest interpretations, but they were not straightforward. François Jacob, who paid a growing interest to the development of this work, was more than skeptical: an operator might sit at either end of an operon, but not in the middle. He advised me to go back to my bench and to look for some bias in the mapping procedure. I did this. The bias was that the strains utilized were heterogeneous in the activity of a galactose transport system. The operator moved back to one end of the galactose operon, supporting one of Jacques Monod's favorite statements according to which "a good model deserves more confidence than one conflicting experiment . . ."

The striking similarity exhibited by the regulatory elements of the lactose and galactose systems strengthened both the repressor hypothesis and the notion that the unit of genetic expression can comprise several genes. I could not help expressing some surprise at how perfectly my results fitted the theory: "you man of little faith!" was the first comment from the boss, soon followed by a straightforward laugh in which one could discern more complicity than boldness.

This docility of the galactose system was indeed reassuring. In the neophyte, it might just as well have given rise to the slightly disappointing feeling of repetitious work, if the puzzling results of experiments involving the transducing phage λ had not initiated a different line of investigations. Clearly, the regulation of the galactose genes obeyed the same regulation, be they in their natural environment, or part of a λ transducing prophage inserted in the bacterial chromosome. But, during the vegetative development of the transducing phage, an intense synthesis of galactokinase was observed, the rate of which was essentially independent of the presence of an inducer. The galactose genes now seemed to obey the regulation common to the phage genes. We had in the past discussed the possibility that the expression of a "structural" gene might be influenced by the overall regulation of the genome in which it is inserted, but this vague hypothesis had now to be reconciled with our evidence that the galactose repressor somehow acted at the level of an operator which remained associated to the galactose structural genes in the transducing particles. We proposed two explanations to this paradox. The first one considered the derepression of the galactose enzymes as the consequence of an imbalance in the ratio of repressor molecules to their operator target sites when multiple copies of the latter were generated by the replication of the transducing phages. The other one postulated a real change in the regulation of the galactose enzymes, arising from the synthesis of a phage transcription enzyme which could displace the bacterial repressor.

The first interpretation was strongly supported by the work of Salvador Luria who, at the same time, analyzed a very similar phenomenon, using a lactose transducing p_1 phage. Taking advantage of the fact that the lactose regulator gene i is close enough to the genes it controls to also remain associated to them in the transducing phages, he could establish that the cointegration of an active i gene was necessary and sufficient to prevent the derepression of the lactose enzymes during the phage vegetative growth. Unfortunately, the structure of the galactose system did not enable one to decide if the same explanation accounted entirely for the derepression of galactokinase.

Yet the most surprising observation arose from the simplest control experiment. When I checked whether the induction of a wild-type λ prophage in a wild-type bacterial strain had any influence on the expression of the nearby galactose genes, an abundant synthesis of galactokinase—weakly stimulated by galactose or D-fucose—was again detected.

A very friendly competition to explain this phenomenon was engaged in with Herbert Wiesmayer and Michael Yarmolinsky who had just observed that epimerase synthesis also escaped its normal control upon λ induction. The naive speculation that the altered expression of host genes caused by the turn-on of prophage functions might have some relevance to the mechanism of animal cell transformation by oncogenic viruses was a strong stimulus. A variety of experiments were carried out, which all showed that a close physical association of the galactose bacterial genes to the λ prophage was a prerequisite to the manifestation of this effect. The kinetics of the constitutive enzyme synthesis suggested that, at least in some cells, the linkage between the viral and host genome was maintained. We were back to considering either phage dependent replication or transcription of the bacterial genes as the basis for this peculiar effect. The conflicting results of experiments devised to clarify this question could be reconciled only much later, when the availability of appropriate phage mutants made it possible to show that both replication and transcription processes initiated on the phage genome could proceed uninterrupted up to the bacterial galactose operon. Even more recently, refined biochemical experiments established that, if λ does not code for a new transcription enzyme, it governs the synthesis of a regulatory factor which makes the bacterial RNA polymerase blind to its stop signals and able to "read-through" a nearby operon.

While I attempted to assemble the pieces of the galactose puzzle, five years had flown by, consisting of days of great excitement, followed by weeks of questionable progress. In the laboratory, a few rites resisted time, like the seminar program, which attracted an increasing number of people from various institutions. I scrupulously attended the seminars, which Jacques Monod considered, with excellent reasons, the necessary basis for the education and recycling of a scientist. But, because most of the talks were delivered in English, for a long time I missed so many of the speakers' points, that I left the room more often dis-

couraged than stimulated. Strengthening my feeling of being handicapped was
the ease with which the boss could join the game ten minutes late and ask within the next ten minutes a first pertinent question about problems very remote
from his actual field of investigation. Another permanent institution was the
lunch ceremony, which from two floors drained André Lwoff, Jacques Monod,
François Jacob, and their colleagues. Over the bread and cheese—or the more
sophisticated masterpieces of a nearby *traiteur*—we talked about scientific
news, political, or artistic events. These discussions showed that whatever the
topic, the very same people were once again the most competant . . .

Some changes were discernible along this period. The *tour d'ivoire* was
infiltrated by a growing number of students who brought their own originality
to a renowned and experienced community which was constantly being enriched by long-term visits of foreign scientists. New rites had also been established, like François Jacob's daily morning visit to our laboratory. On his way to
Jacques Monod's contiguous office, he would stop and either banter, or urge
us to speed up the program, but would always make invaluable comments on
our experiments in progress.

The growing fame of Jacques Monod and his appointment to a professorship
at the University exerted increasing and convergent pressures—which he resisted
remarkably well—to take him away from the laboratory. Then, Saturday afternoons became the best time to join him. The silence of the building contributed
to generating an informal and relaxed atmosphere for discussions which he liked
to pursue while carrying out—perhaps as an antidote to administrative duties—
some experimental work.

The former student today faces, in a very different context, the duties of a
mature scientist. Among the questions which are often raised—even if there are
no answers—on a university campus, two remain for me a major source of
worry. How is one to instill in young people the necessary passion for research?
How can one evaluate a scientist's individual responsibility in the success—or in
the lack of success—of a program with certitude? Perhaps my special concern
when it comes to these problems is nothing but the ransom to be paid for a very
fortunate first contact with the scientific community; and does it perhaps also
illustrate the sly danger of an example?

THE WONDERFUL YEAR

David Perrin

The circumstances in which I met Jacques Monod already reveal something about the man; it was in 1954, when he gave a lecture on Louis Rapkine's esthetic theory at the Philosophical Society. Since childhood a friend and admirer of Louis, I went to listen and was more fascinated by the man than by the subject (the president slept through most of the talk and only woke up to give a brilliant conclusion). Having just finished my "license," majoring in zoology, I went to the not yet famous attic of the Pasteur, to ask Monod if I could work with him. He inquired whether I had any biochemistry, I did; whether I played a musical instrument, I did not, but admitted to singing in the university chorus (to my relief he did not ask for a demonstration). He told me to go learn genetics; I did and that started it all. I worked with him for fifteen years, and discovered later that he too started as a zoologist.

Monod was very conscious that students coming from the French University knew very little. When he designed his lab, he set aside a large room with six benches, which was to be used for a two-month lab course, to be given each year to twelve students. The ideal candidate was defined by Monod as being infinitely ignorant and infinitely intelligent. Actually the course was only given for two years, in 1956, and 1957. It was intended to breach the gap between university teaching and living research. It was our real introduction to what was

to become molecular biology—covering DNA, proteins, physiology, and biochemistry of bacteria and phages, of which we had been taught practically
nothing. For France, the system was completely new. The students helped design the experiments; anything feasible was tried beyond the basic canvass of the
course. The staff of the lab was mixed with the students and everybody learned
together, discussions being general.

This atmosphere prevailed in the lab: the corridor in the evening was the
meeting place where the day's experimental results were submitted for discussion. The weekly seminars were at the same time an informal but important
event. The room was uncomfortable and crowded. Slides were forbidden, since
Monod did not want data "hokus pokused;" curves had to be ploted, tables
laid out, everything in micromoles and milligrams of something, not just in cpm
or activity per milliliter. Slides were introduced only when every speaker was
lost without them, and wanted to show about twenty different sucrose gradients
of the same profile. Monod sat in front. His questions were not only sometimes
quite aggressive but some people could not stand his brilliant and very deliberately logical approach to all subjects. What amazed me most was that he often
embarked on a far-fetched idea, but always managed to land back on his feet by
proposing a feasible experiment that would provide a test for it.

In the lab things were more relaxed and the atmosphere was probably more
like that of an American lab than a French one. We practically lived in, all having
a joyous lunch seated at a table. But it was more like a big family. True respect
for Monod's obvious superior ability was mixed with a deep affection for him.
We, the students, were his children, and he treated us as such, sternly when he
thought it better for us. He wanted each of us to have our own private research
project, and appreciated people who became completely involved. Once a brilliant scientist from another lab gave a seminar, after which I asked Monod what
he thought of it, expecting scientific appreciation. His answer was that the man
really seemed to be inhabited by his problem; it was probably his highest praise
for a scientist.

So 1958 came. I was working on enzyme induction in *Pseudomonas*. One day
Monod came to me and said, "Jacob and I have started a study of the genetics of
galactosidase and permease. The system is ripe, we are getting a lot of new mutants that have to be analyzed and we need more hands. I would like you to
study CRM producing mutants of galactosidase for which there is preliminary
evidence." So I dropped *Pseudomonas* and mutants of catechol oxidase and
joined this extraordinary team for what was to be a fantastic scientific adventure. It was a wonderful year during which every experiment proved what it was
supposed to prove.

The study of CRM was of course prompted by the need to map the structural
gene for galactosidase so it could be distinguished from genes involved in induction. But it was also to understand the obscure relation between that old ghost

Pz and CRM of galactosidase. The experimental approach is interesting in that it reveals how Monod worked. He wanted quantitative results that could be expressed in absolute values. We devised a scheme of competition between galactosidase and CRM in which the only thing measured was enzyme activity. Never did I use an Ouchterlony plate to detect CRM even though it might have been a fast screening procedure. Likewise we practically never looked at bacteria under the microscope. Monod did not have visual intelligence; he saw with his brain, and the only result that really pleased him was a linear plot. His cartesian logic prevailed over everything. Experimental conditions had to be strictly controlled; bacteria were always grown in synthetic medium and had to be exponential. He often made fun of the British who added beef extract and 10% tap water to synthetic media. Still there was available to us as a last resort, when bugs did not grow, a mysterious tube labeled "oligo elements" to be added in case of disaster—I've never seen it work.

We worked following a certain number of Monod's practical aphorisms such as: "bacteria never make mistakes" or "there are no bad experiments." Monod had a knack for extracting from "muddy" data what went wrong and what had to be done to have a significant experiment. Statistics were not used; effects had to be all or none or so great that you only wondered whether they were artifacts, not whether they were meaningful. The last aphorism was the most potent: "autosatisfaction is death."

Monod loved music so much that he could not stand a radio in the lab. He said that when he heard music he could not think. But during that wonderful year Jacob kept whistling a theme from Mozart's clarinet quintet and Monod walked through the corridors booming a trombone theme from a Brahms concerto. Music was with us anyway.

When the different CRM proteins of galactosidase came to be reasonably measurable proteins, Monod asked me to prove that their induction was quantitatively the same as that of galactosidase and that they had no affinity for the inducers. That resulted in a short paper that I have seen quoted in literature as by Perrin and Coll., which gave me a shock for the Coll. were Jacob and Monod. Now, we had two new tools at our disposal: Jacob's Flac episomes which permitted the study of dominance and complementation and CRM which made possible quantitative measurement of the expression of two alleles of the structural gene for galactosidase in a diploid. During that year every experiment added a significant piece to the puzzle. From Flac episomes came 0^c mutants. By measuring CRM and galactosidase in diploid $0^c/0^+$ mutants 0^c was shown to be not only dominant but *cis*-dominant, which was unequivocal proof of the existence of the operator. The i^s mutant which became a cornerstone of the theory of induction by negative control appeared by luck. It was a strange *lac* negative, giving numerous revertants which were all constitutive. It could only be understood if you were prepared for it; it proved to be *trans*-dominant and fit nicely with the theory.

One day shortly after, some Flac heterozygotes were made. There were strange results that could be interpreted as compartmentalization of proteins inside the bacterial cells. For two days "vesicular biology" was rampant in the corridor, then fell flat when a mistake in strains was discovered. Two weeks later, a visitor from the States arrived and excitedly asked about vesicular biology, which was already forgotten. This shows how fast news traveled and the anxious interest of our foreign colleagues in the work in progress. We felt that the theories, the techniques, and the strains at our disposal really put us ahead of many other labs. Therefore we were not involved in a "rat race" and could be somewhat relaxed about publication of results. This resulted in papers that could really be constructed around an idea, with proper controls, and not the hasty unloading of notebooks that is now common.

The wonderful year passed, the chase for the repressor was started, and allostery came. The lab was crowded; on a central bench Changeux and I had only half as much space as Buttin, more advanced and swamped with galactose plates. On the shelf above me stood a large flask with Changeux's "allosteric buffer;" no other buffer worked, and when it was half empty he used to replenish it, neglecting the slime at the bottom which may have been responsible for the miracle.

More years passed. Monod became Director; Jacob moved to mammalia; bacteria seemed less an exciting subject as molecular biologists moved to differentiation and oncogeny. But we still tried to do meaningful work with bacteria following one of Monod's last aphorisms: Remember there is always plenty of room at the bottom."

FROM DIAUXIE TO THE CONCEPT OF
CATABOLITE REPRESSION

Boris Magasanik

I do not remember when I met Jacques Monod for the first time. I was certainly very much aware of his work when I began to study enzymatic adaptation to *myo*-inositol in 1950. I recall that shortly after that time André Lwoff visited J. Howard Mueller, the head of my department at Harvard Medical School, who asked him to talk to me about my work. André Lwoff kindly suggested that my results would interest Jacques Monod and that I should write to him. I was quite abashed at the idea that such a great man would see anything of interest in the modest efforts of a beginner and could not bring myself to take up André Lwoff's suggestion.

It turned out that our efforts to discover, by the use of amino acid auxotrophs, whether the formation of an adaptive enzyme involved synthesis *de novo* of protein paralleled similar efforts of Jacques Monod (1, 2). I am quite certain that we became personally acquainted in 1953 or 1954, but it was a meeting in Boston in the spring of 1956 that has remained most vivid in my memory.

Our studies of inositol metabolism in histidine-requiring mutants of *Aerobacter* (now *Klebsiella*) *aerogenes* had yielded a most unexpected result: the histidine requirement for growth on *myo*-inositol was approximately twenty five times greater than that for growth on glucose (1). We then found that when grown on *myo*-inositol or most other energy and carbon sources, but not when grown on glucose, the cells produced a series of enzymes capable of degrading histidine to ammonia, glutamate, and formamide. Glutamate could be further degraded to serve as a general source of energy and carbon. These enzymes, whose synthesis was induced by histidine, caused the loss of the exogenously supplied histidine, and therefore increased the requirement of the histidine auxotroph for this amino acid (3). Our observation that glucose prevented the formation of these enzymes was thus a rediscovery of the glucose effect identified by Jacques Monod thirteen years earlier as the cause of the diauxic growth of *Escherichia coli* on mixtures of glucose and other carbon compounds (4).

One of my students, Fred Neidhardt, continued the study of this phenomenon. He could show convincingly that glucose did not interfere with the uptake of histidine and did not limit the cell in substances necessary for protein synthesis. He made the completely unexpected, but to us very exciting observation that *K. aerogenes* could grow on glucose with histidine as the only nitrogen source and produced in this case the histidine-degrading enzymes in spite of the presence of glucose; addition of ammonia immediately arrested the synthesis of these enzymes (5).

At this stage, Fred Neidhardt, having completed his dissertation, expressed the wish to be accepted by Jacques Monod for postdoctoral study at the Pasteur Institute; but unfortunately, we were informed that there was no space for him in the coming year. The only hope was that Jacques Monod, who was about to visit Boston, would reverse this verdict upon meeting Fred.

My wife Adele, and I were planning a small reception for Jacques at our house. We decided to take him and Fred to dinner at a well-known seafood restaurant before the reception in the hope that good food and pleasant conversation would soften Jacques' heart toward Fred. During this dinner, Fred told Jacques about our *Klebsiella aerogenes* which, then faced with the dilemma of obeying the command of glucose to stop histidase production, or of disobeying this command, chose to disobey when this disobedience was essential for growth. It became obvious that Jacques considered this an unlikely, perhaps incorrect, but certainly unattractive view. Somewhat crestfallen we finished dinner and drove quickly to our house in order to arrive there before our other guests. While they gathered, Jacques sat quietly in a chair, apparently absorbed in thought. Then suddenly he turned to Fred with a smile and said: "You have proven the existence of God." And he accepted Fred for postdoctoral work at the Pasteur Institut where Fred eventually worked with François Gros.

My own study in Jacques Monod's laboratory as a Guggenheim Fellow in 1959 made me appreciate even more the blend of uncompromising critical rigor and of human concern in Jacques' personality. I began at the Pasteur Institute to study the regulation of the histidine-degrading enzymes in *Salmonella typhimurium*, where the combination of genetic and biochemical techniques developed by Monod and Jacob for the *lac* system of *E. coli* could be used to advantage.

Although Jacques initially did not like Fred Neidhardt's apparently teleological explanation of the escape of histidase from the effect of glucose in cells deprived of ammonia, this explanation was actually based on an earlier discovery by Monod: the inhibition of the formation of an enzyme essential for tryptophan biosynthesis by the addition of tryptophan to the growth medium (6). The *repression* of an enzyme by its product appeared as a rational counterpart to the *induction* of an enzyme by its substrate.

In our analysis of the escape of histidase from the effect of glucose, we made the assumption that the formation of an enzyme may be subject to *both* substrate induction and end product repression. We assumed that such an enzyme would only be produced when the intracellular level of its substrate was high and that of its product low. The ultimate products of histidine degradation are the catabolites, common products of the degradation of all carbon compounds capable of supporting growth, as well as ammonia and glutamate. In a cell growing with glucose as source of carbon and ammonia as source of nitrogen, the intracellular level of catabolites, glutamate, and ammonia would be high enough to repress histidase, overriding the induction by histidine. However, limitation of one of these products by depriving the cell either of ammonia or glutamate or of glucose, an excellent source of carbon catabolites, would permit induction to prevail and histidase to be produced. It is quite easy to see that this hypothesis would also explain why enzymes such as β-galactosidase and the enzymes responsible for inositol degradation would be subject to the effect of glucose, but not be able to escape from this effect when starved for ammonia. The only products of the degradation of lactose or *myo*-inositol are the carbon catabolites more readily available by the degradation of glucose, which would therefore repress the enzymes responsible for the degradation of lactose and of inositol under all conditions. The hypothesis of catabolite repression predicts that energy sources other than glucose should repress glucose-sensitive enzymes in cells grown in media that limit their ability to utilize the catabolites rapidly for the synthesis of macromolecules; and in fact, partial amino acid, purine, pyrimidine, or phosphate starvation has this effect (7).

As the names imply, in a physiological sense, induction is a positive control and catabolite repression a negative control. Nevertheless, for *lac* and *hut* (histidine degradation) and many other systems, induction actually reflects negative control at the molecular level, and in all cases catabolite repression appears to reflect positive control at the molecular level. The postulation by Monod of the existence of a specific *lac* repressor, capable of preventing transcription of the *lac* operon unless neutralized by the specific inducer (8), has been verified completely by the isolation of a repressor protein with these exact attributes (9). The observation by Ullmann and Monod (10) and independently by Perlman and Pastan (11) that the addition of cyclic AMP can overcome the repressive effect of glucose, led to the discovery that the transcription of genes coding for enzymes subject to catabolite repression requires activation by the catabolite activating protein (CAP) charged with cyclic AMP (12). Glucose appears to lower the intracellular level of cyclic AMP by an as yet undiscovered mechanism.

The discovery of a relatively nonspecific molecular mechanism for catabolite repression (CAP recognizes a site located near the promoter of every catabolite sensitive operon or gene), clearly raised anew the question of how the transcription of the *hut* system of *K. aerogenes* could be activated when cells were grown in an ammonia-free medium with glucose as source of energy. Cells growing in such a medium cannot be induced to form β-galactosidase, a clear indication that CAP is not present in its active form. An explanation for the escape of histidase from repression by glucose was finally found, twenty years after Neidhardt had first observed the phenomenon. The transcription of the *hut* genes and of other genes coding for enzymes whose activity can provide the cells with energy, as well as with ammonia or glutamate, can be activated either by CAP charged with cyclic AMP or by nonadenylylated glutamine synthetase (GS) (13, 14). In the presence of excess ammonia, GS is present at a low level and partly in an adenylylated form. Starvation for ammonia results in the deadenylylation of GS and in a rise in its cellular level. This increased amount of nonadenylylated GS is responsible for the activation of the transcription of the *hut* genes in ammonia-starved cells.

In short, the apparent escape from catabolite repression of histidase really reflects a phenomenon distinct from catabolite repression: the activation by GS of the transcription of genes coding for enzymes that can supply the cell with ammonia or glutamate. As expected, the synthesis of an enzyme such as urease, capable of supplying the cell with ammonia but not with catabolites, is activated by GS but not by CAP (15).

In retrospect, Fred Neidhardt and I were stimulated to formulate the hypothesis of catabolite repression by our analysis of the apparent escape of histidase from the effect of glucose. It is this analysis which failed to win Jacques Monod's approval when we first presented it to him. His sensitivity and taste made him aware of a flaw in our analysis that only much more work could elucidate: the apparent escape of histidase was unrelated to the effect of glucose, but reflected a new, unsuspected regulatory mechanism.

References

1.   Ushiba, D. and Magasanik, B. (1952). *Proc. Soc. Exp. Biol. Med.* 80, 626.
2.   Monod, J., Pappenheimer, A. M., Jr., and Cohen-Bazire, G. (1952). *Biochim. Biophys. Acta* 9, 648.
3.   Magasanik, B. (1955). *J. Biol. Chem.* 213, 557.

4. Monod, J. (1942). Recherches sur la croissance des cultures bacteriennes, Paris.
5. Neidhardt, F. C. and Magasanik, B. (1956). *Nature* **178**, 801.
6. Monod, J. and Cohen-Bazire, G. (1953). *C. R. Acad. Sci.* **236**, 530.
7. Magasanik, B. (1961). *CSHSQB* **26**, 249.
8. Pardee, A. B., Jacob, F., and Monod, J. (1959). *J. Mol. Biol.* **1**, 165.
9. Gilbert, W. and Muller-Hill, B. (1966). *Proc. Natl. Acad. Sci. U.S.A.* **56**, 1891.
10. Ullmann A. and Monod, J. (1968). *F.E.B.S.* **2**, 57.
11. Perlman, R. and Pastan, I. (1968). *Biochem. Biophys. Res. Commun.* **30**, 656.
12. Zubay, G., Schwartz, D., and Beckwith, J. (1970). *Proc. Natl. Acad. Sci. U.S.A.* **66**, 104.
13. Magasanik, B., Prival, M.J., and Brenchley, J. E.(1973). *In* " The Enzymes of Glutamine Metabolism" (S. Prusiner and E. R. Stadman, eds.), p. 9, Academic Press, New York.
14. Tyler, B., DeLeo, A. B., and Magasanik, B. (1974). *Proc. Natl. Acad. Sci. U.S.A.* **71**, 225.
15. Friedrich, B. and Magasanik, B. (1977). *J. Bacteriol.* **131**, 446.

PERMEASES AND OTHER THINGS

B. L. Horecker

Early in the 1950s Jacques Monod visited Washington, D. C. and delivered a lecture at the National Academy of Sciences on the subject of enzyme induction in *Escherichia coli*. His earlier careful measurements of the dynamics of growth in microorganisms had led him to describe a phenomenon, which he called diauxie, that characterized growth of *E. coli* on pairs of substrates such as glucose and lactose. He observed that after a period of rapid growth during which the glucose was consumed, there was a leveling-off of the curve before growth resumed on the second substrate. Pursuing this observation and fortified by his early training in genetics in T. H. Morgan's laboratory at the California Institute of Technology, Monod discovered that the second phase of growth was dependent on the synthesis of a specific enzyme, β-galactosidase, whose synthesis was inhibited by the presence of glucose and induced by lactose, the second substrate.

Monod was an inspiring lecturer and his presentation at the National Academy of Sciences was a revelation to those of us who were hearing him for the first time. He described an elegant series of experiments, carried out with his colleagues David Hogness and Melvin Cohn, in which they demonstrated that the appearance of β-galactosidase activity was not due to activation of a pre-existing pro-enzyme but rather to the *de novo* synthesis of the enzyme protein

143

from amino acids. They also observed that the decrease in specific activity of the enzyme, after removal of the inducer, was due to simple dilution by new protein synthesis and not to the degradation of the enzyme protein. Indeed the turnover of *E. coli* proteins under exponential conditions of growth was negligible, so that no radioactivity from prelabeled proteins was used for the synthesis of the induced β-galactosidase.

The one-gene, one-enzyme hypothesis was by then firmly established and the challenging problem of the day was to describe the mechanisms whereby individual genes were turned on and off in response to changes in the environment or in the requirements of the cell. Monod sensed that the phenomenon of enzyme induction in microorganisms such as *E. coli* provided the key to this important question. His studies had already led him to suggest that the inducer did not act directly on the gene, but instead indirectly via a gene product.

During the course of an analysis of the ability of compounds related to lactose to act as inducers of β-galactosidase, Howard Rickenberg, working with Georges Cohen and Gerard Buttin in Monod's laboratory, discovered the inducible transport system ("permease") for β-galactosides. To quote from their classical paper published in the *Annales de l'Institut Pasteur* in 1956,* this discovery:

> donne une solution à de nombreux problèmes que posaient le métabolisme des galactosides et l'induction de la β-galactosidase chez *E. coli*, et apporte une confirmation expérimentale à l'hypothèse, souvent envisagée, que des systèmes catalytiques stériquement spécifiques et fonctionnellement spécialisés, distincts des enzymes métaboliques proprement dits, gouvernent la pénétration de certains substrats dans les cellules microbiennes.

While this work was in progress, Monod visited Bethesda and described these exciting and novel observations in a lecture at the National Institutes of Health. My group had just completed its investigations into the pathway of pentose fermentation and acetic acid production in Lactobacillus, and I was already much impressed with the use of microorganisms as models for the study of basic biological phenomena. I was convinced that the discovery of the permeases in Monod's laboratory had opened the door to the analysis at the molecular level of the mechanisms of cellular transport, and I decided to take advantage of a Rockefeller Public Service award to spend a year at the Pasteur Institute to work on this problem. In September 1957 my family and I sailed for Paris on the liner Statendam.

I could not have chosen a better time. The new science of molecular biology was emerging at the borders of microbial genetics and biochemistry and the Institut Pasteur, with André Lwoff, François Jacob, and Jacques Monod, was at

---

*Rickenberg, H. V., Cohen, G. N., Buttin, G., and Monod, J. (1956). *Annales de l'Institut Pasteur* **91**, 829-857.

the center of the exciting developments in this field. When we arrived, the annual course, "Le Cours," had just begun, and the laboratories were filled with students learning the new techniques of molecular biology, microbial and phage genetics, adaptation, protein synthesis, and immunology. Every day in the tiny library off the refectory, there was a lecture by one of the staff members or by a visitor.

It was during that year that Arthur Pardee, on a sabbatical at the Pasteur Institute, carried out the classical experiment with Monod and Jacob that established the role of the regulator gene, the i gene, in enzyme induction. Pardee, who was one of the discoverers of the phenomena of feedback inhibition and enzyme repression, had come to Paris to work on this problem and the idea, reinforced by Szilard during his frequent visits to the Institute, quickly developed that *induction* of catabolic enzymes by the substrate and *repression* of biosynthetic enzymes by the end product of the biosynthetic pathway were fundamentally similar processes, and that induction was really antirepression. The critical experiment, carried out with Hfr strains constructed for the purpose by Jacob and Elie Wollman, was finally conceived after long and excited discussions in Monod's little office. The experiments of Pardee, Jacob, and Monod also provided evidence that the messenger RNA for β-galactosidase in *E. coli* was unstable.

Monod's earlier studies had shown that the genetic regulation of the galactoside permease was coordinated with that of the β-galactosidase, and indeed that the gene for β-galactosidase (the z gene) and that for the permease (the y gene) were part of the same genetic unit, or operon. Thus both galactosidase and permease were induced coordinately. It was clear from these observations that the product of the permease gene was also a protein. Monod proposed that the permease would have the property of binding its substrate and suggested that we try to identify it by this property. Dietmar Türk, a young organic chemist from Germany, and I, working in a small hood in the hallway next to the refectory, set out to synthesize the lactose analogue, β-thiodigalactoside, labeled with very hot ^{35}S. To measure the binding, we used a simple and clever apparatus for equilibrium dialysis borrowed from Jean-Marie Dubert, designed for measuring the binding of antigen by antibodies. The experiment was negative, although there were a few more counts in the chamber with the extract from the induced cells. When Monod and I recalculated the number of counts expected, it became obvious that our labeled substrate was not of sufficiently high specific activity to allow us to detect the number of permease molecules that might reasonably be expected to be present in the extract. My notebook on this date, October 29, 1957, carries the title from Proust's monumental work "A la recherche du temps perdu." Years later, with much more refined techniques available and with genetically enriched mutants, Walter Gilbert and Benno Müller-Hill, used a similar approach to detect and isolate the *lac* repressor.

The *active* galactoside permease has not yet been isolated, but Fox and Kennedy have isolated and characterized the *y* gene product, which they called the M-protein, after modifying it with the *N*-ethylmaleimide, using a clever modification of the binding idea based on Adam Kepes' observation that the β-galactosidase permease contains essential sulfhydryl groups that are protected by the substrate.

The rest of my year at the Pasteur Institute was spent analyzing the properties of another specific permease that was responsible for the transport of galactose. I was assigned a technician, a charming young lady named Janine Thomas, and from that point my notes were written in French, corrected each evening by Janine, who became my teacher as well as my able and hard-working assistant. The parting greeting each evening became "Est-ce que vous avez mis les souches?" The constitutive galactose permease, measured in a galactokinase-less mutant of *E. coli*, proved to be remarkably specific and able to detect the presence of very low concentrations of galactose in the external medium. Our work also led to the discovery that a specific mechanism, enhanced by DNP, was responsible for the exit of the substrate, which had previously been thought to be a process of passive diffusion. Monod displayed his remarkable versatility by developing a logical, elegant, and simple mathematical formulation that permitted us to calculate the *exit* rate from the kinetics of the initial rate of *uptake*. This was published in the *Journal of Biological Chemistry* in 1958. This simple idea permitted us to analyze the activity of the exit process which, to our surprise, turned out to depend on the constituents of the growth medium. Thus the galactose exit rate was enhanced in cells grown in the presence of galactose, despite the fact that the galactokinase-less cells could not metabolize galactose and the permease was constitutive. The exit of galactose was also found to be inhibited by substances, such as α-methyglucoside and succinate, that were not substrates for the galactose permease. Adam Kepes had already proposed that specific transporters are involved in the movement of substrate across the cell membranes, and his evidence and ours was later supported by the finding of specific binding proteins. Monod's laboratory proved to be a fruitful and stimulating environment for these early studies on transport mechanisms.

Monod was intimately involved in everything that was going on in the laboratory, from sporulation to permeation, and in those days he was always in the laboratory, available for discussion of the work. He was equally ready to talk about music, or art, or the Russian sputnik, the news of which he brought me one Saturday morning. He was full of ideas and he possessed a vast store of information. This always amazed me, because apparently he did not read the literature. Somehow he managed to hear about every important event in science and in that year I came to appreciate the value of the grapevine as a source of information about important new developments.

Jacques Monod's approach to science was the essence of the inductive method, including (1) careful analysis of the facts in hand, (2) development of a suitable model or hypothesis, (3) design and careful execution of appropriate experiments to test the model, (4) revision of the model where necessary and then on to the next round of experiments. It was rare for him to make a serendipic discovery. It was equally rare for an experiment to fail, and when this happened it was likely to be for lack of adequate methodology, rather than because the model was incorrect. Thus, it was fascinating to observe the series of hypotheses and experiments that led his laboratory to the elucidation of the role of the *i* gene in the control of expression of the structural gene. Behind the final conclusion was a carefully constructed logical edifice based on precise genetic and biochemical measurements and broad biological concepts. Another example of his logical approach to the problem of biological regulation was his elaboration of the concept of allosteric proteins. The earlier literature contained many observations that suggested that enzymes and other proteins might possess specific sites, distinct from the catalytic site, for the interaction with specific effector molecules, but it was the classical papers of Gerhart and Pardee that finally provided elegant and convincing evidence for this concept. With Monod's characteristic flair for developing physical and mathematical models, this time with Jeffries Wyman and Jean-Pierre Changeux, who also contributed new experimental evidence, and for articulating these ideas in a stimulating and popular manner, he quickly succeeded in making "allostery" a household word.

Monod's remarkable intellect may have tended to obscure the warm and sensitive human being. His loyalty and devotion to his family and his friends were constant and enduring, but these qualities were very private and were only evident to those who were close to him. His "good works," if made known, would fill many chapters. His qualities as a scientist were more widely recognized and he became the center of discussions at every scientific meeting that he attended. Those of us who had the privilege of working with Jacques Monod on a daily basis were indeed fortunate, and the inspiration that he transmitted will be our lasting legacy.

EARLY KINETICS OF INDUCED ENZYME SYNTHESIS

Adam Kepes

During the many years which I spent in his laboratory (1955-1967), I heard Jacques Monod enunciate a number of aphorisms and sayings. The most universally known and the most often misquoted is "Whatever is true for *E. coli* is true for an elephant." His faith in the universality of the laws and mechanisms of biology contrasting with his provocative attitude of apparent cynicism in front of the great problems "the secrets of life" was fascinating to those of us who surrounded him.

But the cynical attitude was on the surface and I remember him saying that a real researcher must be more or less neurotic. I think he was emphasizing by this comment, the necessity for the researcher to live with his doubt not only until "the experiments are confirmed by the theory," but even beyond that point. The necessity never to consider one's own published statement nor that of anybody else as an irreversible truth, and to be ready at any time to submit them to a revision, implies a strong feeling of insecurity.

One of his expressions which struck me the most at that time and which has since given me ample matter for reflection was the explanation why he chose *E. coli* as the experimental subject. Somehow a liquid culture of *E. coli* reminded him of the perfect gas. Differences between individual bacteria in the culture, just like between molecules in the gas, are averaged out by the large number. An exponential culture remains "homothetic" to itself all the time, the relative increase of population in number, in mass, in optical density remains identical to the relative increase of protein, DNA, and RNA, which can be compared in a gas during compression to the parallel increase in density, pressure, and concentration as well as in partial pressure of each molecular species (if the gas is a mixture). Upon a more detailed analysis of a growing bacterial culture, the relative increase of each individual stable molecular species, or for that matter each unstable molecular species (provided they are in a steady state), also remains identical. This rule is broken, of course, whenever an essential ingredient of the medium becomes limiting during the observation. One very illustrative expression of the impersonal existence of *E. coli* as a perfect gas is that "exponentially growing *E. coli* has no age." This explains the emphasis of the experimental routine in Monod's laboratory on exponential phase bacteria and on conditions of "gratuity" in enzyme induction.

What happens during such an induction, can be described by the analogy with one perfect gas, the uninduced *E. coli*, which is submitted to gradual dilution by the addition of another perfect gas, the induced *E. coli*; all increment in measurable properties is due to the latter. Thus, the total activity of induced enzyme is proportional to the increase of bacterial mass as shown by the classical "Monod plot" $\Delta E = f(\Delta B)$.

The formal linear relationship holds true with astonishing accuracy, in spite of the intuitively obvious fact that during the dilution there is no mixture of uninduced bacteria with induced bacteria, but the whole population is of individuals, partly induced and partly uninduced. This has been beautifully demonstrated by the experiments of Seymour Benzer. Thus it seems that the quality of *E. coli* as a perfect gas is not connected with the division of the matter into the relatively uniformly sized cells, but it is somehow a more profound property. This irrelevance of cell structure to the kinetics of enzyme induction explains (together with the brilliant achievements of phage research made without the help of any direct visual observation) another iconoclastic statement of Jacques Monod's, according to which, "had the use of microscopes been prohibited, biology could have leaped forward fifty years."

Not only the biosynthetic process was independent of the cell's age—its state of division—but the quality, the specificity of the biosynthetic product was independent from the stimulus which brought about its synthesis, the inducer. Jacques Monod showed with Melvin Cohn that the kinetic parameters as well as the immunochemical properties of β-galactosidase did not change when a variety of inducers were utilized with the inducible strain or compared to the enzyme of the constitutive mutants, where no inducer was used. This lack of necessity for outside information led him closer to the idea of a master plan, the genetic information, but also inspired another attempt toward universality, the theory of generalized induction. If every enzyme is manufactured according to genetic information of a common kind, there would also be a common kind of signal to trigger the transfer of information. For constitutive enzymes, the inducer was present in the cytoplasm, presumably as a metabolic intermediate, while for inducible enzymes it had to be added to the medium. This purely intellectual postulate received confirmation with the example of a sequential induction in the mandelic acid metabolic pathway unraveled by Roger Stanier.

Several lines of reasoning started at this point and were solved in the spirit of simple logics, and of universality of mechanisms, by using precisely defined concepts without necessarily naming the underlaying detailed cellular or molecular structures. The inducer is only the signal for biosynthesis; it happens to be a metabolite and a substrate of the inducible enzyme even though these properties might be independent. A search was started to verify this independence and effectively, nonmetabolizable inducers were found, namely, a whole family of thiogalactosides. Also discovered were metabolizable β-galactosides which had no inducing effect, e.g., phenyl β-galactoside. Lactose itself turned out later to be of this kind would it not be for the transgalactosylating activity of β-galactosidase which produces true inducers as shown by Claude Burstein. This distinct function compells postulation that the inducer interacts with a receptor, distinct from the enzyme induced. For this, the inducer must first penetrate into the cell. Hence the discovery of lactose permease by Howard Rickenberg, Georges Cohen, and Gerard Buttin, and generalization of the permease concept, one of the great moments of Jacques' intuition.

The definition of the structural gene of a transport system and the coining of the word permease was perceived as a challenge by the "transport-worker's union." The receptor of the inducer is also genetically determined; its gene being independent from the structural gene of β-galactosidase, it is the gene i. When it is damaged as a signal receptor, its function as a switch is frozen, and the cell is either constitutive i^- or super-repressed i^S. When genes are transferred by conjugation, the structural genes are first expressed constitutively and only later when the i gene is sufficiently expressed becomes the inducer necessary for further synthesis (PaJaMa experiment). Therefore, the i gene codes for a cytoplasmic factor of negative regulatory mode, the repressor. Induction, deinduction, and regulatory mutations of the i gene simultaneously affect the expression of the Z gene, β-galactosidase, of the y gene, lac permease and of the a gene, galactoside transacetylase, discovered in the meantime by Irving Zabin. This parallelism of expression, together with the more restricted coordination in cis in mutants of the operator o locus led to the concept of the operon, the unit of genetic expression.

In the meantime it was demonstrated that DNA, in which genetic information is encoded (Avery, McLeod, et $al.$) assumed the configuration of a double helix with a base pairing principle (Watson and Crick) and this enabled DNA to undergo self-replication (Meselson and Sthal) but apparently DNA was not the template for protein synthesis. Nascent proteins were found in ribosomal fractions containing no DNA and in eukaryotes, DNA was confined in the nucleus while the bulk of protein synthesis took place in the cytoplasm. On the other hand, ribosomes did not fulfill the requirements for an intermediate between gene and its protein product; they remained the same in induced and noninduced, in uninfected and phage-infected bacteria while they got involved in the synthesis of genetically unrelated proteins.

The rapid regulatory switches pointed toward an unstable intermediate embodying the genetic information between gene and protein. The intermediate called "the messenger" soon became the messenger RNA or mRNA. An unstable rapidly labeled RNA fraction, shown first by Volkin and Astrachan in phage T2 infected bacteria and soon in *E. coli* by François Gros, who went to Jim Watson's place at Harvard to fetch the fraction appeared as the right candidate for this role, due to its base composition, its association to ribosomes, and its rapid chase.

Hypotheses were mushrooming about the use and fate of mRNA. Its "exceptionally high rate of turnover," with a half life estimated to less than 15 second suggested the possibility of a stoichiometry of one-to-one (that is to say that one molecule of messenger is destroyed for each molecule of protein synthesized). This possibility expressed by Jacques at the 1961 Cold Spring Harbor Symposium was still in the vein of the perfect gas analogy, but it seemed to meet with serious difficulties. Among other hypotheses which would permit a whole range of copy multiplicity, was the possibility of a predetermined number of protein copies for each kind of messenger (fitted with a copy-counter) or a predetermined lifetime, which would set the range of the copy yield (messenger fitted with a timer like a time bomb). Rather seldom mentioned was the possibility of a random decay with a statistical life expectancy. At any rate, at the start of our kinetic study, nobody was ready to ask questions about the time course of elongation or of degradation of a single macromolecule.

The work outlined below could be qualified as the invention not quite of the time-microscope, but more modestly of a time-magnifying lens which focused attention to molecular events in the 10^0-10^2 second time range, and was one of the several pathways leading beyond the "perfect gas, perfect logic, perfect concept" era. Actually the approach remained mainly on the conceptual rather than on the structural level, the main departure was the abandonment of the punctual molecule-punctual event approach. This work developed between 1961 and 1968. After the reports of Boezi and Cowie and of Pardee and Prestige on the 3-4 minute lag which elapses between the addition of the inducer and the appearance of β-galactosidase, the question arose, what happens if the inducer is removed before it brought about its effect. And I found that the enzyme synthesis occurred all the same, after a lag as usual, but it leveled off as a single wave of synthesis, its final yield being proportional to the duration of the presence of the inducer. I called this the elementary wave with the afterthought, that at the limit an extremely short pulse of inducer would cause a short burst of messenger synthesis substancially a single molecule of messenger per cell. Whatever protein synthesis is forthcoming then, its time course can serve to answer questions about the way the messenger gets inactivated and about its lifespan. Assuming that the rate of protein synthesis at any time reflects the amount of message active at that time, the time bomb model should result in a sudden slowdown of synthesis whereas the progressive slowdown of the wave would be more consistent with a first order, random inactivation of the messenger. Figure I represents the experimental and logical process. The top portion of the figure is the classical Monod plot of β-galactosidase induction taken from M. Cohn (*Bact. Rev.* 1957.) The bottom portion is a reconstitution of the first minutes of the same time course as a sum of consecutive inducer pulses which result in the sum of time-shifted elementary waves. It shows that the contribution of each elementary inducer pulse is identical in amount and in its time program.

It turned out that the decay of the messenger was first order, i.e., exponential with time, with a half life of 1 minute, at 37°, a very reproducible result irrespective of growth rate and metabolic situations. The next question was why a 1.5-minute delay separates the addition of the inducer from the termination (translation) of the first molecule of enzyme. Soon it became clear that the

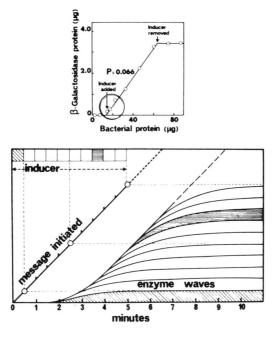

Fig. 1. Represents the experimental and logical process. See text for explanation.

whole of this period was occupied by the translation process, that is to say the elongation of the polypeptide chain. The synthesis of acetylase, the product of the third structural gene of the *lac* operon was terminated only about one minute later. This was the first indication that the structural genes of an operon are expressed in sequence, and the use of rifampicin and actinomycin permitted soon to ascribe this sequential program to the synthesis of a polycistronic messenger. Only one rifampicin sensitive initiation event was followed by two distinct actinomycin sensitive terminations, first that of the Z message and about one minute later of the A message. Knowing the elongation time of mRNA and its lifetime, the problem thus arose: what variants of the integral transcript have coding activity. This question was thoroughly explored by Michel Jacquet at the time, when I already left Pasteur and started an independent group at the laboratory attached to Jacques Monod's chair of Molecular Biology at the Collège de France.

The picture which emerged from these kinetic studies was a highly coordinated sequence of events. Transcription, translation, and messenger RNA breakdown all proceed in the O-Z-Y-A direction. Translation proceeds, making on the average one peptide bond about every 65 milliseconds, and transcription produces three nucleotide bonds in the same time. The initiating end of messenger RNA has a half life of about 60 seconds or in others terms, it has one chance out of 85 to be inactivated the next second, but it has no age; its life expectancy does not decrease with time. The initiation of transcription is independent of previous transcriptions and does start usually before the previous transcription is terminated. The initiation of translation is independent of the length of RNA chain as soon as a sufficient length of RNA is available. The initiation of translation is also independent of previous translations provided a minimum spacing; it only depends on the intact initiating end of mRNA. The progress of translation is independent of both the termination of the transcription and the survival of the initial end of messenger RNA. The survival of the initiating end of messenger RNA is independent of the intracellular concentration of inducer and largely although not completely independent of transcription.

The messenger RNA is polycistronic and stays probably as a single piece for the major part of its functional lifetime. At the steady state of all processes, the polycistronic messenger RNA is however seldom integral. The major part of it should be pieces: some unfinished, some already missing the initiating end, some devoid of both, still growing on one side while losing the other side at the same speed. The weighted average size is calculated as about half the integral size, the unweighted average one-third and the frequency of integral size is about one-eighth of the total population (19% integral for the Z segment).

This detailed kinetic study followed the guidelines of a model largely elaborated in our lab. It gave more coherence to the picture; it helped to make a decision between alternate possibilities, but sometimes it also suggested the existence of steps not suspected before (e.g. a chemically distinct event of peptide chain initiation, inhibited by hydroxylamine, as shown by Simone Beguin). In other instances it brought the first experimental evidence in favor of a postulate, e.g., the polycistronic messenger, the colinear transcription-translation, the "instantaneous" accomplishment of events attributed to conformational changes like the interaction of inducer and repressor. Sometimes the kinetic demonstration preceded, sometimes lagged behind demonstrations by others with other methods, but it remained in permanent dialogue with every step of progress made in the laboratory and in "the world." But Jacques Monod, partly because he was disappointed that permease work, which we started together in joy and excitement, did not lead to the expected triumph through the isolation of the protein, and especially that the acetylase did not keep its promises to be a part of the permease system, partly because very soon he went further ahead to allostery and the "second secret of life," paid a decreasing attention to this finicking work around the first secret (the base pairing principle of genetic conservation and expression).

I personally feel that this piece of work is very much in the line of Jacques Monod's thinking. The elaboration of a rigorous methodology and a patient effort to try and answer all possible questions which that methodology can deal with, just as the formulation of a hypothesis followed by a patient exploration of all its possible predictions, slowly conducted to a new way to conceive pre-existing notions, in this instance the time dimensions of molecular events.

FROM ACETYLASE TO β-GALACTOSIDASE

Irving Zabin

Since graduate student days, I had been working in lipid metabolism, and I wanted to do something different. Monod's name had some magic about it even in the 1950s; he worked in fundamental areas of biology, and he worked in Paris, one of my favorite cities. Therefore in 1957, well in advance of my first sabbatical leave, I wrote asking to spend a year with him at the Pasteur Institute. He answered yes, I obtained a fellowship, and in February 1959, I arrived in Paris.

The *lac* permease in *Escherichia coli* had been discovered a few years earlier (Rickenberg, Cohen, Buttin, and Monod, 1956) and an extensive review summarizing what was known about it had also been published (Cohen and Monod, 1957). *Lac* permease was responsible for transport of lactose and other galactosides into cells. All experiments had been done using whole cells. To go further and get at the mechanism of transport required identification and isolation of the material or materials responsible. The reigning authority on transport in Monod's laboratory then was Adam Kepes who had done some elegant experiments on the kinetics and energy requirements of *lac* permease (Kepes, 1957; Kepes and Monod, 1957). It had to be a membrane protein. Membranes contain lipids as well as proteins. And I had a background in lipid chemistry and metabolism. Therefore what was more logical than to ask me to work with Adam on the permease problem? So Adam patiently introduced me to *E. coli*, and to the mysteries of *lac* permease.

We had a fine time for some months dreaming up and doing experiments designed to help isolate the permease. For example, I remember trying to develop an assay by adding extracts from a permease-positive strain to cultures of a permease-negative strain in the hope of converting them to permease positive. Then, when this didn't work, the recipient cells were pretreated with certain organic solvents to try to pry them open so that the "permease" might be introduced. From time to time we got excited when it looked at first as if there was a small change in ability to transport, but nothing worked.

Monod listened and was available when necessary. He was interested and offered a suggestion now and then; but he let us proceed at our own pace. Then one day in May or June, he said to me, "Why don't you see if you can get the acetylation reaction to work *in vitro*?" The background was as follows: When radioactive substrates like isopropylthiogalactoside (IPTG) or thiomethylgalactoside were transported and accumulated by cells, a small amount of a radioactive derivative was also formed. About a year or so earlier, Herzenberg had been at the Pasteur Institute and had identified the derivative as a 6-*O*-acetyl compound. It was formed by permease-positive but not by permease-negative strains. It was a slow process. For any considerable amount of substrate to be converted to the acetyl form, cultures had to be shaken overnight in air, in the presence of a carbon source. This information was not published until later (Herzenberg, 1961), but it was available in the department. Did acetylation have anything to do with *lac* permease? A permease-negative cell would not transport IPTG into the cell, so IPTG would not be acetylated. Therefore acetylation of the substrate might be only an indirect consequence of the presence of the transport system in *E. coli*. It was foreign: perhaps it was acetylated like foreign amines were in animal tissues. Also acetylgalactosides were not converted to galactosides, and were neither substrates not inducers of *lac* permease. They were inert in *E. coli*. But even with all this, Monod's intuition suggested that acetylation should be examined anyway.

I was reasonably well-suited for the job. I had been a student of Konrad Bloch who had done a great deal of work on acetate metabolism, and I had grown up in biochemistry while "active acetate" was finally identified as acetyl coenzyme A. So I prepared some necessary reagents, repeated some of the whole cell experiments, explored part of the European countryside, and in September found that a cell-free extract of the constitutive strain ML308 would convert IPTG to acetyl-IPTG when supplemented with either acetate, coenzyme A, and ATP, or acetyl-CoA. That was fine, because now we could test for the ability of a strain to carry out acetylation and compare this ability with the presence or absence of permease in that strain. When we did, it turned out that an extract from a strain without *lac* permease could not make acetyl-IPTG, nor could a noninduced wild type make the derivative unless it had first been induced. The correlation was perfect. We were excited about these results. Within a few months we had enough information to publish a short note (Zabin, Kepes, and Monod, 1959). It ended with "The observed correlations constitute strong evidence that the acetylation reaction is carried out by a system closely connected with, or part of, the permease system." At the time, we thought we had a tag for the permease protein. The idea was that the protein which catalyzed the acetylation reaction also carried out transport, or some part of transport *in vivo*. This statement is still literally true in the sense that acetylase is part of the *lac* operon.

Monod said to me one day in November or December, "Why don't you stay another year?" I was due to go back in a few months and the problem had just barely opened up. This was a fine suggestion to all except one small Zabin who missed his friends at home. And, because I felt a whole additional year would be too long to be away, I asked for and arranged a leave of absence for another half-year instead.

I worked pretty hard for the next period of time. There was a lot of biochemistry to do on acetylation. We wanted to examine the properties of the enzyme or enzyme systems responsible for the reaction. We wanted to see what we could find out, if anything, about the permease. And how did this fit in with induced enzyme formation? Now two apparently separate and distinct proteins were turned on by one signal, the addition of inducer to growing cells.

During this time, Monod was more than available. He was often in the lab, bringing up questions, suggesting experiments, waiting for the latest result. He was tremendously stimulating. I was too close then to think of him as a scientific giant or genius; this came later in retrospect, which was perhaps just as well. I have often asked myself what his special qualities were. He had an air of assurance, he was immensely articulate, he was very convincing. He was quick, of course, and he got to the point faster than most. He was imaginative and it always was a logical imaginativeness. But I think he was supremely a synthesizer; this was his great strength. He often looked at things from a quite new point of view; this was part of his ability to put things together. Also, I read somewhere that one quality of genius is the ability to focus intensely on one subject, then at a moment's notice do the same for another. He had that, too.

He had some favorite sayings. I remember one, "You don't do an experiment to prove something, but to disprove it." Of course that didn't prevent him from being highly persuasive. Another, about some experimental result or other, especially if it didn't fit an idea of his, "I don't believe it for a minute." I thought of these, privately, as Monod's "bon-mots." He had great impact on people. At seminars in the small library room, speakers seemed to direct their efforts mostly to him. He was a charmer when and if he wished to be. Few were neutral about him, men or women. I once asked my wife why she thought he was attractive to

women. He was certainly handsome, but that had nothing to do with it. Her answer was "He looks right into your eyes." An old long-time (male) friend of his
said one never had a dull moment in his company. He was easy to be with. I
was always on a first name basis with him. And with all of this, there was a wall
beyond which I, and I suppose all but a very few did not go. Perhaps this was
part of the mystery.

We measured the formation of acetyl-IPTG at first by a chromatographic
method using radioactive IPTG. This was slow. Therefore I worked out a simple
hydroxamate assay and things went much faster. I tested substrate specificities,
affinities, and other properties, and I worked on the purification of the enzyme.
We called it acetylase in the lab. It was also referred to as galactoside acetylase,
galactoside transacetylase and thiogalactoside transacetylase. Adam took part in
some of these experiments and also busied himself with other work, including
measurement of permease and acetylase in more mutant strains. The correlations
we had done at first were with a few well-defined strains. There were many more
available.

We got a lot of information during the next half-year but it soon didn't support the idea that permease and acetylase were the same. For instance, the substrate specificities for transport and for acetylation were different. Though IPTG
worked for both, phenyglucoside was not transported by *lac* permease and was
acetylated. Lactose was accumulated by the cells, but was not a substrate of the
transacetylase. Then, the Michaelis constants were wildly different, high for
acetylation and low for transport. Furthermore, acetylase was not a membrane
protein as presumably the permease was.

Meanwhile, measurements of permease in whole cells vs. acetylase in extracts
went on. From one permease-negative, acetylase-negative strain, a number of
permease-positive revertants were picked out. Every single one was acetylase-
positive. I remember Monod being very impressed with this data. The correlations also held up at first with other strains in the Pasteur Institute's collection.
But then a number of strains were seen to be permease-negative and acetylase-
positive. This didn't fit but it could be explained easily. Acetylase could be only
part of the transport system. Worse, though, was one mutant strain (or maybe
two) which was the reverse: permease-positive and acetylase-negative. This
wasn't a well-characterized mutant and no one seemed to know its origin. We
almost tried to ignore it on this basis.

I think Adam was the first to discard the notion that acetylase had anything
to do with permease. His orientation was that of a kineticist, and the properties
of the acetylase enzyme just weren't right for the permease. Monod hung on
longer; how else could one explain change of two properties by a single nonregulatory mutation unless a single protein was involved in both properties? As
for the rest, the properties of the isolated protein could be different inside the
cell. This last argument was not terribly convincing to a biochemist who had

learned that the way to find out what goes on in the intact cell is to take it apart. But I didn't know. I would have preferred to believe.

There was an excitement in the air. People stopped and talked in the labs and in the hallways of the old building. Monod's group was on the first floor. François Jacob who was two floors up, came down often. I think it was he who was the first to ask me one day how much acetylase was in the cell. The operon model was being unveiled; it was a "groupe de genes à expression coordinée par un operateur." Some of the data to support it came from work on acetylase. The first paper, though, did not mention acetylase, nor was there any need to. In that paper, (Jacob, Perrin, Sanchez, and Monod, 1960), data were presented on levels of β-galactosidase and permease in partial diploids.

In retrospect it seems likely to me that the operon model would have survived and flourished even if acetylase had not been discovered. But the discovery and availability of acetylase must have been an important psychological support to the architects of the model. It would have been hard to convince the outside scientific world that measurement of galactoside transport in whole cells was indeed as valid a measure of gene expression as a direct enzyme assay. Now, whether or not acetylase was permease, definite, quantitative, unarguable data on the expression of two different genes in the *lac* operon could be obtained. So, in the classic review on genetic regulatory mechanisms which appeared the next year in the *Journal of Molecular Biology* (Jacob and Monod, 1961a), acetylase had a prominent part. One important experiment showed the effect of different inducers on the formation of the two enzymes. With effective inducers, high levels of both β-galactosidase and acetylase were formed; with poor inducers, low levels of the two activities were seen.

Of course, some of the evidence for the operon was taken in faith. If assays of two different enzymes were done, then it was necessary to be sure they were direct measurements of quantities of two proteins, and that they were in fact different. By the summer of 1960, I had managed to purify acetylase about 25-fold. This was, though we didn't know it then, less than 10% pure. It was cleanly separated from β-galactosidase and anti-β-galactosidase did not cross-react with acetylease so they were two quite different proteins. But I'm sure this was after-the-fact support of the already mapped-out theory. We had no idea of the subunit composition of β-galactosidase or acetylase. I wondered (later) whether the two proteins might have a common subunit; they don't. But this would have explained coordinate induction in a quite different way.

I wrote a paper after I returned to UCLA in August 1960, but the manuscript went back to Paris once or twice before it was sent to the journal. We presented the enzymological and purification data on acetylase, pointed out some of the difficulties in believing that acetylase was permease or part of it, but left it an open question (Zabin, Kepes, and Monod, 1962). It was open just in case. Before the time of the 1961 Cold Spring Harbor Meeting polarity had been discovered. It was evident that polarity (where a mutation in one gene may affect the expression of a gene or genes further down) could explain why acetylase reappeared in a permease-negative revertant. In their symposium paper, Jacob and Monod pointed this out and suggested that structural gene x (now a) specifies acetylase rather then gene y, the permease gene (Jacob and Monod, 1961b).

Well, if not, what was acetylase doing in the cell? We didn't think it was a detoxifier because the reaction was slow and affinities were low. Years later it was shown that $lac\ a^+$ strains had a selective advantage over $lac\ a^-$ strains when grown under certain conditions because they do detoxify (Andrews and Lin, 1976). This may be the *raison d'etre* of the enzyme. When strains containing the y gene but no a gene were prepared, these carried out the transport process normally (Fox *et al.*, 1966). Therefore there was no longer any reason to believe that acetylase was part of the permease system. However, I can't help but believe that acetylase is still unfinished business.

I left Paris with a feeling of some accomplishment and considerable enthusiasm. In fact I talked with Monod about coming back to the Pasteur Institute, not on another sabbatical, but for an extended period. I didn't do so for a number of reasons both scientific and personal, but I closed down some work on lipids that was still going on in my lab, and switched entirely to the *lac* operon. It was pretty evident to me that the biochemistry of the *lac* proteins could be an important and useful area of work.

One of the first things to do was to get acetylase in pure form, find out how much was made in the cell and measure its size. This took close to two years, but I isolated the enzyme in pure form and also crystallized it (Zabin, 1963). Gene Goldwasser spend a semi-vacation of several months in California and measured the molecular weight (about 60,000) in the ultracentrifuge. The surprise from the purification data was that there was very much less acetylase produced than β-galactosidase, 10-35 times less by weight, depending on conditions of growth. This seemed strange at first. There was some evidence by this time that *lac* DNA was transcribed into a single, polycistronic messenger, so approximately equal amounts of proteins might be expected to be formed.

I spent two or three weeks in Paris in the summer of 1963 and talked about these results. Monod called the finding that more β-galactosidase was made, "wild-type polarity," and also, around the lab, "Zabinism." I didn't mind the publicity but is sounded like the name of a disease.

Wild-type, now often called "natural" polarity in the *lac* operon could be explained or rationalized in a number of ways. One of the most obvious had to do with the subunit composition of these proteins. It wasn't the relative amount by moles that was important in understanding operon function. Or in other words one wanted to know the number, not the size, of polypeptide chains translated by a polycistronic messenger. To get that number it was necessary to find out something about the substructure, not only of acetylase but of β-

galactosidase.

Acetylase was fairly straightforward. By physical and chemical studies it was clearly a dimer of two identical chains, each of about 30,000 daltons (Brown, Brown, and Zabin, 1967; Brown, Koorajian, and Zabin, 1967). Antibody to acetylase did not cross-react with β-galactosidase, nor with anything else in the cell (Berg and Zabin, 1964).

The subunit structure of β-galactosidase was a difficult problem. The molecular weight had been guessed to be 600,000-700,000 but this was revised by a number of physical studies to a value near 500,000. It was generally agreed that the protein was a tetramer; but what was the protomer, a single polypeptide chain or several smaller ones? There were measurements with the ultracentrifuge, end-group analyses and later, complementation experiments which favored the conclusion that there were small chains (cf. Zabin and Fowler, 1970). Also, a single polypeptide as large as 125,000 daltons was unheard of at that time. But when end-group and other studies were carried out, it became clear that β-galactosidase contains long, not short chains. In fact, the polypeptide contains 1021 amino acids (Fowler and Zabin, 1977)!

This put a different picture on polarity of expression in the *lac* operon, because if the molecular weight of the β-galactosidase monomer is four times that of the acetylase monomer, the weight ratios of 10-35:1 must be divided by 4. These molar ratios are not so striking. Deviations from 1:1 ratios can then be explained by a variety of mechanisms including mRNA decay and/or ribosome loading and unloading. In any case natural polarity stimulated a lot of interesting work in many laboratories.

β-Galactosidase has been a challenge, worthy of a lot of work. It still hasn't lost its interest. There were and still are interesting mutants, as well as the structure to wonder about. Though acetylase was and is revisited from time to time, β-galactosidase has been the focus of attention in my lab for many years. With the aid of many collaborators, work has been carried out on gene-protein correlations, on structure-function relationships and on evolution in the *lac* operon. Some of this has been reviewed elsewhere (Zabin and Villarejo, 1975; Zabin and Fowler, 1978) and my purpose here is not to discuss this but to recall my association with Jacques Monod.

I've long since gone my own way, but I'll always be grateful to him for the chance to take part in a major and unique intellectual achievement. I saw Monod from time to time over the years and I spent a half-year sabbatical again at the Pasteur Institute in 1967. I remember, though not why or in what context it came up, he said then that the framework for the study of biology now exists. He meant this to include control of gene expression and allostery. He was right, I think. He set the stage.

References

Andrews, K. J. and Lin, E. C. C. (1976). *J. Bact.* **128**, 510.

Berg, A. and Zabin, I. (1964). *J. Mol. Biol.* **10**, 289.

Brown, J. L., Brown, D. M., and Zabin, I. (1967). *J. Biol. Chem.* **242**, 4254.

Brown, J. L., Koorajian, S., and Zabin, I. (1967). *J. Biol. Chem.* **242**, 4259.

Fowler, A. V. and Zabin, I. (1977). *Proc. Natl. Acad. Sci. U.S.A.* **74**, 1507.

Fox, C. F., Beckwith, J. R., Epstein, W., and Signer, E. R. (1966). *J. Mol. Biol.* **19**, 576.

Herzenberg, L. A. (1961). *Arch Biochem. Biophys.* **93**, 314.

Jacob, F. and Monod, J. (1961a). *J. Mol. Biol.* **3**, 318.

Jacob, F. and Monod, F. (1961b). *Cold Spring Harbor Symp. Quant. Biol.* **26**, 193.

Jacob, F., Perrin, D., Sanchez, C., and Monod, J. (1960). *Comp. Rend.* **250**, 1727.

Kepes, A (1957). *Comp. Rend.* **244**, 1550.

Kepes, A. and Monod, J. (1957). *Comp. Rend.* **244**, 1550.

Rickenberg, H. V., Cohen, G. N., Buttin, G., and Monod, J. (1956). *Ann Inst. Pasteur* **91**, 829.

Zabin, I. (1963). *J. Biol. Chem.* **238**, 3300.

Zabin, I. and Fowler, A. V. (1970). "The Lactose Operon" (J. R. Beckwith and D. Zipser, eds.), p. 27. Cold Spring Harbor Monograph.

Zabin, I. and Fowler, A. V. (1978). "Molecular Aspects of Operon Control" (J. Miller and W. Reznikoff, eds.), in press. Cold Spring Harbor Monograph.

Zabin, I., Kepes, A., and Monod, J. (1959). *Biochem. Biophys. Res. Comm.* **1**, 289.

Zabin, I., Kepes, A., and Monod, J. (1962). *J. Biol. Chem.* **237**, 253.

Zabin, I. and Villarejo, M. R. (1975). *Ann. Rev. Biochem.* **44**, 295.

BEING AROUND

Agnes Ullmann

I arrived too late at the Pasteur Institute to participate in the great adventure: the founding of molecular biology. But I was around long enough to witness many later developments.

How did I get to Pasteur? It all began in Budapest in the late 1940s. As a young student in biochemistry—never trained in genetics—I was attending seminars and film projections on the great discoveries of a genius named Lysenko. Soon afterwards I became suspicious and started wondering why the whole thing seemed monstrous, but I didn't have the elements to judge. One day I decided to confess my doubts to a friend I could trust. Secretly he gave me a page of a French newspaper *Combat,* with an anti-Lysenko article written by the scientist, Jacques Monod. It was a fabulous discovery for somebody to whom western information was unavailable.

A few years later, another paper by the same Jacques Monod impressed me profoundly. This time I could read it openly; it was the BBA article on the *de novo* synthesis of proteins. Once again I was overjoyed because it put an end to the old and very dialectic Schoenheimer myth of the "dynamic state of living matter." This time, I decided that I would do everything to try and go to the Pasteur Institute, in order to work with that man.

In 1958, I managed to go to Paris for six weeks and obtain an appointment with Professor Monod. I was nervously waiting in Madeleine Brunerie's office, when to my surprise a young man came whistling down the corridor and introduced himself as Jacques Monod. He was both friendly and distant. Since Arthur Pardee was waiting for him, the best way he found to get rid of me was to invite me to give a seminar the next day. After the seminar he politely asked me what I was doing in Paris and how long I intended to stay. (He had obviously forgotten our previous evening's talk; at that time I did not yet realize that he always forgot unimportant things.) I gathered all my courage and told him that if he would allow me to work in his lab I could arrange to stay six weeks, and if not I would have to return to Budapest soon. He then took me to his office, told me all about the work going on in the lab and asked me what I would like to do. I said that I would prefer to collaborate on François Gros' project that he had mentioned, and very scared I added—if Monsieur Gros accepts me. He burst out laughing, "François? He is the nicest man on earth; he never says no." It was true; the next morning I started working with François and had a most exciting time during all my stay. François quickly realized that I had personal problems. I felt that I could speak to him safely, and I confided to him that I wanted to leave Hungary for good, come to France and go on working forever in the lab. Somewhat puzzled, François advised me to discuss the problem with Jacques. I answered that I would never dare. He tried to persuade me that Jacques was the most understanding and nicest person on earth, and if I was scared to talk to him myself, he would do so for me. The next day Jacques invited me for dinner at his home and, after a few hour's discussion, told me that he was willing to do everything he could to help me. I asked him why. He answered, "It is a question of human dignity."

In 1960, Jacques arrived in Budapest with a carefully prepared plan for my escape and that of my husband from the country. Three months later I was in Paris. But he would never accept my thanks or agree to talk about all the trouble he had taken to insure the success of our adventure. For him it was a settled affair; at that time the important thing was to isolate the *lac* repressor—the one supposed to be an RNA. I tried hard first with François Gros, then alone with no more success. After a while, I began having doubts about the RNA nature of the repressor; but I did not dare admit them.

However, after hesitating a long time, I knocked at Jacques' office door. He was in discussion with François Jacob and Mel Cohn. Abruptly, I told them that on the basis of the recent data, I thought that the repressor might not be an RNA. I was expecting them to throw me out of the office. But to my greatest surprise after asking for some experimental details Mel said quietly, "After all it may be a nucleo-protein." Then Jacques added, "Why shouldn't it be a protein?" And after a few moments of thought continued, "Of course it is a protein, it can't be anything else." While they were discussing this new possibility, I stood watching them without understanding why they didn't share my torment.

That same evening Jacques came to my lab where I was sadly sitting at my desk and said cheerfully, "You know, you made an important discovery: the repressor *is* a protein." He was right: Benno Müller-Hill and Wally Gilbert proved it.

By the end of 1961, one evening quite late Jacques walked into my lab. His tie was loose and he looked tired and worried. He stood silently at my bench and after a few long minutes he said, "I think I have discovered the second secret of life." I looked at him a bit alarmed; my first impression was that he was not well, so I suggested he should sit down and have a drink. After downing his second or third scotch he started to explain THE discovery to which he had already given a name: allostery. As he realized that I was not quite ready to accept his arguments at once he got up and said, "Believe it or not, the regulatory role of allosteric proteins is absolutely fundamental; it explains everything: hormonal action, repressor function, non-Michaelian enzyme kinetics. . ." and I don't remember the end of the list. During several weeks everybody discussed allostery in the lab—in fact we couldn't help it as any other kind of discussion turned back in a few minutes to this topic. One evening I used a "sentimental" argument concerning his enzyme, β-galactosidase which lacks the virtue of being allosteric. His reply was quick, as usual, "I am sure we can find experimental conditions to make even β-galactosidase allosteric. Since I was skeptical he turned to my technician, Françoise Tillier, and asked her whether she didn't want to try. Of course she did. After a great number of experiments, it turned out that β-galactosidase was completely refractory to allostery! It was the only time his enzyme disappointed him. During this period, Jacques desperately searched for a suitable experimental model, with the idea of doing some benchwork himself. He asked me one day whether it was difficult to prepare muscle phosphorylase and to assay it. I answered that it was a matter of a few days. Ten days later, with Roy Vagelos we obtained experimental evidence that 5-AMP might be an allosteric effector of phosphorylase b. From that time on, new French students arriving at the lab—Marie-Hélène Buc, Maxime Schwartz—were kindly persuaded to choose an allosteric enzyme as their first research project. American postdoctorals were still allowed to do microbial genetics.

In fact, Jacques felt very happy with phosphorylase. Having Eddy Fischer around telling us what not to do, Jacques set up a dye binding technique, and spent hours counting drops from columns and doing binding stoichiometry. After a long and successful experiment I told him that I was amazed to see how good he was at the bench; he answered, "I know everybody thinks I am a theoretician able only to construct hypotheses, and not to do an experiment." In my opinion he was the fastest, the most rigorous, and the most imaginative experimentalist I ever had the opportunity to work with. Moreover he could enjoy an elegant experiment as much as he enjoyed meeting a beautiful woman.

At that time, he was so convinced that only noncovalent interactions are important that at a Gordon Conference on proteins he even remarked that after all, peptide bonds were irrelevant. I remember that Fred Richards got up with consternation, and said, "But Jacques, if you were right, proteins should be gases."

For a few years—in spite of my respect for allostery—I went on being the devil's advocate, by insisting on the importance of covalent modifications. One day, in 1967, I told Jacques that I had decided to look for covalent modifications, triggered by cyclic AMP, in bacteria. After a while I showed him the first data demonstrating that cyclic AMP relieves the glucose effect. His first comment was that it was too bad to get involved with catabolite repression which was too complicated, and certainly had nothing to do with covalent modifications. I was convinced that he was absolutely not interested in this problem. Some weeks later, coming back to the lab after a short leave I saw him working with my technician, both looking very busy. When I asked them what they were doing Jacques proudly answered, "Do you know that cyclic AMP relieves diauxic growth?" Gerard Buttin entering the lab at this point and looking at the growth curves, made the spontaneous remark to Jacques, "How nice, now you can at last finish your thesis."

Jacques was now ready to admit that cyclic AMP plays an important regulatory role, but as far as I was concerned further experiments convinced me that covalent modifications were not involved in this phenomenon. Jacques ironically noticed, "You see where the search for covalent modifications leads? Now you are just about to go on and identify a new allosteric protein: the cyclic AMP receptor. . . ."

The year 1968 was difficult for everybody. The May events stopped all scientific activities in the lab for a while. Jacques was very much involved in various aspects of the students' problems.

Besides, many of the members of the group had decided at that time to assume new directions. This gave Jacques mixed feelings of loneliness, nostalgia, and freedom. He was seriously thinking about a sabbatical leave: "My students don't need me anymore, and I too feel I need a change, a kind of self-renewal," he used to say.

At the beginning of 1970 he was asked to become director of the Pasteur Institute. For weeks and months he discussed this matter over and over with me; on the one hand, his sense of duty and of responsibility, on the other hand, the temptation of having a year of freedom in the States where he could think and write undisturbed (the project of his second book was already born), discuss science, and give lectures.

I tried my hardest to persuade him to leave. Convincing Jacques was nearly always impossible; he listened attentively and generally said, "You may be right but let me think it over." In July 1970, while I attended a meeting in Seattle, he sent me a telegram saying that the decision had been taken: he was not to be director of the Pasteur Institute.

When I got back to Paris, Jacques seemed relieved; he told me about his plans concerning his next book, and among other things about a future transatlantic sail (he even bought a few maps). These dreams did not last long. In the fall, his wife Odette became seriously ill.

Jacques immediately gave up the idea of a sabbatical leave and a few months later he became director of the Pasteur Institute. By accepting this task he wanted to pay a tribute to, and help to save a unique institution which had given him and many others the opportunity to do the kind of research which could have been done nowhere else in France at that time. A feeling of indebtedness certainly played a part in his decision, but in my opinion, the key factor was his Protestant sense of responsibility. He considered that preserving Pasteur from bankruptcy, safeguarding its independence, and insuring the freedom of its scientific activities should be given top priority.

At the beginning of his directorship, Jacques believed his administrative tasks would take him only a few hours a day and that he could spend the rest of his time discussing science, attending seminars, and could even participate personally in some experimental project. After a few months he realized to what extent he had underestimated what administration and business meant. He suddenly became conscious that he was engaged in a different "profession." And by changing profession he had to change his attitude. He became more firm—sometimes harder—and he often regretted being obliged to do so. Gradually he discovered that a gap was widening between him and some of his friends, former collaborators and students.

One day in November 1972, Jacques arrived at my door. Almost shyly, he took out of his pocket a charming little three weeks' old puppy. "May I introduce Vicky?" he said. (I could not have imagined that within a year it would become a sixty-pound Airdale!) I needed some time to understand why he had decided to have a dog: he needed a companion—faithful, loving, and never arguing, except when he wanted to go out for a walk. Jacques took him to the Institute practically everyday. Around 4 P.M. Vicky used to bark at my lab door; according to Jacques he preferred the smell of β-mercaptoethanol to the tediousness of directorial meetings. Vicky knew that Jacques would come along around 8 P.M., a fact some of his friends and former students also knew. It was his moment of relaxation. He wished to be kept informed about the latest results and he was always happy to discuss any detail of a current experiment. He listened and argued with his usual solid logic. But if he happened to discover a mistake in a sophisticated mathematical demonstration of Maxime Schwartz he was as proud as a schoolboy!

In the summer of 1975 during twenty-five days of quite hard sailing, Jacques was in an excellent mood, happy as usual on his boat; his health and physical condition were excellent and he was intellectually impatient to start working on his own. His term as a director would be over in eighteen months, after which he meant to spend part of his time in his house in Cannes working quietly. He then asked me somewhat anxiously, "Do you think I am still capable of doing something worthwhile?" Without waiting for an answer he went on, "I don't mind, I want to learn new things, to feel free to think and write, and also to invite all sorts of people for long discussions on all kinds of topics." Back in Paris he ordered a large number of books and embarked in serious preparation for his future book, *L'homme et le temps*. He discussed experimental work with increased interest and pleasure, was full of ideas and projects; he felt rejuvenated.

Once again these dreams did not last. A few months later he became ill and had to slow down his activities. He still came practically every day to the Institute and continued to assume his functions as director. In the evenings, however, when he came down to the lab to have a short rest and a drink and to pick up Vicky, he looked frightfully tired. But he refused to stay at home and rest unless a high fever kept him in bed. As soon as he could get up he was back at the Institute.

Early in May 1976 his health improved. He told me he was glad to report that even his physician seemed satisfied and had given him the permission to attend the Lactose meeting at Cold Springs Harbor. He regained strength to such a point that he insisted that we should spend some evenings writing an article— his last one.

At the end of May he went to Cannes for a week or so. When we spoke on the phone on May 28 he told me that he was feeling very well and questioned me about several details such as his subscription for the next season's concert programs, his plane reservation for the Lactose meeting, and many other things. Finally he reminded me that I had promised to finish the article for his return on May 31. He ended the conversation by saying, "See you Monday in the lab." I saw him that Monday—not in the lab, but on his bed in Cannes—before he closed his eyes forever.

From this day on, sitting in my lab with Maxime or others, we have understood that nothing would be ever as it was before. Vicky was the only one who for months and months still desperately waited every evening at the door and could not understand why his master did not call for him anymore.

ANOTHER ROUTE

Maxime Schwartz

Often, after a long day, he would go downstairs and have a scotch with Agnes. Almost invariably, he would sit in the red chair, squeezed between the side of Agnes's desk and the small blackboard. This was a good location. Just at hand were the glasses, the ice cubes, and the bottle of scotch, on a small pull-out slide extracted from the desk for that purpose. At hand, too, was the blackboard, on which he could draw straight genes and roundish proteins. He was facing Agnes, sitting at her desk, and also the blue chair. From time to time, somewhat unexpected in the office of an elegant woman, a dirty piece of old bone could be seen on the ground. This meant that Vicky was around. Vicky was an Airdale—not a dog—because dogs were not allowed in the laboratories.

"Tiens, voilà le petit Maxime" Monod would say when I came in. There really was no need to call me "petit." Calling Jacob "le grand François" as some people did, was in a way necessary, because of all the other "François" around. But there was no other Maxime. Well, even if it made no sense, I did not object to being welcomed as "le petit Maxime." This "petit" was one of the very few words expressing the affection which existed between us. Vicky, who was much more outgoing than his master would generally jump on me, to express his feelings in a noisy and damp manner. Monod would then laugh loudly, because he knew I was not so fond of dogs, sorry, Airdales. I would sit

171

in the blue chair and Agnes would ask me, "Vous voulez un verre?" Somewhat reluctantly, because I don't really like scotch, I would say yes, and have some. And then, in spite of the Airdale, and in spite of the scotch, I would spend some very warm moments. We were friends, and it was good to be together. This was during the last years, when Monod was director of the Institut Pasteur. From Agnes and from me he would get a feeling of what was going on at the bench level, so to speak, in what had always been his field of research. It was a deep pleasure for me to tell him about an exciting result, or a new idea, either from my own work, or from others. From him, I was gaining self-confidence, when he agreed with me, but perhaps even more when we disagreed. And this happened more than once. Scotch and Airdales, indeed, were not our sole matters of disagreement—allostery and the mode of gene control were others.

When Monod first asked me what I wanted to work on, in early 1963, I had just completed my first course in genetics, and had seen at the University a beautiful time lapse movie on mitosis. I had marveled at the gracious ballet of chromosomes, and thus answered Monod that I wanted to understand what were the forces driving the chromosomes. Monod laughed, raised his hands to the sky, and this was the end of my first project. Having so destroyed my impetus, he was obliged to provide me with some other idea, and suggested that I work on an ill-defined concept called "allostery." I therefore started to work with Agnes Ullmann, with the aim of demonstrating the existence of an allosteric conformation change in the glycogen phosphorylase b from rabbit muscle. Not that I particularly enjoyed grinding rabbits to extract the enzyme, but I had no choice. Anyway that's how I started to learn the job. Even though Agnes, David Perrin, and Alex Fritsch were my main interlocutors at this time, Monod played a great role in my development. When I look back, I am truly amazed by his patience in answering my somewhat naive questions. If he was in discussion with someone else in the lab, and I wanted to ask something, he always let me speak, answered, and never made me regret my question.

After a few months of rabbit grinding, after a few thousand phosphate assays, I had obtained some results. In particular I had provided kinetic evidence for the existence of what was later called "homotropic" as well as "heterotropic" interactions between various ligands of the phosphorylase. In the fall of 1963, when I started to work full time in the laboratory, I had a discussion with Monod about the orientation of my work. Obviously he expected me to repeat on phosphorylase the same type of work which Jean-Pierre Changeux was finishing on threonine deaminase. Clearly apparent from Jean-Pierre's work, was the importance of working with an enzyme of bacterial origin and therefore open to genetic analysis. Monod therefore suggested that I look for a bacterial glycogen phosphorylase. Since, as everybody knows, what is true for the rabbit is true for *E. coli*, the bacterial phosphorylase had to bee allosteric, and I would only have to study the enzyme produced by the wild-type strain and compare it with that produced by various mutants.

Since I had achieved the unbelievable record of working for six months in Monod's laboratory without growing a single bacterial culture, perhaps even seeing a colony on a plate, Agnes showed me how to inoculate a culture; Michael Malamy, then a postdoctoral fellow in the lab, showed me how to streak bacteria on a plate, and from then on, I was essentially on my own.

One week after drawing my first growth curve, I had found a polysaccharide phosphorylase in *E. coli*, and shown that the synthesis of this enzyme was induced by maltose. A month later I was convinced that this phosphorylase was not an allosteric enzyme. By then my decision had been made. I would not be a second Jean-Pierre Changeux, rather I would be another Gerard Buttin. Gerard had just completed his thesis on the galactose operon, and I had been very impressed by his seminar. I would work on the "maltose operon."

I often wondered about the reasons which lead me to make this decision. For one thing, I saw much more clearly where I was going in a study of the "maltose operon" than in that of an allosteric enzyme, were it of bacterial or mammalian origin. It seemed to me that I could really "prove" things in a study of gene regulation. With an allosteric enzyme, on the other hand, what could I do but accumulate evidence for a somewhat mythical conformation change, which I had no hope to ever see with my eyes. Other factors must also have contributed to my decision. The explosions of hilarity from Jean-Pierre may have scared away the rather shy beginning student that I was. It could also be that the proud young man that I was, felt the necessity of a weaning from Daddy Jacques and Mama Agnes. During the first weeks of my adventure in maltose, Monod made some timid attempts to drive me back to allostery. Was I really sure that this bacterial phosphorylase was not allosteric? The truth was that I simply did not want it to be allosteric, and it is really under Monod's slight, but firm, pressure that I did the minimum number of experiments required to study this point. Had I really wanted to find an allosteric polysaccharide phosphorylase in *E. coli*, I would probably have found the constitutive glycogen phosphorylase described a few years later by Chen and Segel. I never asked Monod what his feelings had been about my change of orientation. Up to a point he was perhaps disappointed that I was not displaying more interest for allostery, his passion at the time. Mainly, I believe, he was secretly pleased that I was paying a tribute to one of his first loves.

Indeed, when he suggested that I look for a bacterial polysaccharide phosphorylase, Monod was not sending me to some *terra incognita*. He knew that such an enzyme was almost certainly involved in maltose metabolism. This was an old story, which brings us back to 1946. Monod then thought that the so-called "adaptive enzymes" could be created by the action of substrates on nonspecific, somewhat "shapeless" protein precursors, according to a kind of "induced fit" mechanism. Enzymes involved in the degradation of substrates similar in structure seemed likely to derive from the same precursor. For this reason Monod decided to study the enzymes involved in the degradation of two similar disaccharides: lactose and maltose. As a result two communications were presented on July 12, 1948 at the French Academy of Sciences. One, signed by J. Monod, A. M. Torriani, and J. Gribetz, described the occurrence, in *E. coli*, of lactase, only present in lactose-grown cells. In the other, signed by J. Monod and A. M. Torriani, was reported the existence of an "amylomaltase," present exclusively in maltose-grown cells. Amylomaltase was an enzyme of a new type. Instead of simply splitting maltose into its two glucose moieties, as anyone might have expected, it transferred one of the glucose moieties to a growing chain of polysaccharide of the amylose type, liberating the other glucose in the free form. One year later (1949) Doudoroff *et al.* demonstrated that the amylose synthesized by amylomaltase was most probably degraded by a phosphorylase. This was the enzyme which Monod sent me to look for.

Why is it that Monod, after the initial characterization of amylomaltase, essentially abandoned it to concentrate on lactase? The reasons, it would seem now, were contingent. First, because the "lactase" was in fact a β-galactosidase of broad specificity, it became possible to synthesize a chromogenic substrate for this enzyme, and therefore to render its assay both very simple and very sensitive, while the assay of amylomaltase still required the use of the cumbersome Warburg apparatus. Then, more importantly perhaps, because analogues of β-galactosides were much easier to synthesize than analogues of maltose, a study of the compared stereospecificity of substrates and inducers of β-galactosidase could be undertaken, leading to the decisive discovery of gratuitous inducers. So deserted by Monod, amylomaltase found a first "cavalier" in H. Wiesmeyer, who, as a student of Melvin Cohn, characterized this enzyme more thoroughly and, in addition, demonstrated the existence of a maltose-inducible maltose permease (1960). By what mechanism did maltose induce the formation of maltodextrin phosphorylase, as I called the enzyme I had characterized, as well as of amylomaltase and maltose permease? This was what I wanted to find out.

To say that I was "on my own" to do so, as I wrote above was somewhat of an exaggeration. To be sure, I was no longer working directly with Monod. Still "Monod était mon maitre, et j'étais son élevè"; "Maitre" and "élevè" in the old European tradition, words which cannot be translated into American English. Jean-Pierre, David, and I would call Monod "Monsieur," even if, according to the American custom, everyone in the lab called each other by their first name. No American word can convey the load of love and respect endowed in the word "maitre." To have Monod as a "maitre" was a real blessing. This I was not long in realizing after meeting so many students complaining either that their boss was always on their back, or that their thesis director had abandoned them. Monod was always available, never on my back. From time to time he would come around and ask me how things were going, and we would always have an interesting discussion. Whenever I had a question, a problem, or a new result, I knew I could knock on his office door, or see him at tea time, when he would regularly come into his lab. If I was depressed, and went to see him, he would invariably cheer me up by showing me how to look at the situation in a positive way.

If Monod's intellectual and moral support were of extreme importance to me, others also had a great influence on me. Jacob was one of them, since I feel that I am most indebted to him for my development as a geneticist. I already mentioned Agnes Ullmann, Michael Malamy, and also David Perrin, who always knew before anyone else what was going on in the laboratory. But there were many others, both among the "permanent" staff of the laboratory, and the crowd of first rate postdoctoral fellows attracted by Monod and Jacob. I say Monod *and* Jacob because their two groups were almost completely mixed. As a matter of fact the maltose saga itself soon became a "coproduction" of the two groups, with Maurice Hofnung, one of Jacob's students, starting to work on the system in 1965.

Alas, with Monod as my "maitre," with Jacob as my adviser, and with all the good angels around, how could I give birth to such an ugly little duckling?

At first, after a few months of work with maltose, I thought I could foresee very well what my thesis seminar would be like. It would take place in the library of the "Service de Biochimie Cellulaire," which served as a meeting and seminar room (as well as a lunch room!). This room contained a small worn out blackboard which displayed "$R \rightleftharpoons T$" when the last discussion had been about allostery, and "iozyAc" when it had been about gene control. For my thesis seminar I would choose a "iozyAc" day and, before a petrified public, I would erase the i, o, z, y and Ac, only to replace them by the symbols representing the gene of the "maltose repressor," the operator sequence, and the structural genes of amylomaltase, phosphorylase, and maltose permease. Indeed, my thesis had started well. I had obtained mutants affected in the structural gene for amylomaltase and phosphorylase, and obtained evidence that these genes were in the same operon. Unfortunately, however, I had also obtained other mutants, which were all monsters! The most frequent class had a pleiotropic negative phenotype, i.e., lacked simultaneously amylomaltase, phosphorylase and permease and, in addition, were resistant to phage lambda. The corresponding mutations generally mapped in the vicinity of the amylomaltase-phosphorylase operon. Some of them, however, mapped in another region, a quarter of the chromosome away. Other mutations, mapping in this second region, led to the most incredible phenotypes. Some mutants were resistant to phage lambda, others were sensitive. Some were pleiotropic negative; others lacked permease, but expressed the amylomaltase-phosphorylase operon in a constitutive manner. And there were still other complications, so much so that even now, to tell the truth, we still haven't quite cleared up this mystery.

At the time, the complication of the system rapidly became a serious hindrance in my communicating with others, Monod included. Every time I wanted to relate even a minor result to someone, it took me half an hour to put him, or her up to date. This very complication in fact, made a very strong impression on Monod. A few years later, when molecular biologists, with "le grand François" as one of the color-bearers, started to leave the world of *E. coli* for new horizons, he often said to me something like "How can they expect to unravel the regulation circuits involved in cell differentiation when you, with all the power of bacterial genetics, can hardly understand the intricacies of the maltose system in *E. coli*." When I came up with all these horrible mutants, Monod's advice was clear. I should first try and isolate the "simple" mutants, i.e., those affecting the repressor and the operator, and then I might be in a position to explain the monsters. He was all the more inclined to give such advice since Germaine Cohen-Bazire and Madeleine Jolit had isolated in 1953 from *E. coli* ML a mutant synthesizing amylomaltase constitutively, and which he believed to be affected in the "maltose repressor." Since nobody knew how to perform genetic crosses with *E. coli* ML, I was unable to analyze this famous mutant. I therefore had to isolate my own, in *E. coli* K12. I failed, in part for technical, but mainly for psychological reasons. I did not find the constitutive mutants (which existed since I found them much later in 1976)*, just for the same reason I did not find the allosteric glycogen phosphorylase of *E. coli*: I didn't really want to find them. The truth was that, rather soon, I started to believe that the maltose system was not regulated in the same way as the lactose system, that the "maltose repressor" simply did not exist.

It must have been in the fall of 1964, or very early in 1965, when a scientist by the name of Ellis Englesberg gave a seminar in the "Service de Biochimie Cellulaire." He spoke of regulation in the L-arabinose system of *E. coli* B. He tried to say that this system was controlled by a "positive" regulator gene. This gene would code for a product, called an "activator" which, once it is itself activated by L-arabinose (the inducer), would promote the expression of the arabinose operon. Being a young student, very susceptible to influence, I was convinced. It is probably fair to say that I was the only one. Not only was I convinced but I was stricken by the many similarities between the L-arabinose system and the maltose system. It is from the day of this seminar, I think, that I must have been working under the secrete hypothesis that the maltose system was positively regulated. Still, at this point, it was only an intuition and I had a long way to go before I would convince myself, not to mention Jacob and Monod. In a way the atmosphere of friendly scepticism which surrounded the idea that the maltose system was positively regulated was very stimulating. Be-

*Note: But they are not affected in a "maltose repressor!"

fore anyone would believe me, I had to try in every possible way to demonstrate that there was no such thing as a "maltose repressor," that what looked like positive regulation involving an activator was not in fact disguised negative regulation, involving a repressor. This was not an easy thing, and Ellis Englesberg had experienced, and was still experiencing the same problem. A positive regulator gene would be mainly defined by mutations which are pleiotropic negative, i.e. which prevent the expression of all the structural genes controlled by its product. The difficulty is that several classes of pleiotropic negative mutations can also be expected in a negatively controlled system. Deletions, polar mutations, "i^S type" mutations leading to super-repression are some, relatively easy to discard. But others, much more vicious, are mutations in a transport system, such that the inducer cannot penetrate and inactivate the repressor; or mutations in an enzyme which might convert the external inducer, added in the medium, into an internal inducer which interacts with the repressor. How could one rigourously exclude all these and a few other possibilities? "Proving" the existence of a regulatory circuit turned out to be more difficult than I originally thought. After all, I was not much better off than if I had chosen to demonstrate the existence of a conformation change in an allosteric enzyme! Nevertheless, I did accumulate evidence that there was a positive regulator gene (malT) in the maltose system, to the point where, some days, Monod would start believing it. One such day he even proposed a name for the product of malT, and of positive regulator genes in general. This name was "provocateur." He thought that "activator" was too general, and often implied the involvement of energy. It was a good word, and I suggested it in a paper for the Annales de l'Institut Pasteur in 1967. However when Dolph Hatfield, Maurice Hofnung, and myself tried to use it in the next paper, which was to be published in an American journal, it was strongly rejected by the editors. I suspect that my friend Ellis was not totally innocent in this affair.

Monod was very difficult to convince about the existence of positive control. In a letter that he sent me in the States, in October 1968, he wrote "Il faudra bien qu'on arrive à savoir un jour si les provocateurs existent réellement. J'avoue que je continue à etre un peu sceptique." In view of this attitude it is not surprising that, when I presented my thesis, in 1967, I thought that Ellis Englesberg and I were more or less the only two persons in the world to believe in positive control.

Why is it that Monod was so reluctant to believe in positive control? One reason can possibly be found in the evolution of his own ideas about regulation in the lactose system. The concept of a regulatory molecule, distinct from the enzyme, and responsible for receiving the induction signal, apparently became clear to him around 1951, after the discovery of gratuitous inducers. It was only in 1958, however, that the famous "Pardee-Jacob-Monod" experiment lead to the idea that the regulatory molecule was a repressor. It had therefore taken seven years for Monod and his colleagues to come up with the hypothesis that "l'inducteur agissait, non pas en provoquant la synthèse de l'enzyme, mais en 'inhibant un inhibiteur' de cette synthèse."* It took seven years to demonstrate that the product of *lac i* was a repressor and not a "provocateur!" No wonder Monod was not immediately willing to accept that the reverse was true for the regulator gene of the maltose system. In addition, Englesberg and his colleagues were soon led to the somewhat unesthetical idea that the product of the arabinose regulator gene was not only an activator in the presence of L-arabinose, but also a repressor in its absence. In the maltose system, on the other hand, the phenotype of many mutants remained unexplained. This unwarranted complexity of the two most well known positively regulated systems made Monod, and many others, suspicious that something basic could be wrong. Still, over the years I could not escape imagining what would have happened if Monod had focused on amylomaltase, rather than on β-galactosidase. I might have had to prove, against an atmosphere of general scepticism that the synthesis of β-galactosidase was regulated in a strictly negative way. And I probably would not have convinced Monod.

*Monod, Nobel Prize Lecture, 1965.

THE LIVELY CORRIDOR

Marie-Hélène Buc

During the spring of 1962, a biochemistry course on "the biosynthesis of macromolecules," presenting experiments which were being done at that very time, was given at the Faculté des Sciences de Paris by Monsieur Jacques Monod.

The courses one usually attended at that time consisted of the boring recitation of formulas, like that of vitamin B_{12} or testosterone—formulas we were more or less bound to learn by heart for the exam—without any reference to the ideas and the experiments which had led to the comprehension of these structures. It was like teaching the precepts of the Bible without referring to the history of the Jewish people.

By contrast, our new teacher appeared personally concerned with the theory of the genetic code. Was the code universal, degenerate? What was the basic unit? What kind of punctuation existed? Rather than trying to simply teach us facts, he had us participate in an intellectual exercise which was his own approach: the hypotheses, the type of methods which could test them, and the actual experimental verifications. I had the impression that he was not teaching, but trying his own logic on us.

His approach had a great power of attraction and even of seduction. Postponing my own aim, medical research, and totally ignorant of the international reputation of my teacher as a scientist, I asked Monsieur Monod for a position in his laboratory.

The interview I had with him one week later was different from what I had imagined: no curriculum vitae, no test of scientific ability. He opened a debate about the potentialities of women and about their place in research. We had a general discussion as if I was not myself a woman asking for a position in his lab. He stated that he very much appreciated the intellectual qualities of women; however, he was totally against women working in research because of their necessary investments outside their work. Moreover, he told me that he was against women in science, especially if they were good, since serious conflicts would develop between their work and their family. How not to agree? I thought I knew what he meant since I already had to organize myself between work at the hospital and a baby at home. In fact, he was not thinking only in terms of time being a limiting factor; he knew that a free mind is an absolute require-ment to do good research, a situation which is unhappily less common among women due to what he called "the necessary investments." At the end of the discussion, I heard that I had to come back the next Friday. When I arrived, I was greeted with, "Here is this ambitious young lady. Come and visit your new lab." I realized then that the word "ambitious" had a different meaning for Monsieur Monod and for me. For him, my main ambition was not, to do research instead of being a physician, but it had been to ask for a position in his group though I was a woman.

I quickly discovered that various aspects of regulation were attacked at the same time in the lab; each student was working hard, trying to analyze "his" operon or "his" regulatory protein. Our results were daily put in the frame of the models which had been elaborated by Jacques Monod and François Jacob, and the models would be modified, after long discussions, according to the experimental data. It seemed to me that most people were working with enthu-siasm and thought they were participating in important issues. It was the golden age of allostery.

Trying to recall that period, I wonder what specific conjunction of people and circumstances had made this group both creative and happy.

The topography of the lab favored communication: it was a long corridor with one pole of attraction, "le labo bleu," which opened to Jacques Monod's office. Another pole of attraction came later at the other end of the corri-dor: François Jacob's door. In between in one room were senior workers tutor-ing a few students; in another a mixture of young students from Jacob and Monod's teams were deliberately placed together with no tutor; and in the largest room, "le grand labo," American postdocs learning French from other students who would in turn learn some science from them. The last room was the kitchen in which Jacques Monod used to come and talk with people or listen to Lucie Barnard sing. All labs opened to the corridor and people therefore had many opportunities to meet. One could see at any time during the day a group of three or four persons in discussion. The composition of the group was constantly changing,but ont of the members very often was David Perrin, who knew everything from the papers in the *J. Mol. Biol.* to the method for getting a specific mutant, to such thing as the number of cattle in Argentina in 1936. There, in this forum, theoretical and technical problems were discussed amiably, and we learned to know and appreciate one another.

Another important and particular place was indeed "le labo bleu." If I remember so well who was sitting at which desk, it means that I probably felt, and I was not the only one, that these individuals were privileged people. They were called "mes enfants" by the boss who many times during the day would open the door between his office and the lab and appear, his glasses in one hand, immediately to start a discussion about a specific point. When I entered the room by chance, I always had mixed feelings. Science was certainly the concern of all these people; at the same time, the atmosphere was clearly different from that in the corridor. I do not mean that everyone wanted to be thought superior by the boss, but it was clear that everyone was very sensitive to his intellectual seduction and wanted to seduce in turn.

I come now to the third important place in the lab: the seminar room. We were supposed to meet there almost every day at noon. The student who was giving the talk had to be prepared for a difficult job: to defend the qualities of the paper as if he were himself the author, and criticize the content and the methods thereby schooling himself in self-confidence. Jacques Monod would manifest his scientific rigor by interrupting at any time to question, or to criticize the questions of others. He was sometimes so hard on us that we hesitated to ask questions. He used to say at the end of the lecture:"It is late; time for just one, but very interesting question." As we were wondering if the question we had in mind was clever enough, he had time to formulate his own comment, which was exasperatingly good.

I have described Jacques Monod's laboratory as objectively as I can trying to put myself in the position of an outsider: admiring, but sometimes irritated and frustrated. But I am not in that position. Day after day, I have lived in this friendly atmosphere where everyone contributed a lot because of Monod's own generosity. He was indeed generous, giving us his time and his warm affection, particularly when we had professional or personal problems. No one knew it, but he was present and efficient. Clearly, he was interested in people; he enjoyed discovering their particular talents and helped develop them. Not only did we tolerate this father-to-child relationship, but I feel we were happy there partly because of it.

May 1968 was the turning point. A picture in *Le Nouvel Observateur* shows Jacques Monod taking care of a young girl wounded by the police. It was for me a symbol of the kind relationship Jacques Monod had with us, but young people did not want any more of it. When Jacques Monod became director of the

Institut Pasteur, he encountered objection to some of his choices for the Institute among those who never fundamentally contested his scientific options. This was certainly difficult for him, and not easy for us. In 1971, when I did not agree with one of his decisions and happened to mention it in public, he was so furious with me that he told me, "you act as an irresponsible. I know better than you what is good for you." I remembered this sentence.

Three weeks before he died, he invited me to his home to have tea with him—again, his presence, his warm smile, his questions ("Are you happy in François' group?"), his suggestions concerning my new work ("Why not try to induce specific differentiation in teratocarcinomas with these new hormones?"). Also he told me, "When I am not too tired, this period of my life is so interesting. I shall die soon, I know it, and because of that, the intensity and the quality of the relations I have with my friends is of another nature." He then spoke about my sons and his sons; and some of his last words to me were: "One never knows what one gives to his children. Did I help them in finding their way?" I was with him for the last time and I knew it. As he accompanied me to the elevator, his eyes followed me for a long while, for he also knew.

TO FOLD OR NOT TO FOLD:
THE WAY TOWARD RESEARCH

Michel Goldberg

I came to Monsieur Monod's laboratory in October 1962, a year or so too late to have known the great excitement of the "operon" and "allostery" periods. Yet, in spite of my total ignorance of biology, I very rapidly became aware of the importance of these two concepts: the main principles governing the regulation of polypeptide chain biosynthesis were understood and the regulation of the enzymatic activity of a protein could be interpreted in terms of subtle changes in the conformation of the polypeptide chains. At that time, these regulation models were far from being universally accepted; but Monsieur Monod was convinced that, though some "refinements" undoubtedly would have to be added, the fundamental principles had been uncovered. He therefore became more and more interested in the single link still missing, at that time, between the genetic message and its expression as a functional protein: the folding of a newly synthesized peptide chain into the specific, three-dimensional structure achieved in the native molecule. How did he involve me in that field of protein folding?

He thought that this problem, like so many others in the then new field of molecular biology, had to be approached with the aid of physical chemistry; and therefore, he tried to attract to his laboratory a few students who had a fairly solid background in physical sciences. I was among his first victims.

183

As soon as we met, he explained to me how he intended to organize my biological training. To start with, a complete brainwashing to erase from my consciousness the academic knowledge I had gained during my studies. Then, some elements of biochemistry would have to be learned by attending the courses in which he participated at the University of Paris. He insisted that these courses were of utmost importance because classical biochemistry was the real, concrete basis of molecular biology. (A few weeks later, I was somewhat surprised to discover that he himself taught essentially the exciting aspects of molecular biology, relying on others, to teach what he claimed to be more basic.) Last but not least, what he considered as essential was the apprenticeship in the laboratory.

He exerted extreme care in choosing the appropriate sponsor for each beginner in his group, and through a subtle combination of intuition, psychology, and reasoning he usually succeeded in reaching an excellent match. In my case, I consider that he reached perfection. When I started working at the bench, Edwin Lennox was spending an extended sabbatical stay in Paris, waiting for the Salk Institute to be completed. When Monsieur Monod asked him to train me as an experimentalist (starting from pipetting and weighing correctly!) Ed was not very happy, since he had expected to be free of such a chore while on sabbatical. Yet he accepted this burden. Because he was so patient, so profoundly generous, he developed a real interest in my evolution and rapidly became a most helpful, exquisite, and efficient adviser. When, after a few months, I told Monsieur Monod how happy I was with Ed Lennox's teaching, he explained the reason for his choice: because Ed himself had undergone a reconversion from physics to biology, nobody better than he could guess, and therefore fill, the gaps in my understanding and knowledge of biochemistry.

Monsieur Monod also considered attending seminars of predominant importance in learning biology; and he literally did not allow anyone to miss a lecture. I once continued an experiment, instead of going to the smoky, overcrowded, uncomfortable library, where what I considered as an uninteresting talk was being given. Monsieur Monod noticed my absence and, in the afternoon, upbraided me in an extremely severe way, insisting that I should never consider my own experiments more important than those of others! Indeed, the seminars were usually quite enlightening and of excellent scientific level. They were also extremely lively, mainly because of Monsieur Monod's sharp, often aggressive and merciless questions to the speaker. It was very noticeable to anybody who regularly attended these noon seminars that Monsieur Monod had a highly variable degree of causticity, depending on who was giving the talk. He obviously could not tolerate an unintelligent or self-satisfied speaker. On the contrary, a graduate student giving a moderately interesting and not too disorganized lecture would frequently be congratulated publicly with some emphasis. I do remember my intense emotion when this first happened to me. Monsieur Monod had asked me to give a talk on van der Waals forces and hydrophobic interactions. I did my best to explain the nature of these interactions without going too much into details concerning their thermodynamics, but I was not certain that I had been understood, nor that I had really captivated the audience with this esoteric subject. As usual, after the seminar, we all went to a neighbôring delicatessen to get some food and, back on the veranda, close to the library, gathered together at a long table to have lunch. Just as I sat down, Monsieur Monod started congratulating me on my talk; these were, as far as I remember, the first compliments I had received from him after six months at the Pasteur Institute. Of course, I tried to hide my emotion, which was so intense that I was unconsciously and nervously squeezing the bag of Italian style spaghetti I had brought with me. And my pride rapidly turned to extreme confusion when I noticed that all the tomato sauce had spread on my trousers. That day, I remained unusually long at the table, and nobody noticed that my clothes had also been blushing!

However, Monsieur Monod was as efficient in condemning as he was in praising. I have a vivid memory of an extremely unpleasant scolding I once received. After Ed Lennox had left to join the Salk Institute, I usually asked David Perrin to teach me any new method I had to use. He thus showed me how to perform sucrose gradient centrifugations and helped me throughout my first experiment. The centrifugation went on overnight. On Friday morning, we stopped the centrifuge, collected the fractions, and analyzed them through a fairly long procedure which kept us busy well after midnight. Because the gates of the Institute closed at 10 P.M. at that time, we had to climb over a wall to escape from the laboratory. When we were about to jump onto the pavement, a police car passed by. The men in the patrol looked at us, smiled, and passed by. A few hours later, I was back at the bench, worked all Saturday, slept about two hours on the sofa in the library, and went on pipetting, assaying, measuring, until Sunday afternoon. Having then finished my experiment, I was so tired that I decided to go home immediately and have a long sleep. When, on Monday morning, I came back to the laboratory, I found a large note, clearly written in huge black letters, hanging above my bench. It said something like: *Michel! This is the last time I tolerate such a mess on your bench. Jacques Monod.*

I was shocked, vexed, and became furious; after having worked so hard, having completed such a nice experiment, all I got was that stern and public humiliation! I rushed into Monsieur Monod's office. He greeted me with a friendly smile; I was about to explode, but he told me, in his deep, quiet, and cheerful voice, "Well, my little Michel, what about your sucrose gradients? I heard you have been working like mad!" I was a bit comforted by the fact that he at least was aware of how hard I had been toiling, and I started explaining why I had left my bench somehow crowded with dirty glassware, pipettes, and tools. His answer came, as sharp as a knife-edge; "I don't care why you *left* your bench messy. You just should never *let* it become filthy like that. The type of work you are doing requires an extreme care and I'll never trust an experiment of yours as long as you are not able to get organized!"

A few days later, having completed the analysis of my experimental results, I carefully and cleanly drew the curves corresponding to the four centrifugations I had performed. To allow for a better comparison of these experiments, I represented the four curves on the same sheet of graph paper, using a different color for each diagram. Proud of my work, I waited for the first occasion to show and explain it to Monsieur Monod. When, at last, I could point out to him the meaning of each curve, I realized that something was wrong; he did not understand what I was explaining. This was quite unusual since he ordinarily would have grasped an idea before I could finish expressing it. So, I tried again, more slowly, "The red curves represent wild type β-galactosidase, the green is U178, the blue is CZ1, and the black one corresponds to the complemented enzyme." A dull, interrogative look showed me that I was not yet clear enough. I was completely baffled, and had no idea why Monsieur Monod could not immediately see the interest of my results. But David Perrin who just had joined us, whispered in my ear, "He is color-blind. How could he sort out your curves?" Understanding the situation was quite a relief and, by reproducing my graphs one by one on the blackboard, I could at last convey my message. While Monsieur Monod was discussing my results, I could not help being amazed by the slight coquetry which led him to conceal his sight defect. The discovery of this weak point in his otherwise apparently monolithic personality was indeed my first insight into his complex, sensitive, and fascinating character.

And that is how, within two years, and by a wise admixture of stimulating compliments, of severe exactingness, of constant scientific interest, of permanent availability to discussion, of total confidence, Monsieur Monod molded me into what he considered an honest biochemist, who could be decently sent out from his laboratory.

This period of introduction to biochemistry came to an end when, on a sunny Saturday morning, Monsieur Monod called me into his office and playing as he often did with my sensitivity, formally asked me to sit down and warned me that he had a very serious matter to discuss with me. I was impressed by his solemn attitude and, when he started telling me that there was nothing more I could learn in his laboratory, I became extremely worried. Judging my deep distress, he then burst into cheerful laughter, and reassured me. What he really meant was that he was no longer able to direct my research, because what I needed at this stage was good training in protein physical chemistry. And this, he said, was far beyond his capabilities. He had come to the conclusion that I should leave his laboratory for some time, and spend one or two years abroad. He just wanted to know whether, in principle, I would agree to such a project. This was a somewhat unexpected question, and I tried deferring the answer by saying that it would depend on where I would go and with whom I would be working. But Monsieur Monod was not caught off guard. He warmly praised

Robert Baldwin, who was just completing a sabbatical year with François Jacob, telling me how he enjoyed discussions with him, and how he admired his sharp mind and acute knowledge of macromolecular physical chemistry. He informed me that Buzz Baldwin had already accepted the offer to sponsor my Ph. D. work; that the "D. G. R. S. T." would support me during my stay in the United States and pay for my fare; that I could apply to NATO to be aided with my wife's travel expenses, that California was a great place. He had organized everything and thought over every little detail. So, a few months later, in October 1964, I left for Stanford University.

When I came back to Paris, many things had changed. The Nobel Prize had drastically modified the status of molecular biology in France. This hitherto minor branch of biology, which itself had been a neglected area when compared to the flourishing fields of mathematics and physics, was now recognized as a real science. And the "Monod-Jacob-Lwoff trio" had become very familiar to people in the street. Yet, as soon as I returned to the laboratory, I could feel that the quality of the intellectual and affective relations between Monsieur Monod and his collaborators had not been altered.

For me, however, the situation was clearly different. He no longer wanted to treat me as a student, and I rapidly discovered that I would be entrusted with some of his scientific preoccupations. Very shortly after my return to Paris, he asked me to give a seminar on the work I had been doing at Stanford. He thought that this was the best way for him to learn about my results. He was apparently happy with them and decided that, after some short experiments which I had to do to complete this work, I should start writing my Ph. D. thesis. At that time a thesis at the University of Paris consisted of two parts: the main one described the examinee's own research, and the minor one was a bibliographical essay which had to be written on a subject chosen by the jury. By deciding that my essay should bear on "prediction of the conformation of a protein from its amino acid sequence," Monsieur Monod hurled me right into the field of protein folding, a theme which has since remained the subject of my research.

When, after a decade, I try to understand why I got so deeply involved in that subject, I can find two main reasons, both related to the fact that Monsieur Monod himself had become particularly interested in protein folding. He was then preparing his first series of lectures at the Collège de France, a very important part of which was devoted to a dissertation on protein structure and evolution. This stimulated endless discussions, which would last for hours, with the help of a glass of Scotch and tens of cigarettes; a huge number of butts thrown on the floor around a stool clearly indicated, the next morning, the bench at which Monsieur Monod had been sitting during the last discussion.

Also, there was an extremely efficient complementarity in our approaches to that problem: he was the biologist, asking questions of physiological importance; and I was the physical chemist, trying to answer these questions in quantitative terms. And this complementarity, because of his exacting confidence, turned me into one of the many facets of an intellectual mirror he had created with several scientists to enrich, through a permanent dialogue, his scientific creativity.

At the risk of boring nonscientists with some words incomprehensible to them, I should like to briefly illustrate the mixture of intuition, common sense, and logic which made so fruitful Monsieur Monod's approach to protein physical chemistry. He was always interested in very general questions dealing with features which could be easily generalized. For instance, one common feature of proteins is that they are very large molecules. Thus, one of the first questions which Monsieur Monod asked in his lectures at the Collège de France was "Why are proteins so large?" To answer this question, he started by emphasizing that a protein, in addition to being a molecule obeying the laws of physics, is an object reflecting the history of millions of years of evolution and that therefore its "function," on which evolution is based, should serve as a guide to the interpretation of its physical properties. Thus to account for the large size of proteins, he tried to analyze the constraints which the functional features of a protein exert on its structure: the existence of a catalytic site requiring the exact relative positioning of half a dozen amino acids; the stability of the protein conformation requiring, according to the "oil drop model," a hydrophobic core; the solubility of the molecule, requiring the presence on its surface of polar residues able to interact with the solvent. By using molecular models, and rather rough energy calculations, we came to the conclusion that a minimum of about 70 to 100 residues were necessary to fulfill these requirements. And surprisingly enough, this is indeed the size of the smallest naturally occurring globular proteins.

Such reasoning was made in the beginning of 1967, when so little was known about protein conformation. Since then, the unraveling of many protein structures by X-ray crystallographers has abundantly confirmed the validity of the then daring assumptions underlying Monsieur Monod's approach to protein conformation.

And today, it may even seem strange that Monsieur Monod could have been so deeply involved in such rough and elementary questions as "Why are proteins so big?" or "Why are proteins so often oligomeric?" or "Are oligomers symmetrical?" or "What is the basis of protein folding and stability?"

In fact, these questions were at the heart of his philosophical preoccupations. It is not by mere coincidence that his lectures at the Collège de France on proteins and evolution were given while he was writing *Chance and Necessity*.

Indeed, he wrote in his book, "By these standards proteins must be deemed the essential molecular agents of teleonomic performance in living beings." Hence, no wonder that he was so much interested in trying to reproduce, *in vitro*, some of the steps of protein evolution. First, as a model for the origin of evolution, he imagined "the precambrian protein" the amino acid sequence of which would have been determined at random. And for years he tried to convince people to construct and study such a protein. Second, as a model for the most elaborate achievements of molecular evolution, (i.e., the acquisition of allosteric properties) he got involved in trying to "allosterize" a nonregulatory enzyme. And I still remember his excitement when I reported some observations I had made on the ion activation of the β-galactosidase produced by a cold-sensitive mutant. When, after a closer examination, it turned out that the observed activation was simply due to an ion-dependent subunit association, Monsieur Monod told me, "You now have the ancestral allosteric transition in your test tube. Try to progress by one more step in evolution."

His interest in protein conformation survived Monsieur Monod's involvement in the direction of the Pasteur Institute. Whenever I entered his directorial office and told him that I had some interesting results, he would sit up in his chair, light up with his deep, affectionate smile and say, "It is so kind of you, Michel, to bring some science into this office." And he would easily spend a whole hour discussing my experiments, while the upper limit for an administrative discussion was about ten minutes.

About two weeks before he died, he felt physically much better than during the preceding months and he told me, "When I retire, I want to write my second book. So many ideas matured during these years. I have so much to say. But do you know, mon petit Michel, what will happen when I am sitting in front of a white page? Shall I ever be able to start again?"

He was not given the chance to face this new challenge. A pity for him. And for science.

A Ph. D. WITH JACQUES MONOD:
PREHISTORY OF ALLOSTERIC PROTEINS

Jean-Pierre Changeux

A beautiful model or theory may not be right; but an ugly one must
be wrong.

Jacques Monod, in "Symmetry and Function of
Biological Systems at the Macromolecular Level."
Nobel Symposium 11, 1969

October 1958: After three years at the Ecole Normale Supérieure and the preparation of the Agrégation des Sciences Naturelles, I was still unacquainted with
Jacques Monod's scientific work. That year, Jacques Dauta, a colleague who was
also preparing the Agrégation, asked me to be present during the defense of his
Diplome d'Etudes Supérieures. His subject, dealing with the biochemistry of bacteria, was quite remote from the concerns of the zoologist and would-be em-
bryologist, that I was. Dauta had spent a few months at the Pasteur Institute, in
the newly created Service de Biochimie Cellulaire, where his sojourn appeared
to have been rather stormy. On the examining board sat a man with severe and
regular features, who used a rich and accurate vocabulary, and expressions that
were sometimes cold and cutting—nothing which could attract a young biologist. This man, nevertheless, was to become my master.

191

Following several prolonged summer stays at the Laboratory of Marine Biology in Banyuls-sur-Mer, I became convinced that the future lay in embryology. I spent a few weeks in Jean Bachet's Laboratory in Brussels and came back to Paris with a subject: the study of the molecular mechanisms of the egg's activation by the spermatozoon. It had been shown that this activation is accompanied by an increase in the activity of several enzymes: different phosphatases and proteases. In Louvain, De Duve had just discovered the lysosome. The hypothesis was that this increase in activity results from the break-down of lysosomes. Working in a small laboratory at the Institut de Biologie Physico-Chimique, I was vainly trying to measure the phosphatases of the sea urchin's egg. These failures leaving me hopeless, I went and talked to Jeanine Yon who was working in a neighboring room. According to her, the only laboratory in Paris where people were both interested in fundamental biological problems and had a profound knowledge of enzymology was Jacques Monod's, at the Pasteur Institute. I had to meet Jacques Monod.

Chance had it that a few days later Jacques Monod called on René Wurmser at the Institut de Biologie. He was a candidate for a vacant professorship at the Faculté des Sciences and, therefore, had to have meetings with each of the current professors. I jumped at the opportunity. Recognizing the person I saw stepping out of René Wurmser's office as the man I had seen at Dauta's thesis defense, I approached him boldly. He looked surprised at first, but his face lit up when I asked him my first question: "Could you teach me how to assay phosphatases?" He asked me why and I started to explain the scientific problem I was facing and the difficulties I was encountering. After the first amusement, interest came. We could not discuss the matter in a hall; I should come and give a seminar at the Pasteur Institute.

A few days later, on a Saturday morning, I found myself in a dusty room on the first floor of the Pasteur Institute. A few books on shelves decorated the room, but most of it was crammed with heaps of jars filled with silkworm cocoons and obsolete machinery. What was to become one of the high places of molecular biology looked more like a thrift shop than a lecture room. Nevertheless, I presented my project enthusiastically, unaware of (as I heard later) the amused but benevolent responses among my small audience. Following the discussion, Jacques Monod, holding my arm, took me to his office, a small and severe place dominated by a beautiful engraving by Piranese. Monod spoke briefly and firmly. Nobody in France was working on chemical embryology. If I wanted to continue my on-going project, I had to emigrate for a while to the United States. Otherwise I had to ". . . choose another path, switch to simpler systems, learn enzymology, genetics, immunology. . ." and then, after a few years, I would be able to come back to my early love.

If I were to choose this latter possibility, Monod would give me the opportunity to come and work at the Pasteur Institute. François Jacob, who had no students at that time, could offer space for me in his laboratory. Jacques Monod gave me two months to think about his proposal. At the moment I did not fully realize what an incredible opportunity had come my way; Jacques Monod's offer did not appeal to me immediately. I read François Jacob's thesis. His theory of episomes, the experiments on chromosome transfer between bacteria and phages reminded me of Briggs and King's embryology experiments. I inquired about the biological material. Gérard Buttin, then one of Monod's students, took me to the 37°C incubator where the coli-bacillus cultures were regularly agitating. The sight of the milklike suspension and its nauseous smell disgusted me to the point that I questioned the whole thing. Reason was stronger, however, and I called Jacques Monod to tell him I had chosen the Pasteur Institute.

FROM BACTERIAL GENETICS TO REGULATORY ENZYMES

A room in the attic, the heat of a Turkish bath without the charms of Oriental perfumes, the rhythmic noise of a waterbath, piles of Petri dishes and, sitting at his desk in the far-away corner of the room in front of the window, François Jacob, his head bent like a car racer's. The first dominant constitutive mutants had just been isolated and identified. The "operon" was in gestation. There was no time to lose. I was, obviously, not needed here. My first experiment consisted in following the infection of a culture of bacteria by a bacteriophage. The experiment succeeded: the culture lysed within the expected time. In the second one I had to establish the growth curve of a bacterial population. The only culture medium available on the third floor was broth: the experiment was carried out in broth. It so happened that the very evening the curve was drawn, Jacques Monod walked into the laboratory and asked for the results. His eyes turned suddenly cold. None of the parameters he was interested in—growth rate, yield, etc.—could be seen on my diagrams. The main part of the analysis he had developed in his thesis could not be applied to this curve which had been established in too complex a medium.

His irritation at the nonquantitative aspect of one of my first experiments in the laboratory made me go down two floors. I found myself in the Service de Biochimie Cellulaire. For the next four months I worked under the direct supervision of Jacques Monod. The proposed subject, which had come out of a discussion between François Jacob and Jacques Monod, consisted of a comparison between the expressions of a gene—that of β-galactosidase—in different cytoplasms, that of coli-bacillus and of *Salmonella*. Every week a protocol was established, remarkably detailed, precise enough to be given to a technical assistant. Week after week I explored each of the main properties of the enzyme synthesized by the strain of *Salmonella*: dissociation constant, thermal stability, immunological properties, etc. Within a few months I had gone through nearly all of enzymology, and even tackled the regulation of the synthesis of β-galactosidase as well as the active transport of β-galactosides across the bacterial membrane. All this was done very concretely on the experimental level, while resting on a sound theoretical basis. Jacques Monod had prepared and organized for me a research training program, the exceptional quality of which I still appreciate today.

Results proved the identity between the coli-bacillus enzyme and the enzyme synthesized by the hybrid *Salmonella*. They had to be written up. The format of a note to the *Compte Rendu* was adopted. I did not know it would be such a painful ordeal. My first text, written in absolute quietude, was violently rejected because of its lack of organization, the looseness and vagueness of style, its excessive length, in short its lack of scientific rigor. For Jacques Monod a note to the *Comptes Rendus* precisely because of its conciseness had to be written up with great care. I should use as a model the "style of a sonnet rather than that of a novel by Proust. As in classical tragedy, everything has to contribute to the action." Rich with these criticisms and comments, I wrote up a second version which, of course, did not receive the imprimatur: I had made but little use of the remarks my first paper had provoked. A third version followed, then a fourth. By the fifth one I could no longer construct a sentence; by the sixth one I was losing my vocabulary.

The ninth version was transmitted to Jacques Trefouel who presented it to the Academy. I started to realize that being a reliable experimenter, or even having inventive genius was not enough to make a research worker. One also had to master one's writing style. Jacques Monod attached as much importance to the manner in which ideas were expressed as to the ideas themselves. I have even heard him say that an idea existed only in so far as it had been written up. Once I had finished this training, Jacques Monod decided the time had come for me to choose a subject for a Ph. D. A meeting with François Jacob took place in Jacques Monod's office in the beginning of September 1959. Jacques Monod gave me a choice of three subjects: (1) the analysis of the fine genetics of double mutations β-galactosidase-permease, a problem the solution of which was to contribute to the concept of operator; (2) the genetic and biological analysis of the enzymes of maltose metabolism, a system from which positive regulation of enzyme synthesis was to be discovered; and (3) the follow-up of the enzymology and biochemistry of β-galactosidase and its different mutants. None of these subjects appealed to me. François Jacob informed us, then, of Umbarger's recent results. He had proven that the synthesis of L-isoleucine in the coli-bacillus was regulated by a negative feedback mechanism. L-Isoleucine, the end product of the biosynthetic pathway, inhibited selectively the activity of L-threonine deaminase, the firse enzyme of the chain, and this effect was preserved *in vitro* after the enzyme's extraction. Moreover, the L-threonine deaminase showed high order kinetics as a function of substrate concentration. No one at the Pasteur Institute had worked on this system. Jacques Monod mentioned a recent conversation with Arthur Pardee who had obtained similar results with another enzyme, the aspartate transcarbamylase, the first enzyme of pyrimidine biosynthesis. It seemed advisable that somebody work on these regulatory enzymes. I was interested in the problem, which reminded me of the activation of the enzymes of the egg during fertilization. The choice was made, but we still had to decide on a specific enzymatic system. We chose, at first, the acetolactate synthetase, the first specific enzyme of the biosynthetic pathway of L-valine, also identified by Umbarger. François Jacob had L-valine-requiring mutants; moreover, the given coli-bacillus was sensitive to this amino acid, and L-valine-resistant mutants had already been selected. According to François Jacob, the best way to tackle the problem was to isolate mutants with an acetolactate synthetase modified on the feedback regulation by valine. Several valine-resistant mutants did happen to possess an acetolactate synthetase insensitive to valine. But it was a difficult enzyme, with a still unidentified cofactor apparently necessary for its activity. We decided to abandon this system in favor of L-threonine deaminase, a very stable protein, simple to assay. My first task was to repeat Umbarger's experiments. The study of regulatory enzymes was becoming one of the research topics of Jacques Monod's laboratory.

THE CONCEPT OF ALLOSTERIC INTERACTION (1960-1962)

My subject had been defined. The task of proceeding was difficult. Isolated in a laboratory crowded with American postdoctoral fellows, it was out of question for me to discuss the protocol of my experiments each week with Jacques Monod. I assume this weaning was done on purpose. Jacques Monod may also have considered my topic of minor importance. He was giving much attention, at that time, to the regulation of protein synthesis, and spent considerable time with François Jacob. Every· once in a while he would visit me. During a conversation with Gérard Buttin, who was sharing my bench, he made a remark underlining the secondary character of the regulation of enzyme activity compared to the regulation of protein biosynthesis. I had to resist.

Several results helped me regain confidence. First, the fact that Umbarger's observations were confirmed: the inhibitory effect of L-isoleucine was specific. Moreover, in spite of an obvious difference in structure with the substrate, L-isoleucine inhibited the activity of the enzyme in a strictly competitive manner. Was this effect due to a steric hindrance following the classical rules of competitive inhibition by a structural analogue of the substrate? An important observation went against this idea. Various chemical treatments of the enzyme, such as heating, exposure to SH reagents, and purification modified its properties in a remarkable way. The threonine deaminase was losing its sensitivity to isoleucine, while keeping its enzymatic activity: the enzyme was becoming "desensitized." Even more important was the fact that along with the loss of the inhibitory effect of isoleucine, disappeared the nonlinear relationship between activity and substrate concentration. A unique structural property of the regulatory enzyme was to account for this phenomenon.

In June 1961, a scientific event took place that was to be of importance in the history of regulatory proteins: the 26th Cold Spring Harbor Symposium on "Cellular Regulatory Mechanisms." The moment had come to present the data collected on L-threonine deaminase. Several weeks before leaving for the United States I wrote up a first paper which I submitted to Jacques Monod. He read it with an interest that surprised me. One conclusion had to be drawn: the classical scheme by steric hindrance could not be maintained; we had to think of a new type of interaction between regulatory ligand and substrate: an interaction between nonoverlapping sites. A discussion was then started on the relationship between the nonhyperbolic shape of the substrate saturation curve and the inhibition by the regulatory ligand. The hypothesis (later verified) of several existing sets of sites for the substrate and for the regulatory ligand was mentioned. Jacques Monod found it needlessly complex. As a rule, he used to tell me, one should always limit oneself to the smallest number of hypotheses. Two sites should be enough, one for the substrate and another for the effector. The few structural analogies between threonine and isoleucine (both are amino acids) would allow the substrate to bind nonspecifically to the site of the inhibitor, and vice versa. This economy of hypotheses actually led to some questioning— although minor—of the fundamental postulate of the existence of two distinct and specific sites. I did not feel satisfied with this model but there was no mention of presenting another one. When the final text was written up I asked Jacques Monod whether he would cosign it. Why did he refuse? Did he consider the results too light for him to engage his scientific reputation, or did he wish to spare my feelings?

The puzzling results on threonine deaminase drew the attention of the participants of the Cold Spring Harbor Symposium. Immediately after the presentation, Bernard Davis stood up to make an important remark. According to him, there was a fundamental analogy between the properties of hemoglobin and of threonine deaminase. Both of them exhibited "cooperative" effects for substrate binding. This property had to be related to their regulatory function, and could result from the presence on the protein molecule, of several sites for each specific ligand. Hemoglobin was becoming the prototype of regulatory proteins.

One of the highlights of the Symposium was, undoubtedly, Jacques Monod's presentation of the concluding remarks. Combining ease with rigor, Monod gave, with his exceptional synthesizing mind, a general review of nearly all of molecular biology in 1961. Dealing with the regulation of enzymatic activity by negative feedback he went back to the paradox of the apparently competitive inhibition by a compound, very different in structure from the substrate. Converging results achieved independently by Gerhart and Pardee on aspartate transcarbamylase (results that were known to him although they had not yet been published) and on L-threonine deaminase led him to draw the general conclusion that the interaction between regulatory signal and substrate was taking place between distinct sites. In his oral report, Jacques Monod used the expression "Novick-Szilard-Umbarger" effect as a tribute to those who had, according to him, first observed negative feedback inhibition. (We actually owe the first description of this phenomenon, in 1941, to Zacharias Dische.) It is in the final text of these concluding remarks, which was written in the course of July and August, that the word "allosteric" appears for the first time—its two Greek roots express the difference in structure between regulatory effector and substrate. In Jacques Monod's writings the word allosteric qualifies nouns such as: inhibition, effect, enzyme or protein; never does the substantive "allostery" appear. To account for the interaction between distinct sites, Jacques Monod mentioned already the possibility of an induced-fit of the enzyme molecule, according to the scheme proposed by Koshland.

These ideas were further elaborated in the *Journal of Molecular Biology,* in a review article entitled "Allosteric proteins and cellular control systems." This text was written by Jacques Monod during 1962. Models of steric hindrance and allosteric effect were being completed by a less plausible model by direct interaction. Actually the introduction of this last model helps better to define the word "allosteric" and to identify this type of interaction as *indirect* interactions, a general definition still entirely valid today. In Chapter 2, Jacques Monod tries to describe more precisely the mechanism of these interactions. A conformational transition—or "allosteric transition"—is postulated. However in almost all the given examples (except hemoglobin) a change in the state of protein aggregation takes place. Indeed it is now known that these molecular weight effects are usually secondary to the allosteric transition triggered by the regulatory ligand. This idea was actually suggested in a footnote about the preliminary results of an ongoing work on phosphorylase *b* by Agnes Ullmann and Roy Vagelos (who was then on a sabbatical year at the Service de Biochimie Cellulaire). Contrary to expectations, the activation of phosphorylase *b* by AMP does not depend directly on the dimerization of the molecule: the allosteric transition is more discrete than a change in the state of aggregation.

Enough progress had been made by Perutz and his associates in their work so as to be able to imagine the extent of the changes accompanying oxygen binding to hemoglobin. First, the oxygen binding sites, the hemes, are about 30 Å apart. Affinity interactions between hemes are therefore allosteric interactions. Secondly, a comparison between the three-dimensional structures of oxygenated and reduced hemoglobin discloses a relative displacement between subunits, minor (about 19% of the distance between subunits), but still significant. Jacques Monod's report of these preliminary results in the 1963 review shows his early interest in the relation between subunits in regulatory proteins. This key idea was to be further developed during the following years, leading to the theory of 1965.

The general discussion in the 1963 review finishes with the generalization of the concept of allosteric protein. These molecules would be the key component of any system of biological control, from the regulation of enzyme activity to enzymatic adaptation, passing by hormone action. The hypothesis is put forward that gene repressors are also allosteric proteins. In 1961, Jacob and Monod thought that the repressor was a polyribonucleotide; as a result of further development of the work on regulatory enzymes, this idea was abandoned.

INTERPRETATION OF ALLOSTERIC TRANSITIONS IN TERMS OF QUATERNARY STRUCTURE (1963-1965)

As soon as it appeared, the 1963 paper gave rise to much controversy. Voices rose, denouncing its lack of originality; the idea was old, only the word "allosteric" was new. Others criticized the idea: "Its ability to explain was so great that it excluded nothing or nearly nothing" (J. Monod, Nobel Lecture), which led Boris Magasanik to quote it as "decadent." Finally, the most serious criticism dealt with the difficulty of distinguishing between a strictly allosteric mechanism and other possible types of direct interactions at the experimental level. Perutz's structural studies on hemoglobin and those of Gerhart and Pardee, and Gerhart and Schachman on aspartate transcarbarmylase brought irrefutable proofs of the existence of interactions at distance between topographically distinct sites.

A wave of publications on regulatory enzymes, nonetheless, began flooding the biochemical literature. Allosteric proteins were fashionable. In the laboratory, Jacques Monod himself was passing phosphorylase *b* through columns of Sephadex equilibrated with bromthymol blue, while Agnes Ullmann followed each of his gestures with warm and apprehensive attention. I was finishing up my thesis work. Kinetic data on threonine deaminase were piling up. Several of its properties were shared by other regulatory enzymes; for example, the existence of "cooperative" phenomena for the binding of substrate and regulatory ligands, etc. I was beginning to feel the temptation to propose a mathematical model accounting for the kinetics observed.

I consulted Adam Kepes who proposed a scheme derived from Michaelis' classical equations. I was put off by its extreme complexity and abstraction. In the course of the year 1963, I presented to Jacques Monod a first draft of my thesis work. The meeting took place in his new and much larger office, which had become vacant following Gabriel Bertrand's death. This room consisted of a desk, a bookcase, and walls of light oak, a comfortable armchair, in a very "rétro" style although this was not yet fashionable; above the desk a beautiful watercolor, a Provencal landscape, reminding one that Jacques Monod's father had been a painter. We started talking. It soon became essential for us to propose a simple molecular mechanism which could account for all the kinetic data on threonine deaminase.

Jacques Monod then launched into a series of very general reflections about the structure of globular proteins. Actually, this was a continuation of old ideas that were close to his heart. As early as 1949 he was already discussing the origin of the specificity of enzymes in a paper entitled "Genetic and Specific Chemical Factors in the Synthesis of Bacterial Enzymes," using terms that were surprisingly presaging the 1965 theory. The matter was quite different though, since the problem was to explain the enzymatic adaptation which Jacques Monod himself later proved to be due to protein synthesis. At that time, however, he considered, among others, a mechanism where the substrate acted as an "enzyme selector." He wrote that

> . . . every hypothesis on the mechanism of enzymatic adaptation implies a choice between a "true adaptative" mechanism and a "selective" one at the intracellular level. If we accept that the structure of the enzyme is determined by a gene, instead of the substrate, then we admit that the role of the substrate is to *select* a certain type of molecule, at least virtually preexisting. How does this selection operate? This is the problem. One assumes naturally that this effect results from the combination of the substrate with the enzyme. This is what Yudkin was the first to suggest, adding the hypothesis—probably hazardous—of an equilibrium between the enzyme and a hypothetical precursor: Precursor ⇌ Enzyme. According to Yudkin, the role of the substrate was to shift the equilibrium toward an increased formation of enzyme. . . .

This excerpt is a good illustration of the basic thought of Jacques Monod to look for the elements of protein structure responsible for the specificity of a biological reaction. It is at the heart of Monod's work on enzymatic adaptation, of his ideas on antibody synthesis (1959), and finally, of his interest for regulatory proteins.

Why did Jacques Monod, in the course of 1963, turn toward the functional organization of proteins? It is quite likely that he was influenced by David Perrin's work on intracistronic complementation, which was done in the laboratory, as well as Crick and Orgel's theoretical paper (1964) on the same topic. Actually, his interest was naturally drawn to homotropic cooperative effects which he considered the fundamental property of allosteric proteins. Did the idea of a correlation between molecular symmetry and cooperative binding develop while he was reading the writings of Jeffries Wyman on hemoglobin (1948-1960)? Did it come out of a conversation with Jeffries Wyman himself? In any case, Wyman had expressed the idea several times, and it had been confirmed by Max Perutz's X-ray work unraveling the symmetry properties of the hemoglobin molecule. Be that as it may, Jacques Monod started studying the various modes of assembly of subunits in a protein molecule, and the relevant properties. He built models—out of cardboard at first, then with balls of clay, and then with dice—which helped him think like a geometer.

First consideration: the three-dimensional folding of a single polypeptide chain gives a fundamentally asymmetrical object on which cannot exist several identical sites for a given ligand. The assembly of several of these objects into a finite structure or "oligomer" offers the possibility to build a molecule possessing several sites for a given ligand, an essential condition for cooperative binding to appear. This assembly can be done in different ways depending upon whether the association between these asymmetrical objects or "protomers" involves the same area (isologous association), or different areas (heterologous association) of the protomer surface. For either esthetic or (more likely) practical reasons, Jacques Monod always preferred the isologous association. It should be noted in this respect that the latter automatically confers a twofold axis of symmetry and, thus, oligomers built by isologous association possess more symmetry properties than those of heterologous association. They always have even numbers of subunits, which explains Jacques Monod's quasi-mystical opposition to trimers and pentamers.

We then had to find a mechanism which would create interactions between identical sites within the oligomer. A purely formal and abstract idea occurred to Jacques Monod: that the conformational transition of the oligomer conserve the symmetry both of the mode of association between subunits, and of the affinity of the binding sites; the cooperative binding then results from a shift in the conformational equilibrium in favor of this state. Without any ambiguity, for Jacques Monod, the postulate of the conservation of symmetry is responsible for the homotropic cooperative effects.

If the allosteric transition takes place between symmetrical states, then these states can only be present in small number. As a consequence, they must be independent from the type of ligand bound, and pre-exist to ligand binding. Therefore, the fundamental postulate of a preexisting conformational equilibrium was the result of a logical reflection required by the model's coherence. As already mentioned, the concept of a "selection" by the ligand can be found in Jacques Monod's writings as early as 1949. In our conversations it had also been mentioned as a simple way of explaining the effect of heterotropic ligands on the cooperativity of substrate binding. Considering the minimum hypothesis of a protein existing under two different states, the allosteric activators would then stabilize the same state as the substrate; conversely, inhibitors would favor the other state. The hypothesis of preexisting states allows a remarkable economy of means and simply explains a large number of kinetic properties. Obviously this concept goes against Koshland's hypothesis of a conformational change induced by the interaction with the ligand, leading to a multiplicity of structural states. We had adopted Koshland's hypothesis in 1961, but after three years it could no longer be considered appropriate.

The writing of the final text took a long time. The first manuscript was written by Jacques Monod during his summer vacation in 1963. If my memory is good, it followed the "historical" approach and began with considerations regarding the structure of oligomeric proteins.

The mathematical model followed, then the fitting of the experimental data by the equation of the model. The manuscript was sent to Jeffries Wyman, and also submitted to Buzz Baldwin, then spending his sabbatical year working with François Jacob. Buzz Baldwin noticed mistakes in the formulation of the equations of the model, and proposed the correct derivation of the "state" and "binding" functions. Version followed version, but Jacques Monod remained unsatisfied. A presentation beginning with the mathematical model was finally adopted, which could not fail to please Jacques Monod by its highly theoretical and formal aspect. In conclusion, speculations on the thermodynamics of allosteric transitions were added. This section did not seem essential to me, but what could I say?

More than a year and half after its conception, the text of the theory was delivered personally to John Kendrew for publication in the *Journal of Molecular Biology*. Jacques Monod made a special trip to Cambridge where he gave a seminar to explain himself. The manuscript was immediately accepted and appeared a few months later.

Reactions were much stronger and often more critical than those which followed the publication of the 1963 text. The Anglo-Saxon audience, always very pragmatic, did not see the logical necessity, and also the experimental basis, of the postulate of symmetry conservation. Rather, they saw in it the delirium of a Frenchman intoxicated by the spirit of geometry. Several months after the publication of the theory, Koshland, Nemethy, and Filmer submitted to the journal *Biochemistry* a paper which clearly expressed this reaction. The authors initially agreed with us upon considering the hypothesis of the "induced fit" as a particular case of a general scheme of two pre-existing states; but then, they postulated that the conformational transition concerns only the protomer and various artificial modes of interaction between subunits are proposed without serious attempt to relate these phenomenological schemes to any concrete protein structure. They wrote

> . . . The "concerted" scheme is represented by a square array merely for convenience, but this model does not depend on the geometry of the interactions since all subunits change simultaneously. The allosteric model of Monod *et al.* (1965) utilizes such a "concerted" change, but it also assumes various symmetry requirements *which are not an essential part* of the "concerted" model shown here. . . .

Biochemists found the symmetry conditions shocking; yet they seduced the solid-state physicist, Charles Kittel, and the cristallographer Max Perutz. The proposed scheme does appear to be an extreme case. Experimental observations may lead to moderate it. It remains true, though, that experimental data on hemoglobin—still the best-known example of allosteric protein—fit both quantitatively and qualitatively with the theory's main postulates.

EPILOGUE

After my Ph.D., I had to leave the laboratory. Military service and a growing interest for pharmacology were distracting me from regulatory enzymes. Daniel Blangy and the Bucs had taken the relay. Allosteric proteins were in good hands at the Pasteur Institute.

During the years I spent at Jacques Monod's laboratory we established a deep relationship. My departure for the United States was truly heart-rending. In the dedication of his book, *Chance and Necessity* Jacques Monod wote, "To my true spiritual and of course slightly parricidal son. . . " This was after I had come back from the United States.

Why would the desire to be independent make me a parricide? Jacques Monod was an exceptional master. He has been much more than that—in many respects, a true father.

DISCUSSIONS ABOUT PROTEINS

Robert L. Baldwin

When I went to the Institut Pasteur in 1963-1964, I was to work with François Jacob. My plan was to learn phage genetics for use in later physicochemical studies of genetic problems. Two surprises were awaiting me. One was a student (Alex Fritsch) who wanted to work with me; he was particularly interested in the uses of the analytical ultracentrifuge. I had wanted to leave both students and the ultracentrifuge behind at Stanford while I learned a new field, but working with Alex proved to be both a pleasure and a big help scientifically.

The second surprise was a manuscript by Jacques Monod on a model for allosteric enzymes. I was taken aback by its contents. It proposed a general model for allosteric enzymes. The particular protein which was discussed in detail was hemoglobin, which was not then known to be an allosteric protein. There were no allosteric ligands for hemoglobin; the Benesch's had not yet found 2,3-diphosphoglycerate, and the role of the Bohr protons in affecting O_2 binding was unclear.

The cooperative binding of O_2 by hemoglobin had intrigued chemists for decades. Such eminent physical chemists as Linus Pauling, G. S. Adair, F. J. W. Roughton, and Jeffries Wyman had studied the "heme-heme interaction." Was it likely that they had missed the answer which would now be supplied by a biologist without formal training in physical chemistry, who had never worked on hemoglobin? The manuscript had no names on it, and I always assumed that Jacques was the sole author of that first draft.

My skepticism grew as I studied the manuscript. It stressed the importance of symmetry: the allosteric transition from an inactive to an active conformation was postulated to be a change from one symmetrical conformation of an oligomeric protein, the R state, to a second symmetrical conformation, the T state. But individual protein chains were notoriously asymmetric objects, and almost nothing was known about the symmetry of their packing arrangements in oligomers. The model was extremely simple in view of the complexity of the problem. There was an equilibrium between molecules in the R and T states; mixed-state intermediates, molecules containing protomers both in the R and T states, were forbidden. All protomers in the R state were assumed to be identical and in equivalent environments, and also in the T state.

In that first draft, the statistical factor for ligand binding, which was well known from the work of Klotz and of Scatchard, was missing. It describes the increase in the probability of binding when a molecule with n binding sites is only partly liganded, caused by the several possible arrangements of i ligands among n binding sites. When I pointed out its omission, Jacques studied the changes that it would produce in the equations. His quick eye caught the fact that the statistical factor rises to a maximum for the half-liganded species and falls off symmetrically for species on either side. He looked down at the set of four dice, glued together, which he used as a model in thinking about the symmetry properties of oligomeric proteins. Then he looked up and smiled, "Well, that makes the equations more symmetrical, doesn't it?"

And so the year began. It progressed through six drafts of the allosteric manuscript. Everyone at the Pasteur enjoyed debate, and I found it easy to take part. But in order to turn it off and sleep nights, I had to resort to strenuous exercise on weekends. I began to climb the tall rocks in the forest of Fontainebleau, a sport in which Jacques once excelled. When I asked him if he had trouble shutting off his thoughts about science when he wanted to sleep, he gave me a surprised look and said, "Why no, do you?"

I was intrigued by Jacques' approach to the problem. First of all I was surprised that he expected to solve the problem of cooperative binding just by thinking about it and studying the clues in the literature. He didn't consider it necessary to have training in physical chemistry. Instead, he studied evidence from genetics on the properties of mutants and crystallographic data (then scanty) on protein structure. A precedent had been set by Crick and Orgel, who had developed a model for intracistronic complementation based on the probable symmetries of protein oligomers. Then too it surprised me that Jacques was convinced that a simple model would provide a general explanation for allosteric enzymes.

At that time the crystal structure of myoglobin was known and the structure of lysozyme was just being completed. The results could be represented by brass rod models with standard bond angles and distances and with every atom locked in place, as in a crystal of NaCl. Most chemists viewed proteins as massive, rigid objects. But the logic of the allosteric model seemed to require that proteins be flexible. A ligand binding at a distant regulatory site had to send a signal through the polypeptide chain to turn on or off the catalytic site. This was the way that transmission of the signal was envisaged in Jacques' manuscript.

I had a slightly different idea. Since the allosteric transition from an active to an inactive conformation was a concerted transition in his model, perhaps the transition was simply a change at the quaternary level between two different packing arrangements of the subunits. The protomers could remain as rigid objects with very little change in tertiary conformation. Also, in a model of this kind, I felt that one could discard the requirement for a transition between two symmetrical conformations, which pleased me. My idea that allosteric transitions might take place at the quaternary rather than at the tertiary level undoubtedly came from the finding in Perutz's lab that the β chains of hemoglobin move substantially closer together on oxygenation. I remember Jean-Pierre Changeux saying, "But the tertiary conformation of the globin chain *must* change on binding O_2." Jacques was intrigued with my idea, and two years later he told me he wished he had adopted it. Today, I'm sure he would be glad he didn't.

Paris weather in winter looked even more inhospitable through the streaked glass walls of the old dining room next to the small library of Biochimie Cellulaire. But the atmosphere at lunch was extraordinarily cheerful. To begin with, one could bring delicious hot food from a nearby *épicerie*, close to the corner of rue du Dr. Roux and rue des Volontaires. Lunch had its proper place in the day, as a time for discussion and reflection. No lunch seminars! François Jacob, Pierre Schaeffer, André Lwoff, and Mme. Lwoff regularly came down from the genetics section on the third floor and joined Sarah Rapkine, Agnes Ullmann, Jacques Monod, and other regulars for a leisurely lunch at the long table. Dr. Lwoff encouraged American visitors to try out their French.

The seminars were lively occasions with a highly responsive audience. A speaker had to choose his words with care. Twice in the year a visiting speaker paused as his next slide came on and mused, "Now what was I going to say about this?", whereupon Jacques, sitting in the front row, promptly answered the question for him.

Jacques became interested in physical chemistry that year and ordered books for the library. He visited Manfred Eigen's laboratory in Göttingen and was deeply impressed by the possibilities of studying allosteric mechanisms by fast-reaction techniques. I was surprised that, until then, molecular biology had developed in Paris with so little contribution from physical chemistry. I asked David Perrin why this had happened. His grandfather (Jean Perrin) and father

(Francis Perrin) had both made notable contributions to physical chemistry. David smiled and replied, "Probably because my grandfather was a poor teacher."

Jacques had earlier discussed his ideas with Jeffries Wyman and a collaboration between them now sometimes brought Wyman to Paris. The physicochemical behavior of the allosteric model was being studied in earnest. Jean-Pierre Changeux arranged for computer simulation studies. At the end of that year Jean-Pierre went off to Berkeley to join John Gerhart and Howard Schachman in their study of the allosteric transition in aspartate transcarbamylase They had just made the remarkable discovery that ATCase had separate catalytic and regulatory subunits. Jacques admitted then that the answers to allosteric mechanisms would probably come from physicochemical studies of purified proteins, together with their crystal structures.

In the spring of 1964, Jacques gave a few seminars on the allosteric model and sparks began to fly. In the autumn, when I had returned to Stanford, he gave a seminar there. Afterward, Dave Hogness turned to me and said, "Well, Jacques has done it again: he has a model which will make a lot of people mad, and they will work on his problem to try to prove him wrong." That certainly is what happened. Hemoglobin, in particular, became one of the most intensively studied molecules known to chemists. One would suppose that today the dust would have settled and one could say definitely whether the change from the oxy to deoxy conformation is a concerted transition without detectable intermediates, as the allosteric model postulates. But no, the controversy goes on. I was told that when Jacques learned in 1970 of the first experiments demonstrating that certain enzymes show negative cooperativity or half-site reactivity, he was pleased and excited although these allosteric enzymes didn't fit his model.

The last time I remember discussing allosteric proteins with Jacques was in the spring of 1968 at Schloss Elmau in the Bavarian Alps. Manfred Eigen had organized a long meeting on relaxation kinetics and molecular biology. Francis Crick was there. Had he thought of doing so, he might easily have applied the concepts of the Crick-Orgel model for intracistronic complementation to the problem of allosteric proteins, and he was keenly interested in Jacques' model from the beginning. At Schloss Elmau he was still thinking about alternative models. But Jacques was beginning to lose interest. He felt that his role in opening up the field was nearing an end. He gave me the set of bonded dice which he had used in his talk and said, "Now, Buzz, if you will admit the importance of symmetry in allosteric enzymes, I will give you these dice. And if you will still not admit it, I will give them to you anyway." Later, in Paris, he inscribed his initials on the, symmetrically, on each die.

When I was at the Institut Pasteur, I was strongly conscious of the difference between Pasteurian science and what I was used to at home—especially the Pasteur emphasis on logical analysis and on the development of alternative models. I was not conscious then of any particular influence on me of Jacques Monod, outside of my sharing the general appreciation of his brilliance in analysis and debate. But later I realized that when I thought about research problems I was attempting to carry on an inner dialogue in a manner inspired by discussions with Jacques, and I am grateful to him for his example.

Jacques once told me his method for choosing a research problem: "The way to do interesting research, Buzz, is to find a paradox; but you must be sure that it is a true paradox." I never asked him which paradox led him to the study of allosteric enzymes, and I can only guess. Certainly he enjoyed the clash of ideas that his model provoked, and it pleased him that physical chemists as well as molecular geneticists and enzyme chemists entered the debate.

SOME MEMORIES OF JACQUES MONOD

D. E. Koshland, Jr.

By his theories and experiments, Jacques Monod permanently altered the thinking of scientists in genetics and molecular biology. He did this largely by cleverly
designed and beautifully written papers in the scientific literature. But perhaps
as important was his impact as a person in private interactions with friends,
visitors to his laboratory, scientists he met on travels, and anyone who enjoyed
logical discourse at a high intellectual level. I was one of those fortunate enough
to have a number of contacts with him over the years, and each was unusually
rewarding on both the scientific and personal level.

One of Jacques most impressive characteristics was his deep joy in discussing
scientific theories. There were many occasions on which I witnessed this deep
commitment to scientific puzzle-solving, but one in Berkeley stands out as
typical. Jacques was visiting the University to give a seminar at a time when
I was home convalescing from an operation. I reluctantly had assumed I would
miss him and had instructed my students to take careful notes which they could
recount to me later. To my surprise, because I knew of his tight schedule,
Jacques phoned the day before and said he'd like to visit with me, a particularly
thoughtful gesture. I was, of course, delighted and my wife cancelled her University appointments and devoted the morning to making a meal worthy of a
distinguished French visitor. Jacques arrived, exchanged pleasantries, and then
we plunged into a discussion of regulation, protein structure, gene expression,

and transport. Suddenly I realized it was very late. He had already missed several appointments and he might even be late for his speech, but the time and our lunch had swept by unnoticed. It was one of Jacques abiding attractions that he became totally intense in the pursuit of scientific problems and as a result swept his listeners along with him in his enthusiasm. Scientific discussions with him always seemed to me like a deep-sea diving expedition in which one plunges into a new world with exciting terrain and a colorful fish flashing by at breathtaking speed. You were never bored and frequently had to sit quietly after he left to assimilate the many ideas that had streamed by in your conversation.

One discussion is particularly memorable to me as illustrating the strong philosophical and Descartian logic which permeated Jacques' thinking. We were discussing our alternate theories of cooperativity which had recently appeared in the literature and in particular the role of symmetry. I was arguing that nature undoubtedly used symmetry but only as a tool to minimize energy, and cooperativity resulted from ligand-induced distortions which altered the energetics between subunits. Jacques argued that symmetry was a ubiquitous characteristic of nature, and conservation laws were pervasive in science. Hence, conservation of symmetry would be an almost inevitable fundamental principle guiding the construction and behavior of protein molecules. At one point Jacques said "I have no formal training in physical chemistry. I'm a geneticist who views the world from principles of evolution." I was impressed not only by the candor of his statement but also because his basic insight and sharp mind had led me to assume he was an expert in the area. He had approached the subject from cosmic generalizations and collected his thermodynamics as he went along. The more we talked the more it became apparent that the two theories were internally consistent but each proceeded from different premises. No logical argument can prove or disprove internally consistent theories anymore than they can prove or disprove Euclidean versus non-Euclidean geometry. Yet in the process of discussion we clarified our thoughts and the discussion, like a fencing match, was a pleasure in itself. I was impressed at the extent to which Jacques utilized philosophical and historical precepts to guide his thinking. And in the end I believe that any theory which attracted him would have to be esthetically appealing as well as logically impeccable.

In New Hampshire in the relaxed science plus leisure atmosphere of a Gordon Conference I remember spending most of one week talking to Jacques on subjects ranging from politics and lifestyles to science and mysticism. One discussion on sailing particularly intrigued me. I enjoy sailing but consider it largely a device to converse with congenial friends in a relaxed and mildly athletic atmosphere. The occasional crises of wind and waves add a pleasant piquance, particularly if it is clear that the danger is surmountable and a happy landing is inevitable. To Jacques sailing offered these virtues but he liked his dangers more intense. He said a crisis that was potentially calamitous excited and stimulated him enormously and sailing in too tepid waters essentially bored him. We discussed at length the analogy between scientific dangers and physical dangers. We both agreed that scientists must venture into uncharted seas to make progress and fear of the turbulence of controversy and the disaster of being wrong inevitably leads to repetitive science. To me, the dangerous adventures of science were enough. To Jacques adventure was part of his blood, not excluded from any facet of his life. He described to me some of his dangers in the French resistance and his attitude was the same. He was a man not seeking danger in a foolhardy way but nevertheless exhilarated and excited by physical as well as intellectual danger.

Jacques enjoyed controversy. He did not seek controversy per se, at least not consciously. However, he had strong convictions both in science and in applying science to philosophical and social phenomena. He discussed his forthcoming storm. *Chance and Necessity* with me at one point saying he knew it would create a strom. The expected attack from those whose religious convictions were threatened he viewed with equanimity. The expected displeasure of scientists worried him more, as those were his intimate peers whom he respected and with whom he broke his daily bread. I asked "Why do you do it if you are so concerned?" He replied, "I must. I have a conviction of the importance of extending scientific reasoning and one cannot turn back because of the expectation of criticism." There was a twinkle in his eye and no shadow of gloom, and I had the distinct impression that he partially welcomed the furor he knew he'd create. He liked the approbation of his peers, but he also liked to be in the center of a rousing intellectual controversy. His assumption of the directorship of the Pasteur Institute was not surprising to me even though many scientists didn't understand his willingness to accept an administrative position. He felt an obligation to help the Pasteur, but perhaps even more he wanted a challenge in a new sphere in which his abilities had not yet been tested.

Jacques' sense of humor added greatly to his charm and to his scientific effectiveness. Humor is always attractive, but it is sometimes absent from individuals of extraordinary scientific dedication. The kind of mind that desires to pursue ideas to their logical extremity is frequently impatient with the nonproductive side paths or illogical juxtapositions that are at the heart of humor. And frequently the most successful scientists become enamored of themselves to the point where the gentle prod of humor becomes an unacceptable irritant. Jacques was more than willing to poke fun at himself. Once when I was talking with him and a number of other scientists during a visit to the Pasteur, I was impressed by his artful use of humor to provide restful interludes during a long and arduous scientific discussion. It was not calculated, but he periodically relieved the tension by a momentary humorous diversion and then quickly brought us back to the pursuit of the elusive scientific problem. And he enjoyed jesting with colleagues and peers. At one session of the 50th anniversary of the Biochemical Society in Paris, he gave me a carefully wrapped present which he told me to deliver to my wife. When she opened it, there was a French cigarette lighter with the admonition "Please help Dan throw some light on his theories."

An interesting sociology develops between scientists who compete in a common area and yet have a deep respect for each other. My relations with Jacques were always tinged with a slight tension based on our interests in similar problems and perhaps they were made special because of it. Whatever the cause, I always found his company unusually exciting and stimulating. He was invariably challenging and penetrating, and I remember our meetings with a special sense that they were rare events which should be prolonged like a good book. His enjoyment of science bubbled over into a world of personal charm and eloquent advocacy. He left contributions of great brilliance in the annals of science and memories of enchanted interludes in the hearts and minds of friends over the whole world.

MOTHER NATURE AND THE DESIGN OF
A REGULATORY ENZYME

Henri Buc

"If we were to follow Plato we would consider such perfect figures
as endowed with more significance and "reality" than any actual
object. Very often indeed, a scientist cannot help feeling a much
closer affinity to Plato, the radical idealist, than to some of the supposedly "realist" or "materialist" thinkers. A beautiful model or
theory may not be right; but an ugly one must be wrong."

Jacques Monod

At the Institut de Biologie physicochimique, scientists used to meet in the library for the Friday afternoon seminar. In 1958, when I had just entered research, an American scientist was presenting her data on the biochemistry of
bacterial cell walls. Suddenly, the course of the seminar was totally diverted.
Somebody whom I could not see (because the tiny place was overcrowded) had
started asking questions which, up to then, I had never considered. He was not
arguing about the experimental facts, but questioning the logical conduct of the
work. Stressing the implicit assumptions made by the speaker, he counterpro-
posed the set of hypotheses he would have formulated; then he showed that no
decisive experiment had yet been performed which could have ruled out either
of the hypotheses. It was obvious that he thought *his* approach to the subject

was more controversial and of a more general interest than the speaker's view. In fact, as soon as the discussion resumed, it focused on the questions this man had posed. I left the seminar, quite puzzled. For the first time I realized that it was possible to openly question the very reasons for which others were doing research.

It was roughly at that time that molecular biology started to be recognized in France as a new attempt to understand the structural basis of biological functions. Yet, most French physicochemists, though deeply interested in biochemistry, had an instinctive scorn for the oversimplifying darings of molecular biologists. Most of them refused to accept the idea that the organization of at least some living systems could be progressively reduced to the complex interplay of macromolecules. They were telling me: "Are you interested in biology? Well, spend ten years to become a good physicochemist, and then find a problem of biological interest. You will become a good biophysicist." The trouble was that I did not understand for what reason they had themselves decided to be physical chemists rather than, for example, embryologists or mathematicians.

In the early 1960s, the arrogant character who had so early ruined my obedient confidence in the work of the scientific establishment was giving a series of lectures on advanced biochemistry. I could not attend the course, but my wife, Marie-Hélène, gave me her notes each week. The excitement around the genetic code was at its peak. Monod's lectures were so logically arranged that students could understand what the specialists in the field were currently trying to demonstrate or to rule out at this very moment. Probably as many others, I was reading these notes as a scientific "roman feuilleton." Looking back at them recently, I realized that part of the excitement came neither from their novelty nor from their logical content. Monod was looking at a nascent science from his peculiar point of view, molecular evolution. Each new result was presented in the lecture as one tiny piece in the puzzle that Mother Nature had solved. We were contemplating "Mother Nature herself in the process of studying new developments for better and finer control of cellular metabolism." Between such a fruitful attitude and the endless studies on "structural features of macromolecules of biological interest," there was no reason to balance.

I had the chance to better understand Jacques Monod's quest when he invited Marie-Hélène and me to his home. He spent the evening explaining the content of the manuscript he had written with Jean-Pierre Changeux and François Jacob. He stressed the type of performances which had to be expected for certain proteins "acting at critical metabolic steps which appeared as electively endowed with specific functions of regulation and coordination." Probably because I had not spent too much time studying the intricacies of classical enzymology, it sounded reasonable to me that when a ligand was binding at a specific place on a protein subunit, this event could be transmitted across a distance to the substrate site, allowing the control to take place.

But Jacques Monod was looking for something else. As he wrote later on: "The disadvantage of this concept is precisely that its ability to explain is so great that it excludes nothing, or nearly nothing. There is no physiological phenomenon so complex and mysterious that it cannot be disposed of, at least on paper, by means of a few allosteric transitions." He agreed with Boris Magasanik to consider the present state of the theory as "decadent" because "there was no *a priori* reason to suppose that allosteric transitions for different proteins need be of the same nature and obey the same rules." As he was actively looking for some unifying principles, he pointed out to me that in some cases the binding of the regulatory signal was affecting the molecular weight of the protein while in other instances no change of molecular weight could be noticed. We therefore discussed possible means of showing that, in this latter case, the conformational change corresponded to a weakening of the noncovalent bonds between the subunits.

Three years later, when I came back from Harvard University, the "model" was written down in its final form. It came to me as a great surprise. If anybody takes care to read in historical order the article by Monod, Changeux, and Jacob and then the reports at the Cold Spring Harbor Symposium of June 1963 devoted to the same topics, he would be struck by the convergence of theoretical reasonings between the main groups engaged in this field. In 1963, everyone was stressing the role of flexibility in enzyme action, the most precise structural analysis being certainly given by D. Koshland. Viewed from outside, the first quantitative theory on allosteric control was expected to be a general induced-fit theory. However, between Pasteur and Berkeley, the prospects were already different. D. Koshland, refuting the argument given above that "the flexibility theory itself is too flexible, i.e., that it can explain anything and hence explains nothing," noted that "the very ease with which a wide variety of phenomena can be explained by this theory is a cogent argument for it," a statement which radically differed from Jacques Monod's objectives. In the same article, Dan Koshland went on to stress in what respect his theory was going to be fruitful: "The detailed arguments lead to predictions of correlation between protein structure and specificity patterns which are verifiable by experiment." Therefore it has always seemed evident to me that the two schools differed, almost from the very beginning, in the very content of what they were trying to explain. Most of the scientists wanted to describe how local, tertiary, and quaternary changes were geared together on a particular protein when a regulatory molecule was binding to it. No general principle was expected to emerge immediately for the rules of the game (i.e., the correlation between protein tertiary structure and specificity patterns) were not even understood. To express this feeling with an image, it seems to me that, for a "realistic" biochemist, Mother Nature was a rather easy-going creature, trying to do her best with the "molecular tinkering" she has at her disposal. This permissive divinity had devoted all her ingenuity in finding out and in maintaining in good order various mechanical devices which allow a regulatory protein to sense the instructions given by the external medium. To understand Mother Nature will take very long because we shall have to become acquainted with a great number of tricks of which we have no idea, for the time being.

Many scientists appreciate the Monod-Wyman-Changeux model because it is a simple, elegant, and imaginative proposal. (Monod liked to call this model a theory since each statement could be independently proved or ruled out on specific examples.) But few people seem to realize that this apparent simplicity had been gained at the cost of painstaking meditations on how evolution could have proceeded at the molecular level. These reflections have extended long after the original manuscript. They have been best expressed in the Nobel symposium on symmetry and functions in biological systems. It is because evolution had been constantly working on allosteric proteins that it was plausible to offer, as early as 1965, a simple theory accounting for their behavior. Mother Nature wanted to have specific devices able to open or to close metabolic pathways with a maximal efficiency; she had thought of proteins and had arranged them into closed structures. The imperious need of obtaining both the maximal sharpness of the regulatory response and the maximal stability of the regulatory proteins imposed the present solution: a concerted transition between two symmetrical states. When Monod was speaking of evolution, Mother Nature looked like a Greek divinity gathering in her hand anarchic monomers and fusing them into platonic figures.

I feel very sad when I see that a very significant confrontation between two different approaches of molecular biology is reduced to a formal conflict between two hypothetical kinetic pathways. What is really at stake is a triple issue. First, it is a good example of classical opposition between informative and selective theories in biology (in the M-W-C model, preexisting states are selected by small metabolites, the concentrations of which reflect the various physiological needs of the cell; according to Koshland and his collaborators, the ligand informs the protein structure and directs its conformational change). Second, they diverge on the basic unity or on the diversity of the structural solutions historically retained by evolution to solve a problem of regulation. Third, Monod's theory is falsifiable: to refute it does not simply mean to show how significantly the real solutions differ from a model. It will demand to gradually put forward a unifying view of the various structural solutions invented by evolution.

I wish to emphasize again that it was this evolutionary point of view which oriented most of the discussions in the laboratory. Monod used to ask: "Suppose you synthesize, according to Merrifield's method, a polypeptide chain, the primary sequence of which is taken completely at random. What is the chance that this pre-cambrian protein will fold with a hydrophobic core inside and with most of its hydrophilic residues outside?" With respect to protein assembly, a constant debate was going on: Was it reasonable to assume that, in a first step, evolution had disfavored those cells where proteins had a large tendency to form aggregates? In such a situation, was it not plausible to assume that only similar monomers would have had the chance to assemble together? More precisely, let us assume that we knew exactly the three-dimensional structure of several monomers and their local flexibility around their equilibrium position: Would it be possible to find a physical criterion which would predict which proteins would polymerize into a symmetrical oligomer, and which ones would lead to closed asymmetrical structures? At what point of a metabolic pathway, enzymes exhibiting negative cooperativity (or functioning according to the "flip-flop" mechanism proposed by Michel Lazdunski) would they be selectively advantageous?

Most of the time, those speculations were initiated according to a well-defined ritual. At around 10 or 11 o'clock in the morning, the door between Monod's office and the "labo bleu" opened. Usually Monod started by spending ten to twenty minutes with Madeleine Jolit, looking at the colonies which had grown overnight. By a smile or a long glance, he made it evident that some new speculations had been going on in his mind overnight. The discussion started on the blackboard in his office. The precise function of this particular type of colloquium was to check with some of us how far one could go from general speculations to logical proposals and eventually to experimental verifications. It is of course impossible for me to describe in English his typical blend of seduction and of demanding logic. In a very personal tempo, rather slow, each logical step was carefully marked and the voice used to adopt a particular impatient vibrato whenever a plausible objection was expected to be raised ("Mais enfin, cela crève les yeux!"). If the whole laboratory worked together for so long, with such an enthusiasm and so few conflicts, it is certainly because he led us to basically adopt his very personal approach to molecular biology, and he managed to reduce the slightly different subjective appreciations of the problem to a few precise alternatives which sometimes could be experimentally solved.

Thus the scientific questions he was raising appealed to us in those days as deep intellectual pleasure. But, as coined by opponents, this attitude would have been at best a dazzling game of fashionable models, at worst "allohystery," a dogmatic oversimplification, if first, Monod had not applied to his own dreams his demanding logic; and second, if the whole permanent staff of the laboratory as well as the numerous postdoctoral fellows and the foreign friends or visitors had not permanently challenged his reductive view with the wealth of their experience. For example, during a long contest with Monod on the proposal that oligomeric proteins are able to react to lower concentrations of ligand than the "equivalent monomer," Francis Crick begins one of his letters with an exasperated call: "Jacques, be reasonable." Monod was sensitive to similar warnings whenever they were justified by strong experimental evidence. Conversely, I fear, he often looked rigid and deaf to logical arguments on extrascientific matters.

It is at this period, as we were all anxious to confront theory and experiment, that another facet of Monod's talent became evident to me: his ability to delineate those dilemmas which were at a given time amenable to solution. Jean-Pierre Changeux had already left for H. Schachman's laboratory to work on the aspartyltranscarbamylase system. Before leaving, he lent me a very precious gift; "la bibliothèque allostérique," an impressive collection of preprints and reprints on regulatory enzymes. He was sending from Berkeley epic letters on his struggle with the ultracentrifuge and on his verbal fights with the misbelievers. We were trying to find out with D. Blangy how to check quantitatively on E. coli phosphofructokinase each theoretical prediction of the model. Passionate attempts to allosterize β-galactosidase were discussed in the long corridor of the laboratory. Monod insisted on two objectives: to find out a reliable method that could directly reveal in solution the point groups of symmetry to which an oligomeric protein could belong, and to be able to determine the elementary steps of the reaction between an allosteric protein and at least one of its regulatory effectors. The first problem is still not really solved; the second one had been previously discussed with Manfred Eigen before I came to the lab. During the spring of 1966, K. Kirschner, a gentleman having the inimitable port of an officer of the British Raj, brought to Paris exciting kinetic data. They allowed for the first time the visualization of a concerted transition of an oligomeric enzyme as the coenzyme was colliding with its stereospecific site. Jacques Monod told me "Enrico, we must go to Göttingen." So we went there, a few months later. I was expecting a rather exotic meeting, something like Haroun-al-Raschid paying a visit to Charlemagne, so distant were the cultures of Manfred Eigen and Jacques Monod at that time. I was really baffled to see, on the contrary, how Manfred Eigen's ability to reduce complex physical problems to a set of binary conjectures was in basic harmony with the scientific approach of the geneticist.

Thus in 1967, a large fraction of the allosteric problems, those related directly to structure were in a fair way to be reduced to specific physicochemical questions, while most of the evolutionary aspects still remain unsolved and challenging.

This period corresponds also to the foundation of the European Organization of Molecular Biology in which M. Eigen, J. Monod, and F. Jacob had taken a very active part, and to Monod's election at the Collège de France, an institution that he liked almost as much as the Pasteur Institute. He opposed these types of institutions to the medieval organization of the French university that he bitterly attacked in several public interviews. In Jacques Monod, as a public man, we recognized our basic need for creative freedom. May 1968 was not very far, another struggle against the stubborn vanity of the establishment, the rise of another creative fancy, the physical solidarity with the students; May 1968, perhaps also for him the tough discovery that the younger generation seemed to reject almost any intellectual leadership. Along the night wanderings through the Quartier Latin, amidst the noise of explosions and hand grenades, I realized that this exceptional relationship was going to take a new course.

RECOLLECTIONS OF JACQUES MONOD

Jeffries Wyman

My first encounter with Jacques Monod was over forty years ago when he gave the Dunham lectures at the Harvard Medical School. But at that time our paths were widely separated. He was largely concerned with genetic adaptations in microorganisms, I with dialectic studies on amino acids and proteins and the physicochemical phenomena involved in ligand binding by respiratory proteins, especially hemoglobin. Little inkling did I then have of the extent to which our interests were to converge in the years to come.

It was some time after this, during the 1950s, that my real friendship with Jacques began. That was when I went to the U.S. Embassy in Paris as science attaché to initiate the program of science advising which had just been established by our State Department. In that role it was incumbent on me (and a pleasant duty it was!) to get to know the community of French scientists and to promote relations between them and their U.S. counterparts in a postwar era of relative isolation. It was the period when the paranoia of McCarthy and his followers was approaching a crescendo and creating a serious barrier between the two countries. Naturally for me, as a biologist, the Pasteur Institute was an obvious place at which to begin my activities. Moreover it so happened that at the time of my arrival in Paris, Alvin Pappenheimer, who was married to a cousin of mine, was spending a sabbatical year at the Institute. As a result of all this I used to walk over to the

221

Institute for an impromptu lunch with a group of which Jacques was a member (this was before the days of the present cafeteria). Others included André Lwoff and François Jacob, as well as another American, the then youthful Mel Cohn. These lunches with their lively conversation about current scientific developments were a pleasant change from the somewhat bureaucratic air of the Embassy. Sometimes during that period, at Jacques' suggestion, I would join another and larger group that used to gather for supper before the seminars held in the library of the Institut de Biologie Physico-Chimique in the rue Pierre Curie. These contacts marked the beginning of a friendship with Jacques which was to extend well beyond the bounds of pure science.

In those years Jacques was an enthusiastic rock climber and I remember his taking me out to a place in the Forest of Fontainebleau where we could practice. I don't think I could find the site today, but the image of those sheer and challenging rocks stands out clear in my memory. This was in Jacques' mountaineering period before he had developed his passion for sailing, although I do remember his glowing accounts of an early voyage to the East Coast of Greenland in an old fashioned square rigger of which he showed me some striking photographs.

A much closer relationship with Jacques, however, came more than a decade later, after I had left the Embassy in Paris as well as a subsequent post in the Middle East, and had returned to scientific work as a guest at the University of Rome. It was in 1965 that Monod and I published our joint paper with J. P. Changeux on what has come to be known as the M-W-C Allosteric Model (or sometimes "the concerted two-state model"). This paper, which appeared in the *Journal of Molecular Biology*, grew out of a seminar I gave in Paris in the autumn of 1964 (a successor of that series of seminars in the rue Pierre Curie which I had frequented earlier in my Embassy days); and this seminar in turn was the result of a talk given the preceding summer at Cold Spring Harbor, which is where I first met Changeux. (Changeux was at that time responsible for the program of the Paris seminars.) Well before this time it had become clear that the interactions, both the homotropic (cooperative) and heterotropic (control) ones, characteristic of many enzymes and respiratory proteins, notable hemoglobin, could be in a large number of cases explained in terms of ligand-linked conformational changes. In particular, in the case of human hemoglobin, there was evidence, drawn partly from kinetic studies involving the uptake of dye but even more from the X-ray work of Max Perutz in Cambridge, that the tetrameric molcule existed in two different quarternary conformations: one characteristic of the deoxy, the other of the oxy form, the transition between them being controlled by the activities of oxygen and proton. The underlying linkage principles, in accordance with which conformational changes can give rise to both hemotropic and heterotropic control, had already been laid down, and it was this subject that formed the basis of the talk I gave in Paris. The paper with Monod and Changeux was really the child of this talk and its prompt publication after the talk bears witness to Jacques' quickness of response to an idea, which was one of his great qualities. The paper as it stands was written almost wholly by him and was presented to me more or less as a *fait accompli* for discussion and criticism. It should be pointed out here that the introductory part dealing with the possible role of symmetry in the assembly of oligometric proteins was largely due to Jacques. Although it is true that I had introduced the concept of symmetry in the case of such systems a good many years before, pointing out that in so far as site interactions were the reflection of the spacing of the sites, symmetry of function as represented by symmetry of the binding curve (fractional saturation vs. chemical potential of the ligand) implied a certain geometric symmetry in a macromolecule. Yet that was before the realization of the role of conformational change and the introduction of the allosteric concept, which greatly changed the picture. It is this part of the paper which is at once perhaps the most intuitively appealing from a physical point of view and at the same time the most open to criticism (and criticism was not wanting). The rest of the paper, based as it is largely on the sure principles of classical thermodynamics, stood on firmer ground.

I vividly remember a meeting Jacques and I had with several of our friends and colleagues at the MRC Laboratory in Cambridge to discuss the manuscript and its suitability for publication in the *Journal of Molecular Biology*. As I recall it, these included Max Perutz, John Kendrew, Francis Crick, and Sydney Brenner, a rather formidable group of critics. The attack mainly centered on the symmetry ideas, and Jacques bore the brunt of it. But afterward, in the calmer atmosphere at tea, we all agreed that the paper, symmetry and all, should be published as it stood, a decision which in retrospect no one I thought could possibly question. That evening John Kendrew and I went to a dinner party at Francis' house, where although there was little further discussion of such a technical matter, some doubts and reservations were further expressed.

Shortly after the paper came out there was an International Congress of Biophysics held in Naples. By that time the paper had been widely read and attracted much attention. Both Jacques and I gave talks based on it at one of the sessions. Jacques stressed the symmetry concept; I the more abstract thermodynamic ideas, taking the occasion also to introduce the closely related concept of the binding potential, which had been developed subsequently to the appearance of the paper. As I look back, that meeting stands out as one of the most exciting and pleasant I have attended. The setting was perfect: in front of us, as we looked westward, the blue expanse of the Bay of Naples with the magic profile of Capri in the distance; behind and to the east, the tangled city rising to the hills crowned by San Martino and Capo di Monte; to the left and south the smok-bulk of Vesuvius; to the right and north, the jagged silhouettes of the islands of Procida and Ischia. At that time Francis Crick was joint owner of a fine cutter which was lying in the port and on which he was living. One afternoon he invited several of us, including Jacques, John Kendrew, and myself, to go for a sail. The day was unexceptionable— a warm sun, a cloudless sky, and a gentle breêze. Soon after we cleared the mooring, Jacques, by that time an accomplished sailor, took the tiller. However, at the end of the afternoon, he gave it back to Francis, who was somewhat less sure of himself and, as we approached the port, showed signs of nervousness—small wonder considering the complications of entering a crowded Italian port. At this point Jacques, evidently enjoying the situation, turned to me with the remark, "It is clear to me that when Jim wrote the opening sentence* of the *Double Helix* he had never seen Francis on a boat"— a fine example of Jacques' wit.

Jacques prided himself, and with reason, on his abilities as a sailor—so far as I know, he did not take up sailing seriously until fairly late in life, though his experiences on the voyage to Greenland must have laid a foundation. I remember, after he had got his first sea-going boat, his speculating about the prudence of a sail from Cannes to Corsica. But later on, in a stouter ship, he had no hesitation in undertaking a voyage from northern France to the Greek islands, though it meant crossing the stormy Bay of Biscay and facing the sometimes furious and capricious winds of the Mediterranean. Jacques' love of the sea and its challenges, like his love of climbing, provided a fine complement, on the human side, to his passions and achievements on the intellectual one.

*"I have never seen Francis Crick in a modest mood."

SAILING WITH JACQUES

Francis Crick

I cannot remember for certain when I first met Jacques Monod. My recollection is that on my first trip to Paris after the war, during the period when I was working with Arthur Hughes at the Strangeways Laboratory, he and I visited the Pasteur Institut together, but to see Dervichian not Jacques. Nor, in 1949, when we were on our honeymoon (which was spent in Italy) did Odile and I pause for any significant time in Paris, although we passed through it. I think my first meeting with Jacques was some years later in the mid 1950s probably after Jim Watson and I had put forward the DNA structure. I clearly recall giving a seminar at the Pasteur in which I suggested the quite erroneous theory that during protein synthesis the inducer was needed to fold up the enzyme correctly. Without inducer, protein synthesis would come to a complete stop. Even at that time I didn't think much of this notion and I came to think even less of it, so it was never published. In those days things moved more slowly and there was less pressure to rush into print.

I believe it was on this occasion (because I recall that there was a certain constraint between us) that I was with Jacques in his laboratory on a Saturday morning. "You'll never guess what I'm trying, my dear," he said to me. (Jacques' English was practically perfect. This use of 'my dear' as the equivalent of 'mon cher' was the only slip I ever remember hearing him make.) He was attempting, in a way that I cannot exactly recall, to see if he could get some sort of an immune response from *E. coli*. I thought it was a silly idea and clearly so did he, but I was impressed that he was prepared to give it a try. It seemed to show a commendable spirit of adventure.

I must, over the years, have had many scientific conversations with Jacques, and I am surprised to discover that I remember hardly any of them. But then I've had many more with Sydney Brenner and almost all those have also been swallowed up by time. I think that, as science advances, one recalls only the results, tending to forget the process of discovery unless it was unexpectedly memorable. Certainly I shall not easily forget the Good Friday morning, in the Gibbs Building in Kings, when François Jacob was talking to us. Suddenly the scales fell from our eyes and we saw that the ribosomal RNA was not the messenger RNA, but that the "Volkin and Astrakan" RNA was. But Jacques was not there on that occasion, although he was present at a lunch Odile prepared for us, some months earlier, in the basement of Portugal Place when Sydney and I were first told about the PaJaMa experiment. I recall how puzzled we were by it and how reluctant to believe it. It was this meeting which sowed the seeds for the eventual conceptual breakthrough. Once it was realized that the ribosome was basically a reading head the world never looked the same again.

There was at least one occasion when we did have a long discussion together. This was in the house in Cannes, where his parents had lived and which the family had kept on as a holiday home. A lovely, solid house, high up on the hillside surrounded by trees, it had a period feeling, partly due to the many paintings by his father on the walls. Jacques had given the Pomona Lectures under the title "Chance and Necessity" and had written, in English, a first draft of his book. He had sent me a copy to read and I stayed with him for a few days, on my way from Greece to the Ile du Levant, to go sailing with him and to discuss the manuscript. During a long morning's conversation together, I remember expressing a number of criticisms and reservations but again time has wiped from my memory exactly what we said. Perhaps my notes on the manuscript still exist somewhere. Jacques eventually rewrote the book in French and I never read it again until the English version (translated by someone else) made its appearance. My impression was that he hadn't changed it very much.

There were a number of topics about which we seldom spoke, though I knew they were important in his life: his experience with the French Resistance, during the war; his friendship with Camus, or any literary topic for that matter; his love of music, though he had told me that at one point he had had to choose between playing the cello professionally and a career in science. Perhaps he sensed that my taste in music was, compared to his, very unsophisticated. He told me once that he greatly admired George Orwell, an author who is not very much to my taste. I nearly said I preferred Proust but thought better of it, which, looking back, was a pity. He did tell me that he was color-blind and produced a striking description of what it felt like—"The word 'green' is a meaningless word to me"–but in spite of this he must have had some interest in the visual arts because I remember once running into him, quite by accident, at an art exhibition in Paris. But most of the time we talked science or gossiped or fussed about the running of The Salk Institute of which we were both nonresident fellows. In fact I saw as much of him in La Jolla as anywhere else. He and I were both appointed in 1962. I served two six-year terms while he was in the middle of his third when he died. We must have met there in the winter (the California winter!) for most of the years from 1962 to 1973, though one or other of us missed a year here and there. I remember writing him a letter from La Jolla with a P. S. "We have just discovered that your head is full of actin." Unfortunately the typist, confronted with an unknown word, wrote "action" and I didn't spot the error before it went off. I can't imagine what Jacques thought when he received it.

The other times we met were connected, in one way or another, with sailing. Jacques was an excellent sailor who could manage his 37 ft. sloop by himself whereas I was always a rather bumbling amateur. One year there was a scientific meeting at Naples. I recall criticizing Jacques' overenthusiasm for symmetry in allosteric reactions, referring to myself, somewhat to the surprise of some of my colleagues, as an "old Jesuit" in these matters and comparing him to a more recent convert. At that time I owned a half share in a splendid sailing boat, a 47 ft. racing cruiser, which was based on Naples. It was crewed by an elderly Italian and as he could speak hardly any English and I spoke less Italian, communication was not always easy. A party of us persuaded Jacques to come out for a sail (not that he needed any real persuasion) and he soon assumed command. The sailor, who had very early spotted my limitations, was soon respectfully taking Jacques' orders. Fortunately the wind was reasonably brisk and we had a pleasant turn outside the harbor and back.

My most rewarding sailing with Jacques was in his own boat. While I was staying with him in Cannes he decided we should run over to Corsica. On the trip out one of his sons and daughter-in-law were with us, so my assistance was hardly required. The trip was uneventful apart from coming close to three whales who frolicked around the boat for a while. On the way back there were just the two of us. We set out in daylight, bound for St. Tropez, intending to sail through the early part of the night. "We'll be there in time for the nightclubs," Jacques told me. It was pleasant enough when we set out, but we ran into a considerable storm. As the waves got higher and the wind blew more strongly I became mildly apprehensive, although trusting in Jacques to get us through, even with the handicap of having me to help him. He was clipping himself on, as he moved about the boat, lit dramatically from above, with darkness all around us. Finally I said to him, "Jacques, exactly what do I do if you fall overboard?" (I didn't think that he would, but I felt I'd better know.) He explained to me what maneuvers to make and I felt a little more relaxed.

Our next problem was to find out where we were. We had a fairly good idea of what our bearing had been but our reckoning of the distance we had covered was far less accurate. This didn't bother Jacques because he had radio direction-finding equipment on board. Unfortunately the electric storm was so severe that as we neared the coast, Jacques found that he couldn't get any proper bearings so we had to look out for the lighthouses and hope we were roughly where we thought we were. Eventually we located the channel and slipped into St. Tropez a little after dawn. The nightclubs were closed, but even if they'd been open we would probably have been too tired to go to one.

It was the sequel, however, which was more revealing. The storm was still blowing strongly. Jacques' motor—he always hated having one—had given up completely so I was confident that we were stuck there till the wind abated. But I had not allowed for Jacques' determination. The following morning it was still blowing strongly from the north. Yachts from St. Tropez are never in a hurry to leave the harbor and on that morning not a single vessel, either motor or sail, made any attempt to leave. We had picked up a passenger and Jacques was determined to get us back to Cannes for the weekend. So he arranged for us to be towed out of the harbor by a local boatman and off we went. Since the wind came from off the shore, the waves, though high, had not had time to grow enormous although the wind was blowing half a gale. Under very light sail we sped along at high speed (or what passes for high speed on a sailboat—that is, rather slower than a bicycle) making the journey, if I recall correctly, in about three hours. It was the best sail I have ever experienced. There was less wind at Cannes and, even with no motor, we managed to berth without too much trouble.

During most of the time Jacques was head of the Institut Pasteur I saw very little of him. He told me, initially, that the job was turning out to be not too difficult, but that was before the real problems started. I was no longer going to La Jolla for winter meetings, looking for sun instead at Marrakesh. In the spring of 1976 Odile and I passed through Paris on our way to Iran. We'd heard that Jacques was seriously ill although now back at work. When we met him he seemed fitter than we expected although sobered somewhat by the threat hanging over him. He was having blood transfusions twice a week. We had a long lunch at his apartment. I broached the question of writing a book about his work and, hopefully, we made plans to meet at The Salk, after Jacques had re-tired from his Pasteur job. I think we both realized how precarious such plans were. Even so his death was a surprise; certainly it came much sooner than I had expected. It produced in me the numb shock one suffers when somebody dies whom one feels is quite irreplacable.

I have written elsewhere (in an obituary for *Nature*) a studied estimate of Jacques' career and character. Here I have tried to convey something of him in a less formal way. He was a few years my senior but his youthful manner and his close friendship made me think of him as a contemporary. He was small in stature, but I never consciously felt of him as being much shorter than I am, though once sitting in the bar of the old Del Charro in La Jolla I was suddenly surprised to notice how small his feet were. Jacques had a natural charm, together with courteous good manners, though less formal than one might expect for a Frenchman in his position. He could be formidable, due to his force and his clarity, and sometimes aggressive, but he never seemed that way to me. In fact, he was very companionable—one always enjoyed an evening when he was there—and it's not everyone that one can go sailing with. Our friendship was not the friendship of those who were young together, nor were we intimate in the sense that we discussed our personal problems with each other. Rather it was based, I think, on a steady admiration, seasoned with an affectionate recognition of each other's failings. Our general attitude to most scientific matters was very similar, yet our backgrounds were sufficiently different to make both of us eager to hear what the other thought. And this is where I feel most strongly a sense of loss. As each new thing comes up, one regrets so much not being able to talk it over with Jacques. He would understand so quickly; he would appreciate the importance of the point; he would say something illuminating that hadn't occurred to one; one could reach agreement together and a deeper understanding. It is for this reason that I find, now that he is gone, that I have no stomach for writing a book about his work even though I still feel a small nagging sense of duty. It would have been such a rewarding experience to write it with his cooperation, his clarifications, and his criticisms—and of how many people could one say *that*?

THE ODE TO OBJECTIVITY

Gunther S. Stent

Einmal dem Fehlläuten der Nachtglocke gefolgt—es ist niemals gutzumachen.

Franz Kafka *(Ein Landarzt)*

(Once having responded to the false alarm of the night bell—it cannot ever be made good.)

Franz Kafka *(A Country Doctor)*

To my ever-lasting regret, the final years of my relations with Jacques Monod were under a cloud because of my critical review in 1971 of his *Chance and Necessity*. During the two years 1948-1950 that Elie Wollman and I collaborated as young postdoctoral fellows in Max Delbrück's laboratory in Pasadena, Elie's description of Jacques (of whom I, an only recently liberated high-polymer chemist, had never heard) caused me to form a mental portrait of Jacques as Superman, straight out of Hollywood Central Casting: handsome, tough, courageous, artistic, brilliant. And when, on my first visit to the now celebrated microbial-physiologic attic, I eventually met Jacques, he did not fall short of the romantic image that I had constructed: he was everything that Elie had claimed on his behalf. I could hardly wait until it was time to move down from Copen-

231

hagen to Paris, to begin my final postdoctoral fellowship year and work down the corridor from that fabulous combination of Darwin and Prince Charming. And again my expectations were not disappointed. Having chosen him for a role model, the year I spent in Jacques' ambience had a profound effect on my formation as a scientist. At the time of leaving Paris for Berkeley to take up my first (and so far, only) job in Wendell Stanley's Virus Laboratory, I considered it as one of the main accomplishments of my sojourn at the Pasteur Institute to have been able to win Jacques as a friend.

The sparkling lunch-time conversations at Jacques' table (to which I was graciously admitted, even though as a member of the *équipe* André Lwoff, I was supposed to eat in François Jacob's lab) covered a broad range of scientific, political, and cultural subjects. But I don't remember the subject of philosophy being discussed much. None of us, Jacques no more than such regulars of his table as Annamaria Torriani, Germaine Cohen-Bazire, Roger Stanier, Mel Cohn, or Alvin Pappenheimer, appeared to be interested in discussing epistemology or the foundations of morality. In 1951-1952 there seemed to be more pressing subjects to think about than the metaphysical nature of man. The only topic that brought us even close to philosophy was the then still festering Lysenko affair. Naturally, everybody was on the side of the angels, and all there was to talk about was how it could be possible for otherwise seemingly intelligent "Free World" scientists to stand up, as some then still did, in defense of the hereditary transmission of acquired characters. Accordingly, the rich intellectual Pasteurian dowry, to which Jacques had so heavily contributed and with which I set up business on my own in Berkeley, did not include much philosophical baggage. And so, when a decade later both Jacques and I began to write in the philosophical domain, our ideas turned out to be rather divergent.

I had chosen philosophy as the required arts "minor" for my undergraduate B.A. degree in chemistry at the University of Illinois. Among my teachers there had been the outstanding philosopher Max Black. But it was only in the early 1960s that two, at first sight wholly unconnected, developments of great affective personal significance caused me to revisit the books of my old "minor." One of these developments was the culmination of molecular genetics in the breaking of the genetic code and in the Jacob-Monod operon model. I had made up my mind to join the search for the physical nature of heredity after learning, while still a chemistry student at Illinois, from Schrödinger's book *What is Life?* that if Delbrück's quantum mechanical model should fail, we would have to give up all attempts to fathom the gene. At the age of twenty-two, the project of proving Delbrück's model true seemed to me to offer scope for a life-long romantic quest. But now, just barely turned forty, I saw that my Holy Grail had been found. The other development was the eruption on the Berkeley campus of the Free Speech Movement, whose trauma caused me and many of my colleagues to perform a critical self-examination of our own motivational infrastructure. As one of the strategies to defuse the explosive situation, the University administration instituted a special category of Professor of Arts and Science, whose only charge was to think big for a year and try to heal the evident cultural breach between students and faculty. For reasons never fully explained, I was given one of the professorships (now long defunct). So *nolens volens*, I was cast into the role of home-town, cracker-barrel philosopher. (My fellow-appointees were a mathematician and an art historian, all three of us of Central European provenance. Curiously, none of the local distinguished bona-fide philosophers or sociologists were called on for this service.) In discharging my duty as a philosophical orator before my campus constituency (later I was gratified to meet a younger colleague who had taken his wife-to-be to one of my speeches on their first date) I managed to connect the denouement of molecular genetics with the Free Speech Movement, showing that both are symptomatic of the inevitable End of Progress.

Thanks to an invitation arranged by François Jacob as Visiting Professor at the Collège de France, I presented a synoptic version of my grandiose apocalyptic, macrohistorical insights in Paris in the summer of 1967. I was rather disappointed that Jacques, to whom I was most eager to expose my views, did not come to hear me, although he did attend the reception that the Collège's Director, Etienne Wolff, gave for me at the conclusion of my course. Word later reached me indirectly that Jacques, just as most of my friends, thought my whole thesis nonsense. His lack of appreciation of my insights should not have been unexpected, though. Just two or three years earlier, on one of Jacques' occasional visits to Berkeley, I had taken him to the Haight-Ashbury district of San Francisco, in order to show him the then brand-new hippie scene. (The word "hippie" had only just been coined, as the diminutive of the earlier San Francisco North Beach "hipster," or "beatnik"; it was then still largely unknown outside of Northern California.) I tried to impress on Jacques my notion that all these unwashed, drugged youths from Squaresville, Middle America loitering on the street were an omen of a coming profound transformation of the human condition. But Jacques was bored, and even slightly annoyed that I had dragged him all the way across the Bay to show him what he saw merely as the Californian homolog of the inebriated *clochards* that have lain under the arches of the Seine bridges since the days of Vercingétorix.

When I was giving my lectures at the Collège, I did not realize that at that very time Jacques himself was getting ready to work the philosophical vineyard, laying the groundwork for his *Inaugural Lesson* as Professor of the Collège. I received the manuscript of the *Lesson* about a year later and was surprised to find Jacques holding views that I had never known to be his. At the very outset of the *Lesson*, Jacques announced his finding that modern man is in a state of alienation. Why? Because, according to Jacques, whereas the present human condition is, in the main, a product of science, "the very source of science, in objective knowledge and in the ethic which grounds it, remains obscure for the majority of mankind." And how is this global "schizophrenia" to be cured? Jacques answers, "by the deepening of knowledge itself, by constantly extending the objective method into new domains." Thus, although I had on previous occasions heard Jacques make disparaging remarks about "scientism" (the ideology holding that the presuppositions and methods of science are valid for the entire sphere of human activity), I suddenly realized that he himself in fact, still embraced the scientistic world view, passed down from Francis Bacon via the Encyclopedists and Marx and Engels. Before setting forth the details of his recommended cure, however, Jacques presented an overview of the contributions of molecular biology to our understnading of the evolution of life, celebrating *en passant* the definitive interment of vitalism. Now with our understanding of the role of DNA as the transmitter of hereditary information, evolution can be seen to be nothing other than a series of accidents. In this connection, however, Jacques exaggerated the claims that can be made on behalf of molecular-biological neo-Darwinism. The stochastic nature of the DNA mutation process notwithstanding, it is by no means certain that the aspect of life to which Jacques referred as "emergence," or the evolutionary creation of increasingly complex structures, is, as he alleges, "pure chance." On the contrary, it is formally possible that there does exist some physicochemical principle that made "emergence" a necessary, rather than contingent, feature of the history of the earth. For instance, as Ilya Progigine once proposed, nonequilibrium thermodynamics might embody a principle to the effect that the flow of solar negative entropy through the earth not merely allows but actually "drives" the emergence of life and the evolution of ever more complex biological structures. Perhaps there is no such principle, but it hardly seemed fair to stigmatize, as did Jacques, persons who are searching for it as "vitalists."

According to Jacques, the most recent of these evolutionary accidents was responsible for the emergence within the biosphere of a new realm, the noosphere, or realm of knowledge. Once the noosphere had come into being there began within it an evolutionary process based on the natural selection, not of genes, but of ideas. Of all the ideas in the noosphere, the most powerful to have emerged is that of objective knowledge. And now Jacques, for the first time, attempts to explicate the concept of objectivity that was to be central to *Chance and Necessity:* for him objective knowledge is that which has no source but the systematic confrontation of logic and experience. Here the *Lesson* already presages a disturbing feature of the later book, namely, the somewhat cavalier usage of its key terms. In either ordinary speech or philosophical parlance "objectivity," or its adjectival form "objective," does not denote anything resembling the meaning that Jacques assigned to it. Moreover, in *Chance and Necessity* he gave it a variety of other, equally unconventional meanings. For instance, sometimes he claimed that objectivity is a property of Nature itself, rather than, as in the *Lesson*, a method of studying Nature. At other times he returned to a methodological meaning, but implied that objectivity is a "principle" that forbids use of "final causes" in the interpretation of natural phenomena. However, as ordinarily understood, the term "objective" has nothing to do with the use of logic or the rejection of final causes, but as the antonym of "subjective," denotes something like freedom from personal bias in the consideration of the external world. Other key terms that Jacques employed with meanings other than those normally understood are "animism," and indeed "science" (to which he explicitly assigned a meaning that is normally covered by the term "metaphysics").

According to the *Lesson*, the practical use of objective knowledge is as old as man himself. But the conscious awareness of the idea of objective knowledge evolved only in Western Europe with the pre-Socratics; "The Chinese never managed to evolve this idea." (Apparently, Jacques was unfamiliar with the history of Chinese philosophy. Socrates' Chinese contemporary Mo Tzu, and the so-called "Logicians" he inspired, knew all about and advocated, objective knowledge. But their more successful Taoist adversaries weighed the idea of objectivity and found it wanting.) But why, if objective knowledge is such a powerful idea, has the modern science that it spawned caused the contemporary condition of schizophrenic alienation? One reason, according to Jacques, is that scientific technique is now beyond the understanding of most men and for them represents a cause of permanent humiliation. A more profound reason, however, is that science has made "man a stranger in the cosmos, without his appointed or necessary place." (In being cited in support of this idea, Kant, whose contributions to the subject under discussion are at least as important as those of the ubiquitous Darwin, makes one of its rare appearances in Jacques' writing.) Moreover, science "has succeeded in destroying the traditional foundations of the various religious ethics [while] it cannot, by its very nature, provide any other." But, fortunately, science embodies within it its own value system, namely, an "ethic of knowledge." And it is that ethic of knowledge which Jacques recommends for general adoption, now that the traditional value systems lie in ruins. What is the supreme good, the *summum bonum*, of the ethic of knowledge? Not the happiness of utilitarian ethics, nor the self-knowledge of deontological ethics. No, it is objective knowledge itself. And immanent in that quest for objective knowledge are such values as the (formerly Christian) scorn for violence and temporal domination, as well as the (formerly Protestant) love of personal and political liberty.

Since Jacques did not solicit my opinion, I did not communicate to him my feeling that his *Lesson* fell short of the stratospheric intellectual standards for which I had always admired him. Moreover, I had no idea that he was planning to expand his lecture into a full-fledged book. No sooner had *Chance and Necessity* appeared than it became an ideal, sitting-duck target for critics of every philosophical stripe (and not merely for those beholden to Jacques' favorite twin targets of Marxism and Judeo-Christianity). Jacques' stridently aggressive tone, his practice of handing out, *ex cathedra*, merits and demerits to a vast cast of characters, from Heraclitus through Hegel, Marx, and Nietzsche, to Chomsky, coupled with the infuriating fact that a recent Nobel Laureate in molecular biology had managed to write a best seller on epistemology and moral philosophy, must have caused itching in the trigger finger of every philosophical hired gun. And so, when the Boston monthly *The Atlantic* (in which Jim Watson's "The Double Helix" had not long before, made its debut in serial form) asked me to review the American edition of Jacques' book, I thought I would try to offset some of the more hysterical attacks by writing a critical, though friendly and respectful, analysis from within molecular biology. In my review, entitled "An Ode to Objectivity," I said that I thought *Chance and Necessity* was an important book. And for this very reason "this philosophical statement by one of the major scientific figures of our time . . . must be subjected to critical analysis, as no doubt (in line with the beliefs he offers here) Monod would be the first to wish it to be."

Unfortunately, I was mistaken. Jacques did not seem to have the wish I attributed to him. In response to the manuscript of my review that I sent him prior to publication, I received from him a five-page letter, the longest he had ever written to me. "My first advice to you, he began, would be to read the book again, and this time read it carefully." But apparently I had read the book sufficiently carefully for Jacques to have found it worthwhile to refute my critique in thirteen specific points. And he closed his letter as follows: "Of course, my dear Gunther, I leave it to you to decide what you wish to make of these remarks. Let me add this: We have had many friendly disagreements in the past. Almost always I have seen you ready to attack my position before you had made any genuine attempt to really understand what I meant. I very strongly believe that the only useful and constructive type of discussion is one when the discussants both feel that what the other party says, even though one may not grasp it right away, contains valid elements. Since you have apparently written your paper even before really reading my book, please, if you have enough time and it is not too much of a bore, read it once more in that spirit. Then perhaps we may be able to talk about it in a significant way."

Naturally, I was crestfallen upon receiving Jacques' letter. It especially pained me to learn that, in all these years, Jacques had interpreted my bent for probing his ideas critically (or, possibly, *hyper*critically), not as I had thought of it, namely, as the best way of showing the authenticity of my esteem, but as perverse eagerness to attack him. Although it certainly transpired from my review that, much to my disappointment, I had perceived some conceptual defects in Jacques' global picture, my essay did in no way intimate that his book was devoid of valid elements, an intimation which would have been totally contrary to what I actually thought. Alas, his letter made me realize too late that, appearances to the contrary notwithstanding, Jacques' scientific lifestyle was not that of my earlier mentor Max Delbrück. In Max's orbit unrelenting criticism really *was* the genuine currency of sincere friendship, and, as the autobiographical essays in the Delbrück Festschrift "Phage and the Origins of Molecular Biology" show, it was hard on the psyche climbing up Mt. Olympus on Max's trail. I responded to Jacques' letter with a ten-page letter of my own, mainly to convince him that, if nothing else, at least I had read his book carefully. I did not hear from Jacques again, and there never presented itself an opportunity to discuss with him his book in some significant way. But two years later, I happened to see him on television being interviewed by Edwin Newman in the "Speaking Frankly" series. It relieved me greatly to hear that, in response to Newman's enquiry about criticism of *Chance and Necessity*, Jacques spoke without rancor of his "friend Gunther Stent" as one of his more substantive critics. Also, while preparing this article I was gratified to discover that in a reply to his critics published posthumously in 1977 under the title "Notes de bas de page" in *Prospective et Santé* Jacques, though not mentioning me by name, did try to deal with many of the very issues I had raised in my review.

I met Jacques one more time, at the 1974 Colloquium "Biology and the Future of Man" held at the Sorbonne. He was drinking coffee at a bar in the foyer of the *Grand Amphitheatre*, a lone and seemingly melancholy figure. I joined him to say hello, and we exchanged a few amicable civilities, without finding words for a substantive conversation. Nevertheless, I could feel that our friendship had survived the unintended offense I had given him, and the souvenir of that friendship will always remain for me a source of pride and inner strength.

JACQUES MONOD: SCIENTIST, HUMANIST, AND FRIEND

S. E. Luria

He had to choose. But it was not a choice
Between excluding things. It was not a choice

Between, but of. He chose to include the things
That in each other are included, the whole,
The complicate, the amassing harmony.

Wallace Stevens

It may seem strange that I should have thought of Jacques Monod as my closest friend even though we lived thousands of miles apart, met only sporadically, and never actually worked together. Ours was a friendship of choice rather than of familiarity. If we had lived in the eighteenth century instead of the twentieth, as I am sure we would both have liked, we might have produced a body of written correspondence, which would now be left for me to reminisce with and perhaps for someone to turn into a postdoctoral thesis. But we did live in our time, the time of telephone and airplane, a time that has made letter writing obsolete. Ours were exciting but tormented times, times when deep friendships were rare

239

and precious.

I first met Jacques in 1946 at Cold Spring Harbor. Immediately I admired his mind, his delight in elegant science. Also I was struck by his unhesitating humanitarian instincts. I recall that there was in Cold Spring Harbor the family of a German-American scientist, desperately worried about the fate of some relatives in French-occupied Germany. When Jacques was apprised of it he immediately undertook (I believe successfully) to help reestablish connections between the members of this family. The former resistance fighter would readily ignore the past enmity when there was a chance of helping human beings.

Jacques and I met again briefly a number of times in the following years. I recall a visit of Jacques to Urbana, Illinois, in the early 1950s, in the course of which we talked of enzyme induction and of host-induced phage modification. A visit of Jacques to MIT in 1958 had a more significant impact of me, as we then planned my visit to the Institute Pasteur in the spring of 1959, a visit that finally brought us closer together in friendship.

It was a brief visit that allowed little time for the experiments I wanted to do. To gain time, I flew to Orly carrying in my pocket some partially grown bacterial cultures and I deposited them in the shaker bath in Jacques' laboratory before checking in at the hotel. After a brief nap I did the first experiment that same afternoon; Monod's *Service* was extremely conductive to work. It was then that I first met many brilliant scientists, residents, and guests, whose dedication to research made that laboratory a joy to work in.

No necessarily pure joy, of course. My experiments at that time dealt with the expression of phage-transduced lactose genes. It was a well-guarded secret (well-guarded from me too) that similar experiments on lactose-transferring episomes were underway in the laboratory, the experiments which later led to the formulation of the operon theory. I suspect that Jacques enjoyed playing a game of cat-and-mouse with me, appearing to predict what my results would be. Only later I found out what had been going on and was a bit angry.

But science was not the most important accomplishment in that brief visit. The windfall was that my real friendship with Jacques started at that time, cemented by the delightful discovery of the close affinity of our intellectual tastes and beliefs. It was a surprising affinity between two persons so different in background and experiences, except in science. It extended beyond science, and was in fact not centered on science as content, but on science as a chosen commitment.

One of our main affinities was our common existentialist persuasion. We shared an intense distrust and dislike of abstract loyalties. We wished our beliefs to be commitments as freely chosen as possible. We viewed loyalties as blank checks, commitments as rationally explored endorsements—endorsements that are acts of will and therefore imply active participation.

Jacques Monod used to assert that an existential philosophy is the only philosophy appropriate to scientists. Later, during a year I spent at the Institut Pasteur and still later when I was lecturing at the Collége de France, the question of the relation between science and existential philosophy was often the topic of our Saturday morning conversations. We insisted that our commitment to science—and more generally to the advancement of rational knowledge—was a choice to be vigorously affirmed but not an absolute value of the human mind. When, in *Chance and Necessity*, Jacques translated this idea of commitment into the formula of an "ethics of knowledge," some confusion arose. The affirmation of commitment to rational knowledge as ethical choice was interpreted by some critics as an affirmation of rational knowledge as an absolute ethical principle. This issue of ethical theory is one that neither this essay not its author is particularly suited to clarify.

I recall a meeting in La Jolla with Jacques when he was preparing the draft of his Pomona College lectures, whose text later became the substance of *Chance and Necessity*. At that time I had become intrigued by Noam Chomsky's ideas about language, and had timidly been "pushing" on Chomsky a genetic and evolutionistic interpretation of the evidence for innate linguistic structures. I was delighted, therefore, when one day at breakfast, as we talked of genetics and anthropology, Jacques blurted out (I paraphrase), "I am absolutely convinced that the evolution of the human language structure was the central driving force in human evolution." (*Je suis absolument convaincu*, incidentally, was a favorite way of Jacques to preface a controversial statement.)

For me it was delightful to discover that our lines of thought, in fact our interest in a new subject, had once more converged by independent and separate ways. Such moments of intellectual convergence are infinitely precious. They are the seals of friendship, just as the kiss of Paolo and Francesca in Dante's *Comedy* was the seal of love. What is friendship but a mutual attraction and affinity of two minds, a mutual valuing and being valued, just as love is made of wanting and being wanted.

In his last years Jacques became concerned with the impact of biology on human society, and, characteristically, tried actively to promote the field of bio-anthropology. He actually involved me and others, through the Royaumont Center, in a number of ventures in the border area between hard and soft science—without, I fear, generating a great deal of solid accomplishment. I believe Jacques was inclined to put more confidence in the ethological and sociobiological approaches than I thought was warranted. Even here, however, he was not dogmatically "biologizing" the human predicament, but simply trying to choose and develop a feasible approach. I suspect that for Jacques these activities actually had an additional function, providing him with an intellectual and social diversion from the concerns of administration and from his separation from day-by-day experimental work.

There was in Jacques' personality a slightly perverse streak. He consciously cultivated a certain ambivalence about issues and about people. He had his vanities, although his sense of humor helped him discriminate attitude from substance, in himself as well as in others. His ambivalence never prevented him, however, from *se prendre au sérieux* when the task at hand warranted it, whether it was war-time resistance, or science, or concern for colleagues and students, or for the Institut Pasteur.

I miss him as a man and a friend. Mature age, even after a full life, is a sad time because one's friends' start to depart. One loses one's partners in discourse, who provide excitement and validation. More important, one loses the actuality of long lasting friendships. Yet the memory of those friendships is the evidence of existence fulfilled.

CONJECTURES AND REFUTATIONS

Antoine Danchin

Contrary to most of the authors who have been asked to contribute to this book, I have been neither a colleague nor a pupil of Jacques Monod. Our encounter occurred after many accidental events which led me from the most formal mathematics to experimental biology. Curiously it is not in Henri Buc's laboratory, where I had many opportunities to see Jacques Monod, that I met him, but at the meetings organized by the Centre de Royaumont pour une Science de l'Homme; and after the first one in 1973 we regularly had numerous conversations. Rather than present here a review article on the various aspects of regulation at the molecular level (this has been done often by Jacques Monod himself, and developed at length in *Chance and Necessity*) or to report anecdotes on the personality of Jacques Monod, I would like to continue in the spirit of the conversations I was lucky to have with Jacques Monod a short time before his death on a subject we began to discuss in detail.

It seems to me—but, clearly, it is my interpretation—that two major themes were present in Jacques Monod's thoughts at that time. The first one was concerned with the methodology necessary for investigating phenomena; it is developed at length in K. Popper's books, and, indeed, Monod has contributed to their diffusion in France: the best way to contribute to building science is to progress by making conjectures and trying to refute them. A self-consistent model, even when it is wrong, is always useful if it is "falsifiable." Oddly enough, the most frequently prevailing attitude, even in the most famous international journals, is a tendency, on the one hand, to produce "irrefutable models" and, on the other, to try to "verify" theories rather than refute them. In this respect the operon as well as the allostery theories are exemplary. In the latter, the Monod-Wyman-Changeux model requires only *two* phenomenological constants in order to describe allosteric regulation, whereas the "equivalent" Koshland-Nemethy and Filmer model asks for at least (in the case of a dimer) *four* such constants in order to describe the same phenomenon. Thus the K-N-F model is practically unfalsifiable (whence its surprising success in the scientific community).

The second theme—as I believe I see it—is clear in the allostery theory. One can explain phenomena using two quite different approaches. Either one assumes the existence of a driving force able to "instruct" (or direct) the evolving of the considered systems, or one attributes to chance alone the ability to display sufficient variety of objects so that interactions with a changing environment are sorted out, and the most stable ones selected (those which last the longest time). Again the M-W-C model is a selective theory whereas the K-N-F model is typically instructive. It is extremely interesting to learn from the published papers, that Monod himself began by an instructive view of allosteric regulation [still found in his reflections on the Maxwell's devil], to end with the selective approach. In this respect I think that the word *teleonomy* used in *Chance and Necessity* carries typical instructive (and even finalist) stereotypes, although it serves to design a concept, still ill-defined in this book, which is of the selective type. The so-called teleonomy law is a kind of contingent necessity (if I dare say so) which expresses necessity *a posteriori* and not *a priori*. And after the last passionate and exciting conversation we have had on this theme, I think that *Chance and Necessity* represented a step toward a thought completely devoid of instructivism, and that the word teleonomy was an inappropriate choice rather than a mistaken concept.

Since this book is mainly devoted to the works of Jacques Monod, it seems unnecessary to consider again the fundamental regulations he has helped elucidate: allosteric regulation and regulations of transcription. I would like only to emphasize the hierarchical order of these regulations: allostery deals with one catalytic activity, the operon, with the coordinate expression of several related activities; and catabolite repression with the coordinate expression (or repression) of several operons. As we had once agreed upon, one may then ask: Is a still more general system, allowing, for instance, the coupling between the cellular metabolism and macromolecular syntheses, possible? In what follows I would like to describe the main lines of a conjecture which would help to state precisely this question, keeping in mind the methodology alluded to above. And if I dare write so, it is in order to follow one of the aspects of the research work Jacques Monod was emphasizing: its exploratory power. We must be bold and daring; we have nothing to lose!

Within the framework of this book I can only give the outlines of the conjecture and questions raised by it. I think however that it is noteworthy to observe that, at the time of Jacques Monod's death, when he had so many important administrative tasks to perform, he was still willing to discuss with a newcomer, as I was, the theoretical lines he was fond of.

The problem was raised by the fact that the models proposed for explaining cell multiplication all involve a *small* number of macromolecular events (e.g., the "replicon" theory). This should result in a Poissonian stochastic distribution of the initiation time which would completely prevent synchronization of cell division. Since synchronization *is* observed, it becomes reasonable to assume that a signal involving a *large* number of molecules takes part in the initiating event. A metabolic signal—which would also couple this initiation to the internal state of the cell—seems quite suitable for such a purpose.

Assuming the existence of such a metabolic signal, several aspects can be described, keeping within the Popperian doctrine often quoted by Jacques Monod:

> We hold that the ideal [of science] can be realized, very simply, by recognizing that the rationality of sciences lies not in its habit of appealing to empirical evidence in support of its dogma—astrologers do so too—but solely in the *critical approach*: in an attitude which, of course, involves the critical use, among other arguments, of empirical evidence (especially in refutations). For us, therefore, science has nothing to do with the quest for certainty or probability or reliability. We are not interested in establishing scientific theories as secure, or certain, or probable. Conscious of our fallibility we are only interested in criticizing them and testing them, hoping to find out where we are mistaken; of learning from our mistakes; and, if we are lucky, of proceeding to better theories.

This means that one does make conjectures and designs experiments capable of refuting them. For instance: How is metabolism organized: acentered or hierarchical? A hierarchy seems most stable and proper, thus the metabolite which controls cell multiplication will derive from metabolic pathways, independent of each other and organized as a hierarchy. Will the control be positive or negative? A teleological line of reasoning will suggest that a negative control is genetically stable when the system under control is rarely employed, whereas a positive control is stable if the system is often used. Thus one will conjecture that the metabolic signal behaves like cyclic AMP. What will be the systems under control? Most probably it is the general cell machinery, which suggests that stable RNA synthesis would reflect the behavior of this control metabolite. What experiments can be designed to detect the metabolic pathways involved in this control? At least two different pathways are involved, corresponding to two different pools of metabolites: an abrupt shift of one of these should both increase the synthesis of the control metabolite and induce starvation in the other pool(s). Then one is led to conclude that the cell must be somehow protected against such an unbalanced effect. The stringent control which couples RNA synthesis to protein synthesis seems a good candidate for such a protecting device. Therefore it appears that strains mutated in this control (the so-called "relaxed" mutants) would be most suitable for this study.

One could multiply the type of questions which can be asked, and the way they are answered. These were the questions I was trying to pose and answer, submitting all the problems for comment to Jacques Monod, just a short time before his death. As he always did, he offered new conjectures and then proposed experiments to refute them.

Although exposed in a brief and awkward fashion, I would like this text to be a tribute to his memory. Up to his last moments, and despite his numerous occupations, he remained available for discussion, and when he did not have free time, he asked me to write the problems in a letter to him, so that he could think about them. This is most remarkable in view of the usual attitude of many scientists. Monod very much liked *ideas*, and I would like, once again, to use the very words of K. Popper whom Monod liked so much. "My answer to the questions; 'How do you know? What is the source of the basis for your assertion? What observations have led you to it?' would be: I do *not* know: my assertion was merely a guess. Never mind the source or the sources, from which it may spring. There are many possible sources, and I may not be aware of half of them; and origins and pedigrees have in any case little bearing upon truth. But if you are interested in the problem which I tried to solve by my tentative assertion, you may help me by criticizing it as severely as you can; and if you can design some experimental test which you think might refute my assertion, I shall gladly, and to the best of my powers, help you to refute it."